Exploring the Meaning of Life

Exploring the Meaning of Life

An Anthology and Guide

Edited by

Joshua W. Seachris

With Section Introductions By

Thaddeus Metz
John Cottingham
Garrett Thomson
Erik J. Wielenberg
John Martin Fischer

A John Wiley & Sons, Ltd., Publication

This edition first published 2013
© 2013 John Wiley & Sons, Inc.

Wiley-Blackwell is an imprint of John Wiley & Sons, formed by the merger of Wiley's global Scientific, Technical and Medical business with Blackwell Publishing.

Registered Office
John Wiley & Sons, Ltd, The Atrium, Southern Gate, Chichester, West Sussex, PO19 8SQ, UK

Editorial Offices
350 Main Street, Malden, MA 02148-5020, USA
9600 Garsington Road, Oxford, OX4 2DQ, UK
The Atrium, Southern Gate, Chichester, West Sussex, PO19 8SQ, UK

For details of our global editorial offices, for customer services, and for information about how to apply for permission to reuse the copyright material in this book please see our website at www.wiley.com/wiley-blackwell.

The right of Joshua W. Seachris to be identified as the author of the editorial material in this work has been asserted in accordance with the UK Copyright, Designs and Patents Act 1988.

Library of Congress Cataloging-in-Publication Data

Exploring the meaning of life : an anthology and guide / edited by Joshua W. Seachris ; with section introductions by Thaddeus Metz ... [et al.].
       p.   cm.
    Includes bibliographical references and index.
    ISBN 978-0-470-65879-6 (pbk.) – ISBN 978-0-470-65878-9 (hbk.)
  1. Life.   2. Meaning (Philosophy)   3. Life–Religious aspects.   I. Seachris, Joshua W.
    BD435.E97 2012
    128–dc23
                                                         2012011203

A catalogue record for this book is available from the British Library.

Set in 10/13pt Minion by SPi Publisher Services, Pondicherry, India
Printed in Singapore by Ho Printing Singapore Pte Ltd

1   2013

Contents

Notes on Contributors

John Cottingham (PhD, Oxford University) is Professor Emeritus of Philosophy at the University of Reading, Professorial Research Fellow at Heythrop College, University of London, and an Honorary Fellow of St. John's College, Oxford. He is an authority on early-modern philosophy, especially Descartes, and has published widely on moral philosophy and the philosophy of religion. His recent titles include *On the Meaning of Life* (Routledge, 2003), The *Spiritual Dimension* (Cambridge University Press, 2005), *Cartesian Reflections* (Oxford University Press, 2008), and *Why Believe?* (Continuum, 2009). He is editor of the international philosophical journal *Ratio*.

John Martin Fischer (PhD, Cornell University) is Distinguished Professor and Chair of the Department of Philosophy at the University of California, Riverside, where he has held a University of California President's Chair (2006–10). He has written on various topics in philosophy, including free will, moral responsibility, normative ethics, death, immortality, and the meaning of life. He is the editor of *The Metaphysics of Death* (Stanford University Press, 1993), and many of his articles on death, immortality, and the meaning of life are collected in his *Our Stories: Essays on Life, Death, and Free Will* (Oxford University Press, 2011).

Thaddeus Metz (PhD, Cornell University) is Research Professor of Philosophy at the University of Johannesburg, South Africa, where he writes on three major topics: resolving controversies in law, politics, business, and medicine by appealing to the value of dignity; interpreting the African ethic of *ubuntu* in an analytic way; and developing and evaluating theoretical approaches to what makes a life meaningful. On the latter topic, Metz has published about two dozen papers, which have appeared in such journals as *American Philosophical Quarterly, Ethics, Ratio, Religious Studies*, and *Utilitas*, as well as in collected volumes such as *New Waves in Philosophy of Religion* (eds. Y. Nagasawa and E. Wielenberg), *Oxford Bibliographies Online* (ed. D. Pritchard), *Philosophy and Happiness* (ed. L. Bortolotti), *Stanford Encyclopedia of Philosophy* (ed. E. Zalta), and *The Moral Life* (eds. N. Athanasoulis and S. Vice). His book, *Meaning in Life: An Analytic Study*, will be published by Oxford University Press in 2012.

Joshua W. Seachris (PhD, University of Oklahoma) is Adjunct Assistant Professor of Philosophy at Wake Forest University in North Carolina, as well as Grant Administrator for The Character Project, which aims to map the contours of the human character by funding key research in philosophy, psychology, and theology. He is the author of peer-reviewed articles on a range of topics in philosophy, including the problem of evil, Confucius and virtue, the meaning of life, and death. His work has appeared in the *International Journal for Philosophy of Religion*, *Asian Philosophy*, *Philo*, *Religious Studies*, and the *Internet Encyclopedia of Philosophy*.

Garrett Thomson (PhD, Oxford University) teaches philosophy at the College of Wooster in Wooster, Ohio, where he holds the Compton Chair. He is the author of several books including *On Kant* (Wadsworth, 2003), *On the Meaning of Life* (Wadsworth 2002), *Una Introducción a la Práctica de la Filosofía* (PanAmericana, 2002), *Bacon to Kant* (Waveland Press, 2001), *On Leibniz*, (Wadsworth, 2001), and *Needs* (Routledge, 1987). He co-edited the six volumes of the *Longman Standard History of Philosophy* with Prof D. Kolak (Longman's Press, 2006). He has also taught at universities in Colombia and the UK. He is chief executive officer of the Guerrand-Hermès Foundation for Peace.

Erik J. Wielenberg (PhD, University of Massachusetts-Amherst) is Associate Professor of Philosophy at DePauw University in Greencastle, Indiana. He works primarily in ethical theory and the philosophy of religion. He is the author of *Value and Virtue in a Godless Universe* (Cambridge University Press, 2005) and *God and the Reach of Reason* (Cambridge University Press, 2007).

Preface

Relative to other philosophical questions, the question of life's meaning received little sustained attention from philosophers within the analytic tradition for most of the twentieth century. Over roughly the last decade, however, this trend has changed. The renewed interest in the meaning of life among analytic philosophers is evidenced by the growing number of journal articles and books on the topic in recent years. And there is a salient optimism that genuine philosophical progress can be made on this question, even if some of the enigma surrounding it will likely always remain.

This anthology contains prominent essays from the resurgence of interest in the topic, and faithfully represents current trajectories in the discussion over life's meaning. It also contains classic essays that no anthology should be without, given that the contemporary dialectic on life's meaning in analytic philosophy shares important affinities with earlier reflection on the question. One will find canonical meaning-of-life texts from Schopenhauer and Tolstoy, for example, alongside contemporary work that is partly inspired by many of the same themes. Each essay has been carefully selected in order to give the reader a deep understanding of the topic. The sections were chosen in order accurately to reflect the dialectical contours that have emerged in the meaning-of-life literature over the past ten years.

This anthology is as much a *guide* as it is a *reader*. It contains an extensive General Introduction that establishes the overarching framework for the 33 essays in the volume. The aim of the General Introduction is to provide readers with several layers of context – historical, experiential, and conceptual – that will help them to situate each essay within the general territory of life's meaning. In addition to the General Introduction, all five sections contain section introductions, each written by an internationally respected philosopher who has advanced the discussion of life's meaning with his own important work. At the end of each section introduction, readers will find a bibliography containing relevant resources if they wish to explore further.

The question of life's meaning is *humanity's* question, not just the *philosopher's* question. It is one that spans time, geography, culture, and academic discipline, and it does so because it is part and parcel of our common *human condition*. Consequently, one can envision an anthology on the topic that comprehensively reflects this expansive reality, but such a volume would be cumbersomely large. As such, one must choose where to focus, and the present anthology does so by including essays that are largely, though not exclusively, (1) western, (2) contemporary, (3) philosophical, and (4) analytic. This fact, however, should not dissuade those with proclivities outside of these four categories from being interested in the volume, as all of the themes found in these essays will be of interest to anyone who, at one time or another, has wondered about the meaning of life.

Intended Audience

Though no doubt focused, the essays in this anthology along with the editorial material have been chosen and written in order to reach a wide and diverse audience. Given the ubiquity and profundity of the question of life's meaning, I envision that this anthology will be of interest to at least the following audiences:

- Advanced undergraduates who want to develop a good understanding of the contemporary dialectic on the meaning of life.
- Philosophy and/or religious studies professors who need a good text on the meaning of life for courses on this and related topics (e.g., human nature, human destiny, life and death).
- Graduate students and faculty whose primary work is in other areas of philosophy but who want to familiarize themselves with contemporary work on the meaning of life.
- Philosophers who are interested in normative theory more broadly and who are curious about the state of normative discussions vis-à-vis the meaning of life.
- Scholars outside the discipline of philosophy whose research may intersect with the meaning of life in important ways (e.g., religious studies scholars, theologians, personality psychologists).
- Others outside of the academy who desire to develop a solid understanding of the contemporary discussion over life's meaning or who are simply curious as to what contemporary analytic philosophers are saying about the meaning of life.

Personal Acknowledgments

My reflection, research, and writing on the topic of life's meaning has spanned roughly the last decade. This anthology constitutes a portion of this experience. Insofar as the experience contains within it the invaluable traces of many individuals, the anthology itself also contains such traces. I cannot possibly remember all of them, and so I here thank everyone who has, in some way, interacted with me on the topic of life's meaning. In addition to these indirect influences, there are many who have had a specific part to play in the realization of this anthology and to whom special recognition is due.

I am very grateful to Jeff Dean at Wiley-Blackwell for his continual guidance throughout this process, which was both efficient and enjoyable under his careful oversight. I extend my thanks to other Wiley-Blackwell staff, including Nicole Benevenia, Sarah Dancy, and Sally Osborn, for their help and professionalism. To the anonymous referees of the prospectus for this volume, I offer my sincere thanks. Many of your suggestions were incorporated, and the anthology is surely stronger as a result. I also thank the University of Oklahoma for a generous subvention to partially cover permission rights.

Special thanks are due to the section introduction writers: Thaddeus Metz, John Cottingham, Garrett Thomson, Erik Wielenberg, and John Martin Fischer. This anthology is unique among anthologies on life's meaning, in part because of their contributions. Their philosophical work has advanced the discipline, both in general and specifically on the meaning of life, and their international presence brings with it an additional layer of depth to this volume. It has been a wonderful privilege working with them on this project. I thank my friend and mentor, Linda Zagzebski, for her encouragement as I envisioned this anthology and for her help with drafting the prospectus. I am deeply thankful for her investment in my life. To my dear friends at Christ Church, I offer my sincere appreciation for your sacrificial support. Finally my parents, Lonnie and Loma Seachris, my parents-in-law, Art and Barbara Sundquist, my two sons, William and Owen, and most importantly my wife, Sarah, were sources of great joy and love during the editing of this volume. My life is more meaningful because of your loving presence.

Joshua W. Seachris
Winston-Salem, North Carolina
May 2012

Acknowledgments

1.1 Paul Edwards (1972) "Why," in Paul Edwards (ed.), *The Encyclopedia of Philosophy*, vols. 7&8, New York: Macmillan Publishing Company, pp. 296–302.

1.2 Garrett Thomson (2002) "Untangling the Questions," Chapter 1 in *On the Meaning of Life*, Belmont, MA: Thomson Wadsworth, pp. 3–14.

1.3 R. W. Hepburn (1966) "Questions about the Meaning of Life," *Religious Studies*, 1(2): 125–40.

1.4 Robert Nozick (1981) "Philosophy and the Meaning of Life," Chapter 6 in *Philosophical Explanations*, Cambridge, MA: Harvard University Press, pp. 571–600.

1.5 Thaddeus Metz (2001) "The Concept of a Meaningful Life," *American Philosophical Quarterly* 38(2): 137–53.

1.6 Arjan Markus (2003) "Assessing Views of Life: A Subjective Affair?" *Religious Studies* 39: 125–43.

2.1 Ecclesiastes, ESV (English Standard Bible) Online Bible, http://www.gnpcb.org/esv/, Wheaton, IL: Crossway.

2.2 C. S. Lewis (1986) "On Living in an Atomic Age," in Walter Hooper (ed.), *Present Concerns*, San Diego, CA: Harcourt, pp. 73–80.

2.3 Jeffrey Gordon (1983) "Is the Existence of God Relevant to the Meaning of Life?" *The Modern Schoolman* 60: 227–46.

2.4 William Lane Craig (2008) "The Absurdity of Life without God," Chapter 2 in *Reasonable Faith: Christian Truth and Apologetics*, 3rd edn., Wheaton, IL: Crossway, pp. 65–88.

2.5 John Haught (2006) "Is Nature Enough?" Chapter 1 in *Is Nature Enough: Meaning and Truth in the Age of Science*, Cambridge: Cambridge University Press, pp. 4–20.

2.6 John Cottingham (2006) "Religion and Value: The Problem of Heteronomy," Chapter 3 in *The Spiritual Dimension: Religion, Philosophy and Human Value*, New York: Cambridge University Press, pp. 37–57.

2.7 Thaddeus Metz (2000) "Could God's Purpose Be the Source of Life's Meaning?" *Religious Studies* 36: 293–313.

3.1 Arthur Schopenhauer (2004) "On the Vanity of Existence," in *Essays and Aphorisms*, trans. R. J. Hollingdale, London: Penguin Books, pp. 51–4.

3.2   Bertrand Russell (1957) "A Free Man's Worship," in *Why I Am not a Christian and Other Essays on Religion and Related Subjects*, New York: Simon and Schuster, pp. 104–16.

3.3   Thomas Nagel (1971) "The Absurd," *Journal of Philosophy* 68(20): 716–27.

3.4   David Benatar (2006) "Why Coming into Existence Is Always a Harm," Chapter 2 in *Better Never to Have Been: The Harm of Coming into Existence*, Oxford: Oxford University Press, pp. 28–59.

3.5   Thomas Nagel (2010) "Secular Philosophy and the Religious Temperament," Chapter 1 in *Secular Philosophy and the Religious Temperament: Essays 2002–2008*, Oxford: Oxford University Press, pp. 3–17.

4.1   John Kekes (2009) "The Human World," *Ratio* XXII: 137–56.

4.2   Richard Taylor (1987) "Time and Life's Meaning," *The Review of Metaphysics*, 40(4): 675–86.

4.3   Susan Wolf (2010) "The Meanings of Lives," in John Perry, Michael Bratman, and John Martin Fischer (eds.), *Introduction to Philosophy: Classical and Contemporary Readings*, 5th edn., New York: Oxford University Press, pp. 794–805.

4.4   Robert Audi (2005) "Intrinsic Value and Meaningful Life," *Philosophical Papers* 34(3): 331–55.

4.5   Erik J. Wielenberg (2005) "God and the Meaning of Life," Chapter 1 in *Value and Virtue in a Godless Universe*, Cambridge: Cambridge University Press, pp. 14–37.

4.6   Richard Norman (2007) "The Varieties of Non-Religious Experience," Chapter 6 in John Cottingham (ed.), *The Meaning of Theism*, Malden, MA: Blackwell Publishing, pp. 91–110.

4.7   Ursula Goodenough (2000) "Emergent Religious Principles," in *The Sacred Depths of Nature*, Oxford: Oxford University Press, pp. 167–74.

5.1   Leo Tolstoy (2006) "A Confession," in *Spiritual Writings*, ed. Charles E. Moore, Orbis Books, pp. 46–58.

5.2   Steven Luper-Foy (1987) "Annihilation," *Philosophical Quarterly* 37(148): 233–52.

5.3   John Martin Fischer (1994) "Why Immortality Is Not So Bad," *International Journal of Philosophical Studies* 2(2): 257–70.

5.4   Thaddeus Metz (2003) "The Immortality Requirement for Life's Meaning," *Ratio* XVI: 161–77.

5.5   Brooke Alan Trisel (2004) "Human Extinction and the Value of Our Efforts," *Philosophical Forum*, XXXV(3): 371–91.

5.6   John Martin Fischer (2005) "Free Will, Death, and Immortality: The Role of Narrative," *Philosophical Papers* 34(3): 379–403.

5.7   Joshua W. Seachris (2011) "Death, Futility, and the Proleptic Power of Narrative Ending," *Religious Studies* 47: 141–63.

5.8   Paul K. Moser (2007) "Divine Hiddenness, Death, and Meaning," Chapter 15 in Paul Copan and Chad Meister (eds.), *Philosophy of Religion: Classic and Contemporary Issues*, Malden, MA: Wiley-Blackwell, pp. 215–27.

General Introduction

Joshua W. Seachris

Two Realities

Sometime around 1940, the French existentialist Albert Camus penned the following words, "Judging whether life is or is not worth living amounts to answering the fundamental question of philosophy. All the rest – whether or not the world has three dimensions, whether the mind has nine or twelve categories – comes afterwards [...] I therefore conclude that the meaning of life is the most urgent of questions."[1] Judging from Camus's corpus of work, he remained faithful to this assessment of philosophy's primary task.

In roughly the same time period, across the English Channel, Bertrand Russell had something quite different to *say* about the question of life's meaning by really saying nothing at all. The story has been told of Russell once being in the back of a cab.[2] As his passenger was arguably the most famous philosopher of his day, the driver of the cab probably saw this as an opportunity to get Russell's thoughts on the perceived quintessential topic of philosophy: the meaning of life. So, he asked him, "What's it all about?" Probably to the driver's shock and disappointment, his famous occupant could give him no answer. If one is familiar with twentieth-century analytic philosophy, Russell's inability to answer speaks volumes. A Russell unable to answer his driver's request was not indicative of one who thought himself ignorant or confused, but rather of one likely deeply suspicious of the meaningfulness of the cab driver's request, or at least of the possibility of answering it during a brief cab ride.

Does philosophy – and, given the focus of many of the essays in this volume, *analytic* philosophy – have anything helpful to say about the meaning of life? With whom do we side, Camus or Russell? Is Camus right, that the question of life's meaning is the most urgent of all questions? Or should we embrace Russell's implied suspicion of the question's basic meaningfulness or suspicion that it has any answer? Could it really be that the most urgent

Exploring the Meaning of Life: An Anthology and Guide, First Edition. Edited by Joshua W. Seachris.
© 2013 John Wiley & Sons, Inc. Published 2013 by John Wiley & Sons, Inc.

question of human existence makes no sense or has no answer? From a different perspective, is Camus's preoccupation with the meaning of life, or anyone else's for that matter, simply a product of an unsatisfied libido, as Freud once famously said about the psychological state of those who feel compelled to ask the question?[3] Is the disparity between Camus and Russell a function of the so-called "Continental-Analytic divide" in philosophy? Is it related to existentialism's perceived idiosyncratic place within philosophy in general (that is, "real" philosophers do not bother with such questions)? Which is more appropriate: Camus's passion-filled assertion or Russell's implied suspicion? Much more than a good story, the cab driver's encounter with Russell, juxtaposed with Camus's bold claim, highlights two salient yet conflicting realities vis-à-vis the question: "What is the meaning of life?"

Philosophical suspicion and neglect

For a large part of the twentieth century, analytic philosophy exhibited two general trends with respect to the question of life's meaning. On the one hand, many analytic philosophers ignored the question because they were likely doubtful that it had an answer, given latent assumptions on the part of many who ask the question about what would have to be the case for life to have a meaning. On the other hand, many were suspicious that it is incoherent and meaningless, much like the question: "What does the color red taste like?" Regarding the trend of neglect, Karl Britton notes:

> Men and women want to read philosophy because they think it will help them to understand the meaning of life: and many philosophers confess that this is what first led them to study philosophy. On the whole, however, the question of the meaning of life does not loom large in the teaching or writing of professional philosophers nowadays.[4]

Though Britton wrote this back in the late 1960s, the trend of ignoring the question continued for at least another two decades, and to a lesser extent is maintained even today. In terms of reference works, the extremely brief entry on the meaning of life in *The Oxford Companion to Philosophy*[5] and the complete lack of an entry in *The Cambridge Dictionary of Philosophy*[6] are telling indicators of this tendency even three or more decades removed from Britton's observation, although a substantive entry written by Susan Wolf is available in *The Routledge Encyclopedia of Philosophy* along with another excellent piece by Thaddeus Metz in *The Stanford Encyclopedia of Philosophy* online.[7] There is some evidence that the trend of neglect is slowing, perhaps even reversing in light of recent work on the topic, including, among others, books by Garrett Thomson,[8] John Cottingham,[9] Julian Baggini,[10] Terry Eagleton,[11] Susan Wolf,[12] and John Kekes,[13] as well as numerous journal articles and special issues of the journals *Philosophical Papers* (2005), *Philo* (2009), and *The Monist* (2010) devoted partly or entirely to the topic.

As for the trend of logical suspicion, it is now generally recognized that the question "What is the meaning of life?" while vague, probably avoids the charge of outright incoherence, though some think that it does so only through reformulation into other questions. The present anthology is further evidence that both trends are, to some extent, reversing.

Perceived importance

The second reality highlighted in the cab driver's encounter with Russell, and placed in juxtaposition with Camus's claim, is that most people consider the question "What is the meaning of life?" to be among the most important that can be asked, if not *the* most important. This, of course, creates a *prima facie* impasse, given that the most pressing question of human existence is one that many of those supposedly functioning as guardians of the canons of reason think is rationally subpar, or at least less deserving of our philosophical energies than is a consideration of, for example, how consciousness and accompanying qualia arise from matter, or whether discussions of epistemic luck and control hold the key to discovering the necessary and sufficient conditions of propositional knowledge.[14] Unfortunately, then, this existentially motivated and infused request, born out of deep yearnings of the human heart, may meet disappointment if one turns to analytic philosophers to illumine the question, let alone point in the direction of possible answers. Alasdair Macintyre laments that such large-scale and existentially important questions receive so little attention by many professional philosophers:

> Yet, while Hume turned away from philosophical questions about the ends of life to the diversions of dining and backgammon, there has developed since a kind of philosophy that sometimes functions for those who engage in it just as dining and backgammon did for Hume. It reduces all questions to technical or semitechnical questions and it has the effect of making the serious and systematic asking of questions about the ends of life, rather than the asking of second-order philosophical questions about those first-order questions, appear if not cold, at least strain'd and ridiculous.[15]

Macintyre's claim is perceptive, and the point he makes is relevant to discussions of the meaning of life. Indeed, much of what is done by philosophers operating under the rubric of "analytic philosophy" has made inquiry into the meaning of life look "strain'd and ridiculous." The publication of this new anthology and the existence of most of the 33 essays contained within it are evidence that not all philosophers who consider themselves analytic philosophers are as suspicious of self-conscious inquiries into the meaning of life.[16]

The challenge

While the trend of neglect is arguably unfortunate, the question "What is the meaning of life?" is undeniably characterized by significant vagueness, such that the trend is partly understandable. Indeed, one cannot plausibly deny that this vagueness makes the question difficult to understand. Philosophically, therefore, the question has seemed unmanageable to many. It is surely not a question about the semantic meaning of the word "life," but what, then, is it a question about? Is it a question about all of existence? Is it asking for a comprehensive explanation of why the universe exists and of our place within it? And if so, is it asked with strong teleological assumptions at the fore, such that a purely efficient, mechanistic causal story would leave the inquirer unsatisfied? Such questions with a holistic focus seem to track a request like: "What is it all about?" There is a profound human impulse to seek a deep explanation, context, or narrative through which to interpret existence, and then to move beyond localized foci by *living into* this universal, totalizing narrative. This first cluster of questions highlights the *cosmic* or *global* dimension of the question of life's meaning, whereby some sort of explanation (perhaps even *narrative* explanation) is sought that will render the universe and our lives within it intelligible. This is an important facet of the question, and one that is underexplored in the current literature.

However, raising questions within the cosmic dimension alone neglects other important questions in the neighborhood of life's meaning. While connected, they are conceptually distinct from the first set; although, depending on how robust is the above explanation of *what it is all about*, one might have good reason to think that it would also encompass this second dimension. In any case, while related to the cosmic or global dimension, these next questions highlight the *individualist* or *local* dimension of the meaning-of-life question. This dimension is more overtly *normative* than is the cosmic dimension. When asking questions within this dimension, we are more concerned with the aim of securing *a meaningful life*. We wonder what we must, or should, or ought to order our lives around so as to render them meaningful. Meaningfulness, then, perhaps supervenes on a life properly ordered around the right stuff.[17] Questions within this dimension include, among others: "Around what purposes should I order my life?" "What confers value on my life?" and "What makes my life worthwhile and not irredeemably futile?"

Most philosophers currently writing on the topic think that the question of life's meaning is somehow a question about all of these and other related topics (within both the cosmic and individualist dimensions), but only insofar as it is viewed as a long disjunctive question or an amalgam of related yet distinct requests about existence, purpose, value, worth, significance, death, and futility, among others. Importantly, those disjuncts (questions) within the individualist dimension are most salient in contemporary discussions. Furthermore, though it is viewed as a request that moves us into normative territory, it is thought to be distinct from purely *ethical* requests about rightness and wrongness, purely *aesthetic* requests about the good and the beautiful, and purely *eudaimonistic* requests about human happiness and flourishing, while bearing some relationship to all three.

Those who read the essays in this anthology will notice that the majority interpret the question in the individualist sense, being primarily concerned with the question of what, if anything, confers meaning (in the normative sense of meaningfulness) on someone's life. This follows the current dialectical trajectory in discussions of life's meaning, as most occur within individualist parameters. The salient asymmetry, in terms of sheer numbers, between cosmic and individualist proposals is a shortcoming, and evidences the reality that discussions of life's meaning within contemporary analytic philosophy remain in relative infancy. Approaches that proceed from a cosmic interpretation of the meaning of life question remain undertheorized, and warrant further reflection.[18]

Though much work remains to be done on the cosmic aspect of the question of life's meaning, it is accurate to say that broad contours have emerged in the discussion, contours that have more clearly demarcated the conceptual boundaries. In order further to contextualize the 33 essays in this anthology, it will be helpful to consider a cluster of factors that contribute to shaping the question of life's meaning, in terms of how it is asked and how it is answered.

The Experiential Context: Perplexity, Angst, and Wonder

The question of life's meaning is born out of uniquely human experiences, capacities, and propensities. The human capacity to *get outside of* ourselves and view our pursuits and very lives both first-personly and distantly from a detached, more-or-less dispassionate, impersonal standpoint is often part of the story for inquiring into the meaning of life. We, unlike butterflies or cats for example, are self-consciously aware, and can take an observational, reflective viewpoint on our lives. We have the ability to shift from mere engagement to reflection. This shift is often accompanied by a salient state of perplexity, perplexity as we ask questions about the universe in relation to ourselves. We are perplexed about the world around us. Is nature all there is, or is there more? We are perplexed about who we are and why we are here. We are perplexed about what we should be doing, and how who we are and what we do cohere with the rest of reality. We are perplexed about whether reality, *all the way down* as it were, in any way *cares* about us and what we do.

Such questions gain existential traction because we can view our lives *sub specie aeternitatis*. From the observational viewpoint of the "eternal," we become spectators of the lives we lead. As provisional bystanders, we may begin to wonder what the meaning of our life is, or worry that it has any meaning at all. Even such pursuits as vocation and raising a family, in which we are often passionately involved, may begin to seem completely arbitrary, thus possibly inducing in us a nagging skepticism about their value and worth. From this distant standpoint, then, our lives and pursuits may appear trivial, insubstantial, or inconsequential.[19] Of course, it may be that regardless of how our lives appear from the distant standpoint, such a standpoint is irrelevant for assessments of life. However, whether in normative appraisals of life it is reasonable to privilege this detached perspective over our immediate, human perspective is beside the point. The fact is that we often do, and this human propensity is strongly correlated with inquiring into the meaning of life.

Inquiring into the meaning of life is also often born out of an experience of existential angst, angst that may or may not be closely connected to adopting the *sub specie aeternitatis* perspective. The source of the angst may be the clash between the passionate-immediate perspective and the detached-distant perspective, it may be intense pain and suffering, or it may perhaps be a perceived incompatibility between a given metanarrative of the universe (e.g., naturalism) and the possibility of there even being a meaning of life. Regardless of its source, existential angst often motivates questions about the meaning of life.

Asking questions and reflecting on concerns closely related to the meaning of life, and born at least partly out of angst, are evidenced in writing as early as the book of Ecclesiastes.[20] This is one reason why the book, in its entirety, is included in this anthology. In Ecclesiastes, we encounter the musings of a wise sage, Qohelet (literally "teacher" or "preacher"), on life, death, injustice, futility, human epistemic limitation, the possibility of a felicitous existence, and the inscrutable economy of God, among others. Some interpretive traditions view Ecclesiastes as thoroughly pessimistic, others as optimistic, though such positions are themselves closely linked with views on a cluster of other issues ranging from debates surrounding authorship to canonicity to the thematic unity of Scripture to biblical inspiration and authority. Regardless of such debates, Qohelet, in relevant ways, sounds like a modern-day existentialist, though he predates them by at least two millennia.[21] Ecclesiastes is concerned with significant meaning-of-life issues, especially death, whether anything in life is truly worthwhile, and whether and how the reality of God may tip the scales in favor of a meaningful, worthwhile existence. Qohelet's musings occur within the context of a visceral and angst-laden search for answers to many of life's most important, yet vexing, questions. Millennia later, angst often remains a salient part of the context for inquiries into life's meaning.

Inquiring into life's meaning is also closely linked with the experience of wonder. Wonder (*thaumazein*) itself is a large motivator for the birth of philosophy within the classical world, as from a state of speechless awe, humans desired a rational, systematic account of the universe and their place within it. Aristotle himself said that philosophy begins in wonder, "For it is owing to their wonder that men both now begin and at first began to philosophize."[22] But there is an earlier, Socratic tradition that predates Aristotle. In the *Theaetetus*, Socrates remarks to the young Theaetetus, "I dare say you do, my dear boy. It seems that Theodorus was not far from the truth when he guessed what kind of person you are. For this is an experience which is characteristic of a philosopher, this wondering: this is where philosophy begins and nowhere else."[23] Both Aristotle and Plato made explicit what was likely a common impetus for philosophy in the classical world: a pathos of astonishment that gave birth to a profound desire to understand and live in the world rightly.

Of relevance is the fact that a significant motivation in classical philosophy born out of a sense of wonder – the desire for a sweeping, holistic account of the world and the related pursuit of how to live well within the world – shares important continuities with generating conditions that often give rise to the question of life's meaning, regardless of one's temporal or geographic location in history. Many of us marvel at various contingent features of the world, wondering why they are as they are. Many of us marvel at the fact that anything exists at all. This marvel often initiates a series of *why questions*, many of which end up being requests in the neighborhood of "What is the meaning of life?"

The ancients sought a comprehensive, coherent narrative through which to live well. The discontinuities between the classical philosophical pursuit of a sweeping account of the world in which to secure the good life and the meaning of life are not significant enough to dismiss what the ancients said on such topics as irrelevant to modern considerations of life's meaning. Salient trajectories exist as one moves from the ancient to the modern world. Themes in Ecclesiastes, for example, are found in Schopenhauer, Camus, and contemporary analytic philosophical discussions of death, futility, and the meaning of life. This should not be surprising because these are prevalent themes of *the human condition*. Qohelet and ancient philosophers share in this common human condition, a condition saliently characterized by perplexity, angst, and wonder.

The Historical Context: A Changing Locus of Authority in the Modern World

Though reflections in the ancient world share important continuities with modern musings on the meaning of life, it also appears to be true that, in some sense, the anxious questioning of life's meaning is more prevalent in the modern world. In his book *The Death of God and the Meaning of Life*, Julian Young opens with an intriguing thesis:

> For most of our Western history we have not talked about the meaning of life. This is because we used to be quite certain that we knew what it was. We were certain about it because we thought we knew that over and above this world of doubtful virtue and happiness is another world: a world Nietzsche calls (somewhat ironically) the 'true world' or, alternatively expressed, 'God'.[24]

Prior to the modern period, life was self-consciously positioned within the context of some such true-world narrative, about which Young states:

> Since journeys have a beginning, a middle and an end, a true-world account of the proper course of our lives is a kind of story, a narrative. And since true-world narratives (that, for example, of Christianity) are global rather than individual, since they narrate not just your life or mine, but rather all lives at all times and places, they are, as I shall call them, 'grand' narratives.[25]

Living within the confines of a grand religious or quasi-religious narrative, humans possessed what they thought were the necessary and sufficient resources to live lives that made sense, that were rationally and existentially satisfying. But this began to change in the modern world, giving rise to generating conditions for the anxiety-laden search for the meaning of life. While the presence of perplexity and wonder may have remained more or less constant between the ancient and modern worlds, it may be the case that the presence of existential angst was significantly on the rise in the modern world.[26]

With the shift away from traditional sources of epistemic authority (e.g., tradition, Scripture) to new ones (i.e., *unaided* reason and science), grand religious or quasi-religious narratives began to lose some of their traction in the Western world. The rise of experimental science, fueled partly by Cartesian and Kantian philosophy, was making less plausible, so it seemed to many, traditional grand religious narratives. Accompanying this diminution of such narratives in the West, people began to question the meaning of life more vigorously, primarily because deeply imbedded narrative elements in the residual cultural consciousness that in some way linked to the meaning of life had supposedly lost intellectual plausibility in a world where science was supplanting teleological-theological explanations with mechanistic-naturalistic ones.[27] Relevant work by Nietzsche, Schopenhauer, Camus, and Sartre, among others, emerged within this progressing naturalistic, mechanistic view of the universe. The pathos in their writings is at least partly a result of having adopted a view of the world where mind, intentionality, and teleology are no longer thought by many to belong to the deepest structure of reality. In some relevant way, correlated with the perceived loss of these elements at the most fundamental ontological level, is the rise of the question of life's meaning.

The Current Analytic Philosophical Landscape

The question's vagueness

Contemporary analytic philosophy has inherited important trajectories from the ancient and modern worlds vis-à-vis the meaning of life. But, understandably, the analytic philosophical impulse toward conceptual clarification has given discussions of the meaning of life within the analytic philosophical tradition a unique shape. Indeed, a significant portion of the discussion within this contemporary context has been primarily concerned with trying to understand the question itself. Is it coherent? Is it meaningful? What is it asking? Does it have an answer? Asking such questions is necessary because the question of life's meaning is vague and has an elusive quality to it. Analytic philosophers have rightly noticed this. There exist a couple of options for addressing this vagueness, short of the outright charge of incoherence that was common for a substantial portion of the twentieth century in the wake of logical positivism's once strong yet now loosened grip.

Nonlinguistic usages of "meaning"

One option is to retain the use of the word "meaning" and secure a usage that applies to nonlinguistic phenomena, given that in asking the question, one is not asking for the *semantic* meaning of the word "life." This strategy is especially concerned with (1) viewing the question as making a *singular* request (contra the amalgam thesis), and (2) finding a natural interpretation of the question through a plausible employment of the term "meaning." "Meaning" has multiple meanings, and at least some of the more prominent ones mitigate its usefulness in the context of trying to formulate the intuitions driving the question of *life's* meaning. Indeed, if one is asking for the semantic meaning of life rather than "life," then the accusation of incoherence is plausible. We rightly ask for the meanings of semantic constructions, but surely not of things like physical entities, events, or life in general. The problem then is that "meaning" is a term that appears to most naturally find its home within linguistic contexts. However, life itself is not such a context. In asking the question, most of us are not asking for any sort of definition of "life" or a description of this term's usage. But, then, what are we asking? This is where the problem lies.

The problem is soluble, though, given that asking what something means need not be a request for a definition or description. There are additional nonlinguistic contexts in which the locution, "What is the meaning of *x*?" makes perfect sense (e.g., intentional signification, nonintentional signification (i.e., natural signs), etc.).[28] Some of them even share family resemblances to the question of life's meaning. One in particular is especially relevant, and tracks *cosmic* interpretations of the meaning of life question.

The locution, "What is the meaning of *x*?" functions naturally in a largely nonlinguistic context where we want to know *how something fits within a larger context or narrative*. We quite naturally and legitimately invoke the formula "What is the meaning of *x*?" in situations where *x* is some fact, event, or phenomenon we encounter and of which we want to know, in the words of N. T. Wright, the fact's or event's or phenomenon's "implication in the wider world within which this notion [or fact, event, or phenomenon] makes the sense it makes."[29] This "wider world" Wright considers to be a worldview or metanarrative or something similar.

To make his point, Wright uses the example of how one comes to understand the Easter event (that is, the putative bodily resurrection of Jesus of Nazareth). For example, a well-educated Roman soldier who comes to learn of the event may contextualize it, and therefore "fix" its meaning, through the myth of *Nero redivivus*, the idea that Nero had come back to life in order to return to Rome in all his glory.[30] The event *means* something different for him than for, say, Saul of Tarsus. The wider worldview framework or narrative (or even simply a more localized narrative that is, itself, part of a larger worldview narrative) will play a heavy interpretive role, then, in "discovering"[31] what any given fact, event, or phenomenon means. Discovering this meaning will be a product of asking and answering questions like: In what larger narrative(s) does the sentence (intended to refer to a fact, event, or phenomenon) belong? What worldviews do such narratives embody and reinforce? What are the universes of discourse within which this sentence and the event to which it refers settle down and make themselves at home – and which, at the same time, they challenge and reshape from within?[32]

In terms of the meaning of *life*, one could reasonably argue that we are trying to find the "wider world" (i.e., worldview, metanarrative) in which the existentially salient elements and accompanying questions of life fit. These existentially salient elements and accompanying questions of life, for which the word "life" is an, admittedly loose, marker, are perennial meaning-of-life themes. They are what often prompt in us the grand question "What is the meaning of life?" and include:

(1) *Fact* – something exists, we [humans] exist, and I exist. *Question* – Why does anything or we or I exist at all?
(2) *Question* – Does life have any purpose(s) and, if so, what are its nature and source?
(3) *Fact* – we are often passionately engaged in life pursuits and projects that we deem valuable and worthwhile. *Question* – Do the worth and value of these pursuits and projects need grounding in something else and, if so, what?
(4) *Fact* – pain and suffering are part of the universe. *Question* – Why?
(5) *Question* – How does it all end? Is death final? Is there an eschatological remedy to the ills of this world?

(1)–(5) constitute the cluster of considerations that track discussions of life's meaning, even though reasonable debate will exist about the details. In asking "What is the meaning of life?" it is plausible to view this as the request for a "wider world" (i.e., worldview, metanarrative) through which to secure answers to these questions. Viewed as such, this renders the question "What is the meaning of life?" coherent and intelligible by securing a usage of "meaning" that fits naturally within a nonlinguistic context.

The amalgam thesis
The interpretive strategy currently in favor for understanding what the question "What is the meaning of life?" means discards the word "meaning" and reformulates the question entirely. On this approach, the question is morphed into a cluster of other, supposedly less vague questions, even if no less difficult to answer. Following precedent in the literature, especially R. W. Hepburn, this approach for addressing the vagueness in the question of life's meaning may be called the *amalgam thesis*.[33] Roughly, the amalgam thesis entails that the original question, framed in terms of *meaning*, is a largely ill-conceived place-holder for a cluster of related requests, and, thus, not really a single question at all. One way of understanding the amalgam thesis is to view it as making the question of life's meaning little more than a disjunctive question that includes, among others, questions like: "*Why does anything exist at all?*" or "*What's it all about?*" or "*What is the purpose of life?*" or "*What makes life*

valuable?" or "*What makes life worthwhile?*" On amalgam thesis premises, then, in asking the question "What is the meaning of life?" we ought to see ourselves as asking a question either about existence or purpose or value or worth or something else.[34] Some of these questions reside within the *cosmic* dimension, others the *individualist* dimension.[35] There is something right about this. Indeed, when you ask both nonphilosophers and philosophers what they take the question to mean, you will likely hear it explicated in terms of value, worth, significance, or purpose.

Due to the dominance of the amalgam thesis as an interpretive strategy and its arguable philosophical merit, most contemporary philosophical treatments of the question consider it in one of its reformulated versions (and most often from within the individualist perspective), such as: "Around what purposes should I order my life?" or "Does my life achieve some good purpose?" "What confers value on my life?" or "What makes my life worthwhile and not irredeemably futile?" or "What brings narrative coherence and intelligibility to my life (or some subset of its parts)?" or "In virtue of what is my life worthy of great esteem?"

So, there exist at least two interpretive levels of the question on the amalgam thesis, one tracking something like the question's formal properties, the other tracking the subsequent questions' material content. In other words, the amalgam thesis implies that the question "What is the meaning of life?" is really just a disjunctive question whereby requests about existence, purpose, value, worth, and significance, among others, are being made.

Of relevance is the fact that the many of the questions most widely discussed, and as enumerated in the amalgam thesis, are normative questions about the concept of meaningfulness. And some of these are meta-ethical questions about what is meant by meaningfulness, not questions about what is, in fact, meaningful. As Thaddeus Metz notes in his introduction to Section I, these are abstract, second-order questions and not first-order normative ethical questions.[36] The latter are primarily concerned with what, if anything, makes life meaningful; the former are about the concept itself, in that they seek to explore what is even being requested in asking what makes a life meaningful. Essays in Section I of this anthology explore these relevant second-order questions.

A meaningful life: extant views

Beyond discussions over the nature of the question itself, one will find competing views on what gives our lives meaning, where by "meaning" something like meaningfulness is meant. That is to say, in virtue of what can life be said to be meaningful, if it all? The four primary competitors are: (1) supernaturalism, (2) objective naturalism, (3) subjective naturalism, and (4) nihilism.[37] Importantly, both objective and subjective naturalism can be categorized as *optimistic* naturalisms, in that these views allow for a meaningful existence in a world devoid of finite and infinite spiritual realities. *Pessimistic* naturalism is what is commonly called "nihilism." Nihilism is generally a view adopted alongside an entirely naturalistic ontology (though vigorous debate exits about whether naturalism entails nihilism), although there is nothing logically impossible with someone adopting nihilism while, at the same time, believing that God exists. It is important to remember that within each of these broad viewpoints one will find multiple theories that often differ substantially from one another. Though there are properties in virtue of which some subset of viewpoints on what makes a life meaningful can be categorized as, say, supernaturalist or objective naturalist, it is a mistake to think that all theories within a category are indistinguishable. My goal here is to provide a brief glimpse of the general properties that permit such categorization.

Supernaturalism

Roughly, supernaturalism maintains that God's existence, along with appropriately orienting one's life toward God, is both necessary and sufficient for securing a meaningful life, although different accounts can be given as to the nature of this relationship.[38] Among countless others, historical representatives of supernaturalism in the ancient Near Eastern world and in subsequent Western history are Qoheleth, Jesus, Paul, Augustine, Aquinas, Edwards, Pascal, Tolstoy, and C. S. Lewis. The supernaturalist position can be plausibly viewed as possessing three distinct yet related dimensions: metaphysical, epistemological, and relational-ethical. Metaphysically, it is argued that God's existence is necessary in order to ground a meaningful life because, for example, conditions necessary for securing a meaningful existence such as objective value are most plausibly anchored in an infinite, essentially good, and necessarily existent person as their ontological ground. In addition to the metaphysical dimension, supernaturalism often requires, at some level, *orthodoxy* (right belief) and *orthopraxy* (right practice), although much debate exists on the details. God's existence may be a necessary condition for securing a meaningful life, but it is generally thought that one must additionally relate to God in relevant ways in the epistemological and ethical dimensions; that is, knowing relevant true propositions about him, and obediently relating to him accordingly in a way consistent with robust knowledge *of a person* (which entails more than simply knowing true propositions about that person). Supernaturalism is summed up well in the now famous words of Augustine and Pascal. In his *Confessions*, Augustine mused, "you have made us for yourself, and our heart is restless until it rests in you."[39] Twelve centuries later, Pascal echoed Augustine:

> What else does this craving, and this helplessness, proclaim but that there was once in man a true happiness, of which all that now remains is the empty print and trace? This he tries in vain to fill with everything around him, seeking in things that are not there the help he cannot find in those that are, though none can help, since this infinite abyss can be filled only with an infinite and immutable object; in other words by God himself.[40]

The supernaturalist position represents, in the minds of many, a serious philosophical and existentially compelling option for securing a meaningful existence, and continues to have able defenders in the contemporary literature. Most of the essays in Section II of this anthology contain expositions and defenses of a supernaturalist viewpoint.

Objective naturalism

Objective naturalism, like supernaturalism, posits that a meaningful life is possible, but denies that the existence of a supernatural being is necessary, in any sense, for such a life. Life in a purely physical world, devoid of finite and infinite spiritual realities, is sufficient for meaning according to objective naturalism. Objective naturalists claim that a meaningful life is a function of appropriately connecting with mind-independent realities that are, contra supernaturalism, entirely natural. Objective naturalism is further distinguished (from subjective naturalism) by its emphasis on *mind independence*. One way of putting this point is to say that *wanting* or *choosing* is insufficient for a meaningful life. For example, choosing to spend one's waking hours counting and recounting blades of grass is likely insufficient for meaning on objective naturalism. Rather, meaning is a function of linking one's life to inherently valuable, mind-independent conditions that are not themselves the sole products of what one wants strongly and chooses (contra subjective naturalism). Put simply, on objective naturalism it is possible to be wrong about what confers meaning on life – something is meaningful, at least partly, in virtue of its intrinsic nature, irrespective of what is believed about it. This is why spending one's entire existence counting blades of grass or reading phone books is probably not meaningful on objective naturalism, even if the person strongly desires this. Experiencing subjective fulfillment alone is not sufficient for a meaningful life, though on hybrid views a subjective-fulfillment component would be necessary. Objective naturalism is an attractive position to numerous contemporary philosophers, as many conclude that the probability of traditional supernaturalist views being true is relatively low on grounds independent of the issue of life's meaning.

Subjective naturalism

Like objective naturalism, subjective naturalism posits that a meaningful life is possible apart from something like supernaturalism being true, but unlike objective naturalism, it differs on what confers meaning on life. According to subjective naturalism, what constitutes a meaningful life varies from person to person, and is a function of one getting what one strongly wants, or by achieving self-established goals, or through accomplishing what one believes to be really important. Caring about or loving something deeply has been thought by some to confer meaningfulness to life.[41] Subjectivism seems most plausible to some in light of perceived failures to ground objective value, either naturally, nonnaturally, or supernaturally.

A worry for subjective naturalism, however, is analogous to ethical worries over moral relativism. Many protest that surely deep care and love *simpliciter* are not sufficient to confer meaningfulness on life. What if someone claims to find meaning in life in counting blades of grass, or reading and rereading the phone book, or, worse, torturing people for fun? Can a life centering on such pursuits be a meaningful life?[42] Though some might think so, the strong, nearly universal intuition here toward objective value in some form inclines in the direction of requiring an objective standard that comes to bear on the meaningfulness of an activity or life in general.[43] Subjectivism still has its defenders, though, with some proposals moving toward grounding value *intersubjectively* – in community – as opposed to in the individual exclusively, and where communal norms would reliably mitigate the possibility of severely deviant activities from being meaningful.

Nuanced forms of naturalism, vis-à-vis meaningfulness in life, make room for both objective and subjective elements, as is captured nicely by Susan Wolf: "Meaning arises when subjective attraction meets objective attractiveness."[44] On such hybrid views, the objective and the subjective must unite to give birth to meaningfulness. Meaningfulness is not present in a life spent believing in, being satisfied by, or caring about worthless projects, but neither is it present in a life spent engaging in worthwhile projects without believing in, or caring about, or being satisfied by them, so the argument goes.

Though they disagree significantly on the conditions for meaningfulness, both objective and subjective naturalism are united in their rejection of supernaturalism, and supernaturalism's insistence that God is necessary in order to secure a meaningful life. In this way, both forms of naturalism can be thought of as optimistic naturalisms; that is, a meaningful life is possible in a godless universe. An optimistic naturalist sees no problem in thinking that a meaningful life can be secured within an entirely naturalistic ontology. The raw materials for meaningfulness are available apart from God. In his reflective essay "Religion and respect," Simon Blackburn expresses well the optimistic naturalist position:

> But there is another option for meaning [...] which is to look only within life itself. This is the immanent option. It is content with the everyday. There is sufficient meaning for human beings in the human world – the world of familiar, and even humdrum, doings and experiences. In the immanent option, the smile of the baby, the grace of the dancer, the sound of voices, the movement of a lover, give meaning to life. For some, it is activity and achievement: gaining the summit of the mountain, crossing the finish line first, finding the cure, or writing the poem. These things last only their short time, but that does not deny them meaning. A smile does not need to go on forever in order to mean what it does. There is nothing beyond or apart from the processes of life. Furthermore, there is no one goal to which all these processes tend, but we can find something precious, value and meaning, in the processes themselves. There is no such thing as *the* meaning of life, but there can be many meanings within a life [emphasis in original].[45]

According to an optimistic naturalist like Blackburn, nothing additional, nothing of the transcendent sort, is needed to ground those things in life that we, pre-philosophically, find to be meaningful. Supernaturalism sets the bar for a meaningful life too high, so the argument goes.

Pessimistic naturalism: nihilism

Against all views where a meaningful existence is thought to be possible is the view of pessimistic naturalism, more commonly called *nihilism*. Roughly, nihilism is the position that denies that a meaningful life is possible because, literally, nothing has any value. If no states of affairs or activities or entities have any value, then neither is life nor any of its parts valuable, and therefore it is very likely meaningless. One way to understand nihilism is by seeing it as the fusion of assumptions and theses drawn from both supernaturalism and naturalism. That is to say, nihilism may be seen as (1) requiring that God or some supernatural realm is likely necessary for value and a meaningful existence, but (2) asserting that no such entity or realm exists, and therefore (3) concluding that nothing is ultimately of value. Other forms of nihilism focus on states like boredom or satisfaction, arguing that boredom sufficiently infuses life so as to make it meaningless, or that human lives lack the requisite amount of satisfaction to confer meaning on them. Another form of nihilism that is logically compatible with the existence of God is one based on a disparity between standpoints. It has been argued that from the most distant, detached viewpoint, nothing we do seems to matter at all. If one thinks that it is possible to view even God and the economy of his workings from some more distant standpoint, then even supernaturalism may face a nihilistic threat of this form.

Death, futility, and a meaningful life

The meaning of life is closely linked with a cluster of related issues surrounding death, futility, and the way life is going to end, both individual lives and the universe as a whole. These are common threads in the meaning-of-life literature, from Ecclesiastes to Tolstoy to Camus to contemporary analytic philosophy. Death (and the end of the universe itself) has often been thought to bear a close relationship with futility. The common pessimistic claim is that *cosmic* futility supervenes on the entirety of human existence, given a naturalistic view of the ultimate fate of life, both human life as well as the universe itself, where death and entropy will likely have the last word.

Why is death in an exclusively naturalistic world thought by many to be a challenge to a meaningful life? One reason may be the widespread view that, *ceteris paribus*, meaningful things last, as in the slogan *diamonds are forever*. With respect to the meaning of life, most people judge various aspects of life, pre-philosophically, to be meaningful. When subsequently engaged in conscious reflection on the necessary conditions for meaningfulness, immortality is often thought to be a transcendental requirement.[46] Most people deeply desire consciousness, memory, personhood, creativity, achievement, and especially loving relationships, among others, to be part of the deep structure of reality, in that the universe, in the long run, makes space for these things – that "it" *cares*.[47] An exclusively naturalistic universe does not.[48] From the perspective of a universe that will very likely become unfavorable to the existence of intelligent life at some point in the distant future, nothing we do seems of any real consequence or value. Death, both our own and the universe's (speaking metaphorically, of course), is a profound barrier to the putatively meaningful properties and activities that populate human existence continuing in any robust sense. And so the threat of futility lingers for many who worry that we live in an exclusively naturalistic universe.

The kind of futility surfacing in this context can either be thought of as *strong futility* or *weak futility*. In the strong sense, it is claimed that if the final state of affairs of the universe (e.g., heat death) is one in which nothing matters, then nothing ever really mattered and everything is irredeemably futile. In the weaker sense, it is claimed that if the final state of affairs of the universe is one in which nothing matters, then the mattering or significance of current states of affairs is in some way mitigated, either minimally or considerably, though not completely destroyed. This futility partly arises, then, through an *asymmetry* between the vantage points of the lifeless, distant future that lacks consciousness of any sort, and the present, filled with conscious life and its various dimensions. A "bad" *ending* is thought to threaten the meaningfulness of the entire story.

Critics of these strong and weak futility claims counter by calling into question what can be called *the arbitrary privileging of the future*. They ask, "Why should the end state of affairs be given such veto power over the worth, significance, and meaning of the here and now?" Maybe the problem is with our normative conclusions about the universe and not the universe itself. In the words of C. S. Lewis, critics of such futility conclusions might contend that "instead of criticizing the universe we may criticize our own feelings about the universe, and try to show that our sense of futility is unreasonable or improper or irrelevant."[49]

It has been noted that the plausibility of appealing to such asymmetry between the future and the present by which to charge naturalism with irredeemable futility is contingent on a suspect assumption; namely, arbitrarily placing an undue amount of importance (perhaps all of the importance) on the final state of affairs to which life leads. But why give the future priority over the present and the past? If life is meaningful now, how can the fact that it will cease to exist at some point in the distant future make it less meaningful now? And, if life is not meaningful now, how could its unending continuation confer meaningfulness to it? Critics of such futility claims argue that the most plausible way to appraise the meaningfulness and worth of life *here and now* is by adopting the *here and now* perspective, not the distant, detached perspective of some indifferent future of a universe in ruins. Of course, one might make the converse claim: "Why privilege the present over the future?" Principled reasons must be offered that will help settle the question of which viewpoint – the *distant future* or the *immediate present* – takes normative priority for appraisals of life as either worthwhile or futile.[50]

The Future of the Discussion

Though the boundaries remain fuzzy, canonical lines of demarcation for the conceptual territory of life's meaning continue to emerge. While discussions of life's meaning are ancient from the perspective of human history or Western philosophical history, they are only in relative infancy if one narrows the focus to contemporary analytic philosophy. There is much work left to be done, and it may connect to progress in other areas of philosophy, including metaphysics, ethics, normative theory more broadly, and philosophy of religion, among others. Below are some areas in need of further exploration.

Within normative theory, one underexplored question is where the concept of *meaningfulness* fits within the normative realm shared by the ethical, aesthetic, and eudaimonistic. Meaning seems closely connected to these other normative categories, but reducible to none (though it is perhaps closest to the third). One can imagine ethical lives that are, for example, profoundly unsatisfying to the one who lives them. Even if the ethical is one component of the meaningful, it seems implausible to think that an apathetic yet morally exemplary life qualifies as fully meaningful, especially if one thinks that meaningfulness is at least partly a function of being subjectively attracted to objective attractiveness.[51] Meaningfulness extends beyond the ethical, while somehow including it. These same sorts of questions can be raised regarding the relationship between meaningfulness and other normative categories. Such questions are second-order questions about the very concept of meaningfulness, and not first-order normative ethical questions concerned with what, if anything, makes life meaningful.

In addition, and in cases where it shares conceptual space with normative territory, the debate between reductive naturalism (roughly, the view that normative properties are fully reducible to states of affairs or properties properly belonging to study within the provinces of biology, chemistry, and, specifically, physics) and nonreductive naturalism (roughly, the view that, while entirely natural, normative properties are not fully reducible to states of affairs or properties that exclusively belong to study within the provinces of biology, chemistry, and, specifically, physics) has direct implications for whether it can be plausibly thought that normative properties are part of the deep structure of reality on naturalism. If they are, then optimistic naturalism of the objective variety may gain the upper hand over subjective optimistic naturalism. So, progress in the debate between objective and subjective naturalism will track progress in discussions within metaphysics more generally (again, as it overlaps with normative theory).

Or consider the problem of evil in philosophy of religion. No doubt the experience of evil links to the meaning of life, especially when one considers death and futility. Quite apart from philosophical reflections on the problem, the experience of evil is often one of those generating conditions for the question of life's meaning born out of existential angst. Is there a rationally and existentially satisfying narrative in which to locate the experience of pain and suffering and to give the sufferer solace and hope? Evil in a *meaningful universe* would not, no doubt, cease from being evil, but it may be more bearable. In this way, the *problem of meaning* may be more foundational than the problem of evil. And one especially thinks of what we might call the *eschatological* dimension of the problem of evil: Is there any hope in the face of pain, suffering, and death, and, if so, what is its nature? Bringing future-oriented considerations of pain and suffering into the philosophical discussion will also naturally link to perennial meaning-of-life topics like death and futility. Additionally, it will motivate more vigorous research and debate over whether the inherent human desire for a felicitous ending to life's narrative, including, for example, post-mortem survival and enjoyment of the beatific vision or some other blessed state, is mere wishful thinking or a cousin to our desire for water, and, thus, a truly natural desire that points to a referent capable of fulfilling it. In any case, discussions over the problem of evil intersect with discussions over the meaning of life, and progress in one might mean progress in the other.

Finally, an underexplored area in contemporary analytic philosophy is how the concept of *narrative* might shed light on the meaning of life. One reason this is important can be seen in the following consideration. Historically, most of the satisfying narratives that in some way narrated the meaning of life were also religious or quasi-religious. Additionally, many of these narratives count as narratives in the paradigmatic sense as opposed to non-narrative modes of discourse. However, with the rise of modern science, both the narratives and the religious or quasi-religious worldviews embedded within them were diminished. This led to the anxious questioning of life's meaning and the fear that a thoroughly scientific-naturalistic narrative of the universe is far from existentially satisfying. This elicits the following important question: "Are such paradigmatic instances of narratives, which in some way narrate the meaning of life, thought to be more existentially satisfying in virtue of their explicitly religious perspective on the world, or in virtue of the fact that they are paradigmatic instances of narrative, or both?" In terms of an interdisciplinary approach, the work of cognitive scientists who are informing us that personal identity has a substantial narrative component may be of benefit here. Perhaps our deep human need to construct meaningful narratives in order to contextualize parts of our lives and our very lives themselves is genetically hardwired. More specifically, perhaps our existential need to locate our lives and the weighty elements that populate human life within grand narratives that are paradigmatic instances of narrative is genetically hardwired. If something like this is correct, then it may become clearer why questioning the meaning of life with such intensity and angst is correlated with the rise of a grand narrative (i.e., naturalism) that is not really a narrative in the paradigmatic sense.

Final Thoughts

Though many commentators consider the question of life's meaning to be the preeminent question of philosophy, it has received relatively little sustained reflection in the analytic philosophical world of the last century. This trend shows some signs of reversing, however. Many of the essays in this anthology are part of a growing and exciting discussion of life's meaning. The question is being approached with an analytic rigor that will hopefully illumine some of the assumptions motivating it and point in the direction of possible approaches for answering it.

This General Introduction concludes where it began: with the juxtaposition of two figures in twentieth-century philosophy who represent very different philosophical approaches, Camus and Russell. Do we side with Camus, who claimed that the meaning of life is the most urgent of all philosophical questions, or with Russell, who could say nothing when asked about the topic?[52] Maybe there is middle ground here: giving the question of life's meaning honest, sustained consideration, while proceeding with an analytic rigor that should illumine and perhaps revise many of the assumptions motivating the question in the first place. When it comes to life's meaning, yes, the philosophical waters are murky, but they are clearing. I hope that the 33 essays in this new anthology on the meaning of life will motivate continued discussion that will clear the waters even further.

Notes

1. Albert Camus (1991) *The Myth of Sisyphus and Other Essays*, New York: Vintage International, pp. 1–2.

2. As recounted in Julian Baggini (2005) *What's It All About? Philosophy and the Meaning of Life*, Oxford: Oxford University Press, p. 1.

3. "The moment a man questions the meaning and value of life, he is sick [...] By asking this question one is merely admitting to a store of unsatisfied libido to which something else must have happened, a kind of fermentation leading to sadness and depression." Letters to Marie Bonaparte of 13 August 1937; in *Letters of Sigmund Freud* (1960), ed. Ernst L. Freud, trans. T. and J. Stern, New York: Basic Books. Interestingly, Freud also reportedly said on multiple occasions that he "heartily abhorred philosophy." Letter of Siegfried Bernfeld to Ernest Jones, June 19, 1951 (Jones Archives).

4. Karl Britton (1969) *Philosophy and the Meaning of Life*, Cambridge: Cambridge University Press, p. 1.

5. Alan Lacey, "The meaning of life," in Ted Honderich (ed.) (2005) *The Oxford Companion to Philosophy*, 2nd edn., New York: Oxford University Press.

6. Robert Audi (ed.) (2001) *The Cambridge Dictionary of Philosophy*, 2nd edn., Cambridge: Cambridge University Press.

7. Susan Wolf (1998) "The meaning of life," in Edward Craig (ed.), *The Routledge Encyclopedia of Philosophy*, London: Routledge; Thaddeus Metz (2007) "The meaning of life," in Edward N. Zalta (ed.), *The Stanford Encyclopedia of Philosophy*, Summer 2007 edn., http://plato.stanford.edu/archives/sum2007/entries/life-meaning/. See also Joshua Seachris (2011) "Meaning of life: The analytic perspective," *The Internet Encyclopedia*

of Philosophy, http://www.iep.utm.edu/mean-ana/, July 6.

8. Garrett Thomson (2003) *On the Meaning of Life*, Belmont, CA: Thomson Wadsworth.

9. John Cottingham (2003) *On the Meaning of Life*, London: Routledge.

10. Julian Baggini (2005) *What's It All About?* Oxford: Oxford University Press.

11. Terry Eagleton (2007) *The Meaning of Life*, Oxford: Oxford University Press.

12. Susan Wolf (2010) *Meaning in Life and Why It Matters*, Princeton, NJ: Princeton University Press.

13. John Kekes (2010) *The Human Condition*, New York: Oxford University Press.

14. I do not intend here to devalue what I consider to be profound philosophical questions in the philosophy of mind and epistemology.

15. Alasdair Macintyre (2006) "The ends of life, the ends of philosophical writing," in his *The Tasks of Philosophy: Selected Essays*, vol. 1, Cambridge: Cambridge University Press, pp. 131–2.

16. I say "most," because not all of the essays contained in this volume are from the analytic philosophical tradition (e.g., *Ecclesiastes*).

17. Note, however, that *meaningfulness* is likely a gradient category such that one's life, or some particular time-slice of one's life, can be *more or less* meaningful. This still allows for one's life to be characterized as meaningful *on balance* if a certain threshold is reached, though determining this threshold may not be easy.

18. For a recent discussion of the question of life's meaning from the *cosmic* perspective, see Joshua Seachris (2009) "The meaning of life as narrative: A new proposal for interpreting philosophy's 'primary' question," *Philo* 12(Spring–Summer): 5–23. One will also find hints of this approach in Thomson (2003), pp. 132–3; Cottingham (2003), pp. 2, 9; John Wisdom (2000) "The meanings of the questions of life," in E. D. Klemke (ed.), *The Meaning of Life*, New York: Oxford University Press, p. 259; and Julian Young (2005) *The Death of God and the Meaning of Life*, London: Routledge, p. 1.

19. Such worries seem to presuppose what Ronald Dworkin calls the "model of impact," which is a metric of the good life that requires a person to make a positive impact to the objective value in the world in order to secure a good life. See Ronald Dworkin (2001) *Sovereign Virtue*, Cambridge, MA: Harvard University Press, Chapter 6.

20. There is debate about the most plausible date for the final composition of Ecclesiastes. For a scholarly discussion of this and other important issues of prolegomena for the book, see especially Craig G. Bartholomew (2009) "Introduction", in *Ecclesiastes* (Baker Commentary on the Old Testament Wisdom and Psalms), Grand Rapids, MI: Baker Academic, pp. 17–100, and Tremper Longman (1997) "Introduction," in *The Book of Ecclesiastes* (New International Commentary on the Old Testament), Grand Rapids, MI: William B. Eerdmans, pp. 1–56.

21. Of course, one must be cautious about the danger of anachronism, reading back into the text existentialist categories and questions that are subtly different from those of Qohelet.

22. *Metaphysics* 982b 12–13, in Richard McKeon (ed.) (1970) *The Basic Works of Aristotle*, trans. W. D. Ross, New York: Random House, p. 692.

23. *Theaetetus* 155d, in John M. Cooper (ed.) (1977) *Plato: The Complete Works*, trans. M. J. Levett, rev. Myles Burnyeat, Indianapolis, IN: Hackett Publishing Company, p. 173.

24. Young (2005), p. 1. A "true-world narrative" is not confined to traditional monotheistic or eastern religions. Young's first example of a true-world narrative is that offered by Plato.

25. Young (2005).

26. However, Qohelet's inquiry into meaning-of-life issues is born out of something akin to existential angst, and he "lived" in the ancient world.

27. Rollo May makes a similar point: "A myth is a way of making sense in a senseless world. Myths are narrative patterns that give significance to our existence [...] Myths are like the beams in a house [...] they are the structure which holds the house together so people can live in it [...] We in the twentieth century are in a [s]ituation of 'aching hearts' and 'repining.' Our myths no longer serve their function of making sense of existence, the citizens of our day are left without direction or purpose in life, and people are at a loss to control their anxiety and excessive guilt feeling." Rollo May (1991) *The Cry for Myth*, New York: Norton, pp. 15–16.

28. There are numerous nonlinguistic contexts in which we naturally and plausibly employ the term "meaning." For example, we often use the locution "What is the meaning of *x*?" when we are puzzled by, say, someone's nonlinguistic behavior. Perhaps a friend *makes a face* at

us, and we are not sure what such a face signifies. In this situation, we may ask her: "What did you *mean* by looking at me that way?" Here, we are trying to ascertain the relevant intentions responsible for producing the configuration of facial muscles, or, in other words, what the face is supposed to signify. The locution "What is the meaning of *x*?" is also plausibly employed in contexts involving *natural signs*, or what Fred Dretske has referred to as "indication" or "indicator meaning." See Fred Dretske (1988) *Explaining Behavior*, Cambridge, MA: MIT Press, pp. 54 ff. Dretske himself credits H. P. Grice for this sense of meaning. Grice's seminal discussion can be found in H. P. Grice (1957) "Meaning," *The Philosophical Review* 66(July): 377–88. Roughly, a natural sign is one whose presence is causally or nomically correlated with the presence of a second event or state of affairs, a state of affairs whose occurrence is not the result of any sort of intentional agency. If one finds the language of causality or some sort of nomic category to be too strong in referring to this relationship, one might take a Humean approach and explain natural signs in terms of regular association or constant conjunction. Regardless of how one understands the relationship between the sign and a second state of affairs to which it "points," nature is full of such signs. Importantly, they may be spoken of in terms of meaning. For example, we can plausibly say that the presence of radiant leaves *means* (nonintentionally signifies) that winter is on its way or that the presence of rain clouds *means* that rain is coming. Another way the locution "What is the meaning of *x*?" may be used is in contexts where we want to know what, for example, an author or poet or playwright *meant* by her book, poem, or production. We may have read all the words or listened to all the lines from beginning to end and yet are puzzled, and so ask what the whole thing *means*. Here, we want to grasp the character or significance of the work that, for whatever reason, still eludes our understanding. We desire a unifying construct, theme(s), or something of this nature that brings coherence and intelligibility to the constituent parts.

29. N. T. Wright (2003) *The Resurrection of the Son of God*, vol. 3, Christian Origins and the Question of God, Minneapolis: Fortress Press, p. 719.

30. Wright (2003), p. 720.

31. Some may think the stronger term "determine" is better than "discover." We need not engage here in debates over the hermeneutical properties of a worldview.

32. Wright (2003), p. 720.

33. See Hepburn's essay in Section I of this anthology. See also Baggini (2005), p. 1, and Thaddeus Metz (2007) "New developments in the meaning of life," *Philosophy Compass* 2(2): 211.

34. One worry with this approach, however, is that these questions are specifically about, for example, purpose and value and worth rather than about the meaning of life.

35. For more on this distinction, see the subsection of this General Introduction titled "The challenge," pp. 3–4.

36. See p. 23.

37. Other views exist, but are less prevalent, for example intersubjectivism and nonnaturalism. However, Robert Audi's essay in Section IV of this anthology ("Intrinsic value and meaningful life") can be placed in the nonnaturalist category, whereby meaning in life is constituted by properties that are neither natural nor spiritual.

38. In addition to these *God-based* theories, there are *soul-based* theories, where meaning in life is thought to be a function, not so much of God, but rather of having an indestructible soul whereby immortality is possible. There are debates about what conditions need to be met in order for immortality to be possible and whether immortality is a possibility even on an exclusively materialist ontology. There are also debates about whether immortality would even be desirable. Perhaps immortality is neither a necessary nor sufficient condition for meaning. According to some commentators, it may even be a sufficient condition for *meaninglessness*. One thinks here of Bernard Williams's famous essay "The Makropulos case: Reflections on the tedium of immortality," in Bernard Williams (1973) *Problems of the Self: Philosophical Papers, 1956–1972*, Cambridge: Cambridge University Press, pp. 82–100.

39. St. Augustine (1998) *Confessions*, trans. Henry Chadwick, Oxford: Oxford University Press, p. 3.

40. Blaise Pascal (1995) *Pensées*, trans. A. J. Krailsheimer, London: Penguin Books, p. 45.

41. See Harry Frankfurt (1988) "The importance of what we care about," in *The Importance of What We Care About*, New York: Cambridge University Press, pp. 80–94.

42. For a recent discussion of this question, see Iddo Landau (2011) "Immorality and the meaning of life," *Journal of Value Inquiry* 45(November): 309–17.

43. Of course, some subjectivists might respond by noting that one can lead a meaningful, *yet morally blameworthy* life.

44. Susan Wolf (1997) "Happiness and meaning: Two aspects of the good life," *Social Philosophy and Policy* 14(Winter): 211.

45. Simon Blackburn (2007) "Religion and respect," in Louise M. Antony (ed.), *Philosophers Without Gods: Meditations on Atheism and the Secular Life*, Oxford: Oxford University Press, p. 190.

46. Immortality is not, however, generally considered to be sufficient for a meaningful life in light of putative counter-examples to a given instance of unending life being meaningful. For example, consider a case where the last-existing human being in the universe has two pills, one that will end his life, and one that will prolong it for ever. The prudent decision seems clear to this person – living for ever in a state devoid of all contact with any other human beings is highly undesirable. After carefully weighing the options, he swallows what he thinks is the pill that will end his life, only to discover, to his horror, that he has swallowed the pill that has, instead, brought him immortality. He will now live for ever, completely *alone*. To many commentators, this is clearly a case where an immortal life lacks the property of meaningfulness, especially if meaningfulness is thought to require, among other things, that life be satisfying. For a fuller version of this story, see William Lane Craig's essay in Section II of this anthology.

47. These are not merely surface desires, but profound desires anchored in the core of our being, perhaps every bit as strong as our desire, indeed our *need*, for water.

48. Although it must be admitted that immortality is not logically impossible in an exclusively naturalistic universe. However, attempting to secure personal immortality within a naturalistic ontology is tenuous at best.

49. C. S. Lewis (1995) *De Futilitate* in *Christian Reflections*, Grand Rapids, MI: Eerdmans, p. 59. See also Ronald Dworkin's discussion of the model of challenge metric of the good life as a criticism of strong and weak futility claims: Dworkin (2001), Chapter 6.

50. My suspicion is that deciding which viewpoint is more salient in normative appraisals of the meaningfulness, significance, value, and worth of life is not a simple *either/or* matter.

51. Cf. footnote 17.

52. This is not entirely true, because one of Russell's own pieces is included in this anthology, though he may not have taken himself to be answering the question "What is the meaning of life?" as he understood it.

Section I

Understanding the Question of Life's Meaning

Introduction

Thaddeus Metz

If you are reading this book, then you are probably interested in answering the question of what (if anything) makes life meaningful. You no doubt have *some* sense of what this question means, having elected to read this book instead of one about some other value such as justice or virtue. However, there are two reasons why a reader should want to become *extremely clear and precise* about what is being asked when posing the question of life's meaning. First, doing so would be useful; differentiating inquiry into the meaning of life from related sorts of intellectual investigation should help to prevent conflation and to ensure that interlocutors are debating the same thing, rather than speaking past one another. Second, those with a developed philosophical sensibility might want to know for its own sake what talk of "meaning" means. Some will find it intrinsically interesting to specify what the difference is between asking about what makes life meaningful, on the one hand, and about what makes life sacred or worthwhile (for example), on the other.

The contributions to this section take up this abstract, "second-order," or "meta-ethical" issue. Instead of principally seeking to answer the "first-order" or "normative ethical" question of in virtue of what (if anything) life is or can be meaningful, as many of the essays in the other sections do, the present texts are *about* this question, in that they seek to explicate what posing it essentially involves. Articulating the sense of the question of life's meaning is much more than merely pointing out its synonyms; it is not sufficiently revealing to be told that talk of "life's meaning" is equivalent to talk of "a significant existence." These phrases indeed connote the same thing, but one naturally wonders what they both connote. After working through the essays in this section, the reader can expect to acquire a firm grasp of what professional philosophers are talking about when they theorize about the meaning of life.

More carefully, the reader can expect to become familiar with *different views* about what theorists have in mind when inquiring into life's meaning. Just as there is substantial

Exploring the Meaning of Life: An Anthology and Guide, First Edition. Edited by Joshua W. Seachris.
© 2013 John Wiley & Sons, Inc. Published 2013 by John Wiley & Sons, Inc.

controversy in other fields of philosophy, so there is about the philosophical issue of how talk of "meaning" essentially differs from talk of other goods in life. In the rest of this Introduction, I lay out and critically discuss some of the divergent perspectives on this topic that philosophers working in the Anglo-American tradition have taken over the past 50 years.

Some philosophers maintain that the question of life's meaning is primarily a "holistic" one, asking something about the universe or about the human race as a species, while others deem it to be much more "individualist," that is, about one of us. In his contribution, Paul Edwards is naturally read as addressing the former approach to meaning talk when he discusses what people have in mind when posing what he calls the two major "cosmic why-questions": "Why are we here?" and "Why is there something rather than nothing?"

According to Edwards, asking what the point of human life is or why the human race exists normally invites a theological answer, one appealing to a creator who intentionally brought us about, either through a long process of natural selection or by intelligent design. Edwards points out that it is natural to ask the further question of why this creator exists, which in turn prompts the "super-ultimate" question of why anything exists.

Edwards contends that this latter question, which may also be expressed by asking "What is the point of it all?" or "Does everything have a meaning?," is "devoid of sense" or "meaningless." A sensible or meaningful question is one that in principle admits of an answer, and Edwards maintains that the super-ultimate why-question does not; when one asks for an explanation of why everything exists, no answer is conceivably possible, as there is nothing beyond everything that could account for it.

It is worth wondering whether Edwards is correct to claim that the super-ultimate why-question is nonsensical. Even if he turned out to be correct about that, note that comparatively little of the field of life's meaning would be undercut. A large majority of work that describes itself as being about "the meaning of life" does not seek to explain why there is something rather than nothing, a question that is not straightforwardly understood to be evaluative. Instead, most of the field has been aiming to account theoretically for a salient respect in which our lives can be valuable.

Now, there are ways of interpreting the question of life's meaning as being both cosmic (about a whole) and evaluative (about something desirable), but, as Joshua Seachris notes in his General Introduction, this is an undertheorized approach, one that I agree warrants more reflection.[1] For the most part, when the field has construed the question of life's meaning to be about something we should want to exist, it has deemed the primary sense of the question to be individualist; that is, to be about whether, and if so how, one of our lives can acquire a certain kind of desirability. All the remaining contributions to this section interpret the question of life's meaning in this way.

One way to distinguish the evaluative-individualist construals of the question of life's meaning is with regard to whether they are simple or complex. The most simple analysis of the question invokes a single property to spell it out, while a more complex analysis appeals to many properties. R. W. Hepburn and Robert Nozick tend toward simple analyses,

---

[1]   See also Joshua Seachris (2009) "The meaning of life as narrative: A new proposal for interpreting philosophy's 'primary' question," *Philo* 12: 5–23.

suggesting that talk of "life's meaning' is about one or two features that our lives can exhibit, while Arjan Markus, Garrett Thomson, and I maintain that such talk is about at least three distinguishable conditions.

Hepburn maintains that asking whether life is meaningful is just a matter of asking whether a person has achieved worthwhile goals in a way that is satisfying to her.[2] To inquire into how life can be meaningful, on his view, is to investigate which ends not only merit pursuit in life, but also would energize or otherwise interest a given individual.

One problem with this view is that it would be *logically impossible* for a depressed person to have a meaningful life. Hepburn's analysis implies that Vincent van Gogh, at least in our stereotypical understanding of him, *by definition could not* have had a meaningful life, which seems counterintuitive; after all, many believe that van Gogh actually did have a meaningful life, in virtue of the great works of art he created and their posthumous reception.

On Hepburn's behalf, one might suggest dropping the idea that meaning-talk is in part essentially about what makes a person feel satisfied. Perhaps asking whether life is meaningful is merely asking whether a person has achieved worthwhile goals. However, that analysis is arguably much too broad, as I contend in my essay. Consider these goals: scratching an itch, rearing a child with love and insight, waiting in a queue to deposit money in the bank, eating ice cream, acquiring an education, staying alive. All of these goals are worth pursuing, but not all of them are *prima facie* candidates for conferring meaning on one's life.

Nozick is also naturally read as providing a simple analysis of the question of life's meaning. For him, meaning-talk essentially connotes the idea of one's exhibiting a relationship to something valuable beyond oneself. To ask whether life is meaningful, for Nozick, is basically to ask whether a person is connected in certain ways to something greater than herself. Insofar as Hepburn is correct that to inquire into the meaning of a person's life is to investigate the purposes that she ought to pursue (or, in Nozick's terms, the "life-plan" that she ought to adopt), Nozick would suggest that the relevant ends are those that involve self-transcendence.

Nozick's account of what theorists have in mind when investigating the meaningfulness of life has been the most influential.[3] The idea of positively relating to something valuable apart from one's person does appear to capture a large part of what (at least) philosophers mean by "meaning in life" and cognate phrases. However, one might reasonably wonder whether it captures all of what they have in mind. As I contend in my essay, Nozick's analysis rules out, *by definition*, the possibility of certain internal states conferring meaning on life. Those friendly to Aristotle have thought that virtues such as courage and integrity would make one's existence significant; those who like Kant have believed that performing right acts because they are right at least partly constitutes one's final purpose; and those who appreciate Hume have maintained that fulfilling one's strongest desires is what gives one sufficient reason to live (and to die). If Nozick's account of meaning-talk were correct, then,

---

[2]   For a recent, sophisticated advancement of this view, see Susan Wolf (1997) "Happiness and meaning: Two aspects of the good life," *Social Philosophy and Policy* 14: 207–25.

[3]   For some clear followers, see, e.g., David Cooper (2005) "Life and meaning," *Ratio* 18: 125–37; Neil Levy (2005) "Downshifting and meaning in life," *Ratio* 18: 176–89; Joe Mintoff (2008) "Transcending absurdity," *Ratio* 21: 64–84.

oddly, these views *could not be about* the meaning of life (a much more contentious claim than that they are *false* views about the meaning of life).

Impressed by the persistence of counterexamples to promising monistic analyses, in my essay I ultimately conclude that the field is unlikely to be able to specify necessary and sufficient conditions for the question of life's meaning. That is, I argue that we probably cannot point to one property, or even a handful of them, that captures all and only theories of life's meaning. Instead, when we ask about the meaning of life, I suggest that we are asking about a cluster of ideas that are similar to one another, overlap with one another, and do not admit of a bright line between them and ideas related to other value-theoretic categories such as excellence, well-being, morality, and the like. So, I maintain that to ask about meaning is to pose questions such as what is worth pursuing beyond one's own pleasure, how to transcend one's animal nature, and what merits great esteem or admiration. I do not say that these are the only questions that are involved, leaving space open for still more that might be found to capture salient facets of self-described theoretical debate about meaning. And I do not deny that these questions are germane to other, related sorts of inquiry into valuable aspects of life. Such an account of the concept of life's meaning is sometimes called a "family resemblance" view.[4]

Some, including Thomson and Markus, would maintain that I have given up the attempt to articulate and demarcate precisely the content of meaning-talk too soon. They reject simple analyses of the sort proffered by Hepburn and Nozick, but they also, unlike me, think that the concept of meaning has a complex essence that is specifiable. Thomson and Markus, then, are "in between" the theorists canvassed so far, in maintaining that when we use words such as "meaningful" or "significant" and the like, we are connoting a specific number of ideas. Thomson believes that "meaningful" and cognate terms are associated solely with ideas of the degree to which a life: achieves some purpose, contains value, is intelligible; and Markus maintains that they are just about the extent to which a life: is purposive, is worth living, has parts that cohere in some way. I take the three recurrent themes here to be *purpose, value, pattern*.

Neither Thomson nor Markus is particularly clear about whether he believes that, to be speaking about meaning in life, one must be discussing *all* three properties at the same time or merely *at least one* of them. It is worth considering both readings; namely, whether either version is plausible. Concerns about narrowness arise if Thomson and Markus are read as maintaining that to ask about meaning in life is just to ask whether a life has purpose, value, *and* pattern. Imagine a person who did a lot of good for humanity, but whose life were chaotic and failed to admit of a readable biography. Would meaning be utterly absent? Conversely, concerns about broadness arise if Thomson and Markus are read as believing that asking about life's meaning is equivalent to asking whether a life has purpose, value, *or* pattern. Imagine a person whose life made sense and could be narrated in a compelling way, but did not achieve this by virtue of adopting choice-worthy goals; suppose her life had been completely manipulated by another agent (hypothetically, by a mad scientist

---

[4]   For a similar perspective, which emphasizes the "persistent vagueness" and "polyvalence" of the question of life's meaning, see Timothy Mawson, "Sources of dissatisfaction with answers to the question of the meaning of life," *European Journal for the Philosophy of Religion* 2 (2010): 19–41.

determining her neural states by remote control), or that her life story had obtained purely because of luck. Would some meaning necessarily be present?

I do not answer these questions here, but leave them open for the reader to consider. Is there a way to interpret the pluralist view of Thomson and Markus that explicitly accounts for all and only meaning-talk? Or might it still be worth trying to find a defensible monistic view? In particular, is there a way to interpret Nozick's relational account that can avoid counterexamples? Or what about the suggestion, underexplored here, that asking about what (if anything) makes life meaningful is asking about which facets of life (if any) merit certain responses such as esteem, admiration, awe, devotion, unconditional commitment, and the like?[5] Finally, has a family resemblance model best captured talk about values beyond the sphere of life's meaning, suggesting that it, by analogy or generalization, would be suitable there as well?

The lack of consensus in the field about these issues means that readers have much to think about for themselves and that they have a real opportunity to come up with fresh ideas that would advance the literature. Although it would be worth obtaining an even firmer grasp than is currently available of how to understand the question of life's meaning, I conclude by pointing out that readers could also, on becoming acquainted with the texts included in this section, sensibly move on to more substantive issues, which the other sections of this book address. What the field does, by and large, agree on is that most of the literature on life's meaning is about a facet of a human person's life that is desirable for its own sake, where this final value is at least to some large degree analytically captured by considerations of choice-worthy goals, self-transcendence, life stories, and related properties. Although that construal of the question of life's meaning is vague in some respects, I submit that it is clear and precise enough both to explain why readers chose to pick up this book rather than one about some other value, and to enable them to understand what the contributions to this book are about.

Suggestions for Further Reading

Baggini, Julian (2005) *What's It All About? Philosophy and the Meaning of Life*, Oxford: Oxford University Press.

Baier, Kurt (1997) *Problems of Life and Death: A Humanist Perspective*, Amherst, NY: Prometheus.

Benatar, David (ed.) (2010) *Life, Death, and Meaning: Key Philosophical Readings on the Big Questions*, Lanham, MA: Rowman and Littlefield.

Cooper, David E. (2003) "The meaning of life," in David E. Cooper (ed.), *Meaning*. Chesham: Acumen.

Cottingham, John (2003) *On the Meaning of Life*, London: Routledge.

Klemke, E. D., and Steven M. Cahn (eds.) (2008) *The Meaning of Life: A Reader*, New York: Oxford University Press.

Lacey, Alan (2005) "The meaning of life," in Ted Honderich (ed.), *The Oxford Companion to Philosophy*, 2nd edn., New York: Oxford University Press.

Landau, Iddo (1997) "Why has the question of the meaning of life arisen in the last two and a half centuries?" *Philosophy Today* 41(Summer): 263–9.

Landau, Iddo (2011) "Immorality and the meaning of life," *Journal of Value Inquiry* 45(November): 309–17.

Levy, Neil (2005) "Downshifting and meaning in life," *Ratio* 18(June): 176–89.

---

[5]   I take up this view briefly in my contribution, but it was first spelled out with care in Charles Taylor (1989) *Sources of the Self: The Making of the Modern Identity*, Cambridge, MA: Harvard University Press, pp. 3–90. For a very recent proponent, see Antti Kauppinen (forthcoming) "Meaningfulness and time," *Philosophy and Phenomenological Research* (DOI: 10.1111/j.1933-1592.2010.00490.x): 8–11.

Lurie, Yuval (2006) *Tracking the Meaning of Life: A Philosophical Journey*, Columbia, MO: University of Missouri Press.

Mawson, Timothy J. (2010) "Sources of dissatisfaction with answers to the question of the meaning of life," *European Journal for Philosophy of Religion* 2(Autumn): 19–41.

Metz, Thaddeus (2002) "Recent work on the meaning of life," *Ethics* 112(July): 781–814.

Metz, Thaddeus (2007) "The meaning of life," in Edward N. Zalta (ed.), *The Stanford Encyclopedia of Philosophy (Summer 2007 Edition)*, http://plato.stanford.edu/archives/sum2007/entries/life-meaning/.

Metz, Thaddeus (2009) "Happiness and meaningfulness: Some key differences," in Lisa Bortolotti (ed.), *Philosophy and Happiness*, London: Palgrave Macmillan, pp. 3–20.

Munitz, Milton K. (1993) *Does Life Have a Meaning?* Buffalo, NY: Prometheus Books.

Nielsen, Kai (2008) "Linguistic philosophy and 'the meaning of life,'" in E. D. Klemke and Steven M. Cahn (eds.), *The Meaning of Life*, New York: Oxford University Press, pp. 203–19.

Oakley, Tim (2010) "The issue is meaninglessness," *The Monist* 93(January): 106–22.

Perrett, Roy W. (2010) "Ineffability, signification and the meaning of life," *Philosophical Papers* 39(July): 239–55.

Rescher, Nicholas (1990) "The meaning of life," in *Human Interests: Reflections on Philosophical Anthropology*, Stanford: Stanford University Press, pp. 151–65.

Runzo, Joseph, and Nancy M. Martin (eds.) (2000) *The Meaning of Life in the World Religions*, Oxford: Oneworld Publications.

Seachris, Joshua (2009) "The meaning of life as narrative: A new proposal for interpreting philosophy's 'primary' question," *Philo* 12(Spring–Summer): 5–23.

Seachris, Joshua (2011) "Meaning of life: The analytic perspective," in *Internet Encyclopedia of Philosophy*, http://www.iep.utm.edu/mean-ana/, August 15.

Singer, Irving (1996) "The meaning of life: Rephrasing questions," in *Meaning in Life*, vol. 1, The Creation of Value, Baltimore: Johns Hopkins University Press, pp. 17–47.

Taylor, Charles (1990) *Sources of the Self*, Cambridge, MA: Harvard University Press.

Thomson, Garret (2003) *On the Meaning of Life*, South Melbourne: Wadsworth.

Wolf, Susan (1998) "The meaning of life," in Edward Craig (ed.), *The Routledge Encyclopedia of Philosophy*, London: Routledge.

1.1

Why

Paul Edwards

Lack of clarity about the uses of the word "why" is responsible for confusion on a number of philosophical fronts. In this article we shall confine ourselves to two groups of topics where greater attention to the proper and improper behavior of this word might well have avoided the adoption of misguided theories. There is, first, the contrast, or the alleged contrast, between the "how" and the "why" and the view, shared by writers of very different backgrounds, that science can deal only with how-questions. Second, there are certain "ultimate" or "cosmic" questions, such as "Why do we exist?" or, more radically, "Why does the world exist?" or "Why is there something rather than nothing?" Some, like Schopenhauer and Julian Huxley, regard these questions as unanswerable; others, like Gilson and Copleston, believe that they can be answered; but whether these questions can be answered or not, it seems to be widely agreed that they are very "deep." These questions, in the words of the British astro-physicist A. C. B. Lovell, raise problems "which can tear the individual's mind asunder" (*The Individual and the Universe*, New York, 1961, p. 125). Speaking of the question "Why is there something rather than nothing?," Heidegger first remarks that it is "the fundamental question of metaphysics" and later adds that "with this question philosophy began and with this question it will end, provided that it ends in greatness and not in an impotent decline" (*An Introduction to Metaphysics*, p. 20).

How and Why

The contrast between the how and the why has been insisted on for two rather different reasons. Some writers have done so in the interest of religion or metaphysics. Their position

Paul Edwards (1972) "Why," in Paul Edwards (ed.), *The Encyclopedia of Philosophy*, vols. 7&8, New York: Macmillan Publishing Company, pp. 296–302.

seems to be that while science and empirical research generally are competent to deal with how-questions, the very different and much deeper why-questions are properly the concern of religion or metaphysics or both. Thus, in a widely read book the British psychiatrist David Stafford-Clark insists that the confusion between the how and the why is the "fundamental fallacy" behind "the whole idea that science and religion are really in conflict at all" (*Psychiatry Today*, Harmondsworth, England, 1952, p. 282). Freud in particular is accused of committing this fallacy in his antireligious writings. Stafford-Clark is not at all opposed to Freudian theory so long as it confines itself to the how of psychological phenomena. Psychoanalysis cannot, however, "begin by itself to answer a single question as to why man is so constructed that they should happen in this way" (*ibid.*, p. 287). Although he repeatedly expresses his own fervent belief in God, Stafford-Clark unfortunately does not tell us how religion answers the question why man is "constructed" the way he is. Perhaps he would answer it along the lines in which Newton answered a similar question about the sun. "Why is there one body in our system qualified to give light and heat to all the rest," Newton wrote in his first letter to Richard Bentley, "I know no reason, but because the author of the system thought it convenient" (*Opera*, London, 1779–85, Vol. IV, pp. 429 ff.).

Similar views are found in the writings of many professional philosophers. Thus, writing of Newton's work on gravitation, Whitehead observes that "he [Newton] made a magnificent beginning by isolating the stresses indicated by his law of gravitation." But Newton "left no hint, why in the nature of things there should be any stresses at all" (*Modes of Thought*, New York and Cambridge, 1938, pp. 183–4). Similarly, discussing the limitations of science, Gilson declares that "scientists never ask themselves *why* things happen, but *how* they happen. … Why anything at all is, or exists, science knows not, precisely because it cannot even ask the question" (*God and Philosophy*, New Haven, 1959, p. 140). For Gilson the two topics mentioned at the beginning of this article appear to merge into one. The why of particular phenomena, he seems to argue, cannot be determined unless we answer the question "why this world, taken together with its laws … is or exists" (*ibid.*, p. 72).

Among those who have asserted that science can only deal with how-questions there are some who are not at all friendly to metaphysics or religion. These writers usually add to their remarks that science cannot handle why-questions the comment that no other enterprise fares any better. This "agnostic positivism," as we may call it, goes at least as far back as Hume. We know, he writes, that milk and bread are proper nourishment for men and not for lions or tigers, but we cannot "give the ultimate reason why" this should be so (*An Inquiry Concerning Human Understanding*, Sec. IV, Part I). Hume seems to imply that this unhappy state can never be remedied, regardless of the advances of physiology or any other science. Several writers in the second half of the nineteenth century advanced this position under the slogan "The task of science is to describe phenomena, not to explain them." Ernst Mach, Gustav Kirchhoff, and Joseph Petzoldt were among the best-known figures in central Europe who advocated this view. In England, Karl Pearson, its most influential exponent, conceded that there was no harm in speaking of "scientific explanations" so long as "explanation" is used "in the sense of the descriptive-*how*" (*The Grammar of Science*, Everyman edition, 1937, p. 97). We can indeed "describe how a stone falls to the earth, but not why it does" (*ibid.*, p. 103). "No one knows why two ultimate particles influence each other's motion. Even if gravitation be analyzed and described by the motion of some simpler particle or ether-element, the whole will still be a description, and not an explanation, of motion. Science would still have to content itself with recording the *how*." No matter how far physics may progress, the why will "remain a mystery" (*ibid.*, p. 105).

It is important to disentangle purely verbal from substantive issues in all of this. Insofar as the various writers we have quoted merely wish to assert that causal statements and scientific laws in general are contingent and not logically necessary propositions, little exception could be taken to their remarks. However, they are, or at least they appear to be, saying a great deal more. They all seem to agree that there is a class of meaningful questions, naturally and properly introduced by the word "why" in one of its senses, which cannot be answered by the use of empirical methods. Writers belonging to the first group claim that the answers can be obtained elsewhere. The agnostic positivists maintain that human beings cannot obtain the answers at all.

It is this substantive issue which we shall discuss here, and it is necessary to point out that there are numerous confusions in all views of this kind. To begin with, although this is the least important observation, "how" and "why" do not always have contrasting functions but are in certain situations used to ask the very same questions. Thus, when we know or believe that a phenomenon, *A*, is the cause of another phenomenon, *X*, but at the same time are ignorant of the "mechanics" of *A*'s causation of *X*, we indifferently use "how" and "why." We know, for example, that certain drugs cure certain diseases, but our knowledge is in a medical sense "purely empirical." Here we would be equally prepared to say that we do not know "why" the drug produces the cure and that we do not know "how" it does this. Or, to take a somewhat different case, it is widely believed that cigarette smoking is causally connected with lung cancer. It is also known that sometimes two people smoke the same amount and yet one of them develops lung cancer while the other one does not. In such a case the question naturally arises why cigarette smoking, if it is indeed the cause at all, leads to cancer in one case but not in the other. And we would be just as ready to express our ignorance or puzzlement by saying that we do not know how it is as by saying that we do not know why it is that smoking produced cancer in the first man but not in the second. In all such cases it is clear that science *is* in principle competent to deal with the "why" no less than with the "how," if only because they are used to ask the very same questions.

It is undeniable, however, that in certain contexts "how" and "why" are used to ask different questions. This contrast is most obvious when we deal with intentional, or more generally with "meaningful," human actions. What seems far from obvious, what in fact seems plainly false, is that empirical methods are not in principle adequate to determine the answers to why-questions in these contexts. Let us take as our example the recent in 1964 theft of the Star of India sapphire and other gems from the Museum of Natural History in New York. We can here certainly distinguish the question why the burglary was committed from the question how it was carried out. The latter question would concern itself with the details of the act – how the thieves got into the building, how they immobilized the alarm system, how they avoided the guards, and so on. The why-question, by contrast, would inquire into the aim or purpose of the theft – were the thieves just out to make a vast amount of money, or were there perhaps some other aims involved, such as proving to rival gangs how skillful they were or showing the incompetence of the police force? Now, the aim or purpose of a human being is surely not in principle undiscoverable, and frequently we know quite well what it is.

The person himself usually, though not always, simply knows what his aim is. An orator, for example, who is advocating a certain policy, ostensibly because it is "for the good of the country," may at the same time know perfectly well that his real aim is personal advancement. It used to be said that in such situations a human being knows his own purpose by means of "introspection," where introspection was conceived of as a kind of "inner sense." This way of talking is not inappropriate to situations in which somebody is confused about his own motives, for then special attention to his own feelings, resembling in some ways the effort to discriminate the detailed features of a physical scene, may well be necessary in order to ascertain his "true" aims. Much more commonly, however, a human being simply knows what his aims are, and it would be much better to say that he knows this "without observation" than that he knows it by introspection. In order to find out the purpose of somebody else's action, it is in countless instances sufficient to ask the person a direct question about his aim. Where the agent's veracity is suspect or where a person is the victim of self-deception, it is necessary to resort to more elaborate investigations. In the former type of case one might ask the agent all kinds of other questions (that is, questions not directly about the purpose of his action), one might interview his friends and acquaintances and other witnesses of his conduct, one might tap his telephone and employ assorted bugging devices, and one might perhaps go so far as to question him after the administration of "truth" drugs. In the latter type of case it may not be possible to ascertain the real purpose unless the person undertakes psychiatric treatment. While the practical difficulties in the way of discovering the purpose of an action are no doubt insurmountable in many cases of both these types, empirical procedures are clearly in principle adequate to this task.

We also contrast how- and why-questions when the latter are not inquiries into the purpose of any agent. Here, however, "how" has a different meaning from any previously discussed. In all examples so far considered, how-questions were in one way or another *causal* questions – "How did the thieves carry out their plan of stealing the Star of India?" is a question about the means of achieving a certain goal, and "How is it that smoking produces cancer in one man but not in another?," although not a question about means, is nevertheless about the processes leading to a certain result. These causal "hows" should be distinguished from what one may call the "how" of "state" or "condition." "How cold does it get in New York in the winter?" "How does the decline in his powers manifest itself?" "How is his pain now – is it any better?" are examples of the "how" of state or condition, and it is how-questions of this kind which we contrast with non-teleological why-questions – "Why does it get so cold in New York in the winter?" "Why did his powers decline so early in life?" "Why is his pain not subsiding?"

It is sometimes maintained or implied, as in the remarks of Stafford-Clark quoted earlier, that why-questions are invariably inquiries about somebody's purpose or end – if not the purpose of a human being, then perhaps that of some supernatural intelligence. This is clearly not the case. There can be no doubt that "why" is often employed simply to ask questions about the cause of a phenomenon. Thus the question "Why are the winters in New York so much colder than in Genoa, although the two places are on the same geographical latitude?" would naturally be understood as a request for information about the cause of this climatic difference, and it is not necessary for the questioner to suppose that there is some kind of plan or purpose behind the climatic difference in order to be using the word "why" properly. In saying this, one is not begging any questions against the theory that natural phenomena like the cold of the winter in New York are the work of a supernatural being: one is merely calling attention to what is and what is not implied in the ordinary employment of "why" in these contexts.

Let us briefly summarize the results obtained so far: in some situations "how" and "why" are naturally employed to ask the very same questions; when we deal with intentional human actions, we naturally use "why" to inquire about the purpose or goal of the agent and "how" to learn about the means used to achieve that goal; finally, how-questions are frequently used to inquire about the state or condition of somebody or something, while why-questions inquire about the cause of that state or condition without necessarily implying that any purpose or plans are involved. In all these cases it appears to be in principle possible to answer why-questions no less than how-questions, and this without the aid of religion or metaphysics.

The Theological "Why"

Let us turn now to what we earlier called "cosmic" why-questions. Two such cosmic "whys" need to be distinguished, the first of which, for rather obvious reasons, will be referred to as the theological "why." Here the questioner would be satisfied with a theological answer if he found such an answer convincing in its own right. He may or may not accept it as true, but he would not regard it as irrelevant.

Gilson, whose remarks on the limitations of science were quoted earlier, immediately supplies the answer to the "supreme question" which science "cannot even ask." Why anything at all exists must be answered by saying:

> [Each] and every particular existential energy, and each and every particular existing thing depends for its existence upon a pure Act of existence. In order to be the ultimate answer to all existential problems, this supreme cause has to be absolute existence. Being absolute, such a cause is self-sufficient; if it creates, its creative act must be free. Since it creates not only being but order, it must be something which at least eminently contains the only principle of order known to us in experience, namely, thought. (*God and Philosophy*, p. 140)

There is no doubt that many people who ask such questions as "Why does the universe exist?" or "Why are we here?" would also, at least in certain moods, be satisfied with a theological answer, though they would not necessarily accept all the details of Gilson's Thomistic theology. It should be emphasized that one does not have to be a believer in God to be using "why" in this way. The American playwright Edward Albee, for example, recently remarked, "Why we are here is an impenetrable question." Everyone in the world, he went on, "hopes there is a God," and he later added, "I am neither pro-God nor anti-God" (New York *Times,* January 21, 1965). Albee's question "Why are we here?" evidently amounts to asking whether there is a God and, if so, what divine purposes human beings are supposed to serve. He does not definitely accept the theological answer, presumably because he feels unsure of its truth, but he does regard it as very much to the point.

It should be observed in passing that people frequently use the word "why" to express a kind of cosmic complaint or bewilderment. In such cases they are not really asking for an answer, theological or otherwise. This use of "why" is in some respects similar to the theological "why" and may not inappropriately be referred to as the quasi-theological "why." A person who is and regards himself as a decent human being, but who is suffering a great deal, might easily exclaim "Why do I have to suffer so much, when so many scoundrels in the world, who never worked half as hard as I, are having such a lot of fun?" Such a question may well be asked by an unbeliever who is presumably expressing his regret that the workings of the universe are not in harmony with the moral demands of human beings. Even when believers ask questions of this kind, it may be doubted that they are invariably requesting information about the detailed workings of the Divine Mind. In the deeply moving first-act monologue of *Der Rosenkavalier*, the Marschallin reflects on the inevitability of aging and death:

> I well remember a girl
> Who came fresh from the convent to be
>   forced into holy matrimony.
> Where is she now?
>
> .   .   .   .
>
> How can it really be,
> That I was once the little Resi
> And that I will one day become the old woman?

How, she exclaims, can something like this be? She is far from doubting the existence of God and proceeds to ask:

> Why does the dear Lord do it?

And worse, if he has to do it in this way:

> Why does He let me watch it happen
> With such clear senses? Why doesn't He
>   hide it from me?

The Marschallin obviously does not expect an answer to this question, not, or not merely, because she thinks that the world's metaphysicians and theologians are not quite up to it. She is not, strictly speaking, asking a question but expressing her regret and her feeling of complete helplessness.

However, let us return from the quasi-theological to the theological "why." The difficulties besetting an answer like Gilson's are notorious and need not be reviewed here at length. There are the difficulties, much stressed by recent writers, of saying anything intelligible about a disembodied mind, finite or infinite, and there are further difficulties of talking meaningfully about the creation of the universe. There are the rather different difficulties connected not with the intelligibility of the theological assertions but with the reasoning used to justify them. Schopenhauer referred to all such attempts to reach a final resting place in the series of causes as treating the causal principle like a "hired cab" which one dismisses when one has reached one's destination. Bertrand Russell objects that such writers work with an obscure and objectionable notion of explanation: to explain something, we are not at all required to introduce a "self-sufficient" entity, whatever that may be. Writing specifically in reply to Gilson, Nagel insists that it is perfectly legitimate to inquire into the reasons for the existence of the alleged absolute Being, the pure Act of existence. Those who reject such a question as illegitimate, he writes, are "dogmatically cutting short a discussion when the intellectual current runs against them" (*Sovereign Reason*, Glencoe, Ill., 1954, p. 30). Without wishing to minimize these difficulties, it is important to insist that there is a sense in which the theological why-questions *are* intelligible. The question can be answered for such a person if it can be shown that there is a God. If not, it cannot be answered. Albee and Gilson, for example, do not agree about the truth, or at any rate the logical standing, of the theological assertion, but they agree that it is relevant to *their* cosmic why-question. There is thus a sense in which the questioner here knows what he is looking for.

The Super-ultimate "Why"

The theological "why" must be distinguished from what we are here going to call the super-ultimate "why." A person who is using "why" in the latter way would regard the theological answer as quite unsatisfactory, not (or not just) because it is meaningless or false but because it does not answer *his* question. It does not go far enough. For granting that there is a God and that human beings were created by God to serve certain of his purposes, our questioner would now ask "Why is there a God of this kind with these purposes and not another God with other purposes?" or, more radically, he would ask "Why was there at some time God rather than nothing?" The Biblical statement "In the beginning God created heaven and earth," Heidegger explicitly remarks, "is not an answer to … and cannot even be brought into relation with our question." The believer who stops with God is not pushing his questioning "to the very end" (*An Introduction to Metaphysics*, pp. 6–7). (It is not certain how somebody pressing the super-ultimate why-question would react to the rejoinder of those theologians who maintain that God exists necessarily and that hence the question "Why was there at some time God rather than nothing?" is illegitimate. In all likelihood he would support the view, accepted by the majority of Western philosophers since Hume and Kant, that it makes no sense to talk about anything, natural or supernatural, as existing necessarily.)

There are times when most people would regard these super-ultimate why-questions as just absurd. Stafford-Clark himself speaks with impatience of the "rumination" and the tedious and interminable speculations of obsessional patients. " 'Why is the world?' was a question to which one patient could find no answer but from which he could find no relief" (*Psychiatry Today*, p. 112). Yet, at other times, most of us are ready to treat these why-questions as supremely profound, as riddles to which it would be wonderful to have the answer but which, because of our finite intellects, must forever remain unsolved. It is true that certain philosophers, like Schelling and Heidegger, who have frequently been denounced as obscurantists, have laid special emphasis on super-ultimate why-questions; but it would be a total misunderstanding of the situation to suppose that more empirical philosophers, or indeed ordinary people, are not given to asking them or to treating them with great seriousness. It is almost unavoidable that any reasonably intelligent and reflective person who starts wondering about the origin of the human race, or animal life, or the solar system, or our galaxy and other galaxies, or about the lack of justice in the world, the brevity of life, and seeming absolute finality of death, should sooner or later ask "Why this world and not another – why any world?" The scientist Julian Huxley is as far removed in temperament and philosophy from Heidegger as anybody could be. Yet he also speaks of the "basic and universal mystery – the mystery of existence in general ... why does the world exist?" For Huxley it is science which "confronts us" with this mystery, but science cannot remove it. The only comment we can make is that "we do not know." We must accept the existence of the universe "and our own existence as the one basic mystery" (*Essays of a Humanist*, London, 1964, pp. 107–8). Ludwig Büchner was a materialist and an atheist, and yet he repeatedly spoke of the "inexplicability of the last ground of things." Nor are super-ultimate why-questions confined to those who do not believe in God or who have no meta-physical system. Schopenhauer was supremely confident that his was the true metaphysic, but he nevertheless remarks in the concluding chapter of his main work that his "philos-ophy does not pretend to explain the existence of the world in its ultimate grounds. ... After all my explanations," he adds, "one may still ask, for example, whence has sprung this will, the manifestation of which is the world. ... A perfect understanding of the existence, nature, and origin of the world, extending to its ultimate ground and satisfying all demands, is impossible. So much as to the limits of my philosophy, and indeed of all philosophy" (*The World As Will and Idea*, 3 vols., translated by R. B. Haldane and J. Kemp, London, 1883, Ch. 50). Similarly, Voltaire, who was a firm and sincere believer in God and who never tired of denouncing atheists as blind and foolish, nevertheless asked, at the end of the article "Why?" in his *Philosophical Dictionary*, "Why is there anything?," without for a moment suggesting that an appeal to God's creation would be a solution. William James, too, although he repeatedly defended supernaturalism, never claimed that it provided an answer to the question "How comes the world to be here at all instead of the non-entity which might be imagined in its place?" Philosophy, in James's opinion, whether it be naturalistic or supernaturalistic, "brings no reasoned solution" to this question, "for from nothing to being there is no logical bridge" (*Some Problems of Philosophy*, New York, 1911, pp. 38–40). "The question of being," he observes later in the same discussion, is "the darkest in all philosophy. All of us are beggars here, and no school can speak disdainfully of another or give itself superior airs" (*ibid.*, p. 46).

Having pointed out how widespread is this tendency to ask and take seriously the super-ultimate why-question, it is necessary to explain why, in the opinion of a number of contemporary philosophers, it must nevertheless be condemned as meaningless. It is the mark of a meaningful question, it would be urged, that not all answers can be ruled out *a priori*; but because of the way in which the super-ultimate why-question has been set up, it is *logically* impossible to obtain an answer. It is quite clear that the questioner will automat-ically reject any proposed answer as "not going back far enough" – as not answering *his* why, "All explanation," in the words of Peter Koestenbaum, an American disciple and expositor of Heidegger, "occurs within that which is to be explained … so the question applies to any possible answer as well" ("The Sense of Subjectivity," p. 54), that is, there *cannot* be an answer. If, however, a question can be put at all, to quote Wittgenstein,

> then it *can* also be answered … doubt can only exist where there is a question; a question only where there is an answer, and this only where something *can* be *said*. (*Tractatus Logico-philosophicus*, 6.5 and 6.51)

It must be emphasized that the super-ultimate "why" does *not* express ignorance about the "early" history of the universe. Büchner, for example, had no doubt that matter was eternal and that nothing which could be called "creation" had ever occurred; Voltaire similarly had no doubt that the physical universe was created by God and that God had always existed – yet both of them asked the super-ultimate "why" and regarded it as unanswerable. No doubt, some who have asked super-ultimate why-questions would, unlike Büchner and Voltaire, declare themselves ignorant of the remote history of the universe, but it is not this ignorance that they are expressing by means of the super-ultimate "why."

Those who insist that the super-ultimate why-question is meaningful do not usually deny that it very radically differs from *all* other meaningful why-questions. To mark the difference they occasionally refer to it by such labels as "mystery" or "miracle." Thus Koestenbaum remarks that "questions of this sort do not lead to answers but to a state of mind that appreciates the miracle of existence," they call attention to "the greatest of all mysteries" (*op. cit.*, pp. 54–5). Heidegger writes that the question "is incommensurable with any other" (*An Introduction to Metaphysics*, p. 4) and subsequently observes that "not only what is asked after but also the asking itself is extraordinary" (*ibid.*, p. 10).

Calling the super-ultimate why-question a "mystery" or a "miracle" or "incommensurable" or "extraordinary" does not in any way remove the difficulty: it is just one way of acknowledging that there is one. If it is granted that in all other situations a question makes sense only if an answer to it is logically possible, one wonders why this principle or criterion is not to be applied in the present case. If the defender of the meaningfulness of the super-ultimate why-question admits that in the "ordinary" sense the question is meaningless but that in some other and perhaps deeper sense it is meaningful, one would like to be told what this other and deeper sense is.

The point of the preceding paragraphs is sometimes expressed in a way that is not totally satisfactory. It is maintained that a question does not make sense unless the questioner knows what kind of answer he is looking for. However, while the fact that the questioner knows the "outline" of the answer may be a strong or even conclusive reason for supposing that the question is meaningful, the converse does not hold. One can think of examples in which a question is meaningful although the person asking it did not know what a possible answer would look like. Thus somebody might ask "What is the meaning of life?" without being able to tell us what kind of answer would be relevant and at a later time, after falling in love for the first time, he might exclaim that he now had the answer to his question – that love was the meaning of life. It would be much better to say in such a case that the question, as originally asked, was not clear than to say that it was meaningless. It is not objectionable to condemn a question as meaningless on the ground that the questioner does not know what he is looking for if in the context this is a way of saying that he has ruled out all answers *a priori;* and very probably those who express themselves in this way do not mean to point to some *contingent* incapacity on the part of the questioner but, rather, to a disability consequent upon the logical impossibility of obtaining an answer to the question. It is similar to saying that it is inconceivable that 3 plus 2 should equal 6 when we do not mean to assert a contingent fact about a certain incapacity on the part of human beings but, rather, that "3 plus 2 equals 6" is a self-contradiction.

The conclusion that the super-ultimate why-question is meaningless can also be reached by attending to what has here happened to the word "why." A little reflection shows that in the super-ultimate question "why" has lost any of its ordinary meanings without having been given a new one. Let us see how this works when the question is put in the form "Why does the universe exist?" and when the "universe" is taken to include everything that in fact exists. In *any* of its familiar senses, when we ask of anything, x, why it happened or why it is what it is – whether x is the collapse of an army, a case of lung cancer, the theft of a jewel, or the stalling of a car – we assume that there is something or some set of conditions, other than x, in terms of which it can be explained. We do not know what this other thing is that is suitably related to x, but unless it is in principle possible to go beyond x and find such another thing, the question does not make any sense. (This has to be slightly modified to be accurate. If we are interested in the "why" of a state of x at a certain time, then the answer can certainly refer to an earlier state of x. This does not affect the issue here discussed since, in the sense with which we are concerned, reference to an earlier state of x is going beyond x.) Now, if by "the universe" we mean the totality of things, then our x in "Why does the universe exist?" is so all-inclusive that it is *logically* impossible to find anything which could be suitably related to that whose explanation we appear to be seeking. "The sense of the world," wrote Wittgenstein, "must lie outside the world" (*Tractatus Logico-philosophicus*, 6.41), but by definition nothing can be outside the world. Heidegger, who avoids the formulation "Why does the universe exist?" and who instead inquires into the why of *das seiende* (the official translation of this term is "the essent," but Koestenbaum and others quite properly translate it as "things"), nevertheless makes it clear that *das seiende* here "takes in everything, and this means not only everything that is present in the broadest sense but also everything that ever was or will be." "Our question," he writes a little later, presumably without seeing the implications of this admission, "reaches out so far that we can never go further" (*An Introduction to Metaphysics*, p. 2).

For anybody who is not clearly aware of what we may call the logical grammar of "why," it is very easy to move from meaningful why-questions about particular things to the meaningless why-question about the universe. This tendency is aided by the picture that many people have of "the universe" as a kind of huge box which contains all the things "inside it." Voltaire's article "Why?," from which we quoted earlier, is a good example of such an illegitimate transition. Voltaire first asks a number of why-questions about specific phenomena, such as

Why does one hardly ever do the tenth part good one might do? Why in half Europe do girls pray to God in Latin, which they do not understand? Why in antiquity was there never a theological quarrel, and why were no people ever distinguished by the name of a sect?

He then gets more and more philosophical:

> Why, as we are so miserable, have we imagined that not to be is a great ill, when it is clear that it was not an ill not to be before we were born?

A little later we have what may well be a theological "why":

> Why do we exist?

Finally, as if there had been no shift in the meaning of "why," Voltaire asks:

> Why is there anything?

It should be noted that the argument we have just presented is not in any way based on an empiricist meaning criterion or on any question-begging assumptions in favor of naturalism. Anybody who uses the word "universe" in a more restricted sense, so that it is not antecedently impossible to get to an entity that might be the explanation of the universe, may be asking a meaningful question when *he* asks "Why does the universe exist?" Furthermore, even if "universe" is used in the all-inclusive sense, what we have said does not rule out the possibility that God or various divine beings are part of the universe in this sense. The point has simply been that the word "why" loses its meaning when it becomes logically impossible to go beyond what one is trying to explain. This is a matter on which there need not be any disagreement between atheists and theists or between rationalists and empiricists.

It will be well to bring together the main conclusions of this article:

(1) There is a sense in which "how" and "why" have roughly the same meaning. In this sense science is perfectly competent to deal with the "why."

(2) There are certain senses in which "how" and "why" serve to ask distinct questions, but here too both types of questions can in principle be answered by empirical procedures.

(3) One of the cosmic "whys" – what we have called the theological "why" – is used to ask meaningful questions, at least if certain semantic problems about theological utterances are disregarded. It was pointed out, however, that this does not imply that the theological answers are true or well supported.

(4) Some apparent questions introduced by "why" are really complaints and not questions, and for this reason unanswerable.

(5) What we have called the super-ultimate "why" introduces questions that are devoid of sense, whether they are asked by ordinary people in their reflective moments or by philosophers.

1.2

Untangling the Questions

Garrett Thomson

In medieval Europe it was generally assumed that humans were a special creation, with an immortal soul made in the image of God. According to this conception, humans were essentially different from the animals and the rest of the natural, physical world. Furthermore, in this world picture, it was thought that the earth occupied a central position at rest in the cosmos and that the heavens move around it. In both a literal and metaphorical sense, the universe revolved around us. It was also thought that nature was full of special signs revealing divine purpose, for us to guide our earthly lives by. The natural world was full of hidden meanings.

Compare this to the modern scientific view of the universe. The universe is incredibly large: there are billions of galaxies and our galaxy has billions of stars and our solar system is located towards the outer part of one of the spiral arms of this galaxy. All life on our planet, including our own, is no more than the product of blind causal processes, and the whole universe consists only of material or physical things. We humans are not so different in kind from the other animals.

The universe has existed for about 18 billion years, but it has no special objective or plan, and thus human life has no special purpose. Furthermore, because everything is made of matter, we have no immaterial soul and so, very soon, each one of us shall die. There is probably no God, and there are no special signs, just inert matter.

These two conceptions of the cosmos and human life are very different from each other. This change took place more or less in two jumps: one in the seventeenth century following the invention of physics, and the other, at the end of the nineteenth century following Darwin's theory of evolution.

Garrett Thomson (2002) "Untangling the Questions," Chapter 1 in *On the Meaning of Life*, Belmont, MA: Thomson Wadsworth, pp. 3–14.

Exploring the Meaning of Life: An Anthology and Guide, First Edition. Edited by Joshua W. Seachris.

Our purpose is not to evaluate in what ways the advent of science has been beneficial or harmful, but rather to evaluate its consequences for our conception of the meaning of life. In a relatively short historical time span, the question of life's meaning has acquired a new urgency. This is partly because the modern scientific view has largely replaced the medieval view and in the process has acquired an incredible authority. Yet to challenge that modern scientific account is not to necessarily endorse the medieval view. Sometimes, we set the two in opposition as if there were no third or fourth or more alternatives. …

Preliminary Obstacles

I would like to start by clearing out of the way some of the obstacles we might have to approaching this question in a real or authentic way. We need to establish some attitudes and the general approach to this investigation before going on to examine the question itself. First, the question 'Does life have a meaning?' is surrounded by a host of others, such as 'How did the universe come into being?' 'In what sense does life evolve?' 'What significance does death have?' 'Does anything matter?' We shall examine these associated disputes only in so far as they are relevant to the original query, which is difficult enough as it stands without help from its cousins.

The difficulty of the original question arises mostly because it needs clarification. It is not a straightforward empirical question that can be settled by observation. The question itself needs to be analyzed and better understood, because it is not clear what it means and what would count as an answer. We need to make it specific, so that it can be answered. Without such clarity, it would be premature to study different replies; they might be addressed to distinct questions.

The question 'What is the meaning of life?' may seem naive. In part, this is because of the word 'the'. With that single word, we make the assumption that life has either one meaning or else none at all. It claims uniqueness. It is in part because of this, that the whole phrase has become a battleground for ideologies or world-views. By apparently gaining the right to use this phrase, a thinker can seem to declare exclusivity for his or her evaluations. We tend to assume that the negative reply to the question, 'What is the meaning of life?' will imply that life is meaningless. However, the greatest challenge to the idea that life has a meaning is that it has many rather than none.

Also, the question is inhibiting, because it appears to be a request for some short formula, such as 'To obey God' or 'To find happiness,' which could be put in a fortune cookie or on the back of a matchbox. It is naive to think that some simple formula could be a suitable reply. The question is complex in many ways and, therefore, we should not expect nor aim for a simplistic answer, which in any case would not provide real insight.

For reasons such as these, the meaning of life is the subject of some not so funny jokes. The whole topic stimulates cynicism. The question and its cousins are often a battleground for ideologies. For example, the paradigmatic Christian and scientist are supposed to have fundamentally opposed theories about the meaning of life. It is easy to fall into the trap of thinking about these issues in such pre-packaged ideological terms. However, we should not allow ourselves to approach this question in such a pre-determined way. We do not want to rule out any ideology without argument, but we do not want to begin the investigation with some set ideological objectives already in mind. Furthermore, ideologies sell their ideas in packets; you have to either accept or reject the whole package. This attitude is not conducive to a deep and careful investigation of the subject matter.

Moreover, many people approach this question with cynicism because they assume that the question is unanswerable, and therefore, presume that it is a waste of time and effort to tackle the issues. However, we cannot assume that the question is unanswerable before we have tried to understand it. The same applies to the distinct claim that any answer to the question is bound to be unknowable.

Unanswerable Questions

Are there any unanswerable questions? Notice that an unanswerable question is one that does not have an answer and this is quite different from a question to which no one knows the answer. I suggest that there are three types of so-called 'unanswerable questions,' but all of which are really pseudo-questions. The first kind consists of questions such as 'What is the answer to this question?' which are somehow logically ill formed. Next, there are questions that are based on false assumptions, such as 'Did you hide the stolen goods at home or at work?' asked of someone who did not receive stolen goods. Third, there are questions that contain many questions rolled into one, such as 'What is the relation between the mind and the brain?' The question 'What is the meaning of life?' might fall into any one of these categories, especially the second and the third. However, in that case it is not so much an unanswerable question, but rather a pseudo-question, which needs to be replaced by others. Indeed, this is what an analysis should do: improve the question.

Improving questions is a very different process from answering them. We can ask new and better questions only if we improve our understanding of the old ones. Better responses require better questions. Much of the work that goes into solving a problem such as 'When is killing wrong?' is clarifying the question, showing what 'morally wrong' means and signifies. Could computers ever think for themselves? Does God exist? Before answering such questions, we have to unpack them and see what they contain. This applies even more so to the important question: What is the meaning of life?

There is another reason why we need to analyze a question such as this one. Suppose there is a meaning to life that we can state in a few sentences. However, even a straightforward and positive short answer would not be satisfying and would probably not illuminate much precisely because we need to understand the question better. What implications would the answer have for the way we live? Suppose that life has no meaning; what would be the implications of this for our lives? Understanding does not just consist in having an answer. It is also necessary to appreciate the significance of the answers.

Unknowable Answers

Another route to cynicism is the prejudice that the answer to questions such as 'What is the meaning of life?' must be unknowable. Notice that claiming that an answer is unknowable is quite different from asserting that no one knows the answer. For example, no one knows whether there are living beings in the Andromeda galaxy, but this is not something unknowable. For something to be unknowable, it must be the case that in principle it is impossible to know it.

To claim that it is in principle impossible to know something is to assert something very strong. For example, to affirm that it is in principle impossible to know whether God exists, it is necessary to say what God is and to show that all arguments in favor of and against the existence of God fail. Actually, one would have to demonstrate even more: namely, all possible arguments for and against the existence of God, including those never thought of before, fail. Consequently, it would rash for us to assume that the meaning of life is unknowable … Instead, keeping our minds open, let us begin to analyze the question.

No Universal Answers

There might be another reason for rejecting the question, 'What is the meaning of life?' It assumes that, at least at some level of generality, there is some universally applicable answer to the question. However, to be clear what this point involves, this assumption does not necessarily rule out individual differences in the meaning of life. For example, suppose that part of the meaning of life is to develop one's talents – this is a universal answer that admits of individual differences.

This assumption is also different from the idea that any answer given in our Western technological culture is bound to be at best incomplete because of the cultural assumptions that it embodies. Despite the qualifications, the question assumes that there is a universally applicable answer, and this assumption would be mistaken, for instance, if the question is culturally specific. As an example, perhaps this question only arises within contemporary Western societies, within that tradition that sometimes claims to be no tradition at all: Western skepticism, which challenges traditional world-views.

However, we should be careful about making an invalid step. Let us assume, for the moment, that people have been concerned only about the meaning of life within our recent Western culture. Even if this is true, then we cannot automatically conclude that any answer to the question is only applicable within that context. The context in which we ask a question is not necessarily the same as the context to which the answer applies.

In his article 'Why the question of the meaning of life has arisen in the last two and a half centuries?' Landau argues that this is because of various changed social factors (Landau, 1997). First, we have lost faith in the absolute nature of both the religious and scientific world-views. Second, he claims that our society or culture emphasizes the ideals of pleasure and comfort, but that many people do not feel that these values are sufficiently important to give life meaning. Our personal expectations do not yet match the ideals advanced by our culture.

Such considerations may explain why we in this culture feel the question of life's meaning is so poignant, but this does not mean that the question does not also apply to other cultures and to the people of other times. In this sense, the question may be universal, even if it has not been universally asked. T. E. Lawrence claimed that it is the

Paradox of our times that we demand great actions of ourselves in a time when we also recognize their utter irrelevance (*quoted in Solomon* (1976), *p.85*).

If our actions are 'utterly irrelevant' today, then they were also so in the past, even though we may not have recognized them as such. Of course, any answer we provide will necessarily be framed in terminology of our culture, and in this way it will be limited. But this does not automatically exclude it from being applicable to other cultures. …

Some Contexts of Questioning

One way to think about the question 'What is the meaning of life?' is to examine the contexts in which it is often asked. By reflecting on these contexts, we may hope to capture the practical points behind the question. Usually people ask about meaning when they feel that their lives lack it, and so we might start by looking at the ways in which life might seem meaningless. For example, a person who is very deeply depressed for a long time would feel despair or hopelessness and may well wonder whether life is even worth living. To give a slightly less extreme example, if one's life is cramped by routine, one might feel that one's life is meaningless because it serves no external important purpose and, because of this, it has no internal purpose. In such circumstances, one's life may feel boring, trivial, and mundane. Additionally, if one feels unreal or that one's life is inauthentic or a lie, then a person may feel that his or her life makes no sense because it is fragmented or perhaps broken. This might happen to a person when he or she becomes unemployed.

Everyday instances of people questioning the meaning of life are not necessarily so dramatic. A person might be living what appears to be a perfectly satisfying and even successful life, and yet underneath, he or she may feel that his or her life is empty or hollow. This need not manifest in a crisis, even though it did in the famous cases of the great Russian novelist, Leo Tolstoy (1828–1910) and the British philosopher and reformer, John Stuart Mill (1806–73). I believe that some people feel that their lives are meaningless, but suppress the feeling and carry on despite this.

Finally, for example, after contemplating the galaxies or seeing a documentary about the birth of the universe, one might feel a sense of value vertigo that generates a genuine puzzlement about the place of humanity in the cosmic scheme. One may conclude that, from this perspective, human life has no real meaning or that it is absurd (see Nagel, 1986).

In summary, there seems to be four distinct kinds of question, which may be combined, one might ask with the question 'What is the meaning of life?'

1. Why should I live when I could commit suicide?
This was the question that haunted Albert Camus, the French existentialist thinker, who called this the most fundamental question of all. …

2. What should I do with the rest of my life?
This is how the question has been understood most often: as seeking guidance for future action. Furthermore, it has usually been taken as a request for a purpose of some kind (or

a set of purposes) around which one should organize one's life. However, this second question does not necessarily have to be understood as the search for a purpose. It can also be a search for non-instrumental value. The question 'How can I improve my life?' can be regarded as a variant of this second question because it is like asking 'What should I do with the rest of my life in order that it be improved (or in order that it be less full of suffering)?'

3.   What sense can I make of my life up to now?

This question is different from the first two, because we can imagine it being asked by a person on his or her deathbed. In such a context, one would not have any interest in asking the first two questions! This third question is apparently asking for a pattern to a person's life, a narrative that makes one's life intelligible. This might take two forms: metaphysical or personal. Traditionally, many metaphysical systems have attempted to give us a generic portrait of human life that would count as its meaning. Also, the question can be a request for a personal narrative that makes sense specifically of one's own life.

4.   What could have been different about my life?

The search for meaning might be construed as an attempt to discover the lost possibilities, or could-have-beens, of one's life. An allied question is 'Would it have been better not to have been born?' One might ask such questions either to reassure oneself that one's life has not been so bad, or else to have a sense of the immense and great possibilities that one could have experienced and did not.

First Steps towards an Analysis

To bring more order to these points, I shall distinguish at least three things that we might be asking with the question 'What is the meaning of life?' However, first, here are some preliminary clarifications. The question can be asked at three levels: of the universe itself, of life in general and of a specific individual's life. The more general forms of the question are probably requests for a metaphysics that makes sense of our existence. A general portrait of the universe might reveal to us some important insight into how we should live. Such a characterization of the universe might shed some new light on what we are and what our lives should consist in. In other words, it provides a connection between what we are and how we should live. For example, the question 'Why does something exist rather than nothing?' would be relevant insofar as its answer has implications for the project of making sense of our own lives. Many of the great metaphysical and religious systems of the past have tried to perform this kind of role. For example, Buddhism offers us a general understanding of the nature of the universe and life, and based on this, offers a set of prescriptions regarding how the individual should live to achieve a state of enlightenment or Nirvana.

In view of the above considerations, we can advance the following principle:

> An understanding of the meaning of life must have some practical implications for the way that we conduct our lives.

This helps us to rule out some readings of the question as irrelevant to our enquiry. For instance, sometimes 'What is the meaning of that?' is a request for information about its causal relationships. As an example, what do these clouds mean? The answer 'Black clouds mean rain' cites the effect of black clouds. What do these spots mean? The answer 'Such spots mean that you have a contagious disease' refers to their cause. In these cases, the meaning of something picks out its causes and effects. However, for this study we are not interested in the causal facts about our lives unless they have practical significance.

We need to distinguish between the meaning of life in general and the meaning that a person's life can have for him or her. In this study we would only be interested in the first insofar as it had important implications for the second. There are two different ways an answer to the question 'Is life meaningful?' might be connected to the practical issue of the way we live.

1. According to the first type of connection, there is some feature or set of features of life in general, or specifically human life, in virtue of which they are meaningful. The meaningfulness is guaranteed by some characteristic of life itself. According to this first way of understanding the question, if life is meaningful, then it is so for everyone regardless of what we actually do. Of course, even if this were true, people may not perceive or feel that meaningfulness. One might feel or consider that one's life is meaningless but, in such a case, one's perceptions would be mistaken or without foundation. According to this idea, whatever we do, our lives are guaranteed to be meaningful; the practical issue is whether we perceive and appreciate that meaningfulness.

2. The second type of connection postulates a feature or set of characteristics that individual lives may or may not have, or may have in varying degrees, in virtue of which a life would be meaningful. For example, if the meaning of life is to live according to one's true or deepest talent, then some people may have meaningful lives and others not. According to this way of interpreting the question, a person's life may actually be meaningless, but he or she may transform it into something meaningful.

There is an important difference between these two kinds of theory and, unfortunately, the language we employ to discuss these issues actually may confuse them. For example, we refer to someone 'having found the meaning of his or her life.' This phrase 'finding the meaning' is ambiguous; it could signify that the person has discovered the meaning that was there all along. Alternatively, it could signify that the person has changed his or her actions or way of life, so that it has actually acquired meaning that was not present before. We find a similar kind of ambiguity in the phrase 'for them' or 'for him.' 'His life has no meaning for him' might signify that it really does have a meaning even if he does not appreciate or recognize that meaning. However, in contrast, it also might indicate the person is living a meaningless existence.

I do not insist on these apparently small points for the sake of pedantry. If we are to make any progress in deepening our understanding of this question, we must know when to be careful with words. …

Let us return to the main point. We should understand the question 'What is the meaning of life?' in a manner that has some practical implications concerning the way we live. Given this, there are three general ways to understand the question:

1. Does life have a purpose or point?

This probably is the way the question is most usually understood and accordingly, a meaningful life would be one which serves or has some kind of purpose, and a meaningless life would be one that is pointless or purposeless. If the question is to be understood in this way then there are important subsidiary questions, such as 'Whose purpose?' and 'What kinds of purpose could constitute the meaning of life?' …

2. Does life have some value?

The question might be asked also as 'Is life worthwhile?' According to this interpretation, something meaningful is non-instrumentally valuable. In other words, there seems to be a conceptual link between the two notions. For example, it might be that meaning is constituted by a certain kind of value or that the meaningfulness of something implies that it has value. Is life absurd?

If the question is to be understood in this way, then there are important subsidiary questions such as 'What kind of value would constitute the meaning of life?' For example, for life to have value, does it have some absolute value (in some as yet unspecified sense of the term 'absolute')? Or rather perhaps for life to be meaningful, its value must be real rather than being no more than a human invention. …

3. Does my life signify something?

Sentences and texts have meaning in the sense of signifying something. Non-linguistic behavior, such as gestures and rituals, also can have a similar type of meaning. Does a person's life have a meaning or significance in an analogous way? We understand the meaning of a person's life by making it intelligible. In this vein, we ask questions such as 'How should we understand human life?' and 'How should a person interpret his or her own life?' which pertain to the idea of making sense of a life. Furthermore, there is also the possibility that the meaning of a person's life might be the message or lesson that it contains for others. In other words, how should other people interpret my life?

I would argue that these are three most basic ways to understand the question, given the principle and qualifications mentioned earlier. This is because there are only three kinds of value: instrumental, non-instrumental and expressive. Of course, this does not preclude there being different kinds of non-instrumental value. Nor does it preclude the possibility that the meaning of life might be some special combination of all three types of value.

References

Landou, Iddo (1997) "Why has the question of the meaning of life arisen in the last two and a half centuries?" *Philosophy Today*, Summer.

Nagel, Thomas (1986) "The absurd", *The Journal of Philosophy*, 68 (1971): 716–27.

Solomon, Robert (1976) *The Passions*, Notre Dame, IN: University of Notre Dame Press.

1.3

Questions about the Meaning of Life

R. W. Hepburn

Claims about 'the meaning of life' have tended to be made and discussed in conjunction with bold metaphysical and theological affirmations. For life to have meaning, there must (it is assumed) be a comprehensive divine plan to give it meaning, or there must be an intelligible cosmic process with a 'telos' that a man needs to know if his life is to be meaningfully orientated. Or, it is thought to be a condition of the meaningfulness of life, that values should be ultimately 'conserved' in some way, that no evil should be unredeemable and irrational. And it may be claimed that if death were to end our experience, meaninglessness would triumph.

Because of this rich metaphysical background, the agnostic or naturalist faces a problem when he asks himself, 'Does life have meaning, for me?': or more formally, 'Can the vocabulary of life as "meaningful" or "meaningless" still play a role in my naturalistic interpretation of things?' The answer is not simple; for the informal logic of the vocabulary itself is not simple. This is a situation in which the naturalistic philosopher is tempted in one of two directions: either to renounce the vocabulary – as too deeply entangled with unacceptable beliefs, or to radically redefine the terms 'meaning', 'meaningful' and their cognates, thereby giving them work to do, but misleadingly different from their traditional work. The task for such a philosopher may be to mediate delicately between these poles, and in the course of trying to do that a good many complexities in the language of 'meaning' may come to light – complexities of interest perhaps not only to the naturalistic philosopher himself.

In the last few years some analytical philosophers have in fact written on the expression 'the meaning of life'; for instance, Kurt Baier, Inaugural Lecture, 'The Meaning of Life' (Canberra, 1957), Antony Flew, 'Tolstoi and the Meaning of Life', *Ethics* (Jan. 1963), Kai Nielsen, 'Linguistic Philosophy and "The Meaning of Life"', *Cross-Currents* (Summer, 1964).

R. W. Hepburn (1966) "Questions about the Meaning of Life," *Religious Studies*, 1(2): 125–40.

Exploring the Meaning of Life: An Anthology and Guide, First Edition. Edited by Joshua W. Seachris.

Their analyses overlap at many points, though not completely. I shall first of all offer a very brief, compressed and somewhat schematised account of these analyses, conflating them where they overlap, and then discuss some of the issues they raise.[1]

According to the interpretations being now worked out, questions about the meaning of life are, very often, conceptually obscure and confused. They are amalgams of logically diverse questions, some coherent and answerable, some neither. A life is not a statement, and cannot therefore have linguistic meaning. But admittedly we do use the word 'meaning' outside linguistic contexts. We speak of the meaning of a gesture, of a transaction, of a disposition of troops; and in such cases we are speaking of the point or purpose or end of an act or set of acts. This usage suggests an equation between meaningfulness and purposiveness. For a life to be meaningful, it must be purposeful: or – to make life meaningful is to pursue valuable ends.

To adopt this schema, however, already involves a shift from traditional ways of speaking about life as meaningful. Meaning is not now something to be found, as awaiting discovery, but is imparted to it by the subject himself. A person looks in vain for meaning and is needlessly frustrated when he cannot find it – if he conceives it as somehow existing prior to his decisions about what policies to pursue.

To say that 'making life meaningful' is a matter of 'pursuing valuable, worthwhile ends' is to say that it is an activity that indispensably involves value judgment. The description of cosmic patterns, tendencies or trends does not obviate the need to make autonomous judgments about the worth-whileness or otherwise of following, or promoting or opposing any of these. This is true no less of statements about God or a hereafter. Since claims about God and hereafter are ultimately claims about what is the case, not what ought to be, no conclusion will follow deductively from them about values. Even in the religious context, the question (as now analysed) still arises, 'What ends are *worthy* of pursuit?' Religious propositions cannot guarantee meaningfulness. Conversely, it is argued, loss of religious or metaphysical belief does not entail the denial of meaningfulness.

If we concentrate on the question 'What is the purpose of life?' rather than on 'What is its meaning?', we are still dealing with the questions 'What ends shall I choose?' 'What purposes shall I hold to?' The analytical philosopher characteristically and quite intentionally changes the question from singular to plural, from 'purpose' to 'purposes'. He will claim that the original question contains a presupposition that must be rejected, the presupposition that life, if purposeful, can have only a single purpose, that only a single policy is worthwhile. Why may not a purposeful existence be a network of many purposes, with trajectories of varying reach, scope and seriousness? 'We are not and cannot always be doing or caring about one big thing.'[2]

The phrase, 'the purpose of human life', can be offensive on a second count, because it may suggest an analogy with the purpose of an instrument, utensil, tool or organ in a living body. The theist, who does take this analogy seriously, sees human life (with its help) as subordinated to the intentions, activities of another being, who 'assigns' (Baier) tasks and roles to men, and thereby imbues his life with purpose. Two senses of 'purpose' must be contrasted: the first, the sense in which one has a purpose if one 'purposes' or plans to do something, perhaps with the help of an artefact, an instrument, or other means: the second is the sense in which an artefact itself has a purpose, that is, a function. Only the first of these senses is compatible with moral autonomy, with being an autonomous purposer. To subordinate oneself wholly to the purposes of another is to forfeit moral status. This amounts to a moral argument against the manner in which theism seeks to secure purpose for human life. We must resist the temptation to translate 'What is the purpose of life?' into 'What are people *for?*'

We have seen two ways in which recent analyses of questions about the meaning of life seek to disconnect those questions from metaphysical and religious claims, or at least try to deprive such claims of any unique, privileged importance in the handling of the questions. Religious and metaphysical statements are still statements of fact, and therefore logically cannot in themselves be answers to questions about meaning. Second: if human life is given purpose by virtue of man's fulfilling the task assigned him by God, it will be 'purpose' in the autonomy-denying, dignity-destroying sense. Two further arguments tend to the same general conclusion.

Consider the familiar claim that life is meaningless if death ends all, that a necessary condition of life being meaningful is immortality or resurrection. Against this it is argued that there is no entailment between temporal finiteness and disvalue, futility. We can and do love flowers that fade; and the knowledge that they will fade may even enhance their preciousness. To be everlasting, that is, is no necessary or sufficient condition of value and worth-whileness, nor therefore of meaningfulness. An eternity of futility is not logically impossible.

Again, the quest for the meaning of life is very often thought of, but thought of confusedly, as a quest for *esoteric wisdom*, metaphysical or theological. On this, Flew's discussion of Tolstoi is interesting and relevant. First, we find in Tolstoi's *A Confession* (O.U.P. ed., 1940) an account of a period of 'arrest of life', the loss of a sense that life has any meaning or purpose, an inner deadness and disorientation. Tolstoi asked, 'What is it for?' 'What does it lead to?' His reflection took various pessimistic turns, including notably a refusal to account anything worthwhile, if death ends all. It struck him eventually, however, that the vanity and brevity of life were well enough known to very simple and unreflective people: yet in their cases there was seldom any 'arrest of life'. Tolstoi concluded that these people must know the meaning of life, the meaning that eluded the learned Tolstoi himself: it must be, not a piece of rational knowledge, but some non-rational or supra-rational knowledge to which they somehow had access. Flew now contests the assumption that these people necessarily had any esoteric, mystical knowledge that Tolstoi lacked. 'What we surely need here is Ryle's distinction between knowing *how* and knowing *that;* the peasants may indeed know how to live their lives free of all sophisticated psychological disabilities, but this by no means presupposes the possession of any theoretical knowledge' hidden from such a man as Tolstoi. In fact, the characters in Tolstoi's novels know better. In *War and Peace* Pierre's 'mental change' is a coming to have (a learning how to have) peace of mind, not a matter of acquiring new information, new dogma. The same is true of Levin and Hadji Murad. In so far as this kind of discovery of meaning is religious, it is so in a way that may be 'analysable in terms of ethics and psychology only'. Crucially, to know the meaning of life is to know how to live, as at one stage Tolstoi did not.

If we continue thus and develop these last themes, it becomes clear that the first-mentioned schematic account of the meaning of life is quite misleadingly oversimple. To give life meaning cannot be just a matter of pursuing worthy projects, for that account fails to cope with phenomena like Tolstoi's arrest of life – or John Stuart Mill's during his mental crisis of 1826. More generally, it is quite possible to make various value-judgments in cold blood, while yet suffering from a sense of meaninglessness. One may fill one's days with honest, useful and charitable deeds, not doubting them to be of value, but without feeling that these give one's life meaning or purpose. It may be profoundly boring. To seek meaning is not just a matter of seeking justification for one's policies, but of trying to discover how to organise one's vital resources and energies around these policies. To find meaning is not a matter of judging these to be worthy, but of seeing their pursuit as in some sense a fulfil-ment, as involving self-realisation as opposed to self-violation, and as no less opposed to the performance of a dreary task. Baier's account of 'meaning' includes reference to the pursuit of worthwhile projects, both in the sense of 'projects that afford satisfaction to the pursuer', and in the sense of 'morally worthwhile projects' – concerning, for instance, the well-being of others. Questions of the meaning of life, I suggest, are typically questions of how these two sorts of pursuit can be *fused*. I do not think that the use of such words as 'fulfilment' and 'self-realisation' need force one into a refined form of egoism, nor that the price of avoiding such is to empty the words of all sense. It need not be claimed that the values, duties, etc. involved *derive their force* from their ability to gratify the agent. If a particular agent fails to see the pursuit of moral and social goals as conferring meaning on his life, he need not be lamenting that he has failed to envisage how their pursuit could yield gratification for him. Nor is he necessarily revealing *Akrasia*. He may actually rise to his duty, but he rises to it as one rises from a warm bed to a chill morning's tasks. If he is asking how his duties (and other pursuits) can be represented as of 'interest' to him, it need not be in the sense of 'interest' that egoism requires, but in the sense *of concern* to him. What one often finds, on reading the reflective autobiographies and semi-autobiographies that are undoubtedly our best source-books here, is that in asking questions about the meaning of his life, the author is asking how he can relate the pursuit of various valuable ends to the realising of a certain kind or form of life, the thought of which evokes in him the response: 'The pursuit of these goals really concerns me, matters to me!' He may achieve this by way of an imaginative vivifying of the objectives (moral, social, religious …) of his policies and pursuits, by sum-moning up and dwelling upon a vision of the ideal that facilitates self-identification with it. The writer may be helped in this by some extant public myth (compare R. B. Braithwaite on religious belief), or he may elaborate a private myth in which he casts himself in the role of a person dedicated to the pursuit of the valuable ends, whatever they are.[3]

I have kept the plural – 'goals', 'ends' – following the tendency (noted above) to repudiate 'monolithic' accounts of the good life. But it needs to be remarked that there are perfectly intelligible occurrences of the singulars in many contexts; occurrences that do not stem from bad metaphysics or bad moral philosophy. A life may be said to acquire 'new meaning' through the rallying and ordering of resources that have hitherto been dispersed and conflicting in disunity. This is a sort of 'integrating' that is independent of any claims about all goods being ultimately one. Vronsky, in love with Anna Karenina, 'felt that all his powers, hitherto dissipated and scattered, were now concentrated and directed with terrible energy toward one blissful aim … He knew that … all the happiness of life and the only meaning of life for him now was in seeing and hearing her' (I, ch. XXXI). In the same novel, Levin, having seen Kitty passing in a coach, reflects: 'in the whole world there was only one being able to unite in itself the universe and the meaning of life for him. It was Kitty' (III, ch. XII).

All these complexities are reflected in the complexity of the criteria we are likely to use in commenting upon or appraising discourse about the meaning a person's life has for him. Where we are moved to disapproval, our criticism may certainly be in part a *moral* criticism: one may disapprove, for instance, of a person's commitment to the Don Juan pattern of life, its goals and priorities. But such criticism may involve other factors besides the moral. Suppose someone does take the Don Juan pattern as fitting his life as lived at present and as setting 'tasks' for his future. But suppose also that in this particular case, the life as it is being lived is totally ineffectual in the relevant respects. We shall want to say, '*This* meaning cannot be given to *this* life'; and the cost of trying to impose it is a falsification of the course the life is taking in fact. The effect of such blunders in self-commitment to a pattern of life may be grotesque or pathetic, or, as in the case of the other Don – Don Quixote – it may be richly comic. Or again, although we might not wish to speak of falsification, of events and pattern at loggerheads, we might detect that there is a self-conscious, self-dramatising and only half-sincere playing-out of a role. Whereas, on the other hand, we should count integrity, the refusal of stereotyped, paste-board *personae*, as pre-eminent among grounds for approval in this domain. The agent himself may come to see, in a dawning self-knowledge, that some attempt to give meaning or purpose has been proceeding on the wrong lines. Once more, in *Anna Karenina* (Part II, ch. XXXV), Kitty's attempt to find meaning through adopting Varenka's religious way of life ends unhappily. She decides it has not risen above the level of an imitation, and has involved pretence and self-deception. Some pages later, Anna reflects on her efforts to love Karenin: 'Have I not tried, … with all my might, to find a purpose in my life? Have I not tried to love him …? But the time came when I could no longer deceive myself …' (Part III, ch. XVI). Where we can estimate them, the ease or difficulty, 'slickness' or strenuousness involved in the quest for meaning may figure in criticism. We sometimes say that someone has found meaning in too facile or superficial a way, or that an autobiography discloses a 'lack of probing', 'a relaxed mood' or a cocksureness that replaces the tension of real self-exploration.[4]

The pursuit of meaning, in the senses we have been examining, is a sophisticated activity, involving a discipline of attention and imagination. Is this true of *all* relevant senses? The case of Tolstoi and the peasants, as discussed by Flew, suggests otherwise. To look back at that may help to plot further ramifications.

What makes it plausible to say that the peasants knew the meaning of life, and in what sense, if any, did they *not* know it? On Flew's Rylean account (*ibid.* p. 116) 'the secret of the peasants … [is] knowledge of *how* to go on living, [and this is] only another way of saying that they … enjoy rude mental health'. This 'no nonsense' analysis relies on a very weak sense of 'knowing how'. It is not being claimed that the peasants had mastered techniques for banishing depression – for they did not suffer from it; nor even rules, skills by which to steer their lives round the hazards of depression and mental arrests. They could hardly know of such states of mind as Tolstoi's or J. S. Mill's or Coleridge's in 'dejection'. They are unaware of the perils they have missed. If for the peasants 'knowing the meaning of life' equals 'knowing how to live', it amounts to no more than this: that as a matter of fact the peasants were not vulnerable to the malaise that Tolstoi suffered. One might want to say,

'This is surely not a "knowing" *at all*', but just a fortunate combination of circumstances *happening* to produce 'rude mental health'. It is true, however, that ordinary language allows this weak sense of 'knowing how', a sense that is consistent with Flew's account of the peasants. It is applicable, for instance, to the baby who 'knows how to cry', even to the bird who 'knows how to build a nest'.

On the other hand, if one's aim is (like Flew's) 'to throw light upon the meaning of the question: "What is the meaning of life?"' (*ibid.* p. 110), one must keep in mind that a quite important element of meaning is not covered by this weak sense of 'knowing how …', 'knowing how to live', etc. Tolstoi may well have been mistaken in thinking that the peasants had an esoteric knowledge that he lacked, a knowledge that gave a key to the problem of life's meaning. But, in thinking so, he was testifying to that side of the logic of 'the meaning of life' that has to drop out in the case of the peasants: namely, that questions about the meaning of life involve a problem, see life as a problem, and involve a search for an answer. This is so frequently presupposed in discourse about the meaning of life, that such discourse is felt as curiously attenuated, if it is thought away. If we do take the problematic context as built in to the logic, then the sense of 'knowing how to live' that is correlative with solving the problem and coming to know that meaning, will be a stronger sense than can be used of the peasants. It will involve awareness of the hurdles, the threats of futility, and the devising of tactics to overcome them.

Could a man's life have or fail to have meaning, without his knowing that it did or did not have meaning? This question could be answered either way, according to the interpretation given to 'the meaning of life'. We can answer Yes: his own awareness of his life's meaning is not a necessary condition for its being meaningful. This is so, if 'having meaning' is equated with 'contributing to valuable projects', 'achieving useful results'. But it may be felt, again, that such an answer goes against the grain of language: that it is too odd to say, for instance, 'White did not himself find the meaning of his life: but Black (White's biographer, writing after White's death) did find it'. Finding the meaning of White's life may be deemed to be something only White is logically able to do. The giving of meaning to life is seen as essentially a task for the liver of it. Conversely, in the case of people who have not worked at it, seen it as a task, who have been unreflectively happy or unhappy, it would be most natural to say that they have neither found nor failed to find the meaning of life.

It must, of course, be admitted that the peasants had something Tolstoi wanted to have but did not have. In the sense we have been elucidating, if Tolstoi succeeded in getting it, he could be said to have found the meaning of life, but we should not say the same of the peasants, since they had never been conscious of a problem. If this is logically curious, it is not unintelligible. Were life never problematic, were people never subject to arrests of life, it is unlikely that we should ever have acquired the expressions we are discussing. But having once acquired them in the problematic context, they can be extended to other and non-problematic contexts. The former seem to remain primary, however, and it distorts the logic of 'the meaning of life' if we take as paradigmatic instances of success in discovering meaning, people who have never been troubled by the problematic aspects of life, its limits, contingency and the like.

(Two smaller, related points may be mentioned in passing. Flew's statement that the characters in Tolstoi's novels know better than Tolstoi is contestable. In the case of Levin there is a good deal about the revelation of 'a knowledge unattainable by reasoning'. The knowledge of 'what we should live for … cannot be explained by reason' (Part VIII, chs. XIX, XII, etc.). Again, Tolstoi does permit himself to use the expression, 'the meaning of life' in a remarkably different sense from that on which our discussion, and Flew's, has centred. When Anna, just before her suicide, discerned the hopelessness of her position, 'she saw it clearly in the piercing light which now revealed to her the meaning of life and of human relations' (Part VII, ch. XXX) – a diabolical, not a benign, pattern being revealed. To have seen this 'meaning' was not to be enabled to live, but was to judge, on the contrary, that a continuance of life was unendurable. This is an eccentric but noteworthy usage.)

On the highly particularised problems of giving meaning to an individual life, philosophy may not have much to say: but it is certainly concerned with what seem to be general threats to meaningfulness arising out of the human situation as such. For the non-theist, the chief threat may well appear to come from the realisation of mortality. The relation between meaning and mortality is, as we have noted, a focus of attention in current discussions. On the one side are writers (Tolstoi is again among them – as Flew brings out) who in some contexts virtually identify the question of meaningfulness with the question of immortality: deny immortality and you necessarily deny meaningfulness. This account plainly distorts the logic of the question about the meaning of life, not least by reducing its complexity to a single issue of fact. On the other side, a naturalistic account oversimplifies and dogmatises if it claims that 'death is irrelevant' (Baier) to questions of value, worthwhileness – and hence to meaningfulness. The argument that values are not devalued by mortality, although unassailable on grounds of logic, may be used to express a naturalism that is more optimistic and brash than it is entitled to be. For a person may heed the argument that mortality and value are compatible, and yet may be burdened with a sense of futility that the argument cannot dispel. His malaise may range from occasional vague misgivings over the worthwhileness of his activities, to a thoroughgoing arrest of life.

We can most usefully consider this sort of malaise at a still more general level. A complaint of meaninglessness can be a complaint about a felt disproportion between preparation and performance; between effort expended and the effect of effort, actual or possible. Yeats expressed the complaint in well-known words: 'When I think of all the books I have read, wise words heard, anxieties given to parents, … of hopes I have had, all life weighed in the balance of my own life seems to me *a preparation for something that never happens*.' (Compare again, Tolstoi's question, 'What does it *lead* to?')

A useful vocabulary in which to discuss this can be borrowed from aesthetics. In Monroe Beardsley's book, *Aesthetics* (New York, 1958, pp. 196 f.), he distinguishes, in a musical composition, passages that have 'Introduction quality' and passages that have 'Exhibition quality': the one is felt as leading up to the other, the first as preparation and the second as fulfilment. He quotes, *apropos*, an amusing criticism by Tovey of Liszt's tone poem, *Ce qu'on Entend sur La Montagne*. The work consists of 'an introduction to an introduction to a connecting link to another introduction …, etc.' Beardsley adds: 'When [the tone poem] stops it is still promising something that never arrives.'

In music this sort of disappointment can be due to more causes than one. It may be the listener's expectations, not the music, that are at fault. He may be simply misinformed about the programme he is to hear; expecting a symphony, but getting only a concert overture.

A musical idiom may disappoint him: he awaits a fully-fashioned melody in the style of Brahms, but – since the music happens to be in the style of Webern – it provides none. In different cases, different kinds of correction are required: to study the programme, to familiarise himself with musical development after Brahms. What sounded prefatory can come to sound performatory. But, as in the Liszt-Tovey case, the fault may lie with the music, and nothing the listener can do can give it an exhibition quality.

How far can the analogy be applied? To draw first its limits: a piece of music is 'given' to a listener in a way that his life, being partly shaped by his choices, is not given. The nearest to a given in the latter case is an awareness of the general conditions and scope of human existence, of what is it open for men to do and to be, of what they can reasonably count on doing and being. Suppose a person who has lost belief in immortality has a sense of futility due to the feeling that life is all prefatory, has no exhibition quality. An analytical philosopher points out to him that things can be valuable although not eternal, and so on. This is rather like pointing out that a symphony was never on the programme, but that other valuable things were. The implication is that just as a satisfactory short piece of music can be heard as having exhibition quality, so can life within the limits of earthly existence be perceived as having it.

This suggestion may dispel the sense of futility, or it may not. It may dispel it, because to some considerable extent it does lie within our power to take a particular experience either in a prefatory or exhibitory way, although how this is done we cannot inquire here in any detail. In general, and very obviously, many activities can be understood both as leading to anticipated worthwhile ends, and as worthwhile in themselves also. A person may sometimes successfully counsel himself to dwell less upon the possible future effects of his various activities, and relish the present activities themselves. (To do so, there must, admittedly, be something relishable about the activities.)

Suppose, then, the suggestion does not dispel the sense of futility. To follow the analogy a step further: life may be found recalcitrant in the way that Liszt's tone-poem was recalcitrant to Tovey. Clearly there are experiences, of prolonged and unrelievable ill-health, for instance, that can be regarded as valuable, in the sense of disciplinary, only so long as death is not believed to be the end. Lacking such belief, a person cannot simply be counselled to endow a life pervaded by pain with exhibition quality. It is of such suffering that people tend to use words like 'pointless' and 'senseless'. If this experience is followed by no 'exhibition-section', it is unredeemably futile.

What follows? The existence of unsuccessful musical compositions exposed to the Tovey criticism does not devalue those that are not exposed. Must one say any more, in the case of lives, than that some lives are without meaning, in the present sense; but that others are meaningful? Or, in terms of the earlier discussion, that some people are confronted with a stiffer problem than others in giving meaning to their lives, and that the task may sometimes be impossible for them. This would be enough to qualify an over-optimistic naturalism that implies that (where meaning is concerned) everything remains as it was in the days of belief in immortality and Providence.[5] As an index of the difficulty of nicely proportioning prefatory and exhibitory quality in a life, one may instance an aesthetic theory like John Dewey's, according to which the distinctiveness of art is its capacity to provide just such completeness and balance in experience – in contrast to the ordinary experience of life, which seldom can maximise these qualities and can never *guarantee* them.[6]

If it is a condition for life-in-general to be meaningful that these qualities *should* be guaranteed, then life-in-general is without meaning to the naturalist or agnostic – though individual lives may happen to attain it, by practical wisdom and good fortune.

Judgments about the value or futility of human projects are problematic in yet another way. Our appraisal of the value of our activities tends to vary according to the 'backcloth' against which they are viewed. To the naturalist, human endeavour viewed *sub specie aeternitatis*, may seem to shrivel, frighteningly. (Compare Sartre's troubled musings on the heat-death of the sun, in his autobiographical essay, *Les Mots*, p. 208.) He may nonetheless judge as entirely worthwhile some social reform, viewed against the backcloth of a dozen years, or months, of social abuse. Yet it is not only a vestigial romanticism that prompts one to give privileged importance to the widest and broadest backcloth. For the more fully synoptic one's view, the more confident one becomes that one is reckoning with all possible threats of vilification. The movement is towards the discarding of blinkers and frames that artificially confine attention to a narrow context and which might equally artificially boost a sense of importance and worthwhileness. Only: on naturalist assumptions, the *sub specie aeternitatis* view must at least seem to vilify, by revealing human history in an ocean of emptiness before and after. Some of the logical darkness around the meaning-of-life questions comes from the uneasy awareness that there *are* alternative views, perspectives, more or less synoptic or selective in different ways, giving very different answers to questions of value, importance, futility. From this bewildering diversity the questioner seeks some release.

He may come to the problem with the belief or half-belief that there must be an authoritative view; and that if life is to be shown to be meaningful, this authoritative view will also be a value-confirming, value-enhancing view. On authoritativeness, however, I think he is asking for what cannot be given. Either a 'view' is a sheer psychological fact about how someone sees human activity, in which case it has nothing that can properly be called 'authority' – though it may have strikingness and imaginative force. Or, if we judge that a particular view does have authority, this is to make a judgment of value and not simply to describe one's imaginings. Now, the estimate of the importance of human life implied in the 'authoritative' view may or may not conflict with the estimate one makes on other bases. If it does not conflict, there is no further problem: if it does conflict, then we must ask, Which has to yield, the judgment that the perspective is authoritative, or the independent (perhaps workaday) estimate of worthwhileness? The criteria for authoritativeness, crucially, are no less challengeable than the independent value-judgment: only by the agent weighing up, arbitrating between, or oscillating between, the two clashing sets of evaluations, can he deal with his dilemma. If he resolves the dilemma, it is resolved by his own autonomous value-judgments: and therefore the promise of having it resolved for him by some self-evident authoritativeness is not fulfilled.

Despite this argument, the naturalist ought to admit a substantial difference between his position and that of the Christian theist. There must in fact remain, with the naturalist, an uncomfortable tension or conflict between the 'close-up', anthropocentric view or perspective that can sustain his sense of meaningfulness and worthwhileness, and on the other hand his sense of intellectual obligation to the objective, scientific and anti-anthropocentric view – which tends to vilify, if not logically, then psychologically. The Christian is not exposed to this tension in the same way or to the same extent. The doctrines of divine creation and of incarnation combine to rule out the judgment that, in leaving the arena of the human, one is leaving simultaneously the theatre of mind and purpose and value. For the theist, that is, there is the implicit promise of a *harmony* of perspectives. To challenge that is to challenge the ultimate coherence of theism.

Once again, the meaning-of-life vocabulary may be so used (with exacting criteria of application), that only where such a harmony is promised can human life be properly called meaningful. Or at least the reluctance of a theist to concede that life can be meaningful to the unbeliever may reflect this, perhaps unanalysed but sensed, difference between their views of the world.

In the greater part of this discussion we have been assuming that the paradigm case of a satisfactory answer to problems about the meaning of life is contained in Christian theism, and that the question for the non-Christian is whether anything at all can be rescued from a collapse of meaning. This assumption, however, may be questioned in various ways. Two of these must be briefly mentioned.

That Christianity is able to provide a satisfactory answer is implicitly denied by those critics who claim that no hereafter, even of endless beatitude, could compensate for some of the evils actually endured by men here and now.[7] To revert to the musical analogy: in a 'meaningful' work, the exhibition passages fulfil and complete the anticipatory passages, which are unsatisfying by themselves. We can conceive of an anticipatory passage, however, which is so atrocious musically that nothing that followed it, even of high quality, could be said to fulfil or complete it. It may be argued that some 'passages' in some people's lives are so evil that nothing could conceivably justify them. As with a *privatio* theory of evil, so with analysis in terms of 'introductory quality': it makes out evil to be what we cannot by any means always see it to be, as able to be supplemented so as to become ingredient in an aesthetically and morally valuable whole. Here, therefore, the meaning-of-life problem runs into the problem of evil. To the extent that one is baffled by the problem of evil, to the same extent one must be baffled by the meaning of life. We cannot open up that problem here.

Secondly, in his aggressively anti-theistic argument, Kurt Baier claims that theism seeks to give meaning and purpose to human life in a morally objectionable way. Understanding one's life as given purpose by God involves a thoroughgoing self-abasement or self-annulment quite incompatible with the stance of a moral agent. This self-abasement is a correlative of the recognition of God's holiness (on current accounts), the realisation in numinous dread that God is 'wholly other'.

The objection is impressive and serious, and certainly effective against some forms and formulations of theism. If the 'otherness' of God and the *tremendum* side of the mystery are one-sidedly stressed, then human moral judgment and divine purpose are bound to be seen as incommensurable. An attitude of worshipfulness will involve an abrogating of moral autonomy.

It seems equally clear, however, that this is not the only posture a theist can adopt. Worship is by no means a simple, single-stranded concept. To worship is not only to yield to an overwhelming of the intellect or engage in unthinking, undiscerning adulation. Something very different from this is expressed, for instance, in the *B Minor Mass* or Stravinsky's *Symphony of Psalms*. An act of worship need not be a submitting of oneself, without insight, to the wholly inscrutable. Moral perfection and beauty, fused in an intensifying strangeness, are being celebrated, as these are believed to inhere in God. Evaluative reflection is being exercised: it is very far from abdicating. The worshipper is not passively, heteronomously, accepting claims about divine greatness: he is actively and autonomously recognising and relishing them. His worship is not a preface to a life of submission to commands *ab extra*. The very ingredients of his worship itself – in attitude and feeling – become part of his own inner life, the stillness of soul, the wonderment and solemnity.

The element of strangeness, of *mysterium*, has however a further role to play. Without cancelling the values, moral and aesthetic, that are celebrated in the act of worship, it powerfully intimates that they are nonetheless open to further transformation. It forbids thinking that the human vision of the good is precisely congruent with the nature of divine goodness. There is both recognition of affinity and awareness of disparity. But the latter need not be taken as a command to surrender autonomy: rather to extend progressively the zone of 'recognition'.

If it is true that a worshipful stance does not involve abrogating moral autonomy, neither need an acceptance of a divine purpose or meaning to the worshipper's life. This would indeed involve a regulating of one's life, a limiting of one's projects to what, rightly or wrongly, one judged to be compatible with God's will and intention. But such a limiting or circumscribing is a common feature of familiar moral situations, where one acts say, as a member of a trust, or has a special status in a group, a status that prescribes special obligations. In many, if not all such cases – and the case of divine purpose is no exception – the regulating of action is necessary, if some good or goods is to be realised. A rational person will make it his business to understand how the relevant moral institution does bring about that good. In the theistic case one needs reasons for believing that God's wisdom, goodness and power are such that the following of his will is a surer way to achieving goods in general than by carving out patterns of life that ignore or transgress his will.

Nevertheless, this sort of language quickly brings one to difficulties more stubborn than the original problem of autonomy. The fact that some worshipful activity expresses morally and aesthetically valuable states of mind does nothing to guarantee the existence of the God who is the primary object of the worship. It cannot show that God, if he exists, has the qualities celebrated in the act of worship, that these qualities are mutually compatible in a single being or that God can have these qualities and the world be the sort of world it is. And we confront the problem of how one can meaningfully speak of God, an infinite being, as having such features of finite person-hood as willing, intending, purposing. In a word, there remain difficulties enough in the theistic conception of the meaning and purpose of life, but they are the general difficulties of theism itself. The objection that the theist must abdicate his moral status is by no means decisive against all forms of theism, although valid against some.[8]

At the start of this article I mentioned one terse and gruff dismissal of the whole topic, the meaning of life: 'Life is not a statement, is not a linguistic entity, so cannot strictly be said to have or lack meaning.' We evaded this objection by way of a part-equating of 'meaning', in this context, with 'point' or 'purpose'. Yet it is worth asking whether, in discussing the meaning of life, some analogy with linguistic meaning may not often be operative – either in the background or the foreground of attention, helpfully or misleadingly. In what ways could it operate?

The words in a meaningful sentence 'cohere'. Words in a random list do not: like the events of a 'meaningless' life, they merely succeed each other discretely and atomistically, and are no more. The 'past' of a piece of discourse to which one is listening is felt as active and as bearing upon the presently uttered words. It is not a 'lost' past. Neither is it an obsessively dominant past, that imposes a static and completed pattern in place of the developing and novel pattern that the piece of discourse builds up. Certainly life is not a piece of discourse, and the motifs that supply coherence and continuity to it are very different from a rule-governed syntax. But if not pressed to breaking-point, the analogy may have a regulative function in the managing of our relation to our own past. Extreme cases of *failure* in this task can be seen in schizophrenics to whom every day is 'a separate island with no past or future', and who lack all sense of continuity, coherence; and, at the other pole, those who feel 'nailed' to their past, unable to distance it at all.[9]

The vocabulary of 'meaning', however, can obviously do no detailed regulating or managing by itself. If it appears to do much more than hold the bare form of the task before the attention, it may be spellbinding its user into illusion. It may suggest that the pattern of our life as a whole has a unity, and an availability to recollection *in* its unity, beyond what is in fact possible. We may say of apparent unity and coherence in life what Proust said of 'the total value of our spiritual nature': 'At whatever moment we estimate it, … it is more or less fictitious; … notwithstanding the long inventory of its treasures, … now one, now another of these is unrealisable … It is an illusion that our inward wealth is perpetually in our possession.'[10]

The linguistic analogy may lure one on still further. The words of a sentence are uttered as the clock ticks, and the events of a life occur as the clock ticks: but the meaning of the sentence is not an episode in time – and the meaning of the life …? To yield to the suggestion, and to say 'timeless' of the patterns of continuities, overlapping motifs of a life would be no more illegitimate than to say the same thing of logical relations and patterns. Nevertheless, one cannot use the language of 'timelessness', in respect of life, without evoking a whole syndrome of distinctive aspirations, for 'deliverance from time', for experience as a *totum simul*, for 'eternal life': and, seductive though these are, would they not surely be out of place in such reflections?

Yet some writers might not hurry to exorcise them. Santayana, for instance, argued that eternal life cannot be satisfactorily conceived as an endless succession of events, nor, coherently, as a *totum simul;* and concluded that eternity is experienced only in the contemplating of timeless objects and structures.[11] To contemplate the web of one's life's aims, its themes and articulating images, might count, on such a view, as affording as much fulfilment of the longing for eternity as the nature of things affords, everything beyond that being ultimately delusory.

It is natural and not at all absurd for a naturalistic philosopher to seek some (inevitably limited and provisional) substitute for a metaphysical or religious doctrine of eternal life. If he judges that doctrine to be logically incoherent anyway, there is all the less reason to protest if he chooses to savour those facets of experience that give a *partial* backing to the doctrines. The important thing is that he should himself be under no illusions. When he uses the vocabulary of timelessness, the 'metaphysical pathos' of his discourse must be appropriate to his real beliefs and must not borrow illegitimate splendour from the theism and mysticism he rejects.

It is possible (and we have remarked on this briefly already) to take note of all the senses we have been discussing, senses in which life may be held to have meaning within a non-theistic philosophy, to share, at least in outline, the value-theory of the philosophers with whom we started, and yet to insist that life and individual lives are without meaning – 'really'. What is a person doing who insists on this answer?

He may be claiming that life could be thought of as having meaning only so long as that meaning was believed to be a matter for discovery, not for creation and value-decision. He may be claiming that, to be meaningful, life would have to be *comprehensively* meaningful and its meaning invulnerable to assault. Worthwhile objectives must be ultimately realisable, despite appearances. If the Kantian postulates cannot be made, meaningfulness goes: it is for him an all-or-nothing matter. Otherwise expressed, the question about meaning can be put as a question about contingency and fortuitousness. If our attempts to impose or discover coherence and purpose in a life can operate only within the narrow *Spielraum* left by an unplanned and patternless 'facticity', in the end by accidents of birth and death, then the language of meaning is far more misleading (sardonically so) than it is useful.[12] If Nietzsche speaks of how desirable it is to 'die at the right time', of the 'free death' that 'consummates', he succeeds only in throwing into stronger relief the impossibility of guaranteeing anything of the sort, and we recall his own lingering ('meaningless') end as a case in point.

The vocabulary of meaning can thus be rejected *en bloc*, as for instance atheist existentialists have tended to reject it. In criticism, perhaps only this can be said: that it is a pity to expend in one rhetorical gesture a piece of discourse that can be used to express important distinctions between and within individual human lives. The gesture, though impressive, is extravagant and linguistically wasteful. But, so far as the rejection is a piece of (negative) verbal stipulation, one is free to opt for it: the language of the meaning of life is not indispensable. Alternatively, as we saw, one may prune and rationalise and redefine the vocabulary, restricting it to judgments about purposefulness or knowledge how to live. Perhaps there is most to be said for the third option, an elucidatory and conservative tracing of senses of 'the meaning of life' in literature and philosophy, and an attempt to see how differently the tasks of a life can look when they are viewed in the light of the many analogies of meaning.

Our sample of these analogies in this article, if not random, is certainly not complete.

Notes

1. I had completed this article before seeing relevant studies by John Wisdom – *Paradox and Discovery* (1966), Ch. IV, and by Ilham Dilman – *Philosophy*, Oct. 1965.

2. H. D. Aiken, *Reason and Conduct* (New York, 1962), p. 374. See chapter xvi as a whole.

3. Obviously relevant autobiographical quarries include *The Prelude, Dichtung und Wahrheit*, Chesterton's *Autobiography* and Berdyaev's *Dream and Reality*.

I have discussed some other aspects of these topics in 'Vision and Choice in Morality', *Proc. Arist. Soc.* Suppl. vol. 1956, reprinted in *Christian Ethics and Contemporary Philosophy*, ed. I. T. Ramsey (S.C.M. 1966). The present article is generally complementary to that paper.

4. Roy Pascal, *Design and Truth in Autobiography* (1960), pp. 191, 181.

5. In the studies from which this discussion started, Baier and Nielsen, e.g., acknowledge that, on their analysis,

particular lives may, in particular extreme situations, be 'meaningless'.

6. For instance: 'Art celebrates with peculiar intensity the moments in which the past reinforces the present and in which the future is a quickening of what now is' (Dewey, *Art as Experience* (1934), p. 18).

7. Dostoevsky's is the classic statement: see *The Brothers Karamazou*, Book V, chap. 4.

8. Further arguments on this topic can be found in C. C. J. Webb's criticism of N. Hartmann, *Religion and Theism* (1934), pp. 69–86, 87, 144 to end.

9. On these forms of schizophrenia, see R. May, *Existence* (1958), pp. 66 (quoting Minkowski), 68.

10. *Sodome et Gomorrhe*, vol. I. p. 213 (Eng. tr., *Cities of the Plain*, vol. 1, p. 218).

11. *The Philosophy of Santayana*, ed. I. Edman (1953), pp. 206–11.

12. Sartre: 'All existing things are born for no reason, continue through weakness and die by accident. ... It is meaningless that we are born; it is meaningless that we die.'

1.4

Philosophy and the Meaning of Life

Robert Nozick

The question of what meaning our life has, or can have, is of utmost importance to us. So heavily is it laden with our emotion and aspiration that we camouflage our vulnerability with jokes about seeking for the meaning or purpose of life: A person travels for many days to the Himalayas to seek the word of an Indian holy man meditating in an isolated cave. Tired from his journey, but eager and expectant that his quest is about to reach fulfillment, he asks the sage, "What is the meaning of life?" After a long pause, the sage opens his eyes and says, "Life is a fountain." "What do you mean, life is a fountain?" barks the questioner. "I have just traveled thousands of miles to hear your words, and all you have to tell me is that? That's ridiculous." The sage then looks up from the floor of the cave and says, "You mean it's not a fountain?" In a variant of the story, he replies, "So it's not a fountain."

The story is reassuring. The supposed sages are frauds who speak nonsense, nonsense they either never thought to question ("You mean it's not a fountain?") or do not care very much about ("So it's not a fountain"). Surely, then, we have nothing to learn from these ridiculous people; we need not seek their ludicrous "wisdom".

But why was it necessary for the joke to continue on after the sage said "life is a fountain", why was it necessary for the story to include the seeker's objection and the sage's reply? Well, perhaps the sage *did* mean something by "life is a fountain", something profound which we did not understand. The challenge and his reply show his words were empty, that he can give no deep and illuminating interpretation to his remark. Only then are we in a secure position to laugh, in relief.

However, if we couldn't know immediately that his answer "life is a fountain" was ridiculous, if we needed further words from him to exclude the lingering possibility of a deeper meaning to his apparently preposterous first reply, then how can we be sure that his second

Robert Nozick (1981) "Philosophy and the Meaning of Life," Chapter 6 in *Philosophical Explanations*, Cambridge, MA: Harvard University Press, pp. 571–600.

Exploring the Meaning of Life: An Anthology and Guide, First Edition. Edited by Joshua W. Seachris.
© 2013 John Wiley & Sons, Inc. Published 2013 by John Wiley & Sons, Inc.

answer also does not have a deeper meaning which we don't understand? He says "You mean it's not a fountain?"; but who are *you* to mean? If you know so much about it, then why have you gone seeking him; do you even know enough to recognize an appropriate answer when you hear it?

The questioner apparently came in humility, seeking the truth, yet he assumed he knew enough to challenge the answer he heard. When he objects and the sage replies, "so it's not a fountain", was it to gain this victory in discussion that the questioner traveled so far? (The story is told that Gershom Scholem, the great scholar of kabbalism, as a young man sought out practitioners of kabbalah in Jerusalem, and was told he could study with them on the condition that he not ask any questions for two years. Scholem, who has a powerful, critical, and luminous intelligence, refused.)

When he set out on his trip, did the questioner hope for an intellectual formula presenting the meaning of life? He wanted to know how he should live in order to achieve a life with meaning. What did he expect to hear from this meditating man in a cave high in the mountains? "Go back to the posh suburb and continue your present life, but shift to a less pressured job and be more accessible to your children"? Presumably, the man in the cave is following what he takes to be the path to a meaningful life; what else can he answer except "follow my path, be like me"? "Are you crazy; do you think I am going to throw everything over to become a scruffy person sitting in a cave?" But does the seeker know enough to exclude that life as the most (or only) meaningful one, the seeker who traveled to see *him*?

Could *any* formula answer the question satisfactorily? "The meaning of life is to seek union with God" – oh yeah, that one. "A meaningful life is a full and productive life" – sure. "The purpose of life is to pursue the task of giving meaning to life" – thanks a lot. "The meaning of life is love" – yawn. "The meaning of life is spiritual perfection" – the upward and onward trip. "The meaning of life is getting off the wheel of life and becoming annihilated" – no thanks. No one undertakes the trip to the sage who hasn't already encountered all the known formulas and found them wanting. Does the seeker think the sage has some *other* words to tell him, words which somehow have not reached print? Or is there a secret formula, an esoteric doctrine that, once heard, will clarify his life and point to meaning? If there were such a secret, does he think the wise man will tell it to *him*, fresh from Los Angeles with two days of travel by llama and foot? Faced with such a questioner, one might as well tell him that life is a fountain, perhaps hoping to shock him into reconsidering what he is doing right then. (Since he will not understand anything, he might as well be told the truth as best he can understand it – the joke would be that life *is* a fountain. Better yet would be for that to get embodied in a joke.)

If it is not words the questioner needs – certainly no short formula will help – perhaps what he needs is to encounter the person of the sage, to be in his presence. If so, questions will just get in the way; the visitor will want to observe the sage over time, opening himself to what he may receive. Perhaps he will come eventually to find profundity and point in the stale formulas he earlier had found wanting.

Now, let us hear another story. A man goes to India, consults a sage in a cave and asks him the meaning of life. In three sentences the sage tells him, the man thanks him and leaves. There are several variants of this story also: In the first, the man lives meaningfully ever after; in the second he makes the sentences public so that everyone then knows the meaning of life; in the third, he sets the sentences to rock music, making his fortune and enabling everyone to whistle the meaning of life; and in the fourth variant, his plane crashes as he is flying off from his meeting with the sage. In the fifth version, the person listening to me tell this story eagerly asks what sentences the sage spoke.

And in the sixth version, I tell him.

Modes of Meaning(fullness)

As briskly as we can, let us distinguish different senses and kinds of meaning, in order to assess their relevance to our concern.

I.   *Meaning as external causal relationship*: as causal consequences ("this means war"), causal antecedents or causal concomitants that serve as a basis of inference ("those spots mean measles, smoke means fire, red sky at night means fair weather").

II. *Meaning as external referential or semantic relation*: synonomy ("brother" means male sibling), reference ("the man in the corner" means him), standing for a fact (a white flag means they surrender) or symbolizing (the meaning of Yeats' "rough beast").

III. *Meaning as intention or purpose*: intending an action ("he meant well", "what is the meaning of this outburst?" "did you mean to do that?"), purpose ("this play is meant to catch the conscience of the king"), or (Gricean) intending to convey or indicate something via another's recognizing this intention ("by that gesture he meant to insult us").

IV. *Meaning as lesson*: "The Nazi period means that even a most civilized nation can commit great atrocities", "Gandhi's success means that nonviolent techniques sometimes can win over force."

V.   *Meaning as personal significance, importance, value, mattering*: "You mean a lot to me", "the repeal of that legislation means a lot to them". Under this rubric is a completely subjective notion, covering what a person thinks is important to him, and one somewhat less so, covering what affects something subjectively important to him, even if he does not realise this.

These first five notions are not intractable; one might hope they could provide at least some elements for explaining the next two, which are more obscure.

VI. *Meaning as objective meaningfulness*: importance, significance, meaning.

VII. *Meaning as intrinsic meaningfulness*: objective meaning (VI) in itself, apart from any connections to anything else.

VIII. *Meaning as total, resultant meaning*: the sum total and web of something's meaning I–VII.

Using these distinctions, let us consider the question about the meaning of our life or of our existence. A life easily can have meaning as external causal relationships, for example (ignoring adultery, artificial insemination, parthenogenesis, and virgin birth) your life means that your parents had sexual relations at least once, your existence means there will be less room on earth for all the others. On this reading, every life has (multiple) meaning, and if these causally connected things need not be inferable, a life will mean all of its causal antecedents and consequents and concomitants, and perhaps all of theirs as well, in ever widening circles. The meaning of a life, then, would be the whole causal nexus and flow of events; the causal nexus is means by the life's place in it. Thereby is gotten the result that a life certainly means something big and impressive; importance might be attributed to the life due to its role in this impressive web – see how much has prepared the way for it, and how much will flow from it, by the same processes which govern everything. However, this may involve a diminution in relative importance: everything thus connected in the web of events becomes equally important.

It is even easier to establish very impressive semantic meaning to our lives, at least for one sort of semantic meaning. Stipulative definitions can give a word new or altered semantic meaning. For example, I can say that by a *smink* I shall mean a ridiculous example introduced to illustrate a point. To my knowledge, no one else ever has used this word, or used any other word with this meaning. I have just given it this meaning. By stipulation, I have tied the word smink to this meaning; all I need do is use it consistently with this meaning hereafter.

There is no reason of principle why only words or gestures can have semantic meaning. It certainly is convenient that these be the vehicles of meaning – being producible at will, they are easily used for communication. However, some physical objects also are producible at will, while certain words might not be, due to difficulty in pronunciation. So we might stipulate that an event or object (for example, the particular copy of this book you now are reading) will have a specific meaning. And if we can stipulate meanings for objects, we similarly can stipulate meaning for your life or for you, and make this meaning be as exalted as you please. Let your life (be stipulated to) mean the triumph of justice or goodness in the universe. Presto, you life has meaning.

Clearly, this is ridiculous; no such arbitrary connections between a person's life and what it is stipulated to mean can give it the requisite sort of meaning. But we should not leave the topic of semantic meaning without seeing whether there is some nonarbitrary way that a person's life can semantically refer to or mean something. Let us say, following Nelson Goodman, that something exemplifies a property, characteristic, pattern, trait, or attribute, if it both has that property and also refers to it.[1] A life, then, would exemplify those properties it both refers to and has.

It is easy to see how a person's life can have properties. To tell us how a life can refer semantically to these properties we should bring in the third sense of meaning, meaning as intention or purpose. A person can mean something by what he does, or have a certain purpose for what he makes. Similarly, by external design people could have been created as semantic objects, for example, by God to refer to himself. If God's purpose in creating people was to have them refer to himself, and he gave them some properties ("in the image of God") to facilitate this referring, then everyone would be something like a name of God. (Would this be sufficient meaning for us? Is the universe a token through which God reflexively self refers?)

Let us leave theological speculations aside and ask whether a person's life can refer semantically in virtue of his intending or meaning his own life to have certain properties.

The topic of intention is an intricate one; any adequate theory will have to incorporate the directed, focused quality of intention. I intend to bring about only some aspects of what I do, even of what I know will occur when I act. Intending is something like intending to make a particular description true. I can intend to eat vanilla ice cream, and know that if I do so my life will include an incident of vanilla ice cream eating, without thereby intending my life to be that of a sometime vanilla ice cream eater; I need have no such grand intention about my whole life. My intention need not focus upon that aspect of my action.

To intend that my life be a certain way, I must have an intention or desire or goal or plan that focuses upon my life as a whole, or at least upon a significant portion of it. The statement of my intention, its focus, must include some reference to my life. The strongest sort of intention about one's life is a *life plan*,[2] an individual's set of coherent, systematic purposes and intentions for his life. These need not be specified fully, they will leave much open for further detailing, they can be revised, and so on. A life plan specifies the intentional focus of a person's life, his major goals (perhaps partially ordering them), his conception of himself, his purposes, what if anything he dedicates or devotes himself to, and so forth. Unlike the example of intending to eat vanilla ice cream (which would be included as a specific part only in a very strange life plan), a life plan focuses on a person's whole life or a significant chunk of it as a life.

Using this notion of a life plan, we can say that a person's life refers to a property if its having that property is a (weighty) part of the life plan he is engaged in putting into effect. His life exemplifies a property if it both has it and refers to it.

A life plan can have and refer to a property without showing or communicating this. The life of a furtive criminal, in this sense, might mean: steal as much as you can, undetected. In contrast to this, a person's life goals can shine forth. Let us say that a person lives transparently to the extent that the structure and content of what he exemplifies is clear; his life plan (its arrangement and hierarchy of goals, and so forth) is evident to those who take the trouble to notice what he does and says. The surface of his life, its public face, does not hide or cover his life plan. His life is not a mystery, his fundamental motivations and goals are not undetectable. He has made his life an open book.

However, just as empirical data underdetermine a scientific theory, so actions do not uniquely fix the life plan from which they flow. Different life plans are compatible with and might yield the same actions. So, people also state or explain why they act as they do, especially when other prevalent life plans that differ importantly would lead to that same behavior. Some take pains to perform the very actions wherein their life plans and goals significantly diverge from other – they delineate themselves. It is a puzzle how so many people, including intellectuals and academics, devote enormous energy to work in which nothing of themselves or their important goals shines forth, not even in the way their work is presented. If they were struck down, their children upon growing up and examining their work would never know why they had done it, would never know *who* it was that did it. They work that way and sometimes live that way, too.

The next notion of meaning on our list, meaning as lesson to be learned from, can build upon this previous one. People do not want their lives to provide negative lessons ("the lesson of his life is: do not live as he does"); although even here, they may take comfort if they think that lesson is important enough, and that others will act on the moral of their sad story. We hope the lessons to be learned from our lives will be connected more positively with the way we try to live, that the lesson will be based upon a positive evaluation of transparent features of our life plan.

This is recognizable as what some have meant by a meaningful life: (1) a life organized according to a plan and hierarchy of goals that integrates and directs the life, (2) having certain features of structure, pattern, and detail that the person intends his life to have (3) and show forth; the lives transparently so others can see see the life plan his life is based upon (4) and thereby learn a lesson from his life, (5) a lesson involving a positive evaluation of these weighty and intended features in the life plan he transparently lives. In sum, the pattern he transparently exemplifies provides a positive lesson.

Furthermore, the person himself may intend that others learn a lesson from his exemplification, intending also that they learn from it in virtue of recognizing his (Gricean) intention that they do so. In this way, he used his life (partly) to communicate a lesson to others, a lesson about living. This, I suppose, is what is meant by a *teacher*. (Philosophy had one such, Socrates – for how long shall we be able to continue to live off his momentum?) The life of such a person (semantically and nonarbitrarily) means the lesson it exemplifies; it has at least that meaning.

Even of such a shining and exemplary life, however, we can ask what it all amounts to. We can ask whether the lesson itself has any significance or meaning. We can distance ourselves from the life, see it as the particular thing it was, notice its limits, and wonder whether really it has any meaning. We can stand outside it and see it as a thing, as a nonvibrant and meaningless thing, soon to end in death, full of sound and fury, signifying nothing. …

God's Plan

One prevalent view, less so today than previously, is that the meaning of life or people's existence is connected with God's will, with his design or plan for them. Put roughly, people's meaning is to be found and realized in fulfilling the role allotted to them by God. If a superior being designed and created people for a purpose, in accordance with a plan for them, the particular purpose he had for them would be what people are *for*. This is distinct from the view that finds meaning in the goal of merging with God, and also from the view which holds that if you do God's will you will be rewarded – sit at his right hand, and receive eternal bliss – and that the meaning and purpose of life is to achieve this reward which is intrinsically valuable (and also meaningful?).

Our concern now is not with the question of whether there is a God; or whether, if there is, he has a purpose for us; or whether if there is and he had a purpose for us, there is any way to discover this purpose, whether God reveals his purpose to people. Rather, our question is how all this, even if true, would succeed in providing meaning for people's lives.

First, we should ask whether any and every role would provide meaning and purpose to human lives. If our role is to supply CO_2 to the plants, or to be the equivalent within God's plan of fixing a mildly annoying leaky faucet, would this suffice? Is it enough to be an absolutely trivial component within God's grand design? Clearly, what is desired is that we be important; having merely some role or other in God's plan does not suffice. The purpose

God has for us must place us at or near the center of things, of his intentions and goals. Moreover, merely playing some role in a central purpose of God's is not sufficient – the role itself must be a central or important one. If we describe God's central purpose in analogy with making a painting, we do not want to play the role of the rag used to wipe off brushes, or the tin in which these rags are kept. If we are not the central focus of the painting, at least we want to be like the canvas or the brush or the paint.

Indeed, we want more than an important role in an important purpose; the role itself should be positive, perhaps even exalted. If the cosmic role of human beings was to provide a negative lesson to some others ("don't act like them") or to provide needed food for passing intergalactic travelers who *were* important, this would not suit our aspirations – not even if afterwards the intergalactic travelers smacked their lips and said that we tasted good. The role should focus on aspects of ourselves that we prize or are proud of and it should use these in ways connected with the reasons why we prize them. (It would not suffice if the exercise of our morality or intelligence, which we prize, affects our brain so that the intergalactic travelers find it more *tasty*).

Do all these conditions guarantee meaning? Suppose our ingenuity was to be used to aid these travelers on their way, but that their way was no more important than ours. There was no more reason why we were aiding them (and perishing afterwords) than the other way around – the plan just happened to go that way. Would this cruel hoax leave us any more content than if there were no plan or externally given role at all?

There are two ways we individually or collectively could be included in God's plan. First, our fulfilling our role might depend upon our acting in a certain way, upon our choices or cooperation; second, our role might not depend at all upon our actions or choices – willy-nilly we shall serve. (In parallel to the notion of originative value, we can say that under the first our life can have originative meaning.) About the first way we can ask why we should act to fulfill God's plan, and about both ways we can ask why fitting God's plan gives meaning to our existence.[3] That God is good (but also sometimes angry?) shows that it would be good to carry out his plan. (Even then, perhaps, it need not be good *for us* – mightn't the good overall plan involve sacrificing us for some greater good?) Yet how does doing what is good provide meaning? Those who doubt whether life has meaning, even if transparently clearheaded, need not have doubted that it is good to do certain things.

How can playing a role in God's plan give one's life meaning? What makes this a meaning-giving process? It is not merely that some being created us with a purpose in mind. If some extragalactic civilization created us with a purpose in mind, would that by itself provide meaning to our lives? Nor would things be changed if they created us so that we also had a feeling of indebtedness and a feeling that something was asked of us. It seems it is not enough that God have some purpose for us – his purpose itself must be meaningful. If it were sufficient merely to play some role in some external purpose, then you could give meaning to your life by fitting it to my plans or to your parents' purpose in having you. In these instances, however, one immediately questions the meaningfulness of the other people's purposes. How do God's purposes differ from ours so as to be guaranteed meaningfulness and importance? Let me sharpen this question by presenting a philosophical fable.[4]

Teleology

Once you come to feel your existence lacks purpose, there is little you can do. You can keep the feeling, and either continue a meaningless existence or end it. Or you can discover the purpose your existence already serves, the meaning it has, thereby eliminating the feeling. Or you can try to dispose of the feeling by giving a meaning and purpose to your existence.

The first dual option carries minimal appeal; the second, despite my most diligent efforts, proved impossible. That left the third alternative, where, too, there are limited possibilities. You can make your existence meaningful by fitting it into some larger purpose, making yourself part of something else that is independently and incontestably important and meaningful. However, a sign of really having been stricken is that no preexisting purpose will serve in this fashion – each purpose that in other moods appears sufficiently fructifying then seems merely arbitrary. Alternatively, one can seek meaning in activity that itself is important, in something self-sufficiently intrinsically valuable. Preeminent among such activities, if there are any such, is creative activity. So, as a possible route out of my despair, I decided to create something that itself would be marvelous. (No, I did not decide to write a story beginning "Once you come to feel your existence lacks purpose." Why am I always suspected of gimmicks?)

The task required all of my knowledge, skill, intuitive powers, and craftsmanship. It seemed to me that my whole existence until then had been merely a preparation for this creative activity, so completely did it draw upon and focus all of my experience, abilities, and knowledge. I was excited by the task and fulfilled, and when it was completed I rested, untroubled by purposelessness.

But this contentment was, unfortunately, only temporary. For when I came to think about it, although it *had* taxed my ingenuity and energy to make the heavens, the earth, and the creatures upon it, what did it all amount to? I mean, the whole of it, when looked at starkly and coldly, was itself just an object, of no intrinsic importance, containing creatures in a condition as purposeless as the one I was trying to escape. Given the possibility that my talents and powers were those of a being whose existence might well be meaningless, how could their exercise endow my existence with purpose and meaning if it issued only in a worthless object?

At this point in my thoughts I came upon the solution to my problem. If I were to create a plan, a grand design into which my creation fit, in which my creatures, by serving the pattern and purpose I had ordained for them, would find their purpose and goal, then this very activity of endowing their existence with meaning and purpose would be my purpose and would give my existence meaning and point. Also, giving their existence meaning would, retroactively, make meaningful my previous activity of creation, it having issued in something that turned out to be of value and worth.

The arrangement has served. Only occasionally, out of the corner of my mind, do I wonder whether my arbitrarily having picked a plan for them can really have succeeded in giving meaning to the lives of the role-fulfillers among them. (It was necessary, of course, that I pick some plan or other for them, but no special purpose was served by my picking the particular plan I did. How could it have been? For my sole purpose then was to give meaning to my existence, and this one purpose was insufficient to determine any particular plan into which to fit my creatures.) However, lacking any conception of a less defective route to meaningfulness, I refuse to examine whether such a symbiotic arrangement truly is possible, whether different beings can provide meaning and point to each other's existence in a fashion so seemingly circular. Such questions press me toward the alternative I tremble to contemplate, yet to which I find my thoughts recurring. The option of ending it all, by now familiar, is less alien and terrifying than before. I walk through the valley of the shadow of death.

To imagine God himself facing problems about the meaningfulness of his existence forces us to consider how meaning attaches to his purposes. Let us leave aside my fancy that since it is important that our lives be provided with meaning, God's existence is made meaningful by his carrying out that task, so that – since his plans for us thereby become meaningful – our meaning is found in fitting those plans. For if it were possible for man and God to shore up each other's meaningfulness in this fashion, why could not two people do this for each other as well? Moreover, a plan whose *only* purpose is to provide meaning for another's life (or the planner's) cannot succeed in doing the trick; the plan must have some independent purpose and meaning itself.

Nor will it help to escalate up a level, and say that if there is a God who has a plan for us, the meaning of our existence consists in finding out what this plan asks of us and has in store for us. To know the meaning of life, on this view, would consist in our knowing where we came from, why we are here, where we are going. But apart from the fact that many religions hold such knowledge of God's purposes to be impossible (see, for example, *Ecclesiastes* and *Job*), and condemn various attempts to gain such knowledge (such as occult techniques and necromancy), and apart even from the fact that this seems too much a metapurpose, no more satisfying than saying "the purpose of life is the quest for the purpose of life", this view merely postpones the question of wherein God's plan itself is meaningful.

What is it about God's purposes that makes them meaningful? If our universe were created by a child from some other vast civilization in a parallel universe, if our universe were a toy it had constructed, perhaps out of prefabricated parts, it would not follow that the child's purposes were meaningful. Being the creator of all we see is not sufficient to endow his purposes with meaningfulness. Granted, the purposes of God are the purposes of a powerful and important being (as compared to us). However, it is difficult to see why that suffices for those purposes to ground our existence in meaning. Could the purposes of scientists so give meaning to artificially created short-lived animal life they maintained in a controlled laboratory environment? The scientists, creators of the animals' universe and life, would be as gods to them. Yet it would be unbearably poignant if the most intelligent animal, in a leap of intuition, did its equivalent of worshiping the absent scientist.

Various gnostic doctrines have held that our world (or universe) was created by a being who was not the supreme divine being, or who was not the only aspect of the divine being. These doctrines envisaged an even more supreme God above the creator of our universe. If some people were fulfilling (and were committed to fulfilling) the local Lord's commands and plans, would it follow that their lives had meaning? How are things different if it is the plan of the top God (must there be a top to the levels?) which we are fulfilling, and how is it to be determined which lead to follow?

Such speculations about levels, perhaps hidden, beneath levels are bewildering, especially since we shall never be able to claim with certainty of some religious doctrine or scientific theory that it has identified the "ground floor", that there cannot be, underneath the fundamental processes or entities E it identifies, even more fundamental hidden ones of a very different character which give rise to the reality or appearance of E. In his novel *The Magus* John Fowles depicts this: each time the central character comes to a view of what is occurring, this is undercut by a new and different deeper view.[5]

I don't say there is no ground floor (would it be better if there were not?), just that we wouldn't know it if we reached it. Even infinite reflexiveness could have a level underlying it, giving rise to it. My purpose is not to emphasize our limits as knowers but to note the power of our imaginations. We can always imagine a deeper reality, deeper even than what turns out to be the deepest; if we cannot imagine its precise character, nevertheless, we can imagine that there is such a thing. There are or can be mysteries within and behind mysteries. To mention only religious views, the Hindus speak of parabrahman which is beyond even Brahman, and gnostic views posit a God beyond the creator of this universe. Once we are embarked there is no sure stopping; why not a God who created that God, and so forth?

Not only can we not be certain about the ground floor; *it*, if it is the sort of thing that is conscious, cannot be either. For perhaps underneath or apart from everything it knows, is something else that created or underlies it, having carefully covered its tracks. Philosophers have sometimes searched for indicators of a conscious Absolute, in the hopes of making us "at home" and unalienated in the universe, akin to its fundamental character, or somehow favored by it.[6] If there were such an Absolute, it too must occasionally look over its shoulder for a glimpse of a yet deeper, and perhaps not fully friendly, reality. Even the Absolute is a little bit paranoid – so how alien from us can it be?

Yet "like us" does not mean it likes us and is supportive of us and our aspirations, as provided in the vision of a personal God who cares. Is the universe at its fundamental level friendly to our seeking of value; is there some cosmic undergirding so that values, in the phrase of William James, "throw the last stone"? Some have woven science-fiction fantasies of a level that is thus supportive – emissaries from intergalactic civilizations who watch over and guide our progress – and apparently find this comforting. This is not the "ground floor", though. But how important is it anyway that there be a force for value at that level, if it is so distant as effectively to have nothing to do with us? It is not difficult to imagine structures about levels that undercut other levels of reality and their support (or nonsupport) of value. It is less important, though, whether the ground floor exerts a force for value, than whether we do.

There also might turn out to be fewer levels than appear. The gnostic theorists, for example, whatever their evidence for multiple deities, would have had no way to exclude the possibility that there was but one deity who was schizophrenic or possessed different personalities which he alternately showed. On this view, rather than taking sides in a cosmic clash, the task of man for which he was created (by which personality?) might be to act as therapist to bring together the different personalities of God (unifying them or eliminating one?) – the task might be to heal God. This would certainly give man a central mission and purpose in the cosmic structure, but one might question the meaningfulness of harmonizing *that* structure. Another similar theory would see man not as therapist but as therapy, functioning as do patients' drawings in psychological treatment, produced with conflicting impulses to express its maker's nature.[7] When such a deity's products come to think of their maker as psychotic and in need of help and integration, it that a sign of a breakthrough of insight in *it*? (This would provide an ironic version of Hegel's view that in his philosophy Geist comes to full self-awareness.)

These diverse possibilities about the intentional and purposeful creation of our universe – by a child in another dimension, by one of a hierarchy of gods, by a schizophrenic God – press home the question of how, or in virtue of what, a religious view can ground the meaning of our lives. Just as the direct experience of God might unavoidably provide one with a motive to carry out his wishes, so it might be that such an experience (of which type of creator?) always would resolve all doubts about meaning. To experience God might leave one with the absolute conviction that his existence was the fountain of meaning, watering your own existence. I do not want to discount testimony reporting this. But even if we accepted it fully, it leaves unanswered the question of how meaning is possible. What is it about God, as usually conceived, in virtue of which he can ground meaning? How *can* there be a ball of meaning? Even if we are willing to treat the testimony in the way we treat accurate perceptual reports, there still remains the problem of understanding how meaning can be encountered in experience, of how there can be a stopping place for questions about meaning. How in the world (or out of it) can there be something whose nature contains meaning, something which just glows meaning?

In pursuing the question of which aspects of God can provide meaning to our existence, we have presented examples of other more limited imaginable beings who do have those aspects (for example, creator of our universe) yet who obviously fail to give meaning. Perhaps it is in that very step to these examples that we lose the meaning. Perhaps the intrinsic meaningfulness of God's existence and his purposes lies in his being unlimited and infinite, in his being at the ground floor and not undercut or dwarfed or put in a smaller focus by any underlying level or being or perspective. No wonder, then, that the meaning disappeared as we considered other cases that purported to isolate the salient meaning-producing aspect of God. (Still, there would remain questions about why only certain ways of being linked – as creation, worshiper, role-fulfiller, or whatever – transmit meaning to people from God.) If the plausibility of seeing God as providing a stopping place for questions about meaning is grounded in his very infinitude and unlimitedness, in there being no deeper level or wider perspective, we can ask what this shows about the notion of meaning. How must the notion of meaning be structured, what must be its content, for (only) unlimitedness to provide a secure basis for meaning and a stopping place for questions about meaning?

Transcending Limits

Attempts to find meaning in life seek to transcend the limits of an individual life. The narrower the limits of a life, the less meaningful it is.

The narrowest life consists of separated and disparate moments, having neither connection nor unity; for example, the life of an amnesiac who is unable to plan over several days or even moments because he forgets each day (or moment) what came before. Even someone capable of integrating his life may still lead this narrowest life, if he moves to get whatever at any moment he happens to want – provided this is not an overarching policy he will stick to even when specific wants run counter to it.

Integration of a life comes in gradations. The next notable type of life along the dimension of narrowness is one that is well integrated by overarching plans, goals, and purposes. In this case, though, the long term goals do not extend to anything beyond the person, to anything other than his own narrow concerns; for instance, the sole overarching goal that integrates his life plan might be to maximize the sum total of his life's pleasures. Of such lives we ask, "but what does that life add up to, what meaning does it have?" For a life to have meaning, it must connect with other things, with some things or values beyond itself. Meaning, and not merely of lives, seems to lie in such connections. To ask something's meaning is to ask how it is connected, perhaps in specified ways, to other things. Tracking, either of facts or of value, is a mode of being so connected, as is fitting an external purpose. The experience machine, though it may give you the experience of transcending limits, encloses you within the circle of just your own experiences. The phrase "the meaning you give to your life" refers to the ways you choose to transcend your limits, the particular package and pattern of external connections you successfully choose to exhibit.[8]

Mortality is a temporal limit and traces are a way of going or seeping beyond that limit. To be puzzled about why death seems to undercut meaning is to fail to see the temporal limit itself as a limit. The particular things or causes people find make their life feel meaningful all take them beyond their own narrow limits and connect them up with something else. Children, relationships with other persons, helping others, advancing justice, continuing and transmitting a tradition, pursuing truth, beauty, world betterment – these and the rest link you to something wider than yourself. The more intensely you are involved, the more you transcend your limits. World-historical causes link someone with wider concerns but may leave him equally limited along other more personal dimentions. Among personal relations, loving another brings us most outside our own limits and narrow concerns. In love between adults – their mutual openness and trust, the dismantling of the defenses and barriers people carefully have constructed to protect themselves against getting hurt, and the mutual recognition of this (mutual) nondefensiveness – some limits of the self are not merely breached but dissolved. This nondefensiveness is risky. Yet to be less than fully open to growth, because of this, makes the relationship itself a limit rather than a mode of transcending limits, while to preserve some armor, as insurance, constitutes yet another limit.

The problem of meaning is created by limits, by being just this, by being merely this. The young feel this less strongly. Although they would agree, if they thought about it, that they will realize only some of the (feasible) possibilities before them, none of these various possibilities is yet excluded in their minds. The young live in each of the futures open to them. The poignancy of growing older does not lie in one's particular path being less satisfying or good than it promised earlier to be – the path may turn out to be all one thought. It lies in traveling only one (or two, or three) of those paths. Economists speak of the opportunity cost of something as the value of the best alternative forgone for it. For adults, strangely, the opportunity cost of our lives appears to us to be the value of all the forgone alternatives summed together, not merely of the best other *one*. When all the possibilities were yet still before us, if felt to us as if we would do them all.

Some writers have held that we achieve meaning by affirming our limits and living with purpose within them, or (this is Sartre's view, as Arnold Davidson has reminded me) by defining ourselves in terms of what we exclude and reject; the possibilities we choose not to encompass. This living finely within limits may involve a surpassing of what one would have thought those limits entailed, or it may be that such living is valuable, forming a tight organic unity within those limits. Similarly, self-definition by what one chooses to exclude means that one includes and explicitly acts on that principle of rejection, thereby giving one's life greater unified definition. Thus such exclusion is one means to value, not a mode of meaning.

We need not assume there is a complete ordering with respect to the transcending of limits. Our lives contain many dimensions along which it will be clear what is more and what less limited, but this need not be clear for any two arbitrary points in the space of the n dimensions along which one can be limited – the ordering might be only partial. Therefore, it would be difficult to formulate the total meaningfulness of a person's life as a weighted sum or expected value, with the weights being his degree of intensity of involvement, ranging between zero and one, which are multiplied by an interval-scale measure of the meaningfulness of what the person is involved in or connected with, which measure varies inversely with limitedness. For that, we should be thankful.

However widely we connect and link, however far our web of meaningfulness extends, we can imagine drawing a boundary around all that, standing outside looking at the totality of it, and asking "but what is the meaning of that, what does that mean?" The more extensive the connections and linkages, the more imagination it may take to step outside and see the whole web for the particular thing it is. Yet it seems this always can be done. (Whether it will be done or not determines whether there will be a felt problem of meaning.) Consider the most exalted and far-reaching life or role imagined for man: being the messiah. Greater effect has been imagined for no other man. Yet still we can ask how important it is to bring whatever it is the messiah brings to the living beings of the third planet of a minor off-center star in the Milky Way galaxy, itself a galaxy of no special distinction within its particular metagalaxy, one of many in the universe. To see something's limits, to see it as that limited particular thing or enterprise, is to question its meaning.[9]

The intellectual life seems to offer one route across all limits: there is nothing that cannot be thought of, theorized about, pondered. Knowledge of deeper truths, fundamental laws, seems more meaningful since it takes us more significantly beyond our limits. And is the reason for the inadequacy of connecting with possibilities by "living in an imaginary world", that these possibilities don't have sufficient ontological status, or connection to them doesn't, for it to be a transcending of personal limits?

We often estimate the "meaningfulness" of work by the range of things that come within its purview, the range of different factors that have to be taken into account. The (hired) craftsman must take account of more than the assembly line worker, the entrepreneur must look out upon conditions in the wider world, and so forth. To be a technician is not merely to have a technique, but to be restricted to taking account of the narrow range of factors handled by the technique. Even if Socrates had a technique of thought, elenchus, still, as he cast his mind over the range of what was relevant to human concerns he was not a technician.

Via thought, we can be linked to anything and everything. Perhaps this, not professional chauvinism, explains why philosophers often have considered philosophical thought and contemplation the highest activity. Nothing escapes its purview. No assumption constitutes an unquestionable limit. In thought we do not thereby transcend all limits, however. Thought can link to everything, but that is merely one particular kind of link: thinking of. True, we can be connected with other kinds of linkages by thinking of them, too, and including them within our theory; yet this kind of connection with them still remains of one kind only. A unity of theory and practice is not established just by constructing a theory of practice.

In imagination, we stand outside a thing and all it is connected with, and we ask for the meaning of the totality. Connected with X is Y, and it is proposed that Y is the meaning of X. Standing outside, we ask for the meaning of Y itself, or for the meaning of X+Y together. Of each wider and less limited context or entity, we ask for its meaning, in turn. In two ways this can seem to undercut the meaning of the thing, X, with which we began. We can have reached a context Y so wide that X is no longer of any importance to it. The fact that Y has meaning is not placed in question, but the connection of the original X to Y is so attenuated, so insignificant from the perspective of Y, that X does not seem to have or gain any meaning in virtue of that connection. Furthermore, since meaning involves connection to wider context, it seems appropriate, demanded even, to take the widest context as that in which to consider something's meaning. Thus, we find people asking "from the point of view of all of human history, what difference does my life or this contemporary event make?" or "Given the immenstity of the universe and the billions upon billions of galaxies, probably teeming with life elsewhere, is all of human history itself of any significance?"

The second way the widening of the context can seem to undercut the meaning of our original concern is that we can reach a context Y that is so wide that it is not obvious what its meaning is – it just is. But if Y itself has no meaning of its own, then how can any X be provided with meaning by virtue of its connection with that Y? It seems impossible that meaning be based upon or flow from something that itself has no meaning. If meaning is to trickle down from Y to us, mustn't there be some meaning there at the start?

Perhaps this natural picture is mistaken – perhaps the meaning of X can be Y, without Y itself or X+Y having meaning. Must what is the meaning of something itself have a meaning; cannot something's meaning just *be* its meaning without *having* one too? This would be impossible on the picture of something's meaning as had, like a liquid filling it, which we gain via our connection with it – the umbilical theory of meaning. However, if meaning itself is not a thing but a relationship then something can have meaning by standing in that relationship, even to something which itself does not stand further in that relationship. (Not every parent is a grandparent.) Consider the analogy of linguistic meaning. Some recent theories of language have come to see a word or sentence or utterances having meaning not as its being related to a metaphysically special entity, a meaning, but rather as its standing in some type of (functional) relationship.[10] Is it not appropriate, similarly, to view the notion of meaning, applied to someone's life, as relational, so that a life's meaning need not itself have its own further meaning or be intrinsically meaningful?

This view of meaning as explicitly relational helps to loosen the grip of the picture that requires, for there to be any meaning, that something be (but how can it be?) intrinsically meaningful.[11] However, there is no simple mistake or fallacy committed by the person who asks about the meaning of Y, or of X+Y. When the concern is the meaning of our life or existence, when X is our life, we want meaning all the way down. Nothing less will do. This meaning is like importance; to be important for something which itself is unimportant is for these purposes to be unimportant. The person who regards the meaning of X as dissolved when it is shown that the Y that is supposed to be X's meaning itself has no meaning of its own is not shown to be confused simply because there are or might be legitimate relativized or relational notions of importance or meaning. For he is not using and will not be satisfied by such a relativized notion. And do not hasten to argue that there is no conceivable coherent unrelativized notion. For that, if true, is not the solution – it is the problem.

The problem of meaning is created by limits. We cope with this by, in little ways or big, transcending these limits. Yet whatever extent we thereby reach in a wider realm also has its own limits – the same problem surfaces again. This suggests that the problem can be avoided or transcended only by something without limits, only by something that cannot be stood outside of, even in imagination. Perhaps, the question about meaning is stopped and cannot get a grip only when there is nowhere else to stand.

Notes

1. Nelson Goodman, *Languages of Art* (Bobbs-Merrill, Indianapolis, 1968), p. 52.
2. See John Rawls, *A Theory of Justice* (Harvard University Press, Cambridge, 1971), section 63.
3. The question of why we should act to fulfill God's plan, in case it is up to us, may appear foolish. After all, this is God, the creator of the universe, omniscient and omnipotent. But what is it about God, in virtue of which we should carry out our part in his plan? Put aside the consideration that if we do not, he will punish us severely; this provides a prudential reason of the sort a slave has for obeying his more powerful master. Another reason holds that we should cooperate in fulfilling God's plan because we owe that to him. God created us, and we are indebted to him for existence. Fulfilling his purpose helps to pay off our debt of gratitude to him. (See Abraham Heschel, *Who is Man?*, Stanford University Press, 1965, p. 108.) Even if we don't want to play that role, it not being the sort of activity we prize, nevertheless must we do it to repay the debt? We might think so on the following grounds. You were created for the role, and if not for God's desire that you fulfill the role, you wouldn't exist at all; furthermore, existing while performing that role is better than not existing at all, so you should be thankful you were created at all, even if only for that role. Therefore, you are obligated to carry it out.

    However, we do not think this form of reasoning is cogent when it concerns parents and children. The purposes parents have when they plan to have children (provided only these stop short of making the child's life no better than nonexistence) do not fix the obligations of the child. Even if the parents' only purpose was to produce a slave, and a slave's life is better than nonexistence, the offspring does not owe to his parents acquiescence in being enslaved. He is under no obligation to cooperate, he is not owned by his parents even though they made him. Once the child exists, it has certain rights that must be respected (and other rights it can assert when able) even if the parents' very purpose was to produce something without these rights. Nor do children owe to their parents whatever they would have conceded in bargaining before conception (supposing this had been possible) in order to come into existence.

    Since children don't owe their parents everything that leaves their lives still a net plus, why do people owe their ultimate creator and sustainer any more? Even if they owe God no more, still, don't children owe their parents something for having produced and sustained them, brought them to maturity and kept them alive? To the extent that this debt to parents arises from their trouble and labor, since we don't cost an omnipotent God anything, there's nothing to pay back to him and so no need to. However, it is implausible that a child's whole debt to his parents depends merely on the fact that he was trouble. (When a parent takes great delight in his child's growth, so that any inconveniences caused are counterbalanced by the pleasures of parenthood, doesn't this child still owe something to the parent?) Still, at best, these considerations can lead to a limited obligation to our creator and sustainer – there is no arriving at Abraham by this route. To speak of a limited obligation may sound ludicrous here; "we owe everything to him." Everything may come from him, but do we owe it all back?

Our discussion thus far might leave a believer uncomprehending: he might speak as follows. "Why should one do what is wanted by an omnipotent, omniscient creator of you who is wholly good, perfect, and so on? What better reason could there be than that such a being wants you to do it? Catching the merest glimpse of the majesty and greatness and love of such a being, you would want to serve him, you would be filled with an overwhelming desire to answer any call. There would be a surrender rather than a calculation. The question 'why do it?' would not arise to someone who knew and felt what God was. That experience transforms people. You would do it out of awe and love. "I do not want to deny that the direct experience of God would or might well provide an overwhelming motive to serve him. However, there remains the second question: why and how does fitting God's plan and carrying out his will provide meaning to our lives?

4. This first appeared in *Mosaic*, Vol. III, no. 1, Spring 1971 (published by the Harvard-Radcliffe Hillel Society), pp. 27–8, as one of "Two Philosophical Fables", and is reprinted here with only minor changes.

5. See also the Jose Luis Borges story "The Circular Ruins" in his collection *Labyrinths* (New Directions, New York, 1964, pp. 45–50), in which a dreamer realizes that he himself also is dreamt; and note the tale of Chuang Tsu, who wonders if he dreamt the butterfly, or is dreamed by the butterfly. Each of these illustrates

levels undercutting levels, or alternate levels whose ordering is unclear. (Contrast the structure of the traditional detective story, wherein the detective penetrates appearance to reach the underlying, ground-floor reality.) It is as if the universe is or might be constructed according to an unbreakable code via a trapdoor function; we see the encoded message and even if we knew the generating rule we still could not find the plain text. See Martin Hellman, "The Mathematics of Public Key Cryptography", *Scientific American*, Vol. 241, August 1979, pp. 149–57.

6. Some carried out this task too enthusiastically. Fichte's view rendered reality less alien to us, but only by making it so much our product that others (for example Jean Paul, Madame de Staël) justifiably complained that it left us all alone. Would you join any country club that had you as its founder, sole member, and acreage?

7. Carl Jung pursued gnostic themes as revelatory of our psyche, seeing them not as metaphysically accurate but as the self's projections. An alternative theory might view the isomorphism as due to man's being created in the image of (a gnostic) god.

8. It may not be clear always whether there is a connection to something else. If to have the goal of advancing your own knowledge is to connect up with something beyond yourself, namely knowledge or truth, why doesn't the goal of advancing your own pleasure connect you up with something beyond yourself, namely pleasure? Is it the intentionality of knowledge that takes it outside of itself? Would the focused intention to participate in the Platonic Form of Pleasure, rather than merely to have pleasurable experiences, suffice to connect one up with something else?

9. There is a story told that Martin Buber once spoke to a group of Christians saying something like the following: We Jews and you Christians hold many beliefs in common. Both of us believe the messiah will come. You Christians believe he has been here before, so that he will be coming for a second time, while we Jews believe he will be coming for the first time. For the foreseeable future, there is much we can cooperate together on – and when the messiah *does* come, *then* we can ask him whether he's been here before.

There is only one thing to add to Buber's remarks. I would like to advise the messiah, when he comes and is asked the question whether he's been here before or not, to reply that he doesn't remember.

10. See W. V. Quine, "Philosophical Progress in Language Theory", *Metaphilosophy*, Vol. 1, 1970, pp. 2–19; Ludwig Wittgenstein, *Philosophical Investigations, and The Blue and the Brown Books* (Basil Blackwell, Oxford, 1958). In contrast, Jerrold Katz presents an explicitly Platonist interpretation of linguistics in *Languages and Other Abstract Objects* (Rowman and Littlefield, Totowa, New Jersey, 1981). Whatever the merits of Katz's proposal, it is illuminating to have that alternative presented and to see linguistics viewed under the classification of positions in the philosophy of mathematics, so that Chomsky's program is conceptualist, and so on.

11. For illuminating discussions of the latter as the view of Wittgenstein's *Tractatus Logico-Philosophicus*, and of the far-reaching consequences of the undermining in his *Philosophical Investigations* of the notion of an intrinsic terminus for meaning, see Bruce Goldberg, "The Correspondence Hypothesis", *Philosophical Review*, Vol. 77, 1968, pp. 438–54, and "The Linguistic Expression of Feeling", *American Philosophical Quarterly*, Vol. 8, 1971, pp. 86–92.

1.5

The Concept of a Meaningful Life

Thaddeus Metz

Well, my goodness, "What is the meaning of life?" you ask. What is the meaning of "meaning" in your question? And whose life? A worm's?

– John Updike[1]

I.   Introduction: The Meaning of "Meaning"

Compared with the questions of what constitutes happiness or rightness, contemporary normative theorists have done little to address the question of what constitutes meaningfulness.[2] This lack of interest is unjustified, for a theory of life's meaning would help to answer the following important questions, among many others: Why might a good marriage be considered more desirable than a great one-night stand? In what sense do strong candidates for euthanasia have "nothing left to live for"? What disadvantages are there to living in a highly industrialized, consumer society? What makes certain kinds of knowledge worth pursuing? Which attitudes should one have toward the prospect of one's death? Why might people need God in their lives? Is there any independent reason for being moral? What should the goal of psychotherapy be? How do the arts figure into the best life?

This essay does not answer any of these questions or even present a theory of life's meaning that could. Instead, it focuses on the prior issue of what a theory of life's meaning is about. One reason for the lack of systematic answers given to the question of life's meaning is surely that, as Updike notes, this question is imprecise and unclear. What are we asking when we ask whether and how a life is meaningful? Insofar as the answer to this second-order question is murky, theorists will be loathe to address the first-order question.

Thaddeus Metz (2001) "The Concept of a Meaningful Life," *American Philosophical Quarterly* 38(2): 137–53.

To help advance inquiry, then, this paper aims to clarify what we are asking when posing the question of what (if anything) makes a life meaningful.

People associate many different ideas with talk of "meaning," so that one must search for an account of the question that is primary in some way. Therefore, after sketching in section II the major conceptions of life's meaning in 20th century philosophical literature, the remainder of the paper seeks a satisfactory analysis of the concept of a meaningful life that these conceptions all address. In sections III and IV, the paper argues against two major kinds of analysis that are suggested by others' remarks. Next, in section V, the essay develops and critically examines a new analysis that avoids the problems facing the two extant accounts. In section VI, the paper concludes by nothing the ramifications of this discussion for future research into the meaning of life.

II.   Concept and Conceptions of Meaning

To achieve the goal of articulating what we are asking when inquiring into the meaning of life, it of course will not do merely to say that a meaningful life is a life that is "important" or "significant" or that it is an existence that "matters" or "has a point." These terms are synonyms of "meaningful." This paper is pursuing something more revealing than just enumerating terms that have a sense identical (or very similar) to that of the word "meaningful."[3] This essay instead seeks to expound this sense.

However, people associate different senses with the terms "meaningful life," and so this project must specify whose sense is to be articulated. This paper therefore aims to spell out the conceptual element that is at the core of 20th century philosophical discussions about the meaning of life. This essay seeks to analyze the concept that is common to the conceptions of life's meaning to be found in at least the Anglo-American philosophical literature. A *conception* of life's meaning is a theory of what makes a life meaningful. It is a general, fundamental, and systematic account of the conditions that constitute a significant existence. A conception of what makes life meaningful aims to describe the "underlying structure" of a significant existence in as few principles as possible. In contrast, the *concept* of a meaningful life is what the competing conceptions of a meaningful life are about. The concept of life's meaning is that which makes a given theory one of meaningfulness as opposed to, say, one of rightness or happiness.

One might have a prime facie worry about the project of seeking to articulate a concept that is common to the major philosophical conceptions of meaning. Specifically, there may be little reason for thinking that there in fact exists such a concept. Taking a cue from Wittgenstein and contemporary discussions of vagueness, one might reasonably suspect that there are no essential conditions for a theory to be about meaning as opposed to something else.

Perhaps there are not. However, it would be terribly interesting if there did turn out to be a single notion about which the many substantive theories of meaning are in dispute. And one can claim to know with robust justification that there is no unitary concept common to the diverse conceptions of meaning only after throughly searching for one – which has yet to be done. Furthermore, even if there turned out to be no such concept, searching for one would still enrich our understanding of what contemporary philosophical inquiry into life's meaning is about.

So, let us see how far we can get. What follows is an overview of the debate about life's meaning that one finds in 20th century analytic philosophy. The sundry views from the literature can be placed under one of three major headings. These three kinds of theories are not committed to saying that life is in fact significant; rather, they are accounts of what would constitute a meaningful life, were it to exist. Furthermore, these theories are not accounts solely of what would make life as a whole or on balance meaningful. They are instead in the first instance accounts of what would make a life meaningful in some respect or to some degree.[4]

Supernaturalism is one such theory. On this view, one's existence is significant only if one has a certain relation with some purely spiritual being or realm. If neither a god nor a soul existed, or if they existed but one failed to relate to them in the right way, then one's life would be utterly meaningless. There are several familiar types of supernaturalism. For example, justice theory says that meaning lives in conforming to God's purposes, which are the source of justice in this world, or doing good deeds and receiving one's just deserts in the next world. Perfection theory holds that one's life is meaningful by virtue of honoring one's higher, spiritual nature while on earth, or attaining the stage where one will commune with the highest conceivable being upon leaving the earth. Theists in the existentialist tradition, including Leo Tolstoy, Soren Kierkegaard, Emil Fackenheim, and Martin Buber,[5] are the ones who most prominently hold supernaturalism. Several analytically oriented philosophers have recently articulated or espoused the view,[6] and lay people frequently express such ideas. One often hears something like, "What is the point of living (or living in a particular way) if I will not survive the death of my body?"

Naturalism is the contradictory of supernaturalism. A naturalist account denies that life's meaning is contingent on the existence of a purely spiritual order. Naturalists can grant that relating to a god or a soul could confer meaning on a life; they simply dispute that such a relation is a necessary condition of a life's having any meaning.

Subjectivism is one of two sorts of naturalism worth distinguishing. This view holds that meaningful conditions vary, depending on the subject. Subjectivism maintains that what is meaningful for a given person is a function of that toward which she (or her group) has (or would have) a certain pro-attitude, e.g., wanting something and getting it, or setting something as an end and achieving it. William James, A. J. Ayer, Richard Taylor, Bernard Williams, and Stephen Darwall are some 20th century subjectivists about meaning.[7] Of these thinkers, Taylor has been addressed most, his discussion of Sisyphus being particularly engaging. Taylor and other subjectivists often defend their view by appealing to the intuitive claim that a life filled with boredom or frustration could not avoid being meaningless. The problem with Sisyphus, according to Taylor, is that he is not satisfied rolling a rock up a hill. Once we imagine Sisyphus with an intense desire to do what he must do, then it appears to Taylor that this life is filled with as much meaning as anyone could want.

Those who hold naturalistic *objectivism* question this appraisal of Sisyphus. Robert Nozick, David Wiggins, Charles Taylor, Peter Singer, and Susan Wolf are contemporary objectivists about life's meaning.[8] They say that certain features of our natural lives can make them meaningful, but not merely in virtue of any pro-attitude toward them. They tend to find objectivism plausible for two reasons. One thought is that not just any condition could confer meaning on a life, no matter what the pro-attitude toward it; a life simply cannot matter for rolling a rock, however much that is wanted or chosen. The second intuition is that exemplary lives of meaning, say, those of Einstein or Ghandi, do not seem fundamentally to depend on a god or a soul. Instead, supererogatory actions, scientific discoveries, artistic creations, and loving relationships seem able to enhance the significance of a life, even in the absence of a purely spiritual order.

These, then, are the major theories of meaning that one encounters in the literature. Almost all philosophical discussion of meaning can be understood as an articulation, defense, or critique of these three theories. However, not all of it can be. Supernaturalism, subjectivism, and objectivism are accounts of what would make an *individual's* life meaningful. Some philosophers have addressed the different issue of the meaning of the human race or the universe.[9] Furthermore, these three theories are *normative*. Those who hold these theories construe them as accounts of something that would be intrinsically good to have in one's life (or of something that provides a basic reason for action). Some philosophers have addressed a contrasting notion of meaning that is merely descriptive, lacking inherent desirability or choiceworthiness.[10] In sum, to the extent that a discussion of life's meaning does not take meaning to be one aspect of the best life for a person, it gets set aside here. This paper's goal is to analyze the concept of meaning relevant to the normative status of individual lives.

Taking for granted that supernaturalism, subjectivism, and objectivism are the major conceptions of meaning, there are two clear criteria for an analysis of the concept of meaning. First, an analysis of the concept of meaning should allow for the logical possibility of supernaturalism, subjectivism, and objectivism being conceptions of meaning. If any analysis of the concept implied that one of these three theories (or a clear instance of them) were not an account of meaning at all, we would have serious grounds for questioning the analysis.

In addition to giving us conditions that fit *all* theories of meaning, an analysis ideally ought, second, to indicate conditions that fit *only* theories of meaning. An analysis should single out the intrinsic good of meaning from other intrinsic goods. For example, the question of what would make a life meaningful differs from other normative questions such as what would make a life happy or moral. At least in contemporary discourse, inquiring into the nature of happiness is inherently to ask about something substantially mental. The question of what makes a life meaningful is different, as can be gleaned from the common-sensical judgment that time spent in the orgasmatron (a machine inducing the feeling of orgasm) is a prima facie good candidate for happiness but not for meaningfulness. Asking about the nature of dutiful action is, very roughly, to ask about impartial behavior for which the agent would warrant criticism if not done. The extensions of the best answers to the question of what makes an act morally required and the question of what makes life meaningful may overlap (and could even be identical). However, the intensions of these two questions differ, as can be seen from the fact that making a great scientific discovery (that promises no practical benefits) is a prima facie good candidate for being a meaningful action but not for being a morally required action. Therefore, if a proposed analysis failed to indicate the respect in which supernaturalism, subjectivism, and objectivism are all accounts of meaning rather than of happiness or of duty, that would be a strike against the analysis.

III.　Purposiveness

There is an a priori connection between meaning and purpose, at least in that "purposive" is one synonym of "meaningful." Since there are rich associations with the term "purpose," it is worth exploring whether some notion of purposiveness could ground a revealing analysis of the concept of a meaningful life.

Fulfilling God's purpose

According to Bertrand Russell, "Unless you assume a God, the question (of life's meaning) is meaningless, and, like Laplace, 'je n' ai pas besoin de cette hypothèse.'"[11] Of those who have analyzed the concept of meaning in terms of relating to God, most have supposed that inquiring into the meaning of an individual's life is identical to asking how a person is related to a purpose that God has assigned. This view gains plausibility from the fact that the question of life's meaning is often associated with the question, "Why am I here?" and this question, in turn, is naturally understood as asking for the reason for which one was created.

Some might have exclusively theistic ideas in mind when inquiring about the meaning of life, but they will not do as an analysis of the concept that underlies contemporary philosophical dispute about the issue. The obvious problem with the present understanding of the concept of a meaningful life is that it a priori excludes the possibility of naturalist conceptions of meaning (and also supernaturalist conceptions that do not appeal to God). If asking about life's meaning logically involves asking about one's relation to God's purpose, then no naturalist theory of significance is conceptually possible and naturalists and supernaturalists are talking past each other. However, there are many naturalist accounts in the literature, accounts that supernaturalists have argued provide inadequate answers to the question of life's significance. This question therefore cannot itself be understood in supernaturalist terms.

Realizing proper human purposes

Instead of analyzing the concept of a meaningful life in terms of God's purpose, some philosophers have done so in terms of the purposes of human (or rational) beings. Kai Nielsen has most clearly articulated the position that to inquire about the meaning of life is merely to ask which purposes a person should adopt and realize:

> When we ask: "What is the meaning of life?" or "What is the purpose of human existence?" we are normally asking, as I have already said, questions of the following types: "What should we seek?" "What ends – if any – are worthy of attainment?"… . [T]his question is in reality a question concerning human conduct.[12]

On this analysis, the concept of a meaningful life is one of a life that has done well at achieving goals that humans should strive to achieve. This analysis implies that different conceptions of a meaningful life are to be understood as competing theories of the ends that humans should pursue. Roughly, typical supernaturalists say that humans should fulfill the purpose God has assigned them, many subjectivists maintain that people should adopt whatever goals they are inclined to upon reflection, and standard objectivists hold that one should further the ends of truth, beauty, and goodness. It would appear, then, that the present analysis provides a nice account of what the three major theories of life's meaning have in common.

However, this analysis is flawed in not admitting the logical possibility of a person's life being meaningful in virtue of conditions that she cannot control. For example, consider an "aristocratic" theory of meaning according to which one's life is significant by virtue of having been born into a certain family. Being part of a particular bloodline might be thought to make one's life matter, but this is not an end that an individual can pursue. This essentialist view does not seem logically contradictory, which the present analysis implies is the case. For another example, consider people who think their lives are meaningful because they are God's chosen people. Being deemed special by God is not a state of affairs that an individual can bring about (let us suppose), so that the conceptual possibility of its conferring meaning on a life cannot be accommodated by analyzing meaning in terms of ends that should be adopted and realized.

One way to respond on behalf of the present analysis would be to suggest that even these conditions may in a broad sense be said to be "chosen," insofar as a person chooses to stay alive. However, such a response merely buys a little time, since the examples may be effectively reformulated. For instance, this maneuver would not work for the view that meaning comes from God's loving one's immortal soul.

Another response would be to bite the bullet and maintain that it is in fact logically contradictory to suppose that meaning can ever be utterly bestowed rather than chosen. The problem with this response is that a number of people have believed that, say, being considered special by God could conceivably make a person's life more meaningful. Interests in being charitable and in finding an analysis that is historically continuous with the way people have used the term "meaningful" both counsel against denying that a theory is about meaning when many have deemed it to be. For these reasons, if essentialist views seem dubious, then they are better construed as substantively false than as logically contradictory. In any event, it is worth considering whether there is an analysis of the concept of meaning that can accommodate the logical possibility of meaning being something that is endowed instead of pursued.

Producing good states of affairs

Sometimes purposiveness is understood in terms of having a function. So, one might suggest that the concept of a meaningful life is that of an existence that plays a role in the realization of valuable ends. G. E. Moore suggests such a view when he says,

> I have been very much puzzled as to the meaning of the question "What is the meaning or purpose of life?" ... But at last it occurred to me that perhaps the vague words of this question are often used to mean no more than "What is the use of a man's life?" ... A man's life is of some use, if and only if the *intrinsic* value of the Universe as a whole (including past, present, and

future) is greater, owing to the existence of his actions and experiences, than it would have been if, other things being equal, those actions and experiences had never existed.[13]

It is not clear whether Moore's statement about a person's being useful insofar as she promotes intrinsic value is intended to be part of the thin concept of meaning or a thick conception of it. Deeming it to be inherent to the concept is reasonable, since if a meaningful life is one that is useful, it presumbaly will be useful in a relevant sense only insofar as it produces intrinsic value. To think of a meaningful life as one that is useful for ends, regardless of whether they are intrinsically valuable or not, would fail to account for the normative element of meaning. Therefore, it is best to read Moore's remarks as suggesting that we analyze the concept of a significant life in terms of an existence that promotes intrinsically valuable states of affairs.

The present analysis straightforwardly avoids the problems facing the previous two attempts to cash out meaning in terms of purpose. Since it has a wide conception of valuable end in terms of intrinsic goodness that is promoted, the present analysis does not logically tie meaningful conditions to rational choice. It allows for the possibility of a person's life becoming more meaningful merely by constituting or causing a good state of affairs, where this state of affairs need not have been the product of a voluntary decision. Furthermore, the present analysis obviously does not make supernaturalism a priori true. Supernaturalism may instead, on the view under consideration, be seen as a competing substantive account of the intrinsic value that a meaningful life promotes. Very roughly, supernaturalists would think of the relevant intrinsic value in terms of God's will or nature, subjectivists would construe intrinsic value in terms of preference fulfillment, and objectivists would have a mind-independent account of the good. The present analysis therefore provides a prima facie attractive account of the subject matter common to at least central strands of supernaturalism, subjectivism, and objectivism.

Despite these advantages, the present analysis is questionable. First off, it might fail to account adequately for the normative element of meaning. How can this be, when the Moorean account logically ties meaning to intrinsic value? The worry is that it might link these ideas in the wrong way. Recall that meaning theorists typically think of meaning as itself an intrinsic value. Now, the present analysis construes meaning as conceptually a matter of promoting intrinsic value. But to promote intrinsic value is to have extrinsic value. Hence, the present analysis of meaning construes it as a matter of having extrinsic value, which seems not to cohere well with the intuition that meaning has intrinsic value.

The problem is not easily resolved by noting that some things, e.g., eating a meal, are both good for their own sake and good for what they bring about. The puzzle is that the present analysis conceives of meaning as having final value *insofar as* it has instrumental value. In contrast, consuming a meal is not intrinsically good *to the extent that* it is extrinsically good. Eating a green curry dish is good for its own sake in that it is pleasurable, and it is good as a means in that it helps us to stay alive; it is not good for its own sake insofar as it helps us stay alive. But if the concept of a meaningful life is that of a life that promotes intrinsic value, then a meaningful life is intrinsically valuable because it promotes intrinsic value, i.e., because it is extrinsically valuable. That is strange.

Christine Korsgaard and Shelly Kagan have discussed in some detail the idea that intrinsic value might supervene on an object's relational properties.[14] An attractive example of this is an object's having intrinsic value because of its rarity. Kagan takes a further step, noting that if the relational properties of an object can affect whether an object is good for its own sake, then it will be reasonable to expect that instrumentally valuable relational properties can too. Help and creativity are examples that make plausible the idea of an intrinsically valuable extrinsic value. Imagine that one finds a cure for cancer. Supposing this is a meaningful action and hence is intrinsically valuable, it appears that its intrinsic value consists largely in the fact that a cure has the effect of benefiting people. Or imagine that one produces great works of art. Making art-works is simply behavior that produces intrinsically valuable art-objects (or perhaps produces art-objects capable of producing intrinsically valuable experiences). And if one thinks of making art as meaningful and intrinsically worthwhile, then it appears to be an action that is good for its own sake by virtue of the distinct intrinsic good it promotes. If these instances of meaningful activities are plausible examples of intrinsically valuable extrinsic value, then there is no reason to question an analysis that conceives of meaning generally in these terms. So, perhaps there is nothing ultimately paradoxical about the claim that the concept of a meaningful life, and hence of a life with a certain intrinsic value, is just that of a life that promotes intrinsic value.

Although there remains much to question about the coherence of conceiving of a sort of intrinsic value in terms of extrinsic value, there are in fact more serious problems facing the present analysis. For one, it is too broad to be able to distinguish meaningfulness from, say, happiness. Happiness is intrinsically valuable, and is so even if it is not part of a meaningful condition. For example, enjoying an ice cream cone is good for its own sake. Since a happy life is also one that promotes intrinsic value, conceiving of meaning merely as a matter of promoting intrinsic value fails to differentiate the idea of a meaningful life from that of a happy life. A more satisfactory account of the concept of meaning would specify *which* intrinsic values must be promoted in order for meaning to arise.

In addition to having trouble entailing that only theories of meaning count as such, the present analysis has difficulty showing that all theories of meaning count as such. Analyzing the concept of meaning in terms of the promotion of intrinsic value is to think of meaning as an inherently teleological relation, implying that deontological conceptions of meaning are not logically possible. But there are theories that on the face of it are accounts of what makes a life matter but that do not articulate a way to promote intrinsic value. For example, some objectivist views hold that life has significance for treating rational nature with respect.[15] Now, these views usually do think of rational nature as being intrinsically valuable, and they could think of the act of honoring such a nature as promoting intrinsic value. The point is that such views need neither think of meaning as consisting in the bare fact of having such a nature, nor conceive of honoring such a nature as promoting intrinsic value. Instead, these views can and do deem meaning to consist of not degrading the higher self, of treating it as more important than the sensual self, where this treatment is not a matter of promoting intrinsic value. If it is logically possible to conceive of honoring people's intellectual selves as making one's life meaningful *and* to deny that such honoring promotes intrinsic value, then the concept of meaning is not merely the idea of promoting intrinsic value.

In sum, the best version of the purpose analysis has faced two major problems. First, it has been too narrow in being unable to accommodate deontological theories that are about meaning. Second, it has been too broad; conceiving of meaning in terms of the promotion of valuable states of affairs fails to distinguish meaning from happiness. One might try to solve the first problem by suggesting that a meaningful life is one that either promotes or honors intrinsic value; that squarely accommodates deontological theories. The problem with this suggestion is that the analysis is still too narrow. Consider the view that meaning is a matter of engaging in intrinsically worthwhile activities and *enjoying* it.[16] In response, one might propose that the concept of a meaningful life is the idea of one that promotes or honors or likes intrinsic value. But this is unattractive. Such a disjunctive analysis is far from the unitary idea that this essay is seeking. Furthermore, such an analysis seems no longer a function of a notion of purposiveness. The concern also obtains with regard to responses to the second problem. That is, in order to differentiate meaning from happiness and other intrinsic values, one might try to specify exactly which sort of intrinsic value is relevant to meaning. The trouble is that, once this is done, it seems no longer to be an idea of purposiveness that is doing the work. The upshot of this discussion is that an analysis with these two features should be sought: a precise specification of the intrinsic value relevant to meaning and a broad but unified conception of the way to respond to this value.

IV. Transcendence

Another major analysis of the concept of a meaningful life can be gleaned from some of Robert Nozick's remarks.[17] It is not clear that Nozick is intending to provide an analysis of the concept of meaning. However, it does not matter what Nozick's aims are, for his comments provide a prima facie attractive analysis of the concept in terms of transcending limits. The initial motivation for construing theories of meaning as providing substantive accounts of how properly to transcend limits comes from reflection on the use of the word "meaning" (and "significance") in other contexts. If we ask for the meaning of a word, we are told about its relationship with other words or with objects in the world. If we ask what inflation means for the economy, we are told about its effects on something else such as unemployment or interest rates. Robert Nozick proposes that we likewise think of asking for the meaning of a life as a matter of asking how it "connects up to what is outside it."[18]

In order to evaluate this proposal, we need to sharpen it. Exactly which limits are relevant to the issue of life's being significant and how must one cross them? Breaking the speed limit and pinching a stranger are ways of "crossing boundaries" or "transcending limits," but these actions are not prima facie candidates for meaning. Conceiving of meaning as merely a function of connection with something external does not capture the normative dimension of meaning, and, in any event, does not express anything unique to meaning.

Connecting with external value

Consider this proposal: the concept of what makes a life meaningful is the idea of connecting with something intrinsically valuable beyond one's person. As Nozick also says, "meaning is a transcending of the limits of your own value, a transcending of your own limited value."[19] People often think of meaning in terms of an intense relationship with something greater than oneself, where "greater" has a normative dimension.

One way of connecting with superior intrinsic value external to one's person would be to promote it, but this need not be the only way. Supposing that the words "connecting" and "transcending" mean something like responding positively, one could also connect with value beyond oneself by honoring it or by enjoying its production. In addition, since one's happiness is clearly an intrinsic value internal to one's person, the present analysis is able to distinguish meaning from happiness. Hence, the transcendence analysis avoids both of the fundamental problems facing the purpose analysis.

However, there are counterexamples that tell against this version of the transcendence analysis. Consider supernaturalist theories that maintain that a person's life is meaningful insofar as she honors her soul or realizes what she essentially is.[20] Since neither honoring one's higher self nor becoming aware of one's deepest nature is to connect with a value external to oneself, the present analysis counterintuitively implies that these activities are conceptually incapable of making a life meaningful. There are objectivist theories, too that the present analysis wrongly implies are not theories of meaning at all. Consider these examples: publicly standing by what one reflectively believes to be right, being true to one-self, overcoming addiction, and not letting oneself be bossed around. Since integrity, authenticity, autonomy, and self-respect are goods internal to a person, and since these goods are prima facie candidates for a meaningful life, the concept of a meaningful life cannot just be that of an existence that has "a connection with an external value."[21]

Connecting with value beyond the animal self

If a transcendence analysis is going to work, it must allow for the logical possibility of a person's life being meaningful for connecting to both internal and external goods. And such an analysis must carefully specify which internal goods are relevant, to be able to continue to differentiate meaning from happiness.

In light of these concerns, let us go beyond Nozick's remarks and propose the following transcendence analysis: the concept of meaning is the idea of connecting with intrinsic value beyond one's animal self. The animal self is constituted by those capacities that we share with (lower) animals, i.e., those not exercising reason. These include the fact of being alive, the instantiation of a healthy body, and the experience of pleasures. These internal conditions may well be intrinsically valuable, but they do not seem to be the sorts of intrinsic value with which one must connect to acquire significance. To say that the concept of meaning is the idea of relating positively to intrinsic value beyond one's animal self is to say that while merely staying alive or feeling pleasure logically cannot make one's life mean-ingful, connecting with internal goods involving the use of reason, and with all sorts of external goods, can do so.

By virtue of distinguishing between the animal self and the rational self, the present tran-scendence analysis allows conceptual space for internal goods to confer meaning on a life. Realizing one's higher nature and developing excellences, on this account, logically could confer meaning on a life by virtue of being a relevant way to transcend one's animal nature.

Furthermore, the present analysis plausibly specifies which internal goods are conceptually relevant to meaning, namely, those beyond the animal self. This enables the present analysis to differentiate meaning from happiness, since the animal self is the locus of satisfaction. Finally, the present analysis articulates a reasonable understanding of what supernaturalism, subjectivism, and objectivism have in common. On this view, supernaturalists who prescribe communing with God or honoring one's soul, subjectivists who advocate striving to achieve whatever ideals one adopts upon reflection, and objectivists who recommend creating artworks or promoting justice, are all indicating ways to connect with value beyond the animal self. This is the most promising analysis proposed so far.

The biggest difficulty with the present analysis is that it has a hard time accounting for certain subjectivist views. For example, Richard Taylor defends a subjectivist theory that the present analysis must deem not to be a theory of meaning at all. Recall that according to Taylor, one's existence is more significant the more one gets whatever one passionately desires. It does not matter for Taylor how one's desires have been formed, in particular, whether one has reflected on them; he imagines that Sisyphus's life would be as meaningful as it could be if the gods implanted in him a "keen and unappeasable desire to be doing just what he found himself doing."[22] Assuming desire satisfaction is a good at all, it is an internal good that does not fundamentally involve the exercise of reason. Hence, the present analysis of the concept of meaning in terms of connecting with value beyond the animal self cannot count Taylor's view as a theory of meaning.

In reply, one may note that there are several subjectivist views for which the present analysis can account. For example, consider subjectivist theories that conceive of meaning in terms of the realization of ends that agents have adopted upon careful appraisal. These views include a cognitive element, differing from Taylor's purely conative view. For another example, consider the difference between a theory that holds meaning to consist of desire satisfaction and one that holds it to consist of an agent satisfying her desires. The former does not fundamentally involve any exercise of rational choice; a genie or god could fulfill a person's desires. However, the latter account includes a volitional element, the notion that someone must strive to acquire meaning, which would plausibly put it within the ambit of the present analysis. Perhaps it is not a great strike against the present analysis that it cannot accommodate Taylor's theory, at least if it can accommodate many other subjectivist views.

This reply would be stronger if Taylor's discussion of Sisyphus were not probably the most widely read discussion of the meaning of life among contemporary philosophers. His theory lies at the heart of recent debates about what makes a life significant. It is difficult to rest content with an analysis that implies that the many who consider Taylor's theory to be about meaning are conceptually confused. At any rate, it is worth seeing whether there is some other analysis that both has the advantages of the best version of the transcendence analysis and avoids the disadvantage of not accommodating Taylor's theory.

V.   Esteem

We often associate questions of meaning with deathbed reflection. To access whether one's life is meaningful or not, a person often imagines she is at the end of her days on earth and considers how she would appraise her life from that perspective. The next analysis proposes that there is a logical connection between the question of what makes a life meaningful and a question about what kinds of attitudes would be appropriate to have toward it. On this view, there are two kinds of attitudes that are integral to the concept of a meaningful life, depending on whether one takes a first-person or third-person stance with regard to the life. Specifically, the concept of meaning might be this idea: those aspects of a life for which the person whose life it is may sensibly have great esteem and for which others may sensibly have great admiration. For the sake of economy, the following discussion will tend to focus on the first-person perspective and speak of meaning in terms of conditions meriting great esteem.

The terms "esteem" and "pride" are here used interchangeably to denote a certain perceptual-affective response to an object related to oneself. One has both a sense and a feeling of esteem. In taking pride in something, one both perceives that it is worthy and feels satisfaction about it. For example, if a person takes pride in having reared her children, then she judges her behavior to have been all things considered well done and feels pleased for having done it. It would be odd to say that a person has esteem for an action when she deems it on the whole disvaluable or does not feel good for having done it. In short, esteem is a matter of high regard and high spirits about facets of one's life.

One must not confuse esteem with self-esteem. Self-esteem involves having not only a sense that oneself is worthy, but also a sense that one can do something worthy. Esteem differs in that it does not fundamentally involve self-confidence; one can take pride in having done something and still feel incapable of doing much else. One should also not reduce esteem to a mere sense of satisfaction. Esteem includes this, but also includes an element of judgment. A person may be pleased with himself for having finished washing the dishes, but he presumably will not have esteem for doing so, since he does not regard that action to be particularly choiceworthy.

The present analysis does not construe meaning in terms of when people in fact have substantial esteem about their lives. Instead of analyzing a meaningful life as one that results in great pride, it does so in terms of a life in which people would be justified in taking great pride. It conceives of meaning as those conditions of a life warranting the positive responses of great esteem and admiration, regardless of whether such reactions are forthcoming.

Analyzing the concept of meaning in terms of greatly estimable or admirable conditions avoids the major problems facing the purpose and transcendence analyses. Since something other than promoting value or achieving ends could in principle merit great esteem, the esteem analysis allows for deontological and essentialist conceptions of meaning. The esteem analysis also does a good job of differentiating meaning from other values; the idea of a life that warrants great esteem differs from the ideas of happiness and dutiful action. And insofar as it is logically possible for desire satisfaction to constitute the conditions meriting great esteem, the esteem analysis accommodates "cruder" subjectivist theories of meaning.

In fact, the esteem analysis provides a promising way to understand what the three major theories of life's meaning have in common. It construes theories of meaning as providing rival accounts of those aspects of a life in which a person could reasonably take great pride (or for which an outsider could reasonably have great admiration). From this perspective, supernaturalists are contending that if there were no purely spiritual realm, then there would be nothing about one's life in the physical world that could be worthy of substantial esteem. Fulfilling God's purpose, attaining the condition where one could merge with God, or honoring one's soul are plausibly viewed as candidates for great esteem. Subjectivists on this account are maintaining that substantially estimable conditions vary, depending on a person's (or her group's) stronger wants or higher-order ends. Finally, the present analysis construes objectivists as holding that certain features of our natural lives can warrant great pride, but not merely in virtue of the subject's pro-attitude toward them. Roughly, positive responses to the true, the good, and the beautiful are what an objectivist deems to merit great esteem.

Let us question the esteem analysis. One worry about analyzing meaning in terms of greatly estimable conditions is that such an analysis might not in fact be able to single out meaning as a distinct part of the best life. Meaning theorists tend to see meaning as only one aspect of the best life, with other aspects being happiness and morality. However, the best life is surely the one that most warrants great esteem. The esteem analysis therefore apparently fails to differentiate the concept of a meaningful life from that of the best life.

This objection is not fatal. The defender of the esteem analysis can plausibly deny that the notion of the best life is exhausted by the idea of the life most warranting substantial esteem. She can hold that the concept of the best life is analyzed better in terms of a different attitudinal response, namely, desire. The notion of the best life is arguably the idea of the life we have most reason to want. This analysis is prima facie attractive, and it grounds a competing account of the close link between the idea of the best life and that of the life most warranting great pride. There is arguably a synthetic connection between these ideas, such that the notion of the life most warranting great pride is at least part of the best life, i.e., at least part of the life we have most reason to want.

While the esteem analysis might well characterize only theories of meaning, it has a much more difficult time accommodating all of them. If the concept of what makes a life meaningful were the idea of those conditions of a life warranting great esteem or admiration, then it obviously would be logically contradictory to maintain that a condition is meaningful and yet does not warrant great esteem. But there are at least two sorts of cases where it does *not* seem logically contradictory to say that a condition is meaningful but does not warrant great esteem. One kind of counterexample involves cases in which meaning is thought to supervene on happiness (among other conditions). Consider the theory that enjoying worthwhile activities makes a life meaningful. Many subjectivists and objectivists believe that a necessary condition of meaning is not being bored. And think about the view that a person's life is meaningful insofar as she is justly rewarded in an afterlife for having done good deeds. To some it seems that life would make sense only if happiness were ultimately proportioned to virtue. Now, it seems logically consistent to suppose that life would be more meaningful for such conditions *and* to deny that there is anything about enjoyment or reward (as opposed to worthwhile activities and good deeds) in which to take great pride. If these two claims are logically consistent, then the esteem analysis is false; for the esteem analysis implies that it is logically inconsistent to say both that a condition is meaningful and that it does not warrant great esteem.

Another kind of example concerns cases in which living in a certain environment might be thought to confer meaning on an individual's life. Consider the theory that a person's life would be more meaningful if she lived among natural objects than if she lived among plastic replicas of them. Or think about the view that a person's life would be more meaningful for living among old, handworked crafts and architecture than for living among new, mass-produced works. A person could plausibly think that being part of an ecosystem or having a continuity with history confers meaning on a life *and* deny that there is anything worthy of substantial pride about such conditions, particularly since they do not (in these examples) concern a person's identity or self-expression. But the esteem analysis implies that one is conceptually confused to maintain that something could be meaningful and yet not be worthy of great pride.

In sum, the esteem analysis implies that it is a closed question whether a condition warrants great esteem, assuming that it is considered meaningful. The above examples are cases in which a person could intelligibly assert that something is meaningful and yet deny that it warrants great esteem. Therefore, the esteem analysis does not do a good job of explaining what makes these cases theories of meaning. Since the esteem analysis is the most promising one considered and since it cannot account for all theories of meaning, we may at this point reasonably doubt that there is *any* analysis available that can provide a single common denominator among all the diverse theories of meaning.

VI.   Conclusion

This essay began by noting Updike's complaint that the question of what makes a life meaningful is not well formulated. This essay has sought to sharpen the question by finding an analysis of the concept of meaning that underlies the major conceptions of meaning to be found in 20th century philosophical literature. The discussion has progressed dialectically, presenting an analysis, considering counterexamples to it, refining the analysis so that it avoids the counterexamples, considering new counterexamples, and so on. Three major analyses were explored by this means and none was found able to account for all and only extant theories that intuitively seem to be about meaning. A tentative but fair conclusion to draw is that there are no necessary and sufficient conditions for a theory to be about meaning as opposed to something else. If this is true, how can research into the meaning of life proceed?

Here is one plausible answer: the same way that research into dutiful action has been conducted. Analyses of the concept of morality have not captured essential conditions for something to be moral as opposed to something else. Consider, in brief, the major attempted analyses of dutiful action and how they fail to capture all and only extant moral theories. Some suggest that the concept of dutiful action is just the idea of the promotion of human well-being, but this excludes the divine command theory and Kantianism. Others maintain that the concept of morality is just the idea that others provide one a fundamental reason to act, but this omits egoism and instrumental-relativist views. Some construe the moral realm as merely the domain of impartial behavior, but this excludes fundamentally partialist theories (e.g., the views that one owes more to those one cares about or to those who are closest to oneself) and theories that include a self-regarding element (e.g., egoism and Kantianism). Yet a fourth way to understand morality is in terms of norms the violation of which warrants blame, but this does not capture egoism well at all. Although theorists have not been able to specify necessary and sufficient conditions for morality, their attempts to do so have been revealing and moral theory has progressed fine without such conditions. We have arguably learned that moral theories have family resemblances among them, and research has proceeded in light of these characteristics. That is, moral theories are views that are united by virtue of addressing, say, two or more of the following features: other-regarding basic reasons, impartial behavior, promotion of well-being, and norms the violation of which warrants condemnation.

A similar situation is probably true of meaning theory. Having failed to find essential conditions for meaning does not mean that the question of what makes a life meaningful is just as vague as when we started. In the course of searching for a sharp concept that underlies the conceptions of meaning in the literature, our understanding of what these conceptions are about has improved. We have arguably learned that theories of meaning have family resemblances among them. Meaning theories are united by virtue of systematically answering questions such as the following: how may a person bring purpose to her life, where this is not just a matter of pursuing happiness or acting rightly? How should an individual connect with intrinsic value beyond his animal nature? How might one do something worthy of great admiration? Readers should see that these questions are neglected without justification, viz., that they are just as important and amenable of intelligent response as questions about morality and happiness. May this essay spur readers to agree that discussion about what makes a life meaningful is to be continued.

Notes

1. Updike's quotation can be found in Hugh Moorhead, ed., *The Meaning of Life* (Chicago: Chicago Review Press, 1988), p. 200.

2. Although relatively little writing was done in the 1990s, a decent amount was done in the 1960s and 1970s, much of which was anthologized in the 1980s. See Steven Sanders and David Cheney, eds., *The Meaning of Life: Questions, Answers, and Analysis* (Englewood Cliffs, N.J.: Prentice-Hall, 1980); E. D. Klemke, ed., *The Meaning of Life* (New York: Oxford University Press, 1981); and Oswald Hanfling, ed., *Life and Meaning: A Reader* (Cambridge, Mass.: Blackwell, 1987).

3. Although merely listing synonyms does not constitute a revealing articulation of the question of what makes a life meaningful, analyzing the senses of synonyms could do so. For example, "purposeful" seems synonymous with "meaningful," and the possibility that the question of life's meaning is a question about a kind of purposefulness gets explored in section III below.

4. It might seem that talk of a "meaningful life" implies that the only potential bearer of meaning is a person's existence as a biographical whole. In fact, few meaning theorists intend anything so restrictive by such talk. Just as a life is more moral the more it is composed of moral deeds and dispositions, so a life is more meaningful, for most theorists, the more it is composed of meaningful acts and states. There are some, however, who do take life as a whole to be the only possible bearer of meaning. For instance, Thomas Nagel seems to do so in his discussion of meaninglessness from an objective standpoint. See his *What Does It All Mean?* (New York: Oxford University Press, 1987), chap. 10.

5. Leo Tolstoy, "My Confession," trans. Leo Wiener, reprinted in Klemke, *The Meaning of Life*, chap. 1, and *Anna Karenin*, trans. Rosemary Edmonds (Middlesex: Penguin Books, 1954), esp. pp. 373–4, 400, 827–8; Soren Kierkegaard, *Training in Christianity* reprinted in *A Kierkegaard Anthology*, ed. Robert Bretall (Princeton: Princeton University Press, 1946), esp. p. 414;

E. L. Fackenheim, "Judaism and the Meaning of Life," *Commentary* 39 (1965): 49–55; Martin Buber, *I and Thou*, trans. Walter Kaufmann (New York: Simon and Schuster, 1970), esp. part 3.

6. E.g., Robert Nozick, *Philosophical Explanations* (Cambridge: Harvard University Press, 1981), pp. 585–610; William Davis, "The Meaning of Life," *Metaphilosophy* 18 (1987): 288–305; Michael Levine, "What Does Death Have To Do with the Meaning of Life?" *Religious Studies* 23 (1987): 457–65; Thaddeus Metz, "Could God's Purpose Be the Source of Life's Meaning?" *Religious Studies* 36 (2000): 293–313; Philip Quinn, "How Christianity Secures Life's Meanings," in *The Meaning of Life in the World Religions*, ed. Joseph Runzo and Nancy Martin (Oxford: Oneworld Publications, 2000), chap. 3.

7. William James, "What Makes a Life Significant?" in William James, *On Some of Life's Ideals* (New York: Henry Holt and Company, 1900), pp. 49–94; A. J. Ayer, "The Claims of Philosophy," in *Philosophy of the Social Sciences*, ed. Maurice Natanson (New York: Random House, 1963), pp. 475–9; Richard Taylor, *Good and Evil* (London: Macmillan Publishing Company, 1970), chap. 18; Bernard Williams, "Persons, Character, and Morality," in Bernard Williams, *Moral Luck* (Cambridge: Cambridge University Press, 1981), chap. 1; Stephen Darwall, *Impartial Reason* (Ithaca: Cornell University Press, 1983), pp. 164–6.

8. See Nozick, *Philosophical Explanations*, pp. 594–600, 610–19, and *The Examined Life* (New York: Simon and Schuster, 1989), chap. 15; David Wiggins, "Truth, Invention, and the Meaning of Life," revised edition in *Essays on Moral Realism*, ed. Geoffrey Sayre-McCord (Ithaca: Cornell University Press, 1988), chap. 7; Charles Taylor, *The Ethics of Authenticity* (Cambridge: Harvard University Press, 1991), Peter Singer, *Practical Ethics*, 2nd edn. (New York: Cambridge University Press, 1993), chap. 12, and *How Are We to Live?* (Amherst, N.Y.: Prometheus Books, 1995), chaps. 10–11: Susan Wolf, "Happiness and Meaning: Two Aspects of the Good Life," *Social Philosophy and Policy* 14 (1997): 207–25, and "Meaning and Morality," *Proceedings of the Aristotelian Society* 97 (1997): 299–315. In later work Richard Taylor rejects his earlier subjectivist view in favor of a species of objectivism. See "The Meaning of Human Existence," in *Values in Conflict: Life, Liberty, and the Rule of Law*, ed. Burton Leiser (New York: Macmillan, 1981), chap. 1.

9. See, e.g., John Wisdom, *Paradox and Discovery* (Oxford: Basil Blackwell, 1965), pp. 38–42; and Paul Edwards, "Why?" in *The Encyclopedia of Philosophy*, Volume 8, ed. Paul Edwards (London: Macmillan, 1967), pp. 296–302.

10. See, e.g., Paul Edwards, "The Meaning and Value of Life," in Klemke, *The Meaning of Life*, pp. 130–31.

11. Russell is quoted in Moorhead, *The Meaning of Life*, p. 165.

12. Kai Nielsen, "Linguistic Philosophy and the 'The Meaning of Life,'" revised edition in *The Meaning of Life*, ed. Klemke, pp. 186, 193. For a similar claim, see Ayer, "The Claims of Philosophy," pp. 478–9.

13. Moore is quoted in Moorhead, *The Meaning of Life*, pp. 128–9. Cf. G. E. Moore, *Principia Ethica* (London: Cambridge University Press, 1966), p. 35.

14. Christine Korsgaard, "Two Distinctions in Goodness," *The Philosophical Review* 92 (1983): 169–95; Shelly Kagan, "Rethinking Intrinsic Value," *The Journal of Ethics* 2 (1998): 277–97.

15. For a reading of Kant along these lines, see Thomas Pogge, "Kant on Ends and the Meaning of Life," in *Reclaiming the History of Ethics: Essays for John Rawls*, ed. Andrews Reath et al. (New York: Cambridge University Press, 1997), pp. 361–87.

16. For instances of this sort of view, see R. W. Hepburn, "Questions About the Meaning of Life," *Religious Studies* 1 (1965): 125–40; Wolf, "Happiness and Morality," and "Meaning and Morality"; and John Kekes, "The Meaning of Life," in *Midwest Studies in Philosophy: Life and Death*, ed. Peter French and Howard Wettstein, vol. 24 (2000): 17–34.

17. Nozick, *Philosophical Explanations*, chap. 6. and *The Examined Life*, chap. 15.

18. Nozick, *Philosophical Explanations*, p. 601.

19. Nozick, *Philosophical Explanations*, p. 610. See also pp. 594, 611, 618.

20. For instances of such views, see David Swenson, *Kierkegaardian Philosophy in the Faith of a Scholar* (Philadelphia: Westminster Press, 1949); and P. Nagaraja Rao, "Hinduism," in *The Meaning of Life in Five Great Religions*, ed. R. C. Chalmers and John Irving (Philadelphia: The Westminster Press, 1965), pp. 23–36.

21. Nozick, *Philosophical Explanations*, p. 610.

22. Taylor, *Good and Evil*, p. 265.

1.6

Assessing Views of Life
A Subjective Affair?

Arjan Markus

In our postmodern time, people no longer see the established religions as indivisible wholes that you may take or leave, but as multicoloured compositions from which one may take elements when composing one's own view of life. Many people are of the opinion that the quality of views of life is a matter of personal preference. Whether someone seeks the meaning of her life in terms of one religion or a mix of religions, or in terms of a non-religious view of life, is her free choice. However, she should not bother others with her view of life, because they have their own views. If someone is happy with his view of life, then his view is a good one for him, but for others another view may be a better one. A presupposition of this way of thinking is that it is impossible to assess views of life in any objective or interpersonal sense. A view of life is good when you think that it is good for you. The assessment of a framework of meaning seems to be a purely subjective affair, a matter of personal preference.

This pure subjectivity, however, is not satisfactory, I would suggest. Sometimes we will be inclined to judge a framework of meaning as trivial, poor, or even reprehensible. It is the question whether every view of life is equally suitable for the ascription of meaning to life. May be the process of ascribing meaning asks for certain characteristics of a view of life. In this article I will try to discover whether we can deduce from this process requirements for a view of life. For that attempt an analysis is needed of the process of the ascription of meaning to life.

Let us discuss the following three questions in turn. What are we doing when we ascribe meaning? Is the meaning of life something purely subjective (some people talk about objective meaning)? Can we deduce from the process of the ascription of meaning criteria to assess views of life?

Arjan Markus (2003) "Assessing Views of Life: A Subjective Affair?" *Religious Studies* 39: 125–43.

Ascribing Meaning

What do we say about life when we ascribe meaning to it? It seems clear that we make a kind of evaluation when we say that our life, or the life of someone else, or life in general, is meaningful. We can value life as beautiful, useful, exciting, or important, but also as meaningful. Meaning, therefore, is an evaluative term. Should we conclude that meaning is a kind of value, like beauty, usefulness, excitement, and importance? That would mean that meaning is one value amongst other values.[1] This conclusion, however, is too simplistic, because in reality we use the term 'meaning' in a much broader way than only as one of the many possible values. In order to recognize this, let us take a closer look at the use of 'meaning'. An examination of this use can throw light on the question of what kind of evaluation it is to state that life is meaningful.

We use 'meaning' often as a linguistic term, for instance when we talk about the meaning of a word or a text. The meaning of a word depends, among other things, on its coherence with the other words of the text in which it is used. The text itself is meaningful if the words are used in a more or less coherent way. It is a necessary (although not sufficient) condition for a text to be meaningful that the words are used coherently. So the meaning of both part (a single word) and totality (text) has to do with the coherence of the totality. Analogously, the term 'meaning' is used in relation to a human action, or a human life, or life in general. A single human action or an event in human life can be evaluated as meaningful when it coheres with other actions or events, and, ultimately, when it coheres with life as the totality of human actions and events. People can try to give meaning to small and individual aspects of life by connecting them with a larger whole. An individual's life can be experienced as meaningful if it is a more or less coherent totality of actions and events.[2] Furthermore, several people also consider an individual's life or life in general as meaningful when it coheres with an all-embracing whole, like a cosmic process, a divine design, or a world-ideology.[3] In the first place then, when people talk about the meaning of their life, or the meaning of life, we can conclude that meaning has to do with coherence. This is meaning as a coherent whole.

Secondly, we talk about meaningful acts, or a meaningful life, when the acts are performed or the life is lived in light of an intended purpose, goal, end, point, or plan. In this use of meaning, a life is meaningful when it has some overall purpose, or a combination of purposes which give direction to many of one's actions.[4] Additionally, it is also possible to say that life in general is meaningful because it has a purpose. Here, we have meaning as (intended) purpose.

Thirdly, people are looking for the meaning of their lives, or of life in general, when they find themselves asking questions such as 'What makes my life worthwhile?' or 'What makes human life worthwhile?' In answer to such questions people try to describe the meaning of their lives, or the meaning of human life, in terms of values[5] like usefulness, health, prosperity, beauty, love, friendship, or of a combination of such values. This is meaning as value.

This exploration of the concept of meaning makes clear that meaning is not just one value amongst other values like beauty or love. Value appears to be an aspect of meaning, besides coherence and purpose. Moreover, we can also see now what kind of evaluation we make when we decide that a life, or our life, is meaningful. We make an evaluation that consists of three aspects: coherence, purpose, and value. These three aspects make the eval-uation a comprehensive one. We will call it therefore, an overall evaluation. Briefly, to ascribe meaning to life is to provide an overall evaluation of it in terms of coherence, purpose, and value. Accordingly, let us define 'meaning' in the expression 'meaning of (a) life' as *the main set of evaluative aspects* of (that) life.[6]

Thus far we have used 'meaning' in its application to human life without differentiating between the meaning of our own lives, and the meaning of someone else's life, or human life in general. Let us now examine this difference further by taking into consideration the case of the meaning of Mr Jones's life.

Mr Jones is a worker in an enormous washing-machine factory. He is suffering from terminal cancer. For the manager of the factory, Mr Jones's life has no meaning other than the skills he employs in assembling washing machines. Therefore, the manager is not really worried by Mr Jones's illness, for Jones is replaceable by Mr Smith, who is just as skilful. Mrs Jones, however, is devastated now that Mr Jones is lying on his sickbed. For her, Mr Jones's life has a tremendous meaning, because he is such a loving and caring husband. For her, he has a unique value and cannot possibly be replaced. The local clergyman, who visits Jones on a certain day, says: 'Jones, you may believe it or not, but the meaning of life is to serve God forever. This is, therefore, also the meaning of your life.' Mr Jones himself, lying on his bed, thinks a lot about the meaning of his life. He tries to cope with the problems that flow from his illness. He attempts to make sense of existential constraints such as illness and death. As a blue-collar worker, he has always experienced the meaning of his life in terms of a Marxist philosophy of life, and now he is still trying to do so.

In the case of Mr Jones, we encounter several types of meaning. For the factory manager, the meaning of Jones and his life is simply functional. Jones is only valuable because of his skills; he is meaningful in the factory like a screw in a washing machine. To the manager, Jones is a quantity of working power rather than a person. The manager does not know him personally and is not interested in him as an individual. Every Jones could be replaced by a Smith. The only thing that counts is the profitability of the factory. Furthermore, the man-ager's view is an outsider's opinion about the life of another person; it is, therefore, independent of Jones's personal view. The type of meaning we find in the manager's external perspective we will call a 'third-person functional meaning' of Jones's life.

The view of Mrs Jones is another third-person perspective. However, this meaning is surely not functional. Jones's life has unique meaning for Mrs Jones, because she is person-ally related to him as she is to no other. Jones is existentially relevant to her. Jones's life has its meaning because of the person Jones is. Jones is meaningful because of himself. This third-person meaning of Jones's life is therefore 'intrinsic meaning'.

The clergyman's view is also from a third-person perspective. In contrast to the man-ager and Mrs Jones, however, the clergyman is relating the meaning of Jones's life to a universal point of view. The manager and Mrs Jones are talking about the meaning of *Mr Jones's* life. They ascribe meaning to Jones's life only. The clergyman, however, makes a statement about the meaning of life in general, and that is a statement about everyone's life, including Jones's. Here we have a meaning beyond the limits of a particular human existence, a meaning that applies to all human lives. This meaning exists independently of Jones's or everyone else's preferences of ideas because it is inherent within the universe.

With this meaning, therefore, a claim is made about the nature of the universe and of reality. This will be called 'objective meaning'.

A characteristic of objective meaning is that it implies a framework with universal claims about the reality. This makes the clergyman's view different from that of both the manager and Mrs Jones. The manager and Mrs Jones ascribe meaning to Jones's life from personal and limited points of view as wife or factory manager. The clergyman's view, however, states the meaning of Jones's life in terms of a universal framework that embraces the whole of reality. There are, however, different types of frameworks of objective meaning. Objective meaning could be in terms of a framework that relates the inherent meaning of the universe (including human lives) to external powers or a transcendent being – as in the case of the clergyman's meaning. However, such a framework could also focus on our world only with its internal social and political processes, like the framework of Marxism does. As a matter of fact, this framework is not necessarily a complete theory like Marxism; it can also be a more limited framework.

Furthermore, objective meaning could be *functional*: the meaning of Jones's life – and of the lives of everyone else – is serving as a little part in God's plan for the universe; but Jones can be replaced by Smith, who can serve God's purpose as adequately as Jones. Maybe, however, the clergyman aimed at serving as a unique person in a relation of love with God. Then this objective meaning is *intrinsic*.

Jones's own opinion about the meaning of his life is, of course, the view from an internal perspective – it is his own view. In contrast to third-person meaning and objective meaning we will call this 'first-person meaning'. Ascribing first-person meaning, that is to say meaning to your own life, is always an existential concern, because it implies dealing with your experiences of life – positive and negative ones.

Jones opts for a Marxist view when he ascribes first-person meaning, but he could, of course, have chosen the perspective of his wife. Then he would say: 'The meaning of my life is living as a loving and caring husband.' In that case, the intrinsic third-person meaning that his wife ascribed to his life would also be the first-person meaning of his life. He even could have chosen the functional perspective of his manager: 'The meaning of my life is functioning efficiently in the washing-machine factory.' We might judge this as a very poor meaning of one's own life, but in this case the manager's third-person meaning would then be identical with the first-person meaning of Jones's life. Again, Jones could accept the clergyman's objective meaning as the first-person meaning of his life. Furthermore, he could choose as his first-person meaning a combination of third-person meanings, or a combination of a third-person meaning and an objective meaning. He could, for instance, see the meaning of his life in living as a caring and loving husband and in serving God.

In sum, we can conclude that the consideration of the case of Mr Jones's life has brought to light different types of meaning. Ascribing meaning is making an overall evaluation in terms of coherence, purpose, and value, but there are three types of meaning that can be ascribed. There is first-person meaning, ascribed to one's own life; third-person meaning, ascribed to another's life; and objective meaning, ascribed to human life in general. Objective meaning, therefore, is not only ascribed to one's own life, or the life of another, but to all human lives. Furthermore, it appears that these three types of meaning can be functional or intrinsic. We have also seen that first-person meaning includes an existential concern. For our analysis of the ascription of meaning it is important to take first-person meaning and its existential concern into closer consideration.

Ascribing first-person meaning to one's own life is a general characteristic of human beings.[7] Not all people are equally conscious of this process, but all human beings will at some time during their lives try to make sense of events, deeds, a certain phase of life, or of their lives. We all encounter in our lives experiences of positive events like the birth of a child, but also – as in the case of Jones – negative experiences of suffering, illness, death, and the like. Considering all such experiences, we will try to ascribe meaning to our lives. We do this – as noted earlier – with an overall evaluation in terms of coherence, purpose, and value. Why do we make such an evaluation? What is its function? This evaluation is an attempt to unify and clarify our experiences of life.[8] It is an attempt to make our experiences of life understandable to us by means of structuring them.[9] The evaluation of ascribing meaning has this structuring function, not primarily as an intellectual concern but as an existential concern. The ascription of meaning to our own life is an evaluation with which we structure our life-experiences in order to regulate our lives – i.e. to find a way through them. Therefore, the overall evaluation of ascribing first-person meaning in terms of coherence, purpose, and value has two functions: a *structuring function* – structuring and clarifying life-experiences – in consideration of a *regulative function* – finding a life-direction.[10]

The structuring function – which serves the regulating function – implies factual claims about the nature of reality. After all, in order to regulate our lives, we structure events and life-experiences in terms of coherence, purpose, and value. We do so by giving them a coherent place in our lives, by connecting them with our purposes, and by valuing them. We also try to structure our lives themselves and the world in terms of coherence, purpose, and value. By means of our activity of structuring we try to make reality intelligible. All these acts of structuring imply factual claims about our life-experiences, events, our lives, and the nature of reality. The regulative function, in turn, implies a way of life. This way of life follows from the life-direction that the regulative function offers.

If, for example, Jane ascribes as meaning to her life 'living in a relation of mutual love with God who governs the world', this will determine her way of structuring life-events. The birth of her child, for instance, she may see as a gift from God (structuring function), and that may lead her to a thankful way of life towards God (regulative function). This way of structuring implies factual claims about the birth of her child, but also about her life and the nature of the world. To mention some of these claims: her child is God's gift; God influences her life, the world is such that there exists a God who acts in it.

At the end of this section we can draw the following conclusions. When we talk about the meaning of life, meaning can best be defined as the main set of evaluative aspects, because ascribing meaning is making an overall evaluation which includes the aspects of coherence, purpose, and value.

Furthermore, there are three main types of meaning. There is third-person meaning, which is either functional or intrinsic, and there is objective meaning, which also may be either functional or intrinsic. Finally, there is first-person meaning; this may be a functional or an intrinsic meaning, but in any case it has an existential concern. On the basis of the existential involvement of first-person meaning we tracked down two functions of ascribing first-person meaning. The first is a structuring function – which implies factual claims about the nature of reality. The purpose of this function is to serve the second: a regulative function – which leads to a personal way of life.

In this section we used the term objective meaning rather carelessly. However, in a great part of the literature on the ascription of meaning there is discussion about objective meaning. Some authors claim that only objective meaning is worth consideration when it comes to the meaning of life. Others defend the primacy of the meaning that one subjectively gives to his or her life. In the next section we will enter this discussion, starting from the findings we have so far.

Objective Meaning and Subjectively Given Meaning

Is there an objective meaning of human life? The commonly used expressions 'giving meaning to life' and 'ascribing meaning' suggest that the answer must be: No. After all, giving meaning to life seems to suppose that life has no meaning until we give it a meaning. Meaninglessness is here assumed as the state preceding the human act of endowing with meaning.[11] That life has no objective meaning and the universe is absolutely meaningless is emphatically defended by Bertrand Russell. Human beings and all living things are doomed to death and destruction, along with the world on which they live, and there is no reality beyond our finite and accidental existence that can provide a meaningful universal framework for our lives. It is an illusion to think that the human race has some pivotal importance in the universe. Russell argues that a viable view of life can only be construed when this ultimate truth is faced.[12] For some people, the objective meaninglessness of life means that their lives are worthless and absolutely meaningless.[13]

However, the pessimistic conclusion that a life without objective meaning is worthless and absolutely meaningless is not the only possible conclusion. Let us, for the sake of the argument, suppose that life is not endowed with an objective meaning. Even then, it does not necessarily follow that it is not worth living.[14] In fact there are lots of people who, while denying any objective meaning, experience their lives as fully meaningful because of the meaning they give it themselves. In other words, a life that is objectively meaningless can perfectly well be subjectively meaningful. Life with no other meaning than that which we subjectively give it may seem very poor, but it is not necessarily meaningless. Although it may not be satisfying for everyone, it is possible to live with the meaning people subjectively see in their lives.[15]

Some, however, will make the much stronger claim that the only meaning of human life that is worth consideration is the meaning *we give* it. Life without objective meaning can be worthwhile and meaningful because of the meaning humans subjectively give to it, and what is more, apart from this personal and conscious endowing, there is no meaning at all. The defenders of this opinion we will call *subjectivists*. We find a clear example of this in the following quotation of E. D. Klemke:

> It is true that life has no objective meaning. Let us face it once and for all. But from this it does not follow that life is not *worthwhile*, for it can still be subjectively meaningful. And, really, the latter is the only kind of meaning worth shouting about. An objective meaning – that is, one which is inherent within the universe or dependent upon external agencies – would, frankly,

leave me cold. It would not be *mine*. It would be an outer, neutral thing, rather than an inner, dynamic achievement. I, for one, am *glad* that the universe has no meaning, for thereby is *man all the more glorious*. I willingly accept the fact that external meaning is non-existent ..., for this leaves me free to *forge my own meaning*.[16]

Subjectivists like Klemke thus not only claim that a human life can be subjectively meaningful, but also that there exists no objective meaning of human life. According to them, the nature of reality is such that that there is no inherent meaning within reality. This claim about reality evokes a metaphysical debate, which we will not enter here. We will focus on two other suggestions by subjectivists.

Firstly, subjectivists tend to view objective meaning as a rival of subjective meaning. Klemke, in the quotation above, is glad that there is no objective meaning because that leaves room for a subjectively given meaning.[17] However, the idea that objective meaning can exclude the possibility of a subjectively given meaning, or that a lack of objective meaning makes such a meaning possible, is a misconception. This same misconception we find with objectivistic thinkers. *Objectivists* argue for a particular objective meaning, but also claim that we cannot give to our own lives the meaning we like because we must be receptive to the objective meaning. Meaning is not something we can give, and the idea of subjectively given meaning is an illusion, according to them.

As we have seen, however, in the case of the meaning of Mr Jones's life, objective meaning does not exclude the possibility of any other meaning. Jones gives a first-person meaning to his life from a Marxist view. He gives this meaning subjectively to his own life. His ability to do so is not hindered in any way by the fact that other persons give other meanings to his life. Even the objective meaning that was claimed by the clergyman is not incompatible with the fact that Jones could subjectively give meaning. As we have seen, objective meaning is a type of meaning different from first-person meaning that we give subjectively. A defence, therefore, of the possibility of objective meaning is not a denial of the possibility of any subjectively chosen meaning. The assertion that human life has an objective meaning is an assertion about the nature of reality. It is an answer to the question of whether our universe is in itself meaningless, so that humans must create their own meaning out of nothing, or whether the universe has been designed, as it were, for a certain way of giving meaning to life, so that we can subjectively adopt that way.

So our lives may have an objective meaning, but any objective meaning of our lives will leave us cold,[18] unless we appropriate it and thereby make it our own subjectively chosen first-person meaning.[19] This is rightly put forward by subjectivists. If someone declares that the meaning of human life is to serve God, I may shrug my shoulders indifferently and seek the meaning of my life in another perspective; or I may embrace that objective meaning as my first-person meaning. In order to acknowledge a meaning of one's own life, every human subject has to accept subjectively a certain meaning as the meaning of his own life and – in that sense – has to give meaning to his life by an active and intentional act of approval. Let us call this truth of subjectivism the 'subjective aspect of ascribing meaning'.

Secondly, however, there is another suggestion by subjectivists. Some subjectivists seem to claim that we can choose subjectively every meaning we like, and that this act of acceptance or choice is autonomous. On this point, objectivists correctly argue that the autonomy is an illusion. It is an illusion because our lives are constituted by many facts which are not under our control, which are not chosen, and which influence us to a high degree. Objective conditions of human life limit and colour our subjective aspirations. Firstly, we can think of biological conditions as birth, death, and health, or physiological requirements, which are all necessary for a human life and, as a consequence, for a meaningful human life. These conditions endow us with needs and capacities. Secondly, there are psychological conditions – innate or arising out of our lives – that steer our behaviour and way of acting to a certain degree. Thirdly, we are born in a certain social context and live our lives in a certain cultural setting. Social and cultural conditions determine to some extent what we prefer, what we judge as valuable or important to aim at. Our social and cultural context is also the source in which we can find views of life and ideas of objective meaning of human life. Nobody is without tradition.[20]

Of course, these conditions do not fully determine us, but they do limit our options and influence which meaning we subjectively choose for our lives. Human beings are therefore not fully autonomous. This truth of objectivism is the 'objective aspect of ascribing meaning': our attempts at giving meaning are limited and shaped by physiological and psychological conditions, as well as by social and cultural conditions, including traditions of objective meaning. Both aspects, the subjective as well as the objective, are irreducible to each other and are part of the way meaning of life arises.

However, there is more to be said. Although the subjective and objective aspects are necessary parts of the process of deriving and giving meaning, they are not sufficient. We cannot simply decide on a cold grey morning that the meaning of our lives consists in the warmth and light of love and friendship, and then immediately experience that that is in fact the meaning of our lives. In order to have that experience it is also necessary that we are really *inspired* by the idea we adopt as the meaning of our lives.[21] In a similar way as we can be inspired by a beautiful scenery, by an encouraging woman or man, by a delightful piece of music, by a fascinating poem, by a moving painting, or by an exciting novel, we must be inspired by something or somebody to experience meaning, and to live a certain life. We will call this the 'inspirational aspect of ascribing meaning'. This aspect is something beyond our reach – we cannot direct it. We cannot decide that tomorrow at five o' clock we will let ourselves be inspired by the worldview of Marx or the message of Mohammed. The only thing we can do is give attention to a view of life, and hope that it attracts us and will inspire us. It is also possible that we encounter something, somebody, or some thought by chance and are unexpectedly inspired by it.

In light of the above, do we give or find meaning? Both are true. The subjective aspect of ascribing meaning represents the fact that a person intentionally and subjectively gives his own life first-person meaning. The objective aspect makes clear that meaning is also determined and given by objective conditions, even by an idea of objective meaning transmitted by a certain tradition. Finally, the inspirational aspect shows that meaning is also something beyond our reach, something we find.

It is worth noticing that the discussion of these three aspects can be broadened to the question of whether we *choose* our beliefs or whether we *are convinced* to believe things.[22] The subjective aspect here is that *we* are the ones who believe and who can decide whether to take into account certain grounds and considerations. The objective aspect is that we cannot autonomously choose a belief, but are influenced by biological, psychological, social, and cultural conditions. Finally, the inspirational quality of the grounds we consider plays a role: we must be persuaded by something before we can believe it.

With this section we have completed our analysis of the process of ascribing meaning to life. In the next section we will try to answer the question of whether we can deduce from this process requirements for views of life.

Assessing Views of Life

So far we have analysed the process of ascribing meaning. The purpose of this analysis is a search for the requirements that views of life need to fulfil. Before looking for these require-ments, and before translating them into criteria, we first have to analyse the connection between views of life and the process of ascribing meaning – especially first-person meaning. How does the process of ascribing (first meaning) suppose a view of life?

In the foregoing sections we tracked down several characteristics of the process of ascribing meaning:

(1)   Ascribing first-person meaning to life is making an over-all evaluation of one's own life in terms of coherence, purpose and value.
(2)   This overall evaluation has a two-fold function:
    (2a)   a structuring function which implies claims about the nature of life and the nature of reality; this function serves
    (2b)   a regulative function – to find a life-direction – which implies a personal way of life.
(3)   Ascribing first-person meaning has a subjective, an objective, and an inspirational aspect.

The first two facets indicate that we do not ascribe meaning from scratch, but with the help of a complete framework. After all, the overall evaluation in terms of coherence, purpose, and value (1) has on the one side a structuring function (2a) that implies claims about the nature of the whole of reality. These claims form a whole range of beliefs we hold. On the other hand, the evaluation in terms of coherence, purpose and value (1) has the regulative function (2b) to give a life-orientation to a way of life. This life-orientation and personal way of life suppose and imply intentions to live a certain life, moral and non-moral values, norms, and ideals. So when we ascribe meaning to our lives, we do this with a complete framework of intentions, norms, values, ideals, and beliefs about factual reality. This frame-work is a *view of life*.[23] People always formulate the meaning of their lives with the help of their view of life.

Not all people consciously develop their view of life, and several parts of it may be implicit. However, its intentions, norms, values, ideals, and beliefs are always ordered in some way; otherwise the ascription of meaning with the help of a view of life cannot per-form its structuring and its regulative function. If the elements of a view of life are loosely connected or contradict each other, we cannot use it for an overall evaluation to structure reality and thus to give a direction to life. In that case, a more or less coherent and consistent structure is not possible, nor an unambiguous life-orientation.

Usually, however, the fact that we are inspired by something or someone (3) will ensure that this inspiring thing or person causes a certain coherence, consistency, and order in the conceptual forms of our view of life. Brümmer plausibly explains this phenomenon with the help of the concept of a *basic conviction*, in which something or somebody is deemed to be the primary determinant of meaning for all other things. Such basic convictions are

> ... attempts to do the following in some way or other: first, they all define a certain x (an object, or metaphysical entity, or ideal, or person, or something else) as distinct from all other entities. That x is unique in the sense that the attitude appropriate to it differs from attitudes appropriate to any other reality. Secondly, the attitude we ought to adopt to any other thing or situation or event, etc., is ultimately determined by its relation to x. The meaning of all things is therefore determined by their relation to x.[24]

When, for instance, our primary determinant of meaning is the ideal of equal love and respect for all human beings, this has implications for our intentions, our values and norms, and our beliefs. In that case we give our lives meaning in terms of that ideal and in terms of the whole system that coheres with it. However, when our ideal does not really function as a primary determinant, ascribing meaning derails. This would, for instance, be the case if we also had the strong belief that males deserve more love and respect than females, or if we valued educated people far above people without education. A view of life that contains such contradictory beliefs and values cannot adequately function in ascribing meaning. One could object, however, that in everyday life we see many people who have a view of life that has several primary determinants of meaning – and thus, strictly taken, none – and who can apparently live with that view of life. It is true, indeed, that such an incoherent view of life can serve the structuring and regulative function of ascribing meaning to a certain extent. However, problems will arise when the primary determinants come into conflict with each other, or when a crisis in life demands an unambiguous orientation and direction to life. In such situations, a view of life is needed with a clear primary determinant of meaning which creates sufficient coherence. Briefly, from the three facets of ascribing meaning we can proceed to a fourth and a fifth:

(4)   The ascription of first-person meaning implies the use of a view of life, which consists of intentions, values, norms, and beliefs.
(5)   The elements of a view of life need to be ordered and determined by a basic conviction concerning the primary determinant of meaning.

Having explained how the process of ascribing meaning is connected with a view of life, we will turn to the question of whether this process has requirements that can be used to assess views of life. However, it is not obvious beforehand that views of life *can* be assessed. As we have seen in the second section, we are the ones who subjectively give meaning to our own lives, even though within certain objective limits. Furthermore, although meaning is the result of a certain inspiration, we are the ones who must be personally inspired by someone or something. The fact that *we* give meaning and that *we* must be inspired could give rise to the suggestion that the choice of a view of life with which someone gives meaning to her or his life is a matter of mere personal preference. This would mean that we could not judge the view of life with which someone gives meaning to her or his life, for instance, as being trivial, mistaken, or reprehensible. Do judgements about views of life in this way become a matter of mere personal preferences?

This suggestion is very counter-intuitive. Intuitively, we feel that a person who finds the whole meaning of his life in collecting and driving vintage cars has a much poorer view of life than the view that inspired, for instance, Mother Teresa to live her life.[25] In fact we do not judge ascriptions of meaning and views of life only in terms of 'poor', 'rich', or 'interesting'. After all, most of us will judge any ascription of first-person meaning inspired by Nazi ideas about human races as morally reprehensible. We consider it appropriate, I suggest, to challenge each other to expalin why a life lived in accordance with a certain favourite life plan is meaningful. This shows that, in practice, we do make judgements about the views of life people use to give to their lives. The problem, how-ever, is the justification of these judgements. Are there criteria by which one can judge a view of life?

We can distinguish between two ways to develop criteria to assess views of life. We can look for criteria in terms of a certain view of life. The arguments and authority, then, of such criteria come from inside that particular view of life. These are *internal criteria*. These cri-teria only have validity for adherents of that view of life. On the other hand, we can try to find criteria from an external point of view as well, criteria by which we can judge all views of life. In that case we have *external criteria*.[26] Our attempt to derive from the process of ascribing meaning the requirements that views of life need to fulfil is a search for criteria from an external point of view. After all, whatever meaning will be ascribed, the process of ascribing will include the same aspects and conform to the same principles. If this process implies certain requirements, every view of life should meet them.[27]

Let us now turn to conditions and requirements of the process of ascribing meaning in order to find external criteria. We have summarized this process in the five facets men-tioned above. As we have seen, (1), (2), and also (5) ask for consistency and coherence of all elements of the view of life including, of course, the basic conviction. From these two con-ditions we can proceed to the external criteria, *internal consistency* and *internal coherence*. Internal coherence is the fact that the particular elements of the view of life fit together well, so that the view as a whole forms a unity. Internal consistency is the fact that the elements of a view of life do not contradict each other. Both criteria are required for the proper working of the two functions of the overall evaluation in which the ascription of meaning consists. Furthermore, these functions also require consistency and coherence of our view-of-life beliefs with our other beliefs about reality. This leads us to the criteria of *external consistency* and *external coherence*.

As to external consistency, when our religious beliefs contradict our other beliefs about reality, the structuring and regulating functions of our ascription of meaning would only apply to part of our life and to part of reality. This would lead to a rather schizophrenic way of life: beliefs in one area of life contradict the beliefs in another. An example would be a person who has the view-of-life belief that some intelligent beings anywhere in space are governing the earth and his whole life, but who, as a scientist, has the conviction that there probably are no living beings at all in space.

As far as external coherence is concerned, it is difficult to see how our view of life can have an influence – let alone a structuring and regulating influence – on our experience of reality, when the beliefs of our view of life do not cohere with other views we have about that reality. There must be some connection between beliefs belonging to our view of life and our other beliefs about reality to enable us to use our view of life for living in that reality. Suppose, for instance, that we would have in our view of life the belief that it is very important to support financially poor people in the world. When we have outside our view of life no belief at all about poor people – regarding who they are, where they live, how they can be supported, etc. – our belief about supporting poor people cannot have any structuring or regulating function.

Briefly, from facets (1), (2), and (5) we can conclude that the view of life by which we ascribe meaning to our life is adequate for the structuring and regulative function when it is internally as well as externally consistent and coherent. It must be noted here that these criteria do not require full consistency and coherence. If only absolutely consistent and coherent views of life are adequate, no view can count as such, I am afraid. These criteria ask for a sufficient consistency and coherence because the more consistent and coherent a view of life is, the more adequate it is in the process of ascribing meaning.[28] This need for consistency and coherence is also emphasized by psychology. K. I. Pargament, for instance, writes about religious views of life:

> Built into most religious perspectives, however, is a tolerance for some inconsistency and fragmentation. People can hold on to themselves and their religions, imperfect orienting systems and all. But if there are too many holes and inconsistencies – if the religious realm is too disconnected from the secular, if practices are unrelated to beliefs, if motivations have little to do with practices – the orienting system loses its ability to guide the individual through troubled times.[29]

With his remarks about fragmentation, however, Pargament points not only to the framework of a view of life itself, but also to the connection between the view of life and the practices of living with that view. This leads us to another set of criteria for adequacy. A view of life must not only be adequate in a formal sense but also in a practical sense, that is to say, it must be successful in the practice of our lives. One type of this practical adequacy is *existential suitability*: a view of life must be adequate considering the demands of our human existence. This condition is implied by (2b): the regulative function of providing a life-orientation in our life. The demand of existential suitability is also implied by the objective aspect of ascribing meaning (3): the ascription of meaning with a view of life must fit the objective conditions of our life; these conditions were discussed in the previous section. A view of life is existentially suitable only when it helps us to deal with the demands with which life confronts us, and thus gives us an orientation for living it. In a similar way, it is argued in psychological and pastoral literature that not every (religious) view of life is likewise successful in helping to deal with the problems of life. Especially in hard times, it becomes clear whether a view of life is a help or a hindrance in coping with the problems of life.[30] The requirement of existential suitability will have a much wider scope when our view of life implies an objective meaning. In that case the view of life not only must be existentially suitable within our own lives, but it must in principle be applicable in the lives of everyone.

Mere existential suitability, however, is not sufficient. A view of life must be existentially suitable for persons in *all* situations of life. We need a universally successful use of it for coping with the ever-changing demands of life through several times. We will call this adequacy *universalizability*. A view of life is still more universalizable, when it could in principle provide us with a life-orientation in various cultures. Furthermore, when our view of life implies an objective meaning, it must not only meet the demand of universalizability in our own lives, but it must also have the capacity to be universally existentially suitable in the lives of everyone.

In order to be practically adequate, the elements of our view of life must also actually be integrated with our way of life. In other words, our actual lifestyle must correspond with the way of life implied by our ascription of meaning (2b). We will call this requirement the criterion of *integrity*. We might, for instance, say that our way of life is inspired by mountain climbing and that the highest goal of our life is climbing Mount Everest. The view of life, in terms of which this meaning (mountain climbing) is ascribed, could be formally adequate, but may nevertheless fail to fit within our actual way of life. That would be the case when we completely failed to exhibit the behaviour implied by our first-person meaning: climbing mountains, reading books about mountaineering, buying the necessary equipment, training, etc., etc. In such a case, our view of life has no integrity.

The importance of this type of integrity also emerges from the psychological research of Pargament. He argues, on the ground of empirical evidence, that a lack of integration of a (religious) view of life with the practice of away of life has a negative effect on one's psychological competence. By this competence he means things like personal control, self-esteem, trust in others, and coping skills.[31]

A final criterion of practical adequacy arises from (3) (especially the inspirational aspect). If we ascribe a certain first-person meaning because we decide that something or someone is inspiring to the greatest degree, that someone or something must indeed have the capacity to be inspiring and to continue being so. This capacity is required by the criterion of *inspirational quality*. Even though it cannot be decided by external criteria whether a particular source of inspiration should be our primary determinant of meaning, the criterion of inspirational quality is an external criterion. Other people, even if they disagree with our view of life, can ask us to account for the inspirational quality of the primary determinant of meaning of our view of life. In such a case they can assess our account in an external way, because they assess the inspirational quality of our view of life without accepting our view of life.

When, however, our view of life implies an objective meaning, then the criterion of inspirational quality becomes a universal demand. In that case, our view of life must be capable of shaping the ascription of first-person meaning of everybody, and the person or thing who or which is inspiring us, must have the capacity of inspiring everybody.

Accordingly, we can conclude that the requirements of the process of ascribing meaning lead to the following list of external criteria for the assessment of views of life.[32] There are four external criteria of formal adequacy: internal consistency; internal coherence; external consistency; and external coherence. There are four external criteria of practical adequacy:

existential suitability; universalizability; integrity; and inspirational quality. These criteria, however, cannot give us the guarantee that people will easily agree when assessing views of life.[33] Even when we accept the criteria, because they are external to any view of life, applying them may lead to different results because in the application of the criteria our own view may play a role. Moreover, it is very well possible that certain views of life are more or less equally successful in meeting most of the criteria. In that case, if one wants to make a final decision, one's personal preference will be decisive. However, an external discussion about assessing meaning remains possible.

With the external criteria that we have found we can judge whether a particular view of life is adequate for the ascription of meaning. We can answer the question 'Does this view of life work?' With these criteria, however, we cannot decide whether a view of life is rich, trivial, or morally reprehensible. Such assessments cannot be made from an external point of view, by means of external criteria, because in these cases we judge in terms of our own view of life. In other words, in these cases we make an assessment with the help of internal criteria: criteria in terms of a particular view of life. These criteria derive their legitimacy from that particular view of life and are, therefore, normative only for adherents of the view of life to which the criteria belong.[34]

Two important internal criteria are, I suggest: authoritative continuity, and aim-accordance. As to the first internal criterion, the question can be asked whether a certain view of life is sufficiently continuous with its own authoritative sources. If, for instance, a humanist ascribes a certain meaning to his life, this meaning and the way of life that results from it can be judged by means of, for example, normative humanistic moral norms. As to the second internal criterion mentioned above, every view of life has its aims. Therefore, a view of life can be judged in light of these aims by asking: 'Is this view in accordance with its own aims?' Imagine, for instance, an extremist who claimed to be a Christian stating 'According to my view of life, the meaning of my life is serving God by exterminating all godles non-Christians.' The view of life of this extremist could be judged to deviate from the aims of a Christian view of life. Christians could, for example, argue that the extremist, as a follower of Jesus Christ, should accept Jesus' maxim 'Love the Lord your God with all your heart and with all your sould and with all your mind, and love your neighbour as yourself.'[35] Moreover, Christians could argue that the extremist's view is not a Christian view of life at all. In a similar way, elements of a view of life, for instance a certain belief, can be assessed with the criterion of aim-accordance. Suppose that the extremist has the conviction that it is allowed to torture unbelievers that refuse to be converted. Christians could argue that this conviction is not in accordance with the aims of their view of life.

To both of these internal criteria one could object that they are roughly similar to the external criterion of internal coherence. This external criterion requires that the elements of a view of life internally cohere, and the two internal criteria also aim at such coherence. The criterion of authoritative continuity in fact requires that elements of a view of life cohere with that view's authoritative sources, and the criterion of aim-accordance demands coherence of aims with the other elements of a view of life. True as this may be, there is an important difference between the external criterion of internal coherence and both internal criteria. When an outsider of a certain view of life would use both these internal criteria, they would have no authority for her or him, and in that case these internal criteria would be roughly the same as the criterion of internal coherence. For adherents of that view of life, however, these criteria have another weight than the weight of an external criterion. For them these criteria have internal authority because of their view of life. As we have seen above, this characterizes internal criteria in contrast to external criteria.

Finally, let us consider another aspect of internal criteria. In most contemporary societies and cultures several views of life coexist. In spite of all differences, the adherents of various views of life may share fewer or more internal criteria, for instance as a result of a partly shared history of origination or of mutual influencing. This leads to a set of *shared internal criteria* in a certain culture of society, like moral values and norms, and non-moral values and norms. If we restrict ourselves to Western societies, we can discern as shared internal criteria moral values like the protection of human life, human rights, the protection of personal possessions. With regard to non-moral values (as shared Western internal criteria) we can think of self-development. Human autonomy is such a non-moral value as well: taking seriously human beings as responsible persons with a free will. By means of these shared internal criteria, we can assess different views of life from an internal point of view to a certain degree. Shared internal criteria are normative for adherents of more than one view of life.

At the end of this section we can conclude that views of life are not purely person-relative and beyond discussion. We have found four external criteria of formal adequacy and four external criteria of practical adequacy. By means of these external criteria we can assess every view of life. Besides assessing from an external point of view it is also possible to judge a view of life from an insider's point of view. This can be done with the help of internal criteria. We have also found that there are shared internal criteria by which we can assess a view of life from an internal point of view that is shared by a number of different views of life.

Notes

1. 'Value' is meant here in a general sense as that which makes something worthwile to have, to do etc., cf. E. J. Bond *Reason and Value* (Cambridge: Cambridge University Press, 1983), 2. There are different types of value. An important distinction is that between moral values and non-moral values, such as aesthetic values. See e.g. W. K. Frankena *Ethics* (Englewood Cliffs NJ: Prentice-Hall, 1973), 62.

2. R. W. Hepburn 'Questions about the meaning of life', in E. D. Klemke (ed.) *The Meaning of Life* (Oxford: Oxford University Press, 1981), 209–26, see 223, 224; H. J. Adriaanse 'Sinn, Sinnfrage II', in G. Müller (ed.) *Theologische Realenzyklopädie*, Band XXXI (Berlin: De Gruyter, 2000), 293–8.

3. R. Nozick *Philosophical Explanations* (Oxford: Clarendon Press, 1984), 585–8, 594–600.

4. *Ibid.*, 576, 577; J. E. Heyde 'Vom Sinn des Wortes Sinn: Prolegomena zu einer Philosophie des Sinnes', in R. Wisser (ed.) *Sin und Sein: Ein Philosophisches Symposion* (Tübingen; Max Niemeyer Verlag, 1960), 69–94 (esp. 84–94); Hepburn 'Questions about the meaning of life', 210, 214; P. Edwards 'Life, meaning and value of', in *idem* (ed.) *The Encyclopedia of Philosophy* (New York NY: Macmillan, 1967) vol. 4, 467–77 (esp. 472); Adriaanse 'Sinn', 293.

5. *Ibid.*

6. V. Brümmer *Theology and Philosophical Inquiry: An Introduction* (London: Macmillan, 1981). Brümmer also gathers 'meaning' under the heading of evaluative discourse or value theory (5, 67, 70). He defines the meaning of something as 'the totality of its prescriptive properties'.

7. V. E. Frankl *Man's Search for Meaning: An Introduction to Logotherapy* (Boston MA: Beacon Press, 1992), e.g. 105, 106; M. Stenmark *Rationality in Science, Religion, and Everyday Life: A Critical Evaluation of Four Models of Rationality* (Notre Dame IN: University of Notre Dame Press, 1995), 237–9; K. I. Pargament *The Psychology of Religion and Coping: Theory, Research, Practice* (New York NY: Guilford Press, 1997), 90–95.

8. Stenmark *Rationality*, 257, 263. Stenmark, however, seems only to take account of negative life-experiences of which people try to make sense. In my opinion, however, the same applies in a situation of positive experiences, although negative experiences may lead to questions concerning our existence in a more urgent way.

9. W. Hasker *Metaphysics: Constructing a World View* (Downers Grove IL: InterVarsity Press, 1983), 25, 26, about the function of metaphysical theories.

10. Cf. Stenmark, who distinguishes between a theoretical or perceptual function, and a practical or regulative function of a view of life, *Rationality*, 243.

11. H. J. Adriaanse 'Der klar leuchtende Weltbau', in *idem Von Christentum aus: Aufsätze und Vorträge zur Religionsphilosophie* (Kampen: Kok Pharos, 1995), 50.

12. B. Russell 'The free man's worship', in R. A. Rempel, A. Brink, M. Moran (eds) *Contemplation and Action, 1902–14* (*The Collected Papers of Bertrand Russell, vol. 12*) (London: Allen & Unwin, 1985), 66–72. The title of this paper from 1903, originally 'The free man's worship', is in later reprints changed to 'A free man's worship'.

13. A. Schopenhauer 'Von der Nichtigkeit und dem Leiden des Lebens', in *idem Die Welt als Wille und Vorstellung*, Buch 4, Kapitel 46, *Sämtliche Werke*, Band II (Darmstadt: Wissenschaftliche Buchgesellschaft, 1976), 733–54. English translation: *The World as Will and Representation* (New York NY: Dover Publications, 1969). Cf. L. N. Tolstoy 'A confession', 19, 20, in *idem, A Confession, The Gosepl in Brief and What I Believe* (London: Oxford University Press, 1940), 1–84.

14. K. Baier 'The meaning of life', 115, in Klemke *Meaning of Life*.

15. Thomas Nagel *What Does It All Mean?: A Very Short Introduction to Philosophy* (Oxford: Oxford University Press, 1987), 100; *idem The View from Nowhere* (Oxford: Oxford University Press, 1986), 218–23.

16. E. D. Klemke 'Living without appeal: An affirmative philosophy of life', in *idem Meaning of Life*, 172 (Klemke's italicization). Cf. R. Taylor *Good and Evil: A New Direction: A Forceful Attack on the Rationalistic Tradition in Ethics* (New York NY: Prometheus Books, 1984), 256–68.

17. Klemke 'Living without appeal', 173.

18. Nozick *Philosophical Explanations*, 573.

19. See M. Sarot 'Sisyphus revisited: reflections on the analogy between linguistic meaning and the meaning of life', *Neue Zeitschrift für systematische Theologie und Religionsphilosophie*, 38 (1996), 219–31, 231.

20. For such conditions that limit our possibilities, cf. T. V. Morris *Making Sense of it All: Pascal and the Meaning of Life* (Grand Rapids MI: Eerdmans, 1992), 59–61; but also a subjectivistically orientated writer like J. Kekes explicitly takes account of these sorts of conditions. See his 'The informed will and the meaning of life', *Philosophy and Phenomenological Research*, **47** (1986–7), 75–90, esp. 84–6.

21. See Kekes, who seems to point into the direction of a similar idea: 'Informed will', 84. In a comparable sense Hepburn ('Questions', 212, 213) speaks about 'concern'.

22. See for a discussion of this question, for instance, Descartes' fourth meditation of the *Meditationes De Prima Philosophia* where Descartes stresses the importance of the will and the freedom of choice when it comes to beliefs. David Hume, in contrast, argues in his *Treatise on Human Nature* (book 1, part 3, section 7) that we believe a certain idea because we have become convinced by its superior force, vivacity, solidity, firmness, or steadiness.

23. Cf. Brümmer *Theology and Philosophical Inquiry*, 131–3. Cf. Nozick's description of a life plan, *Philosophical Explanations*, 577.

24. Brümmer *Theology and Philosophical Inquiry*, 133.

25. Cf. A. J. Ayer 'The meaning of life', in *idem The Meaning of Life and Other Essays* (London: Weidenfeld and Nicolson, 1990), 189.

26. See for the distinction between internal and external criteria, Brümmer *Theology and Philosophical Inquiry*, 138.

27. Cf. for other attempts to derive criteria for views of life from the way the ascription of meaning functions: Brümmer *Theology and Philosophical Inquiry*, 138; Stenmark *Rationality*, esp. 253–72.

28. In some cases it will be a matter of discussion whether a view of life is sufficiently consistent and coherent.

29. Pargament *Psychology*, 351; see also 347–51.

30. See e.g. K. I. Pargament *et al.* 'Religion and the problem-solving process: three styles of coping', *Journal for the Scientific Study of Religion*, **27** (1988), 90–104; Pargament *Psychology*, e.g. 90–126; J. A. van der Ven and H. J. M. Vossen 'Pastoral research in theodicy', in *idem* (eds) *Suffering: Why for God's Sake?: Pastoral Research in Theodicy* (Kampen: Kok, 1995), 13–16.

31. Pargament *Psychology*, 349, 350.

32. Some more or less similar criteria can be found in: Brümmer *Theology and Philosophical Inquiry*, 139–43; *idem* 'The inter-subjectivity of criteria in theology' in M. M. Olivetti (ed.) *Intersubjectivité et théologie philosophique* (Padua: Cedam, 2001), 165–90; W. J. Wainwright *Philosophy of Religion* (Belmont CA: Wadsworth, 1988), 171–3; C. Schwöbel *God; Action and Revelation* (Kampen: Kok Pharos, 1992), 17–21; K. E. Yandell *Christianity and Philosophy* (Leicester: Inter Varsity Press, 1984), 272–85. Cf. Pargament who gives keys to assess the process of coping, *Psychology*, esp. 339–58.

33. Cf. Wainwright *Philosophy of Religion*, 174–89, who briefly compares e.g. theism and naturalism, and Christianity and Mahāyāna Buddhism with the help of his external criteria. See also Brümmer *Theology and Philosophical Inquiry*, 142, 143; and *idem* 'Inter-subjectivity', 187–90, about the inter-subjectivity of criteria.

34. When somebody has an individual and purely eclectic view of life, he may be the only adherent of that view, and his internal criteria are valid only for him. A much broader discussion on the basis of internal criteria is possible when it is about a view of life that is a form of one of the more traditional views of life, like world religions or philosophies of life with more adherents. In the following we will mainly have in mind these traditional views of life.

35. Matthew 22, 37, 39.

Section II

What Does God Have to Do with the Meaning of Life?

Introduction

John Cottingham

As Joshua Seachris points out in his General Introduction to this volume, there was a longish period during the twentieth century when the question of life's meaning received little sustained attention from analytic philosophers. For several decades, a very tight and restrictive conception of philosophy was dominant, and questions about the meaning of life were scathingly dismissed either as incoherent or as outside the scope of proper philosophical inquiry. That negative attitude to the grand traditional questions about the purpose of life and its ultimate meaning and value has by no means completely disappeared today. But many people continue to be drawn to philosophy precisely because they are perplexed by such "grand" questions, and the drive to address them is something that cannot be suppressed for long. The publication of the present volume is but one sign, among many others, that the ancient topic of life's meaning has come firmly back onto the philosophical agenda.

But what has God got to do with it all? That is the specific focus of the essays in this present section of the book. They all address, in different ways, the question of how far, if at all, appeals to the existence of God can serve to underwrite or support the meaningfulness of human life. The Judaeo-Christian worldview, which even its sternest contemporary critics would acknowledge to have been enormously influential in shaping the moral and philosophical landscape of the Western world, has of course always maintained that the role of God in this respect is absolutely central. We are, on this view, brought into existence as creatures who can only find their ultimate fulfillment in orienting their lives toward the will of the creator, source of all meaning and value.

Diametrically opposed to this is the outlook that has increasingly come to be referred to under the label of *naturalism*. This is the view that the physical events and processes that arose out of the Big Bang, including the eventual emergence of planetary systems, life, and, in due course, human beings and their activities – that this total set of entirely natural processes and events comprises all the reality there is. There is no transcendent creator, no

Exploring the Meaning of Life: An Anthology and Guide, First Edition. Edited by Joshua W. Seachris.
© 2013 John Wiley & Sons, Inc. Published 2013 by John Wiley & Sons, Inc.

supernatural realm, nothing beyond the natural world in which we find ourselves. One of the main questions addressed in many of the essays that follow is not so much the question of which of these two views, naturalism or its theistic opposite, is *true*; that, of course, is a question of supreme importance, though it may be beyond our human capacity to settle finally. The main issue addressed instead is what *difference* the truth of either view would make to the meaning of life. For example, is the impersonal, godless universe posited by naturalism one in which there is any room for our lives to be truly meaningful? Or again, how exactly would the fact of God's existence, if it is a fact, confer significance on our human existence?

Our selection opens with the book of Ecclesiastes (from the Hebrew Bible or Old Testament), traditionally attributed to Solomon (around 900 BC), though some scholars assign it a somewhat later date. Essentially, it is a powerful lament to the emptiness or futility of the ordinary earthly cycle of human existence. Considered from a mundane point of view, all our frantic endeavors, all our temporary successes and achievements, are ultimately pointless; we die, the cycle relentlessly repeats itself, and there is "nothing new under the sun."

This bleak view forms the starting point (but certainly not the conclusion) of the first essay included here, by the novelist, academic, and great Christian apologist C. S. Lewis. We need to start, Lewis argues, by accepting that "nature is a sinking ship." Although his essay was written in the aftermath of the dropping of the atomic bombs on Hiroshima and Nagasaki, when many thoughtful people were deeply worried about the possibility of human civilization destroying itself in an atomic war, Lewis observes that the danger of atomic destruction is merely a graphic way of bringing home to us what we knew already (though so often prefer to forget): The natural world is slowly running down. "If nature is all that exists – in other words, if there is no God and no life of some quite different sort somewhere outside nature – then all stories will end in the same way: in a universe from which all life is banished with no possibility of return. It will have been an accidental flicker, and there will be no one even to remember it" (p. 134). For Lewis, a purely natural universe is inherently devoid of meaning and value, and therefore profoundly alienating to creatures like us, given our deep human longings for what is true and rational and right – longings that can only be satisfied, in Lewis's view, by accepting the truth of the theistic worldview.

The following essay, by Jeffrey Gordon, seems at first sight to be moving in a quite different direction. The arguments suggesting that God could make a difference to the otherwise bleak human predicament of being stuck in a dying universe are, Gordon argues, "disappointingly weak." Merely giving us immortality might not do the job: "there is nothing self-evident about the connection between a meaningful life and personal immortality" (p. 142). And attempts to show that God can underwrite meaningfulness by generating objective moral value run afoul of the so-called Euthyphro dilemma: Either the edifice of value ordained by God reflects what is already antecedently morally right (in which case God's ordinances are in a sense redundant), or else it arises from a mere divine fiat that would be "no less morally arbitrary than a similar act by a man" (p. 143). Analogous problems beset attempts to ground the meaningfulness of the world in God's designs or purposes. But in spite of all these difficulties, Gordon closes by appealing to our "passion to affirm the world," which might be satisfied by our sense of beauty. Acknowledging this would in a certain way be acknowledging that the meaningfulness of our existence depends crucially on God; for only if there is a God "can we allow ourselves the hope that what appears to be the pointless chaos of our suffering is in fact an essential part of an awesome and magnificent destiny [...] justified in solely aesthetic terms" (p. 149).

In the next essay, the philosopher and Christian apologist William Lane Craig takes up some of the themes broached in the first two essays. Without God, he argues, man and the universe are doomed. Not only is my own life "just a momentary transition out of oblivion into oblivion," but modern science tells us that even the universe itself is "plunging towards extinction," as its energy is inevitably used up. The consequence is that "the life we have is without ultimate significance, value or purpose." For Craig, "[if] man ends in nothing, he is nothing." And this means that "our study, our jobs, our interests, our friendships, all these are in the final analysis utterly meaningless." Without God, Craig goes on to argue, there is no ultimate value. Reason on its own gives us no basis for acting morally rather than immorally, and, what is more, without God there will be no objective standards of right and wrong, "only our culturally and personally relative, subjective judgments." Nor, the argument continues, will there be any purpose to human life without God. Quoting some phrases from the book of Ecclesiastes, Craig insists that without God there will be no more purpose to the life of a human than to the life of a dog or an insect: "all come from the dust and all return to the dust." Perhaps the most urgent question to arise from Craig's position is whether things are indeed as polarized as he suggests. On his view, there is no common ground, no bridging the stark gulf between the implications of naturalism and of theism: Either we accept that the universe is utterly devoid of meaning and value and our human predicament "truly terrible," or else we can choose "life, meaningfulness and happiness" by accepting biblical Christianity (p. 171).

The essay by theologian John Haught makes a useful distinction between the "spiritual adequacy" of naturalism and the question of its truth. If scientific naturalism is true, he argues, then the world is irredeemably bleak for vast numbers of deprived people, since they are living in an ultimately pointless universe where they have no hope of achieving even a minimal fulfillment of their human potentialities, let alone lasting happiness. In this sense, Haught claims, scientific naturalism is "spiritually inadequate," since it cannot claim to respond to humanity's deepest aspirations. But this sobering implication of naturalism, Haught concedes, does not in itself go to show that it is not a reasonable and a true view. The latter question, he proceeds to point out, depends on just how complete a set of explanations the naturalist claims to provide. Haught argues that the typical scientific naturalist "puts too heavy a burden on evolutionary science when they turn it into an *ultimate* explanation." The goal of the naturalist is for a single, economical, "clear and distinct" template (such as "reproductive success") to which all the phenomena in a given domain can be reduced. But Haught suggests that in order to be complete and adequate, explanations must, in the nature of things, be endlessly deep and multilayered. Any conception of science that reduces this complexity to a template that is supposed to offer a "fundamental" or "final" explanation (p. 181) has to be rejected.

In my own contribution, which comes next, I begin by considering some problems in the notion that God can be the *source* of meaning and value in human life. The idea seems to threaten our conception of ourselves as autonomous choosing beings, who find meaning in our own independently formed plans and projects. What the defender of the religious outlook needs to show in answer to this worry, I argue, is that the authentic religious life is not one of servile deference to an alien authority, but a progressive growth toward true freedom informed by knowledge and love of the good. As conceived in the Christian tradition, though we are indeed the creatures of God, and in that sense utterly dependent on a power outside of ourselves, the role of God is nevertheless not that of a controlling tyrant who desires us to conform to his arbitrary will, but rather that of a loving parent who desires above all that we should mature morally so that we seek the good for its own sake. This in turn provides us with the wherewithal to neutralize the Euthyphro problem (mentioned above) – God neither issues arbitrary commands, nor is he subject to prior moral constraints; rather, his commands necessarily reflect his essential nature, as that which is wholly and perfectly good. There follows a discussion of the concept of goodness, which concedes that there is a close connection between goodness and the ordinary natural properties of things in virtue of which they count as good. But it is argued that the theistic picture still makes a crucial difference to the value and meaningfulness we are able to attribute to our human lives. For in pursuing the good, we are not like the talking cows in the final volume of Douglas Adams's *Hitchhiker* trilogy, genetically programmed to accept their imposed destiny of serving the purposes of meat eaters. Instead, the theistic view is one in which there is a moral teleology at work in the universe, and our true fulfillment and peace are not "mere tranquillisation or externally engineered submission to a higher power, but the peace of an autonomous being whose reason has recognised the truth of the ancient religious idea: to serve goodness is the most perfect freedom" (p. 194).

Our final essay, by Thaddeus Metz, takes us into complex theological territory of the attributes or properties traditionally attributed to God. Many theists hold that our human lives are meaningful in so far as they fulfill a purpose that God has assigned. Metz examines and rejects some standard objections to this (of the type we have already considered in the previous paragraph), namely that God's assigning us a purpose threatens our human autonomy and dignity. He plausibly suggests that it is possible for God to assign us a purpose in a way that is noncoercive and fully respectful of our rational agency and moral worth, so such objections do not stand up. But Metz then raises a very radical question that is often ignored or taken for granted in debates in this area: Why exactly does the theist think that relating to God and his purposes should be necessary for a significant human life? Metz maintains that the most plausible explanation is that it is the superior nature of God (the excellent and special quality of the uniquely divine attributes) that is supposed to confer significance on the lives of those who orient themselves toward God, as opposed to anything found in the ordinary physical world. However, if we look at the properties that are special or unique to God (timelessness, immutability, simplicity, and infinity or unlimitedness), then it is by no means clear, Metz argues, that these are compatible with God's having ends or purposes, since the latter notions seem to imply a being who deliberates or acts in time. Metz's objections are here related to a long-standing theological debate about the coherence of the concept of a personal God who wholly transcends the physical world of space and time, and yet who is supposed to be a personal being, and hence to have in some way the characteristics associated with being an agent. What Metz's argument leaves open is whether the theist might more profitably focus on other attributes of God, such as truth, beauty, and goodness, which have often been thought to confer meaning on a human life that is oriented toward them. Although such attributes are not entirely "unique" or special to God, since they are (at least partially or analogously) shared with his creatures, they are arguably much more relevant to the moral and spiritual core of the religious outlook than the more abstract metaphysical properties of the deity such as immutability.

Readers will form their own views concerning the various perspectives and arguments presented in this and the other essays included in this part of the volume. Many of the issues are complex, and those who work through the materials may well find that they are able to accept some claims or some portions of an argument while having reservations about others. Because this part of the volume is devoted to the relation between God and the meaning of life, many aspects of the rival secular approach are necessarily left out, and it will be important for the reader to set the essays contained here against other parts of the volume that include explorations of materialist and nonreligious approaches.

All of these extracts are pieces of the fascinating philosophical jigsaw that is being formed as a result of the current revival of the traditional grand questions concerning the meaning of life. That revival is especially exciting for our contemporary intellectual culture, because it brings into stark relief the clash between religious and secular outlooks that has been gathering speed for over a hundred years, stemming in particular from the revolutionary ideas of Friedrich Nietzsche and Charles Darwin in the nineteenth century, and the challenge they posed for our human self-understanding. Essentially, that challenge is whether we can accept that meaning and value in our lives are the result of a purely contingent chain of events – the series of cosmic accidents and evolutionary pressures that shaped us – or whether we are constrained to acknowledge something cogent and compelling about the traditional religious idea that our deepest aspirations reflect the source of goodness that gives ultimate value and purpose to human life.

These are momentous questions. Our human struggle to achieve meaning and value takes place in a world beset by fragility, and the ever-present threat of alienation, futility, and despair. Of course, these are perils far too great to be overcome by philosophical inquiry alone. But philosophy can perhaps help us to understand the dangers a little better, and to try to discern how we might learn to face them with courage and hope.

Suggestions for Further Reading

Affolter, Jacob (2007) "Human nature as God's purpose," *Religious Studies* 43(December): 443–55.

Adams, Robert Merrihew (1999) *Finite and Infinite Goods: A Framework for Ethics*, New York: Oxford University Press.

Cottingham, John (2005) *The Spiritual Dimension: Religion, Philosophy, and Human Value*. Cambridge: Cambridge University Press.

Cottingham, John (ed.) (2007) *The Meaning of Theism*, Malden, MA: Blackwell.

Cottingham, John (2008) "The self, the good life and the transcendent," in Samantha Vice and Nafsika Athanassoulis (eds.), *The Moral Life: Essays in Honour of John Cottingham*, London: Palgrave Macmillan, pp. 231–74.

Cottingham, John (2009) *Why Believe?* London: Continuum.

Crisp, Roger (2008) "Meaning, morality, and religion," in Samantha Vice and Nafsika Athanassoulis (eds.), *The Moral Life: Essays in Honour of John Cottingham*, London: Palgrave Macmillan, pp. 167–83.

Davis, William H. (1987) "The meaning of life," *Metaphilosophy* 18(July/October): 288–305.

Giussani, Luigi (2006) *The Religious Sense*, Montreal: McGill-Queen's University Press.

Haldane, John (2003) "Religion, value and purpose," in *An Intelligent Person's Guide to Religion*, London: Duckworth, pp. 123–50.

Hartshorne, Charles (1984) "God and the meaning of life," in Leroy S. Rouner (ed.), *On Nature*, Boston University Studies in Philosophy and Religion 6, Notre Dame, IN: University of Notre Dame Press, pp. 154–68.

Haught, John F. (2006) *Is Nature Enough? Meaning and Truth in the Age of Science*, Cambridge: Cambridge University Press.

Metz, Thaddeus (2008) "God, morality, and the meaning of life," in Samantha Vice and Nafsika Athanassoulis (eds.), *The Moral Life: Essays in Honour of John Cottingham*, London: Palgrave Macmillan, pp. 201–30.

Morris, Thomas V. (1992) *Making Sense of It All: Pascal and the Meaning of Life*, Grand Rapids, MI: Eerdmans.

Taliaferro, Charles (2009) "Jesus Christ and the meaning of life," in Paul K. Moser (ed.), *Jesus and Philosophy: New Essays*, Cambridge: Cambridge University Press, pp. 215–29.

2.1

Ecclesiastes

All Is Vanity

1:1 The words of the Preacher, the son of David, king in Jerusalem.

2 Vanity of vanities, says the Preacher,
vanity of vanities! All is vanity.
3 What does man gain by all the toil
at which he toils under the sun?
4 A generation goes, and a generation comes,
but the earth remains forever.
5 The sun rises, and the sun goes down,
and hastens to the place where it rises.
6 The wind blows to the south
and goes around to the north;
around and around goes the wind,
and on its circuits the wind returns.
7 All streams run to the sea,
but the sea is not full;
to the place where the streams flow,
there they flow again.
8 All things are full of weariness;
a man cannot utter it;
the eye is not satisfied with seeing,
nor the ear filled with hearing.

Ecclesiastes, ESV (English Standard Bible) Online Bible, http://www.gnpcb.org/esv/, Wheaton, IL: Crossway.

Exploring the Meaning of Life: An Anthology and Guide, First Edition. Edited by Joshua W. Seachris.
© 2013 John Wiley & Sons, Inc. Published 2013 by John Wiley & Sons, Inc.

9 What has been is what will be,
and what has been done is what will be done,
and there is nothing new under the sun.
10 Is there a thing of which it is said,
"See, this is new"?
It has been already
in the ages before us.
11 There is no remembrance of former things,
nor will there be any remembrance
of later things yet to be
among those who come after.

The Vanity of Wisdom

12 I the Preacher have been king over Israel in Jerusalem. 13 And I applied my heart to seek and to search out by wisdom all that is done under heaven. It is an unhappy business that God has given to the children of man to be busy with. 14 I have seen everything that is done under the sun, and behold, all is vanity and a striving after wind.

15 What is crooked cannot be made straight,
and what is lacking cannot be counted.

16 I said in my heart, "I have acquired great wisdom, surpassing all who were over Jerusalem before me, and my heart has had great experience of wisdom and knowledge." 17 And I applied my heart to know wisdom and to know madness and folly. I perceived that this also is but a striving after wind.

18 For in much wisdom is much vexation,
and he who increases knowledge increases sorrow.

The Vanity of Self-Indulgence

2:1 I said in my heart, "Come now, I will test you with pleasure; enjoy yourself." But behold, this also was vanity. 2 I said of laughter, "It is mad," and of pleasure, "What use is it?" 3 I searched with my heart how to cheer my body with wine – my heart still guiding me with wisdom – and how to lay hold on folly, till I might see what was good for the children of man to do under heaven during the few days of their life. 4 I made great works. I built houses and planted vineyards for myself. 5 I made myself gardens and parks, and planted in them all kinds of fruit trees. 6 I made myself pools from which to water the forest of growing trees. 7 I bought male and female slaves, and had slaves who were born in my house. I had also great possessions of herds and flocks, more than any who had been before me in Jerusalem.

8 I also gathered for myself silver and gold and the treasure of kings and provinces. I got singers, both men and women, and many concubines, the delight of the children of man.

9 So I became great and surpassed all who were before me in Jerusalem. Also my wisdom remained with me. 10 And whatever my eyes desired I did not keep from them. I kept my heart from no pleasure, for my heart found pleasure in all my toil, and this was my reward for all my toil. 11 Then I considered all that my hands had done and the toil I had expended in doing it, and behold, all was vanity and a striving after wind, and there was nothing to be gained under the sun.

The Vanity of Living Wisely

12 So I turned to consider wisdom and madness and folly. For what can the man do who comes after the king? Only what has already been done. 13 Then I saw that there is more gain in wisdom than in folly, as there is more gain in light than in darkness. 14 The wise person has his eyes in his head, but the fool walks in darkness. And yet I perceived that the same event happens to all of them. 15 Then I said in my heart, "What happens to the fool will happen to me also. Why then have I been so very wise?" And I said in my heart that this also is vanity. 16 For of the wise as of the fool there is no enduring remembrance, seeing that in the days to come all will have been long forgotten. How the wise dies just like the fool! 17 So I hated life, because what is done under the sun was grievous to me, for all is vanity and a striving after wind.

The Vanity of Toil

18 I hated all my toil in which I toil under the sun, seeing that I must leave it to the man who will come after me, 19 and who knows whether he will be wise or a fool? Yet he will be master of all for which I toiled and used my wisdom under the sun. This also is vanity. 20 So I turned about and gave my heart up to despair over all the toil of my labors under the sun, 21 because sometimes a person who has toiled with wisdom and knowledge and skill must leave everything to be enjoyed by someone who did not toil for it. This also is vanity and a great evil. 22 What has a man from all the toil and striving of heart with which he toils beneath the sun? 23 For all his days are full of sorrow, and his work is a vexation. Even in the night his heart does not rest. This also is vanity.

24 There is nothing better for a person than that he should eat and drink and find enjoyment in his toil. This also, I saw, is from the hand of God, 25 for apart from him who can eat or who can have enjoyment? 26 For to the one who pleases him God has given wisdom and knowledge and joy, but to the sinner he has given the business of gathering and collecting, only to give to one who pleases God. This also is vanity and a striving after wind.

A Time for Everything

3:1 For everything there is a season, and a time for every matter under heaven:

> 2 a time to be born, and a time to die;
> a time to plant, and a time to pluck up what is planted;
> 3 a time to kill, and a time to heal;
> a time to break down, and a time to build up;
> 4 a time to weep, and a time to laugh;
> a time to mourn, and a time to dance;
> 5 a time to cast away stones, and a time to gather stones together;
> a time to embrace, and a time to refrain from embracing;
> 6 a time to seek, and a time to lose;
> a time to keep, and a time to cast away;
> 7 a time to tear, and a time to sew;
> a time to keep silence, and a time to speak;
> 8 a time to love, and a time to hate;
> a time for war, and a time for peace.

The God-Given Task

9 What gain has the worker from his toil? 10 I have seen the business that God has given to the children of man to be busy with. 11 He has made everything beautiful in its time. Also, he has put eternity into man's heart, yet so that he cannot find out what God has done from the beginning to the end. 12 I perceived that there is nothing better for them than to be joyful and to do good as long as they live; 13 also that everyone should eat and drink and take pleasure in all his toil – this is God's gift to man.

14 I perceived that whatever God does endures forever; nothing can be added to it, nor anything taken from it. God has done it, so that people fear before him. 15 That which is, already has been; that which is to be, already has been; and God seeks what has been driven away.

From Dust to Dust

16 Moreover, I saw under the sun that in the place of justice, even there was wickedness, and in the place of righteousness, even there was wickedness. 17 I said in my heart, God will judge the righteous and the wicked, for there is a time for every matter and for every work. 18 I said in my heart with regard to the children of man that God is testing them that they may see that they themselves are but beasts. 19 For what happens to the children of man and what happens to the beasts is the same; as one dies, so dies the other. They all have the same breath, and man has no advantage over the beasts, for all is vanity. 20 All go to one place. All are from the dust, and to dust all return. 21 Who knows whether the spirit of man goes upward and the spirit of the beast

goes down into the earth? 22 So I saw that there is nothing better than that a man should rejoice in his work, for that is his lot. Who can bring him to see what will be after him?

Evil Under the Sun

4:1 Again I saw all the oppressions that are done under the sun. And behold, the tears of the oppressed, and they had no one to comfort them! On the side of their oppressors there was power, and there was no one to comfort them. 2 And I thought the dead who are already dead more fortunate than the living who are still alive. 3 But better than both is he who has not yet been and has not seen the evil deeds that are done under the sun.

4 Then I saw that all toil and all skill in work come from a man's envy of his neighbor. This also is vanity and a striving after wind.

5 The fool folds his hands and eats his own flesh.

6 Better is a handful of quietness than two hands full of toil and a striving after wind.

7 Again, I saw vanity under the sun: 8 one person who has no other, either son or brother, yet there is no end to all his toil, and his eyes are never satisfied with riches, so that he never asks, "For whom am I toiling and depriving myself of pleasure?" This also is vanity and an unhappy business.

9 Two are better than one, because they have a good reward for their toil. 10 For if they fall, one will lift up his fellow. But woe to him who is alone when he falls and has not another to lift him up! 11 Again, if two lie together, they keep warm, but how can one keep warm alone? 12 And though a man might prevail against one who is alone, two will withstand him – a threefold cord is not quickly broken.

13 Better was a poor and wise youth than an old and foolish king who no longer knew how to take advice. 14 For he went from prison to the throne, though in his own kingdom he had been born poor. 15 I saw all the living who move about under the sun, along with that youth who was to stand in the king's place. 16 There was no end of all the people, all of whom he led. Yet those who come later will not rejoice in him. Surely this also is vanity and a striving after wind.

Fear God

5:1 Guard your steps when you go to the house of God. To draw near to listen is better than to offer the sacrifice of fools, for they do not know that they are doing evil. 2 Be not rash with your mouth, nor let your heart be hasty to utter a word before God, for God is in heaven and you are on earth. Therefore let your words be few. 3 For a dream comes with much business, and a fool's voice with many words.

4 When you vow a vow to God, do not delay paying it, for he has no pleasure in fools. Pay what you vow. 5 It is better that you should not vow than that you should vow and not pay. 6 Let not your mouth lead you into sin, and do not say before the messenger that it was a mistake.

Why should God be angry at your voice and destroy the work of your hands? 7 For when dreams increase and words grow many, there is vanity; but God is the one you must fear.

The Vanity of Wealth and Honor

8 If you see in a province the oppression of the poor and the violation of justice and righteousness, do not be amazed at the matter, for the high official is watched by a higher, and there are yet higher ones over them. 9 But this is gain for a land in every way: a king committed to cultivated fields.

10 He who loves money will not be satisfied with money, nor he who loves wealth with his income; this also is vanity. 11 When goods increase, they increase who eat them, and what advantage has their owner but to see them with his eyes? 12 Sweet is the sleep of a laborer, whether he eats little or much, but the full stomach of the rich will not let him sleep.

13 There is a grievous evil that I have seen under the sun: riches were kept by their owner to his hurt, 14 and those riches were lost in a bad venture. And he is father of a son, but he has nothing in his hand. 15 As he came from his mother's womb he shall go again, naked as he came, and shall take nothing for his toil that he may carry away in his hand. 16 This also is a grievous evil: just as he came, so shall he go, and what gain is there to him who toils for the wind? 17 Moreover, all his days he eats in darkness in much vexation and sickness and anger.

18 Behold, what I have seen to be good and fitting is to eat and drink and find enjoyment in all the toil with which one toils under the sun the few days of his life that God has given him, for this is his lot. 19 Everyone also to whom God has given wealth and possessions and power to enjoy them, and to accept his lot and rejoice in his toil – this is the gift of God. 20 For he will not much remember the days of his life because God keeps him occupied with joy in his heart.

6:1 There is an evil that I have seen under the sun, and it lies heavy on mankind: 2 a man to whom God gives wealth, possessions, and honor, so that he lacks nothing of all that he desires, yet God does not give him power to enjoy them, but a stranger enjoys them. This is vanity; it is a grievous evil. 3 If a man fathers a hundred children and lives many years, so that the days of his years are many, but his soul is not satisfied with life's good things, and he also has no burial, I say that a stillborn child is better off than he. 4 For it comes in vanity and goes in darkness, and in darkness its name is covered. 5 Moreover, it has not seen the sun or known anything, yet it finds rest rather than he. 6 Even though he should live a thousand years twice over, yet enjoy no good – do not all go to the one place?

7 All the toil of man is for his mouth, yet his appetite is not satisfied. 8 For what advantage has the wise man over the fool? And what does the poor man have who knows how to conduct himself before the living? 9 Better is the sight of the eyes than the wandering of the appetite: this also is vanity and a striving after wind.

10 Whatever has come to be has already been named, and it is known what man is, and that he is not able to dispute with one stronger than he. 11 The more words, the more vanity, and what is the advantage to man? 12 For who knows what is good for man while he lives the few days of his vain life, which he passes like a shadow? For who can tell man what will be after him under the sun?

The Contrast of Wisdom and Folly

7:1 A good name is better than precious ointment,
and the day of death than the day of birth.
2 It is better to go to the house of mourning
than to go to the house of feasting,
for this is the end of all mankind,
and the living will lay it to heart.
3 Sorrow is better than laughter,
for by sadness of face the heart is made glad.
4 The heart of the wise is in the house of mourning,
but the heart of fools is in the house of mirth.
5 It is better for a man to hear the rebuke of the wise
than to hear the song of fools.
6 For as the crackling of thorns under a pot,
so is the laughter of the fools;
this also is vanity.
7 Surely oppression drives the wise into madness,
and a bribe corrupts the heart.
8 Better is the end of a thing than its beginning,
and the patient in spirit is better than the proud in spirit.
9 Be not quick in your spirit to become angry,
for anger lodges in the bosom of fools.
10 Say not, "Why were the former days better than these?"
For it is not from wisdom that you ask this.
11 Wisdom is good with an inheritance,
an advantage to those who see the sun.
12 For the protection of wisdom is like the protection of money,
and the advantage of knowledge is that wisdom preserves the life of him who has it.
13 Consider the work of God:
who can make straight what he has made crooked?

14 In the day of prosperity be joyful, and in the day of adversity consider: God has made the one as well as the other, so that man may not find out anything that will be after him.

15 In my vain life I have seen everything. There is a righteous man who perishes in his righteousness, and there is a wicked man who prolongs his life in his evildoing. 16 Be not overly righteous, and do not make yourself too wise. Why should you destroy yourself? 17 Be not overly wicked, neither be a fool. Why should you die before your time? 18 It is good that you should take hold of this, and from that withhold not your hand, for the one who fears God shall come out from both of them.

19 Wisdom gives strength to the wise man more than ten rulers who are in a city.

20 Surely there is not a righteous man on earth who does good and never sins.

21 Do not take to heart all the things that people say, lest you hear your servant cursing you.
22 Your heart knows that many times you yourself have cursed others.

23 All this I have tested by wisdom. I said, "I will be wise," but it was far from me. 24 That which has been is far off, and deep, very deep; who can find it out?

25 I turned my heart to know and to search out and to seek wisdom and the scheme of things, and to know the wickedness of folly and the foolishness that is madness. 26 And I find something more bitter than death: the woman whose heart is snares and nets, and whose hands are fetters. He who pleases God escapes her, but the sinner is taken by her. 27 Behold, this is what I found, says the Preacher, while adding one thing to another to find the scheme of things – 28 which my soul has sought repeatedly, but I have not found. One man among a thousand I found, but a woman among all these I have not found. 29 See, this alone I found, that God made man upright, but they have sought out many schemes.

Keep the King's Command

8:1 Who is like the wise?
And who knows the interpretation of a thing?
A man's wisdom makes his face shine,
and the hardness of his face is changed.

2 I say: Keep the king's command, because of God's oath to him. 3 Be not hasty to go from his presence. Do not take your stand in an evil cause, for he does whatever he pleases. 4 For the word of the king is supreme, and who may say to him, "What are you doing?" 5 Whoever keeps a command will know no evil thing, and the wise heart will know the proper time and the just way. 6 For there is a time and a way for everything, although man's trouble lies heavy on him. 7 For he does not know what is to be, for who can tell him how it will be? 8 No man has power to retain the spirit, or power over the day of death. There is no discharge from war, nor will wickedness deliver those who are given to it. 9 All this I observed while applying my heart to all that is done under the sun, when man had power over man to his hurt.

Those Who Fear God Will Do Well

10 Then I saw the wicked buried. They used to go in and out of the holy place and were praised in the city where they had done such things. This also is vanity. 11 Because the sentence against an evil deed is not executed speedily, the heart of the children of man is fully set to do evil. 12 Though a sinner does evil a hundred times and prolongs his life, yet I know that it will be well with those who fear God, because they fear before him. 13 But it will not be well with the wicked, neither will he prolong his days like a shadow, because he does not fear before God.

Man Cannot Know God's Ways

14 There is a vanity that takes place on earth, that there are righteous people to whom it happens according to the deeds of the wicked, and there are wicked people to

whom it happens according to the deeds of the righteous. I said that this also is vanity. 15 And I commend joy, for man has no good thing under the sun but to eat and drink and be joyful, for this will go with him in his toil through the days of his life that God has given him under the sun.

16 When I applied my heart to know wisdom, and to see the business that is done on earth, how neither day nor night do one's eyes see sleep, 17 then I saw all the work of God, that man cannot find out the work that is done under the sun. However much man may toil in seeking, he will not find it out. Even though a wise man claims to know, he cannot find it out.

Death Comes to All

9:1 But all this I laid to heart, examining it all, how the righteous and the wise and their deeds are in the hand of God. Whether it is love or hate, man does not know; both are before him. 2 It is the same for all, since the same event happens to the righteous and the wicked, to the good and the evil, to the clean and the unclean, to him who sacrifices and him who does not sacrifice. As the good one is, so is the sinner, and he who swears is as he who shuns an oath. 3 This is an evil in all that is done under the sun, that the same event happens to all. Also, the hearts of the children of man are full of evil, and madness is in their hearts while they live, and after that they go to the dead. 4 But he who is joined with all the living has hope, for a living dog is better than a dead lion. 5 For the living know that they will die, but the dead know nothing, and they have no more reward, for the memory of them is forgotten. 6 Their love and their hate and their envy have already perished, and forever they have no more share in all that is done under the sun.

Enjoy Life with the One You Love

7 Go, eat your bread with joy, and drink your wine with a merry heart, for God has already approved what you do.

8 Let your garments be always white. Let not oil be lacking on your head.

9 Enjoy life with the wife whom you love, all the days of your vain life that he has given you under the sun, because that is your portion in life and in your toil at which you toil under the sun. 10 Whatever your hand finds to do, do it with your might, for there is no work or thought or knowledge or wisdom in Sheol, to which you are going.

Wisdom Better than Folly

11 Again I saw that under the sun the race is not to the swift, nor the battle to the strong, nor bread to the wise, nor riches to the intelligent, nor favor to those with knowledge, but time and chance happen to them all. 12 For man does not know his time. Like fish that are

taken in an evil net, and like birds that are caught in a snare, so the children of man are snared at an evil time, when it suddenly falls upon them.

13 I have also seen this example of wisdom under the sun, and it seemed great to me. 14 There was a little city with few men in it, and a great king came against it and besieged it, building great siegeworks against it. 15 But there was found in it a poor, wise man, and he by his wisdom delivered the city. Yet no one remembered that poor man. 16 But I say that wisdom is better than might, though the poor man's wisdom is despised and his words are not heard.

17 The words of the wise heard in quiet are better than the shouting of a ruler among fools. 18 Wisdom is better than weapons of war, but one sinner destroys much good.

> **10:1** Dead flies make the perfumer's ointment give off a stench;
> so a little folly outweighs wisdom and honor.
> 2 A wise man's heart inclines him to the right,
> but a fool's heart to the left.
> 3 Even when the fool walks on the road, he lacks sense,
> and he says to everyone that he is a fool.
> 4 If the anger of the ruler rises against you, do not leave your place,
> for calmness will lay great offenses to rest.

5 There is an evil that I have seen under the sun, as it were an error proceeding from the ruler: 6 folly is set in many high places, and the rich sit in a low place. 7 I have seen slaves on horses, and princes walking on the ground like slaves.

> 8 He who digs a pit will fall into it,
> and a serpent will bite him who breaks through a wall.
> 9 He who quarries stones is hurt by them,
> and he who splits logs is endangered by them.
> 10 If the iron is blunt, and one does not sharpen the edge,
> he must use more strength,
> but wisdom helps one to succeed.
> 11 If the serpent bites before it is charmed,
> there is no advantage to the charmer.
>
> 12 The words of a wise man's mouth win him favor,
> but the lips of a fool consume him.
> 13 The beginning of the words of his mouth is foolishness,
> and the end of his talk is evil madness.
> 14 A fool multiplies words,
> though no man knows what is to be,
> and who can tell him what will be after him?
> 15 The toil of a fool wearies him,
> for he does not know the way to the city.
>
> 16 Woe to you, O land, when your king is a child,
> and your princes feast in the morning!
> 17 Happy are you, O land, when your king is the son of the nobility,
> and your princes feast at the proper time,

for strength, and not for drunkenness!
18 Through sloth the roof sinks in,
and through indolence the house leaks.
19 Bread is made for laughter,
and wine gladdens life,
and money answers everything.
20 Even in your thoughts, do not curse the king,
nor in your bedroom curse the rich,
for a bird of the air will carry your voice,
or some winged creature tell the matter.

Cast Your Bread upon the Waters

11:1 Cast your bread upon the waters,
for you will find it after many days.
2 Give a portion to seven, or even to eight,
for you know not what disaster may happen on earth.
3 If the clouds are full of rain,
they empty themselves on the earth,
and if a tree falls to the south or to the north,
in the place where the tree falls, there it will lie.
4 He who observes the wind will not sow,
and he who regards the clouds will not reap.

5 As you do not know the way the spirit comes to the bones in the womb of a woman with child, so you do not know the work of God who makes everything.

6 In the morning sow your seed, and at evening withhold not your hand, for you do not know which will prosper, this or that, or whether both alike will be good.

7 Light is sweet, and it is pleasant for the eyes to see the sun.

8 So if a person lives many years, let him rejoice in them all; but let him remember that the days of darkness will be many. All that comes is vanity.

9 Rejoice, O young man, in your youth, and let your heart cheer you in the days of your youth. Walk in the ways of your heart and the sight of your eyes. But know that for all these things God will bring you into judgment.

10 Remove vexation from your heart, and put away pain from your body, for youth and the dawn of life are vanity.

Remember Your Creator in Your Youth

12:1 Remember also your Creator in the days of your youth, before the evil days come and the years draw near of which you will say, "I have no pleasure in them"; 2 before the sun and the light and the moon and the stars are darkened and the clouds return after the rain, 3 in the day when the keepers of the house tremble, and the strong men are bent, and the grinders cease because they are few, and those who look through the windows are dimmed, 4 and the doors on the street are shut – when the sound of the grinding is low, and one rises up at the sound of a bird, and all the daughters of song are brought low – 5 they are afraid also of what is high, and terrors are in the way; the almond tree blossoms, the grasshopper drags itself along, and desire fails, because man is going to his eternal home, and the mourners go about the streets – 6 before the silver cord is snapped, or the golden bowl is broken, or the pitcher is shattered at the fountain, or the wheel broken at the cistern, 7 and the dust returns to the earth as it was, and the spirit returns to God who gave it. 8 Vanity of vanities, says the Preacher; all is vanity.

Fear God and Keep His Commandments

9 Besides being wise, the Preacher also taught the people knowledge, weighing and studying and arranging many proverbs with great care. 10 The Preacher sought to find words of delight, and uprightly he wrote words of truth.

11 The words of the wise are like goads, and like nails firmly fixed are the collected sayings; they are given by one Shepherd. 12 My son, beware of anything beyond these. Of making many books there is no end, and much study is a weariness of the flesh.

13 The end of the matter; all has been heard. Fear God and keep his commandments, for this is the whole duty of man. 14 For God will bring every deed into judgment, with every secret thing, whether good or evil.

2.2

On Living in an Atomic Age

C. S. Lewis

In one way we think a great deal too much of the atomic bomb. "How are we to live in an atomic age?" I am tempted to reply: "Why, as you would have lived in the sixteenth century when the plague visited London almost every year, or as you would have lived in a Viking age when raiders from Scandinavia might land and cut your throat any night; or indeed, as you are already living in an age of cancer, an age of syphilis, an age of paralysis, an age of air raids, an age of railway accidents, an age of motor accidents."

In other words, do not let us begin by exaggerating the novelty of our situation. Believe me, dear sir or madam, you and all whom you love were already sentenced to death before the atomic bomb was invented: and quite a high percentage of us were going to die in unpleasant ways. We had, indeed, one very great advantage over our ancestors – anaesthetics; but we have that still. It is perfectly ridiculous to go about whimpering and drawing long faces because the scientists have added one more chance of painful and premature death to a world which already bristled with such chances and in which death itself was not a chance at all, but a certainty.

This is the first point to be made: and the first action to be taken is to pull ourselves together. If we are all going to be destroyed by an atomic bomb, let that bomb when it comes find us doing sensible and human things – praying, working, teaching, reading, listening to music, bathing the children, playing tennis, chatting to our friends over a pint and a game of darts – not huddled together like frightened sheep and thinking about bombs. They may break our bodies (a microbe can do that) but they need not dominate our minds.

"But," you reply, "it is not death – not even painful and premature death – that we are bothering about. Of course the chance of *that* is not new. What is new is that the atomic bomb may finally and totally destroy civilization itself. The lights may be put out for ever."

C. S. Lewis (1986) "On Living in an Atomic Age," in Walter Hooper (ed.), *Present Concerns*, San Diego, CA: Harcourt, pp. 73–80.

This brings us much nearer to the real point; but let me try to make clear exactly what I think that point is. What were your views about the ultimate future of civilization *before* the atomic bomb appeared on the scene? What did you think all this effort of humanity was to come to in the end? The real answer is known to almost everyone who has even a smattering of science; yet, oddly enough, it is hardly ever mentioned. And the real answer (almost beyond doubt) is that, with or without atomic bombs, the whole story is going to end in NOTHING. The astronomers hold out no hope that this planet is going to be permanently inhabitable. The physicists hold out no hope that organic life is going to be a permanent possibility in any part of the material universe. Not only this earth, but the whole show, all the suns of space, are to run down. Nature is a sinking ship. Bergson talks about the *élan vital*, and Mr Shaw talks about the "Life-force" as if they could surge on for ever and ever. But that comes of concentrating on biology and ignoring the other sciences. There is really no such hope. Nature does not, in the long run, favour life. If Nature is all that exists – in other words, if there is no God and no life of some quite different sort somewhere outside Nature – then all stories will end in the same way: in a universe from which all life is banished without possibility of return. It will have been an accidental flicker, and there will be no one even to remember it. No doubt atomic bombs may cut its duration on this present planet shorter than it might have been; but the whole thing, even if it lasted for billions of years, must be so infinitesimally short in relation to the oceans of dead time which precede and follow it that I cannot feel excited about its curtailment.

What the wars and the weather (are we in for another of those periodic ice ages?) and the atomic bomb have really done is to remind us forcibly of the sort of world we are living in and which, during the prosperous period before 1914, we were beginning to forget. And this reminder is, so far as it goes, a good thing. We have been waked from a pretty dream, and now we can begin to talk about realities.

We see at once (when we have been waked) that the important question is not whether an atomic bomb is going to obliterate "civilization". The important question is whether "Nature" – the thing studied by the sciences – is the only thing in existence. Because if you answer *yes* to the second question, then the first question only amounts to asking whether the inevitable frustration of all human activities may be hurried on by our own action instead of coming at its natural time. That is, of course, a question that concerns us very much. Even on a ship which will certainly sink sooner or later, the news that the boiler might blow up *now* would not be heard with indifference by anyone. But those who knew that the ship was sinking in any case would not, I think, be quite so desperately excited as those who had forgotten this fact, and were vaguely imagining that it might arrive somewhere.

It is, then, on the second question that we really need to make up our minds. And let us begin by supposing that Nature is all that exists. Let us suppose that nothing ever has existed or ever will exist except this meaningless play of atoms in space and time: that by a series of hundredth chances it has (regrettably) produced things like ourselves – conscious beings who now know that their own consciousness is an accidental result of the whole meaningless process and is therefore itself meaningless, though to us (alas!) it *feels* significant.

In this situation there are, I think, three things one might do:

(1)   You might commit suicide. Nature which has (blindly, accidentally) given me for my torment this consciousness which demands meaning and value in a universe that offers neither, has luckily also given me the means of getting rid of it. I return the unwelcome gift. I will be fooled no longer.

(2)   You might decide simply to have as good a time as possible. The universe is a universe of nonsense, but since you are here, grab what you can. Unfortunately, however, there is, on these terms, so very little left to grab – only the coarsest sensual pleasures. You can't, except in the lowest animal sense, be in love with a girl if you know (and keep on remembering) that all the beauties both of her person and of her character are a momentary and accidental pattern produced by the collision of atoms, and that your own response to them is only a sort of psychic phosphorescence arising from the behaviour of your genes. You can't go on getting any very serious pleasure from music if you know and remember that its air of significance is a pure illusion, that you like it only because your nervous system is irrationally conditioned to like it. You may still, in the lowest sense, have a "good time"; but just in so far as it becomes very good, just in so far as it ever threatens to push you on from cold sensuality into real warmth and enthusiasm and joy, so far you will be forced to feel the hopeless disharmony between your own emotions and the universe in which you really live.

(3)   You may defy the universe. You may say, "Let it be irrational, I am not. Let it be merciless, I will have mercy. By whatever curious chance it has produced me, now that I am here I will live according to human values. I know the universe will win in the end, but what is that to me? I will go down fighting. Amid all this wastefulness I will persevere; amid all this competition, I will make sacrifices. Be damned to the universe!"

I suppose that most of us, in fact, while we remain materialists, adopt a more or less uneasy alternation between the second and the third attitude. And although the third is incomparably the better (it is, for instance, much more likely to "preserve civilization"), both really shipwreck on the same rock. That rock – the disharmony between our own hearts and Nature – is obvious in the second. The third seems to avoid the rock by accepting disharmony from the outset and defying it. But it will not really work. In it, you hold up our own human standards against the idiocy of the universe. That is, we talk as if our own standards were something *outside* the universe which can be contrasted with it; as if we could judge the universe by some standard borrowed *from another source*. But if (as we were supposing) Nature – the space-time-matter system – is the only thing in existence, then of course there can be no other source for our standards. They must, like everything else, be the unintended and meaningless outcome of blind forces. Far from being a light from beyond Nature whereby Nature can be judged, they are only the way in which anthropoids of our species feel when the atoms under own own skulls get into certain states – those states being produced by causes quite irrational, unhuman, and non-moral. Thus the very ground on which we defy Nature crumbles under our feet. The standard we are applying is tainted at the source. If our standards are derived from this meaningless universe they must be as meaningless as it.

For most modern people, I think, thoughts of this kind have to be gone through before the opposite view can get a fair hearing. All Naturalism leads us to this in the end – to a quite final and hopeless discord between what our minds claim to be and what they really must be if Naturalism is true. They claim to be spirit; that is, to be reason, perceiving universal intellectual principles and universal moral laws and possessing free will. But if Naturalism is true they must in reality be merely arrangements of atoms in skulls, coming about by irrational causation. We never think a thought because it is true, only because blind Nature forces us to think it. We never do an act because it is right, only because blind Nature forces us to do it. It is when one has faced this preposterous conclusion that one is at last ready to listen to the voice that whispers: "But suppose we really are spirits? Suppose we are not the offspring of Nature …?"

For, really, the naturalistic conclusion is unbelievable. For one thing, it is only through trusting our own minds that we have come to know Nature herself. If Nature when fully known seems to teach us (that is, if the sciences teach us) that our own minds are chance arrangements of atoms, then there must have been some mistake; for if that were so, then the sciences themselves would be chance arrangements of atoms and we should have no reason for believing in them. There is only one way to avoid this deadlock. We must go back to a much earlier view. We must simply accept it that we are spirits, free and rational beings, at present inhabiting an irrational universe, and must draw the conclusion that we are *not derived from it*. We are strangers here. We come from somewhere else. Nature is not the only thing that exists. There is "another world", and that is where we come from. And that explains why we do not feel at home here. A fish feels at home in the water. If we "belonged here" we should feel at home here. All that we say about "Nature red in tooth and claw", about death and time and mutability, all our half-amused, half-bashful attitude to our own bodies, is quite inexplicable on the theory that we are simply natural creatures. If this world is the only world, how did we come to find its laws either so dreadful or so comic? If there is no straight line elsewhere, how did we discover that Nature's line is crooked?

But what, then, is Nature, and how do we come to be imprisoned in a system so alien to us? Oddly enough, the question becomes much less sinister the moment one realizes that Nature is not all. Mistaken for our mother, she is terrifying and even abominable. But if she is only our sister – if she and we have a common Creator – if she is our sparring partner – then the situation is quite tolerable. Perhaps we are not here as prisoners but as colonists: only consider what we have done already to the dog, the horse, or the daffodil. She is indeed a rough playfellow. There are elements of evil in her. To explain that would carry us far back: I should have to speak of Powers and Principalities and all that would seem to a modern reader most mythological. This is not the place, nor do these questions come first. It is enough to say here that Nature, like us but in her different way, is much alienated from her Creator, though in her, as in us, gleams of the old beauty remain. But they are there not to be worshipped but to be enjoyed. She has nothing to teach us. It is our business to live by our own law not by hers: to follow, in private or in public life, the law of love and temperance even when they seem to be suicidal, and not the law of competition and grab, even when they seem to be necessary to our survival. For it is part of our spiritual law never to put survival first: not even the survival of our species. We must resolutely train ourselves to feel that the survival of Man on this Earth, much more of our own nation or culture or class, is not worth having unless it can be had by honourable and merciful means.

The sacrifice is not so great as it seems. Nothing is more likely to destroy a species or a nation than a determination to survive at all costs. Those who care for something else more than civilization are the only people by whom civilization is at all likely to be preserved. Those who want Heaven most have served Earth best. Those who love Man less than God do most for Man.

2.3

Is the Existence of God Relevant to the Meaning of Life?

Jeffrey Gordon

Are we not straying through an infinite nothing? Do we not feel the breath of empty space?

Friedrich Nietzsche

The question whether life has a meaning – elemental, profound, irresistible as it may seem – is by no means a perennial concern of Western philosophy. The similar inquiry initiated by the ancients, "What is the good life?" is nevertheless a very different matter. Questions of the meaning of life are radical: they leave open the possibility that even the good life is trivial. In fact, these latter questions – primarily "Does life have a meaning?," "If so, what is that meaning?," and "If not, how should we contend with this truth?" – do not become frequent and explicit themes in philosophy until modern times and especially in the present twentieth century. Why is this? It has often been suggested that the secularization of the modern world is responsible for their emergence, that the "death of God" has created an atmosphere of disillusionment that has made these questions inevitable. Only so long as people are confident of the existence of God, so this analysis assumes, can their questions about the meaning of life be positively answered. It may be a fact of psychology that human beings need God in order to be assured that their lives can have meaning, but this fact (if it is a fact) may nevertheless be perplexing. For psychology aside, when we consider what rational grounds there may be for maintaining this intimate connection between God and meaning, we discover that the arguments traditionally entrusted with the demonstration of this connection are disappointingly weak. Can it be that so deep-seated an association as that between God and the meaningfulness of human life is in fact a mere atavism to a pre-rational

Jeffrey Gordon (1983) "Is the Existence of God Relevant to the Meaning of Life?" *The Modern Schoolman* 60: 227–46.

Exploring the Meaning of Life: An Anthology and Guide, First Edition. Edited by Joshua W. Seachris.

age, that those who have maintained the necessity of God to meaning – a number that includes such unremitting enemies of theism as Russell, Camus, and Sartre – have simply not thought the matter through, that the disillusionment of our time, so far as its source is the death of God, can find no support from the quarter of reason? In this paper, I want to reconsider the relation between God and meaning. Psychological associations aside, is the existence of God relevant to the meaning of human life?

I

I want to begin by clarifying the question I am asking. What can it mean to ask whether a given state of affairs is or is not relevant to the meaning of life?

There are two broad senses in which we can speak of such relevance, and these are correlates of the two senses in which we can speak of the meaning of life – the subjective and objective senses. "The loss of his son," we might say, "undermined the meaning of his life." Here the phrase "the meaning of life" denotes a subjective conviction. We intend to convey in this sentence the man's own assessment of the value, point, and purpose of his life, not our own assessment of these, nor an objective one. In contrast, consider the following sentences. "The history of human achievement is a history of vainglory disguised as noble ambition. To see this is to realize the vanity and meaninglessness of human life." Whatever we may think of this observation about human motivation or of the legitimacy of deriving this conclusion from it, it is clear that the notion of the meaning of life is used here very differently than in the first example. There is a consideration, this imaginary speaker would say, in virtue of which *any* human life, however satisfactory to the person living it, is in fact without meaning. I call this second sense "objective" and distinguish it from the first, "subjective" sense, in which all that is meant by "the meaning of life" is the subject's own explicit or implicit perception of the purpose and value of the life he is living.

Still, just what sort of consideration allows the speaker in the second example to pronounce the meaninglessness of all human lives despite the contrary assessment of (at least some) individuals living those lives? He would probably respond as follows:

> It is natural and proper for human beings to believe that on at least some important occasions they can transcend motives of self aggrandizement and act with genuine honor. In fact, however, we can approach this ideal only in myth and in self-delusion, and therefore our lives are absurd. They are absurd because the discrepancy in them between pretense and reality is an affront to rational expectation, and because neither the pretense nor the reality is subject to alteration. Given our nature as human beings, we can no more extirpate the dream of nobility than we can the all-determining drive for glory. We can no more abide a world without honor than we can make a world with it, and the clash between these two facts renders us ludicrous creatures and our lives correspondingly vain and meaningless.

To speak of the meaning of life in the objective sense is, as our imaginary speaker illustrates, to (try to) provide rationally compelling conditions for the possibility of there being a point, purpose, and value in individual human lives – conditions that may or may not be met.

If we were asking the relevance of God to the meaning of life in the subjective sense, we would be asking either the cultural-historical question, "Has the existence of God been taken by cultures to serve an important role in defining the significance of the lives of its members?" or the biographical question, "Have individuals believed that the existence of God served an important role in defining the significance of their lives?" In both cases, the answer would certainly be yes, and all our interest would converge on the effort to understand the precise connection between God and meaning that these cultures or individuals affirmed. But that is not the sense of the question I am asking it here. I am raising the question not as a point of cultural-historical interest but as a matter of philosophical truth. I am asking whether it can be said truly that the existence of God is relevant to the meaning of life objectively understood. And the word "relevant" here is also intended restrictively, so that God will be relevant to the meaning of life if life cannot be meaningful without him (and can be with him). The question I am asking, then, is whether, however satisfactory their lives may seem to any number of non-believers, an objectively defensible affirmation of the meaningfulness of human life in fact requires that God exist.

II

Three principal beliefs have been held about the relevance of God to the meaning of life. I will first set them out briefly, then examine each in greater detail. One has to do with immortality; another, with morality; and the third, with design.

Tolstoy provides a classic example of the first case. His *Confession*[1] gives moving expression to a conviction with deep roots in Christian faith: if this passionate will directed upon the world hall be cut off abruptly at the point of death and consigned thereafter to infinite oblivion, then all our efforts and achievements here are idle and empty, an indecipherable jot in cosmic time. God, the immortal father, is thus on this view our redeemer from meaninglessness, for he is our assurance of everlasting life.

In regard to the connection between God and morality, no one has spoken more confidently than has Nietzsche: Belief in the Judeo-Christian God was the very foundation of our Western morality, and now that that belief has been undermined, it cannot be long before that entire system of laws and ideals must crumble.[2] Sartre has echoed this analysis: "There can no longer be an *a priori* Good, since there is no infinite and perfect consciousness to think it."[3] God on this view is the fount and deliverer of moral truth, the authority to whom we once could appeal for the validation of our moral principles. If life can be meaningful only so long as our highest ideals have this validation (a view emphatically not held by Nietzsche, though Sartre's case is more ambiguous), then God's role in establishing the meaning of life is unmistakable.

In regard to the third consideration, the matter of design, Russell's Mephistophelean account of Creation is instructive. Finding only suffering and contingency in this world, but imbued with the will to affirm his life, man declares that there is, after all, a purpose to his misery, that the purpose is good, though hidden from view and beyond his ability to fathom.[4] Human life is meaningful on this view only if it is part of a benign scheme, an episode in a larger drama that ultimately redeems our earthly woes. As God is the author of this design, the benefactor in this drama, his relation to the meaning of life is again established.

III

Now one may think to have an easy way with all three of these claims. How, one may ask, can an otherwise meaningless existence be transformed into a meaningful one merely by being allowed to continue forever? Bestowing eternality on an empty life might yield an infinity of emptiness. Is it not, then, a mistake to give so high a place to immortality in our determination of a meaningful life? Similarly with respect to morality: How is an otherwise idle existence made less idle by the fact that one's moral principles have external validation? Precisely those universal moral verities may condemn his life as universally worthless. And again in regard to design: How could one's role in God's larger drama redeem his lowly role in the human one? If a life is without value here on earth, what possible divine scheme can expunge or alter this? The objection is the same in each case and all three criticisms can be expressed in a single argument: If it is possible to imagine a perfectly meaningless existence which is nevertheless favored with immortality, an objective standard of moral truth, and the certainty of purpose in the cosmos, then these qualities, either singly or collectively, cannot determine the meaningfulness of human life.

This argument makes a simple but important error. It assumes that what is being asserted in each of the three claims for the relevance of God to the meaning of life is a *sufficient* condition of meaningfulness, when in fact it is only a *necessary* one.[5] Human life can be meaningful, so the first claim goes, only if an already valuable and purposeful existence is not blotted out forever by death. It can be meaningful, says the second claim, only if the ideals to which we commit our honor are not arbitrary conventions. And it can be meaningful, the third claim asserts, only if our achievements here on earth resound in a higher realm. None of these claims presents a formula for the meaningfulness of life; each rather is content to set down a prerequisite, a *sine qua non* of meaning.

IV

If not vulnerable to this line of criticism, however, these claims may be vulnerable to others, and each of these candidates for a necessary connection between God and the meaning of life has had its eager and formidable opponents.

To begin with, it is not self-evident that meaningful human life requires personal immortality. Although many thinkers in Western philosophy have associated transiency with meaninglessness, what many of these same thinkers have sought as deliverance from the transitory is the *transcendence* of time, not its infinite extension. And this should clarify for us their conception of the transient. Insofar as it was something to be loathed, the transient was not for these thinkers a primarily temporal phenomenon at all, but a flimsy, momentarily seductive substitute for truth in the mind's quest for absolute knowledge. The life that Plato, for example, exalted was one devoted to the vision of the Good, for someone successful in this quest experienced eternity – the *release from time* – however brief his years on earth. And at least one Western thinker has extolled the fleeting as against the everlasting: "Against the value of the eternal," Nietzsche wrote, "the value of the briefest, most transitory, seductive speck of gold on the belly of the serpent *vita*."[6] The point here is not to dispute one position by citing assertions of its contrary, but rather to support my claim that there is nothing self-evident about the alleged connection between meaningful human life and personal immortality. Neither Plato's nor Nietzsche's position on this is obviously false.

Assuming, however, that we are persuaded by Kierkegaard[7] or Tolstoy or James[8] that personal immortality *is* a necessary condition of the meaningfulness of life, must we then concede the necessity of God to meaning? Only if God alone could assure that the individual soul survives the death of the body, only if this survival could be secured in no other way, and this would seem an especially difficult thesis to verify.

If there is personal immortality, the dualist thesis that the human mind is separable from the human body must, of course, also be true. It may be argued that this latter thesis, the object of a relentless assault in contemporary philosophy, has been by now so thoroughly discredited as to banish any lingering hope on the matter of immortality. But suppose we grant the truth of dualism, so that the possibility of immortality is again secured. In order now to establish the necessity of *God* to immortality (and hence to meaning), we would have to show that the soul, left to its natural course, would suffer decline and death; we would have to show that something external to the soul would be required to prevent this, and that this something could only be God. Given the nature of the case, it would, of course, be extremely difficult to show any of this. But worse, it is far from clear that any sense at all could be made of the death of the soul. All the processes associated with death – decay, deterioration, decomposition – would seem to have no application to a non-physical entity. Between a dualist who maintained that personal immortality was assured by the single fact of the soul's essential independence of the body and a dualist who postulated the necessity of God to sustain the soul, against the forces of decay, the presumption would seem to be in favor of the first. In any case, the necessity of God to the meaning of life cannot be established merely by the need for immortality. Given that immortality is necessary, it must still be shown that the soul, too, is subject to death and that only God can save it.

V

The presumption is against the sort of dualism that would demonstrate the necessity of God to personal immortality, hence against the case for the relevance of God to the meaning of human life as based upon the alleged need for immortality. When we turn to the argument for this relevance as based upon the need for moral truth, we see that the obstacles in the theist's path are even more forbidding. The argument is that human life can be meaningful only if the principles and ideals that govern our moral choices have objective validity, and that since God alone can provide this, the existence of God is necessary to the meaningfulness of life. But the first premiss is dubitable, and the second, disastrous.

Is it necessary to the meaning of life that our moral ideals have objective validation? As with the insistence on immortality, this alleged prerequisite of meaningfulness can be and has been challenged. A thinker who maintained, for example, that no exemplary moral life whatsoever but rather vitality and strength of spirit were the highest values attainable by man, who held these values to be paradigmatic and therefore in principle beyond external validation,[9] and who furthermore judged every moral code according to the single standard of conduciveness to the creation of these qualities – such a thinker would find no cause for despair in the thought that the moral beliefs of men are without objective confirmation. Nietzsche understood how natural it is for men to seek external validation for their values, but he regarded this itself as a weakness of spirit, a hunger for duty and subordination of the will. The strong spirit, in his view, recognized that in the moral realm no less than in the aesthetic, the point, was not to conform but to create.

But if even so relentless a critic of Western morality as Nietzsche felt the need to postulate absolute values, someone may now say, perhaps we ought not to dismiss so quickly the claim that the irremediable subjectivity of values would condemn much if not all human endeavor to ludicrousness. What judgment would Nietzsche render of his own life's work – a work charged with moral ambition – were he convinced that the value he accorded vitality and strength was not a function of insist but of idiosyncrasy? It is not on the face of it unreasonable to demand that the values that give direction to a life ring with something stronger than the sound of one's own voice if human aspiration is to be saved from absurdity.

Even granting the aptness of this demand, however, we must ask whether the argument we are considering is right to assume that the objective validity of a value requires confirmation "from the outside" – that is, in terms of a principle or authority more certain than the value itself. Is it not a mistake to suppose that the only alternative to arbitrary values are values externally confirmed?

Acknowledging the response to this question that an intuitionist would assuredly make, but conceding for the sake of argument not only the necessity of objective moral truth to the meaningfulness of human life but also the necessity of external validation to the objectivity of moral values, we must nevertheless come to see that the desired confirmation cannot be provided by God. However indivisible morality and God have become in Christian culture, the futility of appealing to gods to establish the authority of moral claims was seen as early as the *Euthypro*. According to what lights will God construct the edifice of morality? Will he not be guided by the intrinsic nature of the Good? But if so, there is an *a priori* Good independent of God's will, and the alleged link between them is broken. If now it is asserted that God's will *establishes* moral truth, that moral law exists only insofar as there is God to think it, this will indeed restore the relation of necessity between the existence of God and morality, but it will not avoid the specter of arbitrariness, for nothing in the caprice of God lifts it above caprice. Either God is inspired in his dicta to man by the vision of an eternal Good that would thus exist without him, or the Good is established in an act of fiat no less morally arbitrary than a similar act by man.

VI

This argument of Socrates' has often been disputed, so it may be well to dwell on it a moment. It has been argued, for example, that it is no mark against God's perfection that he choose without reason, that this is precisely what we should expect of an infinitely sovereign being, so that it is completely compatible with his sovereignty and perfection that he determine the moral law without, a justification for his choices.[10] But this observation is beside the point. The question is not whether God's perfection is consistent, with his acting arbitrarily. The question is whether *any* morally arbitrary act – of either man or God – could establish an *objective* truth in matters of morality, and the answer to this question must, certainly be no.

Still, it might be further argued, God might well *have* reasons for his choices, in which case these choices would not be arbitrary, but *his* reasons need nevertheless not provide reasons for *us* to obey his moral dicta.[11] Hence, God commands that we not kill, and his reason may be, for example, that he wishes to reserve for himself among all conscious entities the power to destroy human life. If so, his commandment will not be arbitrary in the sense of being without rationale, but this rationale of God's can hardly serve as a ground for us to respect and obey his proscription against murder. Since this is so (the argument will proceed), we can see that a key premiss of the argument in the *Euthyphro* is false. For Socrates assumed that if God has reasons for his moral decrees, these same reasons must provide a ground for our practicing the moral life independent of the fact that God wills us to do so. The example, however, demonstrates a possibility Socrates failed to consider, and that is that the reason for God's decree may be something other than the intrinsic moral value of the state of affairs he is commanding. *His* reasons for commanding a certain behavior, contrary to the assuption of the *Euthyphro*, need not be reasons for *us* to adopt it.

This argument fails to grasp the thrust of Socrates' case. It is true that the argument in the *Euthyphro* requires that God's reasons for his moral commandments also be capable of serving as reasons for us to practice the code enjoined in those commandments. This is required because Socrates rightly recognized that only *such* reasons could establish the moral validity of God's decrees. If God's reasons are not morally relevant, then whatever reasons he may have can do nothing to abjure the charge that he acts with moral arbitrariness when he wills the moral law. What is needed to silence this charge is the certainty that God acts with moral discretion when he proclaims this law. What is needed, in other words, is the certainty that God has a *moral justification* for his decrees. But it should go without saying that whatever serves as a moral justification for God should certainly be capable of serving as a moral justification for man.

One may attempt to shore up this argument against Socrates' key assumption. He may try to show that God can have *morally relevant* reasons for defining the moral law as he does, but that these need not be such as to demonstrate the existence of an *a priori* Good independent of God's will. Again, let us use the example of the commandment against murder. Assume that God's reason for asserting it is that killing is destruction of God's purpose for man, which is that man complete his creation by freely developing his soul.

In this case, God has a reason for his proscription that is morally relevant (since his purpose for man has moral value), but the reason does not provide a demonstration of the existence of an objective truth in matters of morality that is independent of God's will (since the reason itself involves God's will, his will to provide an opportunity to man to build his soul on earth). Has Socrates been refuted? I think not. If we are convinced that such a reason does indeed establish the moral validity of God's commandment, "Thou shalt not kill," it is because we are convinced that God's reason is objectively good. If we believe it is good solely in virtue of the fact that it is God's, there would have been no need for a reason in the first place, since the decree itself would have been good in virtue of the same fact. Hence, what it means for us to be convinced that God's reason is objectively good is that it reflects or expresses a moral truth that is independent of God.

Finally, it may be said that no theist has ever argued that the fact of God's will *alone* establishes the objective validity of his moral decrees.[12] There is an implicit assumption in all claims for a relation between God and morality (it will be argued), and Socrates' case is destroyed when that assumption is made explicit. In the theist's view, after all, we bear a certain relationship to God; we are his creatures, his children, and therefore owe him obedience. It is, then, both the fact of his willing a certain course of conduct and the fact that we are his creatures that make his moral law binding, and this will be true whether God has reasons for his commandments or not.

As an attempt to derive moral truths from religious ones, this can hardly succeed. A moment's inspection shows us that this argument is not really deducing moral truths from the dual religious "facts" of God's will and our relationship to him, but rather from the *moral claim* that we owe God obedience. Yes, but does not this moral claim establish the necessity of God to moral truth? On the contrary: there would have to be moral truth independently of God in order for this claim (that we owe God obedience) to be true. The truth of *this claim*, after all, cannot be established by appeal to the fact that God wills our obedience to him since it is precisely our obligation to obey the will of God that is in question. But the truth of this claim must first be established before we can deduce moral law from the fact that God wills a certain sort of conduct.

If we are inclined to grant the truth of the claim, it is not merely in virtue of our belief that we bear a certain relationship to God, the relationship of creature to Creator. We can bear such a relationship to an evil genius, and in this case we would renounce the claim that we owed our creator obedience. If we are inclined to grant the truth of the claim in respect to God, it is because we are convinced that this Creator is infinitely *good*. I am not saying that the goodness of God itself *establishes* the validity of the claim that we owe him obedience; I am saying that the belief in his goodness is an absolutely essential condition of rational assent to this claim. Now what: can it mean to say that God is good? It cannot mean that his will *establishes* the good, for this would merely be to say in different words that his will ought to be obeyed, precisely the principle we are trying to confirm by appeal to his goodness. What else can it mean? Only that there is some criterion of goodness independent of God which his acts of will unfailingly meet. But then if we are to deduce any true moral prescription from the fact, that God wills a certain sort of conduct and the moral claim that we owe him obedience, we must first be convinced that there is a criterion of moral truth that is independent of God, and Socrates is resurrected.

VII

If the argument from immortality is unavailing short of demonstrations of some highly dubious (and possibly meaningless) theses, and the argument from moral truth is decisively flawed, all hope for a necessary connection between God and meaning would seem to rest on the third argument, the argument involving design.

"If at the foundation of all," Kierkegaard wrote, "there lay only a wildly seething power which, writhing with obscure passions, produced everything that is great and everything that is insignificant, if a bottomless void never satiated lay hidden beneath all – what then would life be but despair?"[13] Since man is "the product of causes which had no prevision of the end they were achieving," since "his origin, his growth, his hopes and fears, his loves and beliefs are but the outcome of accidental collocations of atoms," so, Russell thought, a world more void of meaning is unimaginable.[14] If the world is merely a brute given, a blind fact with no purpose, no telos, rhyme or reason, then the advent of man, too, is a pointless eruption in time. Only as the product of divine intention (so the argument goes) can the world escape senseless contingency, and only if the world is thus intelligible can man's life have meaning. Hence, the existence of God as divine artificer is a necessary condition of the meaningfulness of human life.

The key problem here is that the argument sets down as a prerequisite for the meaningfulness of the world a standard that can be satisfied neither by the existence of God nor by anything else. If the world remains senseless so long as our account of the manner and fact of its being ends with brute contingencies, mere givens that are not explainable as the product of will, how shall our knowledge that it is the result of God's design save the world from meaninglessness? Will not this very design stand as a brute given in our explanation of the world? Even if *per impossibile*, God is a logically necessary being,[15] surely this logical necessity does not extend also to his acts of free will. How, then, shall we explain them? If *ex hypothesi* God's is the ultimate will, so that there can be no question of explaining his acts by reference to the purposes of some yet higher being, are we not left in our quest for the meaning of the world with the blind fact of his purpose, a brute given? It seems that all the existence of God can assure in our quest for the world's intelligibility is that we forestall by one step our resignation to its contingency. The argument postulates as a necessary condition of the meaningfulness of human life the intelligibility of the world. In order for the world to be intelligible, the argument insists, it must be susceptible of an explanation that does not end with brute givens. Since, however, as we have seen, no such explanation of the world is possible, the consequence of adopting the argument's conception of intelligibility is that we are forced to conclude that neither God nor anything else whatsoever can save human life from meaninglessness.

Now it may be argued that I have misinterpreted this argument's condition for the intelligibility of the world. When the argument insists that our account of an intelligible world cannot end with brute facts, it is demanding only that it end instead with conscious intention, design. To adduce design as the source of the world *is* to deny its contingency. Hence, to say that the world is the product of God's will is to say that the manner and the fact of its being are not mere contingencies.

Now it is true (this rejoinder will continue), that God's design will itself be inexplicable, but this does not imply that we must resign ourselves to the contingency of the world. To say that an explanation of the world in terms of God's design itself ends with brute contingency is to imply that some coherent question about the purpose of all things remains unanswered by this explanation. But once we have said that God's design is the source of the universe, no meaningful question remains as to the world's purpose. God's design, after all, pertains to everything that is, in heaven and earth. The purposes of God, then, provide the ultimate teleological explanation because there is nothing outside God and his Creation to which we can address the (illegitimate) question of the purpose of God's purposes. God's design is not part of a larger scheme, because God's design is the purpose in the totality of all things, and no larger scheme can exist outside this totality. It is true, then, that God's design will itself be inexplicable, but this is because it is logically insusceptible of explanation. It would be better to say that God's purposes are neither explainable nor unexplainable, since the demand for their explanation is incoherent.

This rejoinder does not, however, demonstrate the incoherence in the question, "What is the purpose of God and his Creation?" It proves only that this question must remain unanswered. It provides a reason that an answer cannot be given; it does not provide a reason that the question cannot be asked. That it is a matter of logical necessity that this question remain unanswered does not mitigate the fact that we end our explanation of the world with an inexplicable datum, a brute given that we must accept without any possible explanation. The rejoinder does nothing to remedy the brute contingency of the world; it shows instead that brute contingency is absolutely unavoidable.

But suppose we waive this criticism and accept the argument of the rejoinder that the purposes of God, themselves neither explainable nor unexplainable, provide the ultimate teleological explanation of the world and in doing so banish its contingency. It will soon be seen that this is not enough to establish the intelligibility of the world in the relevant sense and that the argument we are presently considering for the necessity of God to the meaningfulness of human life still faces insuperable difficulties.

It is only as a *necessary* condition of the intelligibility of the world that this argument requires a teleological explanation of its nature and being. It will not be sufficient to establish its intelligibility merely by showing it to be the product of will, and a moment's reflection will demonstrate why this is so. The world will not be intelligible in the relevant sense (that is, the sense in which its intelligibility can allow for the meaningfulness of human life) if, for example, the will which creates it is the desire to be amused at the spectacle of human folly. If the world is to be intelligible, the will that is its source must be one whose meaningfulness – whose value, point, and purpose – can itself be defended. Even if it is illegitimate to demand an explanation of God's will in terms of a yet higher will, are we not nevertheless left with the task of *justifying* his creative enterprise? In the name of what motives did God act? Why did he choose to undertake the creation of a world at all and why of this particular world? If God is to close the fissures and gaps in our understanding of the world, then we must be able to provide a justification for his prodigious undertaking. But here it would seem that we embark upon a vicious regress, for if even the purposes of God must be justified, what will prevent us from making this same demand of every proposed justification? God created the world in order that there would be man, the creature designed in his image. But why should he have wished man to be and why should he have placed him in this world? The existence of man he willed so there would be a creature responsive to his love, and the world would provide the opportunity for the continuance of God's Creation through man's freedom. But why should he have wished that there be a creature responsive to his love and why should he have willed. ... The questions could never end. The task of making sense of the world could never be completed.

If the world is meaningless so long as its intelligibility has not been established, it would seem that we assure the meaninglessness of human life when we demand as a prerequisite of the contrary the intelligibility of the world. Realizing this may prompt us to re-examine the legitimacy of the alleged prerequisite. The re-examination, however, can only deliver us to the horns of the following dilemma: If we abandon the prerequisite of intelligibility, we withdraw this argument for the necessity of God to the meaning of life – the argument which was to be the last hope of this thesis. And if we retain the prerequisite, we are forced to conclude that neither God nor anything else can save human life from meaninglessness.

VIII

These are the leading arguments for the relevance of God to the meaning of life. The first, involving immortality, requires auxiliary proofs about the human soul that would be well-nigh impossible to provide. The second, involving moral truth, is hopelessly flawed. And the third, involving design or purpose, postulates a prerequisite of intelligibility that not even God could help to meet. In view of these facts, the conclusion that the existence of God is *not* essential to the meaning of human life would seem to be very likely. But this is much too important a conclusion to be advanced in haste. Are there considerations we failed to take into account in our examination of these arguments? Are there other stronger arguments in favor of the thesis that we have not considered at all?

I want to return to the last of the arguments, because this one of the three may seem to have the greatest intuitive force, a force that may seem to persist despite the apparent cogency of my argument against it. It may not seem unreasonable, after all, to require that the world be intelligible if human life is to have meaning, to require that the origin of all we know be something other than a wild, seething, unconscious force, that the passions that define mankind be something other than a random collection of atoms. But the mistake this argument made, I think, was to confuse our quite natural repulsion for a vision of the world as a congeries of blind accidents with the demand for its ultimate explanation, an explanation that would silence all questions. Once the quest for intelligibility is understood in this way, the dead ends I described are indeed inevitable.

But the demand for the intelligibility of the world may be of a very different order. Rather than regard its goal on the model of cognitive clarity, we might better approach it on the model of aesthetic coherence. When we say of a piece of music, for example, that it is meaningful, intelligible, we mean that it presents itself to us as a unified and moving whole, that each of its themes enriches the others and articulates a profound aesthetic intent. Similarly, when we ask for the intelligibility of the world, we may not at all be asking for its ultimate rationale, but merely for the assurance that it is, in itself and in all its parts, informed with unified aesthetic purpose – an intent which, furthermore, is both profound and benign. And it is not as though once convinced of such a vision of the world, we would be forced to justify our conviction of its beauty and thus initiate a new regress. We do not fetter the creative potential of a new work of art by insisting that it conform to a standard of beauty established by the works that preceded it. Just as in approaching a work of art, so in confronting an aesthetic depiction of the world, we would have to stand ready to abandon all previous standards of merit, to be instructed to a new conception of beauty by the power of the vision itself. The aesthetic vision must be allowed to create the very terms by which it is to be judged.

The last of these arguments for the necessity of God seems to me to be the strongest because it is based upon a datum few of us can deny, since it is demonstrated in our own case: the passion to affirm the world. This datum alone, however, does not advance our discussion far, because passions are notoriously elusive of clarification. But what I am suggesting here is that this passion be understood not as a quest for the explanation that silences all questions, but for a vision of the world as profound aesthetic object, or as part of a larger aesthetic design whose justification, like that of all such works, is finally contained within itself. I am suggesting that the demand for the intelligibility of the world be understood not exclusively as a demand of the mind, but primarily as a demand of the heart.

A world without God is a world with no aesthetic purpose whatsoever, a world in which wrenching misfortune and terrible injustice wear the armored face of indifference, a world in which the evening desire to feel a kinship with the universe is mocked by a treachery of silence. It is, in short, a world, of incurable ugliness, an offense not to our craving for clarity but to our passion for beauty. And it is this terrible vision, I am suggesting, that is being resisted in the grave demand for the world's intelligibility. Only if we are convinced of the existence of a divine artificer can we allow ourselves the hope that what appears to be the pointless chaos of our suffering is in fact an essential part of an awesome and magnificent destiny, a destiny justified in solely aesthetic terms. My conclusion, then, is that God *is* necessary to the meaningfulness of human life, when meaningfulness is understood to require the aesthetic coherence of the world.

IX

Now, my proposal may seem open to at least two powerful objections. First, although it may seem plausible to require that the world be intelligible if human life is to have meaning, it does not seem plausible to require that it be beautiful. Are there not many things – certain sentences, gestures, even (arguably) works of art – that we recognize as meaningful but which we regard at the same time as aesthetically neutral or positively ugly? What, then, is the relevance of beauty to the meaningfulness of the world? As I seem to reduce the demand for intelligibility to the desire for beauty, have I not in fact conflated two very different things, only the first of which may be a legitimate prerequisite of meaningful human life?

And is there not a second sense in which my proposal is irrelevant? For even if my readers accept what they may understand as a substitution of beauty for intelligibility as a prerequisite of the meaningfulness of the world, does not the criterion of beauty fail to establish a necessary role for *God* in determining the meaning of life? That, role *would* be established only if in every instance the beautiful were inseparable from an agent creator. We are familiar, however, with many counterexamples: beautiful things that are not the product of conscious design but of wholly mechanical forces. One need not see divine intention in the symmetry of a mineral crystal or the grasses in a twilit field in order to appreciate their beauty, and this ought to teach us not to confuse the beauty of a thing with the nature of its origin. But if beauty and origin are independent, how is the case for the necessity of God advanced by requiring of a meaningful world that its order have the quality of beauty?

I must certainly concede that the world could be beautiful without God, that there is nothing in the concept of a beautiful world that requires the existence of God. Indeed, I suspect that if the overmastering beauty of the world were evident, the need for God would be much less acute than it is. One need not be blind to the grandeur of nature, however, to recognize that her work is not uniformly beautiful, that predation and plague are as much nature's products as are mountains and verdant fields. Precisely the horrors of nature (and of man) are the occasion of the demand for aesthetic order, the devout wish that despite the appearance of indifference and discord, the world may be ultimately beautiful. Seeing that the whole of their experience gives evidence only of a blind nature,[16] men have turned to the unseen in the hope that they may be taught otherwise. It is, in other words, because the world is on the face of it *not* beautiful that men have felt the need for God. Still, although it may be understandable why it is, given the evident facts of the world, that men would feel the necessity for a God to set it right, the question remains whether he is necessary to the ultimate beauty of the world, and I have already answered *this* question in the negative. Since the concept of beauty is logically independent of the concept of artifice, it is possible that a beautiful universe would have no God. It is possible that the discordance in this life is redeemed in the next, but that this situation is not the product of conscious design. What, then remains to be said on behalf of my proposal?

What remains to be said is that even an unquestionably beautiful world would not necessarily be an *intelligible* one, and just as my imaginary objector points out, it is intelligibility and not beauty that is the issue here. The intention of my proposal is not to substitute an aesthetic criterion for the criterion of intellibility, but rather to analyze the demand for the intelligibility of the world in aesthetic rather than cognitive terms. It is still the intelligibility of the world that must be established. The product of random forces may indeed be beautiful, but a beautiful accident is no more *meaningful* than is a hideous one. A beautiful and accidental world could not satisfy the demand for intelligibility.

Perhaps I can best convey my point here with an example. Suppose I am walking along a desolate beach in a mood of dejection. At one point I stop absentmindedly and watch the ocean, and at just this moment small pebbles cast by the now receding waves form unmistakably the letters of the word "HOPE." I will find this an astonishing occurrence, to be sure. But if I do not take it as a sort of sign, a kind of message, the expression of a conscious intention, if I think it merely a remarkable *accident*, then the word will have *no meaning*; the letters will convey nothing, they will be an empty design. Analogously, the wind and waves may be beautifully musical. Perhaps they will form some unspeakably gentle and haunting chords. But unless I understand this as some sort of response, a reminder, a question, or a call – the communication of some conscious intent – the music will not diminish my solitude: beautiful and soothing, it will remain also random and dumb, devoid and innocent of *meaning*. Similarly, now, with respect to the world as such. A random collocation of atoms could indeed be beautiful, but since that beauty would express no aesthetic purpose (let alone the profound and benign aesthetic intent sought in the quest for the world's intelligibility), it would have *no meaning*.

I have proposed that the demand for the intelligibility of the world be understood as a demand for aesthetic order. But beauty alone is not the equivalent of aesthetic order. The latter is possible only for a *work* or *creation*, and this must be one informed throughout with discernible aesthetic *intent*. Aesthetic order is possible only in a work that *communicates a meaning* from one soul to another. Thus, it is no point against my proposal that the beautiful and the meaningful are separable. It is precisely on account of this separability that the mere beauty of the scheme of things – wholly accidental and hence inexpressive – could not by itself establish the *intelligibility* of the world. It is precisely for this reason that God as cosmic artificer is imperative to the *meaningfulness* of life.

The world is intelligible in aesthetic terms when we can see it as object of *art* – that is, when we can respond to it as the articulation of a *meaning*. Both the objections mistake the point of my proposal. It is not that we substitute beauty for sense as a prerequisite of the meaningfulness of the world, but that we understand sense as *aesthetic* sense – the elaboration of an aesthetic purpose. And since aesthetic *purpose* requires conscious agency, the conclusion to which our reflections have led us is that God as supernal craftsman is necessary to an intelligible world.

If the world has aesthetic order, then it is intelligible in the sense that a purpose may be discerned in it. But the discerning of this purpose does not lead to an endless quest for its justification, the demonstration of its meaningfulness. If the purpose that shapes the world is an articulation of the beautiful, then it, like the ground-breaking work of art, justifies itself.

If the world is unintelligible, then the life of man is the solitary, anguished, homeless venture depicted in Kafka and Beckett.[17] He is a creature imbued with passions remarkably inappropriate to the universe in which he is immersed – the passion for justice, for communion, for aesthetic order, and what is perhaps the cruelest of his drives, the will to celebrate without reserve the very world that mocks him. If God is dead, then the world is hopelessly unintelligible, and if this is so, then man's situation has its strict linguistic equivalent in the word "absurdity" – and no dream of the Dionysius he might become can mitigate or after this truth.

Notes

1. Leo Tolstoy, *My Confession*, trans. Leo Wiener (London: J. M. Dent and Sons, 1905).

2. Friedrich Nietzsche, *The Gay Science*, trans. Walter Kaufmann (New York: Vintage, 1974), pp. 279, 280.

3. Jean-Paul Sartre, *Existentialism*, trans. Bernard Frechtman (New York: Philosophical Library, 1947), p. 26.

4. Bertrand Russell, "A Free Man's Worship," in *The Basic Writings of Bertrand Russell,* ed. Robert E. Egner and Lester E. Denonn (New York: Simon and Schuster, 1961), p. 67.

5. Thomas Nagel is guilty of this error in his treatment of certain of the "inadequate arguments" in defense of the

conviction that human life is absurd. See his *Mortal Questions* (Cambridge Univ. Press, 1979), p. 12.

6. See Friedrich Nietzsche, *The Will to Power*, trans. Walter Kanfmann and R. J. Hollingdale (New York: Vintage, 1968), Section 577, p. 310. I have used here William Earle's translation of the aphorism in Section 577. See his "What is Man?" in *Triquarterly*, Winter, 1965, p. 74.

7. See Søren Kierkegaard, *Fear and Trembling and The Sickness unto Death*, trans. Walter Lowrie (Princeton: Princeton Univ. Press, 1974), p. 30.

8. See William James, *The Varieties of Religious Experience* (New York: Mentor, 1964), pp. 120–22. See also *The Will to Believe and Human Immortality* (New York: Dover, 1956), p. 44 of *Human Immortality*.

9. See Friedrich Nietzsche, *Twilight of the Idols, II, 2* in *The Portable Nietzsche*, trans. Walter Kaufmann (New York: Viking Press, 1963), pp. 473, 474.

10. Cf. Baruch Brody, "Morality and Religion Reconsid-ered," in *Readings in the Philosophy of Religion*, ed. Baruch Brody (Englewood Cliffs, NJ: Prentice-Hall, 1974), p. 593.

11. Cf. Brody, p. 594.

12. Cf. Brody, p. 594.

13. Kierkegaard, p. 30.

14. Russell, p. 67.

15. For the contrary view, see e.g., J. J. C. Smart, "The Existence of God", in *New Essays in Philosophical Theology*, ed. A. Flew and A. MacIntyre (New York: Macmillan, 1955), pp. 35–9.

16. Cf. David Hume, *Dialogues Concerning Natural Religion* (New York: Hafner Publishing Co., 1948), p. 79.

17. I am referring here to the entire *oeuvre* of each of these writers, but see especially Franz Kafka, *The Castle*, trans. Willa and Edwin Muir (New York: Alfred A. Knopf, 1964) and Samuel Beckett, *Waiting for Godot* (New York: Grove Press, 1954).

2.4

The Absurdity of Life without God

William Lane Craig

One of the apologetic questions that contemporary Christian theology must treat in its doctrine of man is what has been called "the human predicament," that is to say, the significance of human life in a post-theistic universe. Logically, this question ought, it seems to me, to be raised prior to and as a prelude to the question of God's existence.

Historical Background

The apologetic for Christianity based on the human predicament is an extremely recent phenomenon, associated primarily with Francis Schaeffer. Often it is referred to as "cultural apologetics" because of its analysis of post-Christian culture. This approach constitutes an entirely different sort of apologetics than the traditional models, since it is not concerned with epistemological issues of justification and warrant. Indeed, in a sense it does not even attempt to show in any positive sense that Christianity is true; it simply explores the disastrous consequences for human existence, society, and culture if Christianity should be false. In this respect, this approach is somewhat akin to existentialism: the precursors of this approach were also precursors of existentialism, and much of its analysis of the human predicament is drawn from the insights of twentieth-century atheistic existentialism.

Blaise Pascal

One of the earliest examples of a Christian apology appealing to the human predicament is the *Pensées* of the French mathematician and physicist Blaise Pascal (1623–62). Having

William Lane Craig (2008) "The Absurdity of Life without God," Chapter 2 in *Reasonable Faith: Christian Truth and Apologetics*, 3rd edn., Wheaton, IL: Crossway, pp. 65–88.

come to a personal faith in Christ in 1654, Pascal had planned to write a defense of the Christian faith entitled *L'Apologie de la religion chrétienne*, but he died of a debilitating disease at the age of only thirty-nine years, leaving behind hundreds of notes for the work, which were then published posthumously as the *Pensées*.[1]

Pascal's approach is thoroughly Christocentric. The Christian religion, he claims, teaches two truths: that there is a God whom men are capable of knowing, and that there is an element of corruption in men that renders them unworthy of God. Knowledge of God without knowledge of man's wretchedness begets pride, and knowledge of man's wretchedness without knowledge of God begets despair, but knowledge of Jesus Christ furnishes man knowledge of both simultaneously. Pascal invites us to look at the world from the Christian point of view and see if these truths are not confirmed. His *Apology* was evidently to comprise two divisions: in the first part he would display the misery of man without God (that man's nature is corrupt) and in the second part the happiness of man with God (that there is a Redeemer).[2] With regard to the latter, Pascal appeals to the evidences of miracle and especially fulfilled prophecy. In confirming the truth of man's wretchedness Pascal seeks to unfold the human predicament.

For Pascal the human condition is an enigma. For man is at the same time miserable and yet great. On the one hand, his misery is due principally to his uncertainty and insignificance. Writing in the tradition of the French skeptic Montaigne, Pascal repeatedly emphasizes the uncertainty of conclusions reached via reason and the senses. Apart from intuitive first principles, nothing seems capable of being known with certainty. In particular, reason and nature do not seem to furnish decisive evidence as to whether God exists or not. As man looks around him, all he sees is darkness and obscurity. Moreover, insofar as his scientific knowledge is correct, man learns that he is an infinitesimal speck lost in the immensity of time and space. His brief life is bounded on either side by eternity, his place in the universe is lost in the immeasurable infinity of space, and he finds himself suspended, as it were, between the infinite microcosm within and the infinite macrocosm without. Uncertain and untethered, man flounders in his efforts to lead a meaningful and happy life. His condition is characterized by inconstancy, boredom, and anxiety. His relations with his fellow men are warped by self-love; society is founded on mutual deceit. Man's justice is fickle and relative, and no fixed standard of value may be found.

Despite their predicament, however, most people, incredibly, refuse to seek an answer or even to think about their dilemma. Instead, they lose themselves in escapisms. Listen to Pascal's description of the reasoning of such a person:

> I know not who sent me into the world, nor what the world is, nor what I myself am. I am terribly ignorant of everything. I know not what my body is, nor my senses, nor my soul and that part of me which thinks what I say, which reflects upon itself as well as upon all external things, and has no more knowledge of itself than of them.
>
> I see the terrifying immensity of the universe which surrounds me, and find myself limited to one corner of this vast expanse, without knowing why I am set down here rather than elsewhere, nor why the brief period appointed for my life is assigned to me at this moment rather than another in all the eternity that has gone before and will come after me. On all sides I behold nothing but infinity, in which I am a mere atom, a mere passing shadow that returns no

more. All I know is that I must soon die, but what I understand least of all is this very death which I cannot escape.

As I know not whence I come, so I know not whither I go. I only know that on leaving this world I fall for ever into nothingness or into the hands of a wrathful God, without knowing to which of these two states I shall be everlastingly consigned. Such is my condition, full of weakness and uncertainty. From all this I conclude that I ought to spend every day of my life without seeking to know my fate. I might perhaps be able to find a solution to my doubts; but I cannot be bothered to do so, 1 will not take one step towards its discovery.[3]

Pascal can only regard such indifference as insane. Man's condition ought to impel him to seek to discover whether there is a God and a solution to his predicament. But people occupy their time and their thoughts with trivialities and distractions, so as to avoid the despair, boredom, and anxiety that would inevitably result if those diversions were removed.

Such is the misery of man. But mention must also be made of the greatness of man. For although man is miserable, he is at least capable of *knowing* that he is miserable. The greatness of man consists in thought. Man is a mere reed, yes, but he is a *thinking* reed. The universe might crush him like a gnat; but even so, man is nobler than the universe because he *knows* that it crushes him, and the universe has no such knowledge. Man's whole dignity consists, therefore, in thought. "By space the universe encompasses and swallows me up like a mere speck; by thought I comprehend the universe." Man's greatness, then, lies not in his having the solution to his predicament, but in the fact that he alone in all the universe is aware of his wretched condition.

What a chimaera then is man, what a novelty, what a monster, what chaos, what a subject of contradiction, what a prodigy! Judge of all things, yet an imbecile earthworm; depositary of truth, yet a sewer of uncertainty and error; pride and refuse of the universe. Who shall resolve this tangle?[4]

Pascal hopes that by explaining man's greatness as well as his misery, he might shake people out of their lethargy to think about their condition and to seek a solution.

Pascal's analysis of the human predicament leads up to his famous Wager argument, by means of which he hopes to tip the scales in favor of theism.[5] The founder of probability theory, Pascal argues that when the odds that God exists are even, then the prudent man will gamble that God exists. This is a wager that all men must make – the game is in progress and a bet must be laid. There is no opting out: you have already joined the game. Which then will you choose – that God exists or that he does not? Pascal argues that since the odds are even, reason is not violated in making either choice; so reason cannot determine which bet to make. Therefore, the choice should be made pragmatically in terms of maximizing one's happiness. If one wagers that God exists and he does, one has gained eternal life and infinite happiness. If he does not exist, one has lost nothing. On the other hand, if one wagers that God does not exist and he does, then one has suffered infinite loss. If he does not in fact exist, then one has gained nothing. Hence, the only prudent choice is to believe that God exists.

Now Pascal does believe that there is a way of getting a look behind the scenes, to speak, to determine rationally how one should bet, namely, the proofs of Scripture of miracle and prophecy, which he discusses in the second half of his work. But for now, he wants to emphasize that even in the absence of such evidence, one still ought to believe in God. For given the human predicament of being cast into existence and facing either eternal annihilation or eternal wrath, the only reasonable course of action is to believe in God: "for if you win, you win all; if you lose, you lose nothing."[6]

Fyodor Dostoyevsky

Another apologetic based on the human predicament may be found in the magnificent novels of the great nineteenth-century Russian writer Fyodor Dostoyevsky (1821–81). (May I add that I think the obsession of contemporary evangelicals with the writings of authors like C. S. Lewis to the neglect of writers like Dostoyevsky is a great shame? Dostoyevsky is a far, far grander writer.) The problem that tortured Dostoyevsky was the problem of evil: how can a good and loving God exist when the world is filled with so much suffering and evil? Dostoyevsky presented this problem in his works so persuasively, so poignantly, that certain passages of his, notably "The Grand Inquisitor" section from his *Brothers Karamazov*, are often reprinted in anthologies as classic statements of the problem of evil. As a result, some people are under the impression that Dostoyevsky was himself an atheist and that the viewpoint of the Grand Inquisitor is his own.

Actually, he sought to carry through a two-pronged defense of theism in the face of the problem of evil. Positively, he argued that innocent suffering may perfect character and bring one into a closer relation with God. Negatively, he tried to show that if the existence of God is denied, then one is landed in complete moral relativism, so that no act, regardless how dreadful or heinous, can be condemned by the atheist. To live consistently with such a view of life is unthinkable and impossible. Hence, atheism is destructive of life and ends logically in suicide.

Dostoyevsky's magnificent novels *Crime and Punishment* and *The Brothers Karamazov* powerfully illustrate these themes. In the former a young atheist, convinced of moral relativism, brutally murders an old woman. Though he knows that on his presuppositions he should not feel guilty, nevertheless he is consumed with guilt until he confesses his crime and gives his life to God. The latter novel is the story of four brothers, one of whom murders their father because his atheist brother Ivan had told him that moral absolutes do not exist. Unable to live with the consequences of his own philosophical system, Ivan suffers a mental collapse. The remaining two brothers, one of whom is unjustly accused of the parricide and the other a young Russian orthodox priest, find in what they suffer the perfection of their character and a nearness to God.

Dostoyevsky recognizes that his response to atheism constitutes no positive proof of Christianity. Indeed, he rejects that there could be such. Men demand of Christ that he furnish them "bread and circuses," but he refuses to do so. The decision to follow Christ must be made in loneliness and anxiety. Each person must face for himself the anguish of a world without God and in the solitude of his own heart give himself to God in faith.

Søren Kierkegaard

The Danish existentialist of the mid-nineteenth century, Søren Kierkegaard (1813–55), also presents a sort of negative apologetic for the Christian faith. He thinks of life as being lived on three different planes or stages: the aesthetic stage, the ethical stage, and the religious stage. Man in the aesthetic stage lives life only on the sensual level, a life that is self- and pleasure-centered. This need not be a gross hedonism. Man on this level could be very cultivated and even circumspect; but nevertheless his life revolves around himself and those material things – whether sex, art, music, or whatever – that bring him pleasure. The paradox of life on this level is that it leads ultimately to unhappiness. The self-centered, aesthetic man finds no ultimate meaning in life and no true satisfaction. Thus, the aesthetic life leads finally to boredom, a sort of sickness with life.

But this is not the end, for only at this point is a person ready to live on the second plane of existence, the ethical plane. The transition to the ethical stage of life is a sort of leap motivated by dissatisfaction to a higher level, where one affirms transpersonal moral values and guides life by those objective standards. No longer is life lived only for self and for pleasure; rather one is constrained to seek the ethical good and to change one's conduct to bring it into conformity with that good. Thus, man in the ethical stage is the moral man. But life on this level, too, ends in unhappiness. For the more one tries sincerely to bring one's life into conformity with the objective standards of the good, the more painfully aware one is that one cannot do it. Thus, the ethical life, when earnestly pursued, leads ultimately to guilt and despair.

But there is one more stage along life's way: the religious stage. Here one finds forgiveness of sins and a personal relationship with God. Only here, in intimate communion with one's Creator, does man find authentic existence and true fulfillment. Again, Kierkegaard represents the transition to this stage from the ethical as a leap. The decision to believe is a criterionless choice, a leap of faith into the dark. Although man can be given no rational grounds to leap, unless he does so, he will remain in despair and inauthentic existence.

Francis Schaeffer

As I remarked earlier, Francis Schaeffer (1912–84) is the thinker most responsible for crafting a Christian apologetic based on the so-called modern predicament. According to Schaeffer, there can be traced in recent Western culture a "line of despair," which penetrates philosophy, literature, and the arts in succession. He believes the root of the problem lies in Hegelian philosophy, specifically in its denial of absolute truths. Hegel developed the famous triad of thesis-antithesis-synthesis, in which contradictions are seen not as absolute opposites, but as partial truths, which are synthesized in the whole. Ultimately all is One, which is absolute and non-contradictory. In Schaeffer's view, Hegel's system undermined the notion of particular absolute truths (such as "That act is morally wrong" or "This painting is aesthetically ugly") by synthesizing them into the whole. This denial of absolutes has gradually made its way through Western culture. In each case, it results in despair, because without absolutes man's endeavors degenerate into absurdity. Schaeffer believes that the Theater of the Absurd, abstract modern art, and modern music such as compositions by John Cage are all indications of what happens below the line of despair. Only by reaffirming belief in the absolute God of Christianity can man and his culture avoid inevitable degeneracy, meaninglessness, and despair.

Schaeffer's efforts against abortion may be seen as a logical extension of this apologetic. Once God is denied, human life becomes worthless, and we see the fruit of such a philosophy in the abortion and infanticide now taking place in Western society. Schaeffer warns that unless Western man returns to the Christian world and life view, nothing will stop the trend from degenerating into population control and human breeding. Only a theistic worldview can save the human race from itself.

Assessment

The loss of God and immortality

Man, writes Loren Eiseley, is the Cosmic Orphan. He is the only creature in the universe who asks, "Why?" Other animals have instincts to guide them, but man has learned to ask questions.

"Who am I?" he asks. "Why am I here? Where am I going?" Since the Enlightenment, when modern man threw off the shackles of religion, he has tried to answer these questions without reference to God. But the answers that have come back were not exhilarating, but dark and terrible. "You are the accidental by-product of nature, a result of matter plus time plus chance. There is no reason for your existence. All you face is death."

Modern man thought that when he had gotten rid of God, he had freed himself from all that repressed and stifled him. Instead, he discovered that in killing God, he had only succeeded in orphaning himself.

For if there is no God, then man's life becomes absurd.

If God does not exist, then both man and the universe are inevitably doomed to death. Man, like all biological organisms, must die. With no hope of immortality, man's life leads only to the grave. His life is but a spark in the infinite blackness, a spark that appears, flickers, and dies forever. Compared to the infinite stretch of time, the span of man's life is but an infinitesimal moment; and yet this is all the life he will ever know. Therefore, everyone must come face to face with what theologian Paul Tillich has called "the threat of non-being." For though I know now that I exist, that I am alive, I also know that someday I will no longer exist, that I will no longer be, that I will die. This thought is staggering and threatening: to think that the person I call "myself" will cease to exist, that I will be no more!

I remember vividly the first time my father told me that someday I would die. Somehow, as a child, the thought had just never occurred to me. When he told me, I was filled with fear and unbearable sadness. And though he tried repeatedly to reassure me that this was a long way off, that did not seem to matter. Whether sooner or later, the undeniable fact was that I would die and be no more, and the thought overwhelmed me. Eventually, like all of us, I grew to simply accept the fact. We all learn to live with the inevitable. But the child's insight remains true. As the French existentialist Jean-Paul Sartre observed, several hours or several years make no difference once you have lost eternity.

Whether it comes sooner or later, the prospect of death and the threat of non-being is a terrible horror. I met a student once who did not feel this threat. He said he had been raised on the farm and was used to seeing the animals being born and dying. Death was for him simply natural – a part of life, so to speak. I was puzzled by how different our two perspectives on death were and found it difficult to understand why he did not feel the threat non-being. Years later, I think I found my answer in reading Sartre. Sartre observed that death is not threatening so long as we view it as the death of the other, from a third-person standpoint, so to speak. It is only when we internalize it and look at it from the first-person perspective – "my death: I am going to die" – that the threat of non-being becomes real. As Sartre points out, many people never assume this first-person perspective in the midst of life; one can even look at one's own death from the third-person standpoint, as if it were the death of another or even of an animal, as did my friend. But the true existential significance of my death can only be appreciated from the first-person perspective, as I realize that I am going to die and forever cease to exist.

And the universe, too, faces a death of its own. Scientists tell us that the universe is expanding, and the galaxies are growing farther and farther apart. As it does so, it grows colder and colder, and its energy is used up. Eventually all the stars will burn out, and all matter will collapse into dead stars and black holes. There will be no light at all; there will be no heat; there will be no life; only the corpses of dead stars and galaxies, ever expanding into the endless darkness and the cold recesses of space – universe in ruins. This is not science fiction. The entire universe marches irreversibly toward its grave. So not only is the life of each individual person doomed; the entire human race is doomed. The universe is plunging toward inevitable extinction – death is written throughout its structure. There is no escape. There is no hope.

The absurdity of life without God and immortality

If there is no God, then man and the universe are doomed. Like prisoners condemned to death, we await our unavoidable execution. There is no God, and there is no immortality. And what is the consequence of this? It means that life itself is absurd. It means that the life we have is without ultimate significance, value, or purpose. Let's look at each of these.

No ultimate meaning without God and immortality

If each individual person passes out of existence when he dies, then what ultimate meaning can be given to his life? Does it really matter whether he ever existed at all? It might be said that his life was important because it influenced others or affected the course of history. But this shows only a relative significance to his life, not an ultimate significance. His life may be important relative to certain other events, but what is the ultimate significance of any of those events? If all the events are meaningless, then what can be the ultimate significance of influencing any of them? Ultimately it makes no difference.

Look at it from another perspective: Scientists say that the universe originated in an explosion called the "Big Bang" about thirteen billion years ago. Suppose the Big Bang had never occurred. Suppose the universe had never existed. What ultimate difference would it make? The universe is doomed to die anyway. In the end it makes no difference whether the universe ever existed or not. Therefore, it is without ultimate significance.

The same is true of the human race. Mankind is a doomed race in a dying universe. Because the human race will eventually cease to exist, it makes no ultimate difference whether it ever did exist. Mankind is thus no more significant than a swarm of mosquitoes or a barnyard of pigs, for their end is all the same. The same blind cosmic process that coughed them up in the first place will eventually swallow them all again.

And the same is true of each individual person. The contributions of the scientist to the advance of human knowledge, the researches of the doctor to alleviate pain and suffering, the efforts of the diplomat to secure peace in the world, the sacrifices of good people everywhere to better the lot of the human race – all these come to nothing. In the end they don't make one bit of difference, not one bit. Each person's life is therefore without ultimate significance. And because our lives are ultimately meaningless, the activities we fill our lives with are also meaningless. The long hours spent in study at the university, our jobs, our interests, our friendships – all these are, in the final analysis, utterly meaningless.

In his poem "The End of the World" Archibald MacLeish portrays life as an idiotic circus, until one day the show is over:

> Quite unexpectedly, as Vasserot
> The armless ambidextrian was lighting
> A match between his great and second toe,
> And Ralph the lion was engaged in biting
> The neck of Madame Sossman while the drum
> Pointed, and Teeny was about to cough
> In waltz-time swinging Jocko by the thumb
> Quite unexpectedly the top blew off:
>
> And there, there overhead, there, there hung over
> Those thousands of white faces, those dazed eyes,
> There in the starless dark, the poise, the hover,
> There with vast wings across the cancelled skies,
> There in the sudden blackness the black pall
> Of nothing, nothing, nothing – nothing at all.[7]

This is the horror of modern man: because he ends in nothing, he is nothing.

But it's important to see that it is not just immortality that man needs if life is to be meaningful. Mere duration of existence does not make that existence meaningful. If man and the universe could exist forever, but if there were no God, their existence would still have no ultimate significance. I once read a science-fiction story in which an astronaut was marooned on a barren chunk of rock lost in outer space. He had with him two vials: one containing poison and the other a potion that would make him live forever. Realizing his predicament, he gulped down the poison. But then to his horror, he discovered he had swallowed the wrong vial – he had drunk the potion for immortality. And that meant that he was cursed to exist forever – a meaningless, unending life. Now if God does not exist, our lives are just like that. They could go on and on and still be utterly without meaning. We could still ask of life, "So what?" So it's not just immortality man needs if life is to be ultimately significant; he needs God and immortality. And if God does not exist, then he has neither.

Twentieth-century man came to understand this. Read *Waiting for Godot* by Samuel Beckett. During this entire play two men carry on trivial conversation while waiting for a third man to arrive, who never does. Our lives are like that, Beckett is saying; we just kill time waiting – for what, we don't know. In a tragic portrayal of man, Beckett wrote another play in which the curtain opens revealing a stage littered with junk. For thirty long seconds, the audience sits and stares in silence at that junk. Then the curtain closes . That's all.

French existentialists Jean-Paul Sartre and Albert Camus understood this, too. Sartre portrayed life in his play *No Exit* as hell – the final line of the play are the words of resignation, "Well, let's get on with it." Hence, Sartre writes elsewhere of the "nausea" of existence. Man, he says, is adrift in a boat without a rudder on an endless sea. Camus, too, saw life as absurd. At the end of his brief novel *The Stranger*, Camus's hero discovers in a flash of insight that the universe has no meaning and there is no God to give it one. The French biochemist Jacques Monod seemed to echo those sentiments when he wrote in his work *Chance and Necessity*, "Man finally knows he is alone in the indifferent immensity of the universe."

Thus, if there is no God, then life itself becomes meaningless. Man and the universe are without ultimate significance.

No ultimate value without God and immortality

If life ends at the grave, then it makes no difference whether one has lived as a Stalin or as a saint. Since one's destiny is ultimately unrelated to one's behavior, you may as well just live as you please. As Dostoyevsky put it: "If there is no immortality, then all things are permitted." On this basis, a writer like Ayn Rand is absolutely correct to praise the virtues of selfishness. Live totally for self; no one holds you accountable! Indeed, it would be foolish to do anything else, for life is too short to jeopardize it by acting out of anything but pure self-interest. Sacrifice for another person would be stupid. Kai Nielsen, an atheist philosopher who attempts to defend the viability of ethics without God, in the end admits,

> We have not been able to show that reason requires the moral point of view, or that all really rational persons, unhoodwinked by myth or ideology, need not be individual egoists or classical amoralists. Reason doesn't decide here. The picture I have painted for you is not a pleasant one. Reflection on it depresses me. … Pure practical reason, even with a good knowledge of the facts, will not take you to morality.[8]

But the problem becomes even worse. For, regardless of immortality, if there is no God, then any basis for objective standards of right and wrong seems to have evaporated. All we are confronted with is, in Jean-Paul Sartre's words, the bare, valueless fact of existence. Moral values are either just expressions of personal taste or the by-products of socio-biological evolution and conditioning. In the words of one humanist philosopher, "The moral principles that govern our behavior are rooted in habit and custom, feeling and fashion."[9] In a world without God, who is to say which actions are right and which are wrong? Who is to judge that the values of Adolf Hitler are inferior to those of a saint? The concept of morality loses all meaning in a universe without God. As one contemporary atheistic ethicist points out, "To say that something is wrong because … it is forbidden by God, is perfectly understandable to anyone who believes in a law giving God. But to say that something is wrong … even though no God exists to forbid it, is *not* understandable. …" "The concept of moral obligation [is] unintelligible apart from the idea of God. The words remain but their meaning is gone."[10] In a world without a divine lawgiver, there can be no objective right and wrong, only our culturally and personally relative, subjective judgments. This means that it is impossible to condemn war, oppression, or crime as evil. Nor can one praise brother-hood, equality, and love as good. For in a universe without God, good and evil do not exist – there is only the bare valueless fact to existence, and there is no one to say that you are right and I am wrong.

No ultimate purpose without God and immortality

If death stands with open arms at the end of life's trail, then what is the goal of life? To what end has life been lived? Is it all for nothing? Is there no reason for life? And what of the universe? Is it utterly pointless? If its destiny is a cold grave in the recesses of outer space, the answer must be yes – it is pointless. There is no goal, no purpose, for the universe. The litter of a dead universe will just go on expanding and expanding – forever.

And what of man? Is there no purpose at all for the human race? Or will it simply peter out someday, lost in the oblivion of an indifferent universe? The English writer H. G. Wells foresaw such a prospect. In his novel *The Time Machine* Wells's time traveler journeys far into the future to discover the destiny of man. All he finds is a dead earth, save for a few lichens and moss, orbiting a gigantic red sun. The only sounds are the rush of the wind and the gentle ripple of the sea. "Beyond these lifeless sounds," writes Wells, "the world was silent. Silent? It would be hard to convey the stillness of it. All the sounds of man, the bleat-ing of sheep, the cries of birds, the hum of insects, the stir that makes the background of our lives – all that was over."[11] And so Wells's time traveler returned. But to what? – to merely an earlier point on the purposeless rush toward oblivion. When as a non-Christian I first read Wells's book, I thought, "No, no! It can't end that way!" But if there is no God, it will end that way, like it or not. This is reality in a universe without God: there is no hope; there is no purpose. It reminds me of T. S. Eliot's haunting lines:

> This is the way the world ends
> This is the way the world ends
> This is the way the world ends
> Not with a bang but a whimper.[12]

What is true of mankind as a whole is true of each of us individually: we are here to no purpose. If there is no God, then our life is not fundamentally different from that of a dog. I know that's harsh, but it's true. As the ancient writer of Ecclesiastes put it: "The fate of the sons of men and the fate of beasts is the same. As one dies so dies the other; indeed, they all have the same breath and there is no advantage for man over beast, for all is vanity. All go to the same place. All come from the dust and all return to the dust" (Eccles. 3:19–20 AT). In this book, which reads more like a piece of modern existentialist literature than a book of the Bible, the writer shows the futility of pleasure, wealth, education, political fame, and honor in a life doomed to end in death. His verdict? "Vanity of vanities! All is vanity" (1:2 ESV). If life ends at the grave, then we have no ultimate purpose for living.

But more than that: even if it did not end in death, without God life would still be without purpose. For man and the universe would then be simple accidents of chance, thrust into existence for no reason. Without God the universe is the result of a cosmic accident, a

chance explosion. There is no reason for which it exists. As for man, he is a freak of nature –
a blind product of matter plus time plus chance. Man is just a lump of slime that evolved
rationality. There is no more purpose in life for the human race than for a species of insect;
for both are the result of the blind interaction of chance and necessity. As one philosopher
has put it: "Human life is mounted upon a subhuman pedestal and must shift for itself alone
in the heart of a silent and mindless universe."[13]

What is true of the universe and of the human race is also true of us as individuals.
Insofar as we are individual human beings, we are the result of certain combinations of
heredity and environment. We are victims of a kind of genetic and environmental roulette.
Biologists like Richard Dawkins regard man as an electro-chemical machine controlled by
its mindless genes. If God does not exist, then you are just a miscarriage of nature, thrust
into a purposeless universe to live a purposeless life.

So if God does not exist, that means that man and the universe exist to no purpose –
since the end of everything is death – and that they came to be for no purpose, since they
are only blind products of chance. In short, life is utterly without reason.

Do you understand the gravity of the alternatives before us? For if God exists, then there
is hope for man. But if God does not exist, then all we are left with is despair. Do you understand why the question of God's existence is so vital to man? As Francis Schaeffer aptly put
it, "If God is dead, then man is dead, too."

Unfortunately, the mass of mankind do not realize this fact. They continue on as though
nothing has changed. I'm reminded of Nietzsche's story of the madman who in the early
morning hours burst into the marketplace, lantern in hand, crying, "I seek God! I seek
God!" Since many of those standing about did not believe in God, he provoked much
laughter. "Did God get lost?" they taunted him. "Or is he hiding? Or maybe he has gone on
a voyage or emigrated!" Thus they yelled and laughed. Then, writes Nietzsche, the madman
turned in their midst and pierced them with his eyes.

> "Whither is God?" he cried, "I shall tell you. *We have killed him* – you and I. All of us are his
> murderers. But how have we done this? How were we able to drink up the sea? Who gave us the
> sponge to wipe away the entire horizon? What did we do when we unchained this earth from
> its sun? Whither is it moving now? Away from all suns? Are we not plunging continually?
> Backward, sideward, forward, in all directions? Is there any up or down left? Are we not stray-
> ing as through an infinite nothing? Do we not feel the breath of empty space? Has it not become
> colder? Is not night and more night coming on all the while? Must not lanterns be lit in the
> morning? Do we not hear anything yet of the noise of the gravediggers who are burying God?
> … God is dead . …. And we have killed him. How shall we, the murderers of all murderers,
> comfort ourselves?"[14]

The crowd stared at the madman in silence and astonishment. At last he dashed his lantern to the ground. "I have come too early," he said. "This tremendous event is still on its
way – it has not yet reached the ears of man." People did not yet truly comprehend the consequences of what they had done in killing God. But Nietzsche predicted that someday
people would realize the implications of their atheism; and this realization would usher in
an age of nihilism – the destruction of all meaning and value in life. The end of Christianity,
wrote Nietzsche, means the advent of nihilism. This most gruesome of guests is standing

already at the door. "Our whole European culture is moving for some time now," wrote Nietzsche, "with a tortured tension that is growing from decade to decade, as toward a catastrophe: restlessly, violently, headlong, like a river that wants to reach the end, that no longer reflects, that is afraid to reflect."[15]

Most people still do not reflect on the consequences of atheism and so, like the crowd in the marketplace, go unknowingly on their way. But when we realize, as did Nietzsche, what atheism implies, then his question presses hard upon us: how *shall* we, the murderers of all murderers, comfort ourselves?

The practical impossibility of atheism

About the only solution the atheist can offer is that we face the absurdity of life and live bravely. Bertrand Russell, for example, wrote that we must build our lives upon "the firm foundation of unyielding despair."[16] Only by recognizing that the world really is a terrible place can we successfully come to terms with life. Camus said that we should honestly recognize life's absurdity and then live in love for one another.

The fundamental problem with this solution, however, is that it is impossible to live consistently and happily within such a worldview. If one lives consistently, he will not be happy; if one lives happily, it is only because he is not consistent. Francis Schaeffer has explained this point well. Modern man, says Schaeffer, resides in a two-story universe. In the lower story is the finite world without God; here life is absurd, as we have seen. In the upper story are meaning, value, and purpose. Now modern man lives in the lower story because he believes there is no God. But he cannot live happily in such an absurd world; therefore, he continually makes leaps of faith into the upper story to affirm meaning, value, and purpose, even though he has no right to, since he does not believe in God. Modern man is totally inconsistent when he makes this leap, because these values cannot exist without God, and man in his lower story does not have God.

Let's look again, then, at each of the three areas in which we saw that life is absurd without God, in order to show how modern man cannot live consistently and happily with his atheism.

Meaning of life

First, the area of meaning. We saw that without God, life has no meaning. Yet philosophers continue to live as though life does have meaning. For example, Sartre argued that one may create meaning for his life by freely choosing to follow a certain course of action. Sartre himself chose Marxism.

Now this is utterly inconsistent. It is inconsistent to say that life is objectively absurd and then to say that one may create meaning for his life. If life is really absurd, then man is trapped in the lower story. To try to create meaning in life represents a leap to the upper story. But Sartre has no basis for this leap. Without God, there can be no objective meaning in life. Sartre's program is actually an exercise in self-delusion. For the universe does not really acquire meaning just because *I* happen to give it one. This is easy to see: for suppose I give the universe one meaning, and you give it another. Who is right? The answer, of course, is neither one. For the universe without God remains objectively meaningless, no matter how *we* regard it. Sartre is really saying, "Let's *pretend* the universe has meaning." And this is just fooling ourselves.

The point is this: if God does not exist, then life is objectively meaningless; but man cannot live consistently and happily knowing that life is meaningless; so in order to be happy he pretends that life has meaning. But this is, of course, entirely inconsistent – for without God, man and the universe are without any real significance.

Value of life

Turn now to the problem of value. Here is where the most blatant inconsistencies occur. First of all, atheistic humanists are totally inconsistent in affirming the traditional values of love and brotherhood. Camus has been rightly criticized for inconsistently holding both to the absurdity of life and to the ethics of human love and brotherhood. The two are logically incompatible. Bertrand Russell, too, was inconsistent. For though he was an atheist, he was an outspoken social critic, denouncing war and restrictions on sexual freedom. Russell admitted that he could not live as though ethical values were simply a matter of personal taste, and that he therefore found his own views "incredible." "I do not know the solution," he confessed.[17] The point is that if there is no God, then objective right and wrong cannot exist. As Dostoyevsky said, "All things are permitted."

But Dostoyevsky also showed in his novels that man cannot live this way. He cannot live as though it is perfectly all right for soldiers to slaughter innocent children. He cannot live as though it is all right for dictatorial regimes to follow a systematic program of physical torture of political prisoners. He cannot live as though it is all right for dictators like Pol Pot or Saddam Hussein to exterminate millions of their own countrymen. Everything in him cries out to say these acts are wrong – really wrong. But if there no God, he cannot. So he makes a leap of faith and affirms values anyway. And when he does so, he reveals the inadequacy of a world without God.

The horror of a world devoid of value was brought home to me with new intensity several years ago as I viewed a BBC television documentary called "The Gathering." It concerned the reunion of survivors of the Holocaust in Jerusalem, where they rediscovered lost friendships and shared their experiences. Now I had heard stories of the Holocaust before and had even visited Dachau and Buchen-wald, and I thought I was beyond shocking by further tales of horror. But I found that I was not. Perhaps I had been made more sensitive by the recent birth of our beautiful baby girl, so that I applied the situations to her as they were related on the television. In any case, one woman prisoner, a nurse, told of how she was made the gynecologist at Auschwitz. She observed that pregnant women were grouped together by the soldiers under the direction of Dr. Mengele and housed in the same barracks. Some time passed, and she noted that she no longer saw any of these women. She made inquiries. "Where are the pregnant women who were housed in that barracks?" "Haven't you heard?" came the reply. "*Dr. Mengele used them for vivisection.*"

Another woman told of how Mengele had bound up her breasts so that she could not suckle her infant. The doctor wanted to learn how long an infant could survive without nourishment. Desperately this poor woman tried to keep her baby alive by giving it pieces of bread soaked in coffee, but to no avail. Each day the baby lost weight, a fact that was eagerly monitored by Dr. Mengele. A nurse then came secretly to this woman and told her,

"I have arranged a way for you to get out of here, but you cannot take your baby with you. I have brought a morphine injection that you can give to your child to end its life." When the woman protested, the nurse was insistent: "Look, your baby is going to die anyway. At least save yourself." And so this mother felt compelled *to take the life of her own baby*. Dr. Mengele was furious when he learned of it because he had lost his experimental specimen, and he searched among the dead to find the baby's discarded corpse so that he could have one last weighing.

My heart was torn by these stories. One rabbi who survived the camp summed it up well when he said that at Auschwitz it was as though there existed a world in which all the Ten Commandments were reversed: "Thou shalt kill, thou shalt lie, thou shalt steal …" Mankind had never seen such a hell.

And yet, if God does not exist, then in a sense, our world *is* Auschwitz: there is no right and wrong; *all things* are permitted. But no atheist, no agnostic, can live consistently with such a view of life. Nietzsche himself, who proclaimed the necessity of living "beyond good and evil," broke with his mentor Richard Wagner precisely over the issue of the composer's anti-Semitism and strident German nationalism. Similarly Sartre, writing in the aftermath of the Second World War, condemned anti-Semitism, declaring that a doctrine that leads to extermination is not merely an opinion or matter of personal taste, of equal value with its opposite.[18] In his important essay "Existentialism Is a Humanism," Sartre struggles vainly to elude the contradiction between his denial of divinely pre-established values and his urgent desire to affirm the value of human persons. Like Russell, he could not live with the implications of his own denial of ethical absolutes.

Neither can Richard Dawkins. For although he solemnly pronounces, "There is at bottom no design, no purpose, no evil, no good, nothing but pointless indifference. … We are machines for propagating DNA,"[19] he is a patent moralist. He declares himself mortified that Enron executive Jeff Skilling regards Dawkins's *The Selfish Gene* as his favorite book because of its perceived Social Darwinism.[20] He characterizes "Darwinian mistakes" like pity for someone unable to pay us back or sexual attraction to an infertile member of the opposite sex as "blessed, precious mistakes" and calls compassion and generosity "noble emotions."[21] He denounces the doctrine of original sin as "morally obnoxious."[22] He vigorously condemns such actions as the harassment and abuse of homosexuals, religious indoctrination of children, the Incan practice of human sacrifice, and prizing cultural diversity in the case of the Amish over the interests of their children.[23] He even goes so far as to offer his own amended Ten Commandments for guiding moral behavior, all the while marvelously oblivious to the contradiction with his ethical subjectivism.[24]

A second problem for the atheist is that if God does not exist and there is no immortality, then all the evil acts of men go unpunished and all the sacrifices of good men go unrewarded. But who can live with such a view? Richard Wurmbrand, who has been tortured for his faith in communist prisons, says,

> The cruelty of atheism is hard to believe when man has no faith in the reward of good or the punishment of evil. There is no reason to be human. There is no restraint from the depths of evil which is in man. The communist torturers often said, "There is no God, no Hereafter, no punishment for evil. We can do what we wish." I have heard one torturer even say, "I thank

God, in whom I don't believe, that I have lived to this hour when I can express all the evil in my heart." He expressed it in unbelievable brutality and torture inflicted on prisoners.[25]

The English theologian Cardinal Newman once said that if he believed that all the evils and injustices of life throughout history were not to be made right by God in the afterlife, "Why I think I should go mad." Rightly so.

And the same applies to acts of self-sacrifice. A number of years ago, a terrible mid-winter air disaster occurred when a plane leaving the Washington, DC., airport smashed into a bridge spanning the Potomac River, plunging its passengers into the icy waters. As the rescue helicopters came, attention was focused on one man who again and again pushed the dangling rope ladder to other passengers rather than be pulled to safety himself. Six times he passed the ladder by. When they came again, he was gone. He had freely given his life that others might live. The whole nation turned its eyes to this man in respect and admiration for the selfless and good act he had performed. And yet, if the atheist is right, that man was not noble – he did the stupidest thing possible. He should have gone for the ladder first, pushed others away if necessary in order to survive. But to die for others he did not even know, to give up all the brief existence he would ever have – what for? For the atheist there can be no reason. And yet the atheist, like the rest of us, instinctively reacts with praise for this man's selfless action. Indeed, one will probably never find an atheist who lives consistently with his system. For a universe without moral accountability and devoid of value is unimaginably terrible.

Purpose of life

Finally, let's look at the problem of purpose in life. Unable to live in an impersonal universe in which everything is the product of blind chance, atheists sometimes begin to ascribe personality and motives to the physical processes themselves. It is a bizarre way of speaking and represents a leap from the lower to the upper story. For example, the brilliant Russian physicists Zeldovich and Novikov, in contemplating the properties of the universe, ask, why did "Nature" choose to create this sort of universe instead of another? "Nature" has obviously become a sort of God-substitute, filling the role and function of God. Francis Crick halfway through his book *The Origin of the Genetic Code* begins to spell nature with a capital *N* and elsewhere speaks of natural selection as being "clever" and as "thinking" of what it will do. Sir Fred Hoyle, the English astronomer, attributes to the universe itself the qualities of God. For Carl Sagan the "Cosmos," which he always spelled with a capital letter, obviously fills the role of a God-substitute. Though these men profess not to believe in God, they smuggle in a God-substitute through the back door because they cannot bear to live in a universe in which everything is the chance result of impersonal forces.

Moreover, the only way that most people who deny purpose in life live happily is either by making up some purpose – which amounts to self-delusion as we saw with Sartre – or by not carrying their view to its logical conclusions. Take the problem of death, for example. According to Ernst Bloch, the only way modern man lives in the face of death is by subconsciously borrowing the belief in immortality that his forefathers held to, even though he himself has no basis for this belief, since he does not believe in God. Bloch states that the belief that life ends in nothing is hardly, in his words, "sufficient to keep the head high and to work as if there were no end." By borrowing the remnants of a belief in immortality, writes Bloch, "modern man does not feel the chasm that unceasingly surrounds him and that will certainly engulf him at last. Through these remnants, he saves his sense of self-identity. Through them the impression arises that man is not perishing, but only that one day the world has the whim no longer to appear to him. "Bloch concludes, "This quite shallow courage feasts on a borrowed credit card. It lives from earlier hopes and the support that they once had provided."[26] Modern man no longer has any right to that support, since he rejects God. But in order to live purposefully, he makes a leap of faith to affirm a reason for living.

Finding ourselves cast into a mindless universe with no apparent purpose or hope of deliverance from thermodynamic extinction, the temptation to invest one's own petty plans and projects with objective significance and thereby to find some purpose to one's life is almost irresistible. Thus, the outspoken atheist and Nobel Prize–winning physicist Steven Weinberg at the close of his much acclaimed popularization of contemporary cosmology *The First Three Minutes*, writes:

> However all these problems may be solved, and whichever cosmological model proves correct, there is not much comfort in any of this. It is almost irresistible for humans to believe that we have some special relation to the universe, that human life is not just a more-or-less farcical outcome of a chain of accidents reaching back to the first three minutes, but that somehow we were built in from the beginning. … It is very hard to realize that this is all just a tiny part of an overwhelmingly hostile universe. It is even harder to realize that this present universe has evolved from an unspeakably unfamiliar early condition, and faces a future extinction of endless cold or intolerable heat. The more the universe seems comprehensible, the more it also seems pointless.
>
> But if there is no solace in the fruits of our research, there is at least some consolation in the research itself. Men and women are not content to comfort themselves with tales of gods and giants, or to confine their thoughts to the daily affairs of life; they also build telescopes and satellites and accelerators and sit at their desks for endless hours working out the meaning of the data they gather. The effort to understand the universe is one of the very few things that lifts human life a little above the level of farce, and gives it some of the grace of tragedy.[27]

There is something strange about Weinberg's moving description of the human predicament: *tragedy* is an evaluative term. Weinberg sees the pursuit of scientific research as raising human life above the level of farce to the level of tragedy. But on naturalism, what is the basis for such an evaluative differentiation? Weinberg evidently sees a life devoted to scientific pursuits as truly meaningful, and therefore it's too bad that so noble a pursuit should be extinguished. But why on naturalism should the pursuit of science be any different from slouching about doing nothing? Since there is no objective purpose to human life, none of our pursuits has any objective significance, however important and dear they may seem to us subjectively.

Daniel Dennett recently betrayed a similar inconsistency. Speaking at a conference in New Orleans, Dennett opened his talk by showing a short film that encapsulated what he wanted to convey. It showed a group of young African men playing with a soccer ball, kicking it into the air and adroitly catching it on their feet in quite amazing ways, while never letting the ball touch the ground. Meanwhile a silent narration played across the screen, describing the unfathomable vastness of the cosmos in space and time and contrasting the tininess and brevity of human existence. We are here for a mere twinkling of the eye and then gone forever. The punch line of the film finally came: "We'd better not blow it." That was the end. "What a strange film!" I thought to myself. What does it mean on an atheistic view to "blow it"? If there is no objective purpose for the human race, then how can one miss that purpose? Like *tragedy*, "blowing it" is an evaluative notion which finds no foothold in an atheistic universe. The boys' skill and evident joy in playing football is no more meaningful a pursuit on atheism than some other kid's staying home and drinking himself into a stupor. But even atheists recognize that some of life's pursuits are more objectively meaningful and worthwhile than others.

While participating in a conference on Intelligent Design two years ago, I had the opportunity to have dinner with the agnostic philosopher of science Michael Ruse one evening at an Atlanta steakhouse. During the course of the meal, Michael asked me, "Bill, are you satisfied with where you are in your career as a philosopher?" I was rather surprised by the question and said, "Well, yes, basically, I guess I am – how about you?" He then related to me that when he was just starting out as a philosopher of science, he was faced with the choice of vigorously pursuing his career or just taking it rather easy. He said that he then thought of the anguished words of the character played by Marlin Brando at the close of the film *On the Waterfront*. "I coulda been a contender!" Michael told me that he decided he didn't want to reach the end of his life and look back in regret and say, "I coulda been a contender!" I was struck by those words. As a Christian I am commanded by the Lord "to contend for the faith that was once for all delivered to the saints" (Jude 3 ESV). But what point is there for an atheist or agnostic to be a "contender" – a contender for what? Since there is no objective purpose in life, the only answer can be, to contend for one's own made-up purposes – hence, the irresistible tendency to treat career advancement and fame as though they really were objectively important ends, when in fact they are nothing.

The Human Predicament

The dilemma of modern man is thus truly terrible. The atheistic worldview is insufficient to maintain a happy and consistent life. Man cannot live consistently and happily as though life were ultimately without meaning, value, or purpose. If we try to live consistently within the framework of the atheistic worldview, we shall find ourselves profoundly unhappy. If instead we manage to live happily, it is only by giving the lie to our worldview.

Confronted with this dilemma, modern man flounders pathetically for some means of escape. In a remarkable address to the American Academy for the Advancement of Science in 1991, Dr. L. D. Rue, confronted with the predicament of modern man, boldly advocated that we deceive ourselves by means of some "Noble Lie" into thinking that we and the universe still have value.[28] Claiming that "the lesson of the past two centuries is that intellectual and moral relativism is profoundly the case," Dr. Rue muses that the consequence of such a realization is that one's quest for personal wholeness (or self-fulfillment) and the quest for social coherence become independent from one another. This is because on the view of relativism the search for self-fulfillment becomes radically privatized: each person chooses his own set of values and meaning. "There is no final, objective reading on the world or the self. There is no universal vocabulary for integrating cosmology and morality." If we are to avoid "the madhouse option," where self-fulfillment is pursued regardless of social coherence, and "the totalitarian option," where social coherence is imposed at the expense of personal wholeness, then we have no choice but to embrace some Noble Lie that will inspire us to live beyond selfish interests and so achieve social coherence. A Noble Lie "is one that deceives us, tricks us, compels us beyond self-interest, beyond ego, beyond family, nation, [and] race." It is a lie, because it tells us that the universe is infused with value (which is a great fiction), because it makes a claim to universal truth (when there is none), and because it tells me not to live for self-interest (which is evidently false). "But without such lies, we cannot live."

This is the dreadful verdict pronounced over modern man. In order to survive, he must live in self-deception. But even the Noble Lie option is in the end unworkable. For if what I have said thus far is correct, belief in a Noble Lie would not only be necessary to achieve social coherence and personal wholeness for the masses, but it would also be necessary to achieve one's *own* personal wholeness. For one cannot live happily and consistently on an atheistic worldview. In order to be happy, one must believe in objective meaning, value, and purpose. But how can one believe in those Noble Lies while at the same time believing in atheism and relativism? The more convinced you are of the necessity of a Noble Lie, the less you are able to believe in it. Like a placebo, a Noble Lie works only on those who believe it is the truth. Once we have seen through the fiction, then the Lie has lost its power over us. Thus, ironically, the Noble Lie cannot solve the human predicament for anyone who has come to see that predicament.

The Noble Lie option therefore leads at best to a society in which an elitist group of *illuminati* deceive the masses for their own good by perpetuating the Noble Lie. But then why should those of us who are enlightened follow the masses in their deception? Why should we sacrifice self-interest for a fiction? If the great lesson of the past two centuries is moral and intellectual relativism, then why (if we could) pretend that we do not know this truth and live a lie instead? If one answers, "for the sake of social coherence," one may legitimately ask why I should sacrifice my self-interest for the sake of social coherence. The only answer the relativist can give is that social coherence is in my self-interest – but the problem with this answer is that self-interest and the interest of the herd do not always coincide. Besides, if (out of self-interest) I do care about social coherence, the totalitarian option is always open to me: forget the Noble Lie and maintain social coherence (as well as my self-fulfillment) at the expense of the personal wholeness of the masses. Generations of Soviet leaders who extolled proletarian virtues while they rode in limousines and dined on caviar in their country *dachas* found this alternative quite workable. Rue would undoubtedly regard such an option as repugnant. But therein lies the rub. Rue's dilemma is that he obviously values deeply both social coherence and personal wholeness for their own sakes; in other words, they are objective values, which according to his philosophy do not exist. He has already leapt to the upper story. The Noble Lie option thus affirms what it denies and so refutes itself.

The success of biblical Christianity

But if atheism fails in this regard, what about biblical Christianity? According to the Christian worldview, God does exist, and man's life does not end at the grave. In the resurrection body man may enjoy eternal life and fellowship with God. Biblical Christianity therefore provides the two conditions necessary for a meaningful, valuable, and purposeful life for man: God and immortality. Because of this, we can live consistently and happily. Thus, biblical Christianity succeeds precisely where atheism breaks down.

Now I want to make it clear that I have not yet shown biblical Christianity to be true. But what I have done is clearly spell out the alternatives. If God does not exist, then life is futile. If the God of the Bible does exist, then life is meaningful. Only the second of these two alternatives enables us to live happily and consistently. Therefore, it seems to me that even if the evidence for these two options were absolutely equal, a rational person ought to choose biblical Christianity. It seems to me positively irrational to prefer death, futility, and destruction to life, meaningfulness, and happiness. As Pascal said, we have nothing to lose and infinity to gain.

Notes

1. The definitive ordering and numbering of these notes is that of Louis Lafuma, and the *Pensées* are cited in reference to the number of each fragment.
2. Blaise Pascal, *Pensées* 29.
3. *Ibid.*, 11.
4. *Ibid.*, 217, 246.
5. *Ibid.*, 343.
6. *Ibid.*
7. In *Major American Poets*, ed. Oscar Williams and Edwin Long (New York: New American Library, 1962), 436.
8. Kai Nielse, "Why Should I Be Moral?" *American Philosophical Quarterly* 21 (1984): 90.
9. Paul Kurtz, *Forbidden Fruit* (Buffalo, N.Y.: Prometheus, 1988), 73.
10. Richard Taylor, *Ethics, Faith, and Reason* (Englewood Cliffs, N.J.: Prentice Hall, 1985), 90, 84.
11. H.G. Wells, *The Time Machine* (New York: Berkeley, 1957), chap. 11.
12. T.S. Eliot, "The Hollow Men," in *Collected Poems 1909–1962* (New York: Harcourt, Brace, Jovanovich, 1934). Reprinted by permission of the publisher.
13. W.E. Hocking, *Types of Philosophy* (New York: Scribner's, 1959), 27.
14. Friedrich Nietzsche, "The Gay Science," in *The Portable Nietzsche*, ed. and trans. W.Kaufmann (New York: Viking, 1954), 95.
15. Friedrich Nietzsche, "The Will to Power," trans. W. Kaufmann, in *Existentialism from Dostoyevsky to Sartre*, 2nd edn., ed. with an introduction by W. Kaufmann (New York: New American Library, Meridian, 1975), 130–31.
16. Bertrand Russell, "A Free Man's Worship," in *Why I Am Not a Christian*, ed. P. Edwards (New York: Simon & Schuster, 1957), 107.
17. Bertrand Russell, Letter to the *Observer*, October 6, 1957.
18. Jean-Paul Sartre, "Portrait of the Antisemite," trans. M. Guiggenheim, in *Existentialism*, 330.
19. Richard Dawkins, *Unweaving the Rainbow* (London: Allen Lane, 1998), cited in Lewis Wolpert, *Six Impossible Things before Breakfast* (London: Faber and Faber, 2006), 215. Unfortunately, Wolpert's reference is mistaken. The quotation seems to be a pastiche from Richard Dawkins, *River Out of Eden: A Darwinian View of Life* (New York: Basic, 1996), 133, and Richard Dawkins, "The Ultraviolet Garden," Lecture 4 of 7 Royal Institution Christmas Lectures (1992), http://physicshead.blogspot.com/2007/01/ richard-dawkins-lecture-4-ultraviolet.html. Thanks to my assistant Joe Gorra for tracking down this reference.
20. Richard Dawkins, *The God Delusion* (New York: Houghton-Mifflin, 2006), 215.
21. *Ibid.*, 221.

22. *Ibid.*, 251.

23. *Ibid.*, 23, 313–17, 326, 328, 330.

24. *Ibid.*, 264.

25. Richard Wurmbrand, *Tortured for Christ* (London: Hodder & Stoughton, 1967), 34.

26. Ernst Bloch, *Das Prinzip Hoffnung*, 2nd edn., 2 vols. (Frankfurt am Main: Suhrkamp Verlag, 1959), 2:360–61.

27. Steven Weinberg, *The First Three Minutes* (London: Andre Deutsch, 1977), 154–5.

28. Loyal D. Rue, "The Saving Grace of Noble Lies," address to the American Academy for the Advancement of Science, February 1991.

2.5

Is Nature Enough?

John Haught

At the beginning of his popular *Cosmos* television series scientist and author Carl Sagan declared that "the universe is all that is, all there ever was and all there ever will be."[1] Sagan was a proponent of *naturalism*, the belief that nothing exists beyond the world available to our senses. There is no God, and hence no creative source of the world's existence other than nature itself. Nature, a term derived from the Latin word "to give birth," is self-generating. Nature is quite enough all by itself, and religions professing belief in God or gods are fictitious distractions at best.

To its adherents naturalism is not only intellectually satisfying but also emotionally liberating. It is a breath of fresh air in a world made stale by the obsessive recitations of religion. Naturalism boldly turns our attention toward the immensities of this world even as it embeds us within the cosmic processes that gave birth to life. It rescues adventurous souls from what they take to be the backwardness, irrelevance and oppressiveness of traditional forms of spirituality. Naturalism also has the advantage – or so it would seem – of being completely reconcilable with science.

Naturalism comes in many flavors, but the focus here will be on the specific variety known as scientific naturalism. Scientific naturalism assumes not only that nature is all there is but also that science is the only reliable way to understand it. This latter belief is commonly called "scientism." Scientism, the epistemic soul of scientific naturalism, claims that the experimental method that came to prominence in the modern period is sufficient to tell us everything factual about the universe. It is convinced that all religious visions of nature and humanity are now superseded by a superior way of understanding. Scientism does not always insist that science will answer every important question, but that it has a

John Haught (2006) "Is Nature Enough?" Chapter 1 in *Is Nature Enough: Meaning and Truth in the Age of Science*, Cambridge: Cambridge University Press, pp. 4–20.

better chance of doing so than religion ever will. According to Richard Dawkins, one of the world's most noteworthy scientific naturalists, "it may be that humanity will never reach the quietus of complete understanding, but if we do, I venture the confident prediction that it will be science, not religion, that brings us there. And if that sounds like scientism, so much the better for scientism."[2]

The label "scientific naturalism" is apparently the invention of Charles Darwin's famous advocate Thomas H. Huxley (1825–95).[3] Although for Huxley scientific naturalism may have been more a method of inquiry than a worldview, this restraint is no longer always present. Today the term "naturalism" refers generally to a worldview that questions the existence of anything in principle inaccessible to ordinary experience or science. In fact, many scientific naturalists are now avowed atheists, although some, like Huxley, prefer to be called agnostics. Scientific naturalists, in any case, question whether complete understanding of the world requires reference to a creator or divine action. It seems more likely to them that nature is its own originator and that natural process is the sole author of life and mind as well. Life appeared by accident, as a purely physical occurrence, and then evolution took over. Random genetic changes, natural selection and an enormous amount of time have been enough to cook up all the diversity and complexity of life, including beings endowed with minds. Why then would reasonable people want to look beyond nature, or resort to theology, in order to understand things and events?

Richard Dawkins, going far beyond Huxley in the defense of naturalism, argues that deep cosmic time and blind evolutionary mechanisms are enough to explain life in all its complexity. In *Climbing Mount Improbable* the renowned evolutionist cleverly pictures life on earth as having made its way up a figurative mountain of time. On one side the mountain rises straight up from the plain below, while on the other it slopes gently from bottom to top. It is up the sloped side that life has made its long evolutionary ascent. If life had available to it only a biblical time-slot of several thousand years to mount the vertical side, a miraculous boost would have been needed to produce anything as complex as the eye or human brain so quickly. Natural explanations therefore would not be enough. But if the story of life in fact takes place very gradually, on a path moving back and forth up the gentler slope incrementally over a period of four billion years, then no supernatural assistance is required. Minute changes, together with the relentless weeding out of nonadaptive variations by natural selection in the course of *deep time*, are enough to account for the extraordinary variety and complexity of life. Nature, it would appear, is quite enough.[4] […]

I want to emphasize, that scientific naturalism is not by any means the same thing as science. Science is a fruitful but self-limiting way of learning some things about the world, whereas scientific naturalism is a worldview that goes far beyond verifiable knowledge by insisting on the explanatory adequacy of scientific method. Most reflective scientific naturalists will concede that they are indeed advocating a certain kind of belief, but they would add that their understanding of the world is still much more reasonable and fertile than any others. Indeed, for many inquirers today, scientific naturalism is the undebatable starting point for all reliable knowledge of anything whatsoever.

But does scientific naturalism hold up under careful scrutiny? I shall not be challenging science itself as a *method* of investigating the universe. As far as science itself is concerned, nature is indeed all there is. I agree with scientific naturalists that one should never introduce ideas about God, "intelligent design" or divine action into scientific work itself. As a theologian, I am happy to accept methodological naturalism as the way science works. But suppose there are dimensions of reality that science cannot reach. If there are, then scientific naturalism – the belief that scientifically knowable nature alone is real – is unreasonable since it arbitrarily cuts off access to any such precincts. And if scientific naturalism turns out to be at bottom an irrational set of beliefs, then the universe available to science may not be "all that is, all there ever was, or all there ever will be."

In addition to science there are other reliable ways of putting our minds, and hearts too, in touch with the real world. There may even be deep layers of the real world that we can see or encounter only by cultivating modes of exploration and cognitional habits that are not opposed to science but that are not themselves part of science. Is it possible that religion, even with all its perplexity and failings, still provides at least a dimly lit passage into depths of reality unapproachable by science?

Is Naturalism Spiritually Adequate?

There are, as I have noted, different kinds of naturalism. For example, one may distinguish between hard naturalism and soft naturalism.[5] Hard naturalism is roughly equivalent to scientific materialism. It rules out the existence of anything nonphysical. Soft naturalism, on the other hand, allows that there may be aspects of the real world that hard naturalism leaves out. It proposes that nature consists of complex systems and organic wholes that cannot be accounted for exclusively in terms of their physical antecedents or atomic components. It suggests that "emergent" rules come into play spontaneously as the universe evolves in complexity. Yet these new ordering principles are in no way mystical or in need of theological explanation. They are simply phases of natural process.

A few soft naturalists like to be called *religious* naturalists. Religious naturalists do not believe that anything exists beyond the world of nature, but they often use religious terminology – words such as mystery and sacred – to express their sense that nature by itself is deserving of a reverential surrender of the mind.[6] Still, even to religious naturalists nature is all that exists. In philosophical discourse today the term "naturalism" generally signifies a godless view of the universe. For example, when the philosopher Owen Flanagan states that the mission of contemporary philosophy is to make the world safe for "naturalism," he clearly means safe for atheism.[7] More often than not the term "naturalism" entails the explicit rejection of the personal God of Judaism. Christianity and Islam. It means the denial of any sacred principle of being that is distinct from nature itself.[8]

There are still other ways of understanding naturalism, but most of them adhere minimally to the following core teachings:[9]

1. Outside nature, which includes human and their cultural creations, there is nothing.
2. It follows from #1 that nature is self-originating.
3. Since there is nothing beyond nature, there can be no overarching purpose or transcendent goal that would give any lasting meaning to the universe.

4. There is no such thing as the "soul," and no reasonable prospect of conscious human survival beyond death.
5. The emergence of life and mind in evolution was accidental and unintended.

What I am calling "scientific naturalism" accepts these five tenets, but adds two more:

6. Every natural event is itself the product of other natural events. Since there is no divine cause, all causes must be purely natural causes, in principle accessible to scientific comprehension.
7. All the various features of living beings, including humans, can be explained ultimately in evolutionary, specifically Darwinian, terms. I shall often refer to this belief as "evolutionary naturalism."

From now on I shall use the labels "naturalism" and "scientific naturalism" interchangeably unless otherwise indicated.

As I said earlier, I want to ask whether naturalism is a reasonable set of beliefs. Before beginning my reply to this question, however, I need to raise another. It concerns naturalism's *spiritual* adequacy. Can naturalism respond fully, in other words, to the human quest for meaning? Not all naturalists would consider this to be a relevant question, but it needs to be asked since they themselves sometimes claim that nature is quite enough to give our lives meaning as well as intellectual satisfaction.[10] Consort with nature, they insist, is *spiritually* adequate for humans. Some of the most entrenched naturalists now admit that we humans possess ineradicably spiritual instincts as part of our genetic endowment. That is, we are meaning-seeking beings designed by evolution to seek communion with what is larger than ourselves. Our spiritual instincts need to be satisfied, and that is why our species has been so stubbornly religious, perhaps from the very beginning of the human journey on earth. So why cannot naturalism, a full-fledged belief system of its own, satisfy our native religious cravings for fulfillment? Is not nature itself resourceful enough to bring meaning, happiness and personal satisfaction to our brief life spans? Many naturalists, I have observed, are passionately religious, and their disillusionment with traditional creeds is often the expression of an abundance, not an absence, of spiritual longing.

Within the assembly of naturalists, however, some are sunny and optimistic – these are the religious naturalists – while others are more sober and pessimistic. Sunny naturalists hold that nature's overwhelming beauty, the excitement of human creativity, the struggle to achieve ethical goodness, the prospect of loving and being loved, the exhilaration of scientific discovery – these are enough to fill a person's life. There is simply no good reason to look beyond nature for spiritual contentment. Sober naturalists, on the other hand, are not so sanguine. They agree that nature is all there is, but for them nature is *not* resourceful enough to satisfy the voracious human hunger for meaning and happiness. In fact, they say, our species' religious appetites can never be satisfied since the finite universe is devoid of any discernible meaning, as cosmology and Darwinian science both now seem to confirm. If the universe is all there is, and if it is therefore devoid of purpose, then one must conclude that nature is *not enough* to fill our restless human hearts with the meaning we long for.

A literate representative of sober naturalism is the French writer Albert Camus. This famous novelist and philosopher freely acknowledges that humans have an insatiable appetite for ultimate meaning and eternal happiness. It would be dishonest, he says, to deny it. The hard fact, however, is that the universe can never satisfy such a craving. Eventually the world and each of us will end up in complete annihilation. If death is the final destination of all life, and if God and immortality do not exist – as for Camus they do not – then reality is absurd. Absurdity here means the incongruous union of a death-dealing universe on the one hand and the human passion for life on the other. Since these two sectors of reality will never mesh, their fatal conjunction is the very definition of irrationality. Moreover, no hope can ever surmount this situation. Hence the hero of the human condition is Sisyphus, the exemplar of all striving in the face of futility.[11]

A more scientific representative of sober naturalism is the physicist Steven Weinberg. In *Dreams of a Final Theory* he writes:

> It would be wonderful to find in the laws of nature a plan prepared by a concerned creator in which human beings played some special role. I find sadness in doubting that we will. There are some among my scientific colleagues who say that the contemplation of nature gives them all the spiritual satisfaction that others have found in a belief in an interested God. Some of them may even feel that way. I do not.[12]

Like Camus, Weinberg takes seriously the question of God, and he is distressed that science has made atheism the only reasonable option today. Science provides no evidence of a purposeful universe, so the most one can salvage from our unhappy predicament is a sense of honor in facing up to the finality of tragedy.[13] Weinberg wants nothing to do with sunny naturalism and its shallow compromises with the bitter truth of our actual situation.

Were I to become a naturalist I confess that I would have to side, simply for the sake of logic, with the sober rather than the sunny version. Sober naturalism is at least less cavalier about what all naturalists must acknowledge to be the ultimate truth about the universe and the human condition. As far as naturalism can tell, after all, science has shown the universe to be devoid of meaning. Is it candid, the sober naturalist asks, to pretend that humans could ever find lasting personal fulfillment in a pointless cosmos? If the option were forced, should not a concern for intellectual integrity lead one to take sides with the tragic realism of Camus and Weinberg rather than the groundless optimism of the more sprightly variety of naturalism? Fortunately, as I shall argue at length, there is a reasonable alternative to both sober and sunny naturalism.

The fact that naturalism is spiritually disproportionate to the fact of tragedy, of course, does not make it untrue. Let us concede for the moment that the tenets of naturalism listed above are indeed accurate. But if they are, then the philosopher John Hick is correct in pointing out that naturalism "is very bad news for humanity as a whole."[14] The physical pain, poverty and unbearable suffering of most people throughout history keep them from ever fulfilling their hopes within the limits of nature alone. "Even those who have lived the longest can seldom be said to have arrived, before they die, at a fulfillment of their potential." Naturalists, therefore, are hiding from the truth unless "they acknowledge the fact that naturalism is not good news for much of humanity."[15]

Hick is convinced that, whatever their truth-status, the classic religious traditions can rightly claim to respond to the deepest spiritual aspirations of people:

> We human beings are for so much of the time selfish, narrow-minded, emotionally impoverished, unconcerned about others, often vicious and cruel, but according to the great religions there are wonderfully better possibilities concealed within us … We see around us the different levels that the human spirit has reached, and we know… that the generality of us have a very long way to go before we can be said to have become fully human. But if the naturalistic picture is correct, this can never happen. For according to naturalism, the evil that has afflicted so much of human life is final and irrevocable as the victims have ceased to exist.[16]

Naturalists, therefore, need to be rigorously honest:

> [they] ought frankly to acknowledge that if they are right the human situation is irredeemably bleak and painful for vast numbers of people. For – if they are right – in the case of that innumerable multitude whose quality of life has been rendered predominantly negative by pain, anxiety, extreme deprivation, oppression, or whose lives have been cut off in childhood or youth, there is no chance of ever participating in an eventual fulfillment of the human potential. There is no possibility of this vast century-upon-century tragedy being part of a much larger process which leads ultimately to limitless good.[17]

Is Naturalism Reasonable?

Even if naturalism turns out to be spiritually inadequate, however, this alone does not make it untrue, as Hick would surely agree. But is naturalism true? That is, does it meet the human mind's best standards of understanding and knowing? Can naturalism, even in principle, ever provide an ultimately satisfying framework for making sense of every natural occurrence? Or does human reason have to appeal, at some point in its attempt to make *complete* sense of things, to something deeper than the natural world itself, something beyond the ambience of science?

Are naturalistic explanations ever going to be enough to explain *ultimately* why the universe would give rise to life, mind, ethics, religion and scientific inquiry? Granted, science can say a lot about all of these, but can it say everything? Can one ever be certain that all causes are natural causes? Can science, for example, explain why there is anything at all rather than nothing? Even the astronomer Martin Rees, a devotee of scientific naturalism, places this big question outside the competence of science.[18] If there is nothing that lies beyond or deeper than the scientifically accessible world, then of course natural causes would be the ultimate and exhaustive explanation of everything. Scientific understanding would then amount to final or ultimate enlightenment. There would be no logical space left for theological interpretations of reality, and theology would stand in a competitive relationship to science. In such a set of circumstances it would be best for theology to fade away for good, an outcome that many naturalists fervently desire.

Fortified by the success of science, contemporary naturalists are confident that we can discover in nature alone the sufficient explanation of everything. Life can be completely broken down into chemical terms. Mind is the outcome of natural selection (Cziko). Language (Pinker), ethics (Ruse and Wilson) and even religion (Hinde, Boyer, Atran) can be understood fully in naturalistic terms.[19] Given the fact that naturalists deny the existence of anything other than nature, they are compelled logically to maintain that natural causes provide the final explanation of everything, including intellectual, ethical and religious phenomena. But can naturalism give an ultimate explanation of anything, let alone everything?

Many evolutionists think it can. Today naturalistic confidence flourishes especially among Darwinians. Evolutionary naturalists are certain that the neo-Darwinian recipe – random (contingent) genetic changes (and other natural accidents) plus natural selection, along with a considerable amount of time to experiment – can account entirely for all the features of living beings. Is this confidence justifiable? As a theologian I am eager to have science push evolutionary understanding as far as it can legitimately go. And I agree that evolutionary science has to be an aspect of every serious attempt to understand life, consciousness, ethics and even religion. But are evolutionary explanations enough?

For example, beneath life's evolution there is the larger universe that consists of an exquisite blend of contingent unpredictability, lawful necessity and eons of time, features of nature that Darwinism appeals to but does not and cannot account for by itself. Life's evolution jumps astride this foundational cosmic mix. The essential ingredients for evolution had been laid out on the cosmic table long before life began to stew. Darwinism presupposes a specific cosmic setting, but it does not provide the grounds for it. The physical sciences may have something to say about this cosmic tableau, of course, but even after they are finished, the question will still remain: why is the universe such an exciting, adventurous mix of contingency, predictability and temporality that it can give rise to an evolutionary story at all? Why does the world remain open constantly to a new future? Why does it give rise to subjectivity, feeling and striving? Why does it eventually give birth to an insatiable passion for knowledge? And, of course, why does nature exist at all? Perhaps theology may have at least something to say in response to these questions without in the slightest way interfering or competing with scientific inquiry.

Darwinian naturalists, of course, will protest. Before Darwin came along appeals to theology might have been excusable, they admit, but does not evolutionary biology now provide science with the tools to get to the *ultimate* explanation of living phenomena without having to take flight into the superlunary world of religious understanding?

We shall see. But before going any further, I hope we may at least agree that in the final analysis there can be only one *ultimate* explanation of anything, whereas there can be many intermediate or secondary explanations. Darwinian explanations, I will argue, are intermediate, not ultimate. Naturalists put too heavy a burden on evolutionary science whenever they turn it into ultimate explanation. What I shall propose instead, as a way of giving a place to both science and religion, is *layered explanation*. By this I mean that everything in the universe is open to a plurality of levels of explanation. The alternative to layered explanation, or to explanatory pluralism, is explanatory monism, an approach dear to the heart of most naturalists.

Here is an example of what I mean by layered explanation. Suppose that a wood fire is burning in your backyard. Your neighbor comes over and asks you to explain why the fire is burning. A very good response would be: it is burning because the carbon in the wood is combining with oxygen to make carbon dioxide. This is an acceptable explanation, and for a certain kind of inquiry it is enough. Still, there can be other levels of explanation. For example, you might just as easily have answered your neighbor's question by saying: the fire is burning because I lit a match to it.

And a third answer might be: "The fire is burning because I want to roast marshmallows." Different levels of explanation, as is evident here, can coexist without conflict. "I want to roast marshmallows" does not in any way compete with physical explanations of the burning wood. I do not respond to my neighbor: "The fire is burning because of chemical combustion *rather than* because I want marshmallows." "I want to roast marshmallows," in fact, cannot be squeezed into the explanatory slot that focuses on the chemistry of combustion. And yet, there is no inherent contradiction between the chemistry of combustion and my overarching purpose of wanting something to eat.

Analogously, let us suppose that there is an ultimate reality which for some mysterious reason wants to create a life-bearing universe. We should not expect this divine intentionality to show up within a physical analysis of nature – including scientific speculations on the Big Bang and the origin of life – any more than we should expect to find "I want marshmallows" inscribed on the burning wood or molecules of carbon dioxide. And yet, it is just such direct "evidence" that scientific naturalists almost invariably demand from those who adopt a theological understanding of the universe. The usual reason naturalists give for their opposition to theology is that there is no "evidence" to support the latter's claims. The assumption is that if there were a deeper than natural explanation, it would still have to be *scientifically* available. And since it does not show up at that layer of explanation, it must not exist. Underlying this judgment, of course, is the more fundamental naturalistic assumption that there is really only a single legitimate explanatory slot available, one carved out to fit the contours of scientific method. So, if scientific discoveries now fill this niche, there is no room left over for theology.

Reasonable theology, however, allows for many layers of explanation. It argues that divine action or divine creativity stands in relation to nature – to such occurrences as the emergence of the cosmos, life, mind, ethics and religion – analogously to the way in which "I want marshmallows" stands in relation to the chemistry of burning firewood. [...] It is not a case of God *rather than* nature. It is both. The ultimate explanation of natural phenomena will necessarily be hidden from view when science is focusing on physical explanations. Analogously, even the most painstaking investigation of the molecular movement in the fire will not reveal, at that physical level of scrutiny, the "ultimate" reason why the fire is burring. Likewise, even the most detailed scientific examination of natural processes may not be able to discover, nor indeed rule out, any more profound reason why the universe, life, mind, language, ethics, religion and scientific inquiry have come into existence. There is still plenty of room, logically speaking, for a theological understanding of the natural world alongside scientific accounts.

Of course, the naturalist will immediately reply that my desire for marshmallows can also be accounted for fully in terms of the mindless chemistry that underlies my brain and nervous system. For many a naturalist there can be only one level of explanation, and it must be purely physical at bottom. If this were the case, however, there would be no reason to take the criticism seriously, emanating as it does ultimately from the allegedly mindless physical causes that underlie the brain of my critic. The naturalistic view of reality, if taken consistently, leads to the self-subverting of all truth claims, including those of science.

My wager, then, is that adequate explanation runs endlessly deep and involves many levels. No one science, or even the whole set of sciences, can ever comprehend the rich *totality* of causal ingredients that underlie each cosmic event. Every branch of science, after all, works on the tacit premise that it does not have to account fully for everything. Each field of scientific inquiry, for the sake of clarity, has to leave something out. In fact, the individual sciences can reach toward exactness only by *abstracting from* most of nature's causal depth. The real world is fuzzy and indistinct, so achieving Cartesian clarity in scientific thinking is not a sign that one has arrived at deep understanding.[20] Conversely, the deepest explanations – precisely because they leave less out – will inevitably be the least clear and distinct. This is why theological explanations will always have a vagueness that frustrates the scientific naturalist.

Naturalism (once again, a term that I am using interchangeably with "scientific naturalism" typically insists that ultimate explanation be clear and distinct. In doing so, its devotees often appeal to the idea of Occam's razor, which asserts that explanations should not be multiplied without necessity. Accordingly, since Darwin's recipe can explain life, mind, behavior, language, ethics, religion, and so on, simply in terms of natural selection, the naturalist declares that there no need to appeal to the obscure notion of an unseen divine creativity or purposiveness in order to make ultimate sense of these fascinating developments.

The promise of explaining all the great "mysteries" of life in terms of the economical notion of reproductive success is hard to resist. It has led to the cult of "universal Darwinism" and the belief that natural selection is the bottommost foundation of all the manifestations of life. This exclusionary singleness of mind, however, may be compared to explaining the fire in my backyard by leaving out as completely irrelevant the fact that "I want marshmallows." If we can reach a *simpler* explanation at the level of the fire's chemistry, why bring in the fuzzy idea that I would like something to eat? If one can explain why we have ears, eyes and brains in terms of natural selection, why bring up the possibility that a transcendent creative principle of care wants the universe to become sensitive, conscious and responsive? Would not such a proposal violate Occam's razor?

Occam's razor, I must point out, was never intended to suppress layered explanation as such, even though this is exactly how naturalists often tend to slice up the world with it. If life were as simple as evolutionary naturalists think it is, then of course Darwinian explanation would be adequate. Theological explanations of life would be superfluous. But William of Occam said that explanations should not be multiplied *unless they are necessary*. Sometimes multiple layers of explanation are necessary for deep understanding. So there is no justification, either in Occam's maxim or in science itself, for arbitrarily closing off the road to explanatory depth.

[…] [T]he human mind must look beyond nature, as understood by science, in order to make *ultimate* sense of the world and ourselves. It is not the business of science, but of theology (or religious thought in a broader sense) to look for ultimate explanations.

Notes

1. Carl Sagan, *Cosmos* (New York: Ballantine Books, 1985), p. 1. An earlier version of my reflections on Sagan's claim appears in "Is Nature Enough? No," *Zygon: Journal of Science and Religion* 38 (December, 2003), 769–82.

2. Richard Dawkins, "The Science of Religion and the Religion of Science," *Tanner Lecture on Human Value at Harvard University* (November 20, 2003). Cited on the *Science and Theology* website: http://www.stnews.org/archives/2004_february/web_x_richard.html.

3. Ronald Numbers, "Science without God: Natural Laws and Christian Belief," in *When Science and Christianity Meet*, edited by David C. Lindberg and Ronald Numbers (Chicago: University of Chicago Press, 2003), p. 266.

4. Richard Dawkins, *Climbing Mount Improbable* (New York: W. W. Norton & Co., 1996), pp. 3–37.

5. Holmes Rolston, III, *Science and Religion: a Critical Survey* (New York: Random House), pp. 247–58.

6. Ursula Goodenough, *The Sacred Depths of Nature* (New York: Oxford University Press, 1998); Chet Raymo, *Skeptics and True Believers: the Exhilarating Connection between Science and Religion* (New York: Walker and Company, 1998). There are also soft forms of naturalism that seek an alliance with theistic religion. See, for example, David R. Griffin, *Reenchantment without Supernaturalism: a Process Philosophy of Religion* (Ithaca, N. Y.: Cornell University Press, 2001).

7. Owen Flanagan, *The Problem of the Soul: Two Visions of Mind and How to Reconcile Them* (New York: Basic Books, 2002), pp. 167–8.

8. This is the sense in which C. S. Lewis, for instance, understands naturalism in his passionate critique of it in *Miracles* (San Francisco: HarperSanFrancisco, 2001).

9. This is an adaptation and expansion of Charley Hardwick's understanding of naturalism in *Events of Grace: Naturalism, Existentialism, and Theology* (Cambridge: Cambridge University Press, 1996).

10. See, for example, Flanagan, *The Problem of the Soul* and Goodenough, *The Sacred Depths of Nature*.

11. Albert Camus, *The Myth of Sisyphus, and Other Essays*, translated by Justin O'Brien (New York: Knopf, 1955), pp. 88–91.

12. Steven Weinberg, *Dreams of a Final Theory* (New York: Pantheon Books, 1992), p. 256.

13. *Ibid.*, pp. 255, 260.

14. John Hick, *The Fifth Dimension: an Exploration of the Spiritual Realm* (Oxford: Oneworld Press, 1999), p. 22.

15. *Ibid.*, p. 24.

16. *Ibid.*

17. *Ibid.*, pp. 24–5.

18. Martin Rees, *Our Cosmic Habitat* (Princeton: Princeton University Press, 2003), p. xi.

19. Gary Cziko, *Without Miracles: Universal Selection Theory and the Second Darwinian Revolution* (Cambridge, Mass.: MIT Press, 1995); Steven Pinker, *The Blank Slate: the Modern Denial of Human Nature* (New York: Viking 2002); Michael Ruse and Edward O. Wilson, "The Evolution of Ethics," in *Religion and the Natural Sciences*, edited by James Huchingson (New York: Harcourt Brace Jovanovich, 1993), pp. 308–11; Robert Hinde, *Why Gods Persist: a Scientific Approach to Religions* (New York: Routledge, 1999); Pascal Boyer, *Religion Explained: the Evolutionary Origins of Religious Thought* (New York: Basic Books, 2001); Scott Atran, *In Gods We Trust: the Evolutionary Landscape of Religion* (New York: Oxford University Press, 2002).

20. Alfred North Whitehead, *Process and Reality, corrected edition*, edited by David Ray Griffin and Donald W. Sherburne (New York: The Free Press, 1978), p. 173.

2.6

Religion and Value
The Problem of Heteronomy

John Cottingham

> *Frate, la nostra volontà quieta*
> *virtù di carità, che fa volerne*
> *sol quel ch'avemo, e d'altro no ci asseta . . .*
> *Anzi è formale ad esto beato esse*
> *tenersi dentro a la divina voglia . . .*
> *E'n la sua volontade è nostra pace*
> Brother, our Will can find tranquillity
> Through that true love which makes us to desire
> No more than what we have, nor thirst for more . . .
> And blessedness, for any creature, lies
> In keeping fast within the will of God . . .
> And in His will alone our peace belongs.
>
> Dante Alighieri.[1]

1   Submission to God: An Obsolete Ideal?

Dante's famous lines follow a long religious tradition in seeing submission to the will of God as representing the deepest fulfilment for the human spirit. The thought is not just that religious devotion provides peacefulness of mind, in the sense of securing some kind of tranquillizing or calming effect; rather, the idea is that God is the source of genuine value, and that orienting ourselves towards that source bestows meaning on our human existence and enables us to find true contentment. In the striking words of Augustine, of which

John Cottingham (2006) "Religion and Value: The Problem of Heteronomy," Chapter 3 in *The Spiritual Dimension: Religion, Philosophy and Human Value*, New York: Cambridge University Press, pp. 37–57.

Dante's lines are a clear echo, 'You have made us for Yourself, and our heart is restless until it finds repose in You.'[2]

Yet although this notion is a familiar one, it is not without its difficulties. First, from a metaphysical point of view, one may ask exactly what is involved in the idea of God's being the *source* of meaning and value. We all want our lives to have significance and to be of value, but one might think that these are properties which have to be earned, as it were, by our own efforts, rather than being in the gift of an external power, even a divine one. Are significance and goodness the kinds of property that can be *bestowed* on something, just like that? One might suppose, instead, that if something is meaningful or valuable, it must be meaningful or valuable for a *reason* or *reasons*; and if meaning and value are rationally based in this way, if they arise in virtue of features that make it rational for us to judge a life good or significant, then they are properties that cannot be created by fiat, even divine fiat. So, notwithstanding Dante's resonant phrase, it seems that conformity with the will of God cannot merely of itself be enough to confer meaning and value on our lives.

Even if this metaphysical tangle can be sorted out [...] there seems to be a second, moral, problem with the idea of conformity with God's will as the key to a meaningful and valuable life. Even granting that God somehow functions as an external source of meaning and value, one may ask whether it is consistent with our human dignity and autonomy that we should submit ourselves to his will in the manner envisaged by Augustine and Dante. Are we talking of blind obedience, of the kind of 'humble duty' that a subject was in times past thought to owe to an absolute monarch? This does not on reflection seem a very compelling model for a good and meaningful life; on the contrary, it seems more like an abdication or resigning of responsibility into the hands of another. Just as large sections of the human race pride themselves on having come of age politically, of having freed themselves from subservience to monarchs, so one might think a mature religious sensibility can no longer work with the Dante-esque model of submission to the divine will.

It is certainly the case that if one looks at some of the traditional language of prayer one finds an attitude of self-effacement that borders on the servile. The language of the *Book of Common Prayer* for example, takes us into a sixteenth-century world of absolute monarchs, of subjects offering their duty to rulers whose power is taken to be beyond scrutiny or criticism. 'O Almighty God ... whose power no creature is able to resist, to whom it belongeth justly to punish sinners ... save and deliver us we humbly beseech thee.' And not merely the petitions, but even the thanksgivings have the same note of abject self-abasement: "We thine unworthy servants do give thee most humble and hearty thanks.'[3] In the political arena, we would nowadays find such language totally unacceptable – though an exception, apparently palatable to some, is the quaint ritual in which the British constitution still enshrouds itself, as one sees, for example, in the wording of the traditional motion for debate following the Queen's speech that opens a new legislative session of Parliament:

> Most gracious Sovereign: We, Your Majesty's most dutiful and loyal subjects, the Commons of the United Kingdom of Great Britain and Northern Ireland in Parliament assembled, beg leave to offer our humble thanks to Your Majesty for the Gracious Speech which Your Majesty has addressed to both Houses of Parliament.

Droll perhaps, but if taken seriously it might reasonably call forth the rebuke that this is no way for a responsible legislative body to conceive of itself. Their job is not to grovel, but to exercise their autonomous powers of critical judgment.

But what of the religious person's attitude to the will of God? The feminist theologian Daphne Hampson argues in her recent study *After Christianity* that a similarly suspect self-effacement infects the very structure of Judaeo-Christian religion:

> Within the Judaeo-Christian tradition … the relationship of God is at least potentially heteronomous, such that the human must be obedient to what he or she conceives to be God's will, rather than obeying his or her own conscience.[4]

And again:

> [The Lord's prayer] opens by addressing God as 'father'; the term used is that by which the head of the family was designated in what was a deeply patriarchal society. Our mind is directed not to ourselves but to God. 'He' is conceived to be in heaven, a reality both other than ours and which transcends ours. 'He' is addressed as one would address a sovereign. Christians pray that 'his' kingdom come, 'his' will be done; not that their will should be realised.[5]

To digress for a moment to consider the specifically feminist tone of this critique, it seems fairly uncontroversial that the language of Christianity bears traces of the patriarchal soil from which it sprung. But is not my concern here, even were I competent to do so, to try to assess the extent to which the masculinism is an inherent part of the underlying religious outlook, or only, as it were, part of its cultural expression. C. S. Lewis was one who quite happily embraced the former view, believing that the masculinity of God is absolutely central to Christianity – though his reasons can sometimes appear a little thin: 'only one wearing the masculine uniform can … represent the Lord to the Church; for we are all, corporately and individually, feminine to him'.[6] The idea here seems to be that we need to recognize the active nature of divine creative power in relation to the passiveness or receptivity of creation and the Church; but expressing this thought in terms of the essential *masculinity* of the creator seems to reflect more than a trace of the old Aristotelian biology that takes procreation to involve a toti-potent male seed, with the female component being relegated to that of mere passive receptor. Given that modern micro-biology has long shown such a model to be inaccurate, one might think it makes a somewhat shaky basis for inferring supposedly eternal truths about the nature of divine creativity.

Matters of gender aside, does the addressing of God as a parent put the worshipper into a suspect and heteronomous relationship with the deity in the way Hampson suggests? The analogy of parenthood, it might be said, implies an inherent dependency: the child's relationship to the parent is not that of equal to equal. But as soon as we reflect further, this starts to look like an over-simplification, based, as it were, on a snapshot taken at a particular phase of the child–parent relation. If we look at the phenomenon of parenthood as it actually operates, then to say that X is related to Y as offspring to parent does not imply a fixed and static hierarchy, but points instead to a dynamic relationship that unfolds over time. X begins, to be sure, as an infant, utterly dependent for nutrition and protection on a being of superior wisdom and strength. But as X grows, on any minimally plausible understanding of the obligations of parenthood, it is Y's job to work towards the progressive elimination of the dependency. 'Love is proved in the letting go', says the final line of a fine poem by the other Lewis – C. Day Lewis:

> That hesitant figure, eddying way
> Like a winged seed loosened from its parent's stem
> Was something I never quite grasp to convey
> About nature's give and take, the small, the scorching
> Ordeals which fire one's irresolute clay.
> I've had worse partings but none that so
> Gnaws at my mind still. Perhaps it is roughly
> Saying what God alone could perfectly show –
> How selfhood begins with a walking away
> And love is proved in the letting go.[7]

What this idea implies in not just that a good parent stands back, forbearing to control and dominate, but, more than that, that the very goal of parenthood is to let the child grow to the status of an independent being. The telos, the crown, of the parental relationship is the future hoped-for state when the child itself achieves the status of adulthood, and converses with the parent as an independent being.

2   Autonomy and Dependency

The paradox of our humanity is that we oscillate between two poles: on the one side our contingency and dependency, and on the other our aspiration to independence and autonomy. The admission of dependency which Hampson so dislikes in the Lord's Prayer is simply a religious expression of something fundamental to what it is to be human. For *pace* the existentialists, we are *not* self-creating beings: our fulfilment hinges on a nature and a context we did not create, and cannot radically change. Today's fashionable talk about 'life-style choices' often seems to gloss over this central truth – indeed the legitimate scope of our choice is taken by some to embrace even the supposed 'self-assignments' of gender and bodily appearance that are made possible by modern plastic surgery. But one does not need to pass judgement one way or the other on these costly attempts at self-recreation with the aid of the surgeon's knife in order to believe that there will always remain (irrespective of gender and appearance) an essential structure to our humanity, not of our making, which has to be accepted, like it or not, if we are to function as human beings in the first place. It is *hubris* to think that we can rewrite these fundamental rules – for example the rules of love and vulnerability that determine what we can achieve in relationship to our fellow humans. We can try to force things our way, to demand, to insist, to reject, to rant and rail, but ultimately we can only achieve our goals by conforming to the laws of love: give, not take, fellow-feeling not arrogance, patience not grasping, waiting not insisting. These laws are written deep in our nature as moral beings; and the submission to them which is encapsulated in religious expressions such as 'Thy will be done' is not some strange self-abasement before an alien will, but an expression of objective moral realities to which, like it or not, our lives must conform if they are to flourish.

Despite the phrase 'like it or not', it is important to stress that our relationship to these realities is not one of the animal who is forced by bit and spur to conform to what it cannot properly understand. The other pole of our humanity is our reason, our autonomy (in the sense of our free power of decision-making). It is a complete misunderstanding to suppose that the religious stance – 'Thy will be done' – involves a servile submission to an alien power.[8] The Will that is held up as our destiny is the kind of will that a human parent has for a child – a will that envisages not conformity but open-ended growth. A familiar contrast between the kind of moral teleology that applies to a rational as opposed to a non-rational being may serve to bring out the point. The oak tree or the horse glorifies God – in secular terms, moves towards the perfection of its kind – simply by unfolding its determined nature. The full-grown flourishing oak, stretching out its branches and clothed in the vivid green of high summer, achieves all it is, all it can be, just by being a complete and perfect specimen of its kind; and so for the horse, galloping across the prairie in the full exultant prime of its strength and health: nothing more is needed. But the human is unique in that it cannot glorify God, it cannot achieve the perfection of its kind, just by being a healthy specimen of the species.[9] We need, as the religious mode has it, to complete the work of creation:[10] our autonomy, our rationality, inescapably require us to do something more with our lives, to grow, to learn, not just physically but intellectually and aesthetically and morally, to orient ourselves progressively and ever more closely towards the true, the beautiful, and the good. None of this is a sacrifice of our autonomy properly understood: rather it is its culmination.

The suggestion that the religious ideal of submission to God's will is compatible with the ideal of autonomy is obviously a controversial one. The term 'autonomy' has a long and complex history which there is no space to explore here, other than to draw attention to one particular ambiguity in use of the term: the autonomous person may be construed as either (a) the entirely 'self-legislating' being, who makes up his own rules by a completely independent act of will, subject to no constraints whatsoever – this may be thought of as the extreme existentialist interpretation; or (b) the being who makes decisions independently of the arbitrary will of another, acting in the full light of reason, free from internal or external interference with her rational processes. It is this second sense that I am employing when I speak here of 'autonomy properly understood'. On this account, to act autonomously is to act rationally and freely; and this seems quite compatible with the religious thought that in making my decisions I have to acknowledge that I live in a world I did not create, which contains other free and rational creatures who are entitled to equal respect with me, and that, whether I like it or not, these facts impose constraints on how I may or may not properly exercise my choice.[11]

Iris Murdoch writes: 'How recognizable, how familiar to us, is the man so beautifully portrayed in the *Grundlegung* who, confronted even with Christ, turns away to consider the judgment of his own conscience and to hear the voice of his own reason … this man is with us still, free, independent, lonely, powerful, rational, responsible, brave, the hero of so many novels and books of moral philosophy.'[12] But this noble Kantian vision, properly understood, is not in conflict with the religious vision of our human destiny, but rather is integral to it.[13] The whole history of humankind's religious journey is not, as some critics of theism like to portray it, one of submissive deference to alien authority; rather it is the story of progressive moral growth. The ancient story of Abraham and Isaac (despite Kierkegaard's famous interpretation of Abraham's faith as involving a 'suspension of the ethical'),[14] is perhaps best interpreted not so much as an abject subordination of the will as a progression beyond the dark atavistic imperative of human sacrifice to something more morally enlightened – or at least a lesser evil (the substitution of a ram); later there will be an even more enlightened shift, away from blood sacrifice entirely to the moral conduct that alone is acceptable to God: 'I desire mercy not sacrifice'.[15]

The creative power of God need not foreclose a creature's autonomy, provided the latter term is properly understood – not as subscribing to the dangerous fantasy of total independence, as if we could map out our lives from scratch, but rather as the free and unfettered use of our powers of critical reason. Consider an analogy with how we exercise our independent powers of reason in investigating the physical creation. The theistic claim that the source of the physical cosmos is God does not absolve the scientist from responsibility to use her reason to assess what the cosmos is like. ('It says so in Scripture' is never a good reason for adopting a particular scientific hypothesis.) And similarly for the 'moral creation'. If God has laid down an objective moral order, we still have to use our critical rational powers to determine what it is, and how we should act. 'It says so in Scripture' is never a good reason for following a course of action, nor, *pace* her detractors, need the religious adherent ever think this way. 'Thy will be done' is a way of focusing on the objective moral order towards which our lives need to be oriented if they are to have value and meaning. And the prayer is not to lose sight of that order in some blind act of servility but rather to remain in touch with that order, and to ask that it may be fulfilled in our lives.

3   The Metaphysics of Value

I want to turn to the metaphysical puzzle to which I alluded at the outset – the puzzle of explicating the sense in which God is thought of by the religious adherent as the source of value and meaning in human life.

A familiar objection to the religious position is that it is repugnant to say that God's commands create value. If God's will is simply the will of a powerful being who controls our lives, then this cannot of itself give us *reason* to conform to his will (that is, a moral reason, as opposed to a merely prudential consideration). If God's commands are *worthy* of our obedience, then this must be because they are good. But this in turn suggests that God's will cannot be the source of value; rather it must reflect value. As Bertrand Russell once put it, 'If you are going to say … that God is good, you must then say that right and wrong have some meaning which is independent of God's fiat … If you are going to say *that*, you will then have to say that it is not only through God that right and wrong came into being, but that they are in their essence logically anterior to God.'[16]

This reasoning creates a dilemma for the theist who sees morality as rooted in the will of God (a dilemma whose elements go back to the perplexing 'Euthyphro problem' first articulated by Plato).[17] On the one hand, the mere fact that a supreme being (arbitrarily) wills X cannot provide a moral reason for doing X; on the other hand, if the reason we should obey God's commands is they are antecedently right or good, then God no longer appears to be the source of morality. As Daphne Hampson puts it, the will of God ought not to have any call on our allegiance were it to violate what we perceive to be right; yet if on the other hand God is simply 'one with the ethical', then 'God is of no consequence'.[18]

The standard reply to this dilemma (the line taken by Augustine and Aquinas and by several modern defenders of the idea of divinely based morality)[19] is that goodness is inseparable from God's nature. God neither issues arbitrary commands, nor is he subject to prior moral constraints; rather his commands necessarily reflect his essential nature, as that which is wholly and perfectly good. This need not imply that goodness is 'logically anterior' to God, in Bertrand Russell's phrase: rather, it is thought of as co-existent with God, or as essentially and eternally part of his nature.

This may be theologically unexceptionable (and I shall say something more about its more general appeal in a moment), but it still leaves us with a problem about the sense in which God is the 'source' of morality. Consider a proposition such as 'cruelty is wrong'. We have already seen that this cannot be construed by the theist as an arbitrary command of God; it is better understood as (to use an ancient but useful term) an 'eternal verity', a timeless moral truth or principle held in the mind of God, an inseparable part of the structure of the divine mind. But, someone might object, doesn't this still leave us with an 'is/ought' problem? From the fact that God has these ideas in his mind, it does not seem to follow that they have any normative or evaluative force. We are all familiar with the problems of ethical naturalism, the attempt to equate value or normativity with some feature of the natural world. But isn't there a similar problem with 'ethical *super*naturalism' – the theist's attempt to identify value with some supernatural feature of the mind of God?

The same problem, indeed, seems to go for the eternal truths of logic (and perhaps mathematics). The approach philosophers call 'naturalism' (which broadly speaking attempts to explain everything empirically in terms of the properties of the physical world)[20] has a prima facie problem finding a place for these eternal verities within the architecture of the natural world: the 'mustness' of logical truths, their necessity, and indeed their normativity, does not appear to be derivable from any propositions about what is actually the case.[21] Thus, for example, it seems implausible to explain the laws of logic as empirical truths about how our minds actually work: for we recognize in the laws of logic not just generalizations, however universal, about how we *do* think, but normative principles to which our thought *ought* to conform.[22] Now, the theist, in contrast to the naturalist, locates, the eternal verities of logic within the mind of God; yet although this is to assign them to a realm beyond the domain of mere empirical truth, the same puzzle about their normativity seems to reappear in a different form. For again, if it is just a feature of God that his thought does, as a matter of fact, follow these principles, then it appears there is no more normativity here than there was in the human case.

So it is as if the theist has taken the problematic features of value and necessity, and dumped them (or kicked them upstairs) onto God; but it still remains unexplained how something that *is* the case – even the case about a supernatural being – can yield the required normativity.

The theist, however, can reply along the lines of the traditional approach already referred to – by invoking the essential nature of God. In recognizing the compelling power of values, and of logical principles (their normative, or what is sometimes called their 'magnetic' quality), we humans are plainly recognizing something that goes beyond the observed facts of the natural world. And the theistic outlook now proceeds to interpret these features as signifying the presence, beyond the empirical world, of a transcendent supernatural domain that is by its very nature normative – rational and moral. The two principal categories of the normative, the rational and the good, are features which traditional theology has held to apply to God in virtue of his very nature. God is goodness itself (Aquinas), he is the Logos – ultimate rationality (St John).[23] In short, beyond, or behind, the observable universe – the sequence of events that is simply one contingent happening after another – there is for the theist a domain of eternal value and reason, a domain that impinges on our empirical world, making us respond to something beyond the mere sequence of brute facts.[24] We human creatures (since we are ourselves rational and moral beings, at least in part) are responsive to reason and value, and in being so responsive we participate, however dimly, in the divine nature.

4   God as Source of Morality

Even if one were to be granted the broad outlines of the account just given (an account, clearly, that is more of a statement of the theistic position on normativity than an argument that might be expected to induce the atheistic critic to convert to it), it would still be necessary to clarify what precisely it means for the theist to say that God is the source of value. I began by observing that meaning and value do not seem to be the kinds of things that can be 'bestowed' on our lives – even by a supreme being. Rather, they are properties that depend on, or in the jargon 'supervene on', certain natural features of our lives. So what exactly does the theist claim about God's role here? One bizarre suggestion about this was once made by the distinguished British philosopher John Mackie. Mackie was a strict atheist, and was also a subjectivist about value (he followed the Humean line that goodness is simply a projection of our own inclinations and desires). But in his book *Ethics: Inventing Right and Wrong* he concedes that if there *were* such a thing as objective goodness, then it might provide a good argument for theism. For if objectivism were true, argues Mackie, then there would have to be some objective supervenience relation between a natural empirical property (e.g. an action's alleviating suffering) and the property of its being good:

> If we adopted moral objectivism, then we should have to regard the relations of supervenience which connect values and obligations with their natural grounds as synthetic: they would then be in principle something that god may conceivably create; and since they would otherwise be a very odd sort of thing, the admitting of them would be an inductive ground for admitting also a god to create them ... Moral values, their objectivity and their supervenience would be a continuing miracle ... a constant intrusion into the natural world.[25]

However, the apparently generous concession that Mackie (perhaps ironically) makes to the theist's case is one which the theist would be ill advised to accept. For it is not at all clear how a relation of supervenience could be 'created', even by a divine being. If we consider the analogous case of beauty, and ask how a human artist could create it, it seems the answer must be that she does it by creating objects (sculptures, paintings) which have a certain form and rhythm and harmony. No extra 'decree' of supervenience ('Let beauty arise out of these features!') is needed; rather the ordered generation of the appropriate features *eo ipso* creates a thing of beauty. The traditional Genesis account of the creation of the world has God 'seeing' that what he has created is (*already*, as it were) good,[26] not decreeing (whatever that would mean) that goodness or beauty should supervene on what he has done.

There are many analogous cases. To create a healthy creature is not to create a biological organism and then impose some strange supervenience decree which generates health from the created properties; rather it is to create an organism in which all the organs function harmoniously and efficiently, so as to enable ordered growth and reproduction and resistance to disease and so on. And similarly (though this is of course a more controversial example), to create a conscious being is not to create a complete functioning life form and then be required to 'superadd' to it, in John Locke's phrase, a faculty of thinking or consciousness;[27] rather it is, arguably, just to create a life form with a nervous system intricate enough to enable it to respond appropriately to the environment, and monitor its own internal states, in a sufficiently complex and intelligent way.[28]

It might seem that for a theist to make these kinds of down-to-earth response to Mackie's suggestion of divinely created supervenience relations risks moving too far the other way – towards a reductionistic naturalism: if goodness, or health, or beauty, or consciousness are just appropriately organized natural properties, with no divine 'superadditions' needed, does this not make the deity entirely redundant? I shall argue in a moment that such an implication is too swift: theistic metaphysics will still have a certain kind of role to play with respect to value. But in one sense, I think, the move towards focusing on natural properties, and away from Mackie's (ironically proposed) supernaturalism of value, is a move in the right direction; for when we are deciding if something is healthy, or beautiful, or good, any theistic appeal to divine creation will, as it were, do no real work in our deliberations. The whole argument will quite properly focus on the actual natural features in virtue of which the object in question is claimed to be good, not on the metaphysical truth (if it is one) that the object or its properties were divinely created. A transcendent metaphysics of value still leaves the human moralist or the aesthetician with all the work yet to do, just as a transcendent metaphysics regarding the creation of the material universe still leaves the scientist all the work yet to do in establishing what properties the universe actually has.

It does not follow, however, that the theist's assertion of a benevolent creator is, like Wittgenstein's idle cog wheel,[29] left spinning in the void, completely unconnected to the discourse of morality. For if the theistic outlook is correct, there will be a divine teleology at work in the cosmos, and this will make a radical difference (amongst other things) to the meaningfulness we are able to attribute to our human lives, and their *eudaimonia* (or fulfilment). Consider the graphic and somewhat revolting example in the *Hitchhiker's Guide to the Galaxy*, of the cow genetically engineered to be capable of thought and speech, and to enjoy being killed and eaten for the pleasure of the customers in the 'Restaurant at the End of the Universe'. The animal comes up to the table and recommends to the diners that they might like to choose a piece taken from its rump, pointing out that it has been force-feeding itself to increase the tenderness of the meat. When the Earthman, Arthur Dent, expresses his horror at this performance, his intergalactic friends silence him by coolly asking if he would feel any better if the cow *didn't* enjoy being eaten.[30] Now the author's purpose in sketching this grim little episode is of course to point up the dubious ethical status of our everyday behaviour in ordinary terrestrial steakhouses; but behind the obvious moral is also the thought that Arthur Dent's shocked reaction to the willing bovine victim nevertheless still manifests a valid moral scruple – one that his smart intergalactic friends are the worse for lacking. For the cow's *telos* – its striving to achieve the state where it is killed and eaten – has been cynically imposed on it in such a way that its whole existence is merely instrumental to the pleasure of its owners; and this is clearly morally repugnant.

If the theistic view of our human existence were like this, if our lives were merely of instrumental value to some higher being who had shaped our nature simply and entirely to suit his own purposes, then it is hard to see how our actions and choices in pursuit of our deepest inclinations could, in these circumstances, have any genuine moral meaning. But the theistic conception is of a good and loving creator who desires that his creatures lead lives that are of value to themselves (as well as to him). And this makes a crucial difference – not to the way in which we go about determining what we should do (for that remains within the province of our own rational deliberations), but rather to the *interpretation* we give to our choices, the *significance* which we see them as possessing.[31] The theist believes, sustained by faith, that the careful use of reason, and the sensitive and reflective response to our deepest inclinations, points us towards a life which is the life that a being of the greatest benevolence, goodness, mercy, and love has desired for us, and has destined us to achieve. This will not mean that the theist has access to some magic formula or short cut in ethics, any more than in physical science; metaphysics is never a substitute for science; faith is never a substitute for hard work. But the theistic belief will nonetheless have the capacity to irradiate the believer's life with hope – the kind of hope that the unfortunate rational cow in Douglas Adams' saga must have been unable, in its more reflective moments, to sustain.

For the flavour of Adams' vignette of the restaurant at the end of the universe is, of course, fundamentally absurdist: in the best tradition of Sartre and Camus, it conveys a stark picture of exactly what is involved in a godless universe.[32] Just as, if Hume's account of science is right, there is no ultimate rationality in the universe,[33] and we as human scientists are no better off than the chicken who forms an induction that whenever the barn door opens it will get fed, only to find one morning that it gets its neck wrung;[34] so, if the universe is an utterly impersonal and random process which throws up planets like Earth with living creatures whose deepest inclinations are determined by a kind of genetic roulette, then we as human moralists are no better off than Adams's cow: we can have no faith that our 'reasons' for action are any more than instrumental calculations relative to drives and goals that subserve either an alien purpose, or, to speak more correctly, no purpose at all. For though many modern biologists follow the lead of Richard Dawkins in speaking as if we are lumbering robots programmed to serve the 'purposes' of our genes,[35] this is of course a convenient shorthand for saying that our human nature is the product of completely random mutation and survival pressure. Such a worldview can perhaps allow for human activities being 'meaningful' in some minimal and reduced sense – roughly that of happening to give satisfaction to the agents, or happening to produce certain desired societal goals; but only the theistic worldview can generate a deeper and more fundamental connection between morality and meaning.

In an entirely godless universe, there would be no divine teleology, no supremely intelligent and benevolent purposes, to underwrite our aspirations to moral goodness. Instead, we would just be members of a species who, at a given epoch of evolution, had a particular collection of characteristics and potentialities. Now perhaps some individuals would have more fun developing some of those capacities (for cruelty, let us say), while others would be happier developing others (for generosity, say). Relative to their desires or inclinations, one could say that some had 'reason' to choose cruel acts (a subjective, or instrumental reason, as it were), while others had 'reason' to choose generous acts. But considering the matter independently of the contingent desires of the creatures in question, there would be, so far as I can see, no satisfactory way of assigning to some features of their possible actions the objective property of providing a reason (let alone a conclusive reason)[36] for the agents to act in a certain way.

5   Objectivity and its Basis

This last assertion might be challenged by some modern ethicists who aim to provide an entirely secular account of the metaphysics of (genuine and objective) value.[37] Thus Philip Stratton-Lake (drawing on the work of John McDowell and Tim Scanlon) wholly rejects supernaturalism, but construes the goodness of X as the complex non-natural 'property of having [natural] properties that give us reason to respond in certain positive ways' towards X.[38] This seems to me to be likely to work quite well for non-moral cases (what it is for a raincoat to be good is for it to have natural properties, such as impermeability, that give me reason to give it a preferred place in my suitcase if I am visiting Wales or Ireland). But what of moral properties? Stratton-Lake suggests (in line with his general position) that the wrongness of an act consists in its having (natural) properties that provide us with a reason – but this time a *conclusive* reason, not do not it: 'To say that [an act] is wrong because it is cruel is to say that it is the cruelness of this act that gives us conclusive reason not to do it.'[39] Yet the 'conclusive' seems to me under-supported; for remember that we are supposed to be talking here of *objective* reasons, not just instrumental reasons, or reasons contingent on the particular desires the agents happen to have.

Let us consider in more detail the proposition that cruelty is wrong, for example that bullying the weak or helpless just for personal gratification is wicked. It is unfortunately true that there are people who gain satisfaction from such behaviour – in the words of John Kekes, there are people whose 'resentment, greed, ambition, selfishness and sense of superiority or inferiority gives meaning to their lives and leads them to inflict grievous unjustified harm on others.' 'Such people', observes Kekes, 'may be successfully engaged in their projects, derive great satisfaction from them, and find their lives ... very meaningful.'[40] But despite the grizzly subjective satisfactions so described, such actions are wrong, indeed necessarily wrong: cruelty is wrong in all possible worlds. (Those who doubt this are invited to try to construct a coherent scenario of a possible world in which such behaviour is good or right.)

It is important to note that the idea of the validity of such eternal and necessary moral verities is in no way undermined by the fact that we can point to variations in customs and norms from society to society; nor, more crucially, is it impugned by what Bernard Williams has called the 'radical contingency in our current ethical conceptions', namely that 'they might have been different from what they are'.[41] A widespread shift in attitudes to cruelty, for example as happened in Nazi Germany, could never show, even if it became dominant all over the planet, that cruelty is no longer wrong, only that humanity had become massively corrupted (something, unfortunately that is always a dangerous possibility).[42]

If there are eternal and objective ethical truths such as that cruelty is wrong, they cannot be undermined by the 'radical contingency' in the shifting historical development of human ethical attitudes. Yet, and here is the crucial point, one which I take to be a *reductio* of an atheist metaphysics of value, such objective ethical truths *would be* undermined in the absence of the cosmic moral teleology that theism provides.[43] If it is merely the contingencies of our genetic and cultural makeup that have produced our moral aversion to cruelty, then it is hard to see how we have an objective reason (a reason independent of the contingent set of our desires), let alone a 'conclusive' reason, not to be cruel. For the theist, by contrast, there is a domain of eternal and necessary value, a divine reality that infuses all possible worlds; the purposes of God are necessarily good, and the nature of humans, qua created beings, is such that they can only be truly fulfilled by living in conformity with his moral purposes.

The upshot, paradoxically, is that Mackie's talk of moral objectivism implying the 'irruption' of value into the natural world is in a certain sense correct. It is not that goodness or rightness are 'miraculous' properties, or supernaturally decreed supervenience relations. Rather, as we have seen, goodness is like health: the criteria for its attribution to objects and actions have to do entirely with the presence or absence of certain broadly natural features, such as the tendency to alleviate suffering, the promotion of sympathy and fellow feeling, respectful treatment, and the like. But the normative status of the obligations connected with such types of behaviour is, as Kant famously pointed out, not simply instrumental, or hypothetical: we ought to do these things not just because we have contingently evolved to have certain inclinations, not because our society happens contingently to put a premium on certain goals, but rather because such behaviour is categorically right. Such behaviour is indeed, in the currently fashionable terminology, behaviour we have conclusive reason to pursue. And ultimately, for the theist, such conclusive objective reasons, riding free of the contingencies of our human development, will be interpreted in a way that makes reference to the moral teleology that permeates the whole cosmos.

It is the idea of a moral teleology, or moral cosmology, that finally underlies the maxim of Dante with which we began, 'in his will is our peace'. And the peace envisaged, to come back full circle to our earlier discussion, is not mere tranquillisation or externally engineered submission to a higher power, but is the peace of an autonomous being whose reason has recognised the truth of the ancient religious idea: to serve goodness is the most perfect freedom.[44]

Notes

1. Dante Alighieri, *The Divine Comedy: Paradise* [*La Divina Comedia: Paradiso* c 1310], iii, 70–72, 79–80, 85; transl. J. C.

2. Augustine, *Confessions* [*Confessiones*, c 398], bk. I, ch. 1: 'fecisti nos ad te, et inquietum est cor nostrum donec requiescat in te.'

3. Both these quotations are from 'Prayers and Thanks-givings upon Several Occasions', in the *Book of Common Prayer* [1662]. 1662 is the date of the finally approved version, though most of the formulations date from the previous century, owing much to Thomas Cranmer (1489–1556).

4. Daphne Hampson, *After Christianity* (London: SCM Press 1996; 2nd edn. 2002), p. 137.

5. Hampson, *After Christianity*, p. 129.

6. C. S. Lewis 'Priestesses in the Church' [1948], in *Faith, Christianity and the Church* (London: Harper Collins, 2000), ch. 54, p. 402. Lewis goes on to offer it as an apparently decisive argument against any possible female conceptualisation of God that if *that* were conceivable 'we might just as well pray to "Our Mother which art in Heaven" as to "Our Father"'. (*ibid.*) The shifts in awareness stemming from the gender revolution of the late twentieth century have perhaps rather undermined Lewis's implied *quod est absurdum*.

7. Cecil Day Lewis, 'Walking Away' from *The Gate and Other Poems* (London: Jonathan Cape, 1962).

8. Compare the following: 'God has willed that man remain "under the control of his own decisions" [Sirach/Ecclesiasticus 15:14] so that he can seek his Creator spontaneously, and come freely to utter and blissful perfection through loyalty to Him. Hence man's dignity demands that he act according to a knowing and free choice that is personally motivated and prompted from within, not under blind internal impulse nor by mere external pressure.' *Gaudium et spes* (Rome: Pastoral Constitution on the Church in the Modern World, 1965), §16.

9. My line of thought here is heavily indebted to a passage in Thomas Merton: 'A tree gives glory to God by being a tree. For in being what God means it to be it is obeying him. It "consents" so to speak, to His creative love. It is expressing an idea which is in God and which is not distinct from the essence of God, and therefore a tree imitates God by being a tree.' *Seeds of Contemplation*[1961] (Wheathamstead: Anthony Clarke, 1972), p. 23. As developed by Merton, the thought is not just that natural kinds glorify their creator, but that each individual specimen has a unique role to play: 'the perfection of each created thing is not merely in its conformity to an abstract type but in its own individual identity with itself. This particular tree will give glory to God by spreading out its roots in the earth and raising its branches into the air and the light in a way that no other tree before or after ever did or will do.' The philosophical roots of this idea go back to the notion of *haecceitas* or 'thisness' articulated by the late thirteenth-century Franciscan John Duns Scorns (*Quaestiones in libros metaphysicos*, 7, 13, nos. 9 and 26), which in turn influenced the poet Gerard Manley Hopkins:

As kingfishers catch fire, dragonflies draw flame;
As tumbled over rim in roundy wells
Stones ring; like each tucked string tells, each
    hung bell's
Bow swung finds tongue to fling out broad its name;
Each mortal thing does one thing and the same:
Deals out that being indoors each one dwells;
Selves – goes itself; *myself* it speaks and spells,
Crying: *What I do is me: for that I came.*

From *Poems(1876–1889)*, no. 34,
in Gardner (ed.), *Poems and Prose of Gerard
Manley Hopkins*, p. 51.

10. For the special 'incomplete' nature of human beings, compare Merton: 'Unlike the animals and the trees, it is not enough for us to be what our nature intends. It is not enough for us to be individual men. For us, holiness is more than humanity' (*Seeds of Contemplation*, p. 24).

11. This is very much in the spirit of Kant's account of autonomous moral choice as governed by the categorical imperative, within what he called the 'kingdom of ends' (the entire community of rational agents who are all to be treated with equal dignity and respect). The other main strand in Kant's account of the autonomy of the moral will has to do with its need to be free from internal interferences: moral imperatives cannot be construed as conditional on whatever contingent desires one happens to have, for 'in these cases the will never determines itself directly by the thought of an action, but only by the motivations which the anticipated effect of the action exercises on

the will – *I ought to do something because I want something else.*' (*Groundwork for the Metaphysic of Morals* [*Grundlegung zur Metaphysik der Sitten*, 1785], Akademie edition (Berlin: Reimer/De Gruyter, 1900–), vol. IV, p. 444; trans. T. E. Hill Jr and A. Zweig (Oxford: Oxford University Press, 2003), p. 244.) Because of its dependency on the contingencies of inclination, action of this kind is always for Kant heteronomous. Again, it seems to me that the ideal of autonomous choice to which Kant here aspires is quite consistent with what we find, for example in the Pauline and Augustinian conception of the religious life as freeing the will from the slavery of desire (cf. Romans 7:8–24 and Augustine, *City of God* [*De civitate Dei*, 413–26 CE], ch. 19).

12. Iris Murdoch, *The Sovereignty of the Good* (London: Routledge, 1970), p. 131 (I owe this reference to Sam Vice). Compare Kant on our autonomy, 'the basis of the dignity of human nature and of every rational nature', according to which our will must be considered as *selbstgesetzgebend* ('giving the law to itself'). *Groundwork for the Metaphysic of Morals*, ch. 2; Akademie edition, vol. IV, pp. 436, 431; trans. Hill and Zweig, pp. 236, 232.

13. Why then is Kantian autonomy so often represented as inimical to the religious ideal? Part of the answer may arise from the way Kant often speaks of the will as *self-legislating*: 'whenever the will seeks the law that is to determine it *anywhere else* than in the fitness of its maxims for its *own giving* of universal law, and if therefore it goes outside itself and seeks this law in a property of any of its objects – the result is always heteronomy. In that case the will does not give itself the law; rather, the object gives the law to it, in virtue of its relation to the will' (*Groundwork*, Academie edn. vol. 4, p. 440; Hill and Zweig, p. 241). Certainly the language here, together with Kant's talk of the 'sovereign authority' of the will, may seem to have a very secularising tendency. But it has to be remembered that the context is Kant's insistence that moral action can never be simply a means to the fulfilment of some contingent inclination, or the blind submission to the arbitrary power of another. Nothing here seems intrinsically resistant to being expressed in religious mode: we cannot act rightly by abandoning our (God-given) reason and yielding to the dictates of raw desire, or another's arbitrary power ('blind internal impulse or mere external pressure' – See. n. 8, above).

While (if the above reasoning is correct) the tension between traditional Christian and Kantian conceptions of moral agency may be far less than is often supposed, the respective pictures of the metaphysical foundations of morality do nonetheless turn out to be very different – at any rate if we take the argument of the *Grundlegung* as definitve. This is a point forcefully brought out by Onora O'Neill: 'The Kantian grounding of reason, as of morality, cannot be foundational. Anything that could count as foundation would have to be transcendent, and so alien. Once we make the Copernican turn [the rejection of transcendent metaphysics and the supposition that objects must conform to our human knowledge, rather than vice versa] we cannot expect any such foundations to be available.' ('Reason and Autonomy in *Grundlegung III*', in *Constructions of Reason* (Cambridge: Cambridge University Press, 1989), pp. 64–5). There is however an interesting question (itself later raised by O'Neill) of how far, in his later *Critique of Practical Reason* (*Kritik der Praktischen Vernunft*, 1788), Kant backtracks from his metaphysically 'independent' vindication of morality and freedom.

14. In *Fear and Trembling* [*Frygt og Bœven*, 1843].

15. Hosea 6:6. Cf. Matthew 9:13.

16. Bertrand Russell, 'Why I am Not a Christian' [1927], in *Why I am Not a Christian and Other Essay* (London: Allen and Unwin, 1957), ch. I, p. 8.

17. Plato, *Euthyphro* [c. 390 BCE], 6–10.

18. Hampson, *After Christianity*, p. 137.

19. Compare Aquinas: 'For God alone, [his] essence is his being … And so he alone is good through his essence.' *Summa theologiae* [1266–73], pt. Ia, qu. 6, art. 3. See also pt. Ia, qu. 2, art. 3; pt. Ia, qu. 3, art. 4,7; pt. Ia, qu. 6, art. 3. For the way in which Aquinas' position offers a possible solution to the Euthyphro dilemma, see E. Stump, *Aquinas* (London: Routledge, 2002), pp. 90, 127–8. See also R. M. Adams, 'A Modified Divine Command Theory of Ethical Wrongness', in G. Outka and J. P. Reeder (eds.), *Religion and Morality* (Garden City: Anchor, 1973), pp. 318–47.

20. I am of course giving only a very crude characterization here. For more, see J. Cottingham, 'Our Natural Guide: Conscience, "Nature" and Moral Experience', in D. Oderberg and T. Chappell (eds.), *Human Values* (London: Palgrave, 2005).

21. Compare David Hume's analogous argument about causal necessity: 'when we look about us ... and consider the operation of causes, we are never able, in a single instance, to discover any power or necessary connexion; any quality, which binds the effect to the cause and renders the one an infallible consequence of the other.' *Enquiry concerning Human Understanding* [1748], §7, pt. 1.

22. Compare the view set out by Gottlob Frege: logic must be wholly objective – its laws hold independent of contingent facts about human psychology. They are 'fixed and eternal ... boundary stones set in an eternal foundation, which our thought can overflow, but not dislodge'. *The Basic Laws of Arithmetic* [*Die Grundgesetze der Arithmetik*, vol. I, 1893], trans. M. Furch (Berkeley: University of California Press, 1964), p. 13.

23. See above (n. 19) for references to Aquinas. For the *logos*, see John 1:1. The term has a complex and polyvalent meaning, which embraces notions of 'word', 'significance', and 'reason'; in its Johannine usage it thus becomes a shorthand for the 'dynamic of reason', or 'the creative rationality from which the world has sprung'; see J. Ratzinger, *God and The World [Gott und die Welt, 2000]* (San Francisco: Ignatius Press, 2002), pp. 114, 206.

24. The metaphorical talk of a transcendent domain 'beyond' or 'behind' the empirical world of course raises questions about the legitimacy or possibility of such metaphysical claims.

25. J. Mackie, *The Miracle of Theism* (Oxford: Clarendon, 1982), p. 118.

26. Genesis 1:10, 12, 21, 25, 31.

27. John Locke, *An Essay concerning Human Understanding* [1690], bk. IV, ch. 3, §6.

28. In saying this is 'controversial', I am referring to the fact that many contemporary philosophers maintain that these abilities, however impeccable, would never be sufficient for consciousness without the further presence of mysterious extra items called 'qualia', the supposed episodes of inner awareness of 'what is it like' to see a red rose, or to smell coffee. The locus classicus for this view is Thomas Nagel's article 'What is it like to be a bat?', in T. Nagel, *Mortal Questions* (Cambridge: Cambridge University Press, 1979), ch. 12.

29. Cf. Ludwig Wittgenstein, *Philosophical Investigations* [*Philosophische Untersuchungen*, 1953], I, §271.

30. Douglas Adams, *The Restaurant at the End of the Universe* (London: Pan Books, 1984); the second volume in the *Hitchhiker's Guide to the Galaxy* trilogy.

31. Bernard Williams, in supporting the standard modern view (roughly from Nietzsche onwards) that the traditional project of grand theistic metaphysics has 'irretrievably broken down', nevertheless grants a place for a kind of truth that is not compassed within the robust 'common-sense' species of plain facts. This is the kind of truth involving the *interpretation* of reality (see *Truth and Truthfulness* (Princeton: Princeton University Press, 2002), ch. 1). Yet once this is granted, it is hard to see how a religious metaphysic can automatically be supposed to be untenable; for one plausible way of construing it is as, precisely, an interpretation of reality – of the significance of the existence of the cosmos and of beings such as humans.

32. Compare the conception of human life in a godless universe advanced by Albert Camus in *The Myth of Sisyphus* [*Le Mythe de Sisyphe*, 1943]: our only recourse is the 'refusal to hope and the unyielding evidence of a life without consolation'; trans. J. O'Brian (Harmondsworth: Penguin, 1955), p. 58.

33. Or, at least, if there is any ultimate principle it can never be known: '[T]he utmost effort of human reason is to reduce the principles productive of natural phenomena to a greater simplicity and to resolve the many particular effects into a few general causes ... But as to the causes of these general causes, we should in vain attempt their discovery ... These ultimate springs and principles are totally shut up from human curiosity and enquiry.' *Enquiry concerning Human Understanding* [1748], §4, pt. i. For the sceptical or epistemic as opposed to metaphysical interpretation of Hume, see John Wright, *The Sceptical Realism of David Hume* (Cambridge: Cambridge University Press, 1983).

34. Bertrand Russell's example, in *The Problems of Philosophy* [1912] (Oxford: Oxford University Press, 1967), ch. 6, p. 35.

35. Richard Dawkins, *The Selfish Gene* (Oxford: Oxford University Press, 1976).

36. For this notion, see next section.

37. It is a striking fact that recent work in moral philosophy has reacted powerfully against the kinds of subjectivism and projectivism that were dominant in the closing decades of the twentieth century. Examples

of such neo-objectivism can be found in Paul Bloomfield's *Moral Reality* (Oxford: Oxford University Press, 2001) and Russ Shafer-Landau's *Moral Realism* (Oxford: Oxford University Press, 2003).

If, in common with modern neo-objectivists, we subscribe to the idea that there are genuine objective values (and reject the deflationary accounts of value offered by various kinds of subjectivism and projectivism as flawed), then the philosophical options for giving account of such values are not too numerous. The jury is still out on the project known as 'ethical naturalism', the attempt to reduce values to natural properties of the empirical world, which continues to generate a vast literature (its most ingenious defender is probably Frank Jackson, *From Metaphysics to Ethics* (Oxford: Clarendon Press, 1998)). But if we assume that long-standing doubts about this project (going back to G. E. Moore) turn out in the end to be insurmountable, the only viable alternative would be some form of non-naturalism. Theorists like Shafer-Landau appear content to conceive of such irreducibly non-natural values as 'brute' metaphysical realities (see *Moral Realism*, p. 48) – but this appears to reach a terminus of explanation just a little too soon for comfort. The neo-Aristotelian approach typified by Bloomfield construes moral properties as concerned with human flourishing, and having 'the same ontological status as healthiness' (*Moral Reality*, p. 28); but this appears to require the unacceptably relativistic conclusion that rightness or wrongness depend on the contingencies of species development (compare Bloomfield on how, under different population and survival conditions, sibling rivalry might have turned out to be morally good: p. 39). I shall return to the problem of the 'radical contingency of the ethical' at the end of this chapter. For similar problems with a somewhat different and highly sophisticated form of Aristotelian objectivism, championed by John McDowell, see below, n. 42. If these various approaches to underwriting objectivism fail to deliver a worldview that accommodates the genuine reality of objective values, independent of the contingencies of fluctuating human desire and uncertain historical development, then it seems (against those who appear to rule it out in advance) at least worth considering the possibility that the theistic framework may turn out to offer a way forward.

38. Stratton-Lake, *Ethical Intuitionism*, p. 15, invoking J. McDowell, 'Values and Secondary Properties', in T. Honderich (ed.), *Morality and Objectivity* (London: Routledge, 1985), pp. 110–29, and T. Scanlon, *What we Owe to Each Other* (Cambridge, Mass.: Belknap, 1998), pp. 95 ff.

39. Stratton-Lake, *Ethical Intuitionism*, p. 15. The notion derives from C. D. Broad, who (expounding Joseph Butler) notes that the authority of conscience means that its pronouncements are 'not simply interesting … statements of fact, and not simply … reasons to be balanced against others, but … *conclusive* reasons for or against doing the actions about which it pronounces' (*Five Types of Ethical Theory* [1930], cited in S. Darwall, *The British Moralists and the Internal 'Ought'* (Cambridge: Cambridge University Press, 1995), p. 247. Cf. J. Butler, *Fifteen Sermons* [1726], Sermon II, §8, in D. D. Raphael (ed.), *British Moralists* (Oxford: Clarendon, 1969) §399.

40. John Kekes, *Pluralism in Philosophy: Changing the Subject* (Ithaca: Cornell University Press, 2000), p. 97. Cf. Cottingham, *On the Meaning of Life*, p. 23.

41. Williams, *Truth and Truthfulness*, p. 20.

42. The ever-present possibility of radical corruption in our social fabric seems to me to constitute the main difficulty for John McDowell's form of 'quietist' objectivism about the ethical, notwithstanding the enormous finesse and subtlety with which his account is presented. McDowell insists that moral properties are real properties (not disguised projections of our own), but, taking his cue from Aristotle, construes the process of social acculturation (or ethical education) as providing a mode of access to this reality: 'immersion in a tradition [is] a respectable mode of access to the real'; and thus 'we can stop supposing that the rationality of virtue needs a foundation outside the formed evaluative outlook of a virtuous person' (*Mind and World* (Cambridge, Mass.: Harvard University Press, 1994), p. 98; *Mind, Value and Reality* (Cambridge, Mass.: Harvard University Press, 1998), p. 174). Whether this idea of a formed evaluative outlook (what McDowell calls 'second nature') lacks proper critical resources, or offers too many hostages to cultural conservativism, has generated a considerable critical literature; for spirited attempts to defend McDowell on this issue, see Lovibond,

Ethical Formation, ch. 7, and T. Thornton, *John McDowell* (Chesham: Acumen, 2004), p. 91.

43. Or some substitute for it – perhaps some form of the 'rampant Platonism' that John McDowell summarily dismisses as implying that our human responses to value are 'occult' or 'magical' (*Mind and World*, p. 92).

44. The formula is an extremely old one, found in the ancient 'Collect for Peace': 'Deus, auctor pacis et amator, quern nosse vivere, *cui servire regnare est*'; cf. the fine translation of Thomas Cranmer: 'O God, who art the author of peace and lover of concord, in knowledge of whom standeth our eternal life, *whose service is perfect freedom*' (Morning Prayer, *Book of Common Prayer*). In a more literal rendering of the Latin, God is the one 'whom to serve is to reign.' As with so much in Christianity, the thought has Jewish antecedents; cf. §6 (Vau) of Psalm 119(118): 44–5: 'So shall I keep thy law continually, for ever and ever. And I will walk at liberty: for I seek thy precepts.'

2.7

Could God's Purpose Be the Source of Life's Meaning?

Thaddeus Metz

Introduction: The Status of Purpose Theory

In this paper, I explore the traditional God-centred theory of what can make a human life meaningful. I take the question of what can make life meaningful to be the question of what about our lives (besides bare survival) could be worthy of great esteem.[1] A God-centred theory, as construed here, answers that one's life is worthy of great esteem just insofar as one has a proper relation with a spiritual being who grounds the natural universe. And the traditional God-centred view maintains that at least one proper relation to have with God is to fulfil His purpose. Call this view 'purpose theory'.[2]

Purpose theory is a prima facie attractive account of what could make a life meaningful. It spells out what it would mean to 'exist for a reason' or for 'life to have a point'. It jibes with the fact that 'purpose' is one synonym of 'meaning'. It accounts for the intuition that what confers meaning on one's life is an objective matter, i.e., that meaning is not merely a function of satisfying whatever desires one happens to have. It provides a plausible candidate for what could confer significance on our lives, namely, a holy being. Finally, it squares with the judgment that most (if not all) people are capable of living a meaningful life, but that not everyone in fact does live a meaningful life.

Despite these advantages, several theorists have contended that realizing God's plan could not make our lives meaningful. In fact, many hold that purpose theory, when conjoined with very plausible theses, entails logical contradictions. There are important arguments in the literature purporting to show that purpose theory entails the absurdities that God is not all-good, that God is not all-powerful, and that God is not eternal.

Thaddeus Metz (2000) "Could God's Purpose Be the Source of Life's Meaning?" *Religious Studies* 36: 293–313.

In this paper, I will argue that there are versions of purpose theory which do not entail these absurdities. The three major *reductio* arguments against purpose theory will be shown to fail. However, critical discussion of these arguments will point the way to a more telling objection to purpose theory. I will also argue that reflection on the reason why God might be the key to a meaningful life indicates that purpose theory must be false. The most promising explanation of why a relationship with God could be the sole source of significance implies that something other than achieving a goal assigned by God must constitute this source. In short, the best rationale for God-centred theory in general is incompatible with the particular version of God-centred theory which has dominated religious thinking on the meaning of life. I am not sure that this new objection is sound; I put it forward as something that must be addressed in order for belief in purpose theory to be plausible.

I will begin by spelling out purpose theory in some detail, differentiating what is merely compatible with the view from what is essential to it. Along the way, I will also respond to objections which are based on misunderstandings of purpose theory, clearing the way for a discussion of more substantial criticisms. In the next three sections I will refute the charges that purpose theory oddly entails that God would treat us immorally, lack omnipotence, and fail to be eternal. Then, I will raise a new problem for purpose theory, that it does not square with the best explanation of God-centred theory. After rejecting several accounts of why a relationship with God might be necessary for life to have meaning, I will advance what I take to be the most promising account, an account which will be shown to contradict purpose theory. Hence, I will tentatively conclude that realizing God's purpose could not be what it is about relating to God that would make our lives meaningful. I will end the paper by pointing both to ways that purpose theorists might try to respond to this objection and to avenues of research for religious thinkers who question purpose theory.

An Analysis of Purpose Theory

In this section, my goal is to explicate purpose theory. I will lay out the different basic versions of the view and also clear up common misconceptions.

Purpose theory is the view that a life is meaningful insofar as one fulfils a purpose that God has assigned. Note that purpose theory implies nothing about whether God in fact has a purpose or whether God even exists. Of course, many believers do hold purpose theory, but it would be possible for, say, atheistic existentialists to hold it as well. We may therefore dismiss one objection to purpose theory, namely, the charge that the existence of evil shows that there is no God with a purpose.[3] Evil is not a problem for purpose theory, since it does not contend that there exists a God who has assigned us a purpose. In other words, purpose theory does not imply anything about whether our lives are in fact meaningful. Purpose theory is a thesis about what can confer meaning upon our lives. If atheism were true, then purpose theory would entail nihilism, the view that our lives are meaningless.

It should be instructive to contrast purpose theory with related religious theories of what could make a life meaningful. First, purpose theory is logically distinct from 'justice theory', which says that life is meaningful, say, because God's rules are the source of justice in this world, or because God gives people their just deserts in the next one. The defender of purpose theory may, but need not, hold that God's purposes are the source of morality; she could hold that moral facts obtain independently of God's will, but that meaning facts do not. The purpose theorist can also maintain that life would be meaningful even if there were no ultimate justice; she could hold that doing God's bidding in this imperfect world is sufficient for a significant life.

Second, purpose theory conceptually differs from standard forms of 'perfection theory', the view that a life is meaningful insofar as it is oriented toward a superior nature. Typical versions of perfection theory maintain that one's life is meaningful by virtue of honouring one's higher self as a spiritual, indestructible entity while on earth, or by virtue of attaining the stage where one will commune with a perfect being upon leaving the earth. Purpose theory differs from these forms of perfection theory in that it can hold that life can be meaningful in the absence of a soul which will survive the death of one's body. Merely realizing God's end, without the prospect of an afterlife, could be deemed sufficient for meaning.[4]

Purpose theorists will disagree about whether their account should be conjoined with any of the above perspectives and, if so, which ones. Additional differences among purpose theorists will turn on their conceptions (a) of God, (b) of God's purpose, (c) of the way God assigns it to us, and (d) of the way we are to fulfil it. Let's briefly examine some competing interpretations of these elements.

For the sake of this paper, I will consider God to be at least a spiritual being who is all-powerful, all-knowing, and all-good and who is the ground of the physical world (a). Although most purpose theorists are theists who hold that God is a transcendent, personal being, it is worth noting that pantheist and deist versions of purpose theory are possible, too. And God might also be necessary, infinite, atemporal, immutable, and simple, but I will tend to set such possibilities aside (until the penultimate section).

Many defenders of purpose theory hold that any purpose God assigns to an individual would be part of a larger, single plan for the universe (b). It is thought that if God created the natural world, it was done with one highest-order end in mind, whereby all other ends would be necessary components of or instruments for its realization. However, it is not clear that this is the only possible or plausible account of God's purposes. God could have brought about the universe with several higher-order ends in mind, at least if the ends do not conflict. For example, God arguably could have made the world for the sake of being generous to the creatures in it, maximizing temporal values, glorifying Himself, and enhancing the meaning of His own existence. Perhaps the purpose God assigns to us would be necessary for achieving one (or more) of multiple higher-order ends.

Adherents of purpose theory disagree with one another about the precise content of God's purpose and the way we might come to know it. These are notoriously difficult questions to answer. However, it is a mistake to think, as some objectors have,[5] that purpose theory is unacceptable if it fails to specify our assigned end. The idea behind the objection is that a theory of life's meaning should provide some practical guidance. Now, the purpose theorist can maintain that we do have a reasonable amount of insight into what God's purpose might be. After all, the question of why God would create something rather than nothing, or would create us in particular, is amenable of intelligent reply. But even if the defender of purpose theory could provide no indication as to the content of God's purpose for us, I do not think her view would thereby be disqualified. Utilitarianism has been widely deemed to be a good candidate for a moral theory, despite the enormous difficulty of knowing what course of action would actually produce the best results. Similarly, purpose theory could be an acceptable theory of meaning, even if we do not know how to fulfil God's purpose.

There are further differences among versions of purpose theory regarding the way God might assign a purpose to us (c). For instance, would God command us to realize His end? Might God punish us with eternal damnation if we failed to realize the end assigned to us?

Finally, purpose theorists will disagree about how we ought to fulfil God's purpose (d). Most will hold that it is possible for us not to realize God's end, viz., that we are not predestined to do what God would like. Typical adherents of purpose theory hold that we must freely fulfil the end God assigns. Hence, it is incorrect to say that purpose theory implies that everyone's life would be meaningful merely because God assigned us an end[6] or because we could not avoid realizing it.[7] Purpose theory maintains that one must fulfil the end, not merely be assigned one, and most adherents hold that one must fulfil it by means of a free choice. There arises the further question of how to fulfil God's purpose freely. For example, is one's life (more) meaningful if one takes pleasure in attaining the goal God has assigned, or if one attains it for the basic reason that it is God's goal?

Obviously, many different versions of purpose theory are possible. In the next three sections, my task will be to find versions which do not entail the logical absurdities which have been attributed to purpose theory.

God's Purpose vs. God's Morality

A prominent criticism of purpose theory is that it would be immoral for God to assign a purpose to other agents. Purpose theory arose in the context of a teleological conception of human nature, whereby normativity is understood in terms of a final cause. Modern conceptions of normativity famously reject the idea that persons ought to realize some pre-defined end; they instead tend to hold that we ought to live according to norms which are self-legislated. Now, it appears that being assigned an end conflicts with the dictum that rational beings ought to live by their own choice. Hence, Sartre once said of his subjectivist theory that it 'alone is compatible with the dignity of man; it is the only one which does not make man into an object'.[8]

It is difficult to pin down in exactly what respect a God who assigned us a purpose might degrade our dignity. In order to flesh this out, I will appeal to some Kantian ideas about morality. In characteristically modern fashion, the Kantian standpoint presumes that we are essentially autonomous choosers and proposes that the fundamental moral norm is to respect people's ability to make decisions for themselves. In the following, I will examine the 'Argument from Disrespect', the central claims of which are that it is immoral to treat our capacity for self-determination solely as a means to an end and that God's assigning us an end would do exactly that. These claims together entail that if God assigned us an end, God would be immoral, a logical contradiction since God is by definition morally ideal.

Of course, the purpose theorist could always respond by denying that a Kantian ethics is applicable to us, perhaps favouring utilitarianism instead. Or she could grant that Kantianism applies to us, but deny that it applies to God.[9] Rather than spend time considering how the Kantian might reply to these two claims, I would like merely to set them aside. For the sake of argument, let us suppose that both human and divine wills are morally obliged not to treat rational beings disrespectfully. It would be interesting if it could be shown that purpose theory is consistent with this strong Kantian thesis. In the following, I will explore four ways in which God's assigning us an end might seem to treat our capacity for free choice disrespectfully. I will show that there is nothing inherently disrespectful about God's assigning us a purpose and hence that purpose theory need not absurdly entail that God is immoral.

Coercion

Why hold that God's ascribing us an end would be disrespectful? First, restricting a person's choice by making threats is a quintessential form of disrespect, and it appears that God would threaten us by making eternal damnation the consequence of not realizing His end.[10]

To begin to reply, consider that a threat is not necessarily disrespectful; it depends on why the threat is made. Specifically, a threat made incidentally in the course of maintaining a retributive punishment system is not disrespectful. To fix ideas, suppose that a human society instituted a punishment system for the sake of giving violators of just laws the punishment they deserve. While not intending to deter crime with this punishment system, the society would nonetheless be making incidental threats to those who would break just laws. Regardless of its purpose, the mere existence of a punishment system threatens citizens in saying, 'If you break a law, you will be intentionally harmed'. It does not appear that such threats would be disrespectful, on the plausible assumption that retributive punishment is respectful.

Therefore, if it would not be disrespectful for a state to make threats in the course of maintaining a retributive punishment system, it would not be disrespectful for God to make threats in doing the same. If it would be God's purpose for us to be moral, then our failing to fulfil that purpose would warrant punishment, and any threats God would make incidental to imposing that punishment would be respectful.

Unfortunately, we cannot rest content with this response, since it appears that it is not possible for a human to deserve *eternal* damnation. No finite action can earn an infinite reaction. If so, then even monstrosities such as Hitler and Stalin do not deserve to be in hell forever. Hence, I believe the purpose theorist must reject the idea that God would impose eternal damnation upon those who do not fulfil the purpose He assigns. The purpose theorist can accept that we have souls that live forever. She can also hold that God would impose a finite punishment upon souls that have rejected His (moral) end. However, to avoid the charge that God's assigning us a purpose would be disrespectfully coercive, I suspect that the purpose theorist must reject the postulate that God would send recalcitrants to hell forever. If I am wrong about this, so much the better for the purpose theorist who is enthusiastic about the prospect of eternal damnation for the wicked. The point is that purpose theory can escape the charge that it implies that God would be wrongfully coercive to assign us a purpose.

Exploitation

Even if the purpose theorist rejects the notion of eternal damnation, charges of disrespect may still arise. In fact, God's offering the reward of heaven for realizing His end might seem to be disrespectful. Some could deem this to be a 'coercive offer', or, in terms that I find more applicable, a form of exploitation.

It seems exploitative, and hence disrespectful, to offer a starving person food in exchange for doing what you like. What choice would she have but to conform to your will? By analogy, an objector could maintain that it would be exploitative for God to offer finite creatures an eternity of bliss in exchange for doing His bidding. The God-Father would be making an offer we couldn't refuse.

Of course, one option for the purpose theorist would be to reject the reward of eternal heaven as I have argued she must reject the punishment of eternal hell. She could hold that God would provide either no reward or a moderate reward for realizing His end.

However, I think the purpose theorist can plausibly maintain that God could reward us with eternal bliss for acting according to His will. The charge of 'exploitation' arises most naturally when the purpose of the person making the offer involves degrading or harming the recipient. Most would not hesitate in calling 'exploitative' the offer of food to a starving person in exchange for sex or a kidney. It is not so clear, though, that it would be exploitative to offer such a person food in exchange for maintaining her rational agency or working part-time at a soup kitchen. If this would not be exploitative, then it would likewise not be exploitative for God to offer us heaven forever in exchange for accomplishing His aim that we act morally.

Condescension

There is yet a third version of the Argument from Disrespect, namely, one from Kurt Baier. Baier's rendition interestingly does not turn on God's imposing any scheme of punishment or reward. Since Baier's remarks are important and influential, I quote in full the relevant passage:

> We do not disparage a dog when we say that it has no purpose, is not a sheep dog or a watch dog.... Man is in a different category, however. To attribute to a human being a purpose in that sense is not neutral, let alone complimentary: it is offensive. It is degrading for a man to be regarded as merely serving a purpose. If, at a garden party, I ask a man in livery, 'What is your purpose?' I am insulting him. I might as well have asked, 'What are you for?' Such questions reduce him to the level of a gadget, a domestic animal, or perhaps a slave. I imply that we allot to him the tasks, the goals, the aims which he is to pursue; that his wishes and desires and aspirations and purposes are to count for little or nothing. We are treating him, in Kant's phrase, merely as a means to our ends, not as an end in himself .... [Purpose theory] sees man as a creature, a divine artefact, something halfway between a robot (manufactured) and an animal (alive), a homunculus, or perhaps Frankenstein, made in God's laboratory, with a purpose or task assigned him by his Maker.[11]

Baier's claim is not that God's purpose would be 'selfish', i.e., in His best interest but not ours. Therefore, it will not suffice to point out that God's purpose would be in our objective interests.[12] Baier's concern about God's assigning us a purpose is that it would *degrade* us, not that it would *harm* us. Baier objects that being assigned a purpose would treat one's capacity for rational choice as a mere tool to be used for the realization of a purpose one does not share. It is irrelevant that realizing the purpose would be good for oneself; that would merely add a paternalistic aspect to the degradation.

It is also worth noting that Baier's claim is not that it is disrespectful ever to view someone as being useful. Hence, one cannot respond to Baier by noting cases in which it is not disrespectful to view people as having a use-value. If we ask a stranger what he does for a living, we are in effect asking how he contributes to society, and there is nothing disrespectful about this.[13] Such a case does not tell against Baier, since enquiring about someone's job need not involve treating the person *merely* as a means, which is Baier's concern.

If God were to assign us a purpose, then God would clearly have to regard us as a means, i.e., as being useful for the realization of his end. The question is whether God must thereby regard us *solely* as a means, and that is not so clear. If God did not coerce, exploit, or deceive humans to get them to fulfil a purpose, then God would engage in no manipulation, the central form of treating a person merely as a means. However, Baier's example does not involve the use of force or fraud to get an agent to do something. Baier's case is one in which an agent is *insulted*, rather than *manipulated*. In asking a person what she is for, one offensively expresses the judgment that a person does not exist for her own sake. Must God similarly insult us insofar as He assigns us a purpose? It might seem so. If God has a purpose He wants us to fulfil, it seems that He would have to inform us of it. Hence, if God assigned a purpose to us, He would in some way have to say to each of us, 'There is something I would like you to do with your life, and this is the reason that you exist'. As it stands, this statement does sound a bit patronizing.

However, if we reflect some more on what God's purpose might be and how God might seek to promote it, the statement can be part of a respectful address. For example, suppose that the end God assigned us were to exercise our free will in a moral way. Informing us of such an end need not be condescending. Suppose that we filled out God's statement as follows: 'There is something I would like you to do with your life, and this is the reason that you exist. Specifically, I would like you to be a moral person. Your free will is such that I cannot cajole you into exercising it morally, and your moral choice would be valuable only if it were made freely. Therefore, I must ask you to pursue the fundamental end of pursuing moral ends.' We could even imagine that a 'please' were thrown in.

In short, being assigned a purpose could be a matter of divine request, rather than divine command. If being assigned an end can be a matter of being asked to adopt the end voluntarily, then there need not be anything insulting about being assigned an end. We could well imagine a parent telling his adult daughter that he brought her up for the sake of there being another good person on the planet, an end that he hopes she will freely decide to share with him. There need not be condescension here.

Poorly motivated creation

Baier's invocation of Frankenstein suggests a fourth way that purpose theory might entail that God is disrespectful. We often think that it is possible for parents to be immoral insofar as they create offspring for the wrong reasons, and the same might go for God's creation of us.

To illustrate, suppose that a couple decides to have a child fundamentally because they would like a musician in the family. Now, let us set aside the other elements of disrespect considered so far; assume that the couple neither manipulates the child into becoming a musician nor commands the child to become one. We instead suppose merely that the basic purpose of getting pregnant is to end up with a musically-adept relative, a purpose the parents do not promote in any objectionable way (viz., they observe 'side-constraints' on the pursuit of their end). Merely acting on the maxim of creating a child in order to have a musician might be disrespectful, even if the child is in no way manipulated into being a musician or 'reduced to' her musical aptitude. The same apparently goes for creating a child with the aim of having a worker on the farm or a playmate for a sibling. In contrast, it would not seem disrespectful to make a baby for the sake of promoting a being who will set its own ends. Baier might therefore suggest this principle to govern the creation of rational beings: it is disrespectful to create a rational being for any purpose other than that this being pursues its own purposes.[14]

Now, God's purpose for us would presumably involve living morally, and it therefore appears that God would create us for a purpose other than setting our own ends. By the above principle, then, God would be acting disrespectfully in creating us for the sake of setting moral ends.

Obviously, the purpose theorist must question the principle I have ascribed to Baier. In particular, the purpose theorist must contend that the principle is too broad, i.e., that it can be respectful to create a person for a given purpose in addition to that of adopting her own purposes. It is clear that someone who created a person in order to have another moral agent on earth would be treating that person as a means, but it is not obvious that he would be thereby treating her *merely* as a means. If, as we assume, such a creator did not coerce the created into being moral, did not take advantage of the created's weakness to get her to be moral, and did not condescendingly tell her to be moral, then his creating her to be moral would not dishonour her autonomy. Again, if the creator pursued his end of having the created be moral merely by reasoning and requesting, then the fact that he made the created in order for her to be moral would not appear to treat her capacity for free choice merely as a means to his end.

I conclude that while some versions of purpose theory, particularly those involving eternal damnation, are vulnerable to the Argument from Disrespect, purpose theory as such is not. If we can imagine a God whose end for us includes moral action, who does not threaten us with an eternity in hell to get His way, who does not make offers we cannot refuse, and who does not address us in a patronizing way, then we can imagine a purpose theory which does not entail the absurdity that God is immoral.

On behalf of purpose theory I have often supposed that God's end would require moral action on our part. Note that this does not mean that the purpose theorist must hold divine command theory (or any other religious ethics). The purpose theorist may coherently hold that God's purpose for us would be to act according to moral standards which obtain independently of God's will. Purpose theory might be neater or simpler if it were conjoined with divine command theory. However, divine command theory has notorious problems that we should not want purpose theory necessarily to inherit, and it is worth considering what problems might be thought to arise for purpose theory when it is considered distinct from divine command theory.

God's Purpose vs. God's Omnipotence

The next objection to purpose theory is that it entails that God is not omnipotent, which is a contradiction. If it were possible for us not to fulfil the end assigned to us, and if the end assigned to us were necessary to realize God's plan, then God would need our help. But if God needed our help, then God would not be omnipotent. Therefore, purpose theory implies the absurdity that God would not be omnipotent.[15]

One might reply that purpose theory as such does not imply that we could avoid executing God's plan. Specifically, one may hold a soft determinist view of freedom, and maintain that God would structure causal laws so that we would necessarily freely choose to realize the end God has assigned us. However, to say we 'necessarily freely choose' to realize a particular end is, to many thinkers, to state a contradiction. In addition, with this response purpose theory would lose the ability to say that some human lives are more meaningful than others, for everyone would then be determined to do God's bidding. (Of course, God could make some people choose to attain the ends assigned to them and make others choose not to do so; then it would not be the case that everyone's life is meaningful. However, such a move would introduce an arbitrariness and inequity into God's plan which would presumably undercut its ability to confer meaning at all.)

Therefore, the purpose theorist ought to hold that we have libertarian free will and hence grant that we could avoid realizing the end God assigns us. She should also grant that realizing the end God assigns us would be necessary to fulfil God's higher-order end(s); assuming that God is the source of the universe, we must presume that our existence is an integral part of the reason(s) for which it was created. That means the purpose theorist must admit that there is a sense in which 'God would need our help': the realization of God's higher-order end(s) would depend on our realizing the end He assigns us, something we could freely choose to do or not. Therefore, the purpose theorist must respond to the objection by refuting the claim that God's needing help implies a lack of omnipotence.

Now, it is widely accepted among theologians that we need not conceive of God's omnipotence as implying that God could do what is logically impossible. It is also commonly held that it would be logically impossible for God to bring about by His own power the superior value of a person freely choosing to act morally. Therefore, if one of God's higher-order ends required us to act morally on the basis of free choice, we would have a sense of God 'needing our help' that does not impugn God's omnipotence. God could need our help in that God logically could not by His own efforts fulfil one of His valuable higher-order purposes.

However, this response might raise a new worry. Even if God's omnipotence is not called into question by virtue of God's being logically unable to bring about one of His higher-order ends, we might find such a God to be irrational. It seems incredible that God would create the universe for the sake of an end that might not be realized. How could it be rational to go to the trouble of making a world for a goal, the attainment of which depends on the contingent choice of our un-dependable species?

There are two strong replies to this new concern. First, recall that we can conceive of God making the universe for several higher-order ends. It would certainly seem rational to create nature knowing that, say, two higher-order ends would necessarily be realized but that one would only probably be realized. Second, it could still be rational to bring about a world for the sake of a single highest-order goal which God could not ensure would be achieved. At least if the value of free moral choice were extremely high, then the expected utility of creating a world for the sake of free moral choice, which may or may not materialize, could be greater than that of creating a world without free humans but which necessarily achieves some less valuable goal.

I conclude that God's needing our help to attain His higher-order goal(s) threatens neither God's omnipotence nor His rationality. Let us turn to the third *reductio* against purpose theory.

God's Purpose vs. God's Eternality

The last charge of incoherence in purpose theory claims that there is a tension between claiming that God is beyond space and time, on one hand, and claiming that God sets an end for us, on the other. In the only book-length treatment of life's meaning published in the 1990s, Irving Singer clearly voices the worry about speaking of 'God's purpose':

> … to talk in this way is to assume that one can refer to an intentionality outside of time and space comparable to what occurs within. That is the basic flaw in the analogy… . It is not a question of determining whether we can fathom the cosmic plan, or prove that a cosmic planner exists, or manage to fulfill his purposive program. It is a question of knowing whether our mind is able to formulate these notions with any degree of clarity.[16]

Singer finds the traditional concern about the compatibility of eternality and personality sufficient to disqualify purpose theory.

The most straightforward response, of course, is to deny that eternality must be interpreted in atemporal terms. It appears open to the purpose theorist to maintain that God would exist always in time rather than exist never in time.

To reply on behalf of Singer, one may note that conceiving of God as everlasting has well-known prima facie difficulties for other aspects of theism, e.g., it is unclear that an everlasting God could be the source of space and time. Now, I want to avoid this debate. I would prefer to downplay questions about the coherence of our concept of God, in order to focus on the much more neglected topic of the plausibility of purpose theory.

Therefore, I suggest that a more attractive reply is to say that a merely everlasting God would not be special enough to be a unique source of significance. If a temporal being could not have the right sort of status to be the only source of life's meaning, and if an atemporal being could not be conceived to have a purpose, then the purpose theorist would be caught in a trap. In brief, the purpose theorist potentially faces this dilemma: either (1) God would be atemporal and could be the sole source of meaning, but God could not have a purpose, or (2) God would be temporal and could have a purpose, but God could not be the sole source of meaning.

I believe this is the most important objection facing purpose theory, one that I will develop in the following section. In order to flesh out this dilemma, we must enquire into the underpinnings of God-centred theory.

God's Purpose vs. God-Centred Theory

The objections in the previous three sections contended that purpose theory entails logical absurdities. I have argued that there are versions of purpose theory which can avoid these implications. However, I will now argue that there is a problem facing purpose theory which no version can avoid. Specifically, I will contend that purpose theory as such is incompatible with claims central to a God-centred perspective.

The objection I will develop can be understood in terms of the responses which one might offer to two questions. First, why think that the significance of our lives *essentially depends on a relationship with God*? Second, why think that a relevant relationship with God is a matter of *realizing His purpose*? I will argue that the most promising answer to the first question implies that no satisfactory answer to the second question is available. Specifically, I will argue that the best reason for holding a God-centred theory is that God has qualities such as atemporality, immutability, simplicity, and infinitude, qualities that seem to be incompatible with God's being purposive.

Before presenting the objection, I want to respond to a worry about its form. Someone might be inclined to say the following: 'So what if purpose theory cannot be the correct version of God-centred theory? Whoever supposed that God-centred theory is the proper way to articulate a religious thinker's perspective on the meaning of life?' A God-centred theory, as I construe it, maintains not just that the better one's relationship with God, the more meaningful one's life; it also holds that the existence of God is necessary for one's life to be at all meaningful. A God-centred theory of meaning implies that, if the physical world did not spring from God, then there would be no way to acquire meaning in it. The question is, why think that such a theory should be attractive to theologians? Why not hold instead that, while *some* meaning would be possible if God did not exist, God's existence would potentially make people's lives more meaningful? If Western religious scholars denied the view that God's existence is necessary for a meaningful life, or if such a view were prima facie implausible, then it would not substantially discredit purpose theory to show that it is incompatible with this view.

I have three reasons for thinking that God-centred theory is a relevant standard for appraising purpose theory, at least given a Western context. First, the most influential statements on the meaning of life in the Western religious tradition are clear instances of God-centred theory. Consider Tolstoy's 'Confession',[17] by far the most widely-read religious discussion of the meaning of life. In this work, Tolstoy acutely expresses the worry that life would be meaningless without God. For another instance, think about Kierkegaard's writings on God. In them, he also expresses the judgment that life would be without significance if God did not exist.[18]

In addition to historical prominence, there are strong theoretical reasons for using God-centred theory as a base from which to evaluate purpose theory. Meaningfulness is a value concept, and one would expect a religious theory of meaning to accord with other religious theories of value. Consider, then, that in moral theory a religious view is standardly understood to maintain that moral rules are identical to God's commands and hence that 'if God does not exist, everything is permitted' (Dostoyevsky): For another example, consider the theory of human excellence. Here, many religious thinkers follow Aquinas, holding that God is the unique source of perfection and that other things obtain excellence by virtue of participating in God's. By analogy, then, a religious theory of meaning ought to hold that God is the sole source of meaning and that, without God, there would be no meaning (just as there would be no morality or excellence).

Finally, God-centred theory cuts out philosophically interesting territory. In order for the dispute between naturalists and supernaturalists about life's meaning to be substantive, the latter must hold that a relationship with God is necessary to make our lives meaningful. To see this, suppose that a religious thinker instead maintained the weaker view that while a relationship with God would make our lives more meaningful, it is not necessary for meaning. The problem is that virtually no naturalist would dispute this claim. Very few naturalists would contend that, if God existed, relating to him would fail to enhance the meaning of one's life (and the arguments for this contention are simply unpersuasive).[19] After all, typical naturalists would hardly be displeased if they suddenly discovered God exists; they simply maintain that for a life to be meaningful there need not exist a spiritual being who grounds the universe. Therefore, for religious thinking to carve out a distinct and interesting position, it must maintain that God's existence and a certain relationship with Him are necessary for life to acquire significance.

I conclude, then, that for reasons of tradition, coherence, and relevance, it makes sense to appraise purpose theory in light of God-centred theory. If, as I will contend, purpose theory is not consistent with the underpinnings of God-centred theory, then there is strong reason to reject purpose theory.

My thesis is that if a relationship with God is essential for a meaningful life, then the meaning cannot come by accomplishing a purpose He sets. To defend this thesis, I will now argue in two stages. Step 1 contends that the best explanation of God-centred theory includes the claim that God has certain properties such as immutability and atemporality. Step 2 maintains that these properties are incompatible with a purposive God. These two steps entail (probably) that purpose theory cannot be the correct version of God-centred theory.

Step 1

In looking for an acceptable explanation of why God alone could make our lives meaningful, we must appeal to features that cannot be found anywhere but in God. Again, if our lives acquire significance just to the extent that we have a proper relationship with God, then to explain why God is central to life's meaning we must appeal to features which only God can manifest. Keeping this in mind, let us quickly canvass some common explanations of why life might be meaningless without God.

First, many maintain that God would prevent our lives from being accidental.[20] The idea is that without God as our source and destiny, our lives would be contingent and random matters, which would make them meaningless. Now, it is not entirely clear what it means to speak of a 'contingent' or 'accidental' life. It seems well understood, however, as a life the existence or course of which is not well grounded in the fabric of reality. A life that could not have arisen, or which will perish in a handful of years, seems accidental in this respect. In contrast, a life springing from and returning to a spiritual source of the physical world would seem not to be accidental.

There are two problems with this account. First, if, as many theists believe, God's nature did not require Him to create us, then God would arguably not ground necessity in our lives; it would be His contingent choice to create us. Second, even if God's nature did require Him to create us (or even if His contingent choice to create us prevented our lives from being 'contingent' in the relevant sense), it is not clear that *only* God could prevent contingency. To see this, suppose that the universe were everlasting. In addition, assume that fundamental physical laws dictated only one path for the universe, a path that necessarily resulted in our coming into existence. Finally, imagine that we were somewhat like vampires, able to live indefinitely. Since under these naturalist conditions our lives would be firmly rooted in the structure of reality, it appears that God is not necessary to avoid contingency. Hence, that God could prevent our lives from being contingent cannot explain why a relationship with Him is necessary for meaning.

The same goes for the suggestion that God could make our lives part of a grand scheme, one that encompasses the universe. Some suggest that, from an extremely objective point of view, our lives would be meaningless insofar as they failed to have some large impact on the universe or to play a role crucial to its development.[21] If God did not exist, so the argument goes, we would merely be short-lived beings who exist on the third rock from a star in an enormous sea of stars.

However, God's existence is not necessary to avoid this condition, which a brief reflection on the television series *Star Trek* might indicate. If we could travel near or at the speed of light, then we could enact a plan with an enormous range. Therefore, it cannot be mere scope which explains how God could be the sole source of life's significance.

Now consider justice theory, the relevant version of which maintains that there could be no justice, or more generally no morality, if God did not exist The most famous version of justice theory is divine command theory, the view that God's willing is the source of moral reasons for action, but we may also include here the Thomistic view that God's being is the archetype of goodness. Perhaps a world without God would lack meaning because it would lack moral value.

Philosophers have had a difficult time providing a compelling explanation of why morality is to be identified with God's willing or being. It has seemed to many that morality could be a natural property. It is not my concern to address the responses which religious thinkers have made to their rivals. The point I want to make here is that there is a much *more auspicious* way to explain why God's existence and a relationship with Him might be necessary for life to acquire significance.

I have explored the possibilities that a relationship with God might be necessary for our lives to be meaningful by virtue of His preventing our lives from being contingent, making our lives part of a grand scheme, and grounding morality. Against all three possibilities, I have suggested that nature, independently of God, could perform these functions. In light of this, I suggest that we look to something utterly supernatural in order to explain why God's existence would be necessary for meaning. In particular, perfection theory provides the best explanation of this condition. Perfection theory is the view that a life is meaningful just insofar as it is oriented toward a superior nature. On this view, God alone could be the source of meaning since He has an absolutely unique, supernatural essence, one which alone has the kind of intrinsic value toward which it would be worthwhile contouring one's life.

What is it about God that might make His nature qualitatively different from and more valuable than anything in the natural world? I do not think that God's being all-good, all-powerful, or all-knowing are very plausible candidates. We find goodness, power, and knowledge in our world to some degree. To be sure, God would have these to a superior degree, but this appears to be more of a quantitative difference from human beings, not a qualitative one. It would make most sense to look for features of God that other beings such as humans and angels cannot exhibit; such features would most clearly indicate in what respect God's nature and value would be unique. Four properties readily come to mind: atemporality, immutability, simplicity, and infinitude. Call these the 'qualitative properties'. If God alone had some combination of the qualitative properties, if a being with some combination of these properties had an exceptional excellence, and if we gained significance by contouring our lives toward such a being, then we would have a satisfying explanation of how God alone could be the source of significance.

Now, it is clear that human beings cannot have the qualitative properties. We essentially are spatiotemporal, changeable, decomposable, and limited. Angels, too, are typically understood to be limited and decomposable (at least in thought). Furthermore, there is good reason to believe that important sorts of intrinsic value supervene on the qualitative properties. Classical theists provided many arguments purporting to show that the two values of unity and independence are (partially) constituted by the qualitative properties.[22]

First consider the value of independence, which is a matter of not being confined by or dependent on anything else. All four of the qualitative properties may be deemed instances of independence *par excellence*. A being beyond space and time would be free from the limits of these forms. Such a being would be free not only from decay and death, but also from a point of view restricted to now and here. An immutable being would similarly be something that utterly determines its own nature; if a being which exists in a certain mode can neither have begun to exist nor cease to exist in this mode, then it is free from any influences save itself. A simple being, viz., one without parts, would be free from dependence on these parts for its existence. Such a being would be completely unto itself or *a se*. Finally, an unlimited being would by definition be free of any limits.

Now think about the value of unity. Integrity and oneness are better than disintegration and fragmentation, and the qualitative properties are plausibly manifestations of the former. A being beyond space and time would lack extension or the 'feebleness of division' (Anselm). A simple being, having no parts, forms the ultimate unity in that it cannot even be conceived to dissolve. An immutable being cannot help but remain what it is. Lastly, an unlimited being would be utterly whole.

These have been more argument sketches than full-blown arguments; one could spend an entire paper developing just one of them. My goal is not really to convince the reader that unity and independence are values which supervene on the qualitative properties. My aim is more modestly to show that the *most promising* explanation of why relating to God is essential for a significant life is that God has certain features not found in the physical world and that these features have a superior value which confers significance on us when we orient our lives toward it. Even without a complete analysis of the qualitative properties and of the values of unity and independence, my hope is that the reader will agree that, particularly given the problems facing a supernaturalist ethics, it is fair to say that this perfection theory is the *best* rationale for God-centred theory. Again, explaining why a relationship with God is necessary for one's life to be meaningful is most naturally done by holding that God has some combination of the qualitative properties and that our lives can acquire meaning by being contoured toward an entity with these exceptionally valuable features. Such contouring might take the form of glorifying God in this life or by communing with Him in an afterlife, but, as I will now argue, it cannot be a matter of realizing God's purpose.

Step 2

In Step 1 of the argument, I argued that if God alone could confer meaning on life, this would have to be because He has utterly unique features with a superior worth, viz., the qualitative properties. In Step 2, I need to show that God's having the qualitative properties is incompatible with central tenets of purpose theory.

It is hard to see how a being with the qualitative properties could play the role that purpose theory requires. In fact, this is a common concern among theists; my aim is not to add anything new to this particular issue, but rather to articulate it. So, first off, how could there be an unchangeable being beyond time which is purposive? The worry here is not that it is difficult to conceptualize an immutable, timeless being. While it is difficult, it is not impossible, for, as several philosophers have recently noted, states and dispositions do not seem essentially to be temporal or to involve change. The concern is rather that, to the extent that we can conceive of an immutable being beyond time, such a being appears unable to engage in goal-directed activity. Specifically, the problem is that activities are events, and events seem fundamentally to involve change and time. For God to adopt an end for humans might presuppose some deliberation, and deliberation would appear to be a temporal event involving alteration in God. And even if God adopted an end without prior deliberation, the adoption alone would seem to be something that takes time and that forms something new in God. Furthermore, creating a world according to a plan seems hard to understand as something that does not cover a span of time. Finally, purpose theorists usually hold that God informs us of the end He has set and that He responds to our free decisions of whether to fulfil it or not. Again, these are activities which seem irreducibly to take time to perform and to involve change on God's part.

For another instance of the problem, how could there be an absolutely simple being which has multiple ends, one for humans and one for animals? God presumably would have created bees for a purpose which they do not fail to fulfil. In order to avoid the counterintuitive implication that animal lives can be as meaningful as human lives, the purpose theorist must maintain that we would be assigned a purpose different from and better than those assigned to animals.[23] Now, even if human and animal purposes are components of a single plan for the universe, the fact of there being components would seem to imply a lack of simplicity. The same goes for the different acts mentioned above; more than one act would appear to compromise God's absolute simplicity, and it is difficult to see how a single, grand act could ground purpose theory's conception of what God does.

Finally, how could a being which is unlimited be the sort of entity which has a purpose? As Nozick puts it, 'To be one way and not another is to have limits. It seems, then, that no terms can describe something unlimited, no human terms can truly apply to it.'[24] Analogical reasoning will not get the purpose theorist very far. While I have argued above that purpose theory need not provide much practical guidance to be viable, it must at least be theoretically comprehensible.

There are, of course, responses to these worries in the literature. I do not have the space to explore them here. Instead, my goal at this stage has been to note the prima facie difficulty of reconciling a view of God as timeless, immutable, simple, and unlimited with a view of God as purposive. Summing up: if indeed a God with the qualitative properties cannot be purposive (Step 2), and if God must have the qualitative properties to be the sole source of meaning (Step 1), then it follows that we cannot acquire meaning in our lives by virtue of realizing a purpose God assigns us. I submit that this is the most significant problem facing purpose theory.

Before considering strategies for responding to this objection, I want to clarify it. There is of course a substantial tradition of wondering whether and how God's otherness might be consistent with God's personality. I am not just reiterating points from this tradition, for I am not making a claim about inconsistency within the concept of God. Moreover, my point is not even that purpose theory is inconsistent with the concept of God (this may or may not follow from the account of perfection suggested here).[25] Instead, my thesis is that the most plausible reason for holding a God-centred theory of life's meaning is not consistent with the traditional version of God-centred theory. God alone could be the source of significance just insofar as He has some combination of the qualitative properties, and it is difficult to conceive of a purposive agent which has no limits, is absolutely simple, cannot change, and does not act in time. This argument does not threaten God-centred theory as such. It instead suggests that, if one is sympathetic to God-centred theory, one should reject the version of it which has been central to Western religious thinking about the meaning of life. Rather than hold purpose theory, theologians should adopt the view that a meaningful life consists of, say, worshipping God in this life, or merging with Him in an afterlife.

Conclusion: The End of Purpose Theory

I do not claim that the objection as it has been stated here requires disbelief in purpose theory. However, it would seem that an adequate defence of purpose theory must address it. I will conclude by noting the two aims which purpose theorists might pursue in future work.

First, the purpose theorist could try to show that it is conceivable that a being with some or all of the qualitative properties could be purposive. Aquinas is a promising source of ideas needed to flesh out this strategy. For example, one could contend that atemporal, simple, and immutable knowing is possible, that willing and knowing are not distinct in God, and that having a purpose is part of the concept of willing.[26]

Second, the purpose theorist could grant that purposiveness is indeed incompatible with the qualitative properties, but seek to refute the idea that the latter are the key to meaningfulness. For example, the purpose theorist might join forces with the divine command theorist. If it were plausible to think that God alone could ground morality and that morality is necessary for meaning, then we would have an explanation of how God alone could ground meaning without appeal to qualities such as atemporality and simplicity.

I am at this stage doubtful that either of these two goals is attainable. However, that is something to establish elsewhere, if one is interested in doing so. I suggest that it would also be reasonable, given the objection made here, to develop a God-centred alternative to purpose theory. Suppose God's having some combination of the qualitative properties is part of the best explanation of what would enable Him alone to confer significance on our lives. Exactly which qualitative properties ground God-centred theory? Precisely how would we have to relate to a being with the relevant qualitative properties in order for our lives to acquire significance? These questions, too, are worth considering at this point.

Notes

1. No arguments in this paper depend on this somewhat controversial characterization of the question of life's meaning. I defend this characterization in 'The concept of a meaningful life', *American Philosophical Quarterly*, 38(2001) and constituting the first chapter of a book manuscript in progress, *Meaningful Lives and Politics*. The present essay forms the core of this monograph's second chapter.

2. Explicit adherents of purpose theory include Paul Althaus 'The meaning and purpose of history in the Christian view', *Universitas: A German Review of the Arts and Sciences*, 7 (1965), 197–204; the monotheistic essays in R. C. Chalmers and John Irving (eds) *The Meaning of Life in Five Great Religions* (Philadelphia PA: Westminster Press, 1965), chs 4–6; Delwin Brown

'Process philosophy and the question of life's meaning', *Religious Studies*, 7 (1971), 13–29; Michael Levine 'What does death have to do with the meaning of life?', *Religious Studies*, 23 (1987), 457–65; Lois Hope Walker 'Religion and the meaning of life and death', in Louis Pojman (ed.) *Philosophy: The Quest for Truth* (Belmont CA: Wadsworth Publishing Company, 1989), ch. 16; Philip Quinn 'How Christianity secures life's meanings', in Joseph Runzo and Nancy Martin (eds.) *The Meaning of Life in the World Religions* (Oxford: Oneworld Publications, 2000), ch. 3.

3. For this objection, see Kurt Baier 'The meaning of life', in E. D. Klemke (ed.) *The Meaning of Life* (New York NY: Oxford University Press, 1981), 106–8; Norman Dahl 'Morality and the meaning of life: some first

thoughts', *Canadian Journal of Philosophy*, 17 (1987), n-12 n.; and Oswald Hanfling *The Quest for Meaning* (New York NY: Basil Blackwell Inc., 1987), 50.

4. For explicitly this-worldly versions of purpose theory, see Brown, 'Process philosophy and the question of life's meaning', esp. 24–5; and Levine, 'What does death have to do with the meaning of life?'.

5. Baier 'The meaning of life', 106; and Joseph Ellin *Morality and the Meaning of Life* (Fort Worth TX: Harcourt Brace, 1995), 322.

6. Baier incorrectly states that purpose theory implies the following: 'No human life, however pointless it may seem, is meaningless because in being part of God's plan, every life is assured of significance', (Baier 'The meaning of life', 105; see also 106,115).

7. A. J. Ayer tends to assume that we could not avoid realizing God's plan. See his 'The claims of philosophy', in Maurice Natanson (ed.) *Philosophy of the Social Sciences* (New York NY: Random House, 1963), 475–7.

8. Jean-Paul Sartre *Existentialism and Humanism Philip Mairet* (tr.) (London: Methuen & Co, 1948), 45.

9. For an instance of this argument, see Hanfling *The Quest for Meaning*, 45–6.

10. Baier 'The meaning of life', 107; and Paul Kurtz 'The meaning of life' in *The Fullness of Life* (New York NY: Horizon Press, 1974), 86.

11. Baier 'The meaning of life', 104. For echoes of Baier, see W. D. Joske 'Philosophy and the meaning of life', in Klemke *The Meaning of Life,* 259; and Irving Singer *Meaning in Life, vol. 1: The Creation of Value* (Baltimore MD: Johns Hopkins University Press, 1996), 29.

12. For this response to Baier, see Levine 'What does death have to do with the meaning of life?', 461 n.

13. Brown makes this reply to Baier in 'Process philosophy and the question of life's meaning', 20.

14. Compare Singer's comment: 'If humanity, or life in general, was created to serve a purpose beyond itself, our being would be analogous to that of a manufactured artifact', (Singer *Meaning in Life*, 29).

15. For discussions that prompted me to consider this objection, see Karl Britton *Philosophy and the Meaning of Life* (New York NY: Cambridge University Press, 1969), 31, 34–5; and Hanfling *The Quest for Meaning,* 48.

16. Singer *Meaning in Life*, 31, 32. For the same point, see R. W. Hepburn 'Questions about the meaning of life', in Klemke *The Meaning of Life*, 223.

17. See the selection in Klemke *The Meaning of Life*, 9–19.

18. See, e.g., 'Training in Christianity', in Robert Bretall (ed.) *A Kierkegaard Anthology* (Princeton NJ: Princeton University Press, 1946), 414.

19. The main arguments are these: a life relating to God would be degrading and hence meaningless; and achieving our own subjective ends is alone what confers meaning. For suggestions of both claims, see Baier 'The meaning of life'.

20. For this view, see Tolstoy 'My confession'; Albert Camus *The Myth of Sisyphus* Justin O'Brien (trans.) (New York NY: Knopf, 1955); and William Davis 'The meaning of life', *Metaphilosophy*, 18 (1987), 288–305.

21. Thomas Nagel, while not a supernaturalist has expressed this in a compelling way. See his 'The absurd', in *Mortal Questions* (New York NY: Cambridge University Press, 1979), ch. 2, and 'Birth, death, and the meaning of life', in *The View from Nowhere* (New York NY: Oxford University Press, 1986), ch. 11.

22. Many of the following arguments can be found in Plotinus *The Enneads*; Anseim *Monologion* and *Proslogion*; and Aquinas *Summa Contra Gentiles*, and *Summa Theologica*.

23. For more discussion of human and animal meaning in the context of purpose theory, see Robert Nozick 'Philosophy and the meaning of life', in *Philosophical Explanations* (Cambridge: Harvard University Press, 1981), 586–7; and Hanfling *The Quest for Meaning*, 48–9.

24. Making a very different argument, Nozick also answers the question of why realizing God's purpose might be a source of meaning by appealing to God's being unlimited ('Philosophy and the meaning of life', 593–609). At one point Nozick does not recognize the tension in claiming that God is unlimited and that God has a purpose (606), though at another point. Nozick notes that it would be difficult to predicate anything of an unlimited being (608). For other recent statements of the tension between God's personality and some of the qualitative properties, see Richard Gale *On the Nature and Existence of God* (New York NY: Cambridge University Press, 1991), ch. 2; and Richard Swinburne *The Coherence of Theism* rev. edn. (Oxford: Oxford University Press, 1993), ch. 12.

25. The argument I make in the text is that if God alone could be the source of meaning, this must be because God would have the qualitative properties, perfections

which are incompatible with purposiveness. Darrel Mollendorf and Graeme McLean have wondered whether my argument could be collapsed into the more common contention that God, *qua* perfect, by definition has the qualitative properties and hence cannot be purposive. I do not think that my argument can be easily reduced to this rationale, since God does not, merely *qua* perfect being, have all the perfections. To see this, imagine a quite valuable being who created the universe but who is short of being Anselm's 'thing of which none greater can be conceived'. Such an entity would sensibly be called 'God'. Hence, insofar as the concept of God (or a common one) does not include having all the perfections, God does not (or does not obviously) by definition have the qualitative properties.

26. For interesting work along these general lines, see Norman Kretzmann and Eleonore Stump 'Eternity', *The Journal of Philosophy*, 78 (1981), 429–58, and 'Absolute simplicity', *Faith and Philosophy*, 2 (1985), 353–82; Katherin Rogers 'The traditional doctrine of divine simplicity', *Religious Studies*, 32 (1996), 165–86; and Don Lodzinski 'The eternal act', *Religious Studies*, 34 (1998), 325–52.

Section III

The Loss of Meaning in a World Without God

Pessimistic Naturalism

Introduction

Garrett Thomson

What is pessimistic naturalism? The General Introduction to this book outlined a triad of views: optimistic supernaturalism, pessimistic naturalism, and optimistic naturalism. We can understand this triad in relation to the supernaturalist syllogism:

(1)   God exists.
(2)   The existence of God is sufficient and necessary for the meaningfulness of life.
(3)   Therefore, life is meaningful.

In contrast, pessimistic naturalism rejects the claim that God exists (premise 1) and concludes that life in a godless world is meaningless. Despite the differences, pessimistic naturalism shares a crucial assumption with supernaturalism, namely premise 2. In this regard, we might contrast both views with optimistic naturalism, the topic of the next section, which affirms that life can be meaningful without the existence of God and denies premise 2. In short, pessimistic naturalism stands as an intermediary between optimistic supernaturalism and optimistic naturalism.

However, things are not as simple as that. For a start, pessimistic naturalism is not a single theory. As the variety of essays gathered in this section will testify, it is a loose collection of views, which differ from each other. Roughly, what unifies them is the claim that life is in some sense meaningless or absurd because of some general feature of the natural world. The relevant characteristics do not have to be limited to God's nonexistence. Other features include that we are not immortal souls, that we ourselves are finite (as opposed to infinite) beings, and that we live in time. Pessimistic naturalism maintains that one or more of these characteristics renders our human lives insignificant, meaningless, or absurd; pessimism or nihilism is warranted.

Exploring the Meaning of Life: An Anthology and Guide, First Edition. Edited by Joshua W. Seachris.
© 2013 John Wiley & Sons, Inc. Published 2013 by John Wiley & Sons, Inc.

There is also a second complication. Terms such as "insignificant," "meaningless," or "absurd" differ from each other, as we saw in the first section of this book. For example, life might be absurd and pointless, but it is still worth living. This complication makes pessimistic naturalism a complex and nuanced set of views. For, as we shall see, philosophers of this persuasion sometimes argue for a silver lining, as well as for a dark cloud. For instance, although they accept that life is meaningless or absurd, they may also argue that humans can find this liberating. In this way, pessimistic naturalism can sometimes seem to shade into optimistic naturalism.

We start the section with Arthur Schopenhauer's classic "On the Vanity of Existence," first published in 1851. In the very first sentence, Schopenhauer catalogues the reasons for pessimism:

- The universe is infinite in time and we are finite.
- The present moment is fleeting.
- Everything is contingent.
- Everything in time becomes and never is.
- We have desires that remain unsatisfied.
- Life consists in continual striving.

These all constitute part of the structure of our existence. For example, Schopenhauer argues that our existence is worthless because of the nature of time. The past is nothing because only the present is actual; we only live in the present. However, the present is transient: It becomes the past instantaneously. Schopenhauer argues that something fleeting is not worth serious effort (Section 2).

He also describes our lives as unceasing motion in which happiness is impossible. First, because we strive for rest or repose and cannot attain it, happiness would never be satisfying even if we could achieve it. Second, at the end of a life, it does not matter whether one has been happy or not; it is in the past (Section 3).

Schopenhauer says that we continually live in expectation of better things and, consequently, the present moment is regarded as serving only as the means to our goals. This is also why we feel nostalgia for the past and, at the end of our lives, we feel as if life has passed us by (Section 4). Life consists in striving, but if we attain our goals, the result is boring. Boredom is awareness of the emptiness of existence, and it is direct evidence for the claim that life is valueless (Section 5). Nature declares that all our striving is vain by making our end annihilation; something of intrinsic value would not have nonbeing as its goal. In short, Schopenhauer concludes that it is best to regard life as a process of disillusionment.

The next selection can be regarded as an attempt to accept the intrinsic meaninglessness of the universe, but to show how either human ideals or happiness can still have worth in such a universe. In 1903, the British philosopher Bertrand Russell wrote his famous essay "A Free Man's Worship." In this essay Russell has two main aims. First, he argues that a free person would worship moral ideals, which are our own human creation. His main argument consists in rejecting what he takes to be the only alternative: the slave-like worship of a god of power, which he associates with the major theistic religions. Second, he tries to answer the question: "How can we find a home for our ideals and aspirations in the purposeless and meaningless world described by science?" To do so, he describes a historical process of maintaining these ideals and, through this description, he elaborates the contrast between free and slavish worship, central to his main thesis.

We can discern six steps in Russell's description of the process. The first is that, in a mechanical and apparently hostile universe, people feel impotent before the powers of nature, and therefore, like slaves, they worship gods of power irrespective of whether they are worthy of worship. Second, people begin to feel the claims of moral ideals and construct the conception of God as an all-good and all-powerful being. However, such a conception cannot be maintained because the world is not good, and so humans are still confronted with the choice of worshiping power or goodness. Third, we come to the realization that the worship of force is a failure to maintain our own ideals against an antagonistic universe. Thus, to maintain our moral ideals, we need to defy a hostile universe. However, such Promethean indignation or rebellion is still a form of bondage, and to be free of it, we must pass on to the fourth stage: renunciation, which Russell describes as the gate to wisdom. Through suffering, we realize that the world was not made for us, and we abandon the pursuit of happiness and eager desires. Fifth, we need to shape the temple of our own ideals in our feeling through the contemplation of beauty that we find in music, architecture, and reasoning. Sixth, to enter the temple, we need to pass through a cavern of despair so that we can resign ourselves to Fate (what we cannot control). Having passed through this, we can find in nature reflections of beauty made by our own thoughts. In other words, we can reshape the natural world by projecting our own sense of beauty onto it. In this way, the mind can assert a subtle mastery over the thoughtless forces of nature. The more difficult this process is because of suffering, the greater our achievement.

The next essay, by Thomas Nagel, can be viewed as an attempt to defuse the absurdity of life. Nagel's main aim is to explain why we may feel that life is absurd even though the standard arguments for that claim are weak. Despite their flaws, those arguments express an underlying insight about the nature of the absurd.

Nagel presents two kinds of inadequate arguments. First, he considers the arguments related to space and time; namely, that we are a tiny speck in an immense universe, and that our lives last only a brief instant. He concludes that these arguments are weak because if it were absurd, then life would still be so even if it were everlasting and if we were much bigger in relation to the universe. Second, he examines arguments for the assertion that life is absurd because there are no complete justifications for any value claims; all chains of value justification are incomplete because we die. Nagel criticizes this argument for ignoring the possibility that chains of justification can end within a life.

Nagel argues that life feels absurd because of a discrepancy between two viewpoints. From the internal viewpoint, in the midst of everyday life, we are serious about our concerns. But when we step back from them, our whole system of the justification of values rests on responses and habits that we never question. From this external viewpoint, what we value is arbitrary. The feeling of absurdity arises from the discrepancy between these two inescapable viewpoints.

After showing that such absurdity is inescapable (Section III) and defending his view against objections (Section IV), Nagel compares this view of the absurd to radical epistemological skepticism, the thesis that knowledge claims can never be justified. Skepticism arises because we take an external view of our whole system of beliefs. At the same time, we cannot shed our everyday claims to knowledge. In the case of both skepticism and the absurd, our limitedness joins with our capacity to transcend those limits. Skepticism does not lead us to abandon our everyday beliefs, but it renders them with a special flavor of irony. Likewise with the practical: After encountering the absurd and questioning the seriousness with which we take our lives, we must return to those concerns, albeit with irony.

Now, says Nagel, we can see why the failed arguments for the absurdity of life contain an important insight; the idea that we can view ourselves from a broader perspective is necessary for the discrepancy that constitutes the absurd. Nagel argues that the absurdity of life is not really a problem. It indicates a feature of human life; namely, our capacity to transcend ourselves in thought. Because of this, Nagel advocates irony rather than despair or heroism.

The next selection from a book, *Better to Never Have Been*, published in 2006 by the South African philosopher David Benatar, defends a Schopenhauerian pessimism. The extract contains Benatar's main arguments for the conclusion that coming into existence is always a harm.

The argument for this conclusion is based on an asymmetry between these two claims:

(1)   The absence of pain is a good even if that good is not enjoyed by anyone.
(2)   But the absence of pleasure is not bad unless there is someone for whom this absence is a deprivation.

These two statements define an asymmetry between pain and pleasure with regard to future persons.

Benatar claims that the conjunction of claims (1) and (2) implies that coming into existence is always a harm. First, let us suppose that a future being or person will suffer. Insofar as this will be true then, because of (1), it would be better that such a being or person not come into existence at all. Second, let us suppose that the future being will feel some pleasure and happiness. However, even insofar as this will be true, nevertheless it would not be bad if the future person did not come into existence at all, because of (2). If we put the two results together, we can derive the conclusion that bringing a person into existence is never a good, but it is always bad (because the person will suffer some pain).

Benatar provides several reasons for (1) and (2). The central argument is that the two claims constitute the best explanation of why there is a duty to avoid bringing suffering people into existence, but there is no corresponding duty to bring happy people into being. He adds that one cannot cite sensibly the interests of a potential child as a reason for bringing a child into existence. However, one could cite sensibly those interests as a reason for *not* bringing a child into existence.

In the final essay, Thomas Nagel tries to evaluate strategically the prospects for secular analytic philosophy to satisfy the religious temperament. He outlines three secular responses to the question: "How can one bring into one's individual life a full recognition of one's relation to the universe as a whole?" This question expresses the impulse for a cosmic reconciliation, the desire to be connected to the spiritual sense of the universe as a whole, which marks the religious temperament.

The first secular response is the hardheaded atheistic approach exemplified by Hume, according to which the quest for harmony with the universe is based on an error of applying concepts beyond the conditions that give them meaning (Section III). Nagel challenges this approach (in Section IV), which he says mistakenly implies that the original question is meaningless.

The second response accepts the question as meaningful, but recognizes our inability to answer it from a cosmic point of view. Humanism reframes the question so that it asks about one's meaning in relation to humanity rather than to the universe. According to this view, exemplified by Kant and Sartre, the significance of an individual's life is defined by his or her relation to the community of human or rational beings. Nagel expresses reservations about humanism on the grounds that it is limited.

The third secular response tries to provide a cosmic point of view from which to make sense of our lives that is based on the natural order. This comes in two forms. The first advocates an evolutionary perspective. It tries to make sense of our lives in terms of a process of biological and social evolution (Section VI). This view, which Nagel rejects, is associated with Nietzsche. It relies on a purpose-driven conception of evolution, which is repudiated by contemporary mechanical theories of evolution based on natural selection (Section VII). The second kind of secular cosmic alternative relies on the idea that the universe necessarily generates living beings that can understand it, but without postulating purposes. Nagel characterizes the significance of this Platonic idea as follows: We are part of the process of the universe gradually waking up. Such a view expands our conception of what a human life is without providing a cosmic purpose (Section VIII).

Finally, Nagel expresses severe reservations about all three secular responses to his question. He suggests that if one rejects the Platonic view along with the religious one, then one may be left with the absurd.

In summary, pessimistic naturalism concludes that our lives are meaningless or absurd because of some general natural feature of the world, such as the nonexistence of God or the ever-fleeting nature of the present. Also, it may entreat us to defy this absurdity or to treat it ironically. To evaluate pessimistic naturalism, we must ask: Does the natural feature in question really imply that life is meaningless? As we shall see in the next section, optimistic naturalism usually answers this question in the negative.

Suggestions for Further Reading

Almeida, Michael (2010) "Two challenges to moral nihilism," *The Monist* 93(January): 96–105.

Benatar, David (2009) *Better Never to Have Been: The Harm of Coming into Existence*, Oxford: Oxford University Press.

Camus, Albert (1991) *The Myth of Sisyphus and Other Essays,* trans. Justin O'Brian, New York: Vintage.

Edwards, Paul (1967) "Life, meaning and value of," in Paul Edwards (ed.), *The Encyclopedia of Philosophy*, vol. 4, New York: Macmillan, pp. 467–77.

Feinberg, Joel (1992) "Absurd self-fulfillment," in *Freedom and Fulfillment: Philosophical Essays*, Princeton: Princeton University Press, pp. 297–330.

Gordon, Jeffrey (1984) "Nagel or Camus on the absurd?" *Philosophy and Phenomenological Research* 45(September): 15–28.

Luper-Foy, Steven (1992) "The absurdity of life," *Philosophy and Phenomenological Research* 52(March): 85–101.

Murphy, Jeffrie G. (1982) "Morality, religion, and the meaning of life," in *Evolution, Morality, and the*

Meaning of Life, Totowa, NJ: Rowman and Littlefield, pp. 9–30.

Nagel, Thomas (1986) "Birth, death, and the meaning of life," in *The View from Nowhere*, New York: Oxford University Press, pp. 208–32.

Pritchard, Duncan (2010) "Absurdity, angst, and the meaning of life," *The Monist* 93(January): 3–16.

Smith, Michael (2006) "Is that all there is?" *Journal of Ethics* 10(January): 75–106.

Smith, Quentin (2003) "Moral realism and infinite spacetime imply moral nihilism," in Heather Dyke (ed.), *Time and Ethics: Essays at the Intersection*, Dordrecht: Kluwer, pp. 43–54.

Sommers, Tamler, and Alex Rosenberg (2003) "Darwin's nihilistic idea: Evolution and the meaninglessness of life," *Biology and Philosophy* 18(November): 653–68.

3.1

On the Vanity of Existence

Arthur Schopenhauer

1

The vanity of existence is revealed in the whole form existence assumes: in the infiniteness of time and space contrasted with the finiteness of the individual in both; in the fleeting present as the sole form in which actuality exists; in the contingency and relativity of all things; in continual becoming without being; in continual desire without satisfaction; in the continual frustration of striving of which life consists. *Time* and that *perishability* of all things existing in time that time itself brings about is simply the form under which the will to live, which as thing in itself is imperishable, reveals to itself the vanity of its striving. Time is that by virtue of which everything becomes nothingness in our hands and loses all real value.

2

That which *has been* no longer *is*; it as little exists as does that which has *never* been. But everything that *is* in the next moment *has been*. Thus the most insignificant present has over the most significant past the advantage of *actuality*, which means that the former bears to the latter the relation of something to nothing.

To our amazement we suddenly exist, after having for countless millennia not existed; in a short while we will again not exist, also for countless millennia. That cannot be right, says the heart: and even upon the crudest intelligence there must, when it considers such an idea, dawn a presentiment of the ideality of time. This however, together with that of space,

Arthur Schopenhauer (2004) "On the Vanity of Existence," in *Essays and Aphorisms,* trans. R. J. Hollingdale, London: Penguin Books, pp. 51–4.

Exploring the Meaning of Life: An Anthology and Guide, First Edition. Edited by Joshua W. Seachris.

is the key to all true metaphysics, because it makes room for a quite different order of things than that of nature. That is why Kant is so great.

Every moment of our life belongs to the present only for a moment; then it belongs for ever to the past. Every evening we are poorer by a day. We would perhaps grow frantic at the sight of this ebbing away of our short span of time were we not secretly conscious in the profoundest depths of our being that we share in the inexhaustible well of eternity, out of which we can for ever draw new life and renewed time.

You could, to be sure, base on considerations of this kind a theory that the greatest *wisdom* consists in enjoying the present and making this enjoyment the goal of life, because the present is all that is real and everything else merely imaginary. But you could just as well call this mode of life the greatest *folly*: for that which in a moment ceases to exist, which vanishes as completely as a dream, cannot be worth any serious effort.

3

Our existence has no foundation on which to rest except the transient present. Thus its form is essentially unceasing *motion*, without any possibility of that repose which we continually strive after. It resembles the course of a man running down a mountain who would fall over if he tried to stop and can stay on his feet only by running on; or a pole balanced on the tip of the finger; or a planet which would fall into its sun if it ever ceased to plunge irresistibly forward. Thus existence is typified by unrest.

In such a world, where no stability of any kind, no enduring state is possible, where everything is involved in restless change and confusion and keeps itself on its tightrope only by continually striding forward – in such a world, happiness is not so much as to be thought of. It cannot dwell where nothing occurs but Plato's 'continual becoming and never being'. In the first place, no man is happy but strives his whole life long after a supposed happiness which he seldom attains, and even if he does it is only to be disappointed with it; as a rule, however, he finally enters harbour shipwrecked and dismasted. In the second place, however, it is all one whether he has been happy or not in a life which has consisted merely of a succession of transient present moments and is now at an end.

4

The scenes of our life resemble pictures in rough mosaic; they are ineffective from close up, and have to be viewed from a distance if they are to seem beautiful. That is why to attain something desired is to discover how vain it is; and why, though we live all our lives in expectation of better things, we often at the same time long regretfully for what is past. The present, on the other hand, is regarded as something quite temporary and serving only as the road to our goal. That is why most men discover when they look back on their life that they have the whole time been living *ad interim*, and are surprised to see that which they let go by so unregarded and unenjoyed was precisely their life, was precisely that in expectation of which they lived.

5

Life presents itself first and foremost as a task: the task of maintaining itself, *de gagner sa vie.* If this task is accomplished, what has been gained is a burden, and there then appears a second task: that of doing something with it so as to ward off boredom, which hovers over every secure life like a bird of prey. Thus the first task is to gain something and the second to become unconscious of what has been gained, which is otherwise a burden.

That human life must be some kind of mistake is sufficiently proved by the simple observation that man is a compound of needs which are hard to satisfy; that their satisfaction achieves nothing but a painless condition in which he is only given over to boredom; and that boredom is a direct proof that existence is in itself valueless, for boredom is nothing other than the sensation of the emptiness of existence. For if life, in the desire for which our essence and existence consists, possessed in itself a positive value and real content, there would be no such thing as boredom: mere existence would fulfil and satisfy us. As things are, we take no pleasure in existence except when we are striving after something – in which case distance and difficulties make our goal look as if it would satisfy us (an illusion which fades when we reach it) – or when engaged in purely intellectual activity, in which case we are really stepping out of life so as to regard it from outside, like spectators at a play. Even sensual pleasure itself consists in a continual striving and ceases as soon as its goal is reached. Whenever we are not involved in one or other of these things but directed back to existence itself we are overtaken by its worthlessness and vanity and this is the sensation called boredom.

6

That the most perfect manifestation of the will to live represented by the human organism, with its incomparably ingenious and complicated machinery, must crumble to dust and its whole essence and all its striving be palpably given over at last to annihilation – this is nature's unambiguous declaration that all the striving of this will is essentially vain. If it were something possessing value in itself, something which ought unconditionally to exist, it would not have non-being as its goal.

Yet what a difference there is between our beginning and our end! We begin in the madness of carnal desire and the transport of voluptuousness, we end in the dissolution of all our parts and the musty stench of corpses. And the road from the one to the other too goes, in regard to our well-being and enjoyment of life, steadily downhill: happily dreaming childhood, exultant youth, toil-filled years of manhood, infirm and often wretched old age, the torment of the last illness and finally the throes of death – does it not look as if existence were an error the consequences of which gradually grow more and more manifest?

We shall do best to think of life as a *desengaño*, as a process of disillusionment: since this is, clearly enough, what everything that happens to us is calculated to produce.

3.2

A Free Man's Worship

Bertrand Russell

This essay was first published in 1903 and has since been reprinted in many anthologies. It was the outcome of an experience Russell had early in 1901 which, he later recalled, was "not unlike what religious people call 'conversion.'" He "became suddenly and vividly aware of the loneliness in which most people live, and passionately desirous of finding ways of diminishing this tragic isolation."

In subsequent years Russell gave up some of the theories contained in A Free Man's Worship, but not the materialism implicit in many of its most famous passages. "Fundamentally, my view of man's place in the cosmos remains unchanged," he wrote in 1927. "I still believe that the major processes of the universe proceed according to the laws of physics; that they have no reference to our wishes, and are likely to involve the extinction of life on this planet; that there is no good reason for expecting life after death; and that good and evil are ideas which throw no light upon the nonhuman world. I still believe that, in times of moral difficulty and emotional stress, the attitude expressed in this essay is, at any rate for temperaments like my own, the one which gives most help in avoiding moral shipwreck."

To Dr. Faustus in his study Mephistophelis told the history of the Creation, saying,

The endless praises of the choirs of angels had begun to grow wearisome; for, after all, did he not deserve their praise? Had he not given them endless joy? Would it not be more amusing to obtain undeserved praise, to be worshiped by beings whom he tortured? He smiled inwardly, and resolved that the great drama should be performed.

Bertrand Russell (1957) "A Free Man's Worship," in *Why I Am not a Christian and Other Essays on Religion and Related Subjects*, New York: Simon and Schuster, pp. 104–16.

Exploring the Meaning of Life: An Anthology and Guide, First Edition. Edited by Joshua W. Seachris.

For countless ages the hot nebula whirled aimlessly through space. At length it began to take shape, the central mass threw off planets, the planets cooled, boiling seas and burning mountains heaved and tossed, from black masses of cloud hot sheets of rain deluged the barely solid crust. And now the first germ of life grew in the depths of the ocean and developed rapidly in the fructifying warmth into vast forest trees, huge ferns springing from the damp mold, sea monsters breeding, fighting, devouring, and passing away. And from the monsters, as the play unfolded itself, Man was born, with the power of thought, the knowledge of good and evil, and the cruel thirst for worship. And Man saw that all is passing in this mad, monstrous world, that all is struggling to snatch, at any cost, a few brief moments of life before Death's inexorable decree. And Man said, "There is a hidden purpose, could we but fathom it, and the purpose is good; for we must reverence something, and in the visible world there is nothing worthy of reverence." And Man stood aside from the struggle, resolving that God intended harmony to come out of chaos by human efforts. And when he followed the instincts which God had transmitted to him from his ancestry of beasts of prey, he called it Sin, and asked God to forgive him. But he doubted whether he could be justly forgiven, until he invented a divine Plan by which God's wrath was to have been appeased. And seeing the present was bad, he made it yet worse, that thereby the future might be better. And he gave God thanks for the strength that enabled him to forgo even the joys that were possible. And God smiled; and when he saw that Man had become perfect in renunciation and worship, he sent another sun through the sky, which crashed into Man's sun; and all returned again to nebula.

"Yes," he murmured, "it was a good play; I will have it performed again."

Such, in outline, but even more purposeless, more void of meaning, is the world which science presents for our belief. Amid such a world, if anywhere, our ideals henceforward must find a home. That man is the product of causes which had no prevision of the end they were achieving; that his origin, his growth, his hopes and fears, his loves and his beliefs, are but the outcome of accidental collocations of atoms; that no fire, no heroism, no intensity of thought and feeling, can preserve an individual life beyond the grave; that all the labors of the ages, all the devotion, all the inspiration, all the noonday brightness of human genius, are destined to extinction in the vast death of the solar system, and that the whole temple of man's achievement must inevitably be buried beneath the debris of a universe in ruins – all these things, if not quite beyond dispute, are yet so nearly certain that no philosophy which rejects them can hope to stand. Only within the scaffolding of these truths, only on the firm foundation of unyielding despair, can the soul's habitation henceforth be safely built.

How, in such an alien and inhuman world, can so powerless a creature as man preserve his aspirations untarnished? A strange mystery it is that nature, omnipotent but blind, in the revolutions of her secular hurryings through the abysses of space, has brought forth at last a child, subject still to her power, but gifted with sight, with knowledge of good and evil, with the capacity of judging all the works of his unthinking mother. In spite of death, the mark and seal of the parental control, man is yet free, during his brief years, to examine, to criticize, to know, and in imagination to create. To him alone, in the world with which he is acquainted, this freedom belongs; and in this lies his superiority to the resistless forces that control his outward life.

The savage, like ourselves, feels the oppression of his impotence before the powers of nature; but having in himself nothing that he respects more than power, he is willing to prostrate himself before his gods, without inquiring whether they are worthy of his worship.

Pathetic and very terrible is the long history of cruelty and torture, of degradation and human sacrifice, endured in the hope of placating the jealous gods: surely, the trembling believer thinks, when what is most precious has been freely given, their lust for blood must be appeased, and more will not be required. The religion of Moloch – as such creeds may be generically called – is in essence the cringing submission of the slave, who dare not, even in his heart, allow the thought that his master deserves no adulation. Since the independence of ideals is not yet acknowledged, power may be freely worshiped and receive an unlimited respect, despite its wanton infliction of pain.

But gradually, as morality grows bolder, the claim of the ideal world begins to be felt; and worship, if it is not to cease, must be given to gods of another kind than those created by the savage. Some, though they feel the demands of the ideal, will still consciously reject them, still urging that naked power is worthy of worship. Such is the attitude inculcated in God's answer to Job out of the whirlwind: the divine power and knowledge are paraded, but of the divine goodness there is no hint. Such also is the attitude of those who, in our own day, base their morality upon the struggle for survival, maintaining that the survivors are necessarily the fittest. But others, not content with an answer so repugnant to the moral sense, will adopt the position which we have become accustomed to regard as specially religious, maintaining that, in some hidden manner, the world of fact is really harmonious with the world of ideals. Thus man created God, all-powerful and all-good, the mystic unity of what is and what should be.

But the world of fact, after all, is not good; and, in submitting our judgment to it, there is an element of slavishness from which our thoughts must be purged. For in all things it is well to exalt the dignity of man, by freeing him as far as possible from the tyranny of nonhuman power. When we have realized that power is largely bad, that man, with his knowledge of good and evil, is but a helpless atom in a world which has no such knowledge, the choice is again presented to us: Shall we worship force, or shall we worship goodness? Shall our God exist and be evil, or shall he be recognized as the creation of our own conscience?

The answer to this question is very momentous and affects profoundly our whole morality. The worship of force, to which Carlyle and Nietzsche and the creed of militarism have accustomed us, is the result of failure to maintain our own ideals against a hostile universe: it is itself a prostrate submission to evil, a sacrifice of our best to Moloch. If strength indeed is to be respected, let us respect rather the strength of those who refuse that false "recognition of facts" which fails to recognize that facts are often bad. Let us admit that, in the world we know, there are many things that would be better otherwise, and that the ideals to which we do and must adhere are not realized in the realm of matter. Let us preserve our respect for truth, for beauty, for the ideal of perfection which life does not permit us to attain, though none of these things meet with the approval of the unconscious universe. If power is bad, as it seems to be, let us reject it from our hearts. In this lies man's true freedom: in determination to worship only the God created by our own love of the good, to respect only the heaven which inspires the insight of our best moments. In action, in desire, we must submit perpetually to the tyranny of outside forces; but in thought, in aspiration, we are free, free from our fellow men, free from the petty planet on which our bodies impotently crawl, free even, while we live, from the tyranny of death. Let us learn, then, that energy of faith which enables us to live constantly in the vision of the good; and let us descend, in action, into the world of fact, with that vision always before us.

When first the opposition of fact and ideal grows fully visible, a spirit of fiery revolt, of fierce hatred of the gods, seems necessary to the assertion of freedom. To defy with Promethean constancy a hostile universe, to keep its evil always in view, always actively hated, to refuse no pain that the malice of power can invent, appears to be the duty of all who will not bow before the inevitable. But indignation is still a bondage, for it compels our thoughts to be occupied with an evil world; and in the fierceness of desire from which rebellion springs there is a kind of self-assertion which it is necessary for the wise to overcome. Indignation is a submission of our thoughts but not of our desires; the Stoic freedom in which wisdom consists is found in the submission of our desires but not of our thoughts. From the submission of our desires springs the virtue of resignation; from the freedom of our thoughts springs the whole world of art and philosophy, and the vision of beauty by which, at last, we half reconquer the reluctant world. But the vision of beauty is possible only to unfettered contemplation, to thoughts not weighted by the load of eager wishes; and thus freedom comes only to those who no longer ask of life that it shall yield them any of those personal goods that are subject to the mutations of time.

Although the necessity of renunciation is evidence of the existence of evil, yet Christianity, in preaching it, has shown a wisdom exceeding that of the Promethean philosophy of rebellion. It must be admitted that, of the things we desire, some, though they prove impossible, are yet real goods; others, however, as ardently longed for, do not form part of a fully purified ideal. The belief that what must be renounced is bad, though sometimes false, is far less often false than untamed passion supposes; and the creed of religion, by providing a reason for proving that it is never false, has been the means of purifying our hopes by the discovery of many austere truths.

But there is in resignation a further good element: even real goods, when they are unattainable, ought not to be fretfully desired. To every man comes, sooner or later, the great renunciation. For the young, there is nothing unattainable; a good thing desired with the whole force of a passionate will, and yet impossible, is to them not credible. Yet, by death, by illness, by poverty, or by the voice of duty, we must learn, each one of us, that the world was not made for us, and that, however beautiful may be the things we crave, Fate may nevertheless forbid them. It is the part of courage, when misfortune comes, to bear without repining the ruin of our hopes, to turn away our thoughts from vain regrets. This degree of submission to power is not only just and right: it is the very gate of wisdom.

But passive renunciation is not the whole of wisdom; for not by renunciation alone can we build a temple for the worship of our own ideals. Haunting foreshadowings of the temple appear in the realm of imagination, in music, in architecture, in the untroubled kingdom of reason, and in the golden sunset magic of lyrics, where beauty shines and glows, remote from the touch of sorrow, remote from the fear of change, remote from the failures and disenchantments of the world of fact. In the contemplation of these things the vision of heaven will shape itself in our hearts, giving at once a touchstone to judge the world about us and an inspiration by which to fashion to our needs whatever is not incapable of serving as a stone in the sacred temple.

Except for those rare spirits that are born without sin, there is a cavern of darkness to be traversed before that temple can be entered. The gate of the cavern is despair, and its floor is paved with the gravestones of abandoned hopes. There self must die; there the eagerness, the greed of untamed desire, must be slain, for only so can the soul be freed from the empire of Fate. But out of the cavern, the Gate of Renunciation leads again to the daylight of wisdom, by whose radiance a new insight, a new joy, a new tenderness, shine forth to gladden the pilgrim's heart.

When, without the bitterness of impotent rebellion, we have learned both to resign ourselves to the outward rule of Fate and to recognize that the nonhuman world is unworthy of our worship, it becomes possible at last so to transform and refashion the unconscious universe, so to transmute it in the crucible of imagination, that a new image of shining gold replaces the old idol of clay. In all the multiform facts of the world – in the visual shapes of trees and mountains and clouds, in the events of the life of man, even in the very omnipotence of death – the insight of creative idealism can find the reflection of a beauty which its own thoughts first made. In this way mind asserts its subtle mastery over the thoughtless forces of nature. The more evil the material with which it deals, the more thwarting to untrained desire, the greater is its achievement in inducing the reluctant rock to yield up its hidden treasures, the prouder its victory in compelling the opposing forces to swell the pageant of its triumph. Of all the arts, tragedy is the proudest, the most triumphant; for it builds its shining citadel in the very center of the enemy's country, on the very summit of his highest mountain; from its impregnable watchtowers, his camps and arsenals, his columns and forts, are all revealed; within its walls the free life continues, while the legions of death and pain and despair, and all the servile captains of tyrant Fate, afford the burghers of that dauntless city new spectacles of beauty. Happy those sacred ramparts, thrice happy the dwellers on that all-seeing eminence. Honor to those brave warriors who, through countless ages of warfare, have preserved for us the priceless heritage of liberty and have kept undefiled by sacrilegious invaders the home of the unsubdued.

But the beauty of tragedy does but make visible a quality which, in more or less obvious shapes, is present always and everywhere in life. In the spectacle of death, in the endurance of intolerable pain, and in the irrevocableness of a vanished past, there is a sacredness, an overpowering awe, a feeling of the vastness, the depth, the inexhaustible mystery of existence, in which, as by some strange marriage of pain, the sufferer is bound to the world by bonds of sorrow. In these moments of insight, we lose all eagerness of temporary desire, all struggling and striving for petty ends, all care for the little trivial things that, to a superficial view, make up the common life of day by day; we see, surrounding the narrow raft illumined by the flickering light of human comradeship, the dark ocean on whose rolling waves we toss for a brief hour; from the great night without, a chill blast breaks in upon our refuge; all the loneliness of humanity amid hostile forces is concentrated upon the individual soul, which must struggle alone, with what of courage it can command, against the whole weight of a universe that cares nothing for its hopes and fears. Victory, in this struggle with the powers of darkness, is the true baptism into the glorious company of heroes, the true initiation into the overmastering beauty of human existence. From that awful encounter of the soul with the outer world, renunciation, wisdom, and charity are born; and with their birth a new life begins. To take into the inmost shrine of the soul the irresistible forces whose puppets we seem to be – death and change, the irrevocableness of the past, and the powerlessness of man before the blind hurry of the universe from vanity to vanity – to feel these things and know them is to conquer them.

This is the reason why the past has such magical power. The beauty of its motionless and silent pictures is like the enchanted purity of late autumn, when the leaves, though one breath would make them fall, still glow against the sky in golden glory. The past does not change or strive; like Duncan, after life's fitful fever it sleeps well; what was eager and grasping, what was petty and transitory, has faded away; the things that were beautiful and eternal shine out of it like stars in the night. Its beauty, to a soul not worthy of it, is unendurable; but to a soul which has conquered Fate it is the key of religion.

The life of man, viewed outwardly, is but a small thing in comparison with the forces of nature. The slave is doomed to worship Time and Fate and Death, because they are greater than anything he finds in himself, and because all his thoughts are of things which they devour. But, great as they are, to think of them greatly, to feel their passionless splendor, is greater still. And such thought makes us free men; we no longer bow before the inevitable in Oriental subjection, but we absorb it and make it a part of ourselves. To abandon the struggle for private happiness, to expel all eagerness of temporary desire, to burn with passion for eternal things – this is emancipation, and this is the free man's worship. And this liberation is effected by contemplation of Fate; for Fate itself is subdued by the mind which leaves nothing to be purged by the purifying fire of time.

United with his fellow men by the strongest of all ties, the tie of a common doom, the free man finds that a new vision is with him always, shedding over every daily task the light of love. The life of man is a long march through the night, surrounded by invisible foes, tortured by weariness and pain, toward a goal that few can hope to reach, and where none may tarry long. One by one, as they march, our comrades vanish from our sight, seized by the silent orders of omnipotent death. Very brief is the time in which we can help them, in which their happiness or misery is decided. Be it ours to shed sunshine on their path, to lighten their sorrows by the balm of sympathy, to give them the pure joy of a never-tiring affection, to strengthen failing courage, to instill faith in hours of despair. Let us not weigh in grudging scales their merits and demerits, but let us think only of their need – of the sorrows, the difficulties, perhaps the blindnesses, that make the misery of their lives; let us remember that they are fellow sufferers in the same darkness, actors in the same tragedy with ourselves. And so, when their day is over, when their good and their evil have become eternal by the immortality of the past, be it ours to feel that, where they suffered, where they failed, no deed of ours was the cause; but wherever a spark of the divine fire kindled in their hearts, we were ready with encouragement, with sympathy, with brave words in which high courage glowed.

Brief and powerless is man's life; on him and all his race the slow, sure doom falls pitiless and dark. Blind to good and evil, reckless of destruction, omnipotent matter rolls on its relentless way; for man, condemned today to lose his dearest, tomorrow himself to pass through the gate of darkness, it remains only to cherish, ere yet the blow fall, the lofty thoughts that ennoble his little day; disdaining the coward terrors of the slave of Fate, to worship at the shrine that his own hands have built; undismayed by the empire of chance, to preserve a mind free from the wanton tyranny that rules his outward life; proudly defiant of the irresistible forces that tolerate, for a moment, his knowledge and his condemnation, to sustain alone, a weary but unyielding Atlas, the world that his own ideals have fashioned despite the trampling march of unconscious power.

3.3

The Absurd

Thomas Nagel

Most people feel on occasion that life is absurd, and some feel it vividly and continually. Yet the reasons usually offered in defense of this conviction are patently inadequate: they *could* not really explain why life is absurd. Why then do they provide a natural expression for the sense that it is?

I

Consider some examples. It is often remarked that nothing we do now will matter in a million years. But if that is true, then by the same token, nothing that will be the case in a million years matters now. In particular, it does not matter now that in a million years nothing we do now will matter. Moreover, even if what we did now *were* going to matter in a million years, how could that keep our present concerns from being absurd? If their mattering now is not enough to accomplish that, how would it help if they mattered a million years from now?

Whether what we do now will matter in a million years could make the crucial difference only if its mattering in a million years depended on its mattering, period. But then to deny that whatever happens now will matter in a million years is to beg the question against its mattering, period; for in that sense one cannot know that it will not matter in a million years whether (for example) someone now is happy or miserable, without knowing that it does not matter, period.

What we say to convey the absurdity of our lives often has to do with space or time: we are tiny specks in the infinite vastness of the universe; our lives are mere instants even on a geological time scale, let alone a cosmic one; we will all be dead any minute. But of course

Thomas Nagel (1971) "The Absurd," *Journal of Philosophy* 68(20): 716–27.

none of these evident facts can be what *makes* life absurd, if it is absurd. For suppose we lived forever; would not a life that is absurd if it lasts seventy years be infinitely absurd if it lasted through eternity? And if our lives are absurd given our present size, why would they be any less absurd if we filled the universe (either because we were larger or because the universe was smaller)? Reflection on our minuteness and brevity appears to be intimately connected with the sense that life is meaningless; but it is not clear what the connection is.

Another inadequate argument is that because we are going to die, all chains of justification must leave off in mid-air: one studies and works to earn money to pay for clothing, housing, entertainment, food, to sustain oneself from year to year, perhaps to support a family and pursue a career – but to what final end? All of it is an elaborate journey leading nowhere. (One will also have some effect on other people's lives, but that simply reproduces the problem, for they will die too.)

There are several replies to this argument. First, life does not consist of a sequence of activities each of which has as its purpose some later member of the sequence. Chains of justification come repeatedly to an end within life, and whether the process as a whole can be justified has no bearing on the finality of these end-points. No further justification is needed to make it reasonable to take aspirin for a headache, attend an exhibit of the work of a painter one admires, or stop a child from putting his hand on a hot stove. No larger context or further purpose is needed to prevent these acts from being pointless.

Even if someone wished to supply a further justification for pursuing all the things in life that are commonly regarded as selfjustifying, that justification would have to end somewhere too. If *nothing* can justify unless it is justified in terms of something outside itself, which is also justified, then an infinite regress results, and no chain of justification can be complete. Moreover, if a finite chain of reasons cannot justify anything, what could be accomplished by an infinite chain, each link of which must be justified by something outside itself?

Since justifications must come to an end somewhere, nothing is gained by denying that they end where they appear to, within life – or by trying to subsume the multiple, often trivial ordinary justifications of action under a single, controlling life scheme. We can be satisfied more easily than that. In fact, through its misrepresentation of the process of justification, the argument makes a vacuous demand. It insists that the reasons available within life are incomplete, but suggests thereby that all reasons that come to an end are incomplete. This makes it impossible to supply any reasons at all.

The standard arguments for absurdity appear therefore to fail as arguments. Yet I believe they attempt to express something that is difficult to state, but fundamentally correct.

II

In ordinary life a situation is absurd when it includes a conspicuous discrepancy between pretension or aspiration and reality: someone gives a complicated speech in support of a motion that has already been passed; a notorious criminal is made president of a major philanthropic foundation; you declare your love over the telephone to a recorded announcement; as you are being knighted, your pants fall down.

When a person finds himself in an absurd situation, he will usually attempt to change it, by modifying his aspirations, or by trying to bring reality into better accord with them, or by removing himself from the situation entirely. We are not always willing or able to extricate ourselves from a position whose absurdity has become clear to us. Nevertheless, it is usually possible to imagine some change that would remove the absurdity – whether or not we can or will implement it. The sense that life as a whole is absurd arises when we perceive, perhaps dimly, an inflated pretension or aspiration which is inseparable from the continuation of human life and which makes its absurdity inescapable, short of escape from life itself.

Many people's lives are absurd, temporarily or permanently, for conventional reasons having to do with their particular ambitions, circumstances, and personal relations. If there is a philosophical sense of absurdity, however, it must arise from the perception of something universal – some respect in which pretension and reality inevitably clash for us all. This condition is supplied, I shall argue, by the collision between the seriousness with which we take our lives and the perpetual possibility of regarding everything about which we are serious as arbitrary, or open to doubt.

We cannot live human lives without energy and attention, nor without making choices which show that we take some things more seriously than others. Yet we have always available a point of view outside the particular form of our lives, from which the seriousness appears gratuitous. These two inescapable viewpoints collide in us, and that is what makes life absurd. It is absurd because we ignore the doubts that we know cannot be settled, continuing to live with nearly undiminished seriousness in spite of them.

This analysis requires defense in two respects: first as regards the unavoidability of seriousness; second as regards the inescapability of doubt.

We take ourselves seriously whether we lead serious lives or not and whether we are concerned primarily with fame, pleasure, virtue, luxury, triumph, beauty, justice, knowledge, salvation, or mere survival. If we take other people seriously and devote ourselves to them, that only multiplies the problem. Human life is full of effort, plans, calculation, success and failure: we *pursue* our lives, with varying degrees of sloth and energy.

It would be different if we could not step back and reflect on the process, but were merely led from impulse to impulse without self-consciousness. But human beings do not act solely on impulse. They are prudent, they reflect, they weigh consequences, they ask whether what they are doing is worth while. Not only are their lives full of particular choices that hang together in larger activities with temporal structure: they also decide in the broadest terms what to pursue and what to avoid, what the priorities among their various aims should be, and what kind of people they want to be or become. Some men are faced with such choices by the large decisions they make from time to time; some merely by reflection on the course their lives are taking as the product of countless small decisions. They decide whom to marry, what profession to follow, whether to join the Country Club, or the Resistance; or they may just wonder why they go on being salesmen or academics or taxi drivers, and then stop thinking about it after a certain period of inconclusive reflection.

Although they may be motivated from act to act by those immediate needs with which life presents them, they allow the process to continue by adhering to the general system of habits and the form of life in which such motives have their place – or perhaps only by clinging to life itself. They spend enormous quantities of energy, risk, and calculation on the details. Think of how an ordinary individual sweats over his appearance, his health, his sex life, his emotional honesty, his social utility, his self-knowledge, the quality of his ties with family, colleagues, and friends, how well he does his job, whether he understands the world and what is going on in it. Leading a human life is a full-time occupation, to which everyone devotes decades of intense concern.

This fact is so obvious that it is hard to find it extraordinary and important. Each of us lives his own life – lives with himself twenty-four hours a day. What else is he supposed to do – live someone else's life? Yet humans have the special capacity to step back and survey themselves, and the lives to which they are committed, with that detached amazement which comes from watching an ant struggle up a heap of sand. Without developing the illusion that they are able to escape from their highly specific and idiosyncratic position, they can view it *sub specie aeternitatis* – and the view is at once sobering and comical.

The crucial backward step is not taken by asking for still another justification in the chain, and failing to get it. The objections to that line of attack have already been stated; justifications come to an end. But this is precisely what provides universal doubt with its object. We step back to find that the whole system of justification and criticism, which controls our choices and supports our claims to rationality, rests on responses and habits that we never question, that we should not know how to defend without circularity, and to which we shall continue to adhere even after they are called into question.

The things we do or want without reasons, and without requiring reasons – the things that define what is a reason for us and what is not – are the starting points of our skepticism. We see ourselves from outside, and all the contingency and specificity of our aims and pursuits become clear. Yet when we take this view and recognize what we do as arbitrary, it does not disengage us from life, and there lies our absurdity: not in the fact that such an external view can be taken of us, but in the fact that we ourselves can take it, without ceasing to be the persons whose ultimate concerns are so coolly regarded.

III

One may try to escape the position by seeking broader ultimate concerns, from which it is impossible to step back – the idea being that absurdity results because what we take seriously is something small and insignificant and individual. Those seeking to supply their lives with meaning usually envision a role or function in something larger than themselves. They therefore seek fulfillment in service to society, the state, the revolution, the progress of history, the advance of science, or religion and the glory of God.

But a role in some larger enterprise cannot confer significance unless that enterprise is itself significant. And its significance must come back to what we can understand, or it will not even appear to give us what we are seeking. If we learned that we were being raised to provide food for other creatures fond of human flesh, who planned to turn us into cutlets before we got too stringy – even if we learned that the human race had been developed by animal breeders precisely for this purpose – that would still not give our lives meaning, for two reasons. First, we would still be in the dark as to the significance of the lives of those other beings; second, although we might acknowledge that this culinary role would make our lives meaningful to them, it is not clear how it would make them meaningful to us.

Admittedly, the usual form of service to a higher being is different from this. One is supposed to behold and partake of the glory of God, for example, in a way in which chickens do not share in the glory of coq au vin. The same is true of service to a state, a movement, or a revolution. People can come to feel, when they are part of something bigger, that it is part of them too. They worry less about what is peculiar to themselves, but identify enough with the larger enterprise to find their role in it fulfilling.

However, any such larger purpose can be put in doubt in the same way that the aims of an individual life can be, and for the same reasons. It is as legitimate to find ultimate justification there as to find it earlier, among the details of individual life. But this does not alter the fact that justifications come to an end when we are content to have them end – when we do not find it necessary to look any further. If we can step back from the purposes of individual life and doubt their point, we can step back also from the progress of human history, or of science, or the success of a society, or the kingdom, power, and glory of God,[1] and put all these things into question in the same way. What seems to us to confer meaning, justification, significance, does so in virtue of the fact that we need no more reasons after a certain point.

What makes doubt inescapable with regard to the limited aims of individual life also makes it inescapable with regard to any larger purpose that encourages the sense that life is meaningful. Once the fundamental doubt has begun, it cannot be laid to rest.

Camus maintains in *The Myth of Sisyphus* that the absurd arises because the world fails to meet our demands for meaning. This suggests that the world might satisfy those demands if it were different. But now we can see that this is not the case. There does not appear to be any conceivable world (containing us) about which unsettlable doubts could not arise. Consequently the absurdity of our situation derives not from a collision between our expectations and the world, but from a collision within ourselves.

IV

It may be objected that the standpoint from which these doubts are supposed to be felt does not exist – that if we take the recommended backward step we will land on thin air, without any basis for judgment about the natural responses we are supposed to be surveying. If we retain our usual standards of what is important, then questions about the significance of what we are doing with our lives will be answerable in the usual way. But if we do not, then those questions can mean nothing to us, since there is no longer any content to the idea of what matters, and hence no content to the idea that nothing does.

But this objection misconceives the nature of the backward step. It is not supposed to give us an understanding of what is *really* important, so that we see by contrast that our lives are insignificant. We never, in the course of these reflections, abandon the ordinary standards that guide our lives. We merely observe them in operation, and recognize that if they are called into question we can justify them only by reference to themselves, uselessly. We adhere to them because of the way we are put together; what seems to us important or serious or valuable would not seem so if we were differently constituted.

In ordinary life, to be sure, we do not judge a situation absurd unless we have in mind some standards of seriousness, significance, or harmony with which the absurd can be contrasted. This contrast is not implied by the philosophical judgment of absurdity, and that might be thought to make the concept unsuitable for the expression of such judgments. This is not so, however, for the philosophical judgment depends on another contrast which makes it a natural extension from more ordinary cases. It departs from them only in contrasting the pretensions of life with a larger context in which *no* standards can be discovered, rather than with a context from which alternative, overriding standards may be applied.

V

In this respect, as in others, philosophical perception of the absurd resembles epistemological skepticism. In both cases the final, philosophical doubt is not contrasted with any unchallenged certainties, though it is arrived at by extrapolation from examples of doubt within the system of evidence or justification, where a contrast with other certainties *is* implied. In both cases our limitedness joins with a capacity to transcend those limitations in thought (thus seeing them as limitations, and as inescapable).

Skepticism begins when we include ourselves in the world about which we claim knowledge. We notice that certain types of evidence convince us, that we are content to allow justifications of belief to come to an end at certain points, that we feel we know many things even without knowing or having grounds for believing the denial of others which, if true, would make what we claim to know false.

For example, I know that I am looking at a piece of paper, although I have no adequate grounds to claim I know that I am not dreaming; and if I am dreaming then I am not looking at a piece of paper. Here an ordinary conception of how appearance may diverge from reality is employed to show that we take our world largely for granted; the certainty that we are not dreaming cannot be justified except circularly, in terms of those very appearances which are being put in doubt. It is somewhat far-fetched to suggest I may be dreaming; but the possibility is only illustrative. It reveals that our claims to knowledge depend on our not feeling it necessary to exclude certain incompatible alternatives, and the dreaming possibility or the total-hallucination possibility are just representatives for limitless possibilities most of which we cannot even conceive.[2]

Once we have taken the backward step to an abstract view of our whole system of beliefs, evidence, and justification, and seen that it works only, despite its pretensions, by taking the world largely for granted, we are *not* in a position to contrast all these appearances with an alternative reality. We cannot shed our ordinary responses, and if we could it would leave us with no means of conceiving a reality of any kind.

It is the same in the practical domain. We do not step outside our lives to a new vantage point from which we see what is really, objectively significant. We continue to take life largely for granted while seeing that all our decisions and certainties are possible only because there is a great deal we do not bother to rule out.

Both epistemological skepticism and a sense of the absurd can be reached via initial doubts posed within systems of evidence and justification that we accept, and can be stated without violence to our ordinary concepts. We can ask not only why we should believe there is a floor under us, but also why we should believe the evidence of our senses at all – and at some point the framable questions will have outlasted the answers. Similarly, we can ask not only why we should take aspirin, but why we should take trouble over our own comfort at all. The fact that we shall take the aspirin without waiting for an answer to this last question does not show that it is an unreal question. We shall also continue to believe there is a floor under us without waiting for an answer to the other question. In both cases it is this unsupported natural confidence that generates skeptical doubts; so it cannot be used to settle them.

Philosophical skepticism does not cause us to abandon our ordinary beliefs, but it lends them a peculiar flavor. After acknowledging that their truth is incompatible with possibilities that we have no grounds for believing do not obtain – apart from grounds in those very beliefs which we have called into question – we return to our familiar convictions with a certain irony and resignation. Unable to abandon the natural responses on which they depend, we take them back, like a spouse who has run off with someone else and then decided to return; but we regard them differently (not that the new attitude is necessarily inferior to the old, in either case).

The same situation obtains after we have put in question the seriousness with which we take our lives and human life in general and have looked at ourselves without presuppositions. We then return to our lives, as we must, but our seriousness is laced with irony. Not that irony enables us to escape the absurd. It is useless to mutter: "Life is meaningless; life is meaningless ..." as an accompaniment to everything we do. In continuing to live and work and strive, we take ourselves seriously in action no matter what we say.

What sustains us, in belief as in action, is not reason or justification, but something more basic than these – for we go on in the same way even after we are convinced that the reasons have given out.[3] If we tried to rely entirely on reason, and pressed it hard, our lives and beliefs would collapse – a form of madness that may actually occur if the inertial force of taking the world and life for granted is somehow lost. If we lose our grip on that, reason will not give it back to us.

VI

In viewing ourselves from a perspective broader than we can occupy in the flesh, we become spectators of our own lives. We cannot do very much as pure spectators of our own lives, so we continue to lead them, and devote ourselves to what we are able at the same time to view as no more than a curiosity, like the ritual of an alien religion.

This explains why the sense of absurdity finds its natural expression in those bad arguments with which the discussion began. Reference to our small size and short lifespan and to the fact that all of mankind will eventually vanish without a trace are metaphors for the backward step which permits us to regard ourselves from without and to find the particular form of our lives curious and slightly surprising. By feigning a nebula's-eye view, we illustrate the capacity to see ourselves without presuppositions, as arbitrary, idiosyncratic, highly specific occupants of the world, one of countless possible forms of life.

Before turning to the question whether the absurdity of our lives is something to be regretted and if possible escaped, let me consider what would have to be given up in order to avoid it.

Why is the life of a mouse not absurd? The orbit of the moon is not absurd either, but that involves no strivings or aims at all. A mouse, however, has to work to stay alive. Yet he is not absurd, because he lacks the capacities for self-consciousness and self-transcendence that would enable him to see that he is only a mouse. If that *did* happen, his life would become absurd, since self-awareness would not make him cease to be a mouse and would not enable him to rise above his mousely strivings. Bringing his new-found self-consciousness with him, he would have to return to his meagre yet frantic life, full of doubts that he was unable to answer, but also full of purposes that he was unable to abandon.

Given that the transcendental step is natural to us humans, can we avoid absurdity by refusing to take that step and remaining entirely within our sublunar lives? Well, we cannot refuse consciously, for to do that we would have to be aware of the viewpoint we were refusing to adopt. The only way to avoid the relevant self-consciousness would be either never to attain it or to forget it – neither of which can be achieved by the will.

On the other hand, it is possible to expend effort on an attempt to destroy the other component of the absurd – abandoning one's earthly, individual, human life in order to identify as completely as possible with that universal viewpoint from which human life seems arbitrary and trivial. (This appears to be the ideal of certain Oriental religions.) If one succeeds, then one will not have to drag the superior awareness through a strenuous mundane life, and absurdity will be diminished.

However, insofar as this self-etiolation is the result of effort, will-power, asceticism, and so forth, it requires that one take oneself seriously as an individual – that one be willing to take considerable trouble to avoid being creaturely and absurd. Thus one may undermine the aim of unworldliness by pursuing it too vigorously. Still, if someone simply allowed his individual, animal nature to drift and respond to impulse, without making the pursuit of its needs a central conscious aim, then he might, at considerable dissociative cost, achieve a life that was less absurd than most. It would not be a meaningful life either, of course; but it would not involve the engagement of a transcendent awareness in the assiduous pursuit of mundane goals. And that is the main condition of absurdity – the dragooning of an unconvinced transcendent consciousness into the service of an immanent, limited enterprise like a human life.

The final escape is suicide; but before adopting any hasty solutions, it would be wise to consider carefully whether the absurdity of our existence truly presents us with a *problem*, to which some solution must be found – a way of dealing with prima facie disaster. That is certainly the attitude with which Camus approaches the issue, and it gains support from the fact that we are all eager to escape from absurd situations on a smaller scale.

Camus – not on uniformly good grounds – rejects suicide and the other solutions he regards as escapist. What he recommends is defiance or scorn. We can salvage our dignity, he appears to believe, by shaking a fist at the world which is deaf to our pleas, and continuing to live in spite of it. This will not make our lives un-absurd, but it will lend them a certain nobility.[4]

This seems to me romantic and slightly self-pitying. Our absurdity warrants neither that much distress nor that much defiance. At the risk of falling into romanticism by a different route, I would argue that absurdity is one of the most human things about us: a manifestation of our most advanced and interesting characteristics. Like skepticism in epistemology, it is possible only because we possess a certain kind of insight – the capacity to transcend ourselves in thought.

If a sense of the absurd is a way of perceiving our true situation (even though the situation is not absurd until the perception arises), then what reason can we have to resent or escape it? Like the capacity for epistemological skepticism, it results from the ability to understand our human limitations. It need not be a matter for agony unless we make it so. Nor need it evoke a defiant contempt of fate that allows us to feel brave or proud. Such dramatics, even if carried on in private, betray a failure to appreciate the cosmic unimportance of the situation. If *sub specie aeternitatis* there is no reason to believe that anything matters, then that doesn't matter either, and we can approach our absurd lives with irony instead of heroism or despair.

Notes

1. Cf. Robert Nozick, "Teleology," *Mosaic*, XII, 1 (Spring 1971): 27–8.
2. I am aware that skepticism about the external world is widely thought to have been refuted, but I have remained convinced of its irrefutability since being exposed at Berkeley to Thompson Clarke's largely unpublished ideas on the subject.
3. As Hume says in a famous passage of the *Treatise*: "Most fortunately it happens, that since reason is incapable of dispelling these clouds, nature herself suffices to that purpose, and cures me of this philosophical melancholy and delirium, either by relaxing this bent of mind, or by some avocation, and lively impression of my senses, which obliterate all these chimeras. I dine, I play a game of backgammon, I converse, and am merry with my friends; and when after three or four hours' amusement, I would return to these speculations, they appear so cold, and strain'd, and ridiculous, that I cannot find in my heart to enter into them any farther" (Book 1, Part 4, Section 7; Selby-Bigge, p. 269).
4. "Sisyphus, proletarian of the gods, powerless and rebellious, knows the whole extent of his wretched condition: it is what he thinks of during his descent. The lucidity that was to constitute his torture at the same time crowns his victory. There is no fate that cannot be surmounted by scorn" (*The Myth of Sisyphus*, Vintage edition, p. 90).

3.4

Why Coming into Existence Is Always a Harm

David Benatar

There is a common assumption in the literature about future possible people that, all things being equal, one does no wrong by bringing into existence people whose lives will be good on balance. This assumption rests on another – namely that being brought into existence (with decent life prospects) is a benefit (even though not being brought into existence is not a harm). I shall argue that the underlying assumption is erroneous. Being brought into existence is not a benefit but always a harm. When I say that coming into existence is *always* a harm, I do not mean that it is necessarily a harm. As will become apparent, my argument does not apply to those hypothetical cases in which a life contains only good and no bad. About such an existence I say that it is neither a harm nor a benefit and we should be indifferent between such an existence and never existing. But no lives are like this. All lives contain some bad. Coming into existence with such a life is always a harm. Many people will find this deeply unsettling claim to be counter-intuitive and will wish to dismiss it. For this reason, I propose not only to defend the claim, but also to suggest why people might be resistant to it.

As a matter of fact, bad things happen to all of us. No life is without hardship. It is easy to think of the millions who live a life of poverty or of those who live much of their lives with some disability. Some of us are lucky enough to be spared these fates, but most of us who are, nonetheless suffer ill-health at some stage during our lives. Often the suffering is excruciating, even if it is in our final days. Some are condemned by nature to years of frailty. We *all* face death.[1] We infrequently contemplate the harms that await any new-born child – pain, disappointment, anxiety, grief, and death. For any given child we cannot predict what form these harms will take or how severe they will be, but we can be sure that at least some of them will occur.[2] None of this befalls the non-existent. Only existers suffer harm.

David Benatar (2006) "Why Coming into Existence Is Always a Harm," Chapter 2 in *Better Never to Have Been: The Harm of Coming into Existence*, Oxford: Oxford University Press, pp. 28–59.

Exploring the Meaning of Life: An Anthology and Guide, First Edition. Edited by Joshua W. Seachris.

Optimists will be quick to note that I have not told the whole story. Not only bad things but also good things happen only to those who exist. Pleasure, joy, and satisfaction can only be had by existers. Thus, the cheerful will say, we must weigh up the pleasures of life against the evils. As long as the former outweigh the latter, the life is worth living. Coming into being with such a life is, on this view, a benefit.

The Asymmetry of Pleasure and Pain

However, this conclusion does not follow. This is because there is a crucial difference between harms (such as pains) and benefits (such as pleasures) which entails that existence has no advantage over, but does have disadvantages relative to, non-existence.[3] Consider pains and pleasures as exemplars of harms and benefits. It is uncontroversial to say that

(1) the presence of pain is bad, and that
(2) the presence of pleasure is good.

However, such a symmetrical evaluation does not seem to apply to the *absence* of pain and pleasure, for it strikes me as true that

(3) the absence of pain is good, even if that good is not enjoyed by anyone, whereas
(4) the absence of pleasure is not bad unless there is somebody for whom this absence is a deprivation.

Now it might be asked how the absence of pain could be good if that good is not enjoyed by anybody. Absent pain, it might be said, cannot be good *for* anybody, if nobody exists for whom it can be good. This, however, is to dismiss (3) too quickly.

The judgement made in (3) is made *with reference to the (potential) interests of a person* who either does or does not exist. To this it might be objected that because (3) is part of the scenario under which this person never exists, (3) cannot say anything about an existing person. This objection would be mistaken because (3) can say something about a counterfactual case in which a person who does actually exist never did exist. Of the pain of an existing person, (3) says that the absence of this pain would have been good even if this could only have been achieved by the absence of the person who now suffers it. In other words, judged in terms of the interests of a person who now exists, the absence of the pain would have been good even though this person would then not have existed. Consider next what (3) says of the absent pain of one who never exists – of pain, the absence of which is ensured by not making a potential person actual. Claim (3) says that this absence is good when judged in terms of the interests of the person who would otherwise have existed. We may not know who that person would have been, but we can still say that whoever that person would have been, the avoidance of his or her pains is good when judged in terms of his or her potential interests. If there is any (obviously loose) sense in which the absent pain is good *for* the person who could have existed but does not exist, this is it. Clearly (3) does not entail the absurd literal claim that there is some actual person for whom the absent pain is good.[4]

In support of the asymmetry between (3) and (4), it can be shown that it has considerable explanatory power. It explains at least four other asymmetries that are quite plausible. Sceptics, when they see where this leads, may begin to question the plausibility of these other asymmetries and may want to know what support (beyond the asymmetry above) can be provided for them. Were I to provide such support, the sceptics would then ask for a defence of these further supporting considerations. Every argument must have some justificatory end. I cannot hope to convince those who take the rejection of my conclusion as axiomatic. All I can show is that those who accept some quite plausible views are led to my conclusion. These plausible views include four other asymmetries, which I shall now outline.

First, the asymmetry between (3) and (4) is the best explanation for the view that while there is a duty to avoid bringing suffering people into existence, there is no duty to bring happy people into being. In other words, the reason why we think that there is a duty not to bring suffering people into existence is that the presence of this suffering would be bad (for the sufferers) and the absence of the suffering is good (even though there is nobody to enjoy the absence of suffering). In contrast to this, we think that there is no duty to bring happy people into existence because while their pleasure would be good for them, its absence would not be bad for them (given that there would be nobody who would be deprived of it).

It might be objected that there is an alternative explanation for the view about our procreational duties – one that does not appeal to my claim about the asymmetry between (3) and (4). It might be suggested that the reason why we have a duty to avoid bringing suffering people into being, but not a duty to bring happy people into existence, is that we have negative duties to avoid harm but no corresponding positive duties to bring about happiness. Judgements about our procreational duties are thus like judgements about all other duties. Now I agree that for those who deny that we have any positive duties, this would indeed be an alternative explanation to the one I have provided. However, even of those who do think that we have positive duties only a few also think that amongst these is a duty to bring happy people into existence.

It might now be suggested that there is also an alternative explanation why those who *do* accept positive duties do not usually think that these include a duty to bring happy people into existence. It is usually thought that our positive duties cannot include a duty to create lots of pleasure if that would require significant sacrifice on our part. Given that having children involves considerable sacrifice (at least to the pregnant woman), this, and not asymmetry, is the best explanation for why there is no duty to bring happy people into existence.

The problem, though, with this alternative explanation is that it implies that in the absence of this sacrifice[5] we *would* have a duty to bring happy people into existence. In other words, it would be wrong not to create such people if we could create them without great cost to ourselves. But this presupposes that the duty under discussion is an all-things-considered duty. However, the interests of potential people cannot ground even a defeasible duty to bring them into existence. Put another way, the asymmetry of procreative (all-things-considered) duties rests on another asymmetry – an asymmetry of procreative moral *reasons*. According to this asymmetry, although we have a strong moral reason, grounded in the interests of potential people,[6] to avoid creating unhappy people, we have no strong moral reason (grounded in the interests of potential people) to create happy people.[7] It follows that although the extent of the sacrifice may be relevant to other positive duties, this is moot in the case of a purported duty to bring happy people into existence.

There is a second support for my claim about the asymmetry between (3) and (4). Whereas it is strange (if not incoherent) to give as a reason for having a child that the child one has will thereby be benefited,[8] it is not strange to cite a potential child's interests as a basis for avoiding bringing a child into existence. If having children were done for the purpose of thereby benefiting those children, then there would be greater moral reason for at least many people to have more children. In contrast to this, our concern for the welfare of potential children who would suffer is a sound basis for deciding *not* to have the child. If absent pleasures were bad irrespective of whether they were bad for anybody, then having children for their own sakes would not be odd. And if it were not the case that absent pains are good even where they are not good for anybody, then we could not say that it would be good to avoid bringing suffering children into existence.

Thirdly, support for the asymmetry between (3) and (4) can be drawn from a related asymmetry, this time in our retrospective judgements. Bringing people into existence as well as failing to bring people into existence can be regretted. However, only bringing people into existence can be regretted *for* the sake of the person whose existence was contingent on our decision. This is *not* because those who are not brought into existence are indeterminate. Instead it is because they never exist. We can regret, for the sake of an indeterminate but existent person that a benefit was not bestowed on him or her, but we cannot regret, for the sake of somebody who never exists and thus cannot thereby be deprived, a good that this never existent person never experiences. One might grieve about not having had children, but not because the children that one could have had have been deprived of existence. Remorse about not having children is remorse for ourselves – sorrow about having missed childbearing and childrearing experiences. However, we do regret having brought into existence a child with an unhappy life, and we regret it for the child's sake, even if also for our own sakes. The reason why we do not lament our failure to bring somebody into existence is because absent pleasures are not bad.

Finally, support for the asymmetry between (3) and (4) can be found in the asymmetrical judgements about (a) (distant) suffering and (b) uninhabited portions of the earth or the universe. Whereas, at least when we think of them, we rightly are sad for inhabitants of a foreign land whose lives are characterized by suffering, when we hear that some island is unpopulated, we are not similarly sad for the happy people who, had they existed, would have populated this island. Similarly, nobody really mourns for those who do not exist on Mars, feeling sorry for potential such beings that they cannot enjoy life.[9] Yet, if we knew that there were sentient life on Mars but that Martians were suffering, we would regret this for them. The claim here need not (but could) be the strong one that we would regret their very existence. The fact that we would regret the suffering *within* their life is sufficient to support the asymmetry I am defending. The point is that we regret suffering but not the absent pleasures of those who could have existed.

Now it might be objected that just as we do not regret the absent pleasures of those who could have existed, we do not take joy in the absent pain of those who could have existed. For if we did, the objection goes, we should be overjoyed by the amount of pain that is avoided, given how few of all the possible people ever become actual, and thus how much pain is avoided. But joy is not the appropriate contrast to regret. Although we regret the suffering of distant others, at least when we think about them, we are not usually overcome with melancholy about it.[10] Thus the important question is not whether we feel joy – the opposite of melancholy – about absent pains but whether the absent pain is the opposite of regrettable – what we might call 'welcome' or simply 'good'. The answer, I have suggested, is affirmative. If we are asked whether the absent suffering is a good feature of never existing, we would have to say that it is.

I have shown that the asymmetry between (3) and (4) explains four other asymmetries. Given that these other asymmetries are widely endorsed, we have good grounds for thinking that the asymmetry between (3) and (4) is also widely accepted. That it is so is not evidence of its truth, for the multitude can be and often are wrong. However, it does show that my starting point should have broad appeal.

The judgements supported by the asymmetry of (3) and (4) are not universally shared. For example, positive utilitarians – who are interested not only in minimizing pain but also in maximizing pleasure – would tend to lament the absence of additional possible pleasure even if there were nobody deprived of that pleasure. On their view, there *is* a duty to bring people into existence if that would increase happiness. This is not to say that all positive utilitarians *must* reject the view about the asymmetry of (3) and (4). Positive utilitarians who are sympathetic to the asymmetry could draw a distinction between (i) promoting the happiness of people (that exist, or will exist independently of one's choices) and (ii) increasing happiness by making people. This is the now famous distinction between (i) making people happy and (ii) making happy people. Positive utilitarians who draw this distinction could then, consistent with positive utilitarianism, judge only (i) to be a requirement of morality. This is the preferable version of positive utilitarianism. Taking (ii) also to be a requirement of morality mistakenly assumes that the value of happiness is primary and the value of persons is derivative from this. However, it is not the case that people are valuable because they add extra happiness. Instead extra happiness is valuable because it is good for people – because it makes people's lives go better. To think otherwise is to think that people are mere means to the production of happiness. Or, to use another famous image, it is to treat persons as mere vessels of happiness. But unlike a mere vessel, which is indifferent to how much of a valued substance it contains, a person cares about how much happiness he has.

If my arguments so far are sound, then the view about the asymmetry between harm and benefit is both compelling and widespread. My argument will proceed by showing how, given the asymmetry between harm and benefit, it follows that coming into existence is always a harm. [...]

To show why, given the asymmetry I have defended, it is always a harm to come into existence it is necessary to compare two scenarios, one (A) in which X exists and one (B) in which X never exists. This, along with the views already mentioned, is represented diagrammatically in Figure 3.4.1

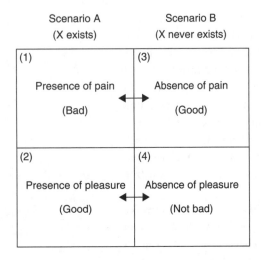

Figure 3.4.1

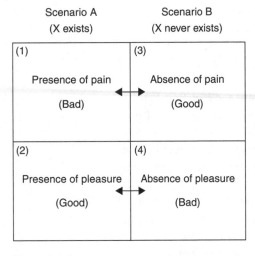

Figure 3.4.2

If I am correct then it is uncontroversially the case that (1) is bad and (2) is good. However, in accordance with the considerations mentioned above, (3) is good even though there is nobody to enjoy the good, but (4) is not bad because there is nobody who is deprived of the absent benefits.

Drawing on my earlier defence of the asymmetry, we should note that alternative ways of evaluating (3) and (4), according to which a symmetry between pain and pleasure is preserved, must fail, at least if common important judgements are to be preserved. The first option is shown in Figure 3.4.2.

Here, to preserve symmetry, the absence of pleasure (4) has been termed 'bad'. This judgement is too strong because if the absence of pleasure in Scenario B is 'bad' rather than 'not bad' then we should have to regret, for X's sake, that X did not come into existence. But it is not regrettable.

The second way to effect a symmetrical evaluation of pleasure and pain is shown in Figure 3.4.3.

To preserve symmetry in this case, the absence of pain (3) has been termed 'not bad' rather than 'good', and the absence of pleasure (4) has been termed 'not good' rather than 'not bad'. On one interpretation, 'not bad' is equivalent to 'good', and 'not good' is equivalent to 'bad'. But this is not the interpretation that is operative in this matrix, for if it were, it would not differ from, and would have the same shortcomings as, the previous matrix. 'Not bad', in Figure 3.4.3, therefore must mean 'not bad, but not good either'. Interpreted in this way, however, it is too weak. Avoiding the pains of existence is more than merely 'not bad'. It is good.

Judging the absence of pleasure to be 'not good' is also too weak in that it does not say enough. Of course the absence of pleasure is not what we would call good. However, the important question, when the absence of pleasure involves no deprivation for anybody, is whether it is also 'not bad' or whether it is 'bad'. The answer, I suggest, is that it is 'not good, but not bad either' rather than 'not good, but bad'. Because 'not bad' is a more informative evaluation than 'not good', that is the one I prefer. However, even those who wish to stick with 'not good' will not thereby succeed in restoring symmetry. If pain is bad and pleasure is good, but the absence of pain is good and the absence of pleasure not good, then there is no symmetry between pleasure and pain.

Comparing Existing with Never Existing

Having rejected alternative evaluations, I return to my original diagram. To determine the relative advantages and disadvantages of coming into existence and never coming to be, we need to compare (1) with (3), and (2) with (4). In the first comparison we see that non-existence is preferable to existence. Non-existence has an advantage over existence. In the second comparison, however, the pleasures of the existent, although good, are not an advantage over non-existence, because the absence of pleasures is not bad. For the good to be an advantage over non-existence, it would have to have been the case that its absence were bad.

To this it might be objected that 'good' *is* an advantage over 'not bad' because a pleasurable sensation is better than a neutral state. The mistake underlying this objection, however, is that it treats the absence of pleasure in Scenario B as though it were akin to the absence of pleasure in Scenario A – a possibility not reflected in my matrix, but which is implicit in (4) of my original description of asymmetry. There I said that the absence of pleasure is not bad *unless there is somebody for whom this absence is a deprivation.* The implication here is

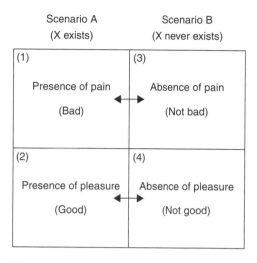

Figure 3.4.3

that where an absent pleasure is a deprivation it is bad. Now, obviously, when I say that it is bad, I do not mean that it is bad in the same way that the presence of pain is bad.[11] What is meant is that the absent pleasure is relatively (rather than intrinsically) bad. In other words, it is *worse* than the presence of pleasure. But that is because X exists in Scenario A. It would have been better had X had the pleasure of which he is deprived. Instead of a pleasurable mental state, X has a neutral state. Absent pleasures in Scenario B, by contrast, are not neutral states of some person. They are no states of a person at all. Although the pleasures in A are better than the absent pleasures in A, the pleasures in A are not better than the absent pleasures in B.

The point may be made another way. Just as I am not talking about intrinsic badness when I say that absent pleasures that deprive are bad, so I am not speaking about intrinsic 'not badness' – neutrality – when I speak about absent pleasures that do not deprive. Just as absent pleasures that do deprive are 'bad' in the sense of 'worse', so absent pleasures that do not deprive are 'not bad' in the sense of 'not worse'. They are not worse than the presence of pleasures. It follows that the presence of pleasures is not better, and therefore that the presence of pleasures is not an advantage over absent pleasures that do not deprive.

Some people have difficulty understanding how (2) is not an advantage over (4). They should consider an analogy which, because it involves the comparison of two existent people is unlike the comparison between existence and non-existence in *this* way, but which nonetheless may be instructive. S (Sick) is prone to regular bouts of illness. Fortunately for him, he is also so constituted that he recovers quickly. H (Healthy) lacks the capacity for quick recovery, but he *never* gets sick. It is bad for S that he gets sick and it is good for him that he recovers quickly. It is good that H never gets sick, but it is not bad that he lacks the capacity to heal speedily. The capacity for quick recovery, although a good for S, is not a real advantage over H. This is because the absence of that capacity is not bad for H. This, in turn, is because the absence of that capacity is not a deprivation for H. H is not worse off than he would have been had he had the recuperative powers of S. S is not better off than H in any way, even though S is better off than he himself would have been had he lacked the capacity for rapid recovery.

It might be objected that the analogy is tendentious. It is obvious that it is better to be Healthy than to be Sick. The objection is that if I treat these as analogies for never existing and existing respectively, then I bias the discussion toward my favoured conclusion. But the problem with this objection, if it is taken alone, is that it could be levelled at all analogies. The point of an analogy is to find a case (such as H and S) where matters are clear and thereby to shed some light on a disputed case (such as Scenarios A and B in Fig. 3.4.1). Tendentiousness, then, is not the core issue. Instead, the real question is whether or not the analogy is a good one.

One reason why it might be thought not to be a good analogy is that whereas pleasure (in Fig. 3.4.1) is an *intrinsic* good, the capacity for quick recovery is but an *instrumental* good. It might be argued further that it would be impossible to provide an analogy involving two existing people (such as H and S) that could show one of the people not to be disadvantaged by lacking some *intrinsic* good that the other has. Since the only unambiguous cases of an actual person lacking a good and not thereby being disadvantaged are cases involving *instrumental* goods, the difference between intrinsic and instrumental goods might be thought to be relevant.

This, however, is unconvincing, because there is a deeper explanation of why absent intrinsic goods could always be thought to be bad in analogies involving only existing people. Given that these people exist, the absence of any intrinsic good could always be thought to constitute a deprivation for them. In analogies that compare two existing people the only way to simulate the absence of deprivation is by considering instrumental goods.[12] Because (3) and (4) make it explicit that the presence or absence of deprivation is crucial, it seems entirely fair that the analogy should test this feature and can ignore the differences between intrinsic and instrumental goods.

Notice, in any event, that the analogy need not be read as proving that quadrant (2) is good and that quadrant (4) is not bad. That asymmetry was established in the previous section. Instead, the analogy could be interpreted as showing how, given the asymmetry, (2) is not an advantage over (4), whereas (1) is a disadvantage relative to (3). It would thereby show that Scenario B is preferable to Scenario A.

We can ascertain the relative advantages and disadvantages of existence and non-existence in another way, still in my original matrix, but by comparing (2) with (3) and (4) with (1). There are benefits both to existing and non-existing. It is good that existers enjoy their pleasures. It is also good that pains are avoided through non-existence. However, that is only part of the picture. Because there is nothing bad about never coming into existence, but there is something bad about coming into existence, it seems that all things considered non-existence is preferable.

One of the realizations which emerges from some of the reflections so far is that the cost-benefit analysis of the cheerful – whereby one weighs up (1) the pleasures of life against (2) the evils – is unconvincing as a comparison between the desirability of existence and never existing. The analysis of the cheerful is mistaken for a number of reasons:

First, it makes the wrong comparison. If we want to determine whether non-existence is preferable to existence, or vice versa, then we must compare the left- and the right-hand sides of the diagram, which represent the alternative scenarios in which X exists and in which X never exists. Comparing the upper and the lower quadrants on the left does not tell us whether Scenario A is better than Scenario B or vice versa. That is unless quadrants (3) and (4) are rendered irrelevant. One way in which that would be so is if they were both valued as 'zero'. On this assumption A can be thought to be better than B if (2) is greater than (1), or to put it another way, if (2) minus (1) is greater than zero. But this poses a second problem. To value quadrants (3) and (4) at zero is to attach no positive value to (3) and this is incompatible with the asymmetry for which I have argued. (It would be to adopt the symmetry of Fig. 3.4.3.)

Another problem with calculating whether A or B is better by looking only at (1) and (2), subtracting the former from the latter, is that it seems to ignore the difference, mentioned earlier, between a 'life worth starting' and a 'life worth continuing'. The cheerful tell us that existence is better than non-existence if (2) is greater than (1). But what is meant by 'non-existence' here? Does it mean 'never existing' or 'ceasing to exist'? Those who look only at (1) and (2) do not seem to be distinguishing between never existing and ceasing to exist. For them, a life is worth living (that is, both starting and continuing) if (2) is greater than (1), otherwise it is not worth living (that is, neither worth starting nor continuing). The problem with this, I have already argued, is that there is good reason to distinguish between them. For a life to be not worth continuing, it must be worse than it need be for it not to be worth starting.[13] Those who consider not only Scenario A but also Scenario B clearly are considering which lives are worth starting. To determine which lives are worth continuing, Scenario A would have to be compared with a third scenario, in which X ceases to exist.[14]

Finally, the quality of a life is not determined simply by subtracting the bad from the good. [...] Assessing the quality of a life is much more complicated than this.

Now some people might accept the asymmetry represented in Figure 3.4.1, agree that we need to compare Scenario A with Scenario B, but deny that this leads to the conclusion that B is always preferable to A – that is, deny that coming into existence is always a harm. The argument is that we must assign positive or negative (or neutral) values to each of the quadrants, and that if we assign them in what those advancing this view take to be the most reasonable way, we find that coming into existence is sometimes preferable (see Fig. 3.4.4).[15]

Quadrant (1) must be negative, because it is bad, and quadrants (2) and (3) must be positive because they are good. (I assume that (3) must be *us* good as (1) is bad. That is, if (1) = −n, then (3) = +n). Since (4) is not bad (and not good either), it should be neither positive nor negative but rather neutral.

Employing the value assignments of Figure 3.4.4 we add (1) and (2) in order to determine the value of A, and then compare this with the sum of (3) and (4), which is the value of B. Doing this, we find that A is preferable to B where (2) is more than twice the value of (1).[16] There are numerous problems with this. For instance, [...], it is not only the ratio of pleasure to pain that determines the quality of a life, but also

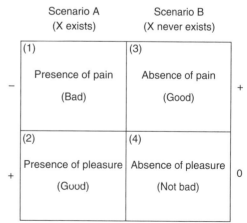

Figure 3.4.4

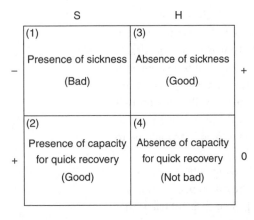

Figure 3.4.5

the sheer quantity of pain. Once a certain threshold of pain is passed, no amount of pleasure can compensate for it.

But the best way to show that Figure 3.4.4 is mistaken is to apply the reasoning behind Figure 3.4.4 to the analogy of H (Healthy) and S (Sick) mentioned earlier.

Following Figure 3.4.5, it would be better to be S than H if the value of (2) were more than twice the value of (1). (This presumably would be the case where the amount of suffering that (2) saves S is more than twice the amount S actually suffers.) But this cannot be right, for surely it is *always* better to be H (a person who never gets sick and is thus not disadvantaged by lacking the capacity for quick recovery). The whole point is that (2) is *good for* S but does not constitute an advantage over H. By assigning a positive charge to (2) and a '0' to (4), Figure 3.4.5 suggests that (2) is an advantage over (4), but it quite clearly is not. The assignment of values in Figure 3.4.5, and hence also in Figure 3.4.4, must be mistaken.[17]

Now it might be asked what the *correct* value assignments are, but I want to resist that question because it is the wrong one to ask. Figure 3.4.1 is intended to show why it is always preferable not to come into existence. It shows that coming into existence has disadvantages relative to never coming into existence whereas the positive features of existing are not advantages over never existing. Scenario B is always better than Scenario A for much the same reason that it is always preferable to be H rather than S. Figure 3.4.1 is not meant to be a guide to determining *how* bad it is to come into existence.

There is a difference, I have indicated, between (a) saying that coming into existence is always a harm and (b) saying how great a harm it is. So far I have argued only for the first claim. The magnitude of the harm of existence varies from person to person, [...] though the harm is very substantial for everybody. However, it must be stressed that one can endorse the view that coming into existence is always a harm and yet deny that the harm is great. Similarly, if one thinks that the harm of existence is not great, one cannot infer from that that existence is preferable to non-existence.

This recognition is important for warding off another potential objection to my argument. One of the implications of my argument is that a life filled with good and containing only the most minute quantity of bad – a life of utter bliss adulterated only by the pain of a single pin-prick – is worse than no life at all. The objection is that this is implausible. Understanding the distinction between (a) coming into existence being a harm and (b) how great a harm it is, enables one to see why this implication is not so implausible. It is true of the person enjoying this charmed life marred only by a single brief sharp pain, that as pleasant as his life is, it has no advantages over never existing. Yet coming into existence has the disadvantage of the single pain. We can acknowledge that the harm of coming into existence is minuscule without denying that it is harm. Setting aside the matter of whether coming into existence is a harm, who would deny that a brief sharp pain is a harm, even if only a minor one? And if one acknowledges that it is a harm – one that would have been avoided had that life not begun – why should one deny that a life begun at that cost is a harm, even if only a minor one? Think again of the analogy of S and H. If S gets sick only once, and then only has a headache that quickly subsides, it is still better to be H (even though not that much better). If all lives were as free of suffering as that of the imagined person who suffers only a pin-prick, the harms of coming into existence would easily be outweighed by the benefits to others (including the potential parents) of that person coming into existence. In the real world, however, there are no lives even nearly this charmed.

Other Asymmetries

I have argued that pleasure and pain are asymmetrical in a way that makes coming into existence always a harm. […]. It should be clear now, that the idea that coming into existence is always a serious harm raises a problem for procreation. Procreation can be challenged in many other ways too, but the arguments of Christoph Fehige[18] and Seana Shiffrin[19] have interesting parallels with my argument.

Consider Seana Shiffrin's argument first. The understanding of benefit and harm implicit in my argument is similar to that which she makes explicit in hers. She understands benefit and harm non-comparatively. That is to say, she understands them not as two ends of a scale or as shifts up and down such a scale. Instead she understands them as absolute conditions of, respectively, a positive and a negative kind. Moreover, her argument, like mine, appeals to an asymmetry between benefits and harms, albeit a different asymmetry. She says that in the absence of evidence of a person's wishes to the contrary, it is permissible, perhaps obligatory, to inflict a lesser harm on that person in order to prevent a greater harm. By contrast, it would be wrong to inflict a harm that would yield a greater (pure) benefit.[20] Thus, we take it to be acceptable to break an unconscious (non-consenting) person's arm in order to prevent a greater harm, such as death, to that person. (This is the 'rescue case'.) However, we would condemn breaking that person's arm in order to secure some greater benefit, such as 'supernormal memory, a useful store of encyclopedic knowledge, twenty IQ points worth of extra intellectual ability, or the ability to consume immoderate amounts of alcohol or fat without side effects'.[21] (Call this the 'pure benefit case'.)

Since all existers suffer harm, procreation always causes harm. Professor Shiffrin is prepared to grant (for the sake of argument?) that 'being created *can* benefit a person.'[22] However, in accordance with the asymmetry just mentioned, we may not inflict the harm in order to secure the benefit. Although existing people can sometimes authorize our inflicting harm in order to secure some benefit for them, we can never obtain the consent of those whom we bring into existence before we create them. Nor can we presume hypothetical consent, she argues. There are four reasons for this.[23] First, the person is not harmed if we fail to create him or her. Secondly, the harms of existence may be severe. Thirdly, the harms of life cannot be escaped without considerable cost. Finally, the hypothetical consent is not based on the individual's values or attitudes towards risk.

There are some interesting differences between Professor Shiffrin's argument and mine. Her argument, at least on the surface, does not preclude treating life's goods as advantages over non-existence (although, as I shall show, it does not require treating

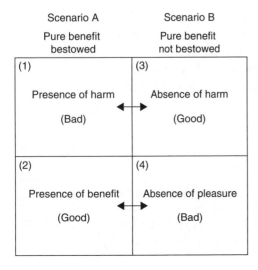

Figure 3.4.6

them as such). On her view, even if pleasures and other goods enjoyed by existers are advantages over non-existence, they are not advantages that we may secure at the costs of existence.[24]

Nor does her basic argument presuppose the asymmetry I have defended. We can see this by comparing two scenarios that involve existing people and that are not characterized by the asymmetry in Figure 3.4.1. The first of these scenarios is one in which a pure benefit is bestowed at the cost of a harm and the other is one in which that harm is avoided at the cost of the pure benefit. Following the pattern of the earlier matrices, we might represent this as shown in Figure 3.4.6.

My asymmetry does not apply in such a case, yet on Professor Shiffrin's asymmetry we would not be warranted in inflicting (1) to secure (2). Put another way, we may not bring about Scenario A over Scenario B (absent the person's consent). Even when applied to cases of procreation, where (I have argued) my asymmetry does apply, Professor Shiffrin's prioritizing of B over A is not based on my asymmetry but rather on hers.

This does not mean that my asymmetry is unconnected with her argument, and it certainly does not mean that my asymmetry is incompatible with it. We find, first, that at least one feature of my asymmetry makes her case against procreation even stronger than her case against other bestowals of pure benefit that cause harm. Professor Shiffrin notes that procreation is not like cases of inflicting a harm in order to rescue somebody because 'if the benefit bestowed by creation is not conferred, the nonexistent person will not experience its absence.' She might have added that in this regard procreation is unlike not only the rescue case, but also non-procreative cases of bestowing pure benefit at the cost of harm. Implicitly recognized here is that the absent benefit when somebody is not brought into existence is not bad (quadrant 4 of Fig. 3.4.1). It is less clear how Professor Shiffrin views the claim in quadrant (3) in Figure 3.4.1 – that the absence of harm when somebody is not created is good. However, I suggest that that claim too would strengthen her case against procreation (although I recognize that she may not be aiming to strengthen this case). Procreation would be more threatened if the absent harms were good and not merely neither bad nor good.

In response to Professor Shiffrin's argument, it has been objected that her asymmetry is not needed to explain the pure benefit case – the case where some benefit is bestowed but at the cost of a harm. It has been suggested[25] that in the pure benefit case Seana Shiffrin describes, somebody's rights have been violated (by having his arm broken without his permission), and *this* explains why the benefit may not be bestowed. It can only be bestowed by violating a right not to be harmed. The implicit assumption here is that in the case of procreation nobody's rights are violated, at least so long as the resultant life is one 'worth living'.

One common basis for denying that procreation violates the rights of the person created is that prior to procreation that person does not exist and thus there can be no bearer of the right not to be created. But this may be an unduly narrow view of rights ascription – one that ignores the special features of procreation. If, as I argued in the opening section of this chapter, one *can* be harmed by being brought into existence, one could argue that the right that protects against this kind of harm is a special kind of right – a right that has a bearer only in the breach. Put another way, we might say that one violates a right by performing some action if, as a result of performing this action, there exists some person who is wrongfully harmed. I acknowledge that this is an unusual kind of right, but coming into existence is an unusual case. If one could make sense of such a right, it would then not be an objection to an argument that a person is wrongfully harmed that there was no right not to be.[26]

Those who agree that there is no logical obstacle to a right not to be created might still argue that the pure benefit case fails to support the (unqualified) asymmetry that Seana Shiffrin wishes to defend. This is because there are actually two kinds of pure benefit cases (which she does not distinguish). First, there are those involving autonomous beings. They have a right not to be harmed without their consent, even for their benefit. Secondly, there are those involving non-autonomous beings. Although they *could* (logically) also have such a right, it could plausibly be argued that they *do not* (morally) have such a right. Although there are limits on the harms parents may inflict on a child for that child's sake, there certainly are cases where a child's best interests (considering both benefits and harms) may warrant the imposition of a harm. Defenders of procreation might argue that although we may not inflict a harm on an autonomous being without his consent even if this will secure a greater benefit for him, we may sometimes do otherwise in the case of children and, a fortiori, of potential children. It is in response to such a criticism that it becomes helpful for Seana Shiffrin to appeal to my asymmetry or, as she implicitly does, at least to part of it. By denying that somebody's best interests can be served by being brought into existence, she can draw the distinction between children and potential children, and thus ward off the paternalistic objection that parents may inflict the harms of life on a potential child for that child's sake. I have argued that making potential people actual is not in their interests.

Christoph Fehige's argument is arguably even closer to mine than Seana Shiffrin's. He defends and then spells out the implications of a view that he calls 'antifrustrationism' (but which is sometimes called what sounds like its opposite – 'frustrationism'). According to this view, a satisfied preference and no preference are equally good. Only an unsatisfied preference is bad. In other words, he argues that although it is good to have fulfilled whatever desires one might have, one is not better off having a fulfilled desire than having no desire at all. By way of example, consider the case in which we 'paint the tree nearest to Sydney Opera house red and give Kate a pill that makes her wish that the tree nearest to Sydney Opera House were red'.[27] Professor Fehige plausibly denies that we do Kate any favour in doing this. She is no better off than had we done nothing. What matters is not that people have satisfied desires but that they do not have unsatisfied ones. It is the avoidance of frustration that is important. There is an asymmetry buried here, as Figure 3.4.7 shows.

Antifrustrationism implies that it would be better not to create people. Their satisfied preferences will not be better than the absence of their preferences had they not existed. However, their unsatisfied preferences – of which there will be many – are worse than the absence of their preferences if they were not created. (1) is worse than B, but (2) is not better than B.

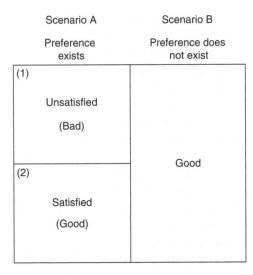

Scenario A Preference exists	Scenario B Preference does not exist
(1) Unsatisfied (Bad)	
(2) Satisfied (Good)	Good

Figure 3.4.7

Scenario A (X exists)	Scenario B (X never exists)
(1) Preference unsatisfied (Bad)	(3) Absent preference that would have been unsatisfied (in A). (Good)
(2) Preference satisfied (Good)	(4) Absent preference that would have been satisfied (in A). (Good)

Figure 3.4.8

We can adapt Figure 3.4.7 to show more clearly its relation to the asymmetry I have defended (see Fig. 3.4.8).

In this adaptation, I have taken the liberty of differentiating (3) from (4) even though Professor Fehige does not do so. He treats all absent preferences alike. However, it does not seem that this differentiation is incompatible with his argument. I have also labelled (2), (3), and (4) all as 'good'. This is because Professor Fehige says that absent preferences and satisfied preferences are 'equally good'.[28] If this is the correct reading of Professor Fehige, then his asymmetry is a little different from mine, even though it yields the same result – that Scenario A is worse than Scenario B.

However, there may be other ways of reading him. When he says that (2) and Scenario B are 'equally good', he might not mean to describe (3) and (4) as good. He might mean only that (2) is no better than Scenario B. This is exactly what I meant when I described (4) in Figure 3.4.1 as 'not bad'. I meant that it was no worse than (2). The problem with describing (4) in Figure 3.4.8 as 'not bad' is that because Professor Fehige seems to treat (3) and (4) as equivalent, (3) would also have to be labelled 'not bad'. If 'not bad' there meant the same as in (4) – that is, 'not worse' – then (3) would not be worse than (1). However, this seems too weak, as I indicated earlier. (3) is better than (1). The alternative, then, is to postulate that if Professor Fehige differentiated (3) and (4) that he would understand them differently. He might understand 'not bad' as meaning something different in the third and fourth quadrants of Figure 3.4.8. In (3) it would mean 'better' than (1), while in (4) it means 'not worse' than (2). On this reading, we might label (3) as 'good', because 'good' is (sufficiently) better than 'bad'. In this way, Christoph Fehige's asymmetry could be interpreted to be the same as mine.

Whichever of these two readings one adopts, (3) is better than (1), and (4) is not worse than (2). The same is true in Figure 3.4.1. In both, coming into existence (Scenario A) is worse than never coming into existence (Scenario B).

Against not Regretting One's Existence

Those who think (with Alfred Lord Tennyson) that it is better to have loved and lost than never to have loved at all[29] might think that they can apply similar reasoning to the case of coming into existence. They might want to say that it is better to have existed and lost (both by suffering within life and then by ceasing to exist) than never to have existed at all. I shall not pass judgement on whether it is indeed better to have loved and lost than never to have loved at all. It suffices to say that even if that claim is true, it does not entail anything about coming into existence. This is because there is a crucial difference between loving and coming into existence. The person who never loves exists without loving and is thus deprived. That, on my account, is 'bad'. (Whether it is *worse* than loving and losing is another question.) By contrast, one who never comes into existence is not deprived of anything. That, I have argued, is 'not bad'.

That coming into existence is a harm is a hard conclusion for most people to swallow. Most people do not regret their very existence. Many are happy to have come into being because they enjoy their lives. But these appraisals are mistaken for precisely the reasons I have outlined. The fact that one enjoys one's life does not make one's existence better than non-existence, because if one had not come into existence there would have been nobody to have missed the joy of leading that life and thus the absence of joy would not be bad. Notice, by contrast, that it makes sense to regret having come into existence if one does not enjoy one's life. In this case, if one had not come into existence then no being would have suffered the life one leads. That is good, even though there would be nobody who would have enjoyed that good.

Now it may be objected that one cannot possibly be mistaken about whether one's existence is preferable to non-existence. It might be said that just as one cannot be mistaken about whether one is in pain, one cannot be mistaken about whether one is glad to have been born. Thus if 'I am glad to have been born', a proposition to which many people would assent, is equivalent to 'It is better that I came into existence', then one cannot be mistaken about whether existence is better than non-existence. The problem with this line of reasoning is that these two propositions are not equivalent. Even if one cannot be mistaken about whether one *currently* is glad to have been born, it does not follow that one cannot be mistaken about whether it is better that one came into existence. We can imagine somebody being glad, at one stage in his life, that he came to be, and then (or earlier), perhaps in the midst of extreme agony, regretting his having come into existence. Now it cannot be the case that (all things considered) it is both better to have come into existence and better never to have come into existence. But that is exactly what we would have to say in such a case, if it were true that being glad or unhappy about having come into existence were equivalent to its actually being better or worse that one came into being. This is true even in those cases in which people do not change their minds about whether they are happy to have been born. Why so few people do change their minds is explained, at least in part, by the unduly rosy picture most people have about the quality of their own lives. […] (With the exception of real pessimists, who may have an accurate view of how bad their lives are) people's lives are much worse than they think.

Notes

1. Here I assume the ordinary view that death is a harm. Those who think that death does not harm the person who dies may simply leave death off my list of harms.

2. Only those who die very soon after coming into existence are spared much of these harms, but obviously are not spared death.

3. The term 'non-existence' is multiply ambiguous. It can be applied to those who never exist and to those who do not currently exist. The latter can be divided further into those who do not yet exist and those who are no longer existing. In the current context I am using 'non-existence' to denote those who never exist. Joel Feinberg has argued that the not yet existent and the no longer existent can be harmed. I embrace that view. What I have to say here applies only to the never existent.

4. One *could* (logically) make symmetrical claims about the absence of pleasure – that, when judged in terms of the (potential) interests of a person who does or does not exist, this absence of pleasure is bad. However, (4) suggests that this symmetrical claim, although logically possible, is actually false. I shall defend (4) later. For now my aim has been only to show that (3) is not incoherent.

5. Or even in its presence, if it is not thought to be great enough to defeat this duty. Just how great must a sacrifice be to prevent a positive duty arising is a complex and hotly disputed matter that I shall not consider here. There are not a few people who think that the extent of the sacrifice that can be required of us is quite considerable. See, for example, Singer, Peter, *Practical Ethics* 2nd edn. (Cambridge: Cambridge University Press, 1993). Notice, by the way, that although Peter Singer's conclusions about the extent of our positive duties are radically counterintuitive, that counterintuitiveness is not usually thought to suffice as an argument against his position. Curiously, though, there is much less hesitance to treat my conclusions as a *reductio* of my argument.

6. The condition that the moral reason (or duty) be grounded in the interests of the potential person is an important one. Those who find plausibility in the claim that we have a reason to create happy people tend to be motivated by impersonal considerations – such as there being more happiness in the world. But these are not considerations about the interests of the potential person.

7. Jeff McMahan says that 'the view that there is no strong moral reason to cause a person to exist just because his life would contain much good ... is deeply intuitive and probably impossible to dislodge.' *The Ethics of Killing: Problems at the Margins of Life* (New York: Oxford University Press, 2002) 300.

8. In other words, it is odd to suggest that one can have a child for that child's sake.

9. That most people do not even think about the absent lives on Mars is itself revealing. Once forced to think about these issues some will claim that they regret absent Martian pleasure. Whether or not they do, I cannot see how one could regret it for the sake of the (non-existent) Martians who would otherwise enjoy that pleasure. It is curious, however, how some people will begin to say that they do feel sorry for the absent Martians once they realize that not doing so supports asymmetry and thus the conclusion that coming into existence is always a harm. However, saying this and its making sense are two different matters.

10. That we do not have the more marked reaction is probably the result of a psychological defence mechanism.

11. The only time it would be bad in that sense is where the absence of pleasure is actually painful.

12. Any instructive analogy for Scenarios A and B would have to involve a comparison of two existing people. An analogy involving an existing and non-existing person would be no clearer than the case we are trying to illuminate. Thus we cannot be required to consider analogies that compare a person's existence with his never existing.

13. Those who consider only Scenario A *could* offer different judgements about when life is 'worth starting' and when it is 'worth continuing'. They could do so by setting different thresholds. Thus, they might say that for a life to be worth continuing, (2) need only just outweigh (1), but for a life to be worth starting, (2) must be significantly greater than (1). Although those who consider only Scenario A could do this, there is no evidence that they are doing it. They seem to treat the judgements alike. In any event, even if they could rectify this, their position would still succumb to the other objections I am raising.

14. In this scenario, which we might call Scenario C, the absence of pain would be 'good' and the absence of pleasure would be 'bad'.

15. I am grateful to Robert Segall for raising this challenge.

16. Where (2) is only twice the value of (1), A and B have equal value and thus neither coming into existence nor never coming into existence is preferable.

17. To take the implications of the value assignments in Fig. 3.4.5 for Fig. 3.4.4 as evidence that the analogy between the two cases must be inapt is another instance of treating the avoidance of my conclusion as axiomatic.

18. Fehige, Christoph, 'A Pareto Principle for Possible People', in Fehige, Christoph, and Wessels, Ulla, eds., *Preferences* (Berlin: Walter de Gruyter, 1998) 508–43.

19. Shiffrin, Seana Valentine, 'Wrongful Life, Procreative Responsibility, and the Significance of Harm', *Legal Theory*, 5 (1999) 117–48.

20. By 'pure benefit' she means 'benefits that are only goods and which are not also removals from or preventions of harm' (*ibid*. 124).

21. *Ibid*. 127.

22. *Ibid*. 119.

23. *Ibid*. 131–3.

24. Or at least not without being prepared to compensate for the harms. Seana Shiffrin is a little reticent about ruling out procreation entirely, although her argument does seem to entail this conclusion and one suspects that she would embrace it. She explicitly defends only the weaker claim that procreation is not a 'straightforward, morally innocent endeavor' (*ibid*. 118).

25. Wasserman, David, 'Is Every Birth Wrongful? Is Any Birth Morally Required?', DeCamp Bioethics Lecture (Princeton, 2004) unpublished manuscript, 8.

26. Obviously much more needs to be said about this. I have sketched only the outline of a response. It is not my aim to prove that there is a right not to come into existence, but rather to show that coming into existence is always a harm.

27. Fehige, Christoph, 'A Pareto Principle for Possible People', 513–14.

28. *Ibid*. 508.

29. Tennyson, Alfred Lord, *In Memoriam*, section 27, stanza 4 (lines 15 and 16).

3.5

Secular Philosophy and the Religious Temperament

Thomas Nagel

I

Analytic philosophy as a historical movement has not done much to provide an alternative to the consolations of religion. This is sometimes made a cause for reproach, and for unfavorable comparisons with the continental tradition of the twentieth century, which did not shirk that task. That is one of the reasons that continental philosophy has been better received by the general public: It at least tries to provide nourishment for the soul, the job by which philosophy is supposed to earn its keep.

Analytic philosophers usually rebuff the complaint by pointing out that their concerns are continuous with the central occupations of Western philosophy from Parmenides onward: metaphysics, epistemology, logic, and ethical theory. Those topics have been pursued in a great tradition of works that are often technical and difficult, and that are not intended for a broad audience. The aim of that tradition is understanding, not edification.

This reply is formally correct, but it fails to acknowledge the significant element of yearning for cosmic reconciliation that has been part of the philosophical impulse from the beginning. Its greatest example is Plato, who had what I would call a profoundly religious temperament – displayed not in what he said about religion, but in his philosophy.

I am using the term "religious temperament" in a way that may seem illegitimate to those who are genuinely religious. Yet I think it is the appropriate name for a disposition to seek a view of the world that can play a certain role in the inner life – a role that for some people is occupied by religion.

Whether anything like this was part of the religion of fourth-century Athens I do not know. But Plato was clearly concerned not only with the state of his soul, but also with his

Thomas Nagel (2010) "Secular Philosophy and the Religious Temperament," Chapter 1 in *Secular Philosophy and the Religious Temperament: Essays 2002–2008*, Oxford: Oxford University Press, pp. 3–17.

relation to the universe at the deepest level. Plato's metaphysics was not intended to produce merely a detached understanding of reality. His motivation in philosophy was in part to achieve a kind of understanding that would connect him (and therefore every human being) to the whole of reality – intelligibly and, if possible, satisfyingly. He even seems to have suffered from a version of the more characteristically Judeo-Christian conviction that we are all miserable sinners, and to have hoped for some form of redemption from philosophy.

The desire for such completion, whether or not one thinks it can be met, is a manifestation of what I am calling the religious temperament. One way in which that desire can be satisfied is through religious belief. Religion plays many roles in human life, but this is one of them. I want to discuss what remains of the desire, or the question, if one believes that a religious response is not available, and whether philosophy can respond to it in another way.

I recognize that this is a conspicuously negative and roundabout way of identifying the subject: What, if anything, does secular philosophy have to put in the place of religion? One answer would be that nothing secular can be put in its place, either because there is something unreal about the question to which religion purports to provide the answer, or because it can be answered only in religious terms. But I do not think this is right. A space remains open if we deny that religion can make sense of everything. And one of the legitimate functions of philosophy is either to try to occupy that place or else to offer a way of assimilating the fact that nothing can occupy it. The subject overlaps with that of the meaning of life, but it is not the same. It is a question of making sense not merely of our lives, but of everything.

II

To better identify the question, we should start with the religious response. There are many religions, and they are very different, but what I have in mind is common to the great monotheisms, perhaps to some polytheistic religions, and even to pantheistic religions that don't have a god in the usual sense. It is the idea that there is some kind of all-encompassing mind of spiritual principle in addition to the minds of individual human beings and other creatures – and that this mind or spirit is the foundation of the existence of the universe, of the natural order, of value, and of our existence, nature, and purpose. The aspect of religious belief I am talking about is belief in such a conception of the universe, and the incorporation of that belief into one's conception of oneself and one's life.

The important thing for the present discussion is that if you have such a belief, you cannot think of yourself as leading a merely human life. Instead, it becomes a life in the sight of God, or an element in the life of the world soul. You must try to bring this conception of the universe and your relation to it into your life, as part of the point of view from which it is led. This is part of the answer to the question of who you are and what you are doing here. It may include a belief in the love of God for his creatures, belief in an afterlife, and other ideas about the connection of earthly existence with the totality of nature or the span of eternity. The details will differ, but in general a divine or universal mind supplies an answer to the question of how a human individual can live in harmony with the universe.

Perhaps religious persons will regard this as a simple-minded caricature, but it is the impression that a nonbeliever gets from the outside, of what it would be like to have a religious world view. In any case, I describe this impression in order to locate my topic, which is a question to which religion provides one type of answer. I want to know what becomes of the question if one does not give it a religious answer.

The question I have in mind is a general one about the relation of individual human life to the universe as a whole. The question is pointed to by its religious answer: namely, that our lives are in some way expressions or parts of the spiritual sense of the universe as a whole, which is its deepest reality, and that we must try to live them in light of this, and not only from the point of view of our local purely individual nature. I believe that the question to which this is one possible response remains to be asked, even if a religious response is not available, namely: How can one bring into one's individual life a recognition of one's relation to the universe as a whole, whatever that relation is?

It is important to distinguish this question from the pure desire for understanding of the universe and one's place in it. It is not an expression of curiosity, however large. And it is not the general intellectual problem of how to combine an objective conception of the universe with the local perspective of one creature within it. It is rather a question of attitude: Is there a way to live in harmony with the universe, and not just in it?

Without God, it is unclear what we should aspire to harmony with. But still, the aspiration can remain, to live not merely the life of the creature one is, but in some sense to participate through it in the life of the universe as a whole. To be gripped by this desire is what I mean by the religious temperament. Having, amazingly, burst into existence, one is a representative of existence itself – of the whole of it – not just because one is part of it but because it is present to one's consciousness. In each of us, the universe has come to consciousness, and therefore our existence is not merely our own.

To live not merely one's own life is also a demand of those forms of morality that take up a universal standpoint as part of their foundation. And something of the kind will very likely form part of a secular response to the religious question. But it is only a part, dealing specifically with recognition of the existence of other people. There is more to the question than this. The extrahuman world that contains and generates all these people also has a claim on us – a claim to be made part of our life. Existence is something tremendous, and day-to-day life, however indispensable, seems an insufficient response to it, a failure of consciousness. Outrageous as it sounds, the religious temperament regards a merely human life as insufficient, as a partial blindness to or rejection of the terms of our existence. It asks for something more encompassing, without knowing what that might be.

My subject is the secular philosophical responses to this impulse. I will (somewhat arbitrarily) call the question to which it seeks an answer the cosmic question. It is a question to which a religion could provide an answer, if one accepted it, but my discussion will concentrate on nonreligious responses. The question, again, is this: How can one bring into one's individual life a full recognition of one's relation to the universe as a whole? It is this quite general question, rather than the more specific search for redemption, that I will focus on.

The secular responses fall into three categories: (a) those that reject the question; (b) those that construct an answer from the inside out, that is, starting from the human point of view; and (c) those that construct an answer from the outside in, that is, starting from a cosmic point of view.

III

Let me begin by discussing the dismissive response that probably fits most comfortably with the analytic tradition. My impression is that most analytic philosophers are devoid of the religious temperament, and that they cannot take seriously the thought that something is missing if it is impossible to make sense of things in that way.[1] Sense, in this outlook, is something to be found within individual human lives, human creativity, human interactions, and human institutions. To take the quest for sense outside the boundaries of those human purposes and aims relative to which all judgments of sense or senselessness must be made is an error, and an error of a philosophically familiar type: an attempt to extend a concept beyond the conditions that give it meaning.

Among great philosophers of the past, I would particularly associate this outlook with Hume, who seems to me a beautiful example of someone perfectly free of religious impulses. His serene naturalism is a deep expression of his temperament, and he obviously feels no yearning for harmony with the cosmos.

This is certainly a possible secular stance: Take life as you find it, and try to play the hand you have been dealt by the contingencies of biology, culture, and history. It is possible to go far beyond these boundaries in the pursuit of pure understanding, but all such understanding will be essentially scientific. It isn't that there is a great absence of sense to the universe as a whole. It is just that there is no way for sense to be either present or absent at that level. And the sense that religious belief confers on everything is entirely gratuitous – an unnecessary add-on whose removal leaves no gap to be filled. If there were a god who was responsible for the existence of the universe and our place in it, the sense of everything would depend on him, but if there is no god, there is nothing by reference to which the universe can either have or lack sense.

Someone who takes this point of view can regard it as a legitimate philosophical task to try to make sense of human life from within – to have something systematic to say about the ends of life, the good life – the meaning of life in one sense of that expression. But it will not seem intelligible to try to make sense of human existence altogether.

This important outlook, probably dominant among atheists, places physical science at the top of the hierarchy of understanding for the universe as a whole. There are other kinds of understanding that are appropriate for local concerns at smaller and more intimate scales. But the universe revealed by chemistry and physics, however beautiful and awe-inspiring, is meaningless, in the radical sense that it is incapable of meaning. That is, natural science, as most commonly understood, presents the world and our existence as something to which the religious impulse has no application. All we can do, and this is a great deal, is extend our knowledge of what the universe contains and of the laws that govern it.

This was not the outlook of religious scientists in the past, who saw themselves as uncovering the wonders of God's creation. And some modern scientists, like Einstein, have taken a quasi-religious attitude toward the natural order and its intelligibility. But the most common secular attitude, I think, is that once we leave the human scale and move to the largest and most general theories, and ultimately perhaps to a theory of everything, we are in a realm of pure description.

One major intellectual task is to describe how the universe generated creatures that find themselves with the need to make some kind of sense of their lives. But this description itself does not have to make sense in the same way. It can be a purely factual account of how sense-seeking creatures – creatures like us, whose lives are capable of significant senselessness – emerged at a certain level of complexity of organization.

The point of the resolutely secular view is that there is nothing missing from this picture. When we look beyond the human world at the universe that contains it and has somehow given rise to it, we are not looking into the abyss. There is no need to carry on about the loneliness of man in the face of the vast impersonality of the universe, no need for the courage to forge a new destiny for ourselves after the death of God. That's just pretentious hand-wringing.

I have set out this view because it is the default or zero position to which I want to explore alternatives; we might call it affectless atheism, or hardheaded atheism. The universe exists and meets a certain description; one of the things it has generated is us; end of story. Of course, a new story begins with our existence, since we find our own lives extraordinarily interesting. But this is a local phenomenon of perfectly understandable self-absorption, unconnected to the big picture. The big picture is of purely theoretical interest.

IV

It is a seductive position, and I do not doubt that many people find it comfortable, as well as intellectually irresistible. To me, it has always seemed an evasion. It requires that we leave the largest question unanswered – in fact, that we leave it unasked, because there is no such question. But there is: It is the question "What am I doing here?" and it doesn't go away when science replaces a religious world view.

The question results from one of those steppings back that constitute the essence of philosophy. We find the familiar unfamiliar by reflecting on features of our situation, or forms of thought and action, so central and pervasive that we are ordinarily submerged in them without paying any notice.[Philosophy in general is the most systematic form of self-consciousness.]It consists in bringing to consciousness for analysis and evaluation everything that in ordinary life is invisible because it underlies and pervades what we are consciously doing.

In this case, the first thing that is brought to notice is that we are parts of the world. We wake up from our familiar surroundings to find ourselves, already elaborately formed by biology and culture, amazingly in existence, in the midst of the contingency of the world, and suddenly we do not know where we are or what we are. We recognize that we are products of the world and its history, generated and sustained in existence in ways we hardly understand, so that in a sense every individual life represents far more than itself. It is a short step, easily taken on a starry night, to thinking that one is a small representative of the whole of existence. That creates in susceptible minds the need to grasp that life and, if possible, to lead it as part of something larger – perhaps even as part of the life of the universe.[2]

So we wrench ourselves from the embedded familiarity of our surroundings and ask whether an understanding of the totality of which we are a part can in turn become part of the self-understanding by which we live. Can we to some extent encompass the universe that has produced us? Whether the answer is yes or no, and whether or not one takes any interest in it, the question, I believe, is real. So although we should keep in mind the default position of hardheaded atheism, according to which the scientific world view abolishes not only cosmic meaning but its absence, I want now to turn to less dismissive secular responses to the question.

V

The minimalist response is that the universe has nothing to offer that we can use, and that we are thrown back on our own resources.[3] This differs from hardheaded atheism because it doesn't reject the question but tells us that we have to come to terms with our inability to answer it. We can't make sense of our lives from the point of view of our place in the universe, and shouldn't expect this to change even if we learn much more about the natural order. And that leaves a gap – the failure of a natural aspiration.

At this point, we may respond with either existentialist despair or existentialist defiance. The latter is particularly well expressed by Camus in *The Myth of Sisyphus*. It consists in making a virtue of the will to go on in spite of the complete indifference of the cosmos – without the kind of sense that religion could give to our lives. Not to be defeated by pointlessness is what gives our lives their point. That is as far as we can go toward living in light of our understanding of everything.

But there is another type of response that tries at least partially to fill the gap left by the death of God, working from the inside out. This is humanism, the view that we ourselves, as a species or community, give sense to the world as a whole. Human beings collectively can fill the place of the world soul. The significance of an individual life does depend on its embeddedness in something larger, but it is the collective consciousness of humanity rather than the cosmos that plays this role. Our self-consciousness and our place in cultural, cognitive, and moral history make membership in the human community a significant larger identity. The universe does not offer any sense to our lives, but we are not alone in it.

This response to the cosmic question does not show us how to live lives that are more than human, but it does argue that living a human life should be something much more than living the life of the individual human being one is. One should think of oneself as a representative of humanity, and live accordingly. Or perhaps a more substantive identity will involve one's particular place in history, and recognition of the origins of one's values and ties in a contingent historical genealogy.

A more abstract analogue of this universal self-conception is the foundation of Kant's moral theory, although Kant proposed that we should regard ourselves as representing the realm of all rational beings, not of anything so contingent and historical as the human species. A more humanist version of the Kantian conception is found in Rawls – see his evocation of the view sub specie aeternitatis at the end of *A Theory of Justice*.[4] Sidgwick's account of the basis of utilitarianism, as an incorporation into our lives of the point of view of the universe, can be regarded as another example of cosmic sense constructed from inside out – since what the point of view of the universe endorses is an impartial concern for the happiness of all sentient creatures. Their individual lives remain the ultimate sources of value.

The thoughts that we should transcend the life of a particular person by taking on the value of humanity, or the value of all rational beings as ends in themselves, or the value of all sentient life, are partial answers to the cosmic question. They go part of the way toward incorporating a cosmic point of view into the life of the individual, and they certainly embed that life in something larger. But they stop with the value of human (and other) life itself, which does not receive endorsement from some higher value. The point of humanism and other "inside-out" answers is that no such endorsement or external support is needed. It is we who give sense to the universe, so there is no need for a higher principle to give sense to us.

Another example is Sartre's existentialism: "There is no universe other than a human universe, the universe of human subjectivity,"[5] he says, summing up his argument that existentialism is a form of humanism. He interprets humanism through a somewhat unstable doctrine of radical freedom constrained by universal prescriptivism: Since God does not exist, everything is permitted, but in choosing what to be, I must think of myself as choosing for everyone. This shares with other humanisms the principle that we are the source of all value, which replaces the value not given to our lives by the nonexistent creator.

William James says, "Were one asked to characterize the life of religion in the broadest and most general terms possible, one might say that it consists of the belief that there is an unseen order, and that our supreme good lies in harmoniously adjusting ourselves thereto."[6] Humanism denies this, and finds our supreme good in harmony not with an unseen but with a visible order – one that is universal in a sense, but not unduly unfamiliar.

VI

Humanism and its relatives take us outside of ourselves in search of harmony with the universe, but not too far outside. Since the universe cannot be identified with the human world, they do not really give us a way of incorporating our conception of the universe as a whole into our lives and how we think of them. Because they take conscious life as a self-contained source of value, their cosmic ambition is limited. In a way, it is more limited than the forms of existentialism that require us to live in the acknowledgment that our lives are senseless, and that there is no harmony possible for us. But perhaps a more ambitious form of harmony, grounded in a larger view of our place in the universe, can be constructed on a secular basis. That is the project of "outside-in" responses to the cosmic question.

When we travel further outside the human perspective than even the universal value of humanity, or of rational or sentient beings, we come to the natural order. The scientific conception of that order is uncompromisingly secular. The question we now have to ask is whether it provides a naturalistic view of our relation to the universe that can be taken on as an essential part of the standpoint from which we lead our lives. Remember, we are talking about possible secular answers to the cosmic question, not about ways of rejecting the question. The development of a naturalistic account of the universe and our appearance in it can be a purely intellectual project, and hardheaded atheism says it has nothing to do with how we are to live – even though scientific knowledge about ourselves may be useful in enabling us to live longer and better. But I am asking now whether it can do something more, namely, provide us with a way of seeing the point or sense of our lives from a perspective larger than the human one from which we naturally start.

The most likely candidate for such a perspective is that of biology, in particular the evolutionary biology of our epoch. More fundamental sciences like physics and chemistry, even though we fall under them, don't seem to offer a perspective from which life can be lived. But biology may, and the evolutionary perspective toward ourselves can seem to offer the possibility of a transformative self-conception – one that is larger than even the universal human perspective.

Evolutionary theory is at the heart of contemporary philosophical naturalism about language, thought, perception, value, ethics, and action, but it often has nothing to do with the cosmic question or the religious temperament. Often, of course, it is associated with the rejection of religion, of its aspirations, and of anything resembling them.

But there is another strain of evolutionary naturalism that can be thought of as a replacement for religion. Its greatest representative is Nietzsche. What is distinctive about Nietzsche is that he turns a genealogical self-understanding, based on both biology and history, into a highly individual project of self-creation. He does not think that an understanding of his place in the natural order leads to moral universalism or anything similar. Instead, he thinks it should lead to freedom from the flattening influence of collective values and collective ideas.

Yet this is pursued in the name of a still larger framework, that of the great biological struggle that is responsible for one's existence and of which one's life is a part.[7] Our freedom and capacity for self-creation depends on our capacity to understand the evolutionary sources of the multiple and conflicting drives that constitute us – sources in both biological and social evolution. The revaluation of values that is Nietzsche's project starts from the values that have been bred into us by our species and its cultural history. The meaning of those values can be understood only through their genealogy – by understanding the functions they performed that led to their survival.

Only on the basis of such genealogical self-understanding can we re-create ourselves – not with the absolute freedom of Sartre's existentialism but by a reordering of our existing drives through a process of lifelong self-selection that is itself a form of evolution. "Valuing freely, as self selecting one's values, is precisely to value in the light of an understanding of why one values. It is to 'incorporate' insight into the selective processes – Darwinian and cultural – that made the values of one's body and spirit."[8] Once we understand how humans have come to be "the sick animal," the animal in which the products of natural and social selection are in conflict, we can in full consciousness re-create ourselves to transcend this conflict. (There is a distinct resemblance here to Freud's diagnosis of the human condition in *Civilization and Its Discontents*, but Freud is much more pessimistic than Nietzsche about the possible extent of our recaptured freedom.)

As Richardson observes, Nietzsche is so multifaceted that one can at best say that the Darwinian theme is one aspect of his views. But exegetical questions aside, this way of understanding and living one's life does seem an important form of naturalistic response to the cosmic question: How can one live in light of an understanding of the universe and one's place in it?

Instead of starting from one's existing values, one steps back and tries first to understand them in virtue of one's place in a much larger natural and historical order, and then to recast one's life from this new, expanded starting point. Nietzsche's ethical and political conclusions are famously radical, but I won't consider them here. It is the general strategy of importing not just historical genealogy but evolutionary biology into the perspective from which one lives that is significant. Nietzsche offers this as a source of enlarged meaning, which replaces the illusory meaning of religion and conventional morality. It is therefore a response to the cosmic question that is distinct from religion, from humanism, and from existentialism.

But can naturalism play this role? How much of one's genealogical, biological, and evolutionary identity does it make sense to assume as one's point of view? A certain measure of such identification is an important antidote to excessive spiritualization. The idea that we humans are really immortal souls temporarily trapped in animal bodies is no longer very attractive, but it has been in the past, and resistance to it has been important in the thought both of Nietzsche and of Freud. Our animality and its history are important aspects of the self that has been built up over eons of genealogical descent. We should not try to escape living our animal life, nor regard it just as a necessary platform for keeping afloat the real life of the higher faculties.

This is not yet a response to the cosmic question. It is a somewhat expanded or enriched conception of our humanity, rather than an expansion of our perspective to include a relation to the universe. But in Nietzsche's case, the connection between evolution and the will to power as the universal explanatory principle makes Darwinism more than a merely biological form of self-understanding. Nietzsche's philosophy is a secular response to the cosmic question, because it tells us how to live on the basis of a comprehensive understanding of our existence as an expression of the fundamental forces of nature. To be sure, what Nietzsche offers in his writings is a very individual response, one that depends specifically on Nietzsche's place in the history of humanity, which he believes gives him a unique understanding of the human genealogy and a unique capacity to make his own life the site for a revaluation of all values that can usher in the next stage of human evolution. But he clearly hoped to offer a choice that others might take up.

For most of us, however, the recognition that we are the products of biological and cultural evolution does not give us a task, a significant role in this larger process. The genealogical facts are interesting, and may lead to some significant self-conscious modifications of what we have been given, but for the most part we take what has resulted from the process as our starting point and live from there forward. Each of us is only a small drop in the evolutionary and historical river. Even if we recognize the importance of our origins to self-awareness, it is hard to see ourselves as expressions of the will to power. Modern evolutionary self-understanding is typically more passive than that.[9]

VII

There is a general reason to think that evolutionary naturalism cannot provide a response to the cosmic question. Nietzsche's conception of evolution, with his underlying power ontology, is very different from the modern Darwinian consensus. As it is usually understood, evolutionary naturalism is radically antiteleological. This implies that it is not suited to supply any kind of sense to our existence, if it is taken on as the larger perspective from which life is lived. Instead, the evolutionary perspective probably makes human life, like all life, meaningless, since it makes life a more or less accidental consequence of physics.

If that is so, then any response to the cosmic question will have to come from within the perspective of human life rather than from the evolutionary perspective toward it. This leads us back either to some form of humanism, to existentialist absurdity, or more likely to hardheaded atheism – the view that there is no way of making the scientific understanding of our place in the universe part of the sense of our lives, and that it doesn't matter.

Darwin's theory of evolution on its own does not have this consequence, because Darwin recognized that it did not explain the origin of life – only the origin of species through natural selection once life and biological heredity were in existence. But the evolutionary naturalism of our day is usually associated with an assumption that both the course of evolution and the origin of life have their basic explanation in the nonbiological sciences, even if the details of that explanation remain to be discovered.

The profoundly nonteleological character of this modern form of naturalism is concealed by the functional explanations that fill evolutionary accounts of the characteristics of living organisms. But any reference to the function or survival value of an organ or other feature is shorthand for a long story of purposeless mutations followed, because of environmental contingencies, by differential reproductive fitness – survival of offspring or other relatives with the same genetic material. It is in the most straightforward sense false that we have eyes in order to see and a heart to pump the blood. Darwinian natural selection could be compatible with teleology if the existence of DNA had the purpose of permitting successive generations of organisms to adapt through natural selection to changes in the environment – but that, of course, is not the naturalistic conception.

That conception, far from offering us a sense of who we are, dissolves any sense of purpose or true nature that we may have begun with. The meaning of organic life vanishes in the meaninglessness of physics, of which it is one peculiar consequence. It is widely thought that, without knowing the details, we now have every reason to believe that life arose from a lifeless universe, in virtue of the basic laws of particle physics or string theory or something of the kind, which did not have life or us "in mind." Hence the description of these ultimate laws as a theory of everything. Hence also the grateful remark of Richard Dawkins that Darwin made it possible for the first time to be an intellectually fulfilled atheist.[10]

A genealogy of this kind gives us nothing to live by. As Daniel Dennett says, it is "universal acid: it eats through just about every traditional concept."[11] To live, we must fall back on our contingently formed desires, reserving the scientific world picture for intellectual and instrumental purposes. If naturalism means that everything reduces to physics, then there is no naturalistic answer to the cosmic question. So the next question is whether there is any secular alternative to this kind of reductive naturalism.

VIII

There may be the radical alternative of some kind of Platonism, according to which there is a nonaccidental fit between us and the world order: In other words, the natural order is such that, over time, it generates beings that are both part of it and able to understand it. Such a nonreductionist conception, though teleological, does not postulate intention or purpose behind one's existence and relation to the universe. Still, it would repudiate the essentially mechanistic conception of nature that has dominated modern thought in the scientific age. I believe there are reasons to doubt the capacity of that conception to account for everything about us, and therefore for everything about the universe. That is not enough by itself to support a Platonist alternative, but if Platonism could be reconciled with the facts, it would offer some sense of what we are that can be internalized in a way that the reductionist, cosmic accident picture cannot. Each of us, on this view, is a part of the lengthy process of the universe gradually waking up. It was originally a biological evolutionary process, and in our species, it has become a collective cultural process as well. It will continue, and seen from a larger perspective, one's own life is a small piece of this very extended expansion of organization and consciousness.

Human life, too, though it is the most advanced version we know of, is only a part of the process. So the identification it encourages is not a form of humanism. In some respects, this is a return to the Nietzschean conception of mere humanity as a stage that we may be in a position to transcend. At the same time, it would share the Nietzschean identification with the prehuman sources that remain embedded in our present nature. We are bound up in many ways with life in general and are ourselves animals, as both Nietzsche and Freud emphasized.

But does it really make any difference whether we are the products of natural teleology or of pure chance? Without an intentional designer, perhaps there is no sense to be made of our lives from the larger perspective in either case: We just have to start from what we contingently are and make what sense we can of our lives from there.

If the question is about whether our lives have a cosmic purpose, I would agree. But that is not the only possibility. The Platonic sense of the world is that its intelligibility and the development of beings to whom it is intelligible are nonaccidental, so our awareness and its expansion as part of the history of life and of our species are part of the natural evolution of the cosmos. This expands our sense of what a human life is. It seems in that case at least somewhat less plausible to say that all sense begins with the contingent desires and choices of the particular individual – that existence precedes essence, in the existentialist formula.

In the Platonic conception, even the biological and cultural evolution that has led to the starting point at which each of us arrives on Earth and reaches consciousness is embedded in something larger, something that makes that entire history less arbitrary than it is on the reductive view. But if the Platonic alternative is rejected along with the religious one, we must go back to the choice between hardheaded atheism, humanism, and the absurd. In that case, since the cosmic question won't go away and humanism is too limited an answer, a sense of the absurd may be what we are left with.

Notes

1. The religious temperament is not common among analytic philosophers, but it is not absent. A number of prominent analytic philosophers are Protestant, Catholic, or Jewish, and others, such as Wittgenstein, clearly had a religious attitude to life without adhering to a particular religion. But I believe nothing of the kind is present in the makeup of Russell, Moore, Ryle, Austin, Carnap, Quine, Davidson, Strawson, or most of the current professoriate.

2. But see Conrad's sardonic observer Marlow for the opposite reaction: "It was one of those dewy, clear, starry nights, oppressing our spirit, crushing our pride, by the brilliant evidence of the awful loneliness, of the hopeless obscure insignificance of our globe lost in the splendid revelation of a glittering, soulless universe. I hate such skies." Joseph Conrad, *Chance*, Oxford World's Classics edition (Oxford: Oxford University Press, 2002), 41.

3. See Steven Weinberg: "The more the universe seems comprehensible, the more it also seems pointless." *The First Three Minutes* (New York: Basic Books, 1977), 155.

4. "The perspective of eternity is not a perspective from a certain place beyond the world, nor the point of view of a transcendent being; rather it is a certain form of thought and feeling that rational persons can adopt within the world. And having done so, they can, whatever their generation, bring together into one scheme all individual perspectives and arrive together at regulative principles that can be affirmed by everyone as he lives by them, each from his own standpoint. Purity of heart, if one could attain it, would be to see clearly and to act with grace and self-command from this point of view." Rawls, *A Theory of Justice* (Cambridge, Mass.: Harvard University Press, 1971), 587.

5. Jean-Paul Sartre, *L'existentialisme est un humanisme (1946)* (Paris: Gallimard, 1996), 76; translated by Bernard Frechtman, *Existentialism* (New York: Philosophical Library, 1947), 60.

6. William James, *The Varieties of Religious Experience* (New York: Longmans, Green and Co., 1902) (Dover reprint, 2002), 53.

7. For this reading of Nietzsche, I am indebted to John Richardson's perceptive study, *Nietzsche's New Darwinism* (New York: Oxford University Press, 2004).

8. Richardson, 107.

9. The use of genealogy to vindicate, rather than undermine, a fundamental human value has recently been proposed by Bernard Williams in his book *Truth and Truthfulness: An Essay in Genealogy* (Princeton, N.J.: Princeton University Press, 2002). Williams believes that history, rather than pure philosophy, provides the enlarged view needed to transcend the unreflective individual perspective – though I should add that Williams, in spite of his admiration for Nietzsche, is quite free of the religious temperament. His humanism is not intended to fill a gap left by the death of God, and he is happy to dismiss the view sub specie aeternitatis as irrelevant to human concerns. See his remarkable essay on humanism, "The Human Prejudice," in his *Philosophy as a Humanistic Discipline* (Princeton, N.J.: Princeton University Press, 2006).

10. Richard Dawkins, *The Blind Watchmaker* (New York: W. W. Norton, 1986), 6.

11. Daniel Dennett, *Darwin's Dangerous Idea* (New York: Simon and Schuster, 1995), 63.

Section IV

Finding Meaning in a World Without God

Optimistic Naturalism

Introduction

Erik J. Wielenberg

What Is the Question?

In Douglas Adams's satirical science fiction story *The Hitchhiker's Guide to the Galaxy*, the computer Deep Thought is tasked with answering the Great Question of "Life, the Universe, and Everything." After seven and a half million years of reflection, Deep Thought provides an answer to the Great Question: "Forty-two." This answer, of course, is entirely unhelpful, and Deep Thought points out the reason why: "I think the problem, to be quite honest with you, is that you've never actually known what the question is."[1]

Questions about the meaning of life are often like the Great Question of Life, the Universe, and Everything, in that they seem to be about something fundamental and deeply important, and yet it is often far from clear just what is being asked. Perhaps this is at least part of the explanation for Bertrand Russell's inability to answer the cab driver's question, "What's it all about?"[2] Deep Thought, the second-greatest computer in all of space and time, somehow had the ability to answer the Great Question without knowing what the Question really was. Russell, a mere human, may have struggled to answer the cabbie's question because he didn't know what he was being asked.

Accordingly, many of the authors represented in this section spend a fair bit of time trying to figure out just what we are asking when we ask whether human life is meaningful, or just what we are claiming when we claim that human life is meaningful (or meaningless). Many of these authors seem to accept the *amalgam thesis*, according to which "the original question, framed in terms of *meaning*, is a largely ill-conceived place-holder for a cluster of related requests, and thus, not really a single question at all."[3]

---

[1] Douglas Adams (2002) *The Ultimate Hitchhiker's Guide to the Galaxy*, New York: Ballantine Books, pp. 113–21.
[2] See Joshua Seachris's General Introduction to this book.
[3] See Joshua Seachris's General Introduction to this book.

Exploring the Meaning of Life: An Anthology and Guide, First Edition. Edited by Joshua W. Seachris.
© 2013 John Wiley & Sons, Inc. Published 2013 by John Wiley & Sons, Inc.

The amalgam thesis has an important implication for the following claim, which is perhaps the central credo of optimistic naturalism:

> Even if there is no God, human life can be meaningful.

The amalgam thesis is grounded at least partially in the idea that the term "meaning" in the question "What is the meaning of life?" is ambiguous; the term has multiple senses. Similarly, the credo above is ambiguous; there are multiple ways of understanding it. Furthermore, it is important to recognize that there are surely some senses in which the thesis is false. This is because there are surely some senses of "meaning" that are inextricably linked with the existence of God. For example, to borrow from my own contribution to this section, one possible sense of "meaning" is *supernatural meaning*. A life has meaning in this sense just in case it has a purpose assigned to it by a supernatural being. If there are no such beings, then of course no human life is meaningful in this sense.

What unites the authors whose work appears in this section is that they all believe that there are at least some important and relevant senses of the credo above that express truths. All of these authors maintain that there are important kinds of meaning that can survive the death of God.

What Do the Squirrels Represent?

One of my favorite comic strips begins with a frame that depicts two stick figures walking past a tree. The first figure says to the second: "There is no God. Our existence is without purpose." The second figure responds: "Oh, definitely. We are adrift in an uncaring void indifferent to all our mortal toil." In the second frame, the second figure is climbing the tree. The first figure, initially oblivious to the second figure's tree climbing, continues: "Exactly! In the end, nothing we do matters. We just […] why are you climbing that tree?" In the third and final frame, the second figure, now up in the tree and obscured by leaves, shouts down to the first figure: "Because the future is an adventure! Come on! Hey! I found *squirrels!*" This comic strip nicely captures the spirit of this section of the book.

In the strip, the discovery of squirrels serves to undermine the pessimistic claims that both figures make earlier in the strip. It is significant that the second figure doesn't find God up in the tree; he finds squirrels. The second figure moves from pessimism to optimism not by finding out that God exists after all, but rather by finding out that there's something worth doing even if God doesn't exist. Of course, the idea that life's meaning lies in squirrels is hardly to be taken seriously. But if not squirrels, then what? What could it be that provides human life with meaning in a godless universe? Each of the authors in this section has something to say about this question. In the remainder of this introduction, I shall try to provide a brief overview of what each author has to say. My goal is merely to provide a kind of a map; as such, it is no substitute for reading the essays themselves.

John Kekes focuses on control, arguing that even if no God or gods exist, our lives are not entirely ruled by chance. He seeks to identify the main boundaries of our control over our lives in a godless universe. Although this control is imperfect and incomplete, the human world "contains and sustains the values that give meaning and purpose to our lives" (p. 293). And even though these values "exist within the human world and there are no values outside of it," they are robust enough to ground an important kind of meaning.

Richard Taylor suggests that the foundation of a meaningful life is a capacity for creative activity. This capacity can be exercised if there is no God. However, Taylor holds that in fact, this capacity is only rarely exercised: "[W]hat gives any human existence its meaning, is the possibility that thus arises of creative power. But it is no more than a possibility, realized here and there, more or less, and fully realized only in exceptional persons" (p. 303). Thus, Taylor defends what might be called *modestly optimistic naturalism*: Human lives can be meaningful even if God does not exist, but most human lives in fact are relatively meaningless.

Susan Wolf distinguishes the claims that (1) human life as a whole is meaningless and (2) individual human lives are meaningless, accepting the former claim but rejecting the latter. To understand what it would be for an individual life to be meaningful, Wolf first considers a series of examples of human lives that are clearly meaningless. Reflection on what is missing from such lives ultimately leads her to the proposal that an individual human life is meaningful when it is "actively and at least somewhat successfully engaged in projects [...] that not just seem to have positive value, but that really do have it" (pp. 308–9). Wolf presses further by asking what reason we might have to care about whether our lives are meaningful. She argues that not to care whether one's life is meaningful is to act as if one's self is the only thing that matters, and that such an attitude flies in the face of the facts. The truth is that each of us is but a tiny speck in a vast universe; each speck is no more or no less significant than any other. According to Wolf, the proper response to this truth is to recognize that while human life as a whole is meaningless, we can still make our own lives meaningful, and that we have good reason to try to do so. By striving for individually meaningful lives, we adopt a practical stance that is "more in accord with the facts" (p. 314).

Robert Audi's contribution focuses largely on the concept of a life being *existentially meaningful*. Audi identifies three factors that contribute to this sort of meaningfulness: (1) creativity and high-level excellence, (2) reduction in the suffering of the lives of others, and (3) rich human relationships. Audi's approach is decidedly pluralistic; he suggests that while none of these three factors may be necessary for a meaningful life, any one of them can be sufficient. He likens this view of meaning to W.D. Ross's view on moral obligation, arguing that "just as, when there are conflicts of duties, an act can be obligatory even when it breaks a promise, a life can be meaningful even when it is bereft of creativity or even persistently painful [...] In both the ethical and the existential cases, there are multiple criteria and there can be tradeoffs among the positive and negative ones" (p. 330).

In my own contribution, I survey some of the arguments that have been advanced for the thesis that without God, all human lives are meaningless, together with various strategies for responding to these arguments. I ultimately endorse a view that I find in Aristotle, according to which some activities are *intrinsically good* and human beings can live meaningful lives by engaging in such activities. Like Audi, I favor a pluralistic approach, suggesting that intrinsically good activities include "falling in love, engaging in intellectually stimulating activity, being creative in various ways, experiencing pleasure of various kinds, and teaching" (p. 348).

Richard Norman focuses on the kinds of experiences that are available to atheists, beginning with the question: "Are atheists missing something important?" Norman discusses five varieties of experience. In each case, he argues that there is an "essential core" of the experience that is "as available to the atheist as to the theist" (p. 353). There is also an additional theistic "gloss" that the theist can put on each experience (p. 366). However, this gloss is not part of the essential core of the experience; even without the theistic gloss, these experiences are "enough to sustain a full, rich, and meaningful life" (p. 366).

Ursula Goodenough's contribution to this section is perhaps best understood in light of Joshua Seachris's suggestion in the General Introduction to this volume that "an under-explored area in contemporary analytic philosophy is how the concept of *narrative* might shed light on the meaning of life" (p. 16). Goodenough is not a philosopher, but her essay seems aimed at quelling the fear "that a thoroughly scientific-naturalistic narrative of the universe is far from existentially satisfying" (p. 16). She claims that "[h]umans need stories – grand, compelling stories – that help to orient us in our lives and in the cosmos. The Epic of Evolution is such a story" (p. 370). In her essay, Goodenough provides a powerful narrative for the contemporary naturalist: "For me, the existence of all this complexity and awareness and intent and beauty, and my ability to apprehend it, serves as the ultimate meaning and the ultimate value" (p. 369).

The Diversity of Optimistic Naturalism

As this overview should make clear, the essays in this section include a number of distinct versions of optimistic naturalism. United in their rejection of the view that the death of God signals the death of all important varieties of meaning in human life, these authors offer different proposals about what kind of meaning might exist in a godless universe, and how lives with that sort of meaning might be attained. Together, these essays constitute a hearty challenge to many of the essays found in Sections II and III of this book. They also have much to offer those who are attracted to the insight expressed by the comic strip I discussed earlier, but are unsure just what can play the role of squirrels in human life.

Suggestions for Further Reading

Belliotti, Raymond Angelo (2001) *What is the Meaning of Human Life?* Amsterdam: Rodopi.

Brogaard, Berit, and Barry Smith (2005) "On luck, responsibility, and the meaning of life," *Philosophical Papers* 34: 443–58.

Frankfurt, Harry G. (1988) "The importance of what we care about," in *The Importance of What We Care About*, New York: Cambridge University Press, pp. 80–94.

Gewirth, Alan (1998) "Ultimate values, rights, reason," in *Self Fulfillment*, Princeton, NJ: Princeton University Press, pp. 159–228.

James, Laurence (2010) "Activity and the meaningfulness of life," *The Monist* 93(January): 57–75.

Landau, Iddo (2011) "The meaning of life *sub specie aeternitatis*," *Australasian Journal of Philosophy* 89: 727–34.

Lotfi, Shidan (2010) "The 'purposiveness' of life: Kant's critique of natural teleology," *The Monist* 93(January): 123–34.

Metz, Thaddeus (2003) "Utilitarianism and the meaning of life," *Utilitas* 15(March): 50–70.

Metz, Thaddeus (2009) "Imperfection as sufficient for a meaningful life: How much is enough?" in Yujin Nagasawa and Erik J. Wielenberg (eds.), *New Waves in Philosophy of Religion*, London: Palgrave Macmillan, pp. 192–214.

Metz, Thaddeus (2011) "The good, the true, and the beautiful: Toward a unified account of great meaning in life," *Religious Studies* 47(December): 389–409.

Sartre, Jean-Paul (2007) *Existentialism Is a Humanism*, trans. Carol Macomber, New Haven, CT: Yale University Press.

Singer, Peter (1995) *How Are We to Live? Ethics in an Age of Self-Interest*, Amherst, NY: Prometheus.

Smith, Quentin (1997) "Normative ethics," in *Ethical and Religious Thought in Analytic Philosophy of Language*, New Haven, CT: Yale University Press, pp. 179–221.

Taylor, Richard (1970) "The meaning of life," in *Good and Evil: A New Direction*, New York: Macmillan, pp. 319–34.

Wielenberg, Erik J. (2006) *Value and Virtue in a Godless Universe*, Cambridge: Cambridge University Press.

Wolf, Susan (1997a) "Meaningful lives in a meaningless world," *Quaestiones Infinitae* 19(June): 1–22.

Wolf, Susan (1997b) "Happiness and meaning: Two aspects of the good life," *Social Philosophy and Policy* 14(December): 207–25.

Wolf, Susan (2010) *Meaning in Life and Why It Matters*, Princeton: Princeton University Press.

Wong, Wai-hung (2008) "Meaningfulness and identities," *Ethical Theory and Moral Practice* 11: 123–48.

4.1

The Human World

John Kekes

I

Our ethical condition, according to Bernard Williams, is that 'we know that the world was not made for us, or we for the world, that our history tells no purposive story, and that there is no position outside the world or outside history from which we can hope to authenticate our activities.'[1] Williams pessimistically concludes that we must accept that even our deepest convictions are conditional, because they are shaped by a historical process that might have been very different. Contingency, rather than objectivity, permeates all of our ethical evaluations. John Cottingham argues that ethical objectivity is possible and Williams' diagnosis of our ethical condition is mistaken. We do not have to accept his 'ethical pessimism,' because it is reasonable to believe that there is 'a teleological framework to give human lives a purpose and meaning'.[2]

I agree with Williams' diagnosis but disagree that ethical pessimism follows from it. I also agree with Cottingham about the possibility of ethical objectivity, but disagree that it depends on a divinely ordered cosmos. This partial agreement and disagreement with both Williams and Cottingham has led me to make a fresh start in struggling with the consequences of contingency for ethics.

Two and a half thousand years ago Euripides asked:

> ... do we, holding that the gods exist,
> deceive ourselves with unsubstantial dreams
> and lies, while random careless chance and change
> alone control the world?[3]

John Kekes (2009) "The Human World," *Ratio* XXII: 137–56.

I will offer an answer to this good and deep question, but I must first discuss the complexities that lurk below its surface. The unsubstantial dream of which Euripides writes is that the world is governed by reason and goodness. Behind our messy daily experience of senseless inhumanity, conflict, unreason, and the tendency of even the best laid plans to go wrong, there is a deeper reality in which reason and goodness rule. The dreamers acknowledge this and explain it by our wilful or ignorant deviation from the very order on which our well-being depends. What Euripides regards an unsubstantial dream is, in fact, the belief that animates the great religions and most metaphysical systems.

As Euripides makes clear in his tragedies, he thinks that random chance and change control the world, and Williams thinks the same. We do not have to agree, of course. We may believe, as Cottingham does, that the unsubstantial dream is true, or accept it for reasons other than its truth. I am with Euripides and Williams in rejecting it, but I do not think that we are therefore driven to believe that chance and change alone control the world. Nor do I think that the dream is a lie. David Stove is right: 'Philosophers are hardly ever cynical manipulators of their readers' minds. They do not produce delusions in others, without first being subject to them themselves.'[4] I have given reasons elsewhere against accepting the dream and I will not repeat them here.[5] What I hope to do is to avoid the dilemma that we must either deceive ourselves and accept the dream even though it is not credible, or resign ourselves to the senselessness of the world. Opting for either has destructive implications for human well-being. If we deceive ourselves, we forfeit responsibility and control over how we live. If we accept that the world is senseless, we must abandon the belief that living reasonably and morally is better than living unreasonably and immorally. The unwholesomeness of these alternatives is a good reason for looking for another possibility, which is what I will now do.

II

To begin with, Euripides' question is too crude. Even if we think that the dream is unsubstantial, we do not have to accept that it is completely false, nor that the only alternative to it is a senseless world. If it were completely false, there would be no order at all and the question of its goodness could not arise. Random chance and change would, then, rule the world. The dream, however, may be only partly false: there is order in the world, but it is not good. This is not to say that it is bad, for it may be neither good nor bad but indifferent. It may hold regardless of what happens to anything that is subject to it, including ourselves.

Indifference is perhaps a misleading way of expressing this, because it leaves open the possibility that the world may change its mind and start caring. But this verges on absurdity. Only sentient beings can care and the world is not a sentient being. Of course we are sentient, part of the world, and we care about our well-being. What is true of a minute part, however, need not be true of the whole. There is caring *in* the world, but no caring *by* the world. This leaves room for the possibility that, although the world's order is indifferent, we may care about what happens in it, especially to us. I will explore the implications of this possibility.

It is not clear, however, that this possibility is anything more than an idle thought we should reject as having no application to the real world. For our caring may be just an illusion we sustain to avoid the unpleasantness of facing the futility of caring about anything. The truth may be that what is senseless is not the world but our caring. Our beliefs about facts and things may be true, but our beliefs about goodness or badness may be false. If this were so, I would have clarified a little Euripides' question, but would not have avoided his answer that reason and morality are illusory. Avoiding it depends on further clarifications about the supposed indifferent order and the illusoriness of our evaluations.

I start with the indifferent order. Let us understand by the world absolutely everything that exists: objects, processes, energy, human constructions, and organisms; ideals and mistakes; acts and omissions; microscopic and macroscopic systems; beliefs and feelings; viruses and galaxies; rainbows and shadows; works of art and inflation. Given this understanding, there can be nothing outside the world. Let us further accept that there is an indifferent order that permeates the world. It may be causal or statistical, but whatever it is, the best guides to understanding at least parts of it are the physical and biological sciences. Human beings, of course, are part of the world and subject to its order.

It is uncontroversial, I think, that the order allows us some control over how we live. One reason for this is that the causal or statistical regularities that constitute the order hold under certain conditions, and we can sometimes change the conditions. We cannot alter the effect of sub-zero temperature on human bodies, but we can dress in protective layers, or stay inside a heated house. Another reason is that although we are always subject to regularities, we can sometimes choose among them. If we want to get from England to the Continent, we can go by plane, boat, train, or try to swim across. The applicable regularities limit each possibility in certain ways, but we can sometimes opt for possibilities we want to pursue and accept limits that go with them. The regularities establish the possibilities and limits of our various endeavours, but they leave us with some control. Necessities do not exhaust our possibilities. We may regard whatever control we have as reward for having done well in the relentless course of evolution.

The fact remains, however, that we cannot completely free ourselves from the regularities, partly because we often cannot change the conditions in which we must act or choose the regularities to which we are subject. And even when we have some control over them, we have it only because preceding regularities had made it possible. This is true of everything we do or might do, including the evaluations we make. Ultimately, therefore, we have no control over how much control we actually have. Since the order is indifferent and our control limited, there is apparently little we can do to direct our lives. This is part of what concerns me.

Another part is the supposed illusoriness of our evaluations. Why might it be an illusion that the rule of law, enjoyment, and kindness are good and lawlessness, misery, and cruelty bad? The answer often given is that *sub specie aeternitatis*, from the point of view of the Universe, as Sidgwick called it, nothing matters. If looked at with complete objectivity, then how it goes for humanity as a whole or for particular individuals has no more or less significance than how it goes for distant galaxies, colonies of ants, or cancelled streetcar tickets. This is not because everything matters equally, but because nothing at all matters. In the vastness of the world, things happen, processes unfold and come to an end, change is ceaseless. There are only things, processes, facts devoid of meaning, significance, or value.

Of course we need not view what happens objectively, *sub specie aeternitatis*. We can view it from our point of view, *sub specie humanitatis*. Things matter, then, because they affect our well-being. The world does not care, but we do. We evaluate facts by asking how they affect us collectively or individually. Such evaluations may be true or false. Everyone may believe that in the long run all manner of things will be well, or that prosperity is good, or that humility is a virtue, and everyone may be wrong. What is good or bad does not depend on what we think or hope; it depends on how it affects our well-being. Our evaluations, therefore, are not objective but subjective in one sense of that much abused term: they proceed from the point of view of the well-being of the subject who does the evaluation. But they are not subjective in the completely different sense of being true or false depending on what the subject happens to believe or feel about them. The beliefs of any subject may be mistaken and the feelings of anyone may be misplaced or inappropriate. Euripides is right about the illusoriness of all *sub specie aeternitatis* evaluations, but he is wrong about the illusoriness of all *sub specie humanitatis* evaluations.

If we approach our evaluations from the point of view of the Universe, we will be driven to conclude that nothing matters. But this is a reason for not approaching them from that point of view, not a reason against taking the human point of view from which many things matter a great deal. Not the least reason for this approach to evaluations is that our well-being depends on it.[6]

Doubts, however, may persist. It may be granted that evaluations need not be illusory, but it may still be thought that they are futile. For the world is what it is, the facts are what they are, and how we evaluate them changes nothing. What, then, is the point of evaluations? Why should we care, if caring makes no difference? Is the preoccupation with things mattering not a pointless exercise that wastes time and energy that would be better used in other ways? The answer is no for two reasons.

One is that we can change some things, because we have some control over our lives. As we have seen, we can sometimes change the conditions in which an adversely evaluated regularity holds in favour of another set of conditions in which a regularity more favourable to us prevails. We need not always freeze in sub-zero weather. And we can sometimes choose among regularities the one that favours us most, such as picking the fastest, or the most convenient, or the cheapest way of travelling from England to the Continent. We have some control over how we live and we can exercise the control we have as our evaluations suggest.

The second reason is that even when we cannot change the facts we can change our attitude toward them. We can respond to the unalterable conditions we face with despair, hope, indignation, irony, rage, resignation, self-deception, surprise, and so forth, and the attitudes we cultivate and those we wean ourselves from have much to do with the quality of our lives.

For these reasons we need not agree with Euripides that if we reject the unsubstantial dream, then we must accept that being guided by reason and morality is futile, that evaluations are pointless, and that we have no control over how we live. Even if the regularities of the world do not allow us to have complete control, they allow us to have some control. And we can exercise that control in good or bad, better or worse ways.

Given these clarifications, can we say that we have found a defensible alternative to Euripides' clarified view that the world is indifferent to our well-being, that deceiving ourselves with unsubstantial dreams is to forfeit responsibility and control, and that it is illusory to rely on reason and morality? We cannot. For even if we have some control over how we live and our evaluations may make our lives better, we must recognize that we have control neither over the extent to which we can control how we live nor over the conditions that influence the evaluations we make. Whether we have the small amount of control I have insisted we have depends on the indifferent order of the world. If this is so, then it may be an illusion that we have any control. Euripides' view then may be restated in a clarified and sharpened form as claiming that our control is an illusion, because indifference rules the world and we are unavoidably subject to it. I will now argue that this view is mistaken.

III

Consider a commercial jet with many people on board flying over the ocean. It runs into a freak storm, lightning strikes, its engines catch fire, the electronic system is disabled, crash is imminent. One scenario is that it crashes and everyone dies. This may be described as bad luck for those who died, for their families and friends, and for the airline. Another scenario is that there is a nearby island with a short runway and the pilot manages to land the plane, because he has had much experience in the air force landing and taking off from aircraft carriers. Everyone is saved. This may be described as good luck for everyone concerned. Such things happen, of course. One interpretation is that contingency is luck. Bad luck harms us, good luck benefits us, but we cannot control either. If we could, it would not be bad luck, but negligence or laziness; nor would it be good luck, but unexpected opportunity or deserved benefit.

Describing anything as luck is a loose shorthand. It stands for various causal chains that intersect and whose intersection we can neither predict nor explain, because we lack the relevant knowledge. In the case of the jet, weather predictions are imperfect, the skill of pilots varies, we cannot make planes safe enough. We are vulnerable, because we are ignorant. And even if we knew enough, we might still not be able to prevent the harm or bring about the benefit. Speaking generally, viruses may assail us, meteorites may destroy us, earthquakes may bury us, or extraterrestrials may tell us about an unlimited source of energy, mutation may make us invulnerable to cancer, and the next great scientific discovery may already be cooking in someone's unusual mind. Luck does not describe how things are; it describes how things seem to us when we are handicapped by ignorance or incapacity. If we were omniscient and omnipotent, or if there were no human beings, there would be nothing describable as luck. Or, to put it differently, *sub specie aeternitatis* there is no luck; there is luck only *sub specie humanitatis*.

If we interpret contingency as luck, then control is an illusion, because how much control we have is a matter of luck: our knowledge and capacities are limited and what we do not know and cannot alter may affect us in ways we cannot predict, explain, or control. If this is how we understand the lines of Euripides that 'careless chance and change alone control the world,' then Euripides is right.

On another interpretation, however, contingency is avoidable, at least to some extent, and on that understanding of what Euripides says, he is wrong. Consider again the stricken jet. Among the hundreds of people on it, there is a torturer going to ply his trade, a paedophile in search of children for rent, and a serial murderer who judged it prudent to remove himself for a time. There is also a physician on his way to work without pay in Africa, a diplomat returning home after having negotiated the end of a murderous civil war, and a policeman escorting the kingpin of a drug cartel whom he arrested and persuaded to testify against the corrupt government that allowed him to function. This time, however, there is no convenient island, the pilot is helpless, and they all die.

The widely shared reaction to this scenario would be that life should not be like that. Good people deserve good things, bad people bad things, but contingency prevented this from happening. The world was indifferent to the merits and demerits of the victims, all fell afoul of the same fate, and this offends our moral sense. What we find offensive is contingency, interpreted as the normative indifference of the world: the regularities to which we are subject affect us without regard to our goodness or badness. We do not want the world to be like that. We agree with Hume's lament that 'such is the disorder and confusion in human affairs, that no perfect or regular distribution of happiness and misery is ever, in this life, to be expected. Not only the goods of fortune, and the endowments of the body (both of which are important), not only these advantages, I say, are unequally divided between the virtuous and the vicious, but even the mind itself partakes, in some degree, of this disorder. … In a word, human life is more governed by fortune than by reason.'[7] This is not sentimental hand wringing provoked by the insensate world, but a realistic description. Nevertheless it does not follow from it that we are helpless and cannot do anything about it. We can and have done so.

We have created and we maintain a human world that is permeated with moral, political, aesthetic, literary, and other values. The human world, of course, is a small part of the world and subject to the regularities that prevail in it. It exists in the space within which we have some control. The space and our control are limited. But they exist and they enable our efforts to make benefits and harms proportional to the goodness and badness of their recipients. The human world and its values are as real as the non-human world and its facts.

The great difference between them is that values exist within the human world and there are no values outside of it. Our values reflect beliefs about what contributes to or detracts from human well-being. These beliefs may be true or false. One reason why many lives are bad is that many of the beliefs are false. There are, of course, also other reasons, which we may or may not be able to alter. But correcting false beliefs about human well-being is something we can do. The proof of that is that we have done it in the past about slavery, the divine right of kings, the persecution of witches, the sinfulness of charging interest for money lent, and stoning adulterers. I stress this as a significant possibility, without wishing to suggest that self-congratulation is warranted. Uncorrected false beliefs abound, and they may do so because we have not discovered that many of them are false. The mere possibility that we can improve our evaluations is not enough to underwrite optimism about human well-being. Nevertheless, the possibility exists and is significant, because it shows that we are not totally at the mercy of contingency. We can do something to control it.

It will be said that all this is an illusion, because, as I have repeatedly acknowledged, we have no control over how much control we have. I acknowledge it once more, but I deny that it makes the control we have illusory. Consider a more personalized example than the stricken jet.

I have accepted a much better job than what I had and my family and I must relocate to take it up. Assume that the family is loving, its tensions are normal, and there are no hidden crises, hatreds, or deep resentments lurking under the placid surface. We must decide whether to live in town or country, in a house or an apartment, close to schools or spend time commuting; how much we should spend on housing; weigh the preferences of everyone in the family; consider how new surroundings might change our customary lives; take into account crime, pollution, likely neighbours, the proximity of stores; try to imagine how life would be if we opted for various possibilities; and so forth. We think, we talk, we weigh, and we arrive at decisions we can all live with. The decisions may still turn out to be mistaken, because we have not foreseen everything, what we have imagined may be unrealistic, we were guided by wishful thinking, or we did not think hard enough.

In the human world decisions like this are ubiquitous. Most of us make them about marriage, family, job, money, health, housing, education, love affairs, politics, and we make them even if those who are immediately affected are not as idyllically related as in my example above. By making such decisions we control how we live and reduce the extent to which contingency rules our lives, even if we have not escaped it altogether.

Contingency, of course, may still interfere with our control either by way of external causes that seem to us to be accidents, disasters, emergencies, epidemics, and so forth, or by internal causes, such as genetic predispositions; internalized early training and education; repressed traumas; or by surrendering our will to religious, political, or nationalistic authorities; or coming under the influence of advertising, propaganda, or charismatic figures.

The objection to what I have been saying is that what appears to us as control is always the effect of internal causes of whose nature and influence we may be unaware. This is what many, but certainly not all, psychologists, sociologists, deconstructionists, ideologues, and other unmaskers are claiming. They think that to see is to see through; that what is on the surface is a misleading indication of depths below; and that appearances systematically misrepresent reality.

I reply with Oscar Wilde: 'it is only shallow people who do not judge by appearances.'[8] This is not just a witticism. Appearances normally reflect what they are appearances of. What seems red is normally red; the voice on the phone that seems to be my wife's is normally hers; the anger I seem to feel is normally anger; and when it seems to me that I have made a considered decision I have normally done just that. If we did not judge by appearances, we could not judge at all. We may suspect that in any particular case our judgment is mistaken and the appearance is misleading. But if the suspicion is reasonable, we must have some reason for it. That what we have made a judgment about is an appearance is not a reason. The reason must be some ground for supposing that the appearance is misleading.

The unmaskers who refuse to take any appearance at its face value often endeavour to offer as such a ground a theory about the supposed deep structure of psychology, sociology, history, language, or whatever. What needs to be said about these theories is what G. E. Moore had said in another context. He held up his finger and said: 'This, after all, you know, really is a finger: there is no doubt about it: I know it and you all know it. And I think we may safely challenge any[one] … to bring forward any argument in favour … of the proposition that it is not true, which does not at some point rest upon some premise which is, beyond comparison, less certain than is the proposition which it is designed to attack.'[9] Even Freud conceded that a cigar is sometimes just a cigar – especially when he smoked it.

Moore's robust common sense is refreshing and only a little overstated. Obviously, there are theories that explain why appearances in some area of life are always misleading: why the Earth seems flat, the Sun rising and setting, the phantom limb aching, and so forth. What Moore should have insisted on is that there could not be a reasonable theory that explains why all appearances are always mistaken. There could not be such a theory, because all theories take for granted some appearances, such as their initial data, confirming or disconfirming observations, instrument readings, the accuracy of their measurements, surprising findings, or the cogency of their quantifications. If they were to deny the reliability of all appearances, they would have to reject the basis on which they rest. If the unmaskers merely said that we are sometimes mistaken when we think that we have achieved some control over our lives, they would be right. But that is not an adequate reason for doubting the appearance that there is a human world with values we have made and prize, that we can sometimes control at least to some extent whether we live according to these values; and that our well-being is not entirely subject to contingency.

IV

The values of the human world are many and varied: among them are moral goodness, political justice, aesthetic beauty, historical understanding, literary classics, philosophical depth, poetic imagination, and personal excellence. Values may be universal, social, or individual; enduring or changing; deeply serious or entertaining; some no society can do without, others vary with contexts; they may be products of reflection, disciplined feeling, or creative imagination; they may be accessible to any moderately intelligent person or only to those with rigorous training of their intellect, character, perception, or taste. Corresponding to these values there are kitschy imitations, as well as disvalues that are impoverishing or demeaning in the same dimension as the values are enriching or ennobling. These values give meaning, purpose, and significance to what we do or try to do once our physical needs are satisfied. They civilize our experiences and responses to the indifferent world when necessity does not compel us to eat, drink, breathe, sleep, or fend off enemies.

This is not the place for a detailed discussion of the contents of the human world, but I do want to say more about an aspect of it to which I have alluded earlier. One main reason for prizing the human world is that it is our attempt to arrange matters, insofar as we can arrange them, so as to make benefits come to good people and harms to bad ones. The world outside the human world is indifferent to goodness and badness. We want to resist this indifference; we want people to have what they deserve and not to have what they do not deserve. This is a very basic moral impulse, analogous to preferring pleasure to pain, enjoyment to misery, and good to bad. Why do we have this preference? Is it a reasonable one? Might it be just a genetically inculcated instinct, like territoriality, acquisitiveness, or the sex drive? I think it is that, but not only that. This preference of ours is based also on a reasonable expectation, which I will now try to describe.

Consider a simple sequence leading to an action. I am hungry, want to eat, decide to go home for lunch, and I walk there. Implicit in the sequence is that I have a set of beliefs (my house is nearby, there is food in the fridge, there are no obstacles in the way, and so on) and I have the required capacities (I can walk, rely on my memory, estimate distance, and the like). The sequence that precedes action, then, has the following elements: motive, belief, capacity, goal, and decision. Each may be defective: motives may be irrational, beliefs false, capacities inadequate, goals unattainable, and decisions wrong-headed. Suppose, however, that they are not defective and I perform the action to which the conjunction of these elements leads. I expect, then, that my action will be successful, that it will achieve its goal. In simple sequences of this sort, normal people in normal circumstances have normally good reason to suppose that the elements are free of defect and no reason to doubt it. Their expectation that their actions will be successful is generally reasonable. If it were otherwise, we would long ago have gone the way of dinosaurs. Our well-being requires that such reasonable expectations be generally met.

It would be comforting if simple sequences were adequate for the business of living, but they are not. Complexities unavoidably arise, because it is often difficult to tell whether an element is defective. Motives conflict and we constantly have to make choices about which of them we should act on. We routinely have to evaluate the reliability of our beliefs on the basis of imperfect knowledge and insufficient evidence. Our capacities are always limited and we have to estimate whether they are adequate for the achievement of difficult goals. We usually have several incompatible goals and must decide about their relative importance. But what seems important at one time may become less so at another. The world changes, we change, and we have to make guesses about how these changes might affect our goals. The choices we make depend on understanding our circumstances and what we want, all things considered, out of life, and both may be unclear at the time we have to choose, and it may be even more unclear how they might be in the future. Coping with complexities requires, therefore, in addition to getting the facts right, also judging the significance of such facts as we have available. Good judgment about such matters is difficult.

Suppose I act on the basis of a complex sequence and my judgment is good. Might I, then, reasonably expect that my action will be successful? No, because even if I act as reasonably as anyone in my position could, I may nevertheless fail, because others justifiably prevent me from succeeding. Most of the time my success depends on the cooperation of others, and they may have more important concerns; or they may also want what I want and are better at getting it; or what I want may run counter to their interests or to the interests of an institution, cause, or collectivity they wish to protect. More is needed, therefore, before I can reasonably expect to get what I want, and the same, of course, is true of everyone else. We all have to take into account that we are participants in the human world and depend on the cooperation of others. The terms of cooperation, therefore, have to be set. In the vast majority of complex sequences, we can get what we want only on the prevailing terms. These terms may be more or less adequate to the purpose of maintaining the optimum conditions in which as many of us as possible can go about getting what we want.

Can we reasonably expect that our actions will be successful if they are based on good judgment and conform to the prevailing terms of cooperation? The answer is still no for two reasons. One is that the terms may be defective. Let us assume, however, that they are adequate, because they set optimal conditions of cooperation. The other reason why the expectation of success may be premature is that not even adequate terms of cooperation can eliminate competition. We may fail to achieve our goals, although we have good judgment and conform to the adequate terms, because we lose out in a competition with others whose judgment is also good and who also conform to the terms. Only one person can win the race, get the job, be the first to make the discovery, and only a few can make the best seller list, get elected, add to the canon, or make a lasting contribution to science. For each of those who succeed, there are many who try and fail. Not all goals are competitive, of course; having a good marriage, enjoying nature, developing a historical perspective, listening to music are not. But many are, and because of them we may have good judgment, conform to the terms, and still fail to achieve our goals.

Putting all this together, the following requirements of successful action emerge: having good judgment; conforming to the prevailing and adequate terms of cooperation; and, if our goals are competitive, winning in the competition. These requirements are the requirements of practical reason, which is the use of reason for making our lives better. Our preference is for a world in which we can confidently expect that our actions will be successful, if we conform to the requirements of practical reason. In such a world we would all have what we deserve and would not have what we do not deserve.

In the actual world, of course, this preference is often frustrated, because contingencies over which we have no control prevent us from conforming to the requirements of practical reason. One main reason for needing and prizing the human world is that it provides the values that motivate us to increase our control by making our judgments better, the prevailing terms of cooperation less inadequate, and conformity to them more likely. The more we succeed, the less we will be subject to contingency and the more we will be in control of our well-being.

Hereabouts, if not much earlier, critics will impatiently charge the account I am defending with superficiality. They will say that it begs the questions raised by the many issues determinists, libertarians, and compatibilists dispute about. I reply that this criticism is the result of endarkenment caused by the heavy metaphysical fog that surrounds these theories. I have ignored them, because they are irrelevant to the account I am giving for two reasons that seem very strong to me. One is that the possibilities of the human world the account explores are readily accepted by all three of these theories. They differ only in how they explain them. I see no reason why I should enter into this hoary dispute. The other is that my concern is not with explaining how the possibilities are possible, but with exploring their significance for human well-being, and that is not what these theories are about. I plead not guilty, therefore, to this charge.

V

In thinking about the human world, we must continually guard against over-reaction. Its limits should not lead us to resign ourselves to the tragic view of Euripides. But no less should its possibilities make us embrace a Whiggish optimism about the human prospect. What I have just finished saying about these possibilities may give the impression that I have succumbed to the latter temptation. In order to correct it, I will now stress that the human world is subject to ineliminable limits. Although we continually attempt to overcome them, we cannot succeed. Nevertheless, these attempts may be reasonable, because they may alleviate some of the adverse effects of contingency.

The limits I will discuss are set by scarcity, conflict, and disproportionality. They are obstacles to realizing one of the values of the human world: that we should have what we deserve and should not have what we do not deserve. Scarcity often makes it impossible to distribute benefits and harms according to our merit or demerit; conflicts among incompatible benefits may be obstacles to having all we deserve even if resources are not scarce; and disproportionality frequently stands in the way of correcting the discrepancy between what we deserve and what we have.

The most obvious way in which scarcity prevents us from having what we deserve is the insufficiency of available resources. If there is not enough money, food, medicine, prison space, police protection, or hospital care, then some of us cannot have what we deserve. It is not only material resources, however, that may be scarce, but also the expertise needed to create and deliver them. Physicians, teachers, administrators, or research scientists may be as scarce as food, shelter, and medicine. The distribution of scarce resources among those who deserve them unavoidably falls short of what we aim at because it forces on us decisions that deprive some of us of what they should have.

It is useless to try to overcome this by distributing scarce resources equally, because the equal distribution of scarce resources may result in the even worse outcome that no one gets enough. If there are not enough oxygen tanks, it does not help to ration the suffocating to the same brief periods of breathing. Furthermore, there are numerous scarce resources whose equal distribution is impossible. Medical specialists, inspiring teachers, or first-rate administrators must restrict their activities to particular contexts, but if there are not enough of them, deserving people outside of those contexts will not get the treatment, education, or efficient service they deserve.

Conflicts among benefits present a further obstacle to having what we deserve. We must often choose between benefits we deserve, because it is impossible to enjoy them simultaneously. Concentration on creative work may be incompatible with cultivating satisfying friendships; early retirement in order to take pleasure in reading and travelling excludes going on with a satisfying job; continued growth in depth makes breadth ranging over several areas unlikely; the price of reflectiveness is diminished spontaneity; carefree enjoyment of well-earned pleasures cannot go with dedication to political activism; and so forth.

Such conflicts force choices not only on the level of individual action, but also on the social level, where choices must be made among incompatible policies. Should limited funding go to support deserving artistic or scientific talent? Are the disabled more or less deserving of resources than those who produce future resources? Do the old deserve to hold on to the jobs they do well or do the young deserve them so that they would have a start in life? Furthermore, liberty and order, justice and patriotism, the free market and high culture, private life and political power are often so related that the more there is of one the scarcer will the other be.

It may be thought that it is possible to correct the adverse effects of scarcity and conflict. This may be so in some cases, but not in many others, because disproportionality may present an insurmountable obstacle. For some of the most adverse effects of scarcity and conflict no correction is possible. The forms of correction are compensation, which provides benefits to correct undeserved deprivation of them, and punishment, which consists in the infliction of deserved harms or in the deprivation of undeserved benefits.

This approach to correction, however, is much too simple. It rests on the mistaken assumption that benefits and harms can be measured on some scale common to them all. Only if this were true would it make sense to speak of adding or removing benefits and harms so as to assure that people have what they deserve. Whether the common scale is based on some objective units, like money, or on subjective judgments involving pair wise comparisons, makes no theoretical difference to the point that the assumption is false, because different types of benefits and harms are often incommensurable. There are some harms suffered for which no benefits can compensate the victim, as there are also harms inflicted for which no punishment is sufficient. Nothing could compensate people who sacrificed their lives for a noble cause, who were blinded or disfigured in an accident for which they were not responsible, who were forced to spend the best years of their lives in concentration camps on trumped up charges, or who contracted AIDS through blood transfusion. Nor is there a proportional punishment for mass murderers, torturers, or fanatics who destroy great works of art. Nothing could redress such imbalances, because no benefit or harm could be commensurate with what created them. Disproportionality, therefore, unavoidably limits our efforts at correction.

Scarcity, conflict, and disproportionality make it impossible to achieve a perfect or even a very close connection between the goodness or badness of people and the benefits they enjoy or the harms they suffer. Hume is right: 'no perfect or regular distribution of happiness and misery is ever … to be expected.' But, although perfection is unattainable, imperfection can be diminished. Doing so is one main aim of the human world. We work toward it through practical reason, which is the use of reason for the betterment of human lives. When it is used well, it increases our control over the conditions under which we cannot help living, reduces the extent to which we are subject to contingency, and makes room for values in an indifferent world. Those who prefer to think in such terms may regard the human world and practical reason as among our most significant evolutionary adaptations.

VI

I have been arguing that our well-being is essentially connected with the human world. For that world contains and sustains the values that give meaning and purpose to our lives. We could live without its values, but we could not live well. The values exist, however, only because we have made them. They are the ways in which we interpret the human significance of the world of things, processes, facts, and of our experience of it. Among those facts are our values and interpretations, which we continually revise in the hope of making them less fallible. The human view of the world, the world *sub specie humanitatis*, is, therefore, unavoidably reflexive. Our fallible and reflexive interpretations and our forever changing values are genuine characteristics of the human world, and therefore of the world of which the human world is a minute part. They really exist, even though we have made them and are perpetuating them.

If we lost the human world, we would lose our humanity. We would still have some control over how we live, but we would not know how to exercise it. Beyond the satisfaction of basic needs, we would have no conception of what is better or worse, nor of what to make of our evolutionary advantages. The human world, therefore, is not a luxury, a dispensable decoration of the physical and biological structure of human existence. It is as much part of that basic structure as any of its other parts.

The human world is causally dependent on our biological constitution, which, in turn, is causally dependent on our physical constitution, which, in turn, is dependent on subatomic particles and forces, or on whatever are the ultimate constituents of the world. The fact that effects are dependent on causes, however, does not make the effects less real than the causes. The human world is the effect of causes, but it is an effect that enables the interpretation both of its own causes and of itself, and therein lies its importance. For such interpretations guide the control that we may wrest from the contingencies of the world. At any rate, so I have argued.

I have not argued and I do not think that we can or should view the world only *sub specie humanitatis*. We can obviously do so *sub specie aeternitatis*. Science and religion are the most obvious attempts in that direction. These alternative viewings, however, are done by us and we do them partly because we care about their significance for us. Perhaps their significance is that human concerns are puny and unimportant in the scheme of things. Perhaps. But the aspirations of science and religion are among those concerns and cannot transcend them, because human concerns are the only concerns we have. The impulse to go beyond the human world and explore what lies outside of it is probably irresistible, and I certainly do not think we should try to resist it. The results of scientific or religious explorations, however, can only alter, but not replace, human concerns. Any attempt to do more is a dangerous denial of our humanity. I share Montaigne's sentiment that 'these transcendental humours frighten me.' They lead to trying to 'escape from ... man. That is madness: instead of changing into angels, they change into beasts. ... We seek other conditions because we do not understand the use of our own.' [10]

Skipping a few centuries, I close with some lines of Wallace Stevens that echo Montaigne's words, although in another medium:

> To say more than human things with human voice,
> That cannot be; to say human things with more
> Than human voice, that, also, cannot be;
> To speak humanly from the height or from the depth
> Of human things, that is acutest speech. [11]

Notes

1. Bernard Williams, *Shame and Necessity*, (Berkeley: University of California Press, 1993), p. 166.
2. John Cottingham, 'The Good Life and the "Radical Contingency of the Ethical" ', in D. Callcut (ed.), *Reading Bernard Williams* (London: Routledge, 2008), Ch. 2, pp. 25–43.
3. Euripides, *Hecuba* [c. 420 BC], in *The Complete Greek Tragedies: Euripides III*, trans. William Arrowsmith,

(Chicago: University of Chicago Press, 1958), pp. 489–92.

4. David Stove, *The Plato Cult and Other Philosophical Follies*, (Oxford: Blackwell, 1991), pp. 121–2.

5. In *Moral Wisdom and Good Lives*, (Ithaca: Cornell University Press, 1995). The whole book is on this point.

6. The conflict between these two points of view is the theme of Thomas Nagel's distinguished body of work, especially of *Mortal Questions*, (Cambridge: Cambridge University Press, 1979) and *The View from Nowhere*, (New York: Oxford University Press, 1986). It is no doubt my fault but I have not been able to understand why he thinks that it is of great importance to take what he calls the objective view of the world. I can see why it is important for the physical and biological sciences to attempt to do this, but not why it is important for ethics, about which he says much, and aesthetics, about which he says very little.

7. David Hume, 'The Sceptic,' in *Essays, Moral, Political and Literary*, (Indianapolis: Liberty Press, 1985/1777), ed. Eugene F. Miller, pp. 178, 180.

8. Oscar Wilde, *The Picture of Dorian Gray*, (Harmondsworth: Penguin, 1949/1891), p. 29.

9. G. E. Moore, 'Some Judgments of Perception,' *Philosophical Studies*, (London: Routledge, 1922), p. 228.

10. Michel de Montaigne, 'Experience' ('De l'experience') from his Essays [*Essais*, 1580], transl. in *The Complete Works of Montaigne*, trans. Donald M. Frame, (Stanford, CA: Stanford University Press, 1943/1588), pp. 856–7.

11. Wallace Stevens, 'Chocorue to Its Neighbor' in *The Collected Poems*, (New York: Vintage, 1982), p. 300.

4.2

Time and Life's Meaning

Richard Taylor

It has been characteristic of metaphysics, since the beginning of philosophy, to deny the reality of time. The characteristics ascribed to it by unreflective people, particularly that of *passage*, have seemed so puzzling and paradoxical that the metaphysical temperament has preferred to banish time altogether rather than embrace those paradoxes. Thus Parmenides, the earliest metaphysician, denied reality to all time and becoming, leaving his bleak and changeless conception of reality to be perfected by his pupil Zeno. Plato, too, declared that reality can only be the eternal, describing the strange passage of time in which we mortals live as nothing but that eternity's moving image. Among modern philosophers Spinoza sounded the same note, being unable to think of any reality in which time, by itself, could make a difference, while Immanuel Kant reduced it to a mere form of sensibility. Among recent thinkers McTaggart comes at once to mind, with his proofs that the concept of time is simply self-contradictory.

Time, which seems to move, but in only one direction and at no assignable rate, *is* paradoxical, to be sure, but no declaration of its unreality can alter the fact that we feel it. With each setting sun we see our lives shortened, see the events that we felt so lively just moments ago begin receding into a fading past, gone forever. And with each rising sun we see hopes unfold in fulfillment or, perhaps more often, collapse with finality, to be replaced by new ones. These things are too close to us, too keenly felt, to be declared illusory. To suggest that our rejoicings and sorrows rest upon illusion, out of deference to metaphysical requirements, would seem to rob our lives of all meaning.

A few philosophical thinkers, aware of this, and starting from experience rather than reason, have found in time and its passage the most basic of realities, real to the point of being unalterable in its course and in its effects. Henri Bergson comes at once to mind, with

Richard Taylor (1987) "Time and Life's Meaning," *The Review of Metaphysics*, 40(4): 675–86.

Exploring the Meaning of Life: An Anthology and Guide, First Edition. Edited by Joshua W. Seachris.

his notorious declaration that "time eats into things and leaves on them the mark of its tooth." The metaphor is an outrage to reason, but perfectly captures the way time is felt. We feel it eating into things, into ourselves, and its marks are all too visible. We are, it has often been noted, the only beings in creation who can contemplate in thought our own graves, make plans upon that anticipated calamity and, it should be added, can actually sense its approach.

Time, then, it would seem, is very real to contemplative beings. But I am going to go farther than this, by suggesting that time is not merely something to be understood and described, as has been done by numberless philosophers and poets. Time, I shall contend, has little significant reality except in the context of beings who not only think and feel, but who *create*. It is this capacity for creation that not only gives time its most fundamental meaning, but gives our lives whatever meaning they have, as well.

I

To begin to see this let us think of the whole of inanimate reality, that is, the entire world, considered as devoid of life. It is a world without history or meaning. What happens in that world has happened before and, considering any event by itself, it makes no difference when it happens, nor even any sense to assign it a date. Time is here irrelevant. The earth turns, for example, but it makes not the least difference whether a given rotation is the millionth, or hundred millionth. Each turning is the same as the others, and no assigning of a number to this one or that has any significance. And so it is with everything else that happens in that lifeless world. A mountain rises gradually and is gradually eroded, but it makes no difference when this happens. And raindrops fall, but that a given raindrop should fall at one time rather than at another does not matter, nor is it even easy to make such temporal distinctions. Each drop is just like any other, and no newness is introduced by supposing that it falls earlier, or later, or even millions of years earlier or later. Such a world is without novelty. Combinations of events might occur which occur at no other time, to be sure, but they are already contained in what has gone before. What happens is but a consequence of what has already happened. Such a world could not, to any god contemplating it and capable of understanding it, contain any surprises. Nothing, in short, would ever be created in such a world. There would be novelties of sorts – for example, a snowflake that resembled no other – but these would not be creations in any sense. They would be but novel combinations of what already existed and then pointlessly fell into those combinations. That lifeless world, in short, resembles a clockwork, but one from which the moving hands are missing. What interests us about a clock is that it tells time, but the lifeless world we are now imagining tells us nothing of the sort. On the contrary, the very image of it is enough to exclude considerations of time. The god we imagined a moment ago would discover nothing from the prolonged contemplation of such a world other than what he already knew, and what he could anticipate in it would be nothing not already implicit in his memories of it. Time, to be sure, would exist for such a god – otherwise his contemplation could not be prolonged, nor would it make sense to speak of his memories. But then, by introducing such a being we have, of course, abandoned our premise of a lifeless world.

II

Let us next, then, add to this lifeless world, in our imaginations, the whole of living creation, excluding only rational beings, that is to say, beings like ourselves who are in the broadest sense capable not only of understanding, but of creative thought and action. What we have now is still a world without history. Except for the long and gradual changes wrought by biological evolution, nothing new or different occurs in this world. The sun that rises one day illuminates nothing that was not there the day before, or a thousand or million days before. It is simply the same world, age after age. The things in it exactly resemble those that went before. Every sparrow is just like every other, does exactly the same things in the same way without innovation, then to be imitated by every sparrow to follow. The robin or squirrel you see today does nothing different from those you saw as a child, and could be interchanged with them without discernible difference. Each creature arises and lives out its cycle with an invariance that is almost as fixed as the clockwork we imagined a moment ago, and it is, again, a clockwork without hands. That such a creature should live today or a hundred years hence makes no difference. There are days in this world, but no dates. And each such creature then perishes, leaving behind it nothing whatsoever except more of the same kind, which will do the same things again, and beget the same, these unchanging cycles then to be repeated over and over, forever.

III

The introduction of living things into our imaginary world has, however, resulted in one significant difference, and that is, the rudimentary *sense* of time, at least among some creatures. Irrational beings do not, of course, contemplate in thought their own graves, reflectively make provision for their descendants, mark anniversaries and so on, but they must nevertheless sometimes feel time's passage. A trapped animal feels its life ebbing and senses the approach of death, and perhaps birds, however mechanical or instinctive their behavior may be, have some anticipation of what is going to be done with the nests they build. Our pets anticipate their meals and look forward to them, and possibly the hours drag for them when we leave them alone for the day.

So to that extent time has, in a significant sense, been introduced into our world by the addition to it of living things. But there still remains this huge difference, that these creatures have no history. Each does today what was done by those that went before, and will be done by those to come. The world we are imagining thus resembles an endless play in which the acts are all identical. Every stage setting is the same as every other, the lines spoken are the same, the costumes the same, and the things done the same. Only the actors change, but none introduces any innovation. It would make no difference to any audience which act they saw, nor would there be any point in numbering the acts, or noting which followed which.

The world just described is not, of course, an imaginary one. It is the very world we live in, considered independently of ourselves and our place in it. It is a world in which there is a before and after – the sun, for example, must have risen in order to set – and it is one in which the passage of time is felt. Yet it is timeless in another significant sense, that it has neither history nor meaning. Its meaninglessness is precisely the meaninglessness of the play we were just imagining. There is never anything new, no purpose, no goal; in a word, nothing is ever created.

IV

This sense of eternal meaninglessness was perfectly captured by the ancients in the myth of Sisyphus. Sisyphus, it will be re-called, was condemned by the gods to roll a stone to the top of a hill, whereupon it would roll back to the bottom, to be moved to the top once more by Sisyphus, then to roll back again, and so on, over and over, throughout eternity. Here, surely, is existence reduced to utter meaninglessness. Nor does that lack of meaning arise from the onerousness of Sisyphus' task. It would not be redeemed if the task were made easier, by representing the stone as a very small one, for example. Nor does that meaninglessness emerge from the sheer boredom of the task. It would still be there even if we imagined Sisyphus to rejoice in it – if we imagined, for example, that he had a compulsive and insatiable desire to roll stones, and considered himself blessed to be able to do this forever.

The meaninglessness exhibited in this myth is precisely the meaninglessness of the world as it has been described up to this point; namely, that of a world without history, a world that is in this significant sense devoid of time. It is, like the cycles of Sisyphus, a world of endless and pointless repetition.

V

If we now modify the story of Sisyphus in certain ways we can take the crucial step needed to transform it from an image of meaninglessness to one of meaning. In so doing, we can finally see what is needed to give the world and human existence, or the life of any individual person, meaning.

Let us first suppose, then, that Sisyphus does not roll the same stone over and over again to the top, but moves a different stone each time, each stone then remaining at the top of the hill. Does this make a difference? Hardly. One stone does not differ from another, so what Sisyphus is now doing is essentially what he was doing before, rolling a stone, over and over, to the top of a hill. The stones, for all we know, merely accumulate there as a huge and growing pile of rubble.

So let us next imagine that this is not so, that the stones, having been moved to the top of the hill, are one by one, over a long period of time, assembled into something beautiful and lasting – a great temple, we might suppose. Has Sisyphus' existence now gained meaning? In a sense it has, for his labor is no longer wasted and pointless. Something important does come of it all. But that existence might still be totally meaningless to Sisyphus, for what we have imagined is consistent with supposing that he is totally ignorant of what is happening, that he is aware only of rolling stones, one after the other endlessly, with no notion at all of what becomes of them, the temple being entirely the work of others and out of his sight and ken. From his point of view, then, nothing has changed at all.

We next imagine, then, that this latter is not so, that Sisyphus sees the fruit of his toil gradually take shape, is aware of its importance and beauty, and thus has at least the satisfaction of understanding what is happening and realizing that what he does is not totally in vain. Something important does come of it all, something that is great and beautiful, and it is something that is understood.

Now have we invested his existence with meaning? In a sense we have, for Sisyphus has been converted from a mere beast of burden to a being who understands. But there is still a lot missing. For what we now have before us is consistent with the idea that Sisyphus is a mere slave, a rational slave up to a point, to be sure, but still one who goes through endless and repetitive motions over which he has no choice, these being entirely dictated by others, and for a result in which he has no hand, but can only passively observe. To revert to our image of the endlessly repetitive stage play, Sisyphus is here like an actor whose luck is to be cast in the leading role, but with this difference: an actor can at least reject the role. Such an existence is not without fulfillment of a sort, but we must remember that it still corresponds to the meaningless and, in a significant sense, timeless existence into which the whole of animal creation is cast. The vast array of living cycles today resemble those of a thousand years ago, and those of a thousand years hence. Nature, so conceived, is not without grandeur and beauty, just as we can imagine the temple that rises from Sisyphus' labors to have the same qualities. But that image still lacks an essential ingredient of meaningfulness, unless, of course, we are willing to ascribe a fully meaningful existence to a merely productive machine, or to a slave who has no voice whatsoever in his own fate or even his own actions from one moment to the next.

One final modification is needed, then, and that is to imagine that Sisyphus not only moves this prodigious quantity of stones to the top of the hill, but that he does so for the very purpose of seeing then converted to a beautiful and lasting temple. Most important of all, this temple must be something of his own, the product of his own creative mind, of his own conception, something which, but for his own creative thought and imagination, would never have existed at all.

VI

It is at this point, then, that the idea of a fully meaningful existence emerges, for the first time. It is inseparable from the concept of creativity. And it is exactly this that was missing from everything we have imagined up until now. Nature, however beautiful and awesome, exhibits nothing of creative activity until we include in it rational beings, that is, beings who can think, imagine, plan, and execute things of worth, beings who are, in the true sense, originators or creators. Rational beings do not merely foresee what will be; they sometimes determine what will be. They do not, like the rest of creation, merely wait to see what nature will thrust upon them. They sometimes impose upon nature herself their own creations, sometimes creations of great and lasting significance. Rational beings are the very creators of time itself, in the historical sense, for without them there would be only a meaningless succession of things and no history at all. An animal can, perhaps, anticipate its own death, as can a person, and an animal can bring about works, sometimes of considerable beauty and complexity, as can a person. But what the animal thus does has been done in exactly that way millions of times before. One thinks of the complex beauty of the spider's web, the intricate basketry of the oriole's nest, the ingenious construction of the honeycomb – all things of impressive intricacy, sometimes arresting and marvellous, but also things that disclose not the least hint of creative power. They are, like Sisyphus' labors, only endless repetitions. Human beings, or at least some of them, are capable of going a crucial step further. What a creative mind brings forth is never something merely learned or inherited, nor is it merely something novel, like the snowflake that resembles no other. It is what a creative mind intends it to be, something to which the notions of success or failure can apply, and sometimes something of such extraordinary originality that no other man or god, no one but its creator himself, could ever have foreseen. And if that creative mind possesses, in addition to this, the rare quality of creative genius, then what is wrought is not merely something that others could neither do nor foresee, it is something they could not even imagine. Thus we see the aptness of Schopenhauer's dictum, that while talent is the ability to hit a target that others miss, genius is the ability to hit a target that others do not even see.

The ancients, in their philosophies, were fond of describing their gods as rational. This idea of divine rationality has persisted among metaphysicians, but the concept of rationality has become narrowed. We think of rationality as care and precision in thought, a due regard for evidence and consistency, and sometimes as mere restraint in conduct. But the ancients quite properly associated it with the contemplative life in the broadest sense. The creation of things beautiful, profound, and unprecedented expressed for them the essense of human rationality. Sisyphus displayed his ultimate rationality, not merely in understanding what he was doing – something that would be within the power of a mere slave – but, as we have modified the myth, in the display of strength and genius that took the form of a beautiful and lasting temple, born first in his own imagination. That was something that no mere slave, and indeed no mere human being, and in fact no other being under the sun except this one, could ever have done. The creative genius of a particular person is something that by its very nature cannot be shared. To the extent that it is shared, such that what it brings forth is also brought forth by others, then it is not only not genius, it is not even a creative power. It is but the capacity for fabrication which, however striking it may be, is quite common throughout nature.

VII

Lest the impression be given that the creative thought and work that I am here praising is something rare, the possession of only a few, let it be noted that it exists in degrees and is, in one form or another, far from rare. What is rare is, I think, the proper appreciation of it. We tend to think of creative works as spectacular achievements, particularly in the arts, but in fact the human capacity to create something new is sometimes found in quite mundane things. Thus, for example, the establishment of a brilliant position in a game of chess is a perfect example of creativity, even though the result is of little value. Things as common as gardening, woodworking and the like give scope to the originality of those who have the knack for them, and are probably the most constant source of life's joys. Intelligent, perhaps witty conversation, and the composition of clear and forceful prose are just as good examples of creativity as the making of a poem of great beauty or depth of meaning, however much they may differ in worth. My own favorite example of a creative work, and one whose value as a creation is rarely appreciated, is the raising of a beautiful family, something that is reserved for the relatively few who can, as a natural gift, do it well. Of course the mere begetting of children is no act of creation at all. It is something that can be done by anyone. And other creatures sometimes with great skill convert their young to self-sufficient adults. They succeed, however, only to the extent that these young exactly resemble themselves, whereas rational human parents should measure their success by the degree to which their children become self-sufficient and capable adults who do *not* resemble their parents, but express instead their own individualities. This is an art that is neither common nor easily learned.

VIII

It would be gratifying if, in the light of what I have been saying, we could now rest upon the comfortable conclusion that our lives derive their meaning from the fact that human beings, and they alone, impose a history upon nature, that the world does not merely persist from age to age, nor does it merely change in the manner of the endless recurrences we see throughout the rest of creation, but that changes are imposed upon it by the creative power of humankind. That would be true, but too general, for in truth, creative power is not something particularly sought and prized by most people. Our culture has taught us to regard all persons as of equal worth, and our religion tells us that this is even God's estimate. Indeed, we are taught that we are, each and every one, created in the very image of that God, so that no one can claim for himself more importance than anyone else. Our lives, it is implied, are invested with great meaning just by virtue of our common humanity. We need only to be born, and our worth is once and for all assured. We are, to be sure, set apart from the remainder of creation, according to this tradition, but what sets us apart is not necessarily anything we do. We are set apart by what is merely given to us, so that a human life, and a valuable and meaningful life, are presumed to be one and the same.

That conception of meaningful existence, which is so familiar, is very sadly at variance with the conception of meaningful existence that I have developed. For in truth, creative power is no common possession. Creative genius is in fact rare. The work of the vast majority of persons does not deviate much from what others have already done and from what can be found everywhere. There seems even to be a determination in most people that this should be so, a determination to pattern their lives after others, to seek as little originality and individual self-worth as possible. People tend, like apes, to mimic and imitate what they already find, absorbing the ideas, manners, values, even, indeed, their religions, from those around them, as if by osmosis. They appropriate virtually everything, returning virtually nothing of their own creative power. The lives of most persons are like the clockwork to which I have so often alluded. They are born, pass through the several stages of life, indulging, for the most part, only trivial thoughts and feelings, absorbing pleasures and distractions, fleeing boredom, conceiving no significant works, and leaving almost nothing behind them. It would be sad enough if this were merely so. What is far sadder is that it is thought not really to matter. Religion then reinforces this by proclaiming that no one can, in God's sight, rise above others anyway, that the fool is already as blessed as the wise, and that the greatest possible human worth has already been bestowed upon us all by our merely being born. It is a hard notion to overcome, and weighs upon us like lead. It tends to render even the exemplary among us weak and hesitant.

We take much comfort in that part of the Bible, the very first book, which assures us that we are all the veritable images of God. We tend to overlook the first five words with which the Bible begins: "In the beginning, God created …" That the result of that act is heaven and earth may be overwhelming, but the emphasis is wrong if we dwell on that. What is significant is that the original description of God is as a *creator*. And it is this, surely, that endows one with the divine quality. That human beings exist is not, in itself, a significant fact. That this or that being is possessed of human form, or is of that biological species, is likewise of no significance, whatever may be the teaching of religion and custom to the contrary. What *is* significant, what gives any human existence its meaning, is the possibility that thus arises of creative power. But it is no more than a possibility, realized here and there, more or less, and fully realized only in exceptional persons.

IX

One brings to consciousness the indescribable worth of creative power by imagining specific instances. Consider, for example, that on a given day the sun rose, as usual, and that throughout that day most of the world was much as it had been the day before, virtually all of its inhabitants doing more or less what they were accustomed to doing; but, in a minute part of that world, a nocturne of Chopin's came into being, or a sonata of Mozart's. On another day, otherwise much like any other, Lincoln composed his address for the visit to Gettysburg, or, Mathew Arnold wrote the concluding lines of his *Dover Beach*, or Grey his *Elegy*, or Plato his *Symposium*. That a little-known woman gave birth to an infant in Malaga, Spain, one October day in 1881 means very little, but that the child was to become Picasso means much. And to complete this kind of imaginative exercise, one needs to fix in his thought some significant creation – something, perhaps, as small but priceless as a prelude of Chopin or a poem of Keats – and then realize that, if a particular person had not at just that moment brought forth that utterly unprecedented thing, then it would never have existed at all. The thought of a world altogether devoid of music or literature or art is the thought of a world that is dark indeed, but if one dwells on it, the thought of a world lacking a single one of the fruits of creative genius that our world actually possesses is a depressing one. That such a world would have been so easy, so inevitable, but for a solitary person, at a single moment, is a shattering reflection.

This, I think, is the verdict of philosophy. One wishes it were the theme of religion as well, for the voice of religion is always louder than that of philosophy. That a world should exist is not finally important, nor does it mean much, by itself, that people should inhabit it. But that some of these should, in varying degrees, be capable of creating worlds of their own and history – thereby creating time in its historical sense – is what gives our lives whatever meaning they have.

4.3

The Meanings of Lives

Susan Wolf

This question, "What is the meaning of life?" was once taken to be a paradigm of philosophical inquiry. Perhaps, outside of the academy, it still is. In philosophy classrooms and academic journals, however, the question has nearly disappeared, and when the question is brought up, by a naïve student, for example, or a prospective donor to the cause of a liberal arts education, it is apt to be greeted with uncomfortable embarrassment.

What is so wrong with the question? One answer is that it is extremely obscure, if not downright unintelligible. It is unclear what exactly the question is supposed to be asking. Talk of meaning in other contexts does not offer ready analogies for understanding the phrase "the meaning of life." When we ask the meaning of a word, for example, we want to know what the word stands for, what it represents. But life is not part of a language, or of any other sort of symbolic system. It is not clear how it could "stand for" anything, nor to whom. We sometimes use "meaning" in nonlinguistic contexts: "Those dots mean measles." "Those footprints mean that someone was here since it rained." In these cases, talk of meaning seems to be equivalent to talk of evidence, but the contexts in which such claims are made tend to specify what hypotheses are in question within relatively fixed bounds. To ask what life means without a similarly specified context, leaves us at sea.

Still, when people do ask about the meaning of life, they are evidently expressing some concern or other, and it would be disingenuous to insist that the rest of us haven't the faintest idea what that is. The question at least gestures toward a certain set of concerns with which most of us are at least somewhat familiar. Rather than dismiss a question with which many people have been passionately occupied as pure and simple nonsense, it seems more appropriate to try to interpret it and reformulate it in a way that can be more clearly and

Susan Wolf (2010) "The Meanings of Lives," in John Perry, Michael Bratman, and John Martin Fischer (eds.), *Introduction to Philosophy: Classical and Contemporary Readings*, 5th edn., New York: Oxford University Press, pp. 794–805.

unambiguously understood. Though there may well be many things going on when people ask, "What is the meaning of life?", the most central among them seems to be a search to find a purpose or a point to human existence. It is a request to find out why we are here (that is, why we exist at all), with the hope that an answer to this question will also tell us something about what we should be doing with our lives.

If understanding the question in this way, however, makes the question intelligible, it might not give reason to reopen it as a live philosophical problem. Indeed, if some of professional philosophy's discomfort with discussion of the meaning of life comes from a desire to banish ambiguity and obscurity from the field, as much comes, I think, from the thought that the question, when made clearer, has already been answered, and that the answer is depressing. Specifically, if the question of the Meaning of Life is to be identified with the question of the purpose of life, then the standard view, at least among professional philosophers, would seem to be that it all depends on the existence of God. In other words, the going opinion seems to be that if there is a God, then there is at least a chance that there is a purpose, and so a meaning to life. God may have created us for a reason, with a plan in mind. But to go any further along this branch of thinking is not in the purview of secular philosophers.[1] If, on the other hand, there is no God, then there can be no meaning, in the sense of a point or a purpose to our existence. We are simply a product of physical processes – there are no reasons for our existence, just causes.

At the same time that talk of Life having a Meaning is banished from philosophy, however, the talk of lives being more or less *meaningful* seems to be on the rise. Newspapers, magazines, self-help manuals[2] are filled with essays on how to find meaning in your life; sermons and therapies are built on the truism that happiness is not just a matter of material comfort, or sensual pleasure, but also of a deeper kind of fulfillment. Though philosophers to date have had relatively little to say about what gives meaning to individual lives, passing references can be found throughout the literature; it is generally acknowledged as an intelligible and appropriate thing to want in one's life. Indeed, it would be crass to think otherwise.

But how can individual lives have meaning if life as a whole has none? Are those of us who suspect there is no meaning *to* life deluding ourselves in continuing to talk about the possibility of finding meaning *in* life? (Are we being short-sighted, failing to see the implications of one part of our thought on another?) Alternatively, are these expressions mere homonyms, with no conceptual or logical connections between them? Are there simply two wholly unconnected topics here?

Many of you will be relieved to hear that I do not wish to revive the question of whether there is a meaning to life. I am inclined to accept the standard view that there is no plausible interpretation of that question that offers a positive answer in the absence of a fairly specific religious metaphysics. An understanding of meaningfulness in life, however, does seem to me to merit more philosophical attention than it has so far received, and I will have some things to say about it here. Here, too, I am inclined to accept the standard view – or a part of the standard view – viz., that meaningfulness is an intelligible feature to be sought in a life, and that it is, at least sometimes attainable but not everywhere assured. But what that feature is – what we are looking for – is controversial and unclear, and so the task of analyzing or interpreting that feature will take up a large portion of my remarks today [in this paper]. With an analysis proposed, I shall return to the question of how a positive view about the possibility of meaning in lives can fit with a negative or agnostic view about the meaning of life. The topics are not, I think, as unconnected as might at first seem necessary for their respectively optimistic and pessimistic answers to coexist. Though my discussion will offer nothing new in the way of an answer to the question of the meaning of life, therefore, it may offer a somewhat different perspective on that question's significance.

Let us begin, however, with the other question, that of understanding what it is to seek meaning in life. What do we want when we want a meaningful life? What is it that makes some lives meaningful, others less so?

If we focus on the agent's, or the subject's, perspective – on a person wanting meaning in her life, her feeling the need for more meaning – we might incline toward a subjective interpretation of the feature being sought. When a person self-consciously looks for something to give her life meaning, it signals a kind of unhappiness. One imagines, for example, the alienated housewife, whose life seems to her to be a series of endless chores. What she wants, it might appear, is something that she can find more subjectively rewarding.

This impression is reinforced if we consider references to "meaningful experiences." (The phrase might be applied, for example, to a certain kind of wedding or funeral.) The most salient feature of an event that is described as meaningful seems to be its "meaning a lot" *to* the participants. To say that a ceremony, or, for that matter, a job, is meaningful seems at the very least to include the idea that it is emotionally satisfying. An absence of meaning is usually marked by a feeling of emptiness and dissatisfaction; in contrast, a meaningful life, or meaningful part of life, is necessarily at least somewhat rewarding or fulfilling. It is noteworthy, however, that meaningful experiences are not necessarily particularly happy. A trip to one's birthplace may well be meaningful; a visit to an amusement park is unlikely to be so.

If we step back, however, and ask ourselves, as observers, what lives strike us as especially meaningful, if we ask what sorts of lives exemplify meaningfulness, subjective criteria do not seem to be in the forefront. Who comes to mind? Perhaps, Gandhi, or Albert Schweitzer, or Mother Teresa; perhaps Einstein or Jonas Salk. Cezanne, or Manet, Beethoven, Charlie Parker. Tolstoy is an interesting case to which I shall return. Alternatively, we can look to our neighbors, our colleagues, our relatives – some of whom, it seems to me, live more meaningful lives than others. Some, indeed, of my acquaintance seem to me to live lives that are paradigms of meaning – right up there with the famous names on the earlier lists; while others (perhaps despite their modicum of fame) would score quite low on the meaningfulness scale. If those in the latter category feel a lack of meaning in their lives – well, they are right to feel it, and it is a step in the right direction that they notice that there is something about their lives that they should try to change.

What is it to live a meaningful life, then? What does meaningfulness in life amount to? It may be easier to make progress by focusing on what we want to avoid. In that spirit, let me offer some paradigms, not of meaning*ful*, but of meaning*less* lives.

For me, the idea of a meaningless life is most clearly and effectively embodied in the image of a person who spends day after day, or night after night, in front of a television set, drinking beer and watching situation comedies. Not that I have anything against television or beer. Still the image, understood as an image of a person whose life is lived in hazy passivity, a life lived at a not unpleasant level of consciousness, but unconnected to anyone or anything, going nowhere, achieving nothing – is, I submit, as strong an image of a meaningless life as there can be. Call this case The Blob.

If any life, any human life, is meaningless, the Blob's life is. But this doesn't mean that any meaningless life must be, in all important respects, like the Blob's. There are other paradigms that highlight by their absences other elements of meaningfulness.

In contrast to the Blob's passivity, for example, we may imagine a life full of activity, but silly or decadent or useless activity. (And again, I have nothing against silly activity, but only against a life that is wholly occupied with it.) We may imagine, for example, one of the idle rich who flits about, fighting off boredom, moving from one amusement to another. She shops, she travels, she eats at expensive restaurants, she works out with her personal trainer.

Curiously, one might also take a very un-idle rich person to epitomize a meaningless life in a slightly different way. Consider, for example, the corporate executive who works twelve-hour, seven-day weeks, suffering great stress, for the sole purpose of the accumulation of personal wealth. Related to this perhaps is David Wiggins' example of the pig farmer who buys more land to grow more corn to feed more pigs to buy more land to grow more corn to feed more pigs.[3]

These last three cases of the idle rich, the corporate executive and the pig farmer are in some ways very different, but they all share at least this feature: they can all be characterized as lives whose dominant activities seem pointless, useless, or empty. Classify these cases under the heading Useless.

A somewhat different and I think more controversial sort of case to consider involves someone who is engaged, even dedicated, to a project that is ultimately revealed as bankrupt, not because the person's values are shallow or misguided, but because the project fails. The person may go literally bankrupt: for example, a man may devote his life to creating and building up a company to hand over to his children, but the item his company manufactures is rendered obsolete by technology shortly before his planned retirement. Or consider a scientist whose life's work is rendered useless by the announcement of a medical breakthrough just weeks before his own research would have yielded the same results. Perhaps more poignantly, imagine a woman whose life is centered around a relationship that turns out to be a fraud. Cases that fit this mold we may categorize under the heading Bankrupt.

The classification of this third sort of case as an exemplification of meaninglessness may meet more resistance than the classification of the earlier two. Perhaps these lives should not be considered meaningless after all. Nonetheless, these are cases in which it is not surprising that an argument of some sort is needed – it is not unnatural or silly that the subjects of these lives should entertain the thought that their lives have been meaningless. Even if they are wrong, the fact that their thoughts are not, so to speak, out of order, is a useful datum. So, of course, would be the sort of thing one would say to convince them, or ourselves, that these thoughts are ultimately mistaken.

If the cases I have sketched capture our images of meaninglessness more or less accurately, they provide clues to what a positive case of a meaningful life must contain. In contrast to the Blob's passivity, a person who lives a meaningful life must be actively engaged. But, as the Useless cases teach us, it will not do to be engaged in just anything, for any reason or with any goal – one must be engaged in a project or projects that have some positive value, and in some way that is nonaccidentally related to what gives them value. Finally, in order to avoid Bankruptcy, it seems necessary that one's activities be at least to some degree successful (though it may not be easy to determine what counts as the right kind or degree of success). Putting these criteria together, we get a proposal for what it is to live a meaningful life: viz., a meaningful life is one that is actively and at least somewhat successfully engaged in a project (or projects) of positive value.

Several remarks are needed to qualify and refine this proposal. First, the use of the word "project" is not ideal: it is too suggestive of a finite, determinate task, something one takes on, and, if all goes well, completes. Among the things that come to mind as projects are certain kinds of hobbies or careers, or rather, specific tasks that fall within the sphere of such hobbies or careers: things that can be seen as accomplishments, like the producing of a proof or a poem or a pudding, the organizing of a union or a high school band. Although such activities are among the things that seem intuitively to contribute to the meaningfulness of people's lives, there are other forms of meaningfulness that are less directed, and less oriented to demonstrable achievement, and we should not let the use of the word "project" distort or deny the potential of these things to give meaningfulness to life. Relationships, in particular, seem at best awkwardly described as projects. Rarely does one deliberately take them on and, in some cases, one doesn't even have to work at them – one may just have them and live, as it were, within them. Moreover, many of the activities that are naturally described as projects – coaching a school soccer team, planning a surprise party, reviewing an article for a journal – have the meaning they do for us only because of their place in the nonprojectlike relationships in which we are enmeshed and with which we identify. In proposing that a meaningful life is a life actively engaged in projects, then, I mean to use "projects" in an unusually broad sense, to encompass not only goal-directed tasks but other sorts of ongoing activities and involvements as well.

Second, the suggestion that a meaningful life should be "actively engaged" in projects should be understood in a way that recognizes and embraces the connotations of "engagement." Although the idea that a meaningful life requires activity was introduced by contrast to the life of the ultra-passive Blob, we should note that meaning involves more than mere, literal activity. The alienated housewife, presumably, is active all the time – she buys groceries and fixes meals, cleans the house, does the laundry, chauffeurs the children from school to soccer to ballet, arranges doctors' appointments and babysitters. What makes her life insufficiently meaningful is that her heart, so to speak, isn't in these activities. She does not identify with what she is doing – she does not embrace her roles as wife, mother, and homemaker as expressive of who she is and wants to be. We may capture her alienated condition by saying that though she is active, she is not actively engaged. (She is, one might say, just going through the motions.) In characterizing a meaningful life, then, it is worth stressing that living such a life is not just a matter of having projects (broadly construed) and actively and somewhat successfully getting through them. The projects must engage the person whose life it is. Ideally, she would proudly and happily embrace them, as constituting at least part of what her life is about.[4]

Finally, we must say more about the proposal's most blatantly problematic condition – viz, that the project's engagement with which can contribute to a meaningful life must be projects "of positive value." The claim is that meaningful lives must be engaged in projects of positive value – but who is to decide which projects have positive value, or even to guarantee that there is such a thing?

I would urge that we leave the phrase as unspecific as possible in all but one respect. We do not want to build a theory of positive value into our conception of meaningfulness. As a proposal that aims to capture what most people mean by a meaningful life, what we want is a concept that "tracks" whatever we think of as having positive value. This allows us to explain at least some divergent intuitions about meaningfulness in terms of divergent intuitions or beliefs about what has positive value, with the implication that if one is wrong about what has positive value, one will also be wrong about what contributes to a meaningful life. (Thus, a person who finds little to admire in sports – who finds ridiculous, for example, the sight of grown men trying to knock a little ball into a hole with a club, will find relatively little potential for meaning in the life of an avid golfer; a person who places little stock in esoteric intellectual pursuits will be puzzled by someone who strains to write, much less read, a lot of books on supervenience.)

The exception I would make to this otherwise maximally tolerant interpretation of the idea of positive value is that we exclude merely subjective value as a suitable interpretation of the phrase.

It will not do to allow that a meaningful life is a life involved in projects that seem to have positive value from the perspective of the one who lives it. Allowing this would have the effect of erasing the distinctiveness of our interest in meaningfulness; it would blur or remove the difference between an interest in living a meaningful life and an interest in living a life that feels or seems meaningful. That these interests are distinct, and that the former is not merely instrumental to the latter can be seen by reflecting on a certain way the wish or the need for meaning in one's life may make itself felt. What I have in mind is the possibility of a kind of epiphany, in which one wakes up – literally or figuratively – to the recognition that one's life to date has been meaningless. Such an experience would be nearly unintelligible if a lack of meaning were to be understood as a lack of a certain kind of subjective impression. One can hardly understand the idea of waking up to the thought that one's life to date has seemed meaningless. To the contrary, it may be precisely because one did not realize the emptiness of one's projects or the shallowness of one's values until that moment that the experience I am imagining has the poignancy it does. It is the sort of experience that one might describe in terms of scales falling from one's eyes. And the yearning for meaningfulness, the impulse to do something about it, will not be satisfied (though it may be eliminated) by putting the scales back on, so to speak. If one suspects that the life one has been living is meaningless, one will not bring meaning to it by getting therapy or taking a pill that, without changing one's life in any other way, makes one believe that one's life has meaning.

To care that one's life is meaningful, then, is, according to my proposal, to care that one's life is actively and at least somewhat successfully engaged in projects (understanding this term broadly) that not just seem to have positive value, but that really do have it. To care that one's life be meaningful, in other words, is in part to care that what one does with one's life is, to pardon the expression, at least somewhat objectively good. We should be careful, however, not to equate objective goodness with moral goodness, at least not if we understand moral value as essentially involving benefiting or honoring humanity. The concern for meaning in one's life does not seem to be the same as the concern for moral worth, nor do our judgments about what sorts of lives are meaningful seem to track judgments of moral character or accomplishment.

To be sure, some of the paradigms of meaningful lives are lives of great moral virtue or accomplishment – I mentioned Gandhi and Mother Teresa, for example. Others, however, are not. Consider Gauguin, Wittgenstein, Tchaikovsky – morally unsavory figures all, whose lives nonetheless seem chock full of meaning. If one thinks that even they deserve moral credit, for their achievements made the world a better place, consider instead Olympic athletes and world chess champions, whose accomplishments leave nothing behind but their world records. Even more important, consider the artists, scholars, musicians, athletes of our more ordinary sort. For us, too, the activities of artistic creation and research, the development of our skills and our understanding of the world give meaning to our lives – but they do not give moral value to them.

It seems then that meaning in life may not be especially moral, and that indeed lives can be richly meaningful even if they are, on the whole, judged to be immoral. Conversely, that one's life is at least moderately moral, that it is lived, as it were, above reproach, is no assurance of its being moderately meaningful. The alienated housewife, for example, may be in no way subject to moral criticism. (And it is debatable whether even the Blob deserves specifically moral censure.)

That people do want meaning in their lives, I take it, is an observable, empirical fact. We have already noted the evidence of self-help manuals, and therapy groups. What I have offered so far is an analysis of what that desire or concern amounts to. I want now to turn to the question of whether the desire is one that it is good that people have, whether, that is, there is some positive reason why they *should* want this.

At a minimum, we may acknowledge that it is at least not bad to want meaning in one's life. There is, after all, no harm in it. Since people do want this, and since there are no moral objections to it, we should recognize the concern for meaning as a legitimate concern, at least in the weak sense that people should be allowed to pursue it. Indeed, insofar as meaningfulness in one's life is a significant factor in a life's overall well-being, we should do more than merely allow its pursuit: we should positively try to increase opportunities for people to live lives of meaning.

Most of us, however, seem to have a stronger positive attitude toward the value of meaningfulness than this minimum concession admits. We do not think it is merely all right for people to want meaning in their lives – as it is all right for people to like country music, or to take an interest in figure-skating. We think people positively ought to care that their lives be meaningful. It is disturbing, or at least regrettable, to find someone who doesn't care about this. Yet this positive assessment ought to strike us, at least initially, as somewhat mysterious. What is the good, after all, of living a meaningful life, and to whom?

Since a meaningful life is not necessarily a *morally* better life than a meaningless one (the Olympic athlete may do no more good nor harm than the idly rich socialite), it is not necessarily better *for the world* that people try to live or even succeed in living meaningful lives. Neither is a meaningful life assured of being an especially happy one, however. Many of the things that give meaning to our lives (relationships to loved ones, aspirations to achieve) make us vulnerable to pain, disappointment and stress. From the inside, the Blob's hazy passivity may be preferable to the experience of the tortured artist or political crusader. By conventional standards, therefore, it is not clear that caring about or even succeeding in living a meaningful life is better *for the person herself.*

Yet, as I have already mentioned, those of us who do care that our lives be meaningful tend to think that it is a positively good thing that we do. We not only want to live meaningful lives, we want to want this – we approve of this desire, and think it is better for others if they have this desire, too. If, for example, you see a person you care about conducting her life in a way that you find devoid of worth – she is addicted to drugs, perhaps, or just to television, or she is overly enthusiastic in her career as a corporate lawyer – you are apt to encourage her to change, or at least hope that she will find a new direction on her own. Your most prominent worry may well be that she is heading for a fall. You fear that at some point she will wake up to the fact that she has been wasting or misdirecting her life, a point that may come too late for easy remedy and will, in any case, involve a lot of pain and self-criticism. But the fear that she will wake up to the fact that she has been wasting her life (and have difficulty turning her life around) may not be as terrible as the fear that she won't wake up to it. If you came to feel secure that no painful moment of awakening would ever come because your friend (or sister or daughter) simply does not care whether her life is meaningful, you might well think that this situation is not better but worse. We seem to think there is something regrettable about a person living a meaningless life, even if the person herself does not mind that she is. We seem to think she *should* want meaning in her life, even if she doesn't realize it.

What, though, is the status of this "should," the nature or source of the regret? The mystery that I earlier suggested we should feel about our value in meaningfulness is reflected in the uneasy location of this judgment. If my own reaction to the woman who doesn't care whether her life is meaningful is typical, the thought that she should, or ought to care is closer to a prudential judgment than it is to a moral one. (If there is a moral objection to a person who lives a meaningless life and is content with that, it is not, in my opinion, a very strong one. The Blob, after all, is not hurting anyone, nor is the idle rich jet-setter. She may, for example, give money to environmental causes to offset the damage she is doing in her SUV, and write generous checks to Oxfam and UNICEF on a regular basis.) The thought that it is too bad if a person does not live a meaningful life (even if she doesn't mind) seems rather to be the thought that it is too bad *for her.*

The closest analogue to this thought in the history of ethics of which I am aware is Aristotle's conception of *eudaimonia*. His conception of the virtuous life as the happiest life is offered as a conclusion of an enlightened self-interest. According to standard conceptions of self-interest, however (either hedonistic or preference-based), it is not obvious why this should be so, and, unfortunately, Aristotle himself does not address the question explicitly. Rather, he seems to think that if you do not just see that the virtuous life, in which one aims for and achieves what is "fine," is a better, more desirable life for yourself, that just shows that you were not well brought up, and in that case, there is no point trying to educate, you.

Our question, the question of whether and what kind of reason there is for a person to strive for a meaningful life, is not quite the same as the question of whether and what kind of reason there is to aspire to virtue – though, when one is careful to interpret "virtue" in the broad and not specifically moral way that Aristotle uses the term, it is closer than it might seem. Still, as I say, Aristotle does not really address the question, and so, though I take my line of thought to be Aristotelian in spirit, a scholarly study of Aristotle's texts is not likely to be an efficient way of finding an answer to the question ourselves.

What reason is there, then, if any, for a person to want to live a meaningful life? I have said that we seem to think it would be better for her, that it is, at least roughly, in her self-interest. At the same time, the thought that she should care about meaning seems to depend on claims from outside herself. Even if there are no desires latent in her psychology which meaningfulness would satisfy, we seem to think, there is reason why she should have such desires. She seems to be making some kind of mistake.

If my analysis of what is involved in living a meaningful life is right, then the question of why one should care about living a meaningful life is equivalent to the question of why one should care that one's life be actively and somewhat successfully engaged in projects of positive value. The source of perplexity seems, in particular, to be about the reason to care that one's projects be positively valuable. As long as you are engaged by your activities, and they make you happy, why should one care that one's activities be objectively worthwhile?

The answer, I believe, is that to devote one's life entirely to activities whose value is merely subjective, to devote oneself to activities whose sole justification is that it is good for you, is, in a sense I shall try to explain, practically solipsistic. It flies in the face of one's status as, if you will, a tiny speck in a vast universe, a universe with countless perspectives of equal status with one's own, from which one's life might be assessed. Living a life that is engaged with and so at least partially focussed on projects whose value has a nonsubjective source is a way of acknowledging one's non-privileged position. It harmonizes, in a way that a purely egocentric life does not, with the fact that one is not the center of the universe.

The basic idea is this: The recognition of one's place in the universe, of one's smallness, one might say, or one's insignificance, and of the independent existence of the universe in which one is a part involves, among other things, the recognition of "the mereness" of one's subjective point of view. To think of one's place in the universe is to recognize the possibility of a perspective, of infinitely many perspectives, really, from which one's life is merely gratuitous; it is to recognize the possibility of a perspective, or rather of infinitely many perspectives, that are indifferent to whether one exists at all, and so to whether one is happy or sad, satisfied or unsatisfied, fulfilled or unfulfilled.

In the face of this recognition, a life that is directed solely to its subject's own fulfillment, or, to its mere survival or towards the pursuit of goals that are grounded in nothing but the subject's own psychology, appears either solipsistic or silly.

A person who lives a largely egocentric life – who devotes, in other words, lots of energy and attention and care toward himself, who occupies himself more specifically with satisfying and gratifying himself, expresses and reveals a belief that his happiness matters. Even if it doesn't express the view that his happiness matters objectively, it at least expresses the idea that it matters to him. To be solely devoted to his own gratification, then, would express and reveal the fact that his happiness is *all* that matters, at least all that matters to him. If, however, one accepts a framework that recognizes distinctions in nonsubjective value, (and if one believes, as seems only reasonable, that what has nonsubjective value has no special concentration in or connection to oneself) this attitude seems hard to justify.

To accept that framework is, after all, to accept the view that some things are better than others. To me, it makes sense partially to understand this literally: Some *things*, it seems to me, are better than others: people, for example, are better than rocks or mosquitoes, and a Vermeer painting is better than the scraps on my compost heap.[5] What is essential, though, is that accepting a framework that recognizes distinctions in nonsubjective value involves seeing the world as value-filled, as containing with it distinctions of better and worse, of more and less worthwhile, if not of better and worse objects per se, then of better and worse features of the world, or activities, or opportunities to be realized. Against this background, a life solely devoted to one's own gratification or to the satisfaction of one's whims seems gratuitous and hard to defend. For, as I have said, to live such a life expresses the view that one's happiness is all that matters, at least to oneself. But why should this be the only thing that matters, when there is so much else worth caring about?

Those familiar with Thomas Nagel's book, *The Possibility of Altruism*, may have recognized an allusion to it in my suggestion that a life indifferent to meaning was practically solipsistic. The allusion is significant, for the argument I am making here, though it is directed to a different conclusion, bears a strong resemblance to the argument of that book. Nagel's argument invites us to see a person who, while evidently trying to avoid or minimize pain to himself, shows total indifference to the pain of others, as a practical solipsist in the sense that he fails, in his practical outlook, to recognize and appreciate that he is one person among others, equally real. Roughly, the suggestion seems to be that if you appreciate the reality of others, then you realize that their pains are just as painful as yours. If the painfulness of your pain is a reason to take steps to avoid it, then, the painfulness of their pain should provide reasons, too. To be totally indifferent to the pain of others, then, bespeaks a failure to recognize their pain (to recognize it, that is, as *really* painful, in the same way that yours is painful to you).

This is not the occasion to discuss the plausibility of Nagel's interpretation of the pure egoist as a practical solipsist, nor even to describe Nagel's complex and subtle position in enough detail to be able fairly to evaluate it. What I want to call attention to has to do not with the substance of the argument but with the type of argument it is: specifically, Nagel's argument suggests that appreciation of a certain fact – in this case, the fact that you are just one person among others, equally real – is a source of practical reason – in this case, it gives you reason to take the pains of others to constitute reasons for action. If Nagel is right, we have reason to care about the pain of others that is grounded, not in our own psychologies (and more specifically, not in any of our own desires), but in a fact about the world. His suggestion is that a person who fails to see the pain of others as a source of reason acts "as if" the pain of others is not real, or not painful. But of course the pain of others *is* real and *is* painful. Such a person thus exhibits a failure not just of morality or sympathy, but of practical reason, in the sense that his practical stance fails to accord with a very significant fact about the world.

My suggestion that we have reason to care about and to try to live meaningful rather than meaningless lives resembles Nagel's in form. Like him, I am suggesting that we can have a reason to do something or to care about something that is, grounded not in our own psychologies, nor specifically in our own desires, but in a fact about the world. The fact in question in this case is the fact that we are, each of us, specks in a vast and value-filled universe, and that as such we have no privileged position as a source of or possessor of objective value. To devote oneself wholly to one's own satisfaction seems to me to fly in the face of this truth, to act "as if" one is the only thing that matters, or perhaps, more, that one's own psychology is the only source of (determining) what matters. By focusing one's attention and one's energies at least in part on things, activities, aspects of the world that have value independent of you, you implicitly acknowledge your place and your status in the world. Your behavior, and your practical stance is thus more in accord with the facts.

Admittedly, this is not the sort of reason that one must accept on pain of inconsistency or any other failure of logic. Just as a person may simply not care whether her life is meaningful, so she may also simply not care whether her life is in accord with, or harmonizes with the facts. (It is one thing to say we should live in accord with the facts of physics, geography, and the other sciences. Living in accordance with these facts has evident instrumental value – it helps us get around in the world. But living in a way that practically acknowledges, or harmonizes with the fact that we are tiny specks in a value-filled world will not make our lives go better that way.) Such a person cannot be accused in any strict sense of irrationality. Like noninstrumental reasons to be moral, the reason to care about living a worthwhile life is not one that narrow rationality requires one to accept. At the same time, it seems appropriate to characterize my suggestion (and Nagel's) as one that appeals to reason in a broader sense. For my suggestion is that an interest in living a meaningful life is an appropriate response to a fundamental truth, and that failure to have such a concern constitutes a failure to acknowledge that truth.

As we have already seen, the truth to which I am proposing a meaningful life provides a response is the truth that we are, each of us, tiny specks in a vast and value-filled universe. Like the truth that we are, each of us, one person among others, equally real, it opposes what children and many adults may have a tendency to assume – namely, that they are the center of the universe, either the possessor or the source of all value. (It is because both Nagel's truth and mine are opposites of that assumption that both might plausibly be understood as alternatives to practical solipsism.) Unlike Nagel's truth, mine is not specifically addressed to our relation to other people. A person may, therefore, appreciate and practically express one of these truths and not the other. Whereas an appropriate response to the equal reality of other people may be, if Nagel is right, an embrace of morality or something relating to morality, my proposal is that an appropriate response to our status as specks in a vast universe is a concern and aspiration to have one's life wrapped up with projects of positive value.

Perhaps, however, I have not made it clear why this is an appropriate response. The question may seem especially pressing because the thought that we are tiny specks in a vast universe, and the sense that it calls for or demands a response has, in the past, tended to move philosophers in a different direction. Specifically, the thought that we are tiny specks in a vast universe was in the past closely associated with that murky and ponderous question to which I referred at the beginning of my [paper] – the question of The Meaning of Life. The thought that we are tiny specks in a vast universe has indeed often evoked that question, and, to those who either do not believe in or do not want to rest their answers in the existence of a benevolent God, it has more or less immediately seemed also to indicate an answer. Considering their answer to the question of the Meaning of Life and contrasting it with my response to the fact of our smallness, may clarify the substance of my proposal.

The train of thought I have in mind is one that has, with variations, been expressed by many distinguished philosophers, including Camus, Tolstoy, Richard Taylor, and, curiously, Nagel himself. For them, the recognition of our place in the universe – our smallness, or our speckness, if you will – seems to warrant the conclusion not only that there is no meaning to life as such but also that each individual life is necessarily absurd.

On the view of these philosophers, a life can be meaningful only if it can mean something *to* someone, and not just to *someone*, but to someone other than oneself and indeed someone of more intrinsic or ultimate value than oneself. Of course, anyone can live in such a way as to make her life meaningful to *someone* other than herself. She can maintain her relationship with parents and siblings, establish friendships with neighbors and colleagues. She can fall in love. If all else fails, she can have a child who will love her, or two children, or six. She can open up an entire clinic for God's sake. But if a life that is devoted solely to yourself, a life that is good to no one other than yourself lacks meaning, these philosophers not implausibly think, so will a life that is devoted to any other poor creature, for he or she will have no more objective importance than you have, and so will be no more fit a stopping place by which to ground the claim of meaningfulness than you. Nor, according to this train of thought, will it help to expand your circle, to be of use or to have an effect on a larger segment of humankind. If each life is individually lacking in meaning, then the collective is meaningless as well. If each life has but an infinitesimal amount of value, then although one's meaning will increase in proportion to one's effect, the total quantity of meaning relative to the cosmos will remain so small as to make the effort pathetic.

From the perspective of these philosophers, if there is no God, then human life, each human life, must be objectively meaningless, because if there is no God, there is no appropriate being *for whom* we could have meaning.

From this perspective, my suggestion that the living of a worthwhile life constitutes a response to a recognition of our place in the universe might seem ridiculously nearsighted, as if, having acknowledged the mereness of my own subjectivity, I then failed to acknowledge the equal mereness of the subjectivity of others. But I think this misunderstands the point in my proposal of living a life that realizes nonsubjective value, a misunderstanding that derives from too narrow a view about what an appropriate and satisfactory response to the fact of our place in the universe must be.

The philosophers I have been speaking about – we can call them the pessimists – take the fundamental lesson to be learned from the contemplation of our place in the universe to be that we are cosmically insignificant, a fact that clashes with our desire to be very significant indeed. If God existed, such philosophers might note, we would have a chance at being significant. For God himself, is presumably very significant and so we could be significant by being or by making ourselves significant to Him. In the absence of a God, however, it appears that we can only be significant to each other, to beings, that is, as pathetically small as ourselves. We want to be important, but we cannot be important, and so our lives are absurd.

The pessimists are right about the futility of trying to make ourselves important. Insofar as contemplation of the cosmos makes us aware of our smallness, whether as individuals or as a species, we simply must accept it and come to terms with it. Some people do undoubtedly get very upset, even despondent when they start to think about their cosmic insignificance.

They want to be important, to have an impact on the world, to make a mark that will last forever. When they realize that they cannot achieve this, they are very disappointed. The only advice one can give to such people is: Get Over It.

Rather than fight the fact of our insignificance, however, and of the mereness of our subjectivity, my proposal is that we live in a way that acknowledges the fact, or, at any rate, that harmonizes with it. Living in a way that is significantly focussed on, engaged with, and concerned to promote or realize value whose source comes from outside of oneself, does seem to harmonize with this, whereas living purely egocentrically does not. Living lives that attain or realize some nonsubjective value may not make us meaningful, much less important, to anyone other than ourselves, but it will give us something to say, to think, in response to the recognition of perspectives that we ourselves imaginatively adopt that are indifferent to our existence and to our well-being.

At the beginning of this paper, I raised the question of how the meaning of life – or the absence of such meaning – was related to the meaningfulness of particular lives. As I might have put it, does it really make sense to think that there can be meaningful lives in a meaningless world? In light of this discussion, we can see how the answer to that question might be "yes" while still holding on to the idea that the similar wording of the two phrases is not merely coincidental.

If I am right about what is involved in living a meaningful life – if, that is, living a meaningful life is a matter of at least partly successful engagement in projects of positive value – then the possibility of living meaningful lives despite the absence of an overall meaning *to* life can be seen to depend on the fact that distinctions of value (that is, of objective value) do not rely on the existence of God or of any overarching purpose to the human race as a whole. Whether or not God exists, the fact remains that some objects, activities and ideas are better than others. Whether or not God exists, some ways of living are more worthwhile than others. Some activities are a waste of time.

People are sometimes tempted to think that if God doesn't exist, then nothing matters. They are tempted to think that if we will all die, and eventually all traces of our existence will fade from all consciousness, there is no point to doing anything; nothing makes any difference. Tolstoy evidently thought this sometimes, and gave eloquent voice to that view. But the reasoning is ridiculous. If one activity is worthwhile and another is a waste, then one has reason to prefer the former, even if there is no God to look down on us and approve. More generally, we seem to have reason to engage ourselves with projects of value whether God exists and gives life a purpose or not.

Putting things this way, however, fails to explain why we use the language of meaning to describe lives engaged in activities of worth. Putting things this way there seems to be no connection at all between the question of whether there is a meaning to life and the question of whether individual lives can be meaningful. I believe, however, that there is a connection, that shows itself, or perhaps that consists in the fact that the wish for both kinds of meaning are evoked by the same thought, and that, perhaps, either kind of meaning would be an appropriate and satisfying response to that thought. The thought in question is the thought (the true thought) that we are tiny specks in a vast universe. It is a thought that is apt to be upsetting when it first hits you – at least in part because, looking back from that position, it may seem that one had until then lived "as if" something opposite were true. One had lived perhaps until then as if one were the center of the universe, the sole possessor or source of all value. One had all along assumed one had a special and very important place in the world, and now one's assumption is undermined. One can see how, in this context, one might wish for a meaning to life. For if there were a meaning – a purpose, that is, to human existence that can be presumed to be of great importance, then, by playing a role, by contributing to that purpose, one can recover some of the significance one thought one's life had. Like the pessimistic philosophers I talked about a few minutes ago, I doubt that that path is open to us. But there seems another way one can respond to the thought, or to the recognition of our relatively insignificant place in the universe, that is more promising, and that can, and sometimes does, provide a different kind of comfort. If one lived one's life, prior to the recognition of our smallness, as if one was the center of the universe, the appropriate response to that recognition is simply *to stop living that way.* If one turns one's attention to other parts of the universe – even to other specks like oneself – in a way that appreciates and engages with the values or valuable objects that come from outside oneself, then one corrects one's practical stance. If, in addition, one is partly successful in producing, preserving, or promoting value – if one does some good, or realizes value, then one has something to say, or to think in response to the worry that one's life has no point.

Only if some suggestion like mine is right can we make sense of the intuitions about meaningfulness to which I called attention in the earlier part of this paper. According to those intuitions the difference between a meaningful and a meaningless life is not a difference between a life that does a lot of good, and a life that does a little. (Nor is it a difference between a life that makes a big splash and one that, so to speak, sprays only a few drops.) It is rather a difference between a life that does good or is good or realizes value and a life that is essentially a waste. According to these intuitions, there is as sharp a contrast between the Blob and a life devoted to the care of a single needy individual as there is between the Blob and someone who manages to change the world for the better on a grand scale. Indeed, there may be an equally sharp contrast between the Blob and the monk of a contemplative order whose existence confers no benefit or change on anyone else's life at all. Ironically, along this dimension, Tolstoy fares exceptionally well.

Thus it seems to me that even if there is no meaning to life, even if, that is, life as a whole has no purpose, no direction, no point, that is no reason to doubt the possibility of finding and making meaning in life – that is no reason, in other words, to doubt the possibility of people living meaningful lives. In coming to terms with our place and our status in the universe, it is natural and appropriate that people should want to explore the possibility of both types of meaning. Even if philosophers have nothing new or encouraging to say about the possibility of meaning of the first sort, there may be some point to elaborating the different meanings of the idea of finding meaning in life, and in pointing out the different forms that coming to terms with the human condition can take.

Notes

1. Thomas Nagel has what might be thought to be an even more pessimistic view – viz, that even if there is a God, there is no reason God's purpose should be our purpose, no reason, therefore, to think that God's existence could give meaning, in the right sense, to our lives.

2. E.g., the day I sat down to begin notes on this article, a review of a book by Monique Greenwood, *Having What Matters: The Black Woman's Guide to Creating the Life You Really Want* was in the paper (*Baltimore Sun*, January 16, 2002). The book is offered as a guide to replace Helen Gurley Brown's 1980s manifesto about having it all. Instead of "she who has the most toys wins," Greenwood says "she who has the most joy wins." She is focused on how to "achieve a life with value and meaning."

3. David Wiggins, "Truth, Invention, and the Meaning of Life," in *Proceedings of the British Academy*, LXII, 1976.

4. It seems to me there is a further condition or qualification on what constitutes a meaningful life, though it does not fit gracefully into the definition I have proposed, and is somewhat peripheral to the focus of this essay: namely, that the projects that contribute to a meaningful life must be of significant duration, and contribute to the unity of the life or of a significant stage of it. A person who is always engaged in some valuable project or other, but whose projects don't express any underlying core of interest and value is not, at least, a paradigm of someone whose *life* is meaningful. Here perhaps there is something illuminating in making analogies to other uses of "meaning," for what is at issue here has to do with their being a basis for "making sense" of the life, of being able to see it as a narrative.

5. *Pace* the creepy scene in the movie *American Beauty* of the garbage bag blowing in the wind.

4.4

Intrinsic Value and Meaningful Life

Robert Audi

Philosophers have often been expected to provide a vision of meaningful life. They have also been expected to clarify the difference between lives that are meaningful and those that are not. The problem of providing an adequate theory of meaningful life is particularly difficult on two important assumptions that many philosophers make. The first assumption is that it is possible for a life to be meaningful even apart from the truth of theism. The second is that 'meaning' and its cognates have their primary home in the semantic domain, or at least are clearest in reference to linguistic elements. I am proceeding on both assumptions. As to the second, however, I do not take it to imply that there are *no* clear non-semantic uses of 'meaningful' and 'meaningless', but the assumption does imply that we must be careful to sort the latter out in their own terms and without importing assumptions proper only or mainly to the semantic domain. I want to begin, then, with some examples that will set the stage for a substantive account of meaningfulness in human life.[1] My account will be objectivistic but at the same time sensitive to the importance of subjective elements in a meaningful life, and it will be non-naturalistic but responsive to the importance of natural properties – particularly psychological properties – that substantially color the lives of individuals.

I. Some Dimensions of Meaningfulness

It should be clarifying to begin with a contrast between meaningfulness in relation to human life and something generically similar which may give rise to expectations that a theory of meaningful life should not be expected to satisfy: meaningfulness as a property of

Robert Audi (2005) "Intrinsic Value and Meaningful Life," *Philosophical Papers* 34(3): 331–55.

a linguistic item. Suppose that a man suffers head injuries in an accident and is uttering sounds in a way that seems to represent an effort to communicate. It might be natural to ask whether the sounds are meaningful. If they are, we may go on to ask what they mean. It is apparently a presupposition of an expression's having linguistic meaning that the question *what* it means is clearly intelligible and even that there is something it means – not in the sense of an entity we may call *a meaning*, but in the sense of a relation to something that is the same *in* meaning. That relation is notoriously difficult to explicate. Worse still, a language may have meaningful expressions for which it contains no synonyms; in that case there may be only a hypothetical expression (or one in another language) having the same meaning as the expression in question.[2] Suppose, however, that the presupposition is correct, i.e., that what has meaning means something in particular. Is there a counterpart of meaningfulness in human life – *existential meaningfulness*, as we might call it?

Consider a case of the kind that above all makes the question of meaningfulness in life urgent. A young woman who is repelled by the triviality of the lives of many around her aspires to lead a truly meaningful life. May we ask her what she wants her life to *mean*? She would doubtless understand the question in a general way, but may we expect her to say something analogous to the semantic point that 'The Latinic word "ergo" means *hence*'? I think not. But there is one important similarity: in both the semantic and existential cases meaningfulness implies that there is a way to *make sense of* the phenomenon in question, indeed to *interpret* it in some way. This point provides a broad constraint on an account of meaningfulness in life, but probably nothing more. To be sure, one can imagine the woman replying. 'I want my life to mean being a great pianist' or 'I want it to mean really great piano playing', but this is surely not a specification of the meaning of her life. It is an best a description of what she thinks will *make* it meaningful.

If we are unduly influenced by the analogy between linguistic and existential meaning, we may find something of a paradox here: unlike a linguistic expression, a life can be meaningful even though there is nothing it means. As our example of the aspiring pianist suggests, however, this *paradox of existential meaningfulness* is not deep. For we do know at least what kinds of things are positively relevant to meaningful life. Let me mention some important ones before beginning to develop an account of existential meaningfulness.

First, on any plausible conception of existential meaningfulness, creativity and high-level excellence, i,e., roughly virtuosity in an important activity such as musical performance or scientific research, counts toward meaningfulness. If a person is creative – in the rich sense entailing the production of things that are *both* novel and 'worthwhile' – or excellent in the way a genuine virtuoso is, this counts toward (existential) meaningfulness. It is at least incompatible with utter meaninglessness.[3] A life's being creative in an overall sense is sufficient at least for its being somewhat meaningful. (A great deal could be said about what it is for a life to be creative or positive in the other ways that concern us here, but all the major points in this paper will be compatible with any of the plausible ways of determining this.)

Second, a substantial contribution to reducing suffering in the lives of others or (less clearly) to enhancing their happiness counts toward meaningfulness and is similarly sufficient for at least a somewhat meaningful life. For brevity we might speak here of contributing to *well-being*; no particular theory of well-being, such as hedonism, need be presupposed.

Third, rich human relationships – those exhibiting (at least) good communication, mutual affection and support, and shared activities felt to be mutually rewarding – are positive for meaningfulness. Whether they can also be sufficient in the same way is less clear. Imagine someone's saying, at the end of life, 'I've had rich friendships, loved and been loved, done things throughout my life that were rewarding for me and the others who participated, but my life has been meaningless.'[4] This is initially incredible. It is clear that there is some dimension of meaningfulness that such a life can lack, for instance the excellence sought by our pianist. But I doubt that such a life could be utterly meaningless. (It will be apparent that I take meaningfulness to admit of degrees; that it does seems evident from, among other things, the idea that certain activities make life 'more meaningful'.) To be sure, the imagined sad comment is quite believable as an expression of commitment to some criterion of meaningfulness that is idiosyncratic or inflated or otherworldly. Some people will not believe their lives have been meaningful unless they think those lives have been 'authentic' in some special way, or that they have done truly great things, or have pleased God. We could treat some such considerations as necessary for a *kind* of meaningfulness or perhaps for a certain high degree of meaningfulness of the general kind I have in mind; but they are not necessary for every instance of that kind.

The fourth criterial element I want to describe has already appeared in characterizing a hypothetical reaction to a life that seems, in a general way, meaningful. It is pleasing God. To some readers this criterion may be of merely theoretical interest; to others it will open up a host of considerations bearing on existential meaningfulness. Let me put the point neutrally. Supposing there is a God who is omniscient and omnibenevolent, pleasing God counts toward meaningfulness (and is indeed apparently sufficient for it, at least as applied to the aspects of one's life in virtue of which divine pleasure is earned).[5] This is at least in part because a being who is both perfectly knowledgeable and wholly good could not be pleased with a life that is not meaningful – on the uncontroversial assumption, anyway, that meaningfulness in a life is desirable overall. There is a further assumption supporting this point, namely, that meaningfulness is a consequential property possessed by a life (ultimately) on the basis of its natural properties, such as being without pains of certain kinds, having pervasive physical health of a certain kind, and containing certain kinds of relations with other persons. An omniscient being could not fail to know all the relevant property-ascribing facts and what is consequential upon them, including meaningfulness; an omnibenevolent being could not be pleased with a life lacking meaningfulness or the properties that underlie it. The criterial point I am suggesting does not imply that the desirability of meaningfulness *in* a life entails that every meaningful life is desirable overall. That God's being pleased with a person at a time entails that the person's life is meaningful at least at that time; it thus entails that the life is not utterly meaningless, but it does not entail either that it is meaningful overall or that it is, on balance, a desirable kind of life.

Two points should be made here for clarity. First, that pleasing God is *sufficient* for meaningfulness in a life does not entail that it *grounds* that property, even in part. A mark of a property need not be a ground of it. Second, there is no reason why a theist must hold that it *is* a ground. Indeed, the basic grounds of normative properties can be seen to be natural properties not only on a theistic world view but (arguably) even on some versions of divine command ethics. That God (as understood in the Abrahamic religions, Christianity,

Judaism, and Islam) exists entails the falsity of naturalism as a comprehensive world view, but it does not entail the falsity of its relatively modest claim that normative properties (including meaningfulness as well as, say, obligatoriness) are consequential on natural properties.[6]

Given what has so far been said, we can raise several questions about existential meaningfulness that are important in understanding the subject. One is whether the property is intrinsic or relational. It would be relational if, for example, pleasing God were a necessary condition for its application. Another question is whether it is social or individual, i.e., whether it can characterize a solitary life. On the assumption that meaningfulness is a good thing in a life, we may also ask whether it is an intrinsic or extrinsic good. Finally, we may ask whether the notion is naturalistically explicable, i.e., explicable as a 'descriptive' property as opposed to one like obligatoriness or intrinsic goodness, which, though consequential upon 'descriptive' properties, are apparently not themselves among them.[7] In what follows I will partially answer all of these questions. They are, however, quite large and it should be enough for my purposes to provide an account that indicates data relevant to full-scale answers.

My aim in bringing into the discussion the theistic assumption that pleasing God is sufficient for meaningfulness is to introduce a critical ideal and to bring into view one prominent position regarding existential meaningfulness. This position has received much attention,[8] and my purpose here is to explore meaningfulness in part from a point of view neutral with respect to theism. In doing this, I will keep in mind the kinds of positive grounds for meaningfulness so far introduced.

II.   Philosophical Naturalism and Existential Meaningfulness

Philosophical naturalism may be the dominant intellectual outlook of our times. It is very roughly the view that nature is all there is and the only basic truths are truths of nature.[9] On a common version of the view, our universe consists of matter and energy, and we ourselves are purely biological systems that die and ultimately rot. There may be deep truths about us and our world, but knowledge of them depends on observation and scientific examination. For philosophical naturalists, scientific method is usually the paradigm of a rational way to achieve knowledge, and philosophy itself is continuous with scientific inquiry. Philosophy, to be sure, raises questions that are more general than scientific ones and treats problems not normally addressed by scientists, but it has no unique method of acquiring knowledge that enables it to reveal truths lying outside the province of science.

For many educated people, and certainly for many intellectuals in the Western world, some version of naturalism is presupposed even if not espoused. Can naturalism answer the question whether, under certain conditions, a human life is meaningful? This question is unmanageably broad unless we give it anchors, as I have done in a preliminary way in Section I. I offer no definition of 'meaningful'; but, in the light of what has emerged so far, I think it is plausible to maintain that if we are convinced we know what kinds of elements make a life *good*, at least with respect to some major dimension of goodness, such as creativity or reducing human suffering, we can rationally conclude that we know at least what kind of thing is *sufficient* to make life meaningful in the senses that interest us. If our outlook is naturalistic, what can we say about the good life?

Suppose we think of human life as above all constituted by experiences. Apart from experiences, say in dreamless sleep, we are only minimally alive. We are most alive when we are intensely experiencing something: beautiful music, good conversation, a zesty round in a favorite sport – the list is open-ended. I choose examples of good experiences because the view I propose is that a good life is one in which good experiences (of a certain kind) predominate. I mean experiences that are *intrinsically good*, hence good in themselves. The intrinsically good is commonly contrasted with the instrumentally good: what is good as a means. Something can of course be good in both ways, as reading a novel can be good in itself *and* a means to relaxing. Clearly, what is good will not help to make life meaningful if the only good things are instrumentally good – say, one thing being a good means to a second, that being a good means to a third, and so on to infinity.[10]

It has not been generally noticed that there are things good in themselves that are not intrinsically good in the way experiences are and that indeed seem to be good only on the basis of their potential role in experience. I am looking at a majestic copper beech tree perhaps 100 feet tall and almost as wide near the ground. Viewing it is aesthetically rewarding. The tree is, however, a constituent in my viewing it; it is not a means (in the instrumental sense) to that viewing. It is valuable *in itself*, because of its *intrinsic* aesthetic properties; but it should not be considered valuable in itself in the way the aesthetically rewarding viewing of it is. Its value is *dependent* on the value – actual or hypothetical – of its being experienced in a certain way; the latter value is not (or certainly not in the same way) dependent on the value of anything else. Instrumental value is of course also dependent; but whereas (on the view I am suggesting) a thing having instrumental value (in the standard sense) is, as such, replaceable without ultimate axiologiocal loss by something equally good for producing the relevant intrinsic value, something valuable in itself in the way aesthetic objects are is not thus replaceable. It figures essentially in, and not just as a contingent producer of, the intrinsically valuable experience of it. Taking a medication may have as much instrumental relaxant value as a listening to a mellifluous sonatina, but the former may have no value in itself.

One way to see the difference here is to think of two worlds, one containing just the rewarding experience and what its existence entails – including the person whose experience it is – and the other containing just the tree (and what its existence entails). The second has something good in itself, but not something *basically* good; if the tree could not figure in intrinsically good experiences, it might be instrumentally good – which is *not* to say that it would not be importantly good – but not (on my view) good in itself. I call this kind of goodness, which is a kind of goodness-in-itself that should be taken into account in the theory of value however one connects value with experience, *inherent goodness*. It is non-relational goodness – since there need be no actual relation to any experience of the thing or its properties – but the goodness is not basic, since it belongs to the thing in virtue of its potential to figure positively in an experience having intrinsic value.[11]

Suppose all this is right. What *sorts* of experiences, on a naturalistic view, can be known to be good in themselves? If we try to be scientific and begin with observation, we find that people virtually universally seek certain pleasures and avoid certain pains. The sources of pleasure are different for different people; but even at that, nearly everyone enjoys fellowship, good food, material comforts, and musical or dramatic entertainments. With pain and suffering, we seem more alike; vulnerable to fire and wind, subject to fear of injury and death, agonized by loss of family and friends. Still, should we assume that our natural desires reveal what is good? Certain theists might justify this, but can naturalists?

One might think we could simply argue: if we don't get what we basically want – pleasures and avoidances of pain – we are frustrated, and that is obviously bad. But why *is* it bad? One answer is that it is unpleasant and the unpleasant is intrinsically bad. But this is apparently not an answer a naturalist can give. For the statement that something is *intrinsically* bad (or good) does not seem to be a candidate to be a truth of nature or, specifically, one answerable through using scientific method. A *moderate naturalism*, to be sure, might allow such substantive non-empirical truths provided they do not require countenancing non-natural *properties*. But intrinsic goodness may be one. I leave this open, but that it is non-natural is strongly supported by its apparently being neither an "observable" property, nor the kind that causally explains phenomena, nor a theoretical property of the sort central in scientific theories.[12]

I have said that intrinsic goodness is *apparently* not a natural property because it is at best difficult to show that it is not one. Moreover, even if this is wrong, what I want to say about meaningfulness in human life is largely unaffected. The view I am presupposing is that the question of what kinds of things are intrinsically good is not empirical. It is a question for philosophical reflection (hence *a priori* in a broad sense of that term). This does not imply that we can answer it without *any* experience. We need the often extensive experience necessary for acquiring the concepts essential to understanding the question; and to justify any definite answers, we need at least the experience constituted by reflection.

III.   Pleasure and Pain as Elements in Meaningfulness

It is time to be more concrete. Imagine a child of two burned in a fire. Think of the screams of agony and the intense pain the child suffers. Does anyone really doubt that this suffering is a bad thing? And is the question whether it is a bad thing *scientific*? Now consider the same child being relieved from the pain and, later, mirthfully laughing as its father bounces it up and down, completely keeping it from any awareness of the bandages. These are good things.

My examples are elemental. We adults are pained by many more things than afflict two-year-olds; we also find pleasure in many more. But I see no reason to doubt that our enjoyable experiences are good and our sufferings are bad.[13]

So far, I may seem to be endorsing hedonism. This is roughly the view that pleasures are the only intrinsic goods and pains are the only intrinsic 'bads'. If we take 'pleasure' and 'pain' broadly enough, hedonism is plausible, but I prefer an even broader view: a conception of the good and the bad as the rewarding and the punishing. I leave open whether all rewards are pleasurable and all punishments painful. I also leave open whether there is a sense in which the rewarding is in some way beneficial to the person; but even if this is so, we cannot say that the punishing is necessarily harmful. It is not only non-harmful suffering that can be punishing; so can even shame and embarrassment that do not cause pain or suffering. This is one reason why, even apart from recognition of 'deontological reasons' for action (such as the kind of negative reason provided simply by an act's being a killing of a person), I would not consider the view I am developing utilitarian.[14]

Suppose, however, that we concentrate on pleasure and pain as the least controversially good and bad things (though not, I shall assume, the only ones[15]). We can know that these have value or disvalue on the basis of reflection. But how will such knowledge help us identify what constitutes a meaningful life?

I have said that a good life is one in which good experiences (of a certain kind) predominate. But must a good life be meaningful, and must a meaningful life be good? I do not see how a good life could fail to be meaningful in *some* important sense. A person living it could *think* it meaningless; but this would be a mistake. It would not be reasonable to believe that one has had a good life and *still* consider it meaningless – as opposed to, say not particularly important. Especially for those with the virtue of humility, it is common to think their contributions are not of great value. This is particularly easy regarding intrinsic value, such as beauty in a poem or profundity in an essay. Even great value can be slow in producing uptake or obscured by minor blemishes.

One could, on the other hand, have a meaningful life that is not good. We might manage to contribute much of value, say to art or philosophy or human well-being, and even see that our contribution is of value, yet suffer constantly and fail to satisfy most of our ideals. There is no doubt that such a life *contributes* to the good, but that does not make it good in itself (overall). Such a life may, however, show something of much importance: that lives are meaningful *in relation to the good*, for instance by *either* being good or contributing significantly to something else that is good. The rough idea here is that a life is meaningful on the basis of the good that is realized *in* it or the good created *by* it.[16] I leave open whether, other things being equal, goodness realized in a life counts more toward its meaningfulness than goodness realized by it. Whatever should be said about that, the suggested distinction between intrinsically and instrumentally good lives is worth observing; and a life can be good in both ways.

Given that I have allowed for the possibility that one might live a good life and mistakenly think it meaningless, one might have the impression that I take the way we view our lives to have no significance for their existential meaningfulness. This is not so. A persistent belief that one's life is meaningless (in the relevant sense) may make it less good and may even reduce its meaningfulness. But I do not see that the absence of such a belief is necessary for meaningfulness, even for a high degree of it. Perhaps I need not stress that *believing* one's life is meaningful is insufficient to make it so; but it may be that a well-grounded conviction to this effect can add a dimension of meaning. The conviction of meaning, and certainly the well-grounded sense of it, can be an element in it, even if a minor one in comparison with the major variables.

IV.   Hedonic Qualities and Meaningful Lives

If pleasure is as important a good as most of us think – even if not the only good – we should ask whether *enough* of it in a painless life suffices to make life good. It does not. This is one reason why a good life is not one in which just *any* kind of good predominates. Even apart from brain manipulation that drastically limits one's capacity for pleasure, a person could simply take pleasure in too few things, and those might themselves be minimally rewarding. One could be so constructed – if only by manipulative training – as to get great pleasure from pretty much the same few decent foods, a few unchallenging games, prosaic conversation, and minimal bodily comforts. This might be a pleasant walk through life, but it has little variation in pace, no passion, and no flights of imagination. It exceeds bestial satisfaction, but is far below human aspiration.

These points might recall John Stuart Mill. Reflecting on the possibility of a person's having a great quantity of pleasure that is intuitively of little value, he distinguished higher from lower pleasures. As an empiricist and naturalist, he needed a criterion for distinguishing the higher ones that did not presuppose any route to their discovery through (*a priori*) reflection. He said, "Of two pleasures, if there be one to which all or almost all who have experience of both give a decided preference, irrespective of any feeling of moral obligation to prefer it, that is the more desirable pleasure" (*Utilitarianism*, Chapter 2). Mill's test is good within limits. Preference grounded on unbiased experience is an important basis of comparison. But we cannot wisely or even safely try out all the things we might enjoy, and even our thoughtful preferences are sometimes untrustworthy.

A different criterion for judging pleasures is suggested in a kind of Aristotelian principle: when other things are equal, we should prefer those experiences that engage our more complex faculties, especially our rational faculties – including the aesthetic – in virtue of which we are beings capable of thought and creativity. This is supported by the intuitive superiority of the pleasures of checkers over those of tic-tac-toe, and of the pleasures or hearing Bach over those of hearing Chopsticks. Do we know this principle *a priori*? This is arguable; but however we may argue for it, it is credible on the basis of reflection on the kinds of cases in question.

What if other things are not equal, however? Suppose there is more variety in an evening pursuing two pleasures at a lower level as opposed to one at a higher level of engagement of the faculties, say those of a swim followed by a soap opera, as opposed to those of a seeing a good performance of *Macbeth*. Here reflection alone does not favor any particular answer. It may permit either choice or, in some cases, as where one simply has not seen *Macbeth* in years, favor one option. But one thing reflection does not support is the view that there is *no* value in either kind of pleasure and that experiencing such pleasures does not conduce at all toward a good life.

Still, why should a life with a predominance of enjoyable experiences, even of a kind that engage our higher faculties, be *meaningful*? Might this kind of life still not be what we want – or should want? It might certainly fail to be what we want in the abstract, since we might happen to have an ideal it fails to fulfill. But is it possible to enjoy something and not want it under some description or other, for instance, as a continuation of a good meal or of watching a play?[17] If this is possible, it is not in general rational. To be sure, it can be rational both to want a certain thing and also to want something else *more*. But for the most part, the rationality of a person's desire rises both with increases in the pleasure that the person can see its object to give and with enhancement of the quality – such as the aesthetic or intellectual quality – of the experience or activity yielding the pleasure.

If I seem to be suggesting that we should cultivate not only our capacities for enjoyment but also our desires – the engines of our conduct – I am. Ideally, we would want (for its own sake) only what is good in itself, and we would want *most* among such things those that are *best* in terms of how rewarding their realization is and how probable it is that they can be realized. To be sure, we can rationally regard as intrinsically good something we think no one can bring about, even something we think not possible given the laws of nature. If this poses a problem for my view, one response would be to say that where we think the probability of realization of something is zero, we should not want it or should at least want it to the lowest degree and less than we want anything realizable. Another response, which I prefer, is that in this case we can only wish it would occur, not want it to.

We should, then, educate not only our intellects, but also our sensibilities. We can then appreciate the best things we can achieve and enjoy a wide range of experiences and activities. Educating our desires should go hand in hand with educating our sensibilities. This multi-faceted quest will not only help us achieve the best ends we can, it will also add to the sense of reward in realizing them. The satisfaction of desire, though not itself an intrinsic good, is commonly attended by both a welcome, often pleasant, sense of relief and a sense of fulfillment that, even if it is not precisely enjoyable, can be rewarding and in that general sense good.

V.   Human Relationships

There is an element in life that I have not so far brought into the picture, but it is indicated by one of the four contributory elements listed in Section I. Its role can be discerned in a poetic passage from Matthew Arnold's 'Dover Beach' in which the poet may be seen as contrasting meaningful with meaningless lives:

> Ah, love, let us be true
> To one another! For the world, which seems
> To lie before us like a land of dreams,
> So various, so beautiful, so new,
> Hath really neither joy, nor love, nor light,
> Nor certitude, nor peace, nor help from pain;
> And we are here as on a darkling plain
> Swept with confused alarms of struggle and flight,
> Where ignorant armies clash by night.[18]

Here love between individuals seems the only refuge in a hostile world – indeed a word in which, in darkness, confusion, and ignorance, there is little or no meaning in the lives of its denizens.

I am not making the vague romantic suggestion that love is the meaning of life. But loving and being loved are (very often) sources of unique and great rewards and, usually, of diverse pleasures, Love is, then, among the things that make life good. Insofar as loving and being loved are experiences, they can indeed be intrinsically good; but love, as an emotion or something like an emotional attitude, can, at least for a large proportion of the time it exists, be non-occurrent ('dispositional') and utterly unexperienced. Even then, it is inherently good, hence good in itself and not just as a means to such ends as peaceful coexistence.

Even apart from being good in itself, love can be experienced in a way that makes life meaningful.[19] To love others entails wanting *their good* for its own sake and tends to help us realize that good. We do not have to think of what we want for them *as* good; but how their life goes in terms of, especially, pleasure and pain, must matter to us. It must, indeed, be *felt* as important even if one's intellectual commitments require taking it to be, in some cosmic sense, insignificant. It seems intuitively clear that if we see life as going well for those we love, we cannot rationally deny that there is some goodness in the world or reasonably hold that life is meaningless.

This point seems clearest where we love deeply and strongly, but it holds for love in general. Its plausibility may be supported in a number of ways, but let me simply connect love with meaningfulness by way of care. Loving implies caring in a particular way; caring about others in that way entails tending to take their well-being as significant in a sense very close to that of meaningfulness understood existentially. If life goes badly for them, and especially if life also goes badly for us, we can rationally hold that there is too *little* goodness in the world, or perhaps none. But even this does not commit one to taking life to be meaningless. On the contrary, if these are the reasons for our disappointment, we might instead say that life has or can have a meaning which, in our own existence, we have failed to realize. We can regard *a* human life as meaningless without regarding human life *itself as* meaningless.

In the last paragraph I have spoken not of meaningfulness *in* life but – as is common – of the meaningfulness *of* life. The latter notion invites us to consider human life *as such* to have a meaning, say on the basis of fulfilling a divine purpose.[20] The former notion has been my focus. One reason for this focus is that I take meaningfulness to be conferred on a life largely (though not entirely) by elements, including activities of our own, that are up to us, at least indirectly. By contrast, the 'meaning of life' sought by some is conferred either by God or by some cosmic or other force beyond our control. For some writers on this topic, it would be plausible to say that human life has meaning if, say, the guilty are duly punished or the human species is evolving toward a higher form.

It is not unnatural to call the kinds of cases I am describing instances of *metaphysical meaningfulness*. This has not been my topic, significant though it is. It may be that if any life is existentially meaningful, then there is some 'metaphysical meaning' in the world. But the striking point is that apparently human life could have metaphysical meaning even if no *individual* life is existentially meaningful. This certainly applies to the case of our species evolving toward a higher level. As the clumsy drawings of a toddler can be a stage on the way to artistic excellence, a whole species could have terrible, meaningless lives on its route to a higher place for their descendants. It also seems possible that, without meaningful lives, there could be wrong-doing of a kind that could be met with cosmic justice. The meaning conferred on human life in the abstract in such cases is not of nearly as great philosophical interest as existential meaningfulness. By contrast, the theistic assumption I have introduced provides a route to metaphysical meaning which, owing to the conditions for an omniscient, omnibenevolent being's being pleased, does not allow the kind of disconnection between existential and metaphysical meaning that my cases portray.

Suppose I have been correct in characterizing meaningfulness in a life. We are then perhaps not far from being able to understand the notion of life as such having meaning – a kind of metaphysical meaning – at least in one of its major aspects. To say that human life has meaning may be to say that it *can* be meaningful in the way I have described. The kind of meaning human life might have entirely by virtue of a relation, such as pleasing God or being a culmination of a grand historical process, is not my main concern. But insofar as the notion is clear, the kind of meaning in question may be plausibly thought to be realizable at least in part on the basis of human life's fulfilling or having the potential to fulfill the sufficient conditions for existential meaningfulness described in this paper. An omniscient, omnibenevolent God, for instance, would tend to be pleased by creativity, by excellence, and by contributions to human well-being, and displeased by the frustration and suffering of the innocent.

To be sure, there are people, including some theists, who may think that life is meaningful only if it has a place in God's plan. There may be other special notions of meaningful life such that a life meaningful on my conception may lack meaning on those notions. My concern here is to do justice to the kinds of data indicated in Section I and to show how the general notion of the meaningfulness of life can be clarified by examining ways in which a given life can be meaningful. Even those who think that life is meaningful only given theism (or some alternative otherworldly metaphysical view) can grant that we have been exploring existential meaning in one important sense of that phrase.[21]

VI.   Unity in Variety

We have seen some sufficient conditions for meaningfulness in life, at least in a certain measure: certain kinds and degrees of creativity or excellence, of contribution to the well-being of others, of interpersonal relations, and (at least hypothetically) of theologically defined success. I have left open that there may be other sufficient conditions; I suggest as a hypothesis that any other sufficient condition will imply at least a significant degree of partial satisfaction of at least one of these criteria. An 'important' life, for instance, might be of necessity meaningful, but I doubt that a life could be important in the relevant sense (the sense rich enough to imply meaningfulness) without being, say, substantially contributory to human well-being or marked by significant creativity or excellence. Might we go so far, then, as to say that some of these criteria are, by themselves, necessary for a meaningful life?

This is not clear. Certainly no significant measure of creativity is necessary, desirable though that is. And could a solitary life not be meaningful? I think it could be, especially given sufficient creativity. If there were great creativity, moreover, but it did not lead to contributions to human well-being, would this not still be sufficient for meaningfulness? I think that it might be. Would we have to say, however, that it contributes to the well-being of the creator? That is likely, but not necessary. My creation could be fraught with pain in the making of it and deeply disappointing to me in the contemplation of it. I might then undervalue it. It is a good *in* my life, whether I see it as such or not. Still, that one good element in my life, even if important enough to make my life meaningful, does not entail a significant contribution to my well-being.

If there are no specific conditions that are necessary for existential meaningfulness, then the hope of arriving at a traditional analysis that provides a set of conditions individually necessary and jointly sufficient is unfulfillable. This need not be a great disappointment. Consider a major approach in ethics. W.D. Ross did not think there is any one characteristic in virtue of which right acts are right, but he did not despair of understanding rightness (in the sense of obligatoriness). Instead, he presented and explicated a set of '*prima facie* duties'.[22] The counterpart idea here is that a number of factors conduce to, and are in some cases sufficient for, meaningfulness, and others, such as persisting pain with no compensating effects, detract from it and in some cases may preclude it. Moreover, just as, when there are conflicts of duties, an act can be obligatory even when it breaks a promise, a life can be meaningful even when it is bereft of creativity or even persistently painful. The person might still contribute substantially to human well-being, love those helped, and find the effort perennially fulfilling. In both the ethical and the existential cases, there are multiple criteria and there can be tradeoffs among the positive and negative ones.

The analogy to the theory of obligation is useful in another way. If Rossian intuitionism succeeds in giving a plausible account of major aspects of the criteria for obligation, it still leaves some reflective people dissatisfied with the lack of a unifying framework. The same kind of reaction may be natural here. I have addressed the unity problem for intuitionism elsewhere, by appeal both to Kantian ethics and to the theory of value,[23] but I am not suggesting any close analogue of Kantian principles to bring into the picture (at least apart from theistic assumptions on which I do not here wish to rely). I have, however, suggested that a sufficiently clear and adequately rich conception of the good life is the best overall idea to bring to the understanding of existential meaningfulness, though I have noted that a sufficiently troubled, pained life might be meaningful yet not, in the overall sense, good. (An Aristotelian view of the good life is one plausible model here, but explicating it would require a paper in itself.) Even here, the notion of the good is still central; the point is that as important as it is in understanding meaningful life, the good realized therein – say, by helping others – may be accompanied by so much that is bad, for instance pain and frustration, that the life in question is not good on the whole.

There is, however, a normative notion somewhat less theoretical than that of the good which can be used both to unify some of what we have seen about the meaningful life and to evoke plausible hypotheses that extend it. The notion is that of the rewarding. Consider the idea that a meaningful life is a rewarding life – one rewarding for the person living it.[24] There is a kind of inconsistency in calling a life rewarding but meaningless. Might a life, however, be meaningful but not (in any way) rewarding?

Recall the case of a person who is perennially creative but frustrated and pained, or consider a person who is a substantial contributor to the well-being of others but deeply unhappy and without friends. Such lives can be meaningful on any plausible view, but are they rewarding? We can say so only if we take objective 'successes' to be rewarding even when not felt as such. I think that sometimes we may. Reward is not desire satisfaction, not even felt desire satisfaction. Moreover, one surely need not *feel* rewarded by a meaningful life or believe such a life to be meaningful. Still, *is* a life rewarding when the person suffers in the ways in question? We may, to be sure, describe some people as unaware of the rewards of their occupation or inappreciative of the rewards of their hard work. But it is not clear that we should describe the kind of painful, frustrated existence I have in mind as a rewarding life even when it is graced with the positive elements I am imagining in relation to vocational achievements.

It may be, however, that we can still say that such a mixed life *contains* rewards and that these are central for its meaningfulness. The pains and frustrations are a misfortune, but not an insurmountable barrier to either the existence of major rewards *in* the lives in question or to the overall meaningfulness of those lives. Perhaps the most we can say by way of summary here is this: the rewardingness of a life is sufficient for its meaningfulness, but rewardingness is necessary for meaningfulness only in application to some important subset of the kinds of good things in a life that, like creativity and rich human relationships, contribute to its meaningfulness. Given how much remains to be said about the rewarding, even this summary does not constitute the core of a traditional analysis. But the notion of the rewarding is clarified by what is said in this paper; it invites many further ideas that help in understanding existential meaningfulness; and it is intuitively useful in discerning the important elements in that concept.

The view of meaningful life I have outlined is not naturalistic, but it is compatible with naturalism. It is also not itself theistic, but is compatible with theism. A theistic perspective, particularly one in which love is central, may add to the grounds for taking many lives – or even human life in general – to be meaningful (and may bring with it a dimension of meaningfulness I have not considered here), but its absence need not subtract anything from the position I have presented. There is a route to meaningful life, and to understanding the concept thereof, available to naturalists. Unlike most theists, they must take life to end with bodily death. But that just limits value and meaning to finitude. Finite values can still be great.

There is, moreover, a kind of immortality of things of value that even non-theists can countenance. Institutions such as universities, practices such as cooperative intellectual inquiry, and love as a unifying fabric in human life, can survive indefinitely. One can found institutions, endow them with programs, and give them ideals; all of these can carry one's memory forward. Intellectual inquiry can go on forever, and the contributions made to it by creative thinkers may take a place among its permanent elements. As long as there are persons, there can be ideas and ideals, joy as well as suffering, excellence in action, and love among people.

These possibilities imply no personal immortality, but they do show one way in which we can try to make a permanently enduring contribution to things we love. They provide, moreover, a naturalistic interpretation for a line from Yeats' 'Sailing to Byzantium' that is perhaps as close as we can come to a kind of naturalist's prayer:

> Gather me into the artifice of eternity.

For those to whom beauty is an anchor of meaning in life, a different kind of reassurance might be felt in Emily Dickinson's poetic credo,

> Estranged from Beauty – none can be –
> For Beauty is Infinity –
> And power to be finite ceased
> Before identity was leased. (c. 1879).

Here is the indomitable faith that we are bound up with the beauty of nature as a condition of our very identity as persons.

For some people, eternity is a possibility for their personal futures. But for anyone, the future need not be finally closed, and the quest to fulfill one's desires, even if short, can be meaningful. Philosophical reflection reveals a plurality of goods to be pursued and a multitude of evils to be avoided. It helps us to see what is worth wanting and to compare the various good and bad things life presents. It does not by itself motivate love, but it can vivify the good things we should want for those we love and it can clarify the evils we should seek to eliminate from their lives. And for some, philosophical reflection itself, like the pursuit of the arts and sciences, is among the things that make life meaningful.

Notes

1. For a wide-ranging discussion of the dimensions of meaningful life that includes a non-denominational treatment of the religious dimension of meaning, see John Cottingham, *On the Meaning of Life* (London: Routledge, 2003). A critical appraisal of this book is provided by Thaddeus Metz, "Baier and Cottingham on the Meaning of Life," *Dispulatio* 1, 19 (2005), 215–28.

2. My wording here may raise the question whether a language can contain expressions that are *not* meaningful. I want to leave this open. But consider 'ugh!' It belongs to English and has a *function*; but although it may be used to express disgust, it does not *mean*, e.g., 'I'm disgusted by that'. A linguistic item with meaning has a function, but the converse is not true.

3. I take 'meaningful' and 'meaningless' to be, in the existential cases, contraries rather than contradictories. Some mixed lives may have elements of meaning mixed with vacuous periods in a way that makes neither term applicable (or at least not clearly so – both are of course vague).

4. Rewardingness is not equivalent to pleasure, though what is rewarding is typically enjoyable. I have characterized the notion in some detail in *The Architecture of Reason* (Oxford: Oxford University Press, 2001), csp, pp. 96–7. Instrumentalists about practical reason might hold a kind of desire-satisfaction view of rewardingness, but in Ch. 5 and (more extensively) in "Prospects for a Naturalization of Practical Reason: Humean Instrumemtalism and the Normative Authority of Desire," *International Journal of Philosophical Studies* 10, 3 (2002), 235–63, I argue that this kind of view cannot account for intrinsic value (of which I take rewardingness to be a kind) or for reasons for action.

5. I leave open here whether the criterion should be taken to provide a necessary condition as well, in part because it would seem that a meaningful life might not be good and the person living it might on that count fail to please God (I here take a criterion, as is not uncommon, to be a consideration that is a basic kind of positive evidence, even if not necessarily by itself a sufficient condition, for what it is a criterion of – it need not be by itself necessary either). 1 also omit the usual third member of the theistic triad, omnipotence, since it does not figure in the points essential here.

6. I argue for this in *Rationality and Religious Commitment* (Oxford: Oxford University Press, 2011).

7. This is not the place to try to clarify the descriptive-normative contrast, and it is enough for my purposes here that there is a *prima facie* distinction. If normative properties are ultimately causal, the distinction is at least less important; that they are not (and, by implication, that the distinction has this much force) is argued in my "Ethical Naturalism and the Explanatory Power of Moral Concepts," in my *Moral Knowledge and Ethical Character* (Oxford: Oxford University Press, 1997).

8. For critical discussion of this theistic view and many references to relevant, literature, see Thaddeus Metz, "Recent Work on the Meaning of Life," *Ethics* 112 (2002), 781–814, and "The Immortality Requirement for Life's Meaning," *Ratio* XVI (2003), 161–77.

9. I have discussed this characterization of naturalism and explored several versions of the position in "Philosophical Naturalism at the Turn of the Century," *Journal of Philosophical Research* (2000).

10. Two points about value should he made here. First, arguably, there cannot be an infinite chain of instrumental values because any chain of instrumental value connections (as opposed to a chain of causes and effects) must terminate in something of intrinsic value (otherwise we have merely a series of means to further means). Second, I omit the apparent possibility of circle since it seems impossible for a thing to be a means to itself in the way it would have to he if, e.g., *A* could be a means to *B*, *B* a means to *C*, and *C* a means to *A*. Cf. Aristotle's point that "we do not choose everything because of something else since, if we do, it will go on without limit, making desire empty and futile ..." (*Nicomachean Ethics*, Book I, 1094a2011). For explication of these valuational notions see my "Intrinsic Value and Reasons for Action," *Southern Journal of Philosophy* 41, Supplement (2003), 30–56.

11. I have explicated inherent goodness and made a case for its non-basic status in "Intrinsic Value and Reasons for Action." As to the problem of why a hallucinatory experience of such a tree is not as good in itself as a veridical one, see Ch. 11 in *Moral Knowledge and Ethical Character*. It should already be plain that a hallucinatory experience may differ from its veridical counterpart in *inherent* value.

12. The nature of normative properties such as intrinsic goodness and the case for their having causal power are explored in my "Ethical Naturalism and the Explanatory Power of Moral Concepts." It may help to note that I there distinguish between the projects of naturalizing *moral explanations* (and by implication other explanations by appeal to normative statements such as that something is intrinsically good) and the project of naturalizing moral (and normative) properties. The former might be naturalized by giving a certain role to the natural properties on which normative ones are consequential; the success of this project would not entail the naturalizability of moral (or normative) properties themselves.

13. The status of pleasure in someone else's pain (*Schadenfreude*) is a difficult case: such pleasure can be good *in* the life of (say) the sadist without being good overall. I have discussed this problem in Ch. 4 of *The Good in the Right: A Theory of Intuition and Intrinsic Value* (Princeton: Princeton University Press, 2004).

14. This is not to say that my view has no affinities with a form of utilitarianism. For a related discussion of utilitarianism in relation to existential meaningfulness, see Thaddeus Meiz, "Utilitarianism and the Meaning of Life," *Utilitas* 15 (2003), 50–70.

15. I have argued for this view in "Intrinsic Value and Moral Obligation," Ch. 11. of *Moral Knowledge and Ethical Character*.

16. This formulation is rough in part because (among other things) it does not take account of wayward causal chains and does not address the question how *much* good is required. It is not clear that a life's creating a great deal of good by just *any* causal process will suffice (though the word 'create' itself tends to rule out wayward chains); and although there is plausibility is holding that the more good a life has, the more meaningful the life is, other things equal, it may he true that there is, for some possible lives, a point at which more good would not add meaningfulness, however significant the addition might be in other respects.

17. There is at least one exception: at the last moment at which one is enjoying something one need not want to continue it. I have discussed this point and the relation between pleasure and desire in some detail in Ch. 4 of *The Architecture of Reasan* (Oxford: Oxford University Press, 2001).

18. Matthew Arnold, "Dover Beach," in A.J.M. Smith (ed.), *Seven Centuries of Verse* (NY: Charles Scribner's Sons, 1947), p. 476. One might wonder how the speaker can address someone its "love" and still say the world contains no love; presumably there is a contrast between the personal relationship, in which the speaker finds meaning in an important sense – which includes their love – and the world at large.

19. In "Recent Work on the Meaning of Life," Metz cites Harry Frankfurt as holding that "One's life is significant if one loves something" (p. 793 in Metz's paper). I am not implying this; one might love something quite without value, for instance. I doubt that loving is intrinsically or even inherently good; my point concerns the ability of some kinds of love to confer value or meaning or both on a life.

20. In "Religion Gives Meaning to life," Lois Hope Walker says, "By 'meaning' in life I mean that life has a purpose. This is some intrinsic rationale or plan to it." See her (pseudonymous) contribution to Louis P. Pojman, ed., *Quest for Truth*, 4th edn. (Oxford: Oxford University Press, 1999).

21. One standard of meaningfulness I have not considered in this connection is autonomy. Those who think that autonomy (or something similar, such as "authenticity") is crucial may, though they need not, take it to succeed in conferring meaningfulness only on the basis of implying the kinds of grounds of meaningfulness I have described. Mere self-government, say in the service of highly whimsical desires with trivial objects, would not significantly count toward meaningfulness. I have presented an account of autonomy and its relation to normative anchoring concepts that supports this conclusion in "Autonomy, Reason, and Desire," *Pacific Philosophical Quarterly* 72, 4 (1992, 247–71), reprinted in *Moral Knowledge and Ethical Character*.

22. See W.D. Ross, *The Right and the Good* (Oxford: Oxford University Press, 1930), Ch. 2. For extensive discussion of Ross's views and a defense of a moderate intuitionism in ethics, see my *The Good in the Right*, esp. Chs. 2 and 3.

23. This unity problem for intuitionism is dealt with in Chs. 3 and 4 of *The Good in the Right*.

24. It should be noted that rewardingness *for* a person is not doxastic, like rewardingness *to* a person (in one main use); it is perspectival. We could have a life meaningful for us even if we believed it was not. I do not speak of meaningfulness for a person, but the same distinction will apply if we use that locution.

4.5

God and the Meaning of Life

Erik J. Wielenberg

1   The Meanings of Life

It is often maintained that if God does not exist then human life is meaningless. There are a number of ways one might interpret this claim, depending on how one understands what it is for a human life to have meaning. Under one interpretation, for a human life to have meaning is for it to have a purpose that is assigned by a supernatural being. When a life has meaning in this sense we can say that it has *supernatural meaning*. Socrates apparently believed that his life had supernatural meaning, and he speculated about what the purpose of his life might be during his famous trial:

> [I]f you put me to death, you will not easily find another who … clings to the state as a sort of gadfly to a horse that is well-bred and sluggish because of its size, so that it needs to be aroused. It seems to me that the god has attached me like that to the state, for I am constantly alighting upon you at every point to arouse, persuade, and reproach each of you all day long.[1]

According to the Christian tradition, the life of Jesus had supernatural meaning: Among its purposes was to atone for the sins of humanity. Indeed, according to some versions of Christianity, every human life shares a common purpose: to glorify God and enjoy Him forever.[2]

Under another interpretation, for a human life to have meaning is for it to bring goodness into the universe. When a life has meaning in this sense, the universe is better than it would

Erik J. Wielenberg (2005) "God and the Meaning of Life," Chapter 1 in *Value and Virtue in a Godless Universe*, Cambridge: Cambridge University Press, pp. 14–37.

have been had the life not been lived. We can say that a life of this sort has *external meaning*. Again according to Christian tradition, the life of Jesus, in addition to having supernatural meaning, had external meaning. According to that tradition, a universe in which Jesus lived the life He did is far better than a universe in which no such life is ever lived.[3]

Under a third interpretation, for a human life to have meaning is for it to be good for the person who lives it and for it to include activity that is worthwhile. When a life has meaning in this sense, the individual is better off having lived than had that person never existed at all. Moreover, the life is one in which something worthwhile is accomplished. It is a life that has a point. It is the urge to live a life like this that is revealed in the expression "I want to *do* something with my life." We can say that a life of this sort has *internal meaning*. This concept may seem similar to external meaning, but the two are distinct. It is possible for a life to have internal meaning yet lack external meaning. Suppose a person engages in worthwhile activity that brings him pleasure and gives his life internal meaning. Suppose further that what gives his activity worth is that through it he accomplishes some meaningful goal. But suppose that if he had never lived, the same goal would have been accomplished by someone else who would have enjoyed accomplishing it just as much as he did. In this case, his life lacks external meaning because the universe would have been just as good if he had never lived. Yet his life has internal meaning. At least initially, it appears that it is also possible for a life to have external meaning but lack internal meaning. Such a life might be lived by someone who sacrifices his own happiness for the sake of others.

These, then, are three of the most natural understandings of what it is for a human life to have meaning. With these in hand, we are ready to consider the oft-made claim that without God, human life is meaningless.

2   Four Arguments that Life Lacks Internal Meaning without God

One way of understanding the claim that the nonexistence of God renders human life meaningless is as the thesis that if God does not exist, then no human life has internal meaning. A wide range of arguments might be offered in support of this thesis. The first of these is the *final outcome argument*. To get the flavor of this argument, consider the following remarks made by William Lane Craig (2004) in a talk called "The Absurdity of Life Without God" delivered at the Academy of Christian Apologetics:

> Scientists tell us that everything in the universe is growing farther and farther apart. As it does so, the universe grows colder and colder, and its energy is used up. Eventually all the stars will burn out, and all matter will collapse into dead stars and black holes. There will be no light at all. There will be no heat. There will be no life, only the corpses of dead stars and galaxies, ever-expanding into the endless darkness and the cold recesses of space, a universe in ruins. The entire universe marches irreversibly toward its grave. So not only is each individual person doomed, the entire human race is doomed. The universe is plunging toward inevitable extinction. Death is written throughout its structure. There is no escape. There is no hope. If there is no God, then man, and the universe, are doomed. Like prisoners condemned to death row, we stand and simply wait for our unavoidable execution. If there is no God, and there is

no immortality, then what is the consequence of this? It means that the life that we do have is ultimately absurd. It means that the life we live is without ultimate significance, ultimate value, ultimate purpose.[4]

Suppose we think of a person's life as a series of events. Some of these events are brought about by the individual, while others are caused by external forces. Roughly, a life may be characterized as the sum total of all the things that happen to an individual while that person is alive. But, goes the argument, the value of a series of events depends entirely on the value of the very last state of affairs to which that series causally contributes. If that final outcome is valuable, then the events that led up to and contributed to it may have value. If that final state of affairs is devoid of value, then similarly all the events that led up to it are worthless.

Without God there is no afterlife of any kind. Consequently, every human life ends with the permanent cessation of the individual's conscious experience and mental activity (at least of any interesting sort). Without God, every human life terminates with the grave and the annihilation of the conscious self. The last outcome to which any human life contributes is an utterly static, lifeless, extropic, frozen universe. Since such an outcome is entirely devoid of value, it follows (according to this argument) that all human lives are entirely devoid of value and hence lack internal meaning. In a Godless universe that ends with a whimper, no human life is worth living.

A second line of reasoning is based on the idea that a life has internal meaning only if it has supernatural meaning. Suppose that your life lacks supernatural meaning. This makes you a man (or woman) without a mission. There is nothing you are supposed to be doing with your life, no higher cause you have been called to serve, no divine quest to which you have been assigned. This means that there are no criteria for evaluating whether your life is a success or a failure – which in turn implies there are no circumstances under which your life would be a successful one. Without some assigned goal, it doesn't much matter what you do: Yours is a pointless existence. A life without an externally assigned goal cannot have internal meaning. In a universe without God, without supernatural beings of any kind, there is no one suitably qualified to assign purposes to human lives. Consequently, in a universe like this, no human life can have internal meaning. We can call this the *pointless existence argument*.[5]

A third type of argument is described (and ultimately rejected) by Susan Wolf in her paper "The Meanings of Lives." Wolf writes:

> [A] life can be meaningful only if it can mean something *to* someone, and not just to *someone*, but to someone other than oneself and indeed someone of more intrinsic or ultimate value than oneself.... If there is no God, then human life, each human life, must be objectively meaningless, because if there is no God, there is no appropriate being *for whom* we could have meaning.[6]

The fundamental premise of this line of reasoning is that a life has internal meaning only if a suitably significant being cares about or takes an interest in that life. More specifically, a life has internal meaning only if an omnipotent, omniscient, morally perfect being cares about it. If no such being exists, then naturally no life is cared about by such a being, and hence no life has internal meaning. We may call this the *nobody of significance cares argument*.

A fourth and final argument, which I shall call the *God as the source of ethics argument*, is based on the idea that God must be the ultimate source of all good and evil and of all right and wrong in the universe. If God does not exist, then nothing can be good or evil and nothing can be right or wrong. [...]

3   Richard Taylor's Way Out: Creating Your Own Meaning

There are at least three interesting ways of responding to the previous three arguments. One of these is proposed by Richard Taylor (2000) in the final chapter of his book *Good and Evil*. In that chapter, titled "The Meaning of Life," Taylor discusses the case of Sisyphus, a tragic figure regularly evoked in discussions of the meaning of life. Sisyphus betrayed the gods by revealing their secrets to humankind and was sentenced to an eternity of frustration. Sisyphus was required to roll a large stone up a hill. Whenever the stone was almost at the top it would roll back down, and Sisyphus would have to begin again. Over and over, up and down the hill, went Sisyphus, accomplishing nothing. The tale is supposed to provide us with a striking example of a life devoid of internal meaning.[7]

Taylor suggests that Sisyphus' life would have internal meaning if the gods gave him a potion that filled him with an overwhelming and unending desire to roll the stone up the hill. This way Sisyphus' existence would be filled with activity of a sort he desires, and he would get to spend eternity doing exactly what he wanted to do. Moreover, this route to internal meaning is available (in principle at least) to anyone. To the question of how to make a life worth living, Taylor answers: Live in precisely the way that you most *want* to live. The chapter and the book end with these inspiring words:

> You no sooner drew your first breath than you responded to the will that was in you to live. You no more ask whether it will be worthwhile, or whether anything of significance will come of it, than the worms and the birds. The point of living is simply to be living, in the manner that it is your nature to be living. ... The meaning of life is from within us, it is not bestowed from without, and it far exceeds in both its beauty and permanence any heaven of which men have ever dreamed or yearned for.[8]

Taylor's proposal, then, is that life can have internal meaning by virtue of a correspondence between a person's desires and that person's activity. The internal value of an individual's life is directly proportional to the degree to which that individual is engaged in desired activity.[9] To the final outcome argument, Taylor would reply that looking to the final situation to which a life causally contributed is not the proper way to assess the value of that life for the one who lived it:

> If the builders of a great and flourishing civilization could somehow return now to see archaeologists unearthing the trivial remnants of what they had accomplished with such effort – see the fragments of pots and vases, a few broken statues, and such tokens of another

age and greatness – they could indeed ask themselves what the point of it all was, if this is what it finally came to. Yet, it did not seem so for them then, for it was just the building, and not what was built, that gave their life meaning.[10]

To the pointless existence argument, Taylor would reply that we ourselves are qualified to assign a purpose to our lives. We do not need a supernatural being to hand down such a purpose to us. A life can have internal meaning even if it lacks supernatural meaning. To the nobody of significance cares argument, Taylor would respond that *we* are sufficiently significant to make our lives meaningful. What is important is not whether God cares about your life but rather whether *you* care about it (in the appropriate way).

Taylor's view of what gives human life internal meaning has an interesting implication for philosophy. Specifically, it implies that there is a real danger involved in reflecting on the question of whether one's life has any meaning. This danger is illustrated by the case of Leo Tolstoy (2000). In *My Confession*, Tolstoy describes how, at the height of his literary success, during a time when he was "on every side surrounded by what is considered to be complete happiness," he found himself increasingly nagged by questions of whether there was any point to his life.[11] As Tolstoy reflected more and more on these questions, he began to view them with increasing seriousness:

> The questions seemed to be so foolish, simple, and childish. But the moment I touched them and tried to solve them, I became convinced, in the first place, that they were not childish and foolish, but very important and profound questions in life, and, in the second, that no matter how much I might try, I should not be able to answer them. Before attending to my Samara estate, to my son's education, or to the writing of a book, I ought to know why I should do that. So long as I did not know why, I could not do anything. I could not live.[12]

Finally, as Tolstoy describes it, he became convinced that nothing was worth doing and lost interest in everything. Tolstoy uses a parable to describe his predicament in the following powerful passage:

> Long ago has been told the Eastern story about the traveler who in the steppe is overtaken by an infuriated beast. Trying to save himself from the animal, the traveler jumps into a waterless well, but at its bottom he sees a dragon who opens his jaws in order to swallow him. And the unfortunate man does not dare climb out, lest he perish from the infuriated beast, and does not dare jump to the bottom of the well, lest he be devoured by the dragon, and so clutches the twig of a wild bush growing in a cleft of the well and holds on to it. His hands grow weak and he feels that soon he shall have to surrender to the peril which awaits him at either side; but he still holds on and sees two mice, one white, the other black, in even measure making a circle around the main trunk of the bush to which he is clinging, and nibbling at it on all sides. Now, at any moment, the bush will break and tear off, and he will fall into the dragon's jaws. The traveler sees that and knows that he will inevitably perish; but while he is still clinging, he sees some drops of honey hanging on the leaves of the bush, and so reaches out for them with his tongue and licks the leaves. Just so I hold on to the branch of life, knowing that the dragon of death is waiting inevitably for me, ready to tear me to pieces, and I cannot understand why I have fallen on such suffering. And I try to lick that honey which used to give me pleasure; but now it no longer gives me joy … the honey is no longer sweet to me. I see only the inevitable dragon and

the mice, and am unable to turn my glance away from them. That is not a fable, but a veritable, indisputable, comprehensible truth. … The two drops of honey that have longest turned my eyes away from the cruel truth, the love of family and of authorship, which I have called an art, are no longer sweet to me.[13]

In Tolstoy's case, philosophical questions and reflection caused the loss of the desire to engage in the activities that had previously sustained him. If Taylor's view about what gives life internal meaning is correct, then philosophical reflection, by taking away Tolstoy's passion for living, rendered him unable to live an internally meaningful life. If Taylor is right, then the moral of the story of Tolstoy is: Don't think too hard about whether your life has meaning, or you may find that the very pondering of the question has given the question a negative answer. Taylor also says, "[Y]ou no more ask whether it [your life] will be worthwhile, or whether anything of significance will come of it, than the worms and the birds."[14] Perhaps we should take this not as a *description* of human life but rather as a *prescription* for how to live. Socrates is famous for, among other things, his assertion that "an unexamined life is not worth living."[15] Taylor might add his own dictum: An *over*-examined life is not worth living. But can this really be right? Some detractors of philosophy might claim that devoting yourself to it entirely is a good way to render your life meaningless, but could it really be true that philosophical reflection could render all of your *other* activities worthless?

I think not; for it turns out that Taylor's view about what gives life internal meaning is mistaken. This may be seen by comparing two cases. The first case comes from an excellent article on Aristotle's views on the good life by Stephen Darwall (1999). Darwall describes a photograph that he clipped from *The New York Times*:

> It shows a pianist, David Golub, accompanying two vocalists, Victoria Livengood and Erie Mills, at a tribute for Marilyn Horne. All three artists are in fine form, exercising themselves at the height of their powers. The reason I saved the photo, however, is Mr. Golub's face. He is positively grinning, as if saying to himself, "And they *pay* me to do this?"[16]

Compare the case of David Golub with a variant of the case of Sisyphus: The case of the grinning excrement-eater.

The grinning excrement-eater, we may suppose, has been condemned to an eternity of eating excrement. As Taylor envisions them being merciful to Sisyphus, however, the gods have shown mercy on the excrement-eater by instilling in him a true passion for eating excrement. He gobbles it down night and day – he simply can't get enough! Both the pianist and the grinning excrement-eater are engaged in activity for which they have a genuine passion; each is doing what he most wants to do. Imagine these two lives, one filled with the sort of activity in which David Golub is engaged in Darwall's photo, the second filled with the grinning excrement-eater's favorite pastime. If we are to accept Taylor's proposal, we must conclude that both lives have internal meaning. But this conclusion is hard to swallow. If you were offered a choice between these two lives, would you be indifferent? Would the two lives seem equally worthwhile to you? If you are like me, the answer is no, in which case you must reject Taylor's proposal. It is simply going too far to say that whether a life has internal meaning is entirely a matter of the attitude of the person who lives the life.[17]

Taylor's view derives some initial plausibility from the way he introduces it. We are asked to compare a Sisyphus who hates stone-rolling with a Sisyphus who loves it. Given such a choice of Sisyphi, any rational person would prefer to be the Sisyphus to whom the gods show mercy and who comes to love stone-rolling.[18] Similarly, given a choice between a life as an excrement-eater who hates eating excrement and a life as a grinning excrement-eater, any rational person would choose the latter. Given that you have to roll stones or eat excrement for an eternity, it is better if you enjoy that sort of thing. Taylor offers a tidy explanation for these intuitions: The internal meaning of a life depends entirely on whether the agent is doing what he wants to do.

But when we make other comparisons – as between pianist Golub and the grinning excrement-eater – it becomes obvious that Taylor's proposal is faulty. A grinning excrement-eater who passes up a pianist's life for the sake of eating excrement is a fool, and if the gods get him to make such a choice by instilling in him a passion for eating excrement, then theirs is a cruel joke rather than an act of mercy. No matter how great his passion, no matter how big his grin as he spoons it down, he should be an object of pity rather than of envy. If we want to find an adequate way of dealing with internal meaning we must look elsewhere.

4   Peter Singer's Way Out: Meaning through Eliminating Pain

In the final two chapters of his book *How Are We to Live? Ethics in an Age of Self-Interest*, Peter Singer (1995) develops and defends an alternative conception of how a human life can have internal meaning. To explain Singer's view, it will be helpful to make use of the familiar distinction between *extrinsic* value on the one hand and *intrinsic* value on the other. Roughly, the intrinsic goodness (or evil) of a thing is the goodness (or evil) it has in virtue of its own nature, in and of itself.[19] In his classic work *Principia Ethica*, G. E. Moore (1903) describes a certain type of thought experiment one can use to determine the intrinsic value, if any, of a given thing. This is the so-called "isolation test," and the method is that of "considering what value we should attach to [something], if it existed in absolute isolation, stripped of all its usual accompaniments."[20] The extrinsic value of a thing, by contrast, is the value a thing has in virtue of how it is related to other things. The most familiar type of extrinsic value is *instrumental* value – the value a thing has in virtue of causing something else that is intrinsically valuable.[21]

Singer holds the view that "[w]e can live a meaningful life by working toward goals that are objectively worthwhile."[22] Singer takes *pain* to be intrinsically evil, and he maintains that the reduction of the total amount of avoidable pain in the universe is objectively worthwhile. So according to Singer, one feature of at least one kind of internally meaningful life is that it reduces the overall amount of avoidable pain in the universe. But this is not a sufficient condition for internal meaningfulness. Elsewhere Singer reminds his readers of "the old wisdom that the way to find happiness or lasting satisfaction is to *aim* at something else, and *try* to do it well."[23] Later, Singer mentions "the need for a *commitment* to a cause larger than the self."[24] These passages indicate that on Singer's view, to live an internally meaningful life, one must *intend* to reduce suffering – one must have this as a conscious goal. A person who pursues only his own pleasure and accidentally reduces the total amount of suffering in the universe is not living an internally meaningful life. Although Singer does not explicitly say so, certain remarks he makes suggest that he would also hold that one must have at least some degree of *success* in achieving one's pain-reducing goal.[25] At the heart of Singer's view, then, is this principle:

(S)   An activity of S's, A, has internal meaning for S just in case (i) in doing A, S is trying to accomplish goal G, (ii) G is objectively worthwhile, and (iii) A in fact leads to G.[26]

According to Singer, one way – in fact the best way – to make your life worth living is to devote it to the reduction of avoidable pain in the universe. Singer calls this "an ethical life," and he declares that "living an ethical life enables us to identify ourselves with the grandest cause of all, and … is the best way open to us of making our lives meaningful."[27] Singer's view seems to be that the reduction of avoidable suffering is the most objectively worthwhile goal there is, and hence devoting one's life to it is the best way to bring internal meaning to one's life. Since this can be done whether God exists or not, the absence of God does not render all human lives internally meaningless.[28]

To establish his position, Singer adopts a method similar to the one used over two thousand years ago by Aristotle (1962) in his masterpiece *Nicomachean Ethics*. Early in the *Ethics*, Aristotle introduces three kinds of lives that humans might live: A life devoted to the pursuit of bodily pleasure; a life devoted to political activity; and a life devoted to contemplation.[29] Aristotle examines each of these and tries to determine which of the three lives is the best. For much of the *Ethics*, it appears that Aristotle has selected the life of political activity as the best, but (in a surprise move that has puzzled commentators for two and a half millennia) Aristotle ultimately selects the life of contemplation as the best.[30] In similar fashion, Singer considers a variety of activities and tries to determine which, if any, hold out the prospect of providing internal meaning. The activities Singer considers include drug and alcohol use, shopping, competition (both financial and athletic), psychotherapy, and, of course, the pursuit of the ethical life. In examining each of these, Singer seems to be concerned mainly with whether the activity produces a lasting sense of fulfillment. Singer reaches the conclusion that only the ethical life meets this condition, hence it alone (of the activities considered) can bring internal meaning to one's life.

It is important not to misunderstand what Singer is up to here. It can appear that we are back to Taylor's view that what gives a life internal meaning is simply one's attitude toward that life. Singer could be misunderstood as maintaining that what makes one's life internally meaningful is that it produces a sense of fulfillment. But Singer's position is more subtle than this. Recall the case of pianist David Golub, whose photograph Stephen Darwall described in a passage quoted in Section 3. The sentence immediately following the passage I quoted reads "Mr. Golub's delight is a *sign* of his activity's value, not what *makes* it good."[31] Similarly, Singer ought to be understood as viewing a lasting sense of fulfillment as a *reliable indicator* of internal meaning – much in the way that Descartes (1960) took clarity and distinctness in his ideas to be a reliable indicator of truth.[32] But what if the gods' potion gave Sisyphus a lasting sense of fulfillment as he rolled stone? And what about a fulfilled excrement-eater? Singer is not committed to the absurd conclusion that such beings live worthwhile lives. His argument does not depend on the claim that a sense of fulfillment is a reliable indicator of internal meaning in every possible world; rather, he needs only the weaker claim that it is a reliable indicator in the actual world. And in the actual world, fruitless stone-rolling and excrement-eating do not, in general, produce feelings of fulfillment, lasting or otherwise.

From time immemorial. Western philosophers have claimed that a life devoted to the acquisition of bodily pleasure is not a particularly worthwhile life for a human being to live. In the Platonic dialogue *Philebus*, Socrates imagines a creature living at the bottom of the ocean with just enough of a mind to experience mild pleasure, but utterly unable to reason, remember, or even form beliefs. Plato (1993) has Socrates say that one who lived such a life "would thus not live a human life but the life of a mollusk or one of those creatures in shells that live in the sea."[33] Aristotle characterizes a life devoted to bodily pleasure as "a life suitable to cattle."[34] Elsewhere he says that "even a slave, can enjoy bodily pleasures. … But no one would grant that a slave has a share in happiness."[35] Aristotle thought of slaves as less than fully human. The consensus, then, of the two greatest ancient Greek philosophers is that a life devoted to pleasure might be acceptable for mollusks, cows, and sub-humans, but it is no way for a human being to live.[36] The tradition continues in the twentieth century with Robert Nozick's (1977) well-known example of "the experience machine," a virtual reality device that produces any desired experience in the mind of someone hooked up to it. Nozick says: "We learn that something matters to us in addition to experience by imagining an experience machine and then realizing that we would not use it."[37]

Even those philosophers traditionally associated with hedonism are careful to make clear that it is not the unbridled pursuit of bodily pleasure alone that they recommend. Epicurus (1964), for example, in his "Letter to Menoeceus" writes:

> When we say that pleasure is the end, we do not mean the pleasure of the profligate or that which depends on physical enjoyment – as some think who do not understand our teachings, disagree with them, or give them an evil interpretation – but by pleasure we mean the state wherein the body is free from pain and the mind from anxiety.[38]

Similarly, in *Utilitarianism*, John Stuart Mill (1979), defending utilitarianism against the charge that it is a "doctrine worthy only of swine," notes that there are different qualities of pleasure, and that bodily pleasure is of the lowest quality and hence is the least valuable kind of pleasure: "[T]here is no known Epicurean theory of life which does not assign to the pleasures of the intellect, of the feelings and imagination, and of the moral sentiments a much higher value as pleasures than to those of mere sensation."[39]

At this point it might be objected that, at least for the purposes of Singer's argument, the testimony of all these philosophers should not be given much weight. After all, they are *philosophers* – precisely the sort of people who *haven't* devoted their lives to the pursuit of bodily pleasure. Wouldn't the testimony of those who have pursued pleasure be more relevant to the question of whether such a life can bring lasting fulfillment?

One of the strengths of Singer's argument is that he considers the testimony of those who have devoted themselves to the various activities he discusses. I will not repeat all of Singer's examples here, but one of the most remarkable bits of testimony comes from Tom Landry, the extremely successful coach of professional football's Dallas Cowboys:

... Even after you've just won the Super Bowl – *especially* after you've just won the Super Bowl – *there's always next year*. If 'Winning isn't everything. It's the only thing', then 'the only thing' is nothing – emptiness, the nightmare of a life without ultimate meaning.[40]

One piece of interesting testimony not discussed by Singer comes from an infamous devotee of bodily pleasure – the Marquis de Sade (1992). Here is a man who surely has some insight into whether the pursuit of bodily pleasure can bring lasting fulfillment! In de Sade's story *Justine*, the heroine falls into the hands of four lascivious friars who hold her captive and take advantage of her. It is telling that de Sade has one of the friars make the following remark to Justine:

Spending the night with one woman always makes me want another in the morning. Nothing is quite as insatiable as our urges; the greater the offerings we make to them, the hotter they burn. Of course, the outcome is always pretty much the same, yet we always imagine that there is better just around the corner. The instant our thirst for one woman is slaked is also the moment when the same drives kindle our desire for another.[41]

The similarity between these remarks and the remarks of Tom Landry is striking. In both cases we get a portrait of men driven by relentless desires that reappear the instant they are satisfied. More significantly, a sense of fulfillment seems to be entirely absent: The desires reappear, often stronger than before, precisely because the satisfaction of the previous desire fails to yield fulfillment.

Turning to the ethical life, Singer discusses the cases of Henry Spira, a life-long activist, and Christine Townend, who, together with her husband, sold her expensive house and flew off to India for five years of volunteer work. According to Singer, both find fulfillment in their devotion to the ethical life. Of Spira, Singer writes: "When, on my occasional visits to New York, I stay with him and his cat in his Upper Westside rent-controlled apartment, I always find him thinking about strategies for getting things moving ahead, and relishing the next challenge. I leave in good spirits."[42] Like Taylor's book, Singer's ends with an inspiring message. Indeed, it is clear that Singer is calling for a kind of ethical revolution:

If 10 percent of the population were to take a consciously ethical outlook on life and act accordingly, the resulting change would be more significant than any change of government. ... Anyone can become part of the critical mass that offers us a chance of improving the world before it is too late. ... You will find plenty of worthwhile things to do. You will not be bored, or lack fulfillment in your life. Most important of all, you will know that you have not lived and died for nothing, because you will have become part of the great tradition of those who have responded to the amount of pain and suffering in the universe by trying to make the world a better place.[43]

In response to the pointless existence argument, Singer, like Taylor, would reply that we do not need a supernaturally bestowed purpose for our lives to have internal meaning. But Singer's basis for this claim is different from Taylor's. Singer's claim is that the presence of avoidable intrinsic evil in the universe takes the place of a supernatural commander as the thing that renders our lives internally meaningful: "There is a tragic irony in the fact that we can find our own fulfillment precisely because there is so much avoidable pain and suffering in the universe, but that is the way the world is."[44] Similarly, it does not matter whether an omnipotent, omniscient, morally perfect being cares about our lives or not. Preventing suffering is worthwhile regardless of whether there is any such being around to pay attention to it. So we should not be concerned by the nobody significant cares argument. In response to the final outcome argument, Singer would reply that such an argument arbitrarily places an undue amount of importance – indeed *all* of the importance – on the *final* state of affairs to which a life leads. But why single out the very last outcome as the only one that matters?

> Suppose that we become involved in a project to help a small community in a developing country to become free of debt and self-sufficient in food. The project is an outstanding success, and the villagers are healthier, happier, better educated, economically secure, and have fewer children. Now someone might say: 'What good have you done? In a thousand years these people will all be dead, and their children and grandchildren as well, and nothing that you have done will make any difference.' … We should not, however, think of our efforts as wasted unless they endure forever, or even for a very long time. If we regard time as a fourth dimension, then we can think of the universe, throughout all the times at which it contains sentient life, as a four-dimensional entity. We can then make that four-dimensional world a better place by causing there to be less pointless suffering in one particular place, at one particular time, than there would otherwise have been. … We will have had a positive effect on the universe.[45]

Regardless of whether we accept all that Singer has to say, we are now in a position to see that the final outcome argument fails. That argument fails because it is based on what Paul Edwards (2000) calls a "curious and totally arbitrary preference of the future to the present."[46] There are a variety of ways of assessing the relative importance of various times. Singer suggests that we ought to view them as being of equal importance. Another view ranks the present and the near future as most important. This point of view lies behind the now-clichéd command to "seize the day." Yes, death awaits us all, and in the end we will turn to nothing more than food for worms – but the proper reaction to this fact is not to give up but rather to get moving! Marcus Aurelius (1805) expressed this idea in the second century c.e. this way: "Do not act as if you had ten thousand years to throw away. Death stands at your elbow."[47] A third perspective views the final moments of time (or, if time has no end, the final *outcome*) as the most important, and it is this perspective that lies behind the final outcome argument. But of the three perspectives, the last is surely the *least* reasonable. A diagnosis of why this manner of thinking can seem reasonable comes later, but for now it is sufficient to see that it is not. Returning to Singer's remarks, the proper response to the question what good have you done? is I've made these villagers happier than they would have been otherwise – and what things will be like a thousand years from now is utterly irrelevant to this fact. Isn't it better that the Nazi Holocaust ended when it did rather than in, say, 1970 – regardless of what the world will be like a million years from now? I can remember occasions in junior high gym class when a basketball or volleyball game became particularly heated and adolescent tempers flared. Our gym teacher sometimes attempted to calm us down with such rhetorical questions as, "Ten years from now, will any of you care who won this game?" It always struck me that a reasonable response to such a query would be, "Does it really matter *now* whether any of us will care in ten years?" In much the same vein, Thomas Nagel (1979) suggests that "it does not matter now that in a million years nothing we do now will matter."[48]

There are many questions that might be asked about Singer's position. Is a sense of fulfillment really a reliable indicator of internal meaning? Is the ethical life as it is characterized by Singer really the *best* way to bring internal meaning to one's life? With respect to the second question, consider that the painless annihilation of all life would drastically reduce the amount of avoidable suffering in the universe – yet surely Singer would not endorse this as an objectively worthwhile goal! Perhaps the ethical life needs to be characterized a bit more carefully. Nevertheless, Singer's position is superior to Taylor's in at least one respect: It provides a straightforward and plausible model that allows us to reject the first three internal meaning arguments from the Section 2. At the heart of Singer's view is the idea that committing oneself to making the universe a better place overall – increasing the amount of intrinsic goodness in the universe (or decreasing the amount of intrinsic evil) – can bring internal meaning to one's life. Since one can do this even if one's life lacks supernatural meaning, and no omnipotent being cares about one's life, and the *final* outcome to which one's life will contribute is valueless, it follows that the final outcome argument, the nobody of significance cares argument, and the pointless existence argument all fail.

5   Aristotle's Way Out: Intrinsically Good Activity

A third view suggests another way of responding to these arguments. This view is the oldest, simplest, and perhaps the most powerful of the responses considered in this chapter. It is found in Aristotle's *Nicomachean Ethics* – and one doesn't have to read very far to find it. The *Ethics* begins with these lines:

> Every art or applied science and every systematic investigation, and similarly every action and choice, seem to aim at some good. … But it is clear that there is a difference in the ends at which they aim: in some cases the activity is the end, in others the end is some product beyond the activity.[49]

At the end of this passage Aristotle divides activities into two categories – those that are good because of what they produce, and those that are good in and of themselves. In this brief remark, Aristotle suggests a possibility not considered by either Taylor or Singer. It is a simple yet profound insight:

> Aristotle's Insight: Some activities are *intrinsically good*.

Activities of this sort are worth engaging in *even if they lead to nothing of value*. They would be worthwhile even if they had no consequences at all. This suggests a third way of bringing internal meaning to one's life: Engage in intrinsically good activities, activities that are worth doing for their own sake. It is part of the very nature of such activities to bring internal meaning to one's life.

In his surprise ending to the *Ethics*, Aristotle singles out contemplation (*theoria*) as the activity with the greatest amount of intrinsic value.[50] This activity may be very roughly characterized as reflection on the basic nature of the universe. This activity is not the acquisition of knowledge; rather, it is reflection upon what one already knows. One of the more interesting arguments Aristotle offers to support his claim that this is the best sort of activity goes like this:

> We assume that the gods are in the highest degree blessed and happy. But what kind of actions are we to attribute to them? Acts of justice? Will they not look ridiculous making contracts with one another, returning deposits, and so forth? Perhaps acts of courage – withstanding terror and taking risks, because it is noble to do so? Or generous actions? But to whom will they give? It would be strange to think that they actually have currency or something of the sort. Acts of self-control? What would they be? Surely, it would be in poor taste to praise them for not having bad appetites. If we went through the whole list we would see that a concern with actions is petty and unworthy of the gods. Nevertheless, we all assume that the gods exist and, consequently, that they are active; for surely we do not assume them to be always asleep. … Now, if we take away action from a living being, to say nothing of production, what is left except contemplation? Therefore, the activity of the divinity which surpasses all others in bliss must be a contemplative activity, and the human activity which is most closely akin to it is, therefore, most conducive to happiness.[51]

Whatever activity the gods engage in is intrinsically the best kind of activity. The gods must engage only in contemplation; therefore, contemplation must intrinsically be the best kind of activity. Thus, Aristotle singles out for the highest praise the activity of the successful philosopher – reflection on what he has learned. In reaching this conclusion, Aristotle outdoes his great teacher, Plato. In the *Republic*, Plato had argued that philosophers *ought to be kings*.[52] Aristotle goes further to suggest that philosophers *are* like *gods*. Alone among the great stinking masses of humanity, philosophers are capable, at least briefly, of rising above their place in the universe and doing the sort of thing that normally is reserved for the gods. It is clear that in the Aristotelian universe philosophers hold a special place indeed!

There is an interesting contrast worth noting between the view expressed here by the great pagan philosopher and the Christian tradition. Aristotle praises the attempt to transcend one's station in the universe and to become like the gods. But according to one strand of thought in the Christian tradition, this sort of thing is harshly condemned. Indeed, according to traditional Christianity, it is precisely this sort of thing that led to the Fall of Man. For instance, in John Milton's (1956) classic *Paradise Lost*, the angel Raphael warns Adam against probing the secrets of the universe:

> But whether these things, or whether not,/Whether the sun predominant in heaven/Rise on the earth, or earth rise on the sun,/… Solicit not thy thoughts with matters hid;/Leave them to God above, him serve and fear;/…Think only what concerns thee and thy being;/Dream not of other worlds, what creatures there/Contented that thus far hath been reveal'd/Not of earth only, but of highest heav'n.[53]

Later, the serpent convinces Eve to eat the fruit from the Tree of Knowledge by telling her that if she and Adam eat the fruit "ye shall be as gods/Knowing both good and evil as they know."[54] And, of course, it is Eve's eating of the fruit that leads to disaster for all of humanity. The message is clear: Mind your own business, be grateful for what God has revealed to you, and, whatever you do, do not, under any circumstances, attempt to transcend your station in the universe.

What, then, are we to make of Aristotle's proposal that contemplation is intrinsically the best sort of activity? In his discussion of the case of Sisyphus, Richard Taylor considers a scenario in which the wretched man's labors *do* produce something. Taylor imagines that Sisyphus' efforts are directed toward the production of a beautiful and enduring temple, and he writes:

> And let us suppose he succeeded in this, that after ages of dreadful toil, all directed at this final result, he did at last complete his temple, such that now he could say his work was done, and he could rest and forever enjoy the result. Now what? What picture now presents itself to our minds? It is precisely the picture of infinite boredom! Of Sisyphus doing nothing ever again, but contemplating what he has already wrought and can no longer add anything to, and contemplating it for an eternity![55]

Taylor suggests that contemplation of the completed temple would be no more worthwhile than Sisyphus' pointless uphill toil in the original version of the story, and I am inclined to agree. Furthermore, the contemplation that Aristotle praises seems to me to have much in common with Sisyphus' contemplation of his completed temple. I don't see much intrinsic worth in either activity. If the gods who condemned Sisyphus were gods of the sort Aristotle envisions, then the fate to which they condemned him was no worse than their own.

Still, even if we reject the details of Aristotle's proposal, we can accept Aristotle's insight. If there are activities available to us during our lifetimes that are intrinsically valuable, then our lives can have internal meaning even if God does not exist. Even if there is no supernatural commander to assign purposes to our lives or a suitably Significant Deity to care about our lives, the existence of intrinsically good activities would make it possible for us to bring internal meaning to our lives. I submit that there are such activities.

What are some intrinsically good activities? And how can I prove that my favored list is the right one? As to the first question, I have nothing particularly insightful or novel to say: My list of intrinsically good activities would include falling in love, engaging in intellectually stimulating activity, being creative in various ways, experiencing pleasure of various kinds, and teaching.[56] To my list it might be objected: Aren't you simply listing things you happen to enjoy doing? The answer is no. There are plenty of things I enjoy doing but do not consider intrinsically worthwhile, and I suspect that a bit of reflection will reveal that the same is true of you. In my own case, playing video games fits the bill. For many years now I have had a passion for video games, and I can spend hour after hour playing them. But I do not regard this activity as intrinsically worthwhile, and I think that a life devoted entirely to it would be a wasted one. In fact, precisely because I enjoy it so much and yet consider it intrinsically worthless, I intentionally refrain from purchasing home video game systems and from installing games on my computer. I know that if video games were readily available to me I would waste countless hours on this frivolous pastime. So the list of activities that I consider to have intrinsic worth is not the same as the list of activities I enjoy.

And how can I justify my list of intrinsically worthwhile activities? I am afraid I have no philosophical proof for, say, the proposition that falling in love is intrinsically good. As has often been pointed out, though, many of the things we know are such that we cannot give an adequate philosophical proof for their truth. The method I recommend for deciding which activities are intrinsically good is a version of G. E. Moore's isolation test described in Section 4: To see if an activity is intrinsically good, consider whether you would find it worthwhile *even if it had absolutely no consequences.* If it seems to you that it *would* be worthwhile, then you have a good candidate for an intrinsically good activity on your hands. Claims about what is intrinsically good are the axioms of ethical theory; they are the starting points, the first principles. As such, they are unlikely to be the sorts of things that can be *proved.* Nevertheless, it is perfectly consistent to say that some activities are intrinsically valuable – and that we *know* what some of these are.

Aristotle's distinction between activities that are good because of what they produce and activities that are intrinsically good helps us to understand why the final outcome argument can seem convincing even though, as I contend, it is a bad argument. The final outcome argument can be made to seem convincing by focusing on activities that are not intrinsically good. If one becomes convinced that all the activities available to us in our earthly lives are of this sort, then the final outcome of all these activities can seem to be of the utmost importance. The reason is that, convinced that the activities that make up our lives are intrinsically worthless, we may believe that the only way they can be worthwhile at all is if they lead to a worthwhile final outcome. Toward the beginning of this chapter I quoted from William Lane Craig's talk "The Absurdity of Life Without God." In that same talk Craig discusses Beckett's play *Waiting for Godot.* Craig uses the play to explain what he thinks human life would be like without God: "During this entire play, two men carry on trivial, mind-numbing, banal conversation while waiting for a third man to arrive who never does. And our lives are like that, Beckett is saying. We just kill time waiting. For what? We don't know."[57]

Notice that the activity in this example is trivial, mind-numbing, and banal. The activity Beckett singles out is obviously *intrinsically* worthless: Any worth it might have would derive only from the arrival of Godot. Because Godot never shows, up the activity is altogether worthless. In likening all of human life to the play, Craig implies that all the activities available to us during our earthly lives are intrinsically worthless. In fact, this is the unstated assumption underlying each of the internal meaning arguments we have been discussing. All three arguments assume that no activity available to us on earth has any intrinsic value. Such activities can have value only if it is bestowed on them from the outside – by being part of a divine plan or an object of concern on the part of a Significant Deity, or by leading to something else of value. But it is precisely this assumption that should be rejected. If the characters waiting for Godot had been in the process of falling in love with each other, would the fact that Godot never showed up have rendered their activity worthless – would the entire evening have been a complete waste? Hardly.

Recall Tolstoy's example of the traveler who falls into a well. The nature of the traveler's predicament depends on what activities are available to him while he is trapped. Recall another part of the story: The traveler sees some drops of honey hanging from a bush and reaches out and licks them. In likening his own situation to that of the trapped traveler,

Tolstoy added the proviso that "the honey is no longer sweet to me" – that is, none of the activities available to him had any intrinsic worth.[58]

Ask yourself this question: If you found yourself in the traveler's predicament, would you have a preference concerning the presence or absence of honey? If the final outcome argument is correct, it should not matter to you. But I suspect you are like me and you do have a preference for honey. As a matter of contingent fact, some humans may be unable to engage in activities that are intrinsically good: They may be like travelers trapped in the well with no honey in sight. But this is hardly an essential feature of the human condition. Since you are reading this book it is likely that you do not face such a situation. There is honey all around you; you have but to reach out and lick it. You do not need God to give your life internal meaning.[59]

The main character of the Spike Jonze (2002) film *Adaptation* is Charlie Kaufman, a screenwriter trying to write a screenplay based on Susan Orlean's book *The Orchid Thief*. At one point in the film, Kaufman, struggling to complete his script, attends a screenwriting seminar. During the seminar Kaufman raises his hand and asks the following question: "[W]hat if a writer is attempting to create a story where nothing much happens, where people don't change, they don't have any epiphanies. They struggle and are frustrated and nothing is resolved. More a reflection of the real world. ..." Kaufman is unable to complete his question because he is interrupted by the seminar's leader. The speaker's response can be construed as a response to Craig and Tolstoy in the spirit of Singer and Aristotle. It also serves as a fitting end to this chapter:

> Nothing happens in the real world? Are you out of your f***ing mind? People are murdered every day! There's genocide and war and corruptionl Every f***ing day somewhere in the world somebody sacrifices his life to save someone else! Every f***ing day someone somewhere makes a conscious decision to destroy someone else! People find love: People lose it, for Christ's sake! A child watches her mother beaten to death on the steps of a church! Someone goes hungry! Somebody else betrays his best friend for a woman! If you can't find that stuff in life, then you, my friend don't know much about life![60]

Notes

1. Plato, *Euthyphro, Apology, Crito*, trans. F. J. Church (New York: Macmillian, 1948), 37.
2. According to the Shorter Scottish Catechism, at any rate.
3. See, for instance, Alvin Plantinga, *Christian Belief*, 489.
4. William Lane Craig, "The Absurdity of life Without God," hisdefense.org/audio/wc_audio.html (accessed March 26,2004). Some of the ideas contained in Craig's talk are also present in a speech given by the character Meursault toward the end of Albert Camus's novel *The Stranger*, trans. Stuart Gilbert (New York: Random House, 1946), 152.

5. For an interesting critical discussion of the view that a life is meaningful to the extent that the one who lives it fulfills some divinely assigned purpose, see Thaddeus Metz, "Could God's Purpose Be the Source of Life's Meaning?" *Religious Studies* 36 (2000), 293–313.
6. Susan Wolf, "The Meanings of Lives," www.law.nyu.edu/clppt/program2003/readings/wolf.pdf (accessed March 26, 2004), 21.
7. The example also suggests that supernatural meaning is not sufficient for internal meaning. Sisyphus has been given a mission by the gods, but it is a mission designed to strip his life of any value for him.

8. Richard Taylor, *Good and Evil* (Amherst, NY: Prometheus Books, 2000), 333–4.

9. In *Atheism, Morality, and Meaning* (Amherst, NY: Prometheus Books, 2002), 201, Michael Martin suggests that Taylor's proposal here is that "[a] life is meaningful if and only if it is lived in the way it is natural to live it." I think my own formulation is preferable because it is clearer and seems to fit better with Taylor's discussion of the case of Sisyphus. Taylor's idea is that the gods could give Sisyphus' life meaning by instilling in him the *desire* to roll stones.

10. Taylor, *Good and Evil*, 332.

11. Leo Tolstoy, "My Confession," in *The Meaning of Life*, 2nd edn., ed. E. D. Klemke (Oxford: Oxford Univ. Press, 2000), 12.

12. *Ibid.*, 12.

13. *Ibid.*, 13–14.

14. Taylor, *Good and Evil*, 333.

15. Plato, *Apology*, 45.

16. Stephen Darwall, "Valuing Activity," in *Human Flourishing*, eds. E. F. Paul, F. D. Miller, Jr., and J. Paul (Cambridge: Cambridge Univ. Press, 1999), 176.

17. Michael Martin reaches a similar conclusion, noting that Taylor's proposal "errs on the side of lenience" because it "allows practically any life … to be meaningful." See Martin, *Atheism*, 205–6. For a related discussion with a similar conclusion, see John Cottingham, *On the Meaning of Life* (New York: Routledge, 2003), 16–18.

18. Taylor, *Good and Evil*, 323.

19. I use the term "intrinsic value" to express what Thomas Hurka calls the "strict definition" of intrinsic value; see Thomas Hurka, "Two Kinds of Organic Unity," *The Journal of Ethics* 2:4 (1998), 301. Some contemporary philosophers have suggested that the term "intrinsic value" can be used to refer to kinds of value that do not depend exclusively on a thing's intrinsic properties. Hurka is open to this suggestion and Shelly Kagan offers an extended argument for it in his "Rethinking Intrinsic Value," *Journal of Ethics* 2:4 (1998), 277–97. For present purposes, I will simply stipulate that "intrinsic value" means intrinsic value in the strict sense.

20. G. E. Moore, *Principia Ethica* (Cambridge: Cambridge Univ. Press, 1903), 91.

21. For a useful discussion of various varieties of extrinsic value, see Ben Bradley, "Extrinsic Value," *Philosophical Studies* 91 (1998), 109–26.

22. Peter Singer, *How Are We to Live? Ethics in an Age of Self-interest* (Amherst, NY: Prometheus Books, 1995), 195.

23. *Ibid.*, 213 (my emphasis).

24. *Ibid.*, 216 (my emphasis).

25. *Ibid.*, 195. For example, in discussing the case of Sisyphus, Singer suggests that Sisyphus could bring meaning into his life by actually *building* a beautiful and enduring temple.

26. A similar (though not identical) conclusion is reached by Wolf (see "Meanings," 6–12). Like Taylor, Wolf approaches the issue of meaningfulness by first considering meaninglessness; instead of Sisyphus, she considers (among others) the case of "The Blob," who "spends day after day, or night after night, in front of a television set, drinking beer and watching situation comedies."

27. Singer, *How?*, 218.

28. A similar proposal is made by Kai Nielsen, who remarks that "A man who says, 'If God is dead, nothing matters,' is a spoilt child who has never looked at his fellowman with compassion" (*Ethics Wihout God*, rev. edn. (New York: Prometheus Books, 1990), 117–18).

29. Aristotle, *Nicomachean Ethics*, trans. Martin Ostwald (Englewood Cliffs, NJ: Prentice Hall, 1962), 8, NE 1095bI5–20.

30. *Ibid.*, NE 10.6–8.

31. Darwall, "Valuing Activity," 176 (my emphasis).

32. Rene Descartes, *Discourse on Method and Meditations*, trans. L. J. Lafleur (New York: Macmillan, 1960), 92.

33. Plato, *Philebus*, trans. D. Frede (Indianapolis: Hackett, 1993), 16, 21d.

34. Aristotle, *Ethics.*, 8, NE 1095b20.

35. Ibid., 288, NB 1177a5–10.

36. The Roman philosopher Boethius concurred (see *The Consolation of Philosophy*, trans. V. E. Watts (New York: Penguin, 1969), 90).

37. Robert Nozick, *Anarchy, State, and Utopia* (New York: Basic Books, 1977), 44.

38. Epicurus, *Letters, Principal Doctrines, and Vatican Sayings* (New York: Macmillan, 1964), 57, 131b.

39. John Stuart Mill, *Utilitarianism* (Indianapolis: Hackett, 1979), 8.

40. Kohn, Alfie. (1986). *No Contest: The case against competition* (Boston: Houghtin Mifflin), 111.

41. Marquis de Sade, *The Misfortunes of Virtue and Other Early Tales*, trans. D. Coward (Oxford: Oxford Univ. Press, 1992), 99–100.

42. Singer, *How?*, 220.

43. *Ibid.*, 235.

44. *Ibid.*, 222.

45. *Ibid.*, 231.

46. Paul Edwards, "The Meaning and Value of life," in *Meaning of Life*, ed. E.D. Klemke, 140.

47. Marcus Aurelius, *Meditations*, trans. J. Collier (London: Walter Scott Publishing Co. Ltd., 1805), 52.

48. Thomas Nagel, *Mortal Questions* (Cambridge: Cambridge Univ. Press, 1979), 11.

49. Aristotle, *Ethics*, 3, NE 1094al–5.

50. This interpretation is somewhat controversial, but for a compelling defense of it see Richard Kraut, *Aristotle on the Human Good* (Princeton; NJ. Princeton Univ. Press, 1989).

51. Aristotle, *Ethics*, 292–3, NE 1178b10–25.

52. Plato, *Republic*, trans. G. M. A. Grube (Indianapolis: Hackett, 1992), 148, 473d.

53. John Milton, *Paradise Lost* (Chicago: The Great Books Foundation, 1956), 187, Book VIII, lines 160–80.

54. *Ibid.*, 222, Book IX, lines 708–9; also see Genesis 3:4–5.

55. Taylor, *Good and Evil*, 331.

56. An activity can be *both* intrinsically and extrinsically good. I should note that my main goal here is not to provide a complete answer to the question "what is the meaning of life?" but instead to make plausible the claim that life can have meaning even if God does not exist. For more systematic secular accounts of the meaning of life, see Paul Kurtz, "The Meaning of life," in *In Defense of Secular Humanism* (Amherst, NY: Prometheus Books, 1983a), 153–68; and Owen Flanagan, *The Problem of the Soul* (New York: Basic Books, 2002), 279–86.

57. Craig, "Absurdity of Life."

58. Tolstoy, "My Confession," 14.

59. See also Wolf, "Meanings," 23.

60. Spike Jonze, dir. *Adaptation*. Film. (Columbia Pictures, 2002).

4.6

The Varieties of Non-Religious Experience

Richard Norman

Are atheists missing something important? If theism does 'make a difference to the flow and perceived significance of someone's life', is it a difference which leaves the atheist at a disadvantage?

The claim that secular humanists are indeed missing something could take two forms – either that the atheist's experience is *incomplete* or that it is *opaque*. The incompleteness claim I shall to some extent concede. There are indeed kinds of experience which theists can have – or at any rate could be having if their beliefs were true – but from which the atheist is debarred. I shall argue, however, that these are only particular and limited aspects of the five fundamental dimensions of human experience which I am going to discuss. The essential core of those five kinds of experience is as available to the atheist as to the theist. Without the core experiences our lives would indeed be diminished and impoverished, but just because they are essentially human, they are experiences in which we can all share. The aspects which are exclusively theistic, on the other hand, may well be kinds of experience which it would be good to have, but they are ones which we can live without. I do not have a precise criterion for distinguishing between experiences which it would be *good to have* – ones which theists think they have and atheists cannot have – and experiences which are *integral components of human life*. I hope however that my discussion of the particular examples will show the distinction to be a plausible one.

The *opacity* claim would be that though human beings do characteristically have the important kinds of experience which I have listed and will discuss, the atheist fails to understand the essentially religious nature of such experiences. The claim thus takes the form of a transcendental argument: that the possibility of such experiences presupposes the existence of a god or gods. I shall aim to show that any such transcendental argument is

Richard Norman (2007) "The Varieties of Non-Religious Experience," Chapter 6 in John Cottingham (ed.), *The Meaning of Theism,* Malden, MA: Blackwell Publishing, pp. 91–110.

unsound. These essential human experiences are just that – forms of *human* experience, integral features of human life, aspects of what it is to be human. We do not need belief in a god in order to make sense of them or to explain their possibility.

The Authority of the Moral 'Ought'

The first suggestion which I want to consider is that we have a distinctive experience of the authoritative character of moral values or moral judgements, and that theism makes best sense of this experience. Though I am not happy with the idea of a sharp divide between moral demands and other kinds of normative reasons, I accept that there is something to be explained here: the sense that we have of something which we ought or ought not to do, regardless of our own wants and inclinations. A theistic transcendental argument may then take the following form. The authority of morality, it may be said, is explicable only as a personal authority, since only persons can make claims on us of a kind which limit or over-ride our own wants and inclinations. The force of moral demands cannot, however, be explained in terms of the claims which finite persons (such as other human beings) make on us; it can only be explained by the authority of a personal god.[1]

My reply to such an argument would be that the authority of the moral 'ought' *can* in fact be sufficiently explained in terms of the limits imposed on our actions by the recognition of other finite persons. The wrong that we do, when we do what morally we ought not to do, is always a wrong done to another person (normally another human being, but perhaps also a non-human animal). To make this reply sufficiently convincing I want to emphasise that when I refer to 'a wrong done to another person', I am not proposing a consequentialist or utilitarian account, in which the wrong perpetrated when, for instance, I tell a lie, or break a promise, is an independently identifiable harm of a generic kind. The position I am taking cuts across the traditional consequentialist/deontological divide. On the one hand, what is wrong about telling a lie is not the violation of some abstract free-floating 'duty'. The wrong is the wrong done *to the person to whom the lie is told*. On the other hand the consequentialist account is unsatisfactory because it fails to recognise the diversity of ways in which we can wrong others, which cannot all be subsumed under a general heading of causing suffering or pain or depriving others of possible happiness or well-being. If I lie to someone, the wrong I do to him is that of deceiving him. If I break my promise to someone, the wrong I do to her is the wrong of letting her down. If I treat someone unjustly or unfairly, the wrong I do to him may be the wrong of exploiting him. If I am ungrateful to someone, the wrong I do may be that of taking her for granted. If I coerce someone, the wrong I do may be that of violating his autonomy, of appropriating his life and treating him as a mere object. And so on.

Why might this be thought not to be a satisfactory account of the authority of the moral 'ought'? Here is one suggestion. Robert Adams, in the context of his defence of a 'modified divine command theory', says:

> In all sin there is offense against a person (God), even when there is no offense against any other human person – for instance, if I have a vice which harms me but does not importantly harm any other human being. Therefore in the Judaeo-Christian tradition reactions which are

appropriate when one has offended another person are felt to be appropriate reactions to any ethical fault, regardless of whether another human being has been offended.[2]

The case of moral wrongs which harm only oneself is the only problematic instance which he mentions. We might respond simply by rejecting the idea of moral duties to oneself – it is, after all, a contentious element in our moral thinking, rather than an integral component of the very idea of morality. Alternatively, if we do want to make sense of the idea, then we shall have to provide some account of how one can morally stand towards oneself as though towards another person – perhaps in terms of a relation of one part of the self to another and better part of oneself. I do not know whether this can be done, but I do think that the idea of moral duties to oneself must stand or fall with the success or failure of such an attempt. Certainly we do not solve the problem by bringing in God, for if we explain moral duties to oneself by saying that they are indeed duties to another person, namely duties to God, then they are not after all duties to oneself, and we have lost precisely what we were supposed to be explaining.

The same response can be made to another argument attempting to show that moral concern cannot be explained simply as a concern for other human persons. Gordon Graham argues that we are committed to an 'absolute conception' of morality, the idea that moral considerations are *overriding*.[3] He takes this to entail that some kinds of action are unconditionally ruled out, whatever the circumstances, and he offers the example of slavery as something which would be generally regarded as absolutely wrong (p. 96). He then acknowledges that there is a problem as to how such a conception can be motivating and can be rational, if it requires us to act in certain ways even in circumstances where this may lead to a worse outcome. In response, he offers a 'transcendental argument' for what he calls 'moral faith' – the faith that acting morally 'is in my interests even when I do not and cannot know this', and that it 'will not ultimately conflict with personal or social well-being, appearances to the contrary notwithstanding' (p. 93).

> There is at least one absolute evil. Therefore we must make our conception of practical reason accord with its possibility. To do this we must presuppose that the conditions of its possibility prevail, and that to abhor this evil is better for us as agents and for the world in general than to accommodate it. We can only reasonably suppose this, however, if we hold that there exists some sort of Providence which makes the maintenance of these conditions its purpose. To believe coherently in the existence of absolute evil therefore requires us to believe in a providential God. (p. 96)

In reply I would want first to distinguish different senses in which moral requirements are 'overriding'. There is first the idea that moral requirements are binding 'irrespective of inclination' (Graham p. 78) and do not derive their force from the desires and purposes which as individuals we may happen to have. This aspect of morality we can perfectly well account for in terms of the constraints imposed on our actions by other persons. That can also generate a stronger notion of overridingness – that morality is not just a matter of the promotion of well-being. A respect for other people's agency, for their autonomy or their rights, may support a strong conception of moral side-constraints, the recognition that certain ways of treating other human beings are ruled out, even though the acceptance of those constraints may lead to less well-being or to greater suffering. Promoting others' well-being, and preventing others' suffering, may not be the only requirements of moral concern and respect for others. We can account for these two senses in which moral requirements are overriding without necessarily having to make a third and still stronger claim – that morality 'absolutely' rules out certain kinds of actions, in any conceivable circumstances. Should we accept that stronger claim? I do not know. I do not see how we can rule out the possibility of some extreme emergency, in which it might be necessary for one group of human beings, for instance, to enslave another in order to prevent total disaster such as the complete destruction of all human life. Suppose, however, we do accept that some moral requirements are overriding in this strongest, 'absolute' sense. If we do, then such a conception is *not* supported by Graham's notion of moral faith, that God will ensure that acting morally is not ultimately in conflict with humans' personal and social well-being. For to make such a move is precisely to reject the very conception of morality which it was supposed to support – that morally requirements are binding in a way which can override the desire to promote human well-being. As with Adams' move, so with Graham's – by re-interpreting moral requirements as duties owed to God, or as duties underpinned by God's guarantees of our well-being, we eliminate precisely those distinctive features of morality which we were supposed to be trying to explain.

The Experience of Beauty

I turn now to the suggestion that the experience of beauty, in art and in nature, has an implicitly religious character. Here is one formulation of that idea, by John Haldane, who claims that 'the experience of the aesthetic may warrant religious beliefs' and that this idea 'stand[s] in opposition to a common humanistic conception of art and the aesthetic as alternative sources of inspiration, consolation and sustenance for those for whom theism is unbelievable.'

> First, then, it is a familiar thought that natural beauty may offer an intimation of creation. Indeed, for many people now detached from traditional religious creeds and practices, the experience of nature may provide the best prospect of any sense of transcendence. ... A second point of relevance ... is that the aesthetic experience of nature has often provided inspiration for the making of works expressing attitudes of 'natural religion'. ... [T]here is the sense of awe at the very being of the world. ... There is also the sense of manifest design felt in observing the beauty of organisms whose parts stand in a fitting relation to one another and to the life of the whole. ... A third consideration is that just as the experience of nature has led some to a belief in God, so has the experience of art: both art in general, as testifying again to the significance of beauty, and religious art in particular, as presenting aspects of the transcendent.[4]

That last sentence alludes to a special point about the experience of religious art to which I will turn in a moment. I shall also say something later about the invoking of the idea of 'transcendence'. But what about the general claim, that the experience of beauty is an intimation of experience of the divine? In contrast to the case of morality, I find it difficult to locate any substantial argument here. Haldane alludes to the argument from design, but I do not see that the experience of beauty in the natural world adds any independent weight to that argument. We may argue that the intricate structure of a living organism, in which the different parts interact with one another to serve the functions of the whole, is evidence of a divine creator. We may also take delight in the beauty of such structures. But if the design argument in the end fails, as for standard reasons I think it does, the experience of beauty cannot shore it up. The experience itself of course remains, but we should accept it for what it is. I want to resist the tendency of some theists to co-opt any experience of mystery and awe and claim it as an experience of the divine. 'Everything is what it is, and not another thing.' We can indeed be transported by experiences of beauty of all kinds, which lift us out of the routine of everyday life and can sustain and inspire us. That is a deep fact about human beings, but we should accept it as such and not try to turn it into something else. What is particularly unsatisfactory about the co-option of the experience of beauty by religious creeds is that, so far from accepting the mystery, it may seek to dispel it. The mystery of aesthetic delight is just that – mysterious – and to attempt to pin it down by interpreting it as an awareness of divine design is to threaten to undermine it by over-interpretation.

Haldane does however pose a genuine problem for the atheist when he turns to the specific case of religious art, and I want to consider this in more detail. He argues that any serious work of art is 'a presentation of the reality and values in which the work seeks to participate', and that in evaluating the work 'we are judging the credibility of what it proclaims' (pp. 171–2). It would seem to follow that if a work presents religious beliefs and values, the atheist is bound to reject those beliefs and values and is therefore committed to judging the work less highly. And this appears to exclude the atheist from fully appreciating and valuing religious works of art. One of Haldane's examples is Piero della Francesca's painting *The Resurrection* in Borgo San Sepolcro. The atheist might try to take refuge in praise of the formal qualities of the work, but as Haldane rightly says, its form and content are inseparable. The arrangement of the figures, with the sleeping soldiers in their poses of disarray 'contrasting with the simple sweeping contour of Christ', who divides the background landscape between the deadness of winter and the new life of spring – all of this serves to point up the content of the painting, and the painting seems to be inescapably religious (pp. 168–9).

I agree with Haldane that, like all Piero della Francesca's work, it is one of the supreme achievements of art. But, as an atheist, can I consistently say this? Haldane's argument could be set out formally as follows.

(1)   'A serious favourable appreciation of the aesthetic value of a work of art carries an implication of the acceptance of its content as constituting a consideration in favour of what is presented.' (p. 172)
(2)   Atheists are precluded from accepting the content of a work of religious art as constituting a consideration in favour of what is presented.
(3)   Therefore atheists are, to that extent, precluded from favourably appreciating the aesthetic value of religious art.

I accept premise (1). It is contentious, and I am not going to open up the matters for contention, but I agree that at least the finest works of art convey truths about our world and our experience, that they provide support for the truths which they convey, and that their doing so is an important part of their value. My quarrel is not with this, but with premise (2). The assumption here is that the truth presented by a religious work of art must itself be a religious truth. That is what I want to question. Of course Piero's painting is a depiction of the resurrection, but it does not give us any reason for believing the claim that Jesus rose from the dead. How could it do so? (It's not as though it were photographic evidence or anything of that sort.) The truths which it conveys are human truths, truths which help us in the understanding of our human condition. Like any great work of art, it conveys such truths by drawing on our own experience and helping us to see a significance in that experience. It says something about the ability of human beings to rise above suffering. And that is specifically a truth about human beings, because the features of the work which convey it are the recognisable human characteristics of the figure rising from the tomb. Typically of Piero, there is a deeply enigmatic quality in the figure, but also a profound stillness, a nobility and a serenity which speaks of suffering overcome through contemplation and understanding. The qualities apparent in the risen Jesus are similar to those of the figures in the right-hand side of Piero's *The Flagellation*, another meditation on suffering and the human response to suffering.

The truths conveyed by *The Resurrection* are also to be found in the figures of the sleeping soldiers at the base of the tomb. Again the truths are conveyed in the significance of the poses and expressions of the human figures. They say something about the propensity of human beings to miss the miracles that are going on in the world around us – in this case, to be oblivious to the transformation and renewal of human life, and to the corresponding transformation and renewal of the natural world, as represented by the change from the bare trees on the left of the picture to the new growth on the right. In these ways, then, the content of the picture provides 'considerations in favour of what is presented', and these considerations are as accessible for the atheist as for the theist. The general point is that the truths conveyed by great religious works of art are human truths. And that is because religious iconography is powerful and compelling when it draws on shared human experience and works to enhance our understanding of that experience.

The Experience of Meaningful Narratives

It is sometimes suggested that without religion we would be bereft of the stories which enrich our lives. In the Christian tradition the relevant stories would be primarily those in the Bible, from the creation story, the Garden of Eden, Noah and the flood, Abraham and Isaac, and so on, through to the Gospel narratives and also including the parables in the Gospels. Some of these stories, in particular the Incarnation, Crucifixion, and Resurrection, also of course have the status of doctrines, but it is their distinctive role as stories, along with the others in the list, that I want to consider. What is special about stories, I take it, is their enactment of important human experiences as they occur in the lives of individuals, and drawing on these can help us to shape our own lives, help us to recognise features of them as exemplifying a universal pattern and thus to make sense of them. The stories of anger and strife and reconciliation, of fear and courage, of love and betrayal and loyalty, of death and despair and new hope, because they are presented as the lived experiences of individuals, bring home to us what these things mean in concrete and particular terms.

It is significant that every religious tradition has its repertoire of stories, of archetypal experiences enacted in the lives of individuals. But if we are considering them not as literal truths but as stories, meaningful fictions which shape our experience, then they are not confined to religions. Every culture has a wealth of stories – myths and sagas, the great epic poems inherited from oral traditions, fairy stories and fables, novels and plays, through to popular fiction and in the modern world the stories offered in profusion by films, television plays and the 'soaps'. The length of the list confirms the ubiquity and depth of the need. By the same token, however, it confirms that religions and their stories are by no means the only source for meeting the need. And if religious stories themselves perform this role as *stories*, as meaningful fictions, they are in that capacity as available to the atheist as to the theist.

Still, it may be said, we have to discriminate. This abundance of stories is all very well, but not just any stories will do, we need the *right* stories. I agree, and when we think of the distorting stereotypes offered by so much popular fiction, in both printed and visual media, we can recognise the importance of getting the story right. But we are talking about the truth appropriate to fictions here, the truth of fictions which honestly capture the reality and complexity of human experience. In that sense we may well judge that, compared with contemporary stories which glamorise power and wealth and violence, stories such as that of a child born in an outhouse to lowly parents and visited by shepherds are preferable – but they can be preferred without being tied to a context of theistic belief.

Some religious traditions, however, including orthodox Christianity, would claim to have 'the right story' in a stronger sense. They would claim to be able to provide an overarching narrative which makes sense of 'the broad sweep of history'.[5] Here I refer to Haldane again. Against the postmodernists, he says, he sides with the modernists and pre-modernists who see the need for so-called 'meta-narratives, overarching accounts of events that subsume other more local narratives' and which locate the 'diversity of cultural forms and life-styles … within a larger picture which gives it a meaning.' For Haldane that larger picture is the Christian meta-narrative, the view of human history as a struggle between good and evil and as the working out of a divine plan, beginning with the Creation and the Fall and leading to some eventual consummation. This, he says, is a narrative which can reconcile the pessimists' acknowledgement of the darker aspects of human history with the need to see in that history a direction which can be a source of hope. He notes that not only the secular grand narratives but also the postmodernists themselves fall back on some form of progressivism (112–13). He suggests however that the need to view human history teleologically, as having a direction and moving towards a goal, cannot be met without a belief in divine agency.

> It is doubtful … whether anything short of real purposeful agency can provide history with a teleology. If that is right, and if the idea of a meta-narrative has rational appeal, then so should the notion that ultimately the course of human history is a religious one, a movement towards or away from God. (p. 122)

As the risk of sounding postmodernist, I have doubts about the need for grand narratives. The idea seems to conflate two different things, the needs for 'stories' in the strict sense, as concrete and particular enactments of aspects of human life which enable us to give them a practical significance, and the need for an objective and literal understanding of the broad features of human history and the human condition. Both are needed, but the latter will not appropriately take the form of an overarching story. Insofar as we need stories, we need them in their diversity, to do justice to the nuances of our experiences and their felt particularity. They cannot all be subsumed into a single story which gives a unique meaning to human history.

Secular humanism has itself been criticised as offering a naïve progressivism, a faith in the onward march of humanity towards an inevitable future from which irrationality and superstition will have vanished. That particular 'grand narrative' is difficult to sustain, especially in the light of the past century's manifestations of the darker side of human behaviour, and to that extent the hopes of the Enlightenment have become tarnished. But if that simplistic progressivism is not available, it does not follow that we have to fall back on a religious teleology in order to sustain our hopes and give meaning to our activities. What we do need, it is true, is some sense of our lives as part of a larger picture, having a meaningful continuity both with the past and with the future. If what will happen after our own deaths does not matter to us, if we have no sense of inheriting things of value from our predecessors and bequeathing them to future generations, then it is difficult to see how what we do with our lives can have any deep significance for us. That necessary sense of continuity across generations can to some extent be fostered by the appropriate stories – novels or plays or films which present the pattern of a whole life, or the lives of successive generations, or which show characters wrestling with contested understandings of their past and their relationship to the previous generation. But the sense of continuity is also of course rooted in our direct experience, of family relationships, and of ties to a wider community, local or national or international, cultural or political.

To sustain our hopes, and to understand our activities as having a point, we need not only a sense of continuity, but also a recognition of the possibilities of change. We do not, I think, need any fiction about the inevitability of progress, or a meta-narrative about the onward march of humanity, or the mission of this or that country to bring freedom, democracy and fast food to the rest of the world, but it is difficult to see how we could maintain much of a commitment to a whole range of human activities unless we had at least realistic hopes in the possibility of progress. For that, however, we need not a meta-narrative but strictly empirical grounds for guarded optimism. Those grounds are, I should say, available. It seems to me undeniable, for instance, that the lives of the great majority of people in this country are substantially better than were the lives of the great majority a century ago, and that this change for the better has come about as a result of the conscious and committed endeavours of countless men and women to achieve it. Clearly this is not the place to argue the point. Here I maintain only that the basis for hope, and thus for the possibility of meaningful activity, does not depend on any meta-narrative which sees our lives as part of a divine plan.

The Experience of Transcendence

It is sometimes said that atheistic humanism cannot be fully satisfying because it cannot meet the need for the experience of transcendence. It is quite unclear what this means, and though the accusation is regularly made I doubt whether there is any one point which it consistently identifies. Sometimes the word 'transcendence' is used in the same vague way as talk of 'spirituality', with the implication that a life without theistic belief is condemned to be shallow and superficial. Perhaps the implication is that atheistic humanism precludes those transfiguring moments which lift us above the humdrum level of everyday life, or that it offers nothing to aim at beyond the pursuit of physical well-being and material goods. Such suggestions are certainly made, but I take them to be too obviously false to merit serious discussion.

Talk of 'transcendence' also draws on the more specifically philosophical, metaphysical sense of the word, with its reference to a possible non-natural world which lies beyond sense-experience. It is true that many versions of theism, including the dominant strand in Christianity, have been tied to a broadly Platonic metaphysics, but to suggest that this points to a lack in atheistic humanism is plainly question-begging. There may or may not be a rational case to be made for the existence of a transcendent realm, but short of such a case, we cannot say that there is a human *need* to hold such beliefs.

There may however be a genuine point to be made by talk of a need for the experience of transcendence, and the best sense that I can make of it is this: that human beings need the experience of the non-human. Without such experience, it may be said, the human world is too limited, too shut in on itself, too cosy. We need a relationship to 'the Other', and that means not just other human beings. We can understand our own humanity only through a relationship to a non-human world.

I think there is something in this, but the source from which such a need is met is most obviously our relationship to the *natural* world rather than to any non-natural realm. There are many dimensions to our experience of nature, and I have already said something about the experience of beauty in nature, but another dimension is certainly the experience of a relationship to something larger than the human world, which in that sense 'transcends' our merely human concerns and puts them into perspective. It can come from the awareness of other living things as having a life of their own, alien and separate and mysterious. Still more strongly is the encounter with the non-human to be found in our experience of the inanimate natural world, and a locus classicus here of course is Wordsworth. Recalling in Book I of *The Prelude* the incident when as a boy he had rowed out onto the moonlit lake and seen the 'huge cliff' rearing up, he says:

> … and after I had seen
> That spectacle, for many days, my brain
> Work'd with a dim and undetermin'd sense
> Of unknown modes of being; in my thoughts
> There was a darkness, call it solitude,
> Or blank desertion, no familiar shapes
> Of hourly objects, images of trees,
> Of sea or sky, no colours of green fields;
> But huge and mighty Forms that do not live
> Like living men mov'd slowly through my mind
> By day and were the trouble of my dreams.[6]

It is the alien and inhuman character of these 'unknown modes of being' that makes them troubling, but for Wordsworth, especially in retrospect, the experience is not just a negative one. By revealing a world beyond the merely human, it is also uplifting. Wordsworth immediately goes on to speak of how 'the passions that build up our human soul' are sustained …

> Not with the mean and vulgar works of Man,
> But with high objects, with enduring things,
> With life and nature, purifying thus
> The elements of feeling and of thought,
> And sanctifying, by such discipline,
> Both pain and fear, until we recognize
> A grandeur in the beatings of the heart.
>
> (435–41)

We can find in this passage, then, an expression of the idea that our human lives need this encounter with the non-human, that such experience puts us in our place and reminds us of our limited importance within a larger universe, and that it can be fed by our relationship to the natural world and does not require any sense of the supernatural or the divine. But in using Wordsworth thus, I have cheated. The passage which I have just quoted is introduced with these lines:

> Wisdom and Spirit of the universe!
> Thou Soul that art the Eternity of Thought!
> That giv'st to forms and images a breath
> And everlasting motion! not in vain,
> By day or star-light thus from my first dawn
> Of Childhood didst Thou intertwine for me
> The passions that build up our human Soul …
>
> (428–34)

Here Wordsworth, looking back on his childhood experience, succumbs to the appeal of the idea that if nature has this capacity to ennoble human passions, this must point to some pre-established harmony between the natural and the human world, to the presence of the same 'spirit' or 'soul' in nature and in the human frame. In these lines the idea is formulated in the language of pantheism, and for Wordsworth himself that pantheism was increasingly transmuted into the espousal of orthodox Christianity.

I see no need to follow Wordsworth down that road. On the contrary, putting it into a theistic framework seems to me, if anything, to negate the original insight. It is precisely the non-human separateness of nature that sustains and nourishes us. To suppose that nature can do this for us because it too is the embodiment of qualities of wisdom and intelligence, of a spirit which has a knowledge of and concern for our own human lives, is ironically to anthropomorphise nature and thereby diminish the experience. The encounter with the non-human is essentially an experience of something alien and indifferent, that is what is important about it, and the atheistic rendering of the experience captures this more accurately than the theistic version.

The Experience of Vulnerability and Fragility

The last form of experience in my list, the experience of fragility, is different from the others. The claim to be considered here is not that the experience of fragility is itself a valuable and essential form of human experience. Rather, the suggestion may be that by accepting the fact of human fragility, by honestly acknowledging it and coming to terms with it, we may be given an intimation of the truth of a religious perspective and may come to see how it can give a meaning to our lives. And the further implication may be that the atheist humanist, wedded perforce to the Promethean assumption that human beings can forge a meaning for their lives from their limited human resources and their own strength of will, are both condemned to futility and debarred from the insights which an acceptance of our fragility can bring.

The acknowledgement of human frailty is a theme explored by John Cottingham. He speaks of 'the sense of possible failure and futility that haunts our quest for meaning', and draws attention to the ways in which our projects may succeed or fail for reasons over which we have no control.[7] Cottingham's response to the fact of our fragility then seems to oscillate between two courses. On the one hand there is the idea that we can come to terms with our vulnerability by what he calls 'some kind of radical interior modification' (p. 79), honestly accepting our dependence, adjusting our values to it and recognising what really matters. But there is also the idea that if our lives are not to be futile, we need some kind of external guarantee, the reassurance of what he refers to as 'the resilience of goodness', and that seems in the end to require a belief that the things over which we have no control are nevertheless guided by a divine power working for good.

The 'radical interior modification' is something which Cottingham sees as essentially religious, something which he equates with the 'spirituality' which 'the great religions have typically aimed to achieve' (p. 79). He also refers to it as

> the insight that through giving up our attachment to the trappings of success, position, money, we become more fully human – more open to the plight of those around us with whom, despite our surface differences, we share so much; such a transformation brings us closer to realising how to live in a world where, sooner or later, we will have to give up everything – our youth, our health, many of those we love, and in the end, even our lives. Status and power temporarily insulate us from our inherent human vulnerability; but in plumbing the depths of that vulnerability we discover what truly matters. (p. 76)

I do not see this insight as a specifically religious one, but as one fully accessible from a secular perspective. In coming to terms with the vicissitudes of life we can, all of us, come to recognise the superficiality of wealth and fame and power and understand what really matters.

But this line of thought also has its limits. It is one thing to talk of 'giving up our attachment to the trappings of success, position, money'. It would be quite another thing to say that our vulnerability to bereavement and loss should lead us to give up our attachment to those we love. The interior modification can only take us so far, it cannot insulate us against grief or loss – or if it did, it would only be by hardening us and deadening our feelings. Perhaps that is why Cottingham's argument seems to move from the need for interior modification to the need for exterior consolation. What I take him to be saying, in fact, is that the interior modification can itself generate an insight into the truth of the relevant belief about an external reality. He acknowledges the difficulties which stand in the way of an acceptance of religious beliefs. Initially, then, he plays down the need for the beliefs. He stresses the importance 'not of doctrines but of *practices*: techniques of meditation and prayer, techniques for self-examination and greater self-awareness' (pp. 87–8). In response to the suggestion that the practices presuppose belief he suggests that 'belief, in the sense of subscribing to a set of theological propositions, is not in fact central to what it is to be religious' (p. 88). In due course, however, he moves to what I take to be a rather different suggestion – that by engaging in the practices we can get 'intimations' of the truth of the beliefs.

What Cottingham appears to propose at this point is a distinctive form of transcendental argument. Drawing on Pascal, he suggests that by engaging in the 'spiritual practices' which embody the religious attitude to life, we may gain insight into the truth of the corresponding beliefs. His example is that of saying grace before meals – a practice which turns the meeting of a mere physical need into an acknowledgement of our finitude and dependence and our place in a larger whole. He suggests that

> … the illuminations that come from the practice of spirituality cannot be accessed by means of rational argument alone, since the relevant experiences are not available to us during those times when we are adopting the stance of detached rationality. … [O]ur human awareness … indisputably includes experiences in which spiritual values are made manifest – experiences in which, arguably, we have intimations of a transcendent world of meaning … (p. 100)

The important claim here seems to be that there are experiences which presuppose the truth of certain beliefs, but that if we start by trying to deciding rationally whether those beliefs are true, we shall cut ourselves off from the experiences. If, however, we open ourselves up to the experiences, and act as though the beliefs were true, we shall come to see that they are indeed true.

There are cases which fit that description. Sometimes, for instance, it is only by trusting someone, by making that leap of faith, that you can establish a relationship of mutual confidence and thereby come to see that the other person can indeed be trusted. Or again, it may be that only in loving someone can we become fully aware of what is lovable about them. In such cases the active commitment brings about a Gestalt switch which enables us to see more clearly the truth on which the commitment depends.

The difficulty for such a position, however, is that we have to be able to distinguish between two kinds of case:

(a)   S acts as though p were true and thereby comes to believe p, where this is a case of self-deception or unthinking habit, inducing a belief which remains ungrounded.
(b)   S acts as though p were true and thereby comes to see what it is that makes p true.

In cases such as that of grace before meals giving us 'intimations of meaning', we need some reason for thinking that they are cases of kind (b) rather than kind (a). In my examples of trust and of love, there is at any rate something that the person can say about what makes p true – what makes the other lovable, how she knows that he is trustworthy. Admittedly, the point of the 'Gestalt switch' account is that what makes p true is more difficult to recognise for someone who has not made the commitment. Still, there has to be *something* which S can say, and which can convey to others what it is that grounds the commitment. Think of the duck-rabbit. Someone who cannot see it as a duck can be told 'Look, that's the beak.' They will not be able to see it as a beak unless they have made the switch to seeing the figure as a picture of a duck; nevertheless, saying to them 'That's the beak' can help them to make the switch. But in the case of the religious believer, if the belief is induced by the practice, and if there is *nothing* that he can say about what it is that he is now aware of which supports his belief, then his position is indistinguishable from that of the self-deceiver in cases of kind (a). Rather than being like that of the person whose love makes them more aware of what is lovable in the other person, it is like that of someone who thinks, perhaps unconsciously, 'I know she doesn't really love me, but if I go on acting as though she did, maybe I'll come to believe that she does.'

Where does this leave the experience of fragility and vulnerability? It leaves it as just that. We are fragile and vulnerable. Accepting that fact may help us to see what is really important, it may open our eyes to what is of real value, such as the enduring beauty of the natural world, and the importance of our relationships to others, in contrast to the superficial trappings of wealth and power. Those ramifications of the experience are as available to the atheist as to the theist. What the experience cannot by itself do is ground the belief in a transcendental realm of meaning, the belief in a divine power and purpose which can sustain us in our vulnerability by assuring us that good will prevail. The experience of vulnerability, and the experience of consolation for our vulnerability, are not the same. This is where I want to distinguish between the kinds of experience which are essential to our humanity, and the kinds of experience which it would be nice to have. Anyone can see the attraction of being able to believe that we are sustained by a higher power, and the attraction of being able to experience our fragility as a confirmation of that belief. But if the belief is to be warranted, there is no short-cutting the need for rational argument. The experience by itself is not enough.

Conclusion

I said at the beginning of this paper that I wanted to distinguish between experiences which it might be good to have and experiences which are an integral part of human life. I hope that my last case has helped to clarify the distinction. The experience of our vulnerability and dependence, and the awareness of what is really important which may be prompted by that experience, are deep features of human life. I suppose there are people who never, or only fleetingly, have that experience and that awareness, but a life without it would lack something. The feeling that, in our times of vulnerability, there is a higher power to sustain us, a guarantee of the resilience of goodness, is different. Atheists cannot have that feeling. They can recognise the attractions of being able to feel it, but it presupposes beliefs which an atheist cannot accept.

The same divergence is apparent in all the areas of experience which I have been surveying. In each of them there is a core experience which is an essential human experience and which is as available to the atheist as to the theist. There is also, in each case, an additional gloss which the theist can put on the experience, and which has its attractions. There is also, as we might expect, an overall pattern to the theistic extras. The theist who believes that there is a personal power which guarantees the resilience of goodness and which sustains us in our vulnerability is also likely to believe that that same personal power is at work in nature – that the transcendence of nature is not sheer otherness but reflects back at us in a higher form our human qualities of intelligence and emotion and will. The belief that that personal power, in nature and in our own lives, is working out some purpose, obscure to us but ultimately making for the triumph of good, provides the theist with a grand narrative, an overall story into which can be fitted the myriad of more particular stories which make sense of our lives. And the theist is also likely to believe that our responsiveness to beauty in art and nature, and our responsiveness to moral values, are intimations of the presence of that same transcendent but personal power.

Where the atheist, then, sees a number of essential but disparate forms of experience, the theist can see them as all manifestations of the same personal power at work in human lives, in human history and in the natural world. If, in each case, the theistic extra has its attractions, the very fact that they all fit into a single overall cohesive picture makes them all the more attractive.

What does the secular humanist have to offer instead? Only, I suppose, a kind of integrity – an insistence that though the prospect of an all-embracing cohesive belief-system is attractive, the attractiveness is not sufficient reason to endorse it. I do not of course suggest that theists necessarily lack integrity. I do not say that they adopt their religious beliefs solely because of the emotional appeal of such beliefs, I simply make the obvious point that the emotional appeal is not a good enough reason to adopt them, and that the secular humanist accepts this. The humanist will add that the various kinds of experience which I have been describing are in any case enough to sustain a full, rich and meaningful life. Humanism does not replace religious belief with some alternative grand narrative, some other synthesising doctrine, or some single supreme value which makes sense of everything. It says that we can live with plurality, with an untidy collection of diverse sources of strength and inspiration which, nevertheless, together are sufficient.

Notes

1. Cf. H. P. Owen, 'Why morality implies the existence of God', in *Philosophy of Religion*, ed. Brian Davies (Oxford: Oxford University Press, 2000).

2. R. M. Adams, 'A Modified Divine Command Theory of Ethical Wrongness', in *Philosophy of Religion: An Anthology*, ed. C. Taliaferro and P. J. Griffiths (Oxford: Blackwell, 2003), p. 466.

3. Gordon Graham, *Evil and Christian Ethics* (Cambridge: Cambridge University Press, 2001), pp. 75–8.

4. John Haldane, *An Intelligent Person's Guide to Religion* (London: Duckworth, 2003), pp. 151–5.

5. *Ibid.* p. 97.

6. William Wordsworth, *The Prelude*, 1805 text, ed. E. de Selincourt (London: Oxford University Press, 1960), Book I, lines 417–27.

7. John Cottingham, *On the Meaning of Life* (London: Routledge, 2003), p. 67.

4.7

Emergent Religious Principles

Ursula Goodenough

When the responses elicited by the Epic of Evolution are gathered together, several religious principles emerge that can, I believe, serve as a framework for a global Ethos.

Taking on Ultimacy

We are all, each one of us, ordained to live out our lives in the context of ultimate questions, such as:

- Why is there anything at all, rather than nothing?
- Where did the laws of physics come from?
- Why does the universe seem so strange?

My response to such questions has been to articulate a covenant with Mystery. Others, of course, prefer to respond with answers, answers that often include a concept of god. These answers are by definition beliefs since they can neither be proven nor refuted. They may be gleaned from existing faith traditions or from personal search. God may be apprehended as a remote Author without present-day agency, or as an interested Presence with whom one can form a relationship, or as pantheistic – Inherent in All Things.

The opportunity to develop personal beliefs in response to questions of ultimacy, including the active decision to hold no Beliefs at all, is central to the human experience. The important part, I believe, is that the questions be openly encountered. To take the

Ursula Goodenough (2000) "Emergent Religious Principles," in *The Sacred Depths of Nature*, Oxford: Oxford University Press, pp. 167–74.

universe on – to ask Why Are Things As They Are? – is to generate the foundation for everything else.

Gratitude

Imagine that you and some other humans are in a spaceship, roaming around in the universe, looking for a home. You land on a planet that proves to be ideal in every way. It has deep forests and fleshy fruits and surging oceans and gentle rains and cavorting creatures and dappled sunlight and rich soil. Everything is perfect for human habitation, and everything is astonishingly beautiful.

This is how the religious naturalist thinks of our human advent on Earth. We arrived but a moment ago, and found if to be perfect for us in every way. And then we came to understand that it is perfect because we arose from it and are a part of it.

Hosannah! Not in the highest, but right here, right now, this.

When such gratitude flows from our beings, it matters little whether we offer it to God, as in this poem, or to Mystery or Coyote or Cosmic Evolution or Mother Earth:

> i thank You God for most this amazing
> day: for the leaping greenly spirits of trees
> and a blue true dream of sky; and for everything
> which is natural which is infinite which is yes
>
> (i who have died am alive again today,
> and this is the sun's birthday; this is the birth
> day of life and of love and wings: and of the gay
> great happening illimitably earth)
>
> how should tasting touching hearing seeing
> breathing any – lifted from the no
> of all nothing – human merely being
> doubt unimaginable You?
>
> (now the ears of my ears awake and
> now the eyes of my eyes are opened)
> *E.E. Cummings, 1950*

Reverence

Our story tells us of the sacredness of life, of the astonishing complexity of cells and organisms, of the vast lengths of time it took to generate their splendid diversity, of the enormous improbability that any of it happened at all. Reverence is the religious emotion elicited when we perceive the sacred. We are called to revere the whole enterprise of planetary existence, the whole and all of its myriad parts as they catalyze and secrete and replicate and mutate and evolve.

Ralph Waldo Emerson invites us to express our reverence in the form of prayer. "Prayer," he writes, "is the contemplation of the facts of life from the highest point of view. It is the soliloquy of a beholding and jubilant soul."

Credo of Continuation

We have thought of evolution as being about prevalence, about how many copies there are of which kinds of genomes. But it is quite as accurate, and I believe more germinative, to think of evolution as being about the continuation of genomes. Genomes that create organisms with sufficient reproductive success to have viable offspring are able to continue into the future; genomes that fail, fail.

Reproductive success is governed by many variables, but key adaptations have included the evolution of awareness, valuation, and purpose. In order to continue, genomes must dictate organisms that are aware of their environmental circumstances, evalute these inputs correctly, and respond with intentionality.

And so, I profess my Faith. For me, the existence of all this complexity and awareness and intent and beauty, and my ability to apprehend it, serves as the ultimate meaning and the ultimate value. The continuation of life reaches around, grabs its own tail, and forms a sacred circle that requires no further justification, no Creator, no superordinate meaning of meaning, no purpose other than that the continuation continue until the sun collapses or the final meteor collides. I confess a credo of continuation.

And in so doing, I confess as well a credo of human continuation. We may be the only questioners in the universe, the only ones who have come to understand the astonishing dynamics of cosmic evolution. If we are not, if there are others who Know, it is unlikely that we will ever encounter one another. We are also, whether we like it or not, the dominant species and the stewards of this planet. If we can revere how things are, and can find a way to express gratitude for our existence, then we should be able to figure out, with a great deal of work and good will, how to share the Earth with one another and with other creatures, how to restore and preserve its elegance and grace, and how to commit ourselves to love and joy and laughter and hope.

It goes back in the end to my father's favorite metaphor. "Life is a coral reef. We each leave behind the best, the strongest deposit we can so that the reef can grow. But what's important is the reef."

Our Religions of Origin

So we extract from reality all the meaning and guidance and emotional substance that we can, and we bring these responses with us as we set out to chart global paths. And then we come back to our religions of origin, the faiths of our mothers and fathers. What do we do with them? What have I done with mine?

Theologian Philip Hefner offers us a weaving metaphor. The tapestry maker first strings the warp, long strong fibers anchored firmly to the loom, and then interweaves the weft, the patterns, the color, the art. The Epic of Evolution is our warp, destined to endure, commanding our universal gratitude and reverence and commitment. And then, after that, we are all free to be artists, to render in language and painting and song and dance our ultimate hopes and concerns and understandings of human nature.

Throughout the ages, the weaving of our religious weft has been the province of our prophets and gurus and liturgists and poets. The texts and art and ritual that come to us from these revered ancestors include claims about Nature and Agency that are no longer plausible. They use a different warp. But for me at least, this is just one of those historical facts, something that can be absorbed, appreciated, and then put aside as I encounter the deep wisdom embedded in these traditions and the abundant opportunities that they offer to experience transcendence and clarity.

I love traditional religions. Whenever I wander into distinctive churches or mosques or temples, or visit museums of religious art, or hear performances of sacred music, I am enthralled by the beauty and solemnity and power they offer. Once we have our feelings about Nature in place, then I believe that we can also find important ways to call ourselves Jews, or Muslims, or Taoists, or Hopi, or Hindus, or Christians, or Buddhists. Or some of each. The words in the traditional texts may sound different to us than they did to their authors, but they continue to resonate with our religious selves. We know what they are intended to mean.

Humans need stories – grand, compelling stories – that help to orient us in our lives and in the cosmos. The Epic of Evolution is such a story, beautifully suited to anchor our search for planetary consensus, telling us of our nature, our place, our context. Moreover, responses to this story – what we are calling religious naturalism – can yield deep and abiding spiritual experiences. And then, after that, we need other stories as well, human-centered stories, a mythos that embodies our ideals and our passions. This mythos comes to us, often in experiences called revelation, from the sages and the artists of past and present times.

Section V

The Meaning of Life and the Way Life Ends

Death, Futility, and Hope

Introduction

John Martin Fischer

In this section of the anthology the authors explore the relationship between the meaning of life and life's ending; if indeed it has an ending. One might say that at least some of the authors here focus on the relationship between the meaning of death and the meaning of life; some argue that the meaning of death is precisely that death helps to give meaning to life. As with the contributions to previous sections, there are some fundamental disagreements represented here. For example, some authors worry that life is meaningless in the absence of immortality, whereas others at least take seriously the contention that an immortal life would be necessarily unappealing to human beings like us. Also, some authors think that life would be meaningless – or, at least, significantly less meaningful – in the absence of God, whereas others resist this view. All of the authors in this section can be understood as presupposing, in some way or another, the importance or at least salience of "endings" in human experience, and they investigate various ways in which the ending of a human life might contribute to its meaning.

In his famous "A Confession," Leo Tolstoy begins with the worry that because our lives will apparently end in death, all our accomplishments along the way are drained of value and, indeed, our lives seem to be meaningless. As he puts it (in a series of disturbing questions [p. 383]), "What will come of what I am doing today or shall do tomorrow? What will come of my life? What is life for? Why should I live, why hope for anything or do anything?" Perhaps the worries can be summed up by a final question: "Does my life have any meaning that death cannot destroy?" The worries behind these questions set the framework for all of the essays in this section.

Tolstoy himself thinks that neither philosophy nor science provides an adequate response to the concerns. He says (p. 385):

> By appealing only to reason I could not get myself out of the quagmire of finitude, and thus life [is] meaningless. But by faith I could find an answer to life's meaning. For faith alone offered the key

Exploring the Meaning of Life: An Anthology and Guide, First Edition. Edited by Joshua W. Seachris.
© 2013 John Wiley & Sons, Inc. Published 2013 by John Wiley & Sons, Inc.

to understanding why life was worth living and why it was we instinctively don't end our own lives. Faith pointed me away from myself to the Infinite, of which I was a part.

Steven Luper-Foy ("Annihilation") provides further reason to suppose that death, understood especially as the Epicureans do, could rob our lives of meaning. This essay is a particularly good example of the interaction between the meaning of death and the meaning of life. Luper-Foy points out that Epicurus and his followers argue that, since (on their view) death is "annihilation," it cannot be a misfortune for the individual who dies. (The Epicurean view seems to depend on various contentious assumptions, including the notion that only events that cause – or could cause – a subject to have unpleasant experiences can be bad for the individual.) In contrast to the Epicurean approach, Luper-Foy argues that it is plausible that death is a bad thing for the individual who dies, insofar as it thwarts certain desires of that individual. More specifically, death is a bad thing for an individual, to the extent that it thwarts his fulfilling his desires. If death really is not bad for one, as the Epicurean supposes, the individual in question must have no such desires. But then it would be hard to see how life itself would have any value or meaning for the Epicurean. As Luper-Foy puts it, "in avoiding all aspirations that can be thwarted by death, Epicureans have had to avoid all desires which are capable of giving Epicureans a reason for living" (p. 394).

Whereas Luper-Foy rejects Epicureanism, he does think that we can gain important insights from a consideration of the view and, further, that we can adjust the view to get to something helpful. More specifically, Luper-Foy endorses the idea that we should take seriously the option of seeking to "Epicureanize our desires." The process of Epicureanizing our desires involves seeking primarily to desire only those goals that can be accomplished within the normal human span of life. Furthermore, it involves attempting to adjust our desires so that insofar as we care about projects that will continue after we die, we have made ourselves "dispensable" to those projects. The basic idea is that if the thwarting of desires is a bad thing, then one wishes to minimize the prospect of one's important desires being thwarted. According to Luper-Foy, a "Neo-Epicurean" (someone who has successfully managed to Epicureanize his desires) can still passionately engage with life while minimizing the way in which death will be a bad thing for him.

In one of my own contributions, "Why Immortality Is Not So Bad," I address the arguments of one of the most salient "immortality curmudgeons," Bernard Williams. Williams argues that immortality – in the sense of embodied existence in "this life" (that is, not in an "after-life" following death) – would be necessarily unappealing to human beings like us. This is a strong claim. The idea is that no matter how a story of putatively appealing immortality involving me is told, Williams will say that it either is not really about "me" at all – the very same person I actually am – or it is unattractive in some way (perhaps involving significant pain, terrible impairment, or boredom). Williams recalls the story of "EM," a character in a play by Karel Capek (and an opera by Leos Janacek), who finally throws away an elixir of eternal life because her life (at 342 years old) has become characterized by boredom and total lack of engagement.

I am willing to concede that many stories of putatively appealing immortality (of the sort in question, that is, not involving an "afterlife") are indeed, on reflection, not choiceworthy for human beings like us. But I argue that such immortality is not necessarily unappealing; I address both the "identity" criterion posited by Williams and also the "attractiveness" condition.

I argue that even with considerable changes in one's personality, the individual in question could still be the very same particular individual – it could still be "me" in a genuine sense. After all, I undergo significant changes in my personality even in a finite life; as long as these changes are "organic" (in a certain difficult-to-specify sense), it can still be "me" (the very same particular person). Furthermore, I argue that infinitely long life need not be boring; to suppose that it necessarily would be boring leaves out certain possibilities for engaging, compelling experiences and activities. In both the case of the identity worry and the attractiveness worry, I urge that we not have a double standard for finite and infinite lives; for example, we are sometimes (or even often) bored in a finite life, so why suppose, as Williams appears to, that boredom could not have any place in a worthwhile immortal life? I suggest that some of the appeal of the view of the Immortality Curmudgeons might come from implicitly – and inappropriately – applying a double standard for finite and infinite lives.

Of course, I do not in any way suggest that immortality is *required* for a good or meaningful life; rather, my view is that immortality is compatible with such a life. Thaddeus Metz ("The Immortality Requirement for Life's Meaning") considers the stronger view to the effect that immortality (appropriately conceived) is *necessary* for life's being valuable for human beings. Again, it is noteworthy that, whereas some philosophers deem immortality incompatible with life's meaningfulness, others view it as necessary for life's meaningfulness.

Metz considers various arguments for what he calls the "immortality requirement," and he points out that these arguments are not valid; that is, they do not adequately support the purported conclusion that immortality is required for meaningfulness in life. But Metz also considers modified versions of these arguments that plausibly do at least get us validly to the immortality requirement. However, he does not defend the soundness of these arguments (that is, the truth of all of the premises as well as the validity of the inferences); he only sketches them and suggests that they are at least initially plausible. His main point here is that, so modified, the arguments also imply that God's existence is a necessary condition for life's being meaningful. So, Metz's view is that insofar as one argues that immortality is necessary for life's having a certain kind of value, one thereby has an argument that God's existence is also necessary for life's having that kind of value.

For Metz, the requirement of immortality goes hand in hand with a requirement of God's existence. One might contrast this view with my own secular arguments to the effect that an immortal life could be choiceworthy. Of course, I am simply offering reasons to suppose that an immortal life could be appealing to creatures like us; I am not offering an argument for the conclusion that, in order for our lives to be choiceworthy, they *must* be immortal.

Brooke Alan Trisel ("Human Extinction and the Value of Our Efforts") considers an interesting extrapolation of the immortality requirement for life's meaningfulness: the requirement that our species continue indefinitely into the future, in order for our lives to be meaningful. Trisel argues against both the immortality requirement and the additional view about the continuation of our species. He suggests that we implicitly and inappropriately shift our standards for what is worthwhile and meaningful when we go from an engaged context (a context of immersion in life) to a more abstract context (such as a perspective from which we look back on stretches of our lives). Trisel points out that it is easy to "increase the standard" or raise the bar that we previously used to evaluate whether our efforts were significant when we engage in a kind of abstract or detached (or perhaps retro-spective) theorizing. But it is not obvious that the higher standard derived from the more abstract perspective is the correct or appropriate standard. Just as I argued that we should not have an inappropriately high standard for judging an immortal life, so Trisel argues that we should not adopt an inappropriately high standard for judging a mortal life.

In my other contribution, "Free Will, Death, and Immortality: The Role of Narrative," I further defend the contention that immortality (not involving an afterlife) could be choiceworthy for human beings. Some philosophers argue in the following way against the notion that we could be immortal (in the relevant sense). Our lives are – or have associated with them – narratives; furthermore, this is not just a contingent fact about us. However, narratives must have endings. Thus, our lives must have endings, and immortality is impossible for creatures like us.

In addressing this kind of argument, I first imagine that immortal lives could be envisaged as corresponding to (say) a series of interlocking short stories or novels. On this sort of approach, each part of our lives could have all the characteristic features of narrativity, including having an ending. Of course, there will not be a single, unified, overarching narrative corresponding to an immortal life with a single ending that brings closure and illumination to the entire life. But still, there will be endings to each of the parts, just as there are endings to each of the novels in a series of novels.

I also distinguish various features of narratives. One important feature is having an ending; this helps the narrative to provide a sense of "totalizing illumination" and a certain distinctive kind of closure. But an equally significant feature of narrativity is "meaning holism": The meaning or value of a particular event in the narrative can depend crucially on its relationship to other events in the narrative. So, for instance, one can change the meaning of a prior event in the narrative; that prior event can acquire a new meaning, depending on what happens subsequently. Even if an immortal life lacks an ending, it can certainly be characterized by meaning holism, both within the parts and across the different parts. For example, frequently in serial novels one finds the same characters who develop both within and across the various novels. So, even if one has to give up the notion of the distinctive kind of illumination and closure provided by a single ending to an overarching story, one can still have meaning holism and thus an important feature of narrativity in an immortal life.

On my view, then, we can have much of what we want from narrativity in an immortal life, even though we must give up on the possibility of an ending. Joshua Seachris ("Death, Futility, and the Proleptic Power of Narrative Ending") can be interpreted in part as showing just how much is lost on a model such as mine. He begins by pointing out that on what he calls a "naturalistic meta-narrative," a story that ends in death and nothing thereafter, it is easy to understand the associated feelings of "cosmic futility." Returning to Tolstoy's original point, on such a naturalist narrative everything we experience will eventually end and (like us) everything we create will eventually turn to dust and ashes. Seachris says (p. 461):

> If we and all the products of our human energies including the immediate building of a family, accomplishments, and the distant traces of progeny will some day cease to

exist *forever*, then our lives and our pursuits, indeed, existence in its entirety, are deeply futile.

Seachris offers an explanation of this sense of deep or cosmic futility by highlighting what he calls the "proleptic power" of a narrative's ending: the power the ending has to elicit a wide range of responses to the narrative as a whole. He states (p. 465):

> The general point [...] is that the way life ends is so important to us, because narrative ending itself is important to us. And, if we view life as whole meta-narratively, it becomes clearer why we are so concerned with how it will all end. Neither naturalist nor theist can avoid the evaluative encroachment of the apocalypse into the present moment of their respective meta-narratives.

Seachris's point is not just that endings are important for us in a host of ways; he also contends that a purely naturalistic ending to a finite human life will lead to feelings of futility and despair. Thus, on this view an immortal life (conceived of naturalistically) would lack something important, and a finite human life that ends in death (with nothing thereafter) would also lack something important – something that can structure and give a distinctive kind of meaning to the whole life.

It might be helpful to pause briefly to consider the insight offered by Seachris. In the end of a naturalistic, finite narrative, death occurs and thus Tolstoy worried that everything is futile. In response, one might wonder why the endpoint of the narrative should be given so much significance. After all, just because a beautiful and rewarding activity will eventually be over, why does that vitiate the meaning of engaging in the activity? Why is the perspective from the endpoint the only relevant perspective or the most important one? Also, simply because one's pain will eventually end, it does not follow that it doesn't matter *now* that one is in pain or that one shouldn't take measures to alleviate it.

Seachris can certainly concede these points, but he will also highlight something deep and significant for human beings: the importance of endings. If our lives are conceptualized as narratives (or corresponding to narratives), we can begin to see the importance of endings. In a narrative, the ending brings a distinctive kind of illumination: All of the events leading up to it are brought together and interpreted in light of the ending. This is the "proleptic" power of the narrative ending, and Seachris counsels us to keep this insight in mind when evaluating different sorts of lives – finite and infinite.

How exactly could a religious view, according to which there is the possibility of eternal life in communion with God (in heaven), provide a suitable "ending"? Here Seachris distinguishes three interpretations of "ending" – termination, telos, and closure. Obviously, eternal life in heaven would not count as "termination." But, Seachris argues, it could count as a telos and also provide a sense of closure. In these senses, Seachris suggests that a certain sort of religious narrative can provide something left out of either a finite or an infinite naturalistic model; whereas the finite naturalistic model terminates in nothingness, the infinite naturalistic model offers an ending in none of the three senses of "ending."

Paul Moser's article ("Divine Hiddenness, Death, and Meaning") provides a further defense of the appeal of the religious narrative in avoiding a sense of the futility of our efforts. Moser (p. 483) says this about death, on a materialist view:

> Our ultimately hopeless destiny, given materialism, is a reality beyond our power to change. We can't save ourselves or anyone else from the abyss of final dispersion and destruction. Our intelligence, however sophisticated, can't save us. Our philosophy, however profound, can't save us. Our willful drive, however resolute, can't save us. Nor can our families, friends, colleagues, or community save us […] Death will leave us in its cold wake, regardless of our cleverness, drive, or acquaintances.

However, whereas it might be conceded by a naturalist that something is indeed lost – something of genuine value – in a purely naturalistic model, he presumably will also point out that his model can nevertheless depict lives of significant value. (Again, as I suggest, there can be crucial features of narrativity, even in a naturalistic model of immortal life.) Furthermore, the naturalist will contend that there must be independent reason to accept the religious narrative; reason apart from simply noting that it would be desirable to achieve a certain sort of narrative closure, lest acceptance of a religious model be driven by wishful thinking. Moser says: "In the face of death, we can reasonably be hopeful only if we have outside help from a power that can overcome death" (p. 483). But presumably, the hope would be reasonable only if there is some independent reason to think that the help is actually available – independent, that is, of the (manifest) desirability of its being available.

Suggestions for Further Reading

Bortolotti, Lisa (2010) "Agency, life extension, and the meaning of life," *The Monist* 93(January): 38–56.

Bovens, Luc (1999) "The value of hope," *Philosophy and Phenomenological Research* 59(September): 667–81.

Chappell, Timothy (2009) "Infinity goes up on trial: Must immortality be meaningless?" *European Journal of Philosophy* March: 30–44.

Fischer, John Martin (1993) "Recent work on death and the meaning of life," *Philosophical Books* 34(April): 65–74.

Fischer, John Martin (2006) "Epicureanism about death and immortality," *Journal of Ethics* 10(December): 355–81.

Fischer, John Martin (2009) *Our Stories: Essays on Life, Death, and Free Will*, New York: Oxford University Press.

Gems, David (2003) "Is more life always better? The new biology of aging and the meaning of life," *The Hastings Center Report* 33(July–August): 31–9.

Haldane, John (2003) "Religion, death and the meaning of life," in *An Intelligent Person's Guide to Religion*, London: Duckworth, pp. 177–206.

Hart, David Bentley (2008) "Death, final judgment, and the meaning of life," in Jerry L. Walls (ed.), *The Oxford Handbook of Eschatology*, Oxford: Oxford University Press, 476–89.

Kamm, F. M. (2003) "Rescuing Ivan Ilych: How we live and how we die," *Ethics* 113(January): 202–33.

Kass, Leon R. (2001) "L'Chaim and its limits: Why not immortality?" *First Things* 113: 17–24.

Leslie, John (1983) "Why not let life become extinct?" *Philosophy* 58(July): 329–38.

Levine, Michael (1987) "What does death have to do with the meaning of life?" *Religious Studies* 23: 457–65.

Lewis, C. S. (1995) "*De futilitate*," in *Christian Reflections*, Grand Rapids, MI: William B. Eerdmans.

Moore, A. W. (2006) "Williams, Nietzsche, and the meaninglessness of immortality," *Mind* 115(April): 311–30.

Nussbaum, Martha C. (1989) "Mortal immortals: Lucretius on death and the voice of nature," *Philosophy and Phenomenological Research* 50: 303–51.

Perrett, Roy W. (1985) "Tolstoy, death and the meaning of life," *Philosophy* 60(April): 231–45.

Perrett, Roy W. (1986) "Regarding immortality," *Religious Studies* 22: 219–33.

Preston, Ted M., and Scott Dixon (2007) "Who wants to live forever? Immortality, authenticity, and living forever in the present," *International Journal for Philosophy of Religion* 61(April): 99–117.

Rouner, Leroy S. (ed.) (2001) *If I Should Die*, Notre Dame, IN: University of Notre Dame Press.

Smuts, Aaron (2011) "Immortality and significance," *Philosophy and Literature* 35(April): 134–49.

Trisel, Brooke Alan (2002) "Futility and the meaning of life debate," *Sorites* 14: 70–84.

Williams, Bernard (1973) "The Makropulos case: Reflections on the tedium of immortality," in *Problems of the Self: Philosophical Papers, 1956–1972*, Cambridge: Cambridge University Press, pp. 82–100.

Wisnewski, J. Jeremy (2005) "Is the immortal life worth living?" *International Journal for Philosophy of Religion* 58(February): 207–14.

5.1

A Confession

Leo Tolstoy

When I got married my search for the meaning of life was completely diverted. My whole life became centered around my family and how to increase our means of livelihood. I tasted the temptation of authorship, as well as the immense monetary rewards and recognition that came with it, and managed to stifle all questions as to the meaning of my own life or life in general.

So I lived, but then something strange began to happen to me. I began to experience moments of perplexity where life "froze," as though I did not know what to do or how to live, and I felt lost and became dejected. But this passed, and I went on living as before. Then these moments of perplexity began to reoccur more and more frequently, and invariably took the same form. When they came, the same questions kept coming to my mind: "Why? What is it for? What does it lead to?"

At first it seemed to me that these were aimless, irrelevant questions. Besides, finding the answers wouldn't be difficult. But these questions kept pressing themselves on me, pounding on me to find an answer. Their persistence was like drops of ink always falling on one place till they ran together into one black blot.

Then something happened to me, which was very much like what occurs to everyone stricken with a mortal disease. At first trivial symptoms of indisposition appear, to which the sick person pays no attention; then these symptoms reappear more and more frequently until they merge into uninterrupted periods of suffering. The suffering increases and, before the sick person can look around, what he took for a mere indisposition has become more important to him than anything else on earth – it is death!

This is exactly what happened to me. I became aware that my condition was not a chance indisposition, but something very serious, and that if all these questions continued to press

Leo Tolstoy (2006) "A Confession," in *Spiritual Writings*, ed. Charles E. Moore, Orbis Books, pp. 46–58.

on me I would have to find an answer to them. But the questions seemed so foolish, so simple, so childish, and yet, no sooner had I taken hold of them and attempted to answer them than I was convinced, first, that they were neither childish nor silly, but were concerned with the deepest problems of life, and, in the second place, try as I would, I was unable to solve them.

I was determined, however, to figure out *why* I was living as I was. As long as I did not know the reason *why* I could not do anything, I could not live. While thinking about the management of my household and estate, which greatly preoccupied me at that time, the question would suddenly occur: "Well, you have five thousands acres of land, and three hundred horses – What then? So what?"

I was absolutely muddled up inside, and did not know what to think. When thinking about how best to educate my children, I would ask myself: "What for?" Or when thinking about how best to promote the welfare of the peasants, I would suddenly say to myself: "But what does it matter to me?" And when I thought about the fame that all my literary works would bring to me, I would say to myself: "Very well, I will become famous. So what? What then?"

I could find no answers, but the questions would not wait. They had to be answered at once, and if I did not answer them, it was impossible for me live. But no answer was being given. I felt that the ground on which I stood was crumbling, that there was nothing for me to stand on, that what I had been living from and for was nothing, that I had no solid reason for living.

My life then came to a standstill. I could breathe, eat, drink, and sleep, for I could not help doing these things. But there was no real life in me because I did not have a single desire, the fulfillment of which I could feel to be reasonable. If I wished for anything, I knew before-hand that, were I to satisfy the wish, or were I not to satisfy it, nothing would come of it. Had a fairy appeared and offered me anything I desired, I wouldn't have known what to say.

I couldn't even wish to know the truth, because I surmised that life was ultimately mean-ingless. Every day of life, every step in it, brought me, as it were, nearer the precipice, and I saw clearly that before me there was nothing but ruin. And to stop was impossible; to go back was impossible; and it was impossible to shut my eyes so as not to see that there was nothing before me but suffering and death, absolute annihilation.

·

So here I was, a healthy, fortunate man, but with no reason for living. As a result, an irresistible power compelled me to rid myself one way or other of life. I cannot say I *wished* to kill myself. The power that drew me away from life was stronger, fuller, and more wide-spread than any mere wish. It was a force similar to that of wanting to live, only in a contrary direction.

All my strength drew me away from life. The thought of self-destruction now came to me as naturally as thoughts of how to improve my life had come formerly. And it was so seductive that I had to be cunning with myself lest I should carry it out too hastily.

Besides, I still wanted to do everything possible to disentangle the matter. "If I cannot unravel these riddles now, there will always be time." And it was then that I, a man blessed by fortune, hid a cord from myself lest I should hang myself from the crosspiece of the partition in my room where I undressed alone every evening. I also ceased to go out shooting with a gun lest I should be tempted by so easy a way of ending my life. I did not know what I wanted: I feared life, desired to escape from it, yet still hoped for something.

There is a tale, told long ago, of a traveler overtaken on a plain by an enraged beast. In trying to escape from the beast he crawls into a dry well, but immediately sees that at the bottom of the well is a dragon with open jaws ready to swallow him. And the unfortunate man, not daring to climb out lest he should be destroyed by the enraged beast, and not daring to leap to the bottom of the well lest he should be eaten by the dragon, seizes a twig growing in a crack in the well and clings to it. His hands are growing weaker and he feels he will soon have to resign himself to the destruction that awaits him above or below; but still he clings on.

Then he sees two mice, a black one and a white one, going regularly around and around the stem of the twig to which he is clinging and gnawing at it. And soon the twig will snap and he will fall into the dragon's jaws. The traveler knows that he will inevitably perish; but while still hanging on he looks around, sees some drops of honey on the leaves of the twig, reaches them with his tongue and licks them.

So I too clung to the twig of life, knowing that the dragon of death was awaiting me, ready to tear me to pieces; and I could not understand why I had fallen into such torment. I tried to lick the honey that formerly consoled me, but the honey no longer gave me pleasure, and the white and black mice of day and night gnawed at the branch by which I hung. I saw the dragon clearly and the honey no longer tasted sweet. I only saw the inescapable dragon and the mice, and I could not tear my gaze from them. And this is not a fable but the real unanswerable predicament that faces every human being.

The deception of the joys of life that formerly relieved my terror of the dragon now no longer deceived me. The two drops of honey that diverted my eyes from the cruel truth of my existence, my love of family and of writing, were no longer sweet to me.

"Family" … I said to myself. But my wife and children are also human. They are placed just as I am: they must either live in a lie or see the terrible truth. Why should they live? Why should I love them, protect them, nurture them? Loving them, I cannot hide the truth from them: each step in knowledge leads them to the truth. And the truth is death.

But what about "writing"? Wasn't this one thing I could do that could escape the clutches of death? But soon I saw that this too was a fraud. As long as I believed that life had meaning, though one I could not express, the reflection of life in writing afforded me pleasure. It was pleasant to look at life in the mirror of literary works. But once I began to seek the meaning of my life, I could no longer soothe myself with what I now saw in the mirror, namely, that my life made no sense and was desperate. Once I grasped how meaningless and terrible my own life was, the play in the mirror could no longer amuse me. No sweetness of honey could be sweet to me once I saw the dragon and saw the mice gnawing away my support.

But this was not all. Had I simply understood that life had no meaning I could have borne it quietly, knowing that this was my lot. But I could not satisfy myself with that. Had I been like a man living in a jungle in which there was no exit, I could have lived. But I was like one lost in a jungle who, horrified at having lost his way, rushes about wishing to find the path. He knows that each step he takes confuses him even more, but still he cannot help rushing about. In my search for answers to life's questions I experienced just what a person feels when lost in a forest. He reaches a glade, climbs a tree, and clearly sees the limitless distance, but sees that his home is not and cannot be there. Then he goes into the dark wood and sees only the darkness; his home is not there.

My life was indeed terrible. And to rid myself of the terror I was ready to kill myself. I felt a horror of what awaited me and knew that it was more horrible than the position I was in. Yet I could not just wait patiently for the end. The horror of the darkness was too great to bear, and I longed to free myself from it as quickly as possible with a rope or a bullet. This was the feeling that, above all, drew me to the brink of suicide.

•

My question – that which at the age of fifty brought me to the verge of suicide – was the simplest of questions, a question lying in the soul of every person. It was a question without an answer to which one cannot live, as I had found by experience. It was: "What will come of what I am doing today or shall do tomorrow? What will come of my life? What is life for?"

Differently expressed, the question is: "Why should I live, why hope for anything, or do anything?" It can also be expressed thus: "Does my life have any meaning that death cannot destroy?"

To this one question, variously expressed, I sought an answer in philosophy and science. According to philosophy, the essence of life and all that exists, is designated as "idea," or "substance," or "spirit," or "will." It's all one and the same: that the essence of life exists and that I am of that same essence.

But why this essence exists the philosopher does not know, and does not say, if he is a careful enough thinker. I ask: "Why should this essence exist? What results from the fact that it is and will be? Philosophy not only cannot answer this question, but can only put forth the same question. If it keeps firmly to its proper sphere, it can only answer the question, "What am I, and what is the universe?" by saying, "All and nothing," and to the question, "Why?" by adding, "I do not know."

When I turned to the study of science the result was the same. "What is the meaning of my life?" "There is none." Or: "What will come of my life?" "Nothing." Or: "Why does everything exist that exists, and why do I exist?" "Because it exists."

I fared no better in turning to the more exact sciences. "What is the meaning of my life?" The biologist answers: "You are what you call your 'life'; you are a transitory, causal cohesion of particles. The mutual interactions and changes of these particles produce in you what you call your 'life'. That cohesion will last some time; afterward the interaction of these particles will cease and what you call 'life' will cease, and so will all your questions. You are an accidentally united little lump of energy. That little lump undergoes decomposition, which we call 'life'; the lump disintegrates, decomposition ends, and with it all the questions."

So answers the scientist.

What I found in philosophy and science I confronted elsewhere among history's sages. For Socrates, life in the body was a deception. Its destruction was thus a blessing, and we should desire it. According to Solomon, everything in the world – folly and wisdom and riches and poverty and mirth and grief – all was vanity and empty. We die and nothing is left of us. It is all very senseless. For the Buddha, we must ultimately free ourselves from life, as life itself consists of suffering. For Schopenhauer, life is something that should not exist at all; it is an evil. Only the passage into Nothingness is good. And what these thinkers have said has been said and thought and felt by millions upon millions of people like them. I too have thought it and felt it.

So my search in philosophy and among the sciences and sages of history, far from freeing me from my despair, only increased it. All was vanity! Happy is he who has not been born. Death is better than life, and one must free oneself from this life.

·

I then turned my attention to the people around me, hoping to find an answer from them. I began to observe how people like myself lived, and what their attitude was to this question that brought me into such despair.

Some simply asserted that life was an absurdity. There was no answer to life's questions. Others, the majority, argued that while life had no ultimate meaning, one should just eat, drink, and be merry. Still others argued that life consisted in strength and power, in destroying life. The absurdity of life could be overcome by taking one's own life in defiance, promptly ending the stupid joke. Though small in number, more and more in our circle were choosing this path. Finally, some admitted that life had no meaning, but in weakness we had to pretend that it did. In short, among my peers the terrible contradiction of life was simply evaded.

I could no longer do this. Had I enough courage I would have ended my life, but I see now that I didn't kill myself because inside me there was a dim awareness that something was not quite right in the way I was approaching my dilemma. I knew that my very act of thinking affirmed the validity of my life. Or to put it another way: were there no life, reason itself would not exist. Reason was life's son. Reason was the fruit of life, yet my reason rejected life itself. Something was wrong here.

There was another thing that nagged me. It was easy to see the pointlessness of living, yet the simplest, most down-to-earth folk around me lived and did so believing that life had meaning. How was this? How did they possess a sense of meaning when all I could conclude was life was pointless?

I instinctively felt that if I wished to live and understand the meaning of life, I must seek this meaning not among my cultured peers, those who lived for no satisfactory reason, but among the masses of those simple, uneducated, and poor people who live and affirm life's meaning, despite the conclusions delivered by reason. Their lives, though rationally groundless, had purpose. They lived by a faith that I, in all my reasonableness, had rejected.

With this realization, however, my situation became even worse. The path of reason led me to reject life. Yet to turn to faith demanded that I deny reason, which was yet more impossible for me than a denial of life. To understand the meaning of life I would have to turn to faith, but to do this I would also have to renounce my reason – the very thing for which alone meaning could be determined. And yet I had to admit that besides rational knowledge there seemed to exist a kind of knowledge – faith – that enabled people to live and that provided them answers to the questions I was asking.

And then it dawned on me that in order to live at all one must believe in something. Faith was the strength of life. Without believing that life was worth living, we would not live. And if I did not acknowledge the illusory nature of the finite, then I had to believe in the finite;

or, if I saw the illusory nature of the finite, then I had to believe in the Infinite. Either way, I realized that no one lives without faith, not even the strictest rationalist.

•

My new realization about the necessity of faith forced me to go back to my original question, which, in turn, helped me to see that the answer I wanted had to do with the Infinite's relation to the finite, and vice versa. What I needed to know was what the meaning of my life had *beyond* time and space, and not what my life meant within the confines of time and space. The answer to that, of course, was: "None."

By appealing only to reason I could not get myself out of the quargmire of finitude, and thus life was meaningless. But by faith I could find an answer to life's meaning. For faith alone offered the key to understanding why life was worth living and why it was we instinctively don't end our own lives. Faith pointed me away from myself to the Infinite, of which I was a part.

What I eventually discovered was that the conception of an infinite God, along with the divinity of the soul, the connection of human affairs with God, the unity and existence of the soul, and our conception of moral goodness and evil – that all of these are hidden in the infinity of human thought. They are the very things without which neither life nor I would exist.

With Solomon, I began to understood that *our* wisdom was folly. I also saw that reason by itself always ran in a vicious circle, like a cogwheel the teeth of which no longer catch in another. However much and however well we may be able to reason we cannot get an answer to our question by reason alone; it will always be $0 = 0$. Finally, I began to grasp that the answers given by faith were stored up in the deepest recesses of human wisdom and that I had no right to deny them on the basis of reason, and that those answers were the only ones that truly solved life's riddle.

So the key to my quest was faith. But not the faith of my self-indulgent peers. These "believers," like myself, lived in comfort and ease while still being gripped by a fear of suffering and death. Like myself, they lived to satisfy their desires and lived just as badly, if not worse, than those who didn't profess any faith. No arguments could convince me of the truth of their faith. Only deeds that would free me from what I dreaded – poverty, sickness, and death – could convince me. And so I turned to the faith of the common people and to those outside the church.

The more I looked at their life the more I became convinced that they were the ones, despite their various superstitions, who had real faith. I found, contrary to those in my own circle, that these folks were content with life – despite a life of heavy labor and hardship. In complete contrast to their ignorance, they knew the meaning of life and death, labored quietly, endured deprivations and suffering, and lived and died seeing therein not vanity but good. And after living among these folks for several years I understood that *that* is life itself, and that the meaning given to that life was truth: and I accepted it.

•

How then was I able to return to my original faith, the one I once held when I was younger but later rejected? What repelled me in the past, as I discovered, was not the faith but the meaninglessness of those lives who lived in contradiction to the faith they professed. This included my own. I went astray not because I erred in my thinking but because I lived badly. It was not an error in my thought that hid the truth from me so much as my life itself, with its epicurean pursuit of satisfying one's pleasures. I asked myself what my life amounted to and got the reply: an evil and an absurdity. And so it was.

But then I made the mistake of concluding that life in general was absurd. I loved the darkness more than the light, but instead of recognizing this I lashed out at life itself. The truth was always as true as that two and two are four, but I refused to acknowledge it, because on admitting two and two to be four I had also to admit that my life was bad and that it was I who had made it so. But I could not do this. I felt I was a good person.

But then I came to love good, honest people. Now everything became clear to me. Compared to them, I had been living as a parasite. My comfort, my welfare, and all my learned discussions were at the expense of those who really earned their living. Yet it was these very people who knew how to live and were happy, not I.

If a naked, hungry beggar has been taken from the crossroads, brought into a building belonging to a beautiful establishment, fed, supplied with drink, and made to move a handle up and down, it is evident that the beggar, before seeking to know why he was taken, why he should work the handle, and whether the arrangements of the establishment are reasonable or not, must first move the handle. If he moves the handle he will understand that it works a pump, that the pump draws water, and that the water irrigates the garden beds. Then he will be taken from the pumping station to another place where he will gather fruits and will enter into the joy of his master, and, passing from lower to higher work, will understand better and better the arrangements of the whole establishment; and he will take part with them without once stopping to ask why he is there, nor will he ever think of reproaching the master of that place.

So it is with those who do the will of their master, the simple, uneducated working folk, whom so many of us educated ones regard as cattle. They do not reproach the master, but we, the wise, eat the master's food but do not do what the master wishes, and instead of doing it sit in a circle and discuss: "Why should that handle be moved? Isn't it stupid to move such a handle?" And when we have thought it all out, what is our conclusion? Why, that the master is stupid or that he doesn't even exist, while we wise ones ultimately feel we are fit for nothing, and that we must somehow or other end our lives.

The conviction that the truth could only be found by living it eventually led me to doubt the rightness of my own life. I began to understand that to grasp life's meaning I had to stop living like a parasite and live a real life. I also had to heed more attentively to my heart, from which my search for God needed to proceed. For I knew that any conception of God I might have would still be but a conception, one that I could evoke or refrain from evoking in myself. That was not what I wanted to seek. I wanted that without which there could be no life. Only then could I truly live. For based on fading memories of my past, I only lived, really lived, when I felt him and sought him with my whole heart.

And then finally, more than ever before, everything within me and around me lit up. "What more did I have to seek?" exclaimed a voice within me. "This is He. God is that without which you cannot live. To know God and to live is one and the same thing! God is life. Live seeking God, and then you will not live without God." This light that had dawned inside and around me never again abandoned me. And I was saved.

I had come full circle. In short, what happened to me was something like this: I was put into a boat and pushed off from an unknown shore, shown the direction to the opposite shore, had oars put into my unskilled hands, and was left alone. I rowed as best I could and moved forward, but the further I advanced toward the middle of the stream, the more rapidly grew the current, bearing me away from my goal. More and more I encounter others, like myself, borne away by the stream.

There were a few rowers who continued to row, but then there were others who had abandoned their oars. There were large boats and immense vessels full of people. Some struggled against the current, others yielded to it. And the further I went, the more, as I watched the long line floating down the current, I forgot the course pointed out to me as my own.

In the very middle of the stream, amid the crowd of boats and vessels floating down, I had altogether lost the course and so threw down my oars. From all sides the joyful and exulting navigators, as they rowed or sailed downstream, assured me – and each other – that no other direction was possible. And I believed them and floated right along. And I was carried far, so far that I heard the roar of the rapids in which I was bound to perish, and I could even see boats that had been shattered from them.

Then I came to my senses. It was long before I clearly comprehended what had happened to me. I saw before me nothing but destruction, toward which I was rushing, which I dreaded. I saw no safety anywhere and did not know what to do!

Yet on looking back, I saw a countless number of boats engaged in a ceaseless struggle against the force of the torrent. Then I remembered the shore, the oars, and the course, and at once I began to row hard up the stream and again toward the shore. That shore was God, that course was the wisdom of the Ages, those oars were the free will given me to make for the shore and unite with God. And so the force of life was renewed in me and I again began to live.

5.2

Annihilation

Steven Luper-Foy

> *I do not want to die – no; I neither want to die nor do I want to want to die; I want to live for ever and ever and ever.*
>
> Miguel de Unamuno, *Tragic Sense of Life*

Like Unamuno, many people find it abhorrent to think that well within 90 years they are going to die and utterly cease to exist. Those who believe that they will *never* cease to exist (perhaps because they think of dying as a transition to an afterlife in which they will live forever) are usually happy about it, and would not willingly forgo the immortality they expect. People who look upon annihilation as a grim prospect certainly may be well aware that under certain circumstances it must be regarded as the lesser of the evils among which choice is limited.[1] They realize that it may be the only escape from a spate of creatively cruel torture, for example, and so a better option than suffering further pain. They may even be willing to say that if their lives were long enough and their possibilities exhausted, then insufferable boredom would set in.[2] And dying after a short life of (say) 100 years might be better than being forced to live on into a future that consists of an eternity of empty, indistinguishable days. But to acknowledge that there are worse fates than annihilation in the near future, is not to deny that it is a terrible fate. Aside from a future filled with the agonies or boredom of the damned, a worse fate than no future at all is difficult to imagine. It *may* be that forever is longer than anyone would voluntarily live; but how many would refuse the chance to drink a potion that would allow them to live as long as they liked?

Even people who argue that dying is not a bad thing do not really seem to believe what they are saying.[3] More often than not, their anxiety to believe in the innocuousness of their

Steven Luper-Foy (1987) "Annihilation," *Philosophical Quarterly* 37(148): 233–52.

demise prevents even brilliant thinkers from realizing that their arguments are inane. Epicurus' famous argument, for example, is about as absurd as any I have seen.

> Death is nothing to us. It concerns neither the living nor the dead, since for the former it is not, and the latter are no more.[4]

Make no mistake about it: when Epicurus speaks here of death, he means *annihilation*, and his claim is that annihilation is *nothing* to us. The self-deception of people like Epicurus is not conscious; we cannot relieve our anxiety by swallowing beliefs of whose inanity we are aware. But deception is nonetheless at work.

Let us assume with Epicurus that death means annihilation. Then can we truthfully say that death is *nothing* to us? I think not. Nor should we *want* to believe that the deaths we shall soon face are nothing to us, I shall argue. Once we see what we would have to be like in order to be truly as unconcerned about dying as Epicurus professed to be, we shall see that we are better off dreading our dying day. However, I shall suggest that there are steps we can take to ensure that if luck is on our side, dying will not be *as* bad a thing for us as it is capable of being. But few are so lucky.

I.   The Misfortune of Dying

Why should anyone believe that dying (thought of as annihilation) is a misfortune? One suggestion begins with the observation that something is a misfortune for us if it thwarts our desires.[5] You would do me an evil if you stole my cherished pet, since thereby you prevent me from fulfilling my desire to live in peace with my pet. On the other hand, if all I wanted for my pet was that it lead a reasonably comfortable life, and it was not my wish that it be *me* who provided for its comfort, then you would do me no harm if you stole my pet so long as you saw to its well-being. In so doing you would not have thwarted my desires.

It seems reasonable to say, then, that whatever prevents me from getting what I want is a misfortune for me. But if something that thwarts my desires is an evil for me, then dying is an evil for me (though perhaps the lesser of all the evils that are inevitable in my circumstances), since it thwarts my desires. Of course, to say that dying thwarts my desires is to understand 'thwarting my desires' liberally. An event can prevent me from fulfilling my desires not just by frustrating my attempts to fulfill them, but also by *removing* my desires. If an event pulls one of my desires out by the roots, it certainly does prevent me from fulfilling it. It is in this sense that dying thwarts my desires. It is a misfortune for me for the same reason that being forced to swallow a drug that washes away my desires (including my desire *not* to have swallowed the drug) is a misfortune for me.

We have said that dying is a bad thing for us since it frustrates our desires. However, a more accurate way to put matters is that dying is bad for us *if* it thwarts our desires. On the strength of the premise that what thwarts my desires is a misfortune for me, we cannot conclude that my dying is a bad thing for me unless I *have* desires that would be thwarted by my death. A death which comes when I have exhausted *all* of my ambitions will be a welcome release from a life destined to be one of excruciating emptiness.

An objection can even be made to the thesis that a death which frustrates its victim's desires is an evil. Suppose that at some point in our lives the only goals we *do* have left would fail to be rewarding or would even make us miserable if we were to achieve them. We would not judge something to be an evil for us if the only goals it frustrated or eradicated were ones which would prove to be unfulfilling or ones which would make us miserable if we were to accomplish them. So dying at a time that interrupts only our pursuit of such goals should not be regarded as a misfortune for us. But an important sort of death, it would seem, remains an evil, namely, one that prevents its victims from fulfilling *fulfilling* desires. Call such a death a *premature* one. Even prematurity as we have defined it is not an infallible sign of a regrettable end; however, it will serve us well enough.

II.   Epicureans

The idea that a premature death is a misfortune for its victim seems rather obvious. I believe that it has been responsible for most of the anxiety which people (such as I) have felt about dying; it seems to them very likely that they are going to die prematurely even if they live to be 120 years old, which they will not. Their plans stretch far out into their futures, and they see no reason why a hundred years from now they would not plan ahead with equal fervor – if it were not for the realization that they cannot survive the inevitable physical breakdown of their bodies which is soon to take place.

Those of us who are uncomfortable or even bitter about dying are appalled by the cheerful indifference of people who are capable of agreeing with Epicurus' absurd claim that "death is nothing to us." What would people have to be *like* to really think that their deaths are nothing to them (assuming that their lack of concern is not simply due to their refusal to dwell upon "morbid" subjects)? The answer, as we shall see, is that to the extent that such people are understandable at all, they are rather coldhearted and passionless. Having said that, I nonetheless want to claim that they are worth careful study. By emulating a certain sort of "Epicurean", as I shall call an individual who is indifferent to dying, it may be possible for others to acquire a measure of equanimity in the face of death without adopting the less desirable characteristics of Epicureans. But before I describe the kind of Epicurean it would behoove us to become, I shall describe others whose ways we should shun.

Virtually the only thing worse than the prospect of spending eternity in unmitigated agony is the prospect of spending eternity in *even more intense* agony. It is obvious that dying would be better than either fate. But Epicureans could agree only if they were not completely indifferent to dying. To agree, they must be willing to admit that under some circumstances dying can be the best of all available alternatives because of the escape it provides. Yet this they cannot do. The fact that the Epicureans are *completely* indifferent to dying means that they never under any circumstances either want to die or want not to die, and that is possible only if under no circumstances do they prefer dying to anything nor anything to dying. This makes Epicureans considered as *completely* indifferent to dying extremely foreign; hence let us try to describe Epicureans whose indifference is somewhat limited. Our Epicureans are capable of thinking that dying is preferable to some alternatives, since it allows them to escape from an unbearable mode of life. But they remain incapable of thinking that there is an alternative than which dying is *worse*. For them, dying is no worse than (i.e., it is at least as good as) remaining alive no matter how utopian life might be. They believe that dying can be a good thing, but they cannot believe that it is ever a bad thing.

Because Epicureans prefer dying to various possibilities, they must be capable of having desires whose form can be expressed as follows:

I want the following to be the case:
Were X not the case at given time *t*, then I would be dead at *t*.[6]

Call desires of this form *escape* desires. They set out conditions under which life is so bad that, according to the Epicureans, death is preferable. If Epicureans had no desires of this form, they would be incapable of ranking dying over living no matter what living entailed, even if living meant torture of the worst sort.

I think that we can make a further assumption about Epicureans, namely, even *they* must agree that a premature death, as we defined it, is a misfortune for its victim. It would be absurd for them to adopt an attitude of indifference when they face premature death, since that would entail being unconcerned about something that prevents them from fulfilling desires which they very much wish to fulfill.

Perhaps, however, it is hasty to think that the prospect of a premature death would dismay the otherwise unflappable Epicureans. Why couldn't they adopt the view that whatever causes us neither pain nor pleasure is a matter of indifference? This, in fact, was Epicurus' own hedonistic view[7]: something can be bad, he believed, only if it causes us pain; and something can be good only if it causes us pleasure. On the strength of the hedonistic criterion, Epicureans could claim that dying is nothing to us even if it does thwart our desires since it causes us neither pain nor pleasure. They would admit that the disease or aging process which causes us to die may be a bad thing; these causes of death may bring us experiences whose unpleasantness is formidable. But dying causes no sensations at all, they would point out. In fact, it brings about an end to all sensing. We lack even the opportunity to regret the fact that death has thwarted our desires; once we die, we experience neither pain, pleasure, nor regret for the simple reason that we experience nothing at all.

But isn't it a tragedy that death deprives us *even of the opportunity to experience, to delight, and to regret*?[8]

Consider the consequences of the hedonistic view. On this view, an event which *would* cause me great pain if I were to find out about it is a matter of indifference so long as I in fact never do. The fact that my spouse and children have fallen for the lies of my enemy and now hate me but are pretending not to is of no concern to me, according to hedonists, if my ignorance prevents that event from causing me any grief. Moreover, hedonists would cheerfully consent to being used in any way we like so long as we promise to precede their treatment with a drug that makes them *enjoy* what we do to them, or at least a drug which suppresses any unpleasant experiences that might otherwise result from the abuses we have planned for them. They could even be made to welcome our drugging away their free will so that they want to be our slaves.

At best, hedonistically inclined Epicureans could say that whatever *would* cause us neither pain nor pleasure if we *were* aware of it while not under the influence of powerful psychotropic drugs (or the like) is neither good nor bad. But this weakened sort of hedonism is not strong enough for their purposes. People who found out that their desires were going to be thwarted *would* be distressed by their discovery; they could not regard it as a matter of indifference. Nor could they be indifferent to that which thwarts their desires, and dying is one of the things that does.[9]

Epicureans never regard dying as a misfortune. But I have said that they would *have* to regard it as a misfortune if dying thwarted desires whose satisfaction would be fulfilling. Hence Epicureans must not *have* any fulfilling desires that can be frustrated by death! Death for them can never be premature or else it *would* be a bad thing; therefore they must be so constituted that any time death comes it is mature. Assuming that Epicureans *have* goals, then either they are unfulfilling ones, or else they are ones that cannot be thwarted by death. If Epicureans had any other sort of goal, they could not be unconcerned about premature death.

But what would a desire that cannot be thwarted by death be *like*? One desire that obviously is impervious to death is the desire to *die*. Rather than being thwarted by my death, my goal to die is *achieved* through my death. Like the death wish, escape desires are also invulnerable to death. They are qualified desires for death: they say that if certain conditions are met, we wish to be dead. But they do not imply that there are any conditions under which we do *not* want to be dead. Hence death presents no obstacle to our satisfying them.

Nor does the list of relevant desires end there. Some of our aims are such that our chances of successfully accomplishing them are not really affected by what we do in the course of our lives or even by whether or not we *are* alive. Being alive does not help us achieve these ends; hence they cannot be thwarted by our deaths. Since the likelihood that such goals will be achieved does not depend on what we do with our lives, let us call these *independent* goals. Ones whose chances of being achieved do depend on our activities we can call *dependent* goals. My desire that the moon continue to orbit Earth, for example, is an independent goal; it cannot provide me any grounds for deploring death since the behaviour of Earth and its satellite is unaffected by what I do in the course of my life.

Goals that have been dependent in the earlier part of my life can become independent as time passes. If at some point I fully accomplish my dependent goal of at least once visiting France, then thereafter it is independent. No matter what I do thereafter, I cannot make it more or less likely that at least once I set foot in France. Even my subsequent death would not reduce my chances of achieving that end. People whose dependent ends once made them vulnerable to premature death could therefore become less vulnerable by rendering those ends independent.

There is another, more interesting, type of desire that is invulnerable to our deaths. Suppose that we care about the situation at some future time, but only on the assumption that we shall be alive at that time; if we think that we shall be dead, we are indifferent about the situation. Suicidal depressants, for example, might take this view. They may strongly wish to be dead, and they may be totally indifferent to anything that may or may not happen once they *are* dead; yet they still may have the attitude that if they *are* to be alive, they should be well fed. They desire something – in this case being well fed – only on the assumption or condition that they will continue to be alive. It will be useful to characterize such conditional desires in a more formal way. My conditional desire concerning some situation X is one that takes the following form:

I want the following to be the case:
Were I alive at *t*, X would be the case at *t*.[10]

Desires that are *not* in this way contingent on our being alive we can call *unconditional*.

Conditional desires are not independent desires. However, both dependent and independent goals are capable of being conditionalized, i.e., converted into conditional goals. Consider the dependent desire to be well fed, for example. As the case of the suicidal depressants mentioned a moment ago shows, it is entirely possible to possess a conditionalized desire to be well fed. My independent desire that the moon continue to orbit the sun can be conditionalized as well. I need only decide that what is important to me is the moon's orbit while I live.

III.   The Epicurean Attitude Toward Life

As far as I can tell, the catalogue of desires which cannot be thwarted by death is limited to escape desires, independent desires, and conditional desires. Not one of the types of goal we have catalogued can be frustrated by death, and any other type of goal *would* be vulnerable to death. Epicureans must possess no fulfilling desires except the sort we have catalogued. This is the secret of their equanimity: since none of their fulfilling desires can be thwarted by death, Epicureans never regard death as a misfortune. Since limiting their desires to the catalogued sorts is the only way Epicureans could ensure that death is no evil for them, however, we shall want to consider what kind of person they have had to become as a result of that limitation. Only then can we decide whether it would be a good idea to follow their example.

Consider their motivation to take up the activities in which we normally engage. Since Epicureans never have any reason to avoid dying, it may appear that they have no reason to do *anything* (with the possible exception of committing suicide). But this is an important mistake. It is true that their independent desires cannot provide Epicureans grounds for any activities, since by definition these are desires about whose fulfillment Epicureans can do nothing of importance. However, conditional desires do provide strong reason for action. Such desires can enable Epicureans to take an interest in things for which life is a precondition. While indifferent to the prospect of dying in their sleep, Epicureans may take the attitude that if they *do* wake, their wakeful days should be spent in vigorous pursuit of an exciting career, in raising a family, etc. And for this to be possible, they will need to seek an education and work long hours in pursuit of a career.

But wouldn't they necessarily be indifferent to their health? No, since it would be eminently reasonable for them to want to spend their days – if days they will indeed spend – in the comparative comfort and convenience of health rather than the discomfort of disease. It is not necessary to want to *avoid* dying in order to want to do things that tend to make dying unlikely. The fact that our goals make our deaths unlikely can be an unintended side-effect. Even Epicureans who are no longer living out of inertia but who have developed a positive wish to die may be unable to commit suicide because of a strong aversion to pain.

Suppose that someone went around injecting Epicureans with painless but deadly poison. Wouldn't an Epicurean society have to be indifferent about that practice, since it would not interfere with any Epicurean's desires? No, precisely because it *would* interfere. It is true that an Epicurean cannot abhor these murders on the grounds that they are bad for their *victims*. But the murders could be abhorred (unless they involve the massacre of entire societies or the entire human race) because they deprive people of their loved ones. The murders are bad for the survivors, who wanted to share their lives (if lives they will lead) with the victims. Still Epicureans could condemn the murder of pariahs who play no positive role in society only on the grounds that if that sort of thing were permitted it might lead people to kill those who *do* have a role to play. Anyone who is inclined to condemn Epicureans on the grounds that they do not appreciate how bad murder is should, however, recall that the victims *themselves* are to their very cores genuinely indifferent to dying. How bad can it be to do something to someone who is incapable of anything except absolute indifference about what you plan to do? We non-Epicureans could object to the murdering of the pariahs on Utilitarian grounds (killing them eliminates future pleasure); just as we could object to the killing of infants and animals that *cannot assess* their fates; but since the pariahs *can*, and are indifferent about future pleasure, shouldn't their rational and informed assessments win out?

So far, adopting the Epicurean approach may not seem terribly unattractive. If something which is a bad thing for us, given our present desires, turns out to be inevitable, then why not alter our desires so that we no longer must regard the inevitable as an evil?[11] Dying is inevitable, so why not disarm it by limiting ourselves to the desires of Epicureans? Unfortunately, the indifference to dying which the Epicurean approach would secure us comes at a price most of us will not be willing to pay. The attraction of the Epicurean way of looking at things is that they do not care whether their lives are shorter than usual or longer than usual; death, whenever it comes, is nothing to them. However, Epicureans think that death is nothing to them only because they think that *life* is nothing to them. They are capable of their indifference to death only because they have pared down their concerns to the point that *life* is now a matter of indifference to them. For in avoiding all aspirations that can be thwarted by death, Epicureans have had to avoid all desires which are capable of giving Epicureans a reason for living. In order to maintain their unconcern about dying, they must avoid having any reason whatsoever for not dying. However, any reason for living is an excellent reason for not dying; so only if they avoid having any reason for living can they avoid having any reason for not dying.

The extent to which Epicureans have sabotaged their motivation for living can be brought out by examining the desires to which they are limited, desires that are invulnerable to death. Independent goals (unlike dependent ones) are incapable of giving us reason to remain alive and to avoid dying, since our lives and the things we do with our lives play no role toward the achievement of such goals. Conditional desires are similarly impotent; because they apply only on the assumption that we are alive, they cannot provide grounds for being alive. Like the other desires Epicureans possess, escape desires (as well as the death wish itself) are incapable of providing any reason to remain alive; on the contrary, escape desires provide reason to *die*. Beyond conditional, independent, and escape desires, the only other desires Epicureans can have are unfulfilling ones, and these are obviously as impotent as the others with respect to motivating Epicureans to live. Out of the desires possessed by Epicureans, then, a case for remaining alive cannot be built. Since they limit their desires to those listed above, and so consider dying at least as good as any other option, it is useful to characterize the Epicurean personality as *death-tolerant*.[12] By contrast, the personality of people who have unconditional desires that make living desirable can be called *life-affirming*.

Since Epicureans cannot allow themselves any motivation to live, they must ensure that they never think that it would be *good* to live. For to say that living is good certainly implies that it is preferable to dying, which is a view Epicureans must eschew. On their view, living no sort of life would be better than dying. A conception of a good or worthwhile life is a description of a life that would be good to live; such a conception Epicureans completely lack. (What they *can* have is a conception of a life such that it is a matter of indifference whether it is lived.) To make sure they do not develop one, moreover, they must be very selective in their activities. If an activity or set of activities promises to be so enjoyable that it threatens to make a life spent in pursuit of that activity *good*, then those who wish to retain a death-tolerant personality must abandon it in haste, or at least take steps which ensure that they do not enjoy what they do so much that they begin to show an interest in living. They must fill their lives with blander fare.

Nothing said here supports the claims, occasionally made, that life's being meaningful or worthwhile is due to the fact that we die,[13] or that life is *meaningless* because we die.[14] Both claims imply that it is due to death that life has the value it does, which is not true. A life can be made neither good nor bad by the fact that it will eventually end, any more than a car can be made good or bad by the fact that it will eventually be scrapped. A life has the value it does quite independently of the fact that it will end. In fact, *death* has the value it does due to the value of the life it ends. Speaking roughly, dying is a bad thing when living on would be good, and when living on would be bad, dying is good.

Because Epicureans are not interested in anything that could lead them to regard living as a good thing, they do not care about *anything* that they believe will happen after they die, ignoring what they care about through their independent desires, which (as we have seen) have no motivational power in the Epicureans' lives anyway. Those with a death-tolerant personality live out of inertia most of the time, acting only under the influence of their conditional desires unless life becomes unpleasant enough to opt out of. But the interest which they take in things through the agency of their conditional desires does not extend beyond what they believe to be the temporal boundaries of their lives. For given that their entire attitude about whether or not a given state of affairs X holds at some time t is conditional, then if they believed that they would be dead at t, then they would be indifferent about whether or not X would hold at t. This makes Epicureans peculiar people indeed. Out of her conditional desire for their well-being, an Epicurean mother may well be concerned about whether her children will survive an imminent catastrophe, but *only* if she assumes that she too will survive. Her conditional desires leave her completely indifferent to their welfare if she assumes that she will die. Nor does the peculiar pattern of her concern for her offspring end here. She may well place herself between a crazed beast and her children since she does not think that her life will be bearable to her if they die, and so is willing to risk her life in their defense. Her life means nothing to her in any case. But she is incapable of writing a will or taking out life insurance out of concern for her children's well-being after she dies, even if she knows that they will lead a horrible existence if she fails to act. Whether their lives go well or poorly after she dies is a matter of utter indifference to her.

Still less could Epicureans desire the welfare of future generations. Because their concern for others is conditional, Epicureans cannot believe that the welfare of future generations matters at all, though the welfare of their contemporaries may be important to them.

Nonetheless, it *is* conceivable that Epicureans have a conditional desire to spend their days working for the benefit of future generations. They could take the attitude that so long as they are to go on, they will work for the benefit of posterity. And an Epicurean mother could decide that, so long as she is alive tomorrow, she will spend it working to ensure that her children flourish after she dies. However, these attitudes are not to be mistaken for concern about what occurs after the Epicureans die. Epicureans just do not care what happens then. They are capable only of indifference about the well-being of posterity, and an Epicurean mother could not care less about the welfare of her children after she believes she will die. Therefore, even if Epicureans take an interest in *working for* the welfare of posterity, they remain indifferent to the welfare of posterity. It takes peculiar people to desire to spend time ensuring that some state of affairs holds in the future even though they are indifferent about whether that state of affairs comes to be. As a matter of psychological fact, it may be impossible. So since Epicureans must sustain their indifference about the future if they are to remain Epicureans, it may be impossible for them to want to spend time influencing the future.

It is worth noting that Epicureans will remain unconcerned about what occurs after their projected dying day if they adopt the hedonist claim that everything which does not actually cause them pain or pleasure is a matter of indifference. Hedonists of this sort are capable of caring about the welfare of their children, but only their welfare at times when the hedonist parents believe that they (the parents) will be alive. For they realize that dead parents can be caused neither pain nor pleasure by the fate of their children. Earlier I argued that hedonism is too implausible to sustain the judgment that premature death is no evil. Here we have a fresh reason to steer clear of hedonism: consistent hedonists exhibit a callousness which renders their view too unsavoury to adopt.

There are still more reasons not to adopt a death-tolerant personality. Quite often, conditionalizing our desires would mutilate them so much that retaining the conditionalized versions of them is something we would not want to do or are psychologically unequipped to do. Consider, for example, the conditionalized form of our altruistic concern for the welfare of others. It is probably not really possible for us to care intensely about someone's welfare up to the point at which we believe that we shall die, yet be entirely indifferent to their welfare thereafter. Some of us could probably manage to be relatively unconcerned about anyone else's welfare at *any* time. Becoming utterly aloof in this way is probably the only way any of us could become death-tolerant, however, since none of us has the capacity to care intensely yet within sharply defined temporal boundaries.

Even the conditionalized form of a purely self-centered desire can be enormously peculiar. Our self-centered projects play an important role in our lives, and most of them can succeed only if we survive, either because we are an essential ingredient in them, as I am in my plan to become President of Money Bank, or my plan to lead a long life of adventure, or else because we play a key role in them. Hence we must conditionalize our concern for these projects if we are to emulate the Epicureans. But is a deep concern about such projects really consistent with the attitude that their failure is a matter of indifference so long as we do not live through their demise? How serious can I be about wanting to discover the cure for cancer if I am just as happy to fail so long as I do not live through my failure? The fact is that a conditionalized passion is not a passion, for we can conditionalize our passions in life only if we no longer take them seriously enough to want to live another day. Once conditionalized, they can no longer play any significant role in what might have been a worthwhile life.

IV.   Epicureanizing Our Desires

Dying is a constant threat to those of us who are unable or unwilling to abandon our concern for projects and lives whose welfare depends crucially on us, and so for us death is an evil. The strategy of the Epicureans, moreover, has proved to be unavailable to those of us who have a life-affirming personality, since they owe their indifference about longevity to their indifference to living. At best, life is a burden for those with a death-tolerant personality, something to be made as free of misery as possible; it is either a bore which they can take or leave, or a curse they would be better off without. Their view is not quite that *nothing* is anything to us, but it comes very close. Instead of succumbing to the despairing attitude that we have nothing to live for, we should be better off immersing ourselves in projects for which we *are* capable of living, and resign ourselves to the fact that we cannot persist in our endeavours for long.

Although we should not emulate the Epicureans we have described, it does seem to me that there *is* a type of Epicurean which we should strive to become. Unlike the ones we have discussed before, the Epicureans I have in mind are anxious to squeeze as much as possible out of life. But these neo-Epicureans (as I will call them) realize that one can squeeze out of a lifetime only as much as a lifetime can hold. If people's life expectancy can be increased, they are certainly in favour of doing so, since more can be squeezed into a longer life. The opportunity to live longer is a bad thing for *no* one. An abundance of life might make us less anxious to pack as much as possible into each moment of our lives, but what would be the harm of living at less frenzied a pace? And of course, if there are people who cannot find anything to do with their extended lives, suicide is always an option. But neo-Epicureans realize that they are forced to accept the life expectancy that is determined by the technology of their era in history. That technology, whether advanced or primitive, determines what for them is a normal lifetime.[15] Neo-Epicureans have impressed upon themselves the fact that unless further advances in life extension techniques can be expected, they cannot possibly expect much more than a normal lifetime, *and so they cannot allow their happiness to require more*. This they accomplish partly by making an effort to commit themselves only to projects which can come to fruition within the confines of a normally extended lifetime. They realize that it is reasonable to live one's life as if on the assumption that one will survive a normal lifetime, but not to plan life as if on the assumption that one will live beyond. Hence they try to make sure that their ambitions do not extend beyond a normal lifetime except in the form of *conditional* desires as well as escape desires.

But the neo-Epicureans could not limit their goals in this way without abandoning much of what makes life worthwhile. For example, they would have to forgo bringing children into the world – or at least avoid developing ties to any children they do produce – since their daughters and sons cannot be counted on to come to an end just as their Epicurean parents die. (Nor, presumably, would Epicurean parents want to ensure that their children would die on schedule if seeing to their demise *were* possible.) The only further alternative for Epicurean parents, caught in the predicament of being unable to reproduce for fear that they may become attached to their issue, is to conditionalize their concern for their children, to adopt the absurd attitude that a child's well-being is important while its parent is alive, but entirely a matter of indifference otherwise.

Rather than adopt one of these absurd approaches, the neo-Epicureans do allow themselves some ventures which will carry over beyond the reach of a normal lifetime. If they set out to raise children, they are prepared to care about the well-being of their families even when all of their children grow into adults. Yet as parents they realize that no matter what they (the parents) do in the course of a normal lifetime, their offspring could come to grief after the parents die. Neo-Epicureans, then, are not unconcerned about everything that happens after they die. But because they are not indifferent, they try to ensure that those of their concerns that their deaths might leave vulnerable are rendered invulnerable. For example, if they plan to have children, neo-Epicurean parents will see to it that the youngsters grow into relatively self-sufficient adults, or at least that the children's well-being does not depend on the survival of their parents beyond a normal lifetime. Neo-Epicureans know that they cannot expect to survive beyond a normal lifetime, and so make sure that well before then they have fully equipped their children for life. Of course, neo-Epicureans also realize that they could die before they have equipped their children; but that does not stop them from reproducing, so long as the odds are in favour of their surviving long enough. To help minimize the possible tragedy of leaving their children parentless, they will resort to devices such as insurance.

Neo-Epicureans have a similar approach to all of their other concerns which might be left vulnerable to what occurs after their deaths. They are not indifferent to these matters; instead, and because of their concern, they see to it that the goals they are concerned about are as invulnerable to their deaths as can be. All such goals neo-Epicureans convert to independent goals, so that the success of these projects is not made less likely by their deaths. In short, as their final years approach, neo-Epicureans make themselves completely dispensable to everything they care about. Not worried that the concerns of their lifetimes will come to a bad end with their deaths, they do not regret passing away. They have, we might say, *epicureanized* their desires. Death which comes before they have done what they have set out to do they hate with all their hearts, since it comes between them and what they consider dear. But death which comes after they have accomplished their goals or rendered their goals independent they do not grudge. It will catch the neo-Epicureans only with independent or conditional desires.

Being dispensable, however, is something that neo-Epicureans carefully postpone to the very end. Early on in life, they begin taking steps that will ensure that they will *be* dispensable, but – like a coffin – dispensability is something they want only when they die. For having our lives deeply intertwined with those of others is part of what makes life worthwhile. What neo-Epicureans want is not that their lives should have made no difference to anybody or anything. What they want is that their *deaths* should make no difference. To the extent that our being alive plays no important role in any of the matters we care about (and to the extent that we care about *nothing*), to that extent we have no reason to value our lives. It is the fact that we are indispensable to people and projects we care about that motivates us to live another day; we should undermine this motivation, therefore, only when we are prepared to die.

The neo-Epicurean approach to life is, I think, an attractive one. It allows those who can assume that their lifetimes will be normal to remain relatively calm about their future deaths without becoming aloof from life. But if I am not already a neo-Epicurean, should I become one? Or should I perhaps be content to admire them from afar? If I *already* take an interest in projects for the success of which I would have to live far beyond a normal lifetime, I can become a neo-Epicurean only if I give up or modify those undertakings. If I find myself engaged in the pursuit of such endeavours, *can* I do what it takes to become a neo-Epicurean even if I want to? Are our desires sufficiently within our control that we can give up certain ones of them if we wish, perhaps replacing them with more desirable ones?

Now of course we have some goals that we cannot modify, no matter how badly we might want to. To say that we should modify them is therefore absurd. (I am assuming that we are not willing to alter our desires using brainwashing or the like. More on that presently.) No one can give up the desire to avoid pure pain, for example, not even masochists. They seek the pleasure which accompanies an otherwise painful experience. Like the aversion to pain, a fondness for pleasures such as gastronomic and orgasmic ones is also something we all have by virtue of our very nature; we are *built* that way. Nor are all of our involuntary desires visceral. Some of them are manifestations in our conscious life of underlying needs. It is human nature, for example, to need the association of other people; that is why solitary confinement is such an effective punishment. Even if we never form the conscious desire for close ties with others – indeed, even if we think we prefer a life of complete solitude – we need them all the same; because of our human nature we would be miserable without them.

But not all desires are so deeply rooted as those which stem from underlying needs. And these shallower ambitions tend to be more malleable. My desire to acquire a cat, for example, is easily abandoned. To drop it, it may be sufficient for me to discover that I am violently allergic to fur. Whether I should change desires that are subject to voluntary manipulation is, therefore, an open question.

Even desires that are to some extent malleable cannot be changed under just any circumstances. Changing a desire is not like changing the position of our hands; we can move our hands at whim, but we cannot desire at whim. But usually we can make substantial changes in our desires when it is clear to us that it is rational for us to do so. The cat was out as soon as I saw that owning it meant suffering.

In speaking about modifications which we can or cannot make in our desires, I have been assuming that we do not resort to measures involving brainwashing or the chemical or surgical manipulation of our brains. However, I see no reason why in principle we should not make desirable changes in our scheme of desires using hypnosis, chemicals, or other sorts of artificial methods. In fact, such artificial methods are constantly invoked already. People who wish to give up smoking are well served by hypnotists who help them conquer their urge for cigarettes, for example. To countenance artificial methods is not to advocate *forced* manipulations of people's desires, of course, any more than to recommend hypnotism to a reluctant smoker is to kidnap and brainwash a smoker who is happy only with tobacco. The suggestion is just that *if* individuals decide that it really would be desirable to epicureanize their aspirations, they may as well use artificial means of doing so rather than limiting themselves to what they can achieve through sheer willpower.

In order for us to avoid forming a desire, or to abandon one we have already formed, it is often sufficient that we come to realize that we cannot possibly fulfill it. But not always. Moreover, the difficulty we have in abandoning desires we just cannot satisfy is sometimes overwhelming even when they are not involuntary. The desire for sight is not wired in, unlike the desire to avoid pain; those who are born blind and always convinced that the condition is irreversible may never develop any serious desire to see. To do so would cause them needless suffering and would be irrational. But I strongly doubt that blind people who have been able to see for most of their lives will ever cease to crave sight. They will always deeply resent their sightless condition. After all, so much of what they value depended on their being able to see, and only if they can completely overhaul their values can they become reconciled to their fate. Of course, the rational thing for them to do is to overhaul their desires, but it is nonetheless tragic that they should have to resort to modification, and the fact that modification is the rational course of action does not mean they can pursue it, or even that they will want to try.

People who are considering whether or not to become neo-Epicureans are in a position in many ways analogous to that of the newly blind. The main difference is that whereas the blind are missing out on something of which most normal human beings are capable, it has never been possible for any human being to live much more than a normal lifetime. The dying are going through something no one has ever been able to escape and which no one may ever be able to escape. In view of the inevitability of death, there can be no question that the rational course is to give up aspirations that we can accomplish only if we live more than a normal lifetime, but it is still tragic that we should have to let these hopes go, tragic that we should have to deal with the misfortune of death by abandoning things we care about. If we nonetheless manage to do so, or better yet, if we can manage to avoid ever forming aspirations that death is certain to defeat, then we shall be a good deal happier. And it is likely that the task of adjusting our desires will become considerably easier if we take seriously the fact that in wishing to do what cannot be accomplished within the confines of a maximally extended lifetime we are trying to attain the impossible. It is conceivable that research will yield life extension techniques; that would call for a readjustment of the plans we make for our lives. But to plan our lives on the assumption that such techniques will be forthcoming would only result in bitter disappointment.

Abandoning desires that cannot be satisfied within the span of a normal lifetime is something we can accomplish only to the extent that we have not already allowed what is dear to us to depend on the impossible being possible. If we have, we face the task of inventing for ourselves a new plan of life that can be realized within the more narrow confines of a normal lifetime, a task that may well prove to be too much for us. It will be those who have been reared with the promise of immortality always before them that will suffer most when they become convinced of their mortality. A good deal of anguish is in store for them unless they never really took that promise so seriously as to let anything dear to them depend on immortality.

Many will find the task of epicureanizing their desires difficult. But some parts of that task are easy to accomplish. Ensuring our own dispensability, for example, is a good deal easier than we perhaps would like to believe. It is rare indeed that people's lives are shattered irretrievably when their parents die, especially when their parents have lived a complete lifetime. It is even more rare that world affairs turn on whether or not particular individuals survive beyond a normal lifetime. For the most part, people are already dispensable; becoming so takes no effort at all. If we are indispensable, it is likely to be because we have developed strong ties to a small number of people in whose lives we play a very important role. It is likely to be because we are united with friends (including those we love) in mutually rewarding activities and our friends value the fact that it is *we* who are taking part in those activities with them.[16]

Even if we succeed in epicureanizing our desires and living long enough to see our projects through, we must still face the usual concomitants of dying: pain and physical breakdown. While it is not accurate to say that dying is a bad thing for us because of the pain and physical decline that lead up to it, this pain and decline certainly are bad things, and even those of us who manage to hold our withering bodies together long enough to achieve what passes as "old age" can rarely hope to avoid suffering terribly before we die.

Still, there is an obvious strategy for minimizing the agony that precedes dying. Supposing that we truly have accomplished our projects on schedule, then instead of waiting for nature to decide the course of events leading up to our death, we are better off taking our fates into our own hands. In many cases, painless suicide will be the best course. But planning for ourselves a painless suicide will require us to make the truly agonizing decision that our ventures are at an end and that further living would not be worthwhile. Making this decision could be the worst experience we shall ever undergo. But we may not be so lucky. What we should experience if we did not make it is likely to be worse.

V.   Summary

We should not be indifferent about dying, any more that we should be indifferent about other misfortunes that will befall us. And a misfortune dying assuredly is for those of us whose endeavours make living a good thing. For dying prevents us from engaging further in those endeavours which we find so rewarding.

Nor should we *want* to be indifferent about dying, in view of what we would have to become in order to be indifferent to death whenever it may come. What we would have to do is to renounce the many ties, concerns and projects that make us life-affirmers. No longer could we pursue any fulfilling desire that would be thwarted if we were to die. But it is precisely *these* goals whose satisfaction makes life worth living. These are the ones that give us a reason to think that living is good. Any aspiration capable of motivating us to live is one we can achieve only if we are alive; inevitably, then, any such hope would be frustrated by our deaths. In the end, then, to become indifferent to death, to adopt a death-tolerant personality, requires that we give up all desires that give us reason to live. It requires that we become indifferent to life. But we are better off thinking that dying is bad than thinking that living cannot be good.

If we are doomed to undergo the misfortune of dying, we can at least make our destiny as tolerable as possible. We can allow ourselves to live life passionately, but according to a plan whereby everything we propose to do can be accomplished within the span of a normal life-time. Concerns which transcend those limits we should occasionally allow ourselves as well, but only if we plan to render them invulnerable to our deaths. If we succeed in moulding the scheme of our desires in this way, and if we die only after accomplishing what we have set out to do, then for us dying will not be such a bad thing. Whether we can say that it will not be a bad thing *at all* depends on what we think we could do with more time than is granted us.

Notes

1. Unamuno is the only person I know of who would insist that there is *nothing* worse than dying:

    And I must confess, painful though the confession be, that in the days of the simple faith of my childhood, descriptions of the tortures of hell, how-ever terrible, never made me tremble, for I always felt that nothingness was much more terrifying. ... It is better to live in pain than cease to be in peace. (*Tragic Sense of Life*, English translation, New York, 1954, pp. 43–4)

    I find his adamancy refreshing.
2. Bernard Williams presses this point in "The Makropu-los Case: Reflections on the Tedium of Immortality," in *Problems of The Self* (Cambridge, 1973).
3. Montaigne gathers a marvellous collection of inanities in "That to Philosophize is to Learn to Die," *The Complete Work of Montaigne*, I, 20, trans. D. Frame (Stanford, 1943), pp. 56–68.
4. *Letter to Menoeceus*.
5. This suggestion is due to Thomas Nagel, "Death", *Nous* 4 (1970), reprinted in *Moral Problems*, ed. J. Rachels (New York, 1971), and in T. Nagel, *Mortal Questions* (Cambridge, 1979).
6. Or alternatively,

    If I (now) believed that X were not the case at a given time *t*, then I would (now) want to be dead at *t*.

    These two possible formulations of escape desires differ in that the first (given in the body of the paper) characterizes escape desires in terms of the form of their *contents*, while the second (given above) characterizes them in terms of the conditions under which we shall *have* them. Both, however, rely on sub-junctive conditionals.
7. According to Epicurus,

    All good and evil consists in sensation, but death is deprivation of sensation. ... For we recognize plea-sure as the first good innate in us, and from plea-sure we begin every act of choice and avoidance, and to pleasure we return again, using the feeling as the standard by which we judge every good. (*op. cit.*)
8. Galileo Galilei is reported by Unamuno (*op. cit.*) to have remarked that

    some perhaps will say that the bitterest pain is the loss of life, but I say there are others more bitter; for whosoever is deprived of life is deprived at the same time of the power to lament, not only this, but any other loss whatsoever.

    No doubt it is confused to support the claim that things exist that are worse than death by adducing a consequence of death, but at least Galileo recognized that loss of the ability to lament would be lamentable.
9. Below I point out that even hedonism cannot help avoid a very unappealing callousness. I might note that there is another reason, often attributed to Epicurus, for denying that dying can be a bad thing for us. The objection is that 'having died' can never correctly be *attributed* to anyone, since before people die, 'having died' is not true of them, and after they die they have ceased to exist, so that nothing remains for 'having died' to be a property of. Hence 'having died' does not refer to a property anyone can have, and so it cannot be

a misfortune for us to have that property. (Arguably, this is what Wittgenstein had in mind when he remarked in *Tractatus*, 6.4311 that "death is not an event in life.")

But this is a mere sophism. Just as I can have properties by virtue of what goes on outside my *spatial* boundaries (for example, being attacked by a cat), so I can have properties by virtue of what is going on outside my temporal boundaries. Thus it is partly due to events that occurred before I came into existence that 'having been conceived' and 'born after Aristotle' are both true of me. And it is partly due to events that will take place after I die that 'will have his will read' and 'will die' are true of me. Death is not an event in a life, but it *is* the event by which a life ends.

10. Alternatively:

If I (now) believed that I would be alive at *t*, then I should (now) want X to be the case at *t*.

Notice that the contents of conditional desires are the contrapositions of escape desires. Contrapositions of subjunctive conditionals are not equivalent to each other, however. (For an explanation, see David Lewis' discussion in *Counterfactuals* (Cambridge, Mass., 1973, p. 35).)

The notion of a conditional desire is essentially Williams'. See his "The Makropulous Case: Reflections on the Tedium of Immortality," *op. cit.*

11. This view has been advocated in one form or another by a great number of people for a good while. It is the third "Noble Truth" of Gautama Siddhartha (563–483 B.C.), and is echoed in the following melancholy advice by the tenth century Buddhist lama Milarepa:

All worldly pursuits have but the one unavoidable and inevitable end, which is sorrow: acquisitions end in dispersion; buildings, in destructions; meetings, in separation; births, in death. Knowing this, one should from the very first renounce acquisition and heaping-up, and building and meeting…. Life is short, and the time of death is uncertain. (From W. Evans-Wentz, *Tibet's Great Yogi: Malarepa* (New York, 1969).)

The Roman Stoic Epictetus (ca. 50–130 A.D.), who lived about three centuries after Epicurus, also suggests that we alter our desires so that we need not regard the inevitable as a bad thing:

Ask not that events should happen as you will, but let your will be that events should happen as they do, and you shall have peace.

If … you try to avoid only what is unnatural in the region within your control, you will escape from all that you avoid; but if you try to avoid disease or death or poverty you will be miserable. (From *The Manual of Epictetus*, in *the Stoic and Epicurean Philosophers*, edited by W. Oates (New York, 1940), pp. 468–84).

12. Indeed, we might just as well call the Epicurean personality death-*wishing* in view of the facts that conditional desires are much like escape desires and the latter are qualified death wishes. What is plausible about Freud's theory is captured by the view that many people are quite death-tolerant.

13. Bernard Williams says this rather casually, *op. cit.*

14. In *My Confessions*, trans. Leo Weiner (London, 1905), Tolstoy seems to suggest that life would be meaningless if we died:

But the answer in this sphere of knowledge to my question what the meaning of my life was, was always: "you are what you call your life; you are a temporal, accidental conglomeration of particles. The inter-relation, the change of these particles, produces in you that which you call life. This congeries will last for some time; then the interaction of these particles will cease, and that which you call life and all your questions will come to an end."

With such an answer it appears that the answer is not a reply to the question. I want to know the meaning of my life, but the fact that it is a particle of the infinite not only gives it no meaning, but even destroys every possible meaning.

15. For a description of the (primitive) status of research into life extension, see R. Parker and H. Gerjouy, "Life-Span Extension: The State of the Art," in *Life Span*, ed. R. Veatch (San Francisco, 1979), pp. 1–27.

16. For an elaboration of the notion of friendship, see my paper "Competing for the Good Life," *The American Philosophical Quarterly* 23 (1986), pp. 167–77.

5.3

Why Immortality Is Not So Bad

John Martin Fischer

I

I shall begin by laying out some of the key elements of Bernard Williams's fascinating and influential discussion of immortality, 'The Makropulos Case: Reflections on the Tedium of Immortality'.[1] Williams discusses a character in a play by Karel Čapek (which was made into an opera by Janáček). This character had various names with the initials EM. When she was 42 years of age, her father gave her an elixir of life which rendered her capable of living forever (at the biological age of 42). At the time of action of the play, EM is aged 342. As Williams puts it, 'her unending life has come to a state of boredom, indifference and coldness. Everything is joyless … In the end, she refuses the elixir and dies, and the formula is destroyed by a young woman (despite the protests of some older men!).'

For my purposes here, it will be useful to begin by distilling from Williams's rich and intriguing discussion his general framework for analyzing models of immortality. This framework involves positing two criteria which must be met if a given model of immortality is to be appealing to an individual. First, the future person (posited by the model) must be genuinely identical to the individual. (This means not just being qualitatively similar or having several identical *properties*; it means being genuinely identical – the same particular person.) Second, the life of the future person must be attractive (in a certain way) to the individual – the life of the future person must be 'suitably related' to the goals and projects of the individual.

This framework is really very simple and natural. It says that, in order for a model of immortality to be attractive to an individual, the model must posit a future scenario in

John Martin Fischer (1994) "Why Immortality Is Not So Bad," *International Journal of Philosophical Studies* 2(2): 257–70.

which the individual can recognize *himself* – someone genuinely identical to the individual. Further, the life of oneself in the future must be appealing; presumably, it cannot involve constant torture, onerous labor, tedium and so forth. The two conditions presented by Williams can be dubbed the 'identity condition' and the 'attractiveness condition'.

Now the problems with EM-type immortality are supposed by Williams to pertain primarily to the second condition, although he also adduces considerations pertinent to the first.[2] With regard to the second condition, Williams constructs a dilemma. Either EM's character (her basic goals, projects, dispositions and interests) remain the same over time, or they change. If they remain the same, then indefinitely many experiences will lead to detachment or boredom: 'a boredom connected with the fact that everything that could happen and make sense to one particular human being of 42 had already happened to her'.[3] But if the character changes, it is unclear whether the second condition is satisfied, because it is unclear how to assess the new projects and goals in light of the old ones.

Williams's point is that it is not merely a contingent fact that eternal life would be unattractive; this unattractiveness is alleged to be an *essential* feature of eternal life.[4] Williams says;

> … perhaps, one day, it will be possible for some of us not to age. If that were so, would it not follow then that, more life being *per se* better than less life, we should have reason so far as that went … to live for ever? EM indeed bears strong, if fictional, witness against the desirability of that, but perhaps she still laboured under some contingent limitations, social or psychological. … Against this, I am going to suggest that the supposed contingencies are not really contingencies; that an endless life would be a meaningless one; and that we could have no reason for living eternally a human life. There is no desirable or significant property which life would have more of, or have more unqualifiedly, if we lasted for ever. In some part, we can apply to life Aristotle's marvellous remark about Plato's Form of the Good: 'nor will it be any the more good for being eternal: that which lasts long is no whiter than that which perishes in a day.' [*Ethica Nicomachea* 1096b4][5]

II

I wish to examine Williams's thesis that immortality is essentially unappealing for creatures like us. First, I shall briefly consider Williams's suggestions about the identity condition. Then I shall turn to the attractiveness condition. Consider the following passage from Williams's essay:

> Some philosophers have pictured an eternal existence as occupied in something like intense intellectual enquiry. … The activity is engrossing, self-justifying, affords, as it may appear, endless new perspectives, and by being engrossing enables one to lose oneself. … But if one is totally and perpetually absorbed in such an activity, and loses oneself in it, then as those words suggest, we come back to the problem of satisfying the condition that it should be me who lives for ever.[6]

Similarly, Williams argues against the appeal of the Spinozistic idea that intellectual activity is the most active and free state that a person could be in. Specifically, Williams argues against Stuart Hampshire's formulation of a doctrine he alleges is shared by both Spinoza and Freud, that

> 'one's only means of achieving this distinctness as an individual, this freedom in relation to the common order of nature, is the power of the mind freely to follow in its thought an intellectual order.' The contrast to this free intellectual activity is 'the common condition of men that their conduct and their judgments of value, their desires and aversions, are in each individual determined by unconscious memories'.[7]

But since Williams believes that such unconscious motivations are indeed part of the self, he accuses the Spinozistic conception of freedom of aspiring to be free from the self, which entails a loss of individuality itself. Thus, again, Williams claims that to lose oneself in intellectual activity is literally to *lose oneself*. If such activity were the dominant component of immortality, it could not be of interest to an individual in the sense in which the individual is especially interested in *his or her own future*; thus, Williams is here primarily concerned with his first criterion for the desirability of immortality – the *identity* criterion. Williams goes on to say:

> As those who totally wish to lose themselves in the movement can consistently only hope that the movement will go on, so the consistent Spinozist – at least on this account of Spinozism – can only hope that the intellectual activity goes on, something which could be as well realised in the existence of Aristotle's prime mover, perhaps, as in anything to do with Spinoza or any other particular man.[8]

But it seems to me that an activity in which it is tempting to say that one 'loses oneself' is one in which the *content* of one's experiences is focused outward: one is thinking about something besides oneself. An engrossing and absorbing activity causes one to 'lose oneself' in the sense that one is not *self-absorbed*. But it is quite another matter to claim that the experiences involved in such activities are themselves not *one's own*. Even though one has 'lost oneself' in something in the sense that one is not narcissistically focused even in part on oneself, it does not follow that one cannot look at a future with such experiences as genuinely *one's own future*.

I would suggest, then, that Williams's remarks about 'losing oneself in the movement' do not call into question the possibility of an immortal life in which a certain particular individual continues to exist (and can envisage him or herself in the future). Even if one's life is heavily invested in activities in which one 'loses oneself', one can still understand these activities to be part of one's own future; the crucial distinction here is between the *content* of the relevant experiences and their *ownership*.

III

I now turn to Williams's second condition – the attractiveness condition. As pointed out above, Williams here constructs a dilemma: either one's character remains fixed, or it is allowed to change over time. I shall begin with the first horn of Williams's dilemma; that is,

I shall be assuming that the individual in question has roughly speaking a fixed character over time.

The specific problem with the first sort of immortality (in which character is held fixed) is its putatively inevitable tendency to become boring and alienating. Williams puts the point as follows:

> In general we can ask, what it is about the imaged activities of an eternal life which would stave off the principle hazard to which EM succumbed, boredom. The Don Juan in Hell joke, that heaven's prospects are tedious and the devil has the best tunes, though a tired fancy in itself, at least serves to show up a real and (I suspect) a profound difficulty, of providing any model of an unending, supposedly satisfying, state or activity which would not rightly prove boring to anyone who remained conscious of himself and who had acquired a character, interests, tastes and impatiences in the course of living, already, a finite life'.[9]

There are various philosophical defenses of the thesis that immortality (of the sort under consideration here) would be necessarily boring and thus would run afoul of the attractiveness condition. I certainly cannot here fully defend the idea that there are some pictures of such immortality which are *not* necessarily unattractive in this (or any other) way, but I wish to make a gesture in this direction by pointing to what appear to me to be some salient errors in Williams's defense of the thesis that such immortality is necessarily boring.

(1) The first error can be seen to come from (or at least be encouraged by) a particular formulation employed by Williams. He says that the defenders of the desirability of immortality must provide a 'model of an unending, supposedly satisfying, state or activity which would not rightly prove boring to anyone who remained conscious of himself and who had acquired a character, interests, tastes and impatiences in the course of living, already, a finite life'.[10] The use of the phrase 'an unending, supposedly satisfying, state or activity', is infelicitous insofar as it suggests (but of course does not strictly speaking *entail*) that the endless life in question must consist in a *single* state or activity. Later, Williams says that the defender of the desirability of immortality must point to 'something that makes boredom *unthinkable* … something that could be guaranteed to be at every moment utterly absorbing. But if a man has and retains a character, there is no reason to suppose that there is anything that could be that'.[11] Again, this passage (especially the use of the singular pronouns 'something' and 'anything') at least suggests that the endless life must consist in some *single* utterly absorbing thing. Finally, Williams considers an eternal existence occupied in activities of intense intellectual inquiry. He says that 'it seems quite unreasonable to suppose that [these activities] would have the fulfilling or liberating character that they do have for [an individual who actually engages in such activities], if they were in fact all he could do or conceive of doing'.[12]

But why suppose that any one *single* supposedly absorbing activity must be pursued *at the expense of all others*? Why can't such activities be part of a *package* in an immortal life, just as we suppose that they should be in a mortal life? Certainly, an immortal life could consist in a certain *mix* of activities, possibly including friendship, love, family, intellectual, artistic and athletic activity, sensual delights, and so forth. We could imagine that any *one* of these would be boring and alienating, pursued relentlessly and without some combination of the others. In general, single-minded and unbalanced pursuit of any single kind of activity will be unattractive. But of course from the fact that one's life will be *unending* it does not follow that it must be *unitary* or *unbalanced*. That one's life is endless clearly does not have the implication that one must endlessly and single-mindedly pursue some particular sort of activity.

(2) It might be useful again to consider Williams's demand for 'something that makes boredom *unthinkable* … something that could be guaranteed to be at every moment utterly absorbing'. His claim is that 'nothing less will do for eternity'.[13] But the justification for this demand is unclear. Why, in particular, should there be an asymmetry (of the sort implied by the demand) in the standards for the attractiveness of a finite life and an infinite life? Surely, we think of certain mortal lives which involve considerable stretches of boredom and even pain nevertheless worth living and even very appealing. Given this, why think that an immortal life with such features would not be on balance appealing? Why think that because a life is *unending*, it must be *uniformly* pleasing in order to be on balance attractive? The inference here is not more compelling than the inference noted above from the unending nature of immortal life to some single *unitary* activity which it putatively must contain.

Suppose one says that one finds some activity 'endlessly fascinating'. This could mean various different things. First, it could mean that whenever one turns to the activity (in the normal course of one's life), one finds it on balance fascinating. Second, it could mean that whenever one turns to the activity (in the normal course of one's life), one finds it *filled with* fascinating moments – perhaps even densely packed with fascinating moments. Finally, I suppose it *could* (just possibly) mean that one pursues the activity *forever* and finds it at every moment fascinating. Thus, with regard to the schema, 'endlessly—', one must distinguish at least three different notions: *reliability, density* and *infinite extensibility*.

Now imagine that an unending life contains some activity which one finds 'endlessly fascinating'. It surely does not follow from the fact that an *unending* life contains an endlessly fascinating activity that the activity must be endlessly fascinating in the sense of infinite extensibility. An unending life can contain an endlessly fascinating activity in the sense of reliability or density. Further, I see no reason simply to *assume* (as Williams seems to) that in order for an endless life to be attractive, it must contain an activity (or even set of activities) that is endlessly fascinating (or endlessly appealing in any way) in the sense of infinite extensibility. I should think that it is even an open question whether in order for an endless life to be attractive, it must contain an activity that is endlessly fascinating (or endlessly appealing in any way) in *any* of the senses.

(3) I wish now to develop a distinction which I believe is important to assessing the appeal of immortality. Having laid out the distinction, I will suggest that the tendency to think that immortality must be boring and alienating may come in part from attending solely to one of the categories involved in the distinction; this is another mistake of the proponents of the thesis that immortality is necessarily boring.

Some pleasurable experiences, it seems, are in some sense 'self-exhausting'. In the case of these pleasures, once (or perhaps a few times) is enough. That is to say, when one experiences such pleasures one tends not to want to repeat them – even at some point relatively far in the future. Some such pleasures are frankly *disappointing*; in the case of these, we find that some highly touted or much anticipated pleasure is just not what it was made out to be, and we simply conclude that it is not worth pursuing these in the future. But there are other such pleasures which are not necessarily disappointing; rather, they may be entirely fulfilling but in some way 'complete in themselves'. More specifically, they seem to be complete in the sense that, having experienced such a pleasure, one has no desire to experience it again at any point in the future.[14]

I take it that everyone has had their share of disappointments, so it is not necessary to dwell on these. But it will be useful to consider some examples of the 'non-disappointing' self-exhausting pleasures. Suppose, for instance, that you have the goal of doing something just (or at least primarily) to prove to yourself that you can do it. Imagine, for example, that you are somewhat afraid of heights, and you have been working hard to overcome this phobia. You form the goal of climbing Mt Whitney just to show yourself that you have overcome the fear – just to show yourself that you can control your life and overcome obstacles. Upon climbing the mountain, you may in fact be very pleased and proud. Indeed, you may be deeply satisfied. But also you may have absolutely no desire to climb Mt Whitney (or any other mountain) again. You have accomplished your goal, but there is no impetus toward repeating the relevant activity or the pleasure that issues from it.

I speculate that there are quite a few activities and resulting pleasures that are relevantly similar to those in the above case. Some of these are activities in which one sets out to prove something to oneself or other people. Others may be activities in which one sets a goal which is essentially 'comparative' in some way – one wants to win a race or some prize, one wants to be the brightest, most productive, most popular, fastest, and so forth (in some given context). Frequently (although certainly not invariably), upon reaching such essentially comparative goals, one finds them either disappointing or 'complete in themselves'; in any case, there is relatively little energy or impetus to repeat the accomplishments. (Of course, the energizing aspect of such accomplishments will vary with the nature of the accomplishment and the individual's personality; for some individuals, such achievements only whet the appetite for more, whereas this is not the case for others.)

I suspect, then, that the class of self-exhausting pleasures (both disappointing and not) is rather large. But these are *not* the *only* sort of pleasures. There are also 'repeatable pleasures'. Here an individual may well find the pleasure highly fulfilling and completely satisfying at the moment and yet wish to have more (i.e., to *repeat* the pleasure) at some point in the future (not necessarily immediately). Certain salient sensual pleasures leap immediately to mind: the pleasures of sex, of eating fine meals and drinking fine wines, of listening to beautiful music, of seeing great art, and so forth. These, or many of them, seem to be – at least for many people – repeatable pleasures. (Note that the distinction between self-exhausting and repeatable pleasures must be *relativized to particular individuals*; this having been said, there will presumably be some similarities across different individuals.)

It is not evident that the distinction between self-exhausting and repeatable pleasures can be understood or explained in terms of other notions. That is, it is not clear that the repeatable pleasures are 'higher', 'more noble', 'more intrinsically compelling', 'more complex', 'more intense', and so forth. It just seems to be a fact about us that we find that some pleasures are self-exhausting and some are repeatable, and it is not clear how even to begin to give an illuminating reductive account of this distinction.[15]

Of course, even repeatable pleasures may become boring or unappealing if distributed too closely (or in an otherwise inappropriate pattern). I suppose that even the most delectable lobster thermidor would quickly become revolting if consumed at every meal. But, as noted above, it is a mistake to suppose that the pleasures must be experienced in this way. Given the appropriate distribution of such pleasures, it seems that an endless life that included some (but perhaps not only) repeatable pleasures would *not* necessarily be boring or unattractive. Perhaps some of the proponents of the 'necessary boredom' thesis tend to attend solely or primarily to the self-exhausting pleasures (and associated activities). But once it is seen that there are also repeatable pleasures, the prospects of a certain sort of immortality are not nearly so grim.

I wish to say a bit more about the distinction between self-exhausting and repeatable pleasures. As the discussion proceeds, I hope it will become evident just how implausible it is to deny that there are repeatable pleasures (or that there can continue to be repeatable pleasures that form part of a mix of pleasurable experiences that extends indefinitely into the future). As a help in further discussing the nature and role of repeatable pleasures, I shall now relate the story of André and his beloved goose liver:[16]

> We had just been served the usual airline fare. The man sitting next to me, call him André, tasted his food deliberately, paused thoughtfully for a moment as if he were extracting what little pleasure could be found in the morsel, and then pronounced judgment: 'Surprising, yes this is really rather nice.' He had a cultured European accent and the appearance of a man dissipated not by wanton and reckless living, but by the civilized excess of too much of the good life. I said something to the effect that I thought all airplane food was awful and this seemed to be no exception. André looked at me with a type of patient parental disappointment. My comment had revealed how little I knew about life. 'Well, of course, this "food" is terrible – not really food at all. But this is an airplane, isn't it? And the point is that this turkey is much superior to what one normally finds in such environs. That is the pleasure in it.' It became clear that André's senses were far more refined than mine. He had trained himself to glean what little enjoyment could be found even in something so bland as a turkey sandwich on United.
>
> He began to relate the various meals he had eaten at different times. And this was how we at last came to the topic of the beloved goose liver. A goose liver, you see, properly nurtured and prepared, simply is better than the best of any other food. André became quiet for a time – lost in reveries like one remembering old and dear friends. He began slowly, reverently to recall for me the rare times when he had found his beloved goose liver. There were the times growing up in Hungary – a country which, as everyone knows, really is the best country at producing goose liver. Later there were great moments when he would return to Hungary to visit his relatives; they would scrimp and save in order to have the week's wages necessary to procure the goose liver. Certainly this was extravagant, but so great was his joy eating the meal that everyone at the table felt it was a small price to pay.
>
> There were other rare occasions in places like Vienna and New York where André would find and become reacquainted with his beloved goose liver in new surroundings. But such moments carried with them tremendous opportunities for disappointment. Not infrequently, the prized liver would be ruined by a clumsy chef who completely lacked the proper respect for the bounty he was preparing. Once, however, André was travelling through a little town in the

Swiss Alps. He happened upon an average-looking restaurant around dinner time. There on the menu was the daily special – goose liver. He inquired after the details of the dish – was it fresh, how was it prepared, and so forth. The answers encouraged him to order the meal. Upon its arrival at his table, André was surprised beyond his wildest dreams. He exclaimed to the waitress that he must meet the chef, for there were only two or three men in the world (he knew them all) who could prepare the beloved goose liver so expertly. How was it possible that the masterpiece could be produced so casually here? Much to André's surprise, when the chef was brought to the table, he turned out to be one of the famous chefs who had prepared André a meal years earlier. (The chef had some family business in the area and was cooking in the restaurant as a favor to the owner who was his friend.) The chef was, of course, delighted to find someone who truly appreciated the treasure which had been laid before him, and the two talked late into the night. André extended his stay in the town three days. He ordered goose liver every night.

Evidently, André's enthusiasm is food. Surely, the pleasures of the goose liver are *repeatable* pleasures for André. And it seems that André does not need such exotic culinary adventures to achieve significant repeatable pleasures; indeed, he gets such pleasures from a wide variety of gastronomic experiences, both elaborate and pedestrian. Further, I see no reason to think that André's pleasures would cease to be repeatable, if part of an immortal life (in which the pleasures are appropriately distributed. Goose liver for breakfast, lunch and dinner would no doubt rather rapidly turn even André's stomach.)

To extend the point. Really, it seems that there are many repeatable pleasures; when one thinks about it – and specific accounts such as that of André help to bring home the point – Williams's necessary boredom thesis becomes very implausible. Think, for instance, of the pleasures of listening to great music. I get extraordinary pleasure from listening to Bach's Second Partita for the Unaccompanied Violin. (Whereas I am certainly not immune to gastronomical delights, Bach's Second Partita is my beloved goose liver.) And I see no reason why it would cease to be a repeatable pleasure, if part of an immortal life (in which there were an appropriate mix of activities and pleasures). Certainly, there are other such pleasures, such as the pleasures of visiting a great art museum, or a great and beautiful city, such as Paris, Venice or San Francisco. (I cannot imagine *ever* getting tired of the view of the city of San Francisco from the Golden Gate Bridge, or the feeling of the fog engulfing me in Golden Gate Park, or the beautiful plaintive sound of the foghorns in the distance. I have *no* tendency to think that these pleasures would become less compelling, unless pursued in a singleminded or compulsive fashion.)

In this section I have in a very sketchy way suggested a distinction between self-exhausting and repeatable pleasures. Although I have not analyzed or developed the distinction in detail, I have suggested that it is a mistake to suppose that all pleasures are relevantly similar to the self-exhausting sort. I wish briefly here to allude to a treatment of these issues which (like Williams's) is insufficiently attentive to the distinction in question. In Kierkegaard's pseudonymous essay 'The Rotation Method', the aestheticist 'A' properly rejects the idea that there must be *one* activity which is the sole source of pleasure and which is pursued relentlessly over the course of a lifetime. Rather, 'A' endorses a system of rotating pleasures just as an efficient farmer might rotate his crops to achieve a better result. But even with the rotation method 'A' finds life boring:

> Starting from a principle is affirmed by people of experience to be a very reasonable procedure; I am willing to humor them, and so begin with the principle that all men are bores. Surely no one will prove himself so great a bore as to contradict me in this.
>
> … All men are bores. The word itself suggests the possibility of a subdivision. It may just as well indicate a man who bores others as one who bores himself. Those who bore others are the mob, the crowd, the infinite multitude of men in general. Those who bore themselves are the elect, the aristocracy; and it is a curious fact that those who do not bore themselves usually bore others, while those who bore themselves entertain others.[17]

But whereas Kierkegaard's hedonist 'A' avoids some of the errors discussed above by adopting the rotation method, he evidently does *not* avoid the error of ignoring or underestimating the repeatable pleasures. Given the existence of such pleasures, a life with a suitable arrangement of them need not be boring. And I do not see why an immortal life with such a mix of repeatable pleasures would necessarily be boring.

Kierkegaard wished to convince us to turn away from hedonism and toward spiritual and religious experiences. I have suggested that he ignored the possibility of a range of pleasures which clearly are accessible even to persons who do not have spiritual or religious experiences. But for those who do indeed have such experiences, there would seem to be even more reason to embrace immortal life; surely, the deep and resonant rewards of spiritual and religious experience would not somehow become wooden or etiolated, if part of an endless life. What reason is there to suppose that such experiences would change their character in such circumstances?

Williams usefully distinguishes between 'conditional' and 'categorical' desires.[18] The conditional desires are desires for certain things, given that one will continue to live. Someone surely will want adequate clothing, food, shelter, and so forth, on the condition that he or she will continue to be alive. But such a person may not prefer to continue to live. Preferences which imply an answer to the question of whether one wishes to be alive are categorical desires. Presumably – although Williams does not explicitly say this – there can be both 'positive' and 'negative' categorical desires. A positive categorical desire implies the desire to continue to live, whereas a negative categorical desire implies the desire not to continue to live.

Perhaps the distinction between self-exhausting and repeatable pleasures can go some distance toward illuminating Williams's claim that one would lose one's positive categorical desires in an immortal life. Granted, this might be true if one focused exclusively on self-exhausting pleasures. After a while – perhaps a long while – these desires would lose their capacity to ground categorical desires and to propel one into the future. But I see no reason to think that the repeatable pleasures would lose their energizing and 'propulsive' character. Further, spiritual and religious experiences would seem to be relevantly similar to the repeatable pleasures in this respect; they seem capable of providing the basis for positive categorical desires, even in an immortal life.[19]

So far I have been concerned to discuss the first horn of Williams's dilemma pertinent to the attractiveness condition (presented above). That is, I have discussed the necessary boredom thesis in the context of a relatively fixed character. Let me now say just a few very brief words about the second horn, according to which the relevant individual's character changes over time. Williams suggests that it is now unclear that the individual will find such immortality attractive, given that it is unclear that there is the appropriate relationship between the individual's current character and future goals, values and interests.

This sort of case notoriously raises fascinating but complex issues.[20] But the basic point is that it seems that an individual could value such an existence if he or she felt that the change in character would result from *certain sorts of sequences*. That is, if I felt that my future character will be different from my present one as a result of appropriate reflection at future times upon my experiences given my 'then-current' character, then I might well value such an existence. One's attitudes toward future changes of character depend on *how* and *why* the changes take place.

Surely in our ordinary, finite lives we envisage certain changes in our values and preferences over time. For example, one may currently value excitement and challenge; thus, one might wish to live in an urban area with many career and avocational opportunities (but with lousy weather and a high crime rate). Still, one might envisage a time in the future when one will be older and will prefer warm weather, serenity and security. One can certainly envisage a time when one will prefer to live in a condominium in a warm, safe place, even if one currently thrives on life in Manhattan. And one need not look at the future stages of one's life (in which significant changes in values and preferences have taken place) as unattractive; certainly, they are not so unattractive as to render death preferable!

Thus, there are quite ordinary cases in our finite lives in which we envisage changes in our characters – our values and preferences – and which are not so unattractive as to render death preferable. Why, then, could not the same be true of immortal existence? As above, why set such radically different standards for immortal life and mortal life?

Granted, if one's character is changed by brainwashing, coercion, deception or various other methods, one might find the resultant existence thoroughly unattractive. But why assimilate all changes of character to these? And a devoted conservative republican may find it unthinkable that she become a liberal democrat, even by rather less exotic means of transformation. But it is not evident to me that such a person would actually prefer death. And even so, there is no reason to assimilate *all* changes of character to such a change; all that is required, in order to defend the thesis that immortality is not necessarily unattractive (on this horn of the dilemma), is that there be certain changes of character plausibly envisaged as part of an immortal life which would not be so unattractive as to render death preferable.

IV

In this paper I have explored some of the philosophical puzzles pertaining to immortality. More specifically, I have used Bernard Williams's important and influential discussion as a springboard for analyzing what I take to be certain problems with the claim that immortality is necessarily unattractive. I have argued that it is unfair to suppose that, in order for immortality to be attractive, it must consist of some *single* activity pursued at the expense of others. Further, it is unfair to demand that, in order for immortality to be attractive, it must consist of *entirely* pleasurable or agreeable experiences; why suppose the standards for immortal life are in this respect different from the standards for mortal life? Also, one may be entirely 'lost' in an engrossing activity in the sense of not *focusing* (primarily) upon one-self; it is quite another matter to say that the relevant experiences are not *one's own*. Finally, it is important to distinguish two different kinds of pleasures: self-exhausting pleasures and repeatable pleasures. A life without repeatable pleasures might well eventually become boring. But it is a mistake to suppose that an immortal life must contain only self-exhausting pleasures at the expense of repeatable pleasures. The repeatable pleasures – perhaps together with spiritual and religious experiences – could provide a reasonable basis for positive categorical desires even in an immortal life. It has been a recurrent theme of my discussion that it is quite unfair to set radically different standards for finite life and immortal life.

Notes

1. Bernard Williams, 'The Makropulos Case: Reflections on the Tedium of Immortality', in Bernard Williams, *Problems of the Self* (Cambridge University Press, 1973), pp. 82–100; reprinted in John Martin Fischer (ed.) *The Metaphysics of Death* (Stanford, CA: Stanford University Press, 1993).

2. For a general taxonomy of models of immortality and a discussion of the bearing of Williams's two criteria on various of these models, see John Martin Fischer and Ruth Curl, 'Philosophical Models of Immortality', George Edgar Slusser (ed.), *Immortal Engines: Life Extension and Immortality: in Science Fiction and Fantasy* (University of Georgia Press, 1996).

3. Williams, *op. cit.* note 1, p. 90.

4. Presumably, the essential boredom thesis is meant to apply to creatures of a certain sort – creatures relevantly similar to us. Otherwise, it would follow from the thesis that God's existence is boring and unattractive (insofar as God is essentially everlasting).

5. Williams, *op. cit.* note 1, p. 89.

6. *Ibid.*, p. 96.

7. *Ibid.*, p. 97.

8. *Ibid.*, p. 98.

9. *Ibid.*, pp. 94–5.

10. *Ibid.*

11. *Ibid.*

12. *Ibid.*

13. *Ibid.*

14. This notion of 'completeness in itself' is different from Aristotle's notion according to which certain activities – *energeiai* – are complete in themselves. Aristotle distinguishes *energeia* from *kinesis*, which are not complete in themselves. Roughly, Aristotle's distinction corresponds to activities which are movements toward a certain product and which are not complete until the production of the product, and activities which are not so understood.

   At *Metaphysics* Theta Six, Aristotle introduces the 'tense test' to distinguish *energeia* and *kinesis*. According to the tense test, if the verb 'X-ing' is an *energeia* verb, then 'I am X-ing' entails 'I have X-ed'. For example, 'I am enjoying myself' entails 'I have enjoyed myself'. If the verb is a *kinesis* verb, 'I am X-ing' entails 'I have not X-ed'. For example, 'I am learning [something]' entails 'I have not learned [the thing]'. There is an analogue of the tense test which is a non-linguistic phenomenon. The proper parts of *energeia* X are also X's: the proper parts of enjoyings are enjoyings. The proper parts of *kinesis* Y are not also Y's: the proper parts of a walking from A to B are are not walkings from A to B. For some discussions of the tense test, see: J.L. Ackrill, 'Aristotle's Distinction Between *energeia* and *kinesis*', in R. Bambrough (ed.) *New Essays in Plato and Aristotle* (New York: Humanities Press, 1965); and Terry Penner, 'Verbs and the Identity of Actions – A Philosophical Exercise in the Interpretation of Aristotle,' in O.P. Wood and G. Pitcher (eds.) *Ryle: A Collection of Critical Essays* (Garden City, NY: Doubleday, 1970).

15. It is an interesting philosophical question: *Why* are some pleasures self-exhausting and others repeatable?

16. For the story of André I am indebted to Mark Ravizza.

17. Soren Kierkegaard, 'The Rotation Method', in *Either/ Or*, in *A Kierkegaard Anthology*, ed. Robert Bretall (New York: The Modern Library, 1946), pp. 21, 23–4.

18. Williams, *op. cit.* note 1, pp. 85–6.

19. It has been brought to my attention that there may indeed be some experiences in life that we savor and value (to the extent we actually do) precisely because we know that we will not enjoy them forever. It is difficult for me to know whether this is really the case, and to what extent (if so). But let me grant that it is true. This admission would not in itself undermine my strategy of argumentation, for even if certain pleasures are expunged or diminished, the repeatable ones may still make immortal life worthwhile. And it is also worth noting that there certainly are painful and unpleasant experiences associated precisely with the fact that we *cannot* have certain relationships and experiences forever: loss and death notoriously impose great pain and suffering upon us. I see no reason to suppose that the diminution in pleasures issuing from immortality would be greater than the diminution in pain and suffering.

20. See, for example, Derek Parfit, *Reasons and Persons* (Oxford: Oxford University Press, 1984).

5.4

The Immortality Requirement for Life's Meaning

Thaddeus Metz

This essay considers the question of what, if anything, makes a life meaningful. This question is roughly equivalent to asking, 'Which conditions of a human's existence are worthy of substantial esteem?' or 'How can a person identify with something great?'[1] Many religious thinkers maintain that for anyone to be oriented toward something higher in the relevant sense, one must possess a soul that will forever survive the death of one's body. This is an instance of a more general view that is here called the 'immortality requirement' (IR). According to the IR, a person's life is meaningless if she is not immortal.

Which sort of immortality is most likely relevant for having a meaningful life? How are immortality and God related, so far as meaningfulness is concerned? Which general conceptions of meaning make the IR plausible? Is the IR in fact true? These questions are obviously worth addressing, but contemporary Anglo-American philosophers have devoted little attention to them. The analytic literature has thoroughly addressed the conditions under which we could survive the death of our bodies and whether such conditions obtain. However, the issues of whether and why an immortal afterlife might be central to meaning have been slighted. There lacks sustained, critical discussion of conceptual distinctions, argumentative strategies, and logical relationships germane to the IR.

This essay aims to help rectify this situation. It would be presumptuous to pronounce the IR to be either true or false, at least at this stage of enquiry into the doctrine. This paper therefore seeks to analyse the IR and to defend a circumscribed yet substantial thesis about it: the immortality requirement is plausible only if the God-centred requirement is plausible to a comparable degree. The God-centred requirement is the view that God's existence is a necessary condition for life to be meaningful. After differentiating what is merely compatible with the IR from what is essential to it, this paper examines three major arguments for

Thaddeus Metz (2003) "The Immortality Requirement for Life's Meaning," *Ratio* XVI: 161–77.

the IR which, on the face of it, are not arguments for the God-centred requirement. It turns out that, as these arguments stand in the literature, they actually fail to support the IR. This essay reconstructs the arguments, and it shows that once they do plausibly support the IR, they comparably support the God-centred requirement. The paper concludes by explaining why we should expect any attractive motivation for holding the IR also to be a good reason for adopting the God-centred requirement.

An Analysis of the Immortality Requirement

The immortality requirement is the view that one's life must be eternal in order for it to be meaningful. The IR is not just the weak claim that immortality could enhance the meaning of one's life; it is instead the strong thesis that life would be meaningless if it were to end. While this is a bold contention, several important thinkers have held it and it will be interesting to examine how it can be supported.

The IR is not so strong as to claim that immortality is sufficient for a meaningful life. Such a thesis would be counterintuitive in at least two respects. First, presuming that everyone is immortal if anyone is, this thesis would imply that either everyone's life is meaningful or no one's life is meaningful. But we seem to think that some people have meaningful lives while others do not. Second, if immortality were sufficient for meaning then an eternal life in hell would be meaningful, which seems incorrect. Hence, immortality is plausibly proposed to constitute merely a necessary condition for meaning, not a sufficient one.

Notice that the IR differs from the claim that people need to believe in an eternal life for their lives to be meaningful.[2] The IR is also different from the view that one can learn about the meaning of life only by getting answers from God in an afterlife.[3] The IR is rather the view that immortality itself (not the belief in it) is a necessary metaphysical (not epistemic) condition of life's meaning.

Several different interpretations of the IR are possible, depending on the way immortality is understood. The concept of immortality at the core is that of a life which will never end. Beyond that, there are several different conceptions of immortality. First, one may conceive of eternal life in temporal or atemporal terms. An immortal life could be one that will never cease to be in time or one that will transcend time altogether. Second, a life that never ends could conceivably be realised in various ontological forms. Consider, on the one hand, a soul that permanently becomes part of a spiritual realm upon bodily death, and, on the other, a life that forever remains embodied in the physical world, e.g., vampires in an infinitely expanding universe. Third, there are sundry ways of thinking about the modal status of immortality. Some think of immortality as a matter of being unable to die, while others think of it merely as a matter of being able to live forever (usefully called 'immortability'[4]).

No version of the IR implies anything about whether we are in fact immortal. Of course, many believers in immortality do hold the IR, but it would be possible to hold the IR and think that we will perish along with the inevitable deaths of our bodies. Hence, the IR also does not imply anything about whether our lives are in fact meaningful; it is compatible with nihilism, the view that our lives are meaningless.

Finally, the IR is logically distinct from the God-centred requirement, which holds that life can be meaningful only if there exists a purely spiritual being who grounds the natural universe and who is all powerful, all knowing, and all good. One can conceptually accept the God-centred requirement while denying the IR, e.g., some think that fulfilling God's purpose or being remembered by God would be sufficient for meaning, even if one were not granted eternal life.[5] Conversely, there is no logical contradiction in believing that immortality but not God is necessary for a life to be meaningful.

Although the immortality requirement and the God-centred requirement are logically distinct, the remainder of this paper defends the view that they are not plausibly distinct. Specifically, the rest of this essay aims to establish that any plausible motivation for adopting the IR is also strong reason to hold the God-centred requirement.

Perfect Justice

One common argument for the immortality requirement is that life would be meaningless if the injustice of this world were not rectified in another world. *Ecclesiastes* expresses the concern that there is no afterlife and hence that life is 'vanity' since both good and evil people share the same fate.

> For what happens to the sons of men happens to animals; one thing befalls them; as one dies, so dies the other. Surely, they all have one breath; man has no advantage over animals, for all is vanity. All go to one place; all are from the dust, and all return to dust. … All things come alike to all: one event happens to the righteous and the wicked. … As is the good, so is the sinner; he who takes an oath as he who fears an oath. There is an evil in all that is done under the sun: that one thing happens to all.[6]

There are two ways in which justice requires different conditions to befall the righteous and the wicked. First, those who have suffered from wrongdoing are owed compensation for their losses. Second, those who have been evil deserve punishment for their wickedness, and those who have been upright deserve reward for their goodness. Obviously, neither compensatory nor retributive justice is perfectly done in this world. Hence, one might think that life could not be meaningful if there were no afterlife in which perfect justice were done. Note that God *qua* ideal judge (i.e., a perfectly impartial, powerful, and omniscient personal being) does not seem to be necessary for just conditions to obtain; both a Karmic, impersonal force or a personal being whose powers are not as robust as God's would be sufficient.[7]

The straightforward problem with the present argument for the IR is that while perfect justice might require an afterlife, it is not clear that it requires an *eternal* afterlife. The immortality requirement is the robust claim that, for our lives to be significant, they must either continue infinitely into the future or enter an atemporal realm where there is no distinction between past and future. It seems that humans would deserve an eternity in heaven only if they did something infinitely good (or an eternity in hell only if they did something infinitely bad). We may reasonably doubt that infinite (dis)values are possible in a finite world. And even if they were, it would not follow that infinity is needed to give people what they deserve. The trouble is that, supposing one can do something infinitely (dis)valuable in a finite amount of time here on earth, it would seem that a response proportionate to this deed requires merely a finite amount of time. If infinitely good or bad deeds are possible in a finite timespan, then so are punishments and rewards matching these deeds. Hence, the immortality requirement apparently gains no support from the view that meaning requires perfect justice to be done.

How might the perfect justice theorist respond to this problem? One way would be to appeal to metaphysical considerations about what could make an afterlife possible. That is, one might argue that if a person were able to survive the death of his body at all, then he would have to be immortal. Perhaps the only way to separate from one's physical self is to have a spiritual self that lacks parts and hence is indestructible. If that were true, then imposing any posthumous scheme of reward and punishment would require immortality.

There are two serious problems with this suggestion. For one, many thinkers view personal identity in terms of a chain of memories, which chain could conceivably outlast a given body and yet not last forever. For another, even if personal identity were constituted by a spiritual substance (and not merely a chain of memories), it is still conceivable that one could have a spirit that outlasts one's body but dissolves at some point. There is no compelling reason to think that there must be an utterly incorruptible aspect of one's identity in order for one to survive the death of one's body.

Let us examine a second response on behalf of the perfect justice rationale for the IR. So far, we have considered the argument that life would be meaningless without perfectly just responses to *imperfect virtue*. The perfect justice theorist might do better if she claimed that life would be meaningless without perfectly just responses to *perfect virtue*. On this view, immortality is necessary not for rewarding relatively good people, but primarily for enabling people to become absolutely good. This view is inspired by some of Kant's remarks:

> The achievement of the highest good in the world is the necessary object of a will determinable by moral law. In such a will, however, the complete fitness of dispositions to the moral law is the supreme condition of a highest good. ... But the perfect fit of the will to moral law is holiness, which is a perfection of which no rational being in the world of sense is at any time capable. But since it is required as practically necessary, it can be found only in an endless progress to that perfect fitness. ... This infinite progress is possible, however, only under the presupposition of an infinitely enduring existence and personality of the same rational being; this is called the immortality of the soul.[8]

We can avoid Kant's technical terminology and theoretical baggage and still find something worth discussing. Kant himself does not speak in terms of life's 'meaning' (any more than the author of *Ecclesiastes* does), but his remarks are relevant for a conception of meaning that promises to ground the IR. When Kant speaks of the 'highest good,' he is referring to the best state of affairs for finite rational beings. For Kant, the highest good is our *final end*, not only in the sense that it must be our foremost goal, but also in that we may conceive of the world as having been created for such a state of affairs. Now, the purpose that we must above all pursue and that is grounded in the order of the universe, according to Kant, is moral perfection and happiness fitting that condition. And since moral perfection is possible only if we are immortal, immortality is necessary for the highest good, for the purpose the fulfilment of which confers meaning on our lives.

The problem with the Kantian response is that it is hard to see why one should think that moral perfection requires immortality. Talk of 'perfection' suggests an intrinsic maximal state, a condition in which the best has been achieved at a given time. Although there would arguably be *more* moral perfection possible if one lived forever, it is not clear that living forever is necessary for moral perfection itself. We seem able to conceive of a morally ideal agent who eventually dies, perhaps an unresurrected Jesus.

How might we motivate the view that an immortal soul is necessary for moral perfection? One possibility is that one's physical nature is incompatible with moral perfection. Some philosophers have held that our sensuous nature interferes with the functioning of our rational, moral nature so much that the latter cannot be perfected until it is free of the former.[9] Others have suggested that a pure moral disposition is one that cannot be corrupted.[10] However, neither view entails that immortality is necessary for moral perfection. Even if it were true that pristine virtue requires a nature that is spiritual or cannot become bad, it does not follow that such a nature must never come to an end. Hence, we still lack a reason for thinking that doing perfect justice to a moral agent (even a saint) requires that agent to have an immortal nature.

Let us explore a third reason why one might think that doing perfect justice to a virtuous agent requires her immortality. To reward a person is to contribute to her well-being. Now, if a person's well-being were a function of satisfying her strongest desires (regarding her own states, experiences, activities, and relationships), and if a person's strongest desires were for eternal bliss of varying degrees, then giving a highly virtuous person her deserved reward would require her immortality.

There are two problems with this response that must be overcome. First, the desire satisfaction theory of human welfare, as construed so far, has counterintuitive implications. Suppose that (for whatever reason) a person strongly wanted to suffer mental anxiety and physical torment for the sake of satisfying no other want. The desire satisfaction theory implies that such a person would be doing quite well for having such a desire fulfilled, which seems absurd.

Second, this appeal to the desire satisfaction theory of welfare fails to buttress the immortality requirement in the right way. Immortality theorists hold that immortality is 'necessary' for a meaningful life in a sense much stronger than the claim that immortality is required, given certain contingent desires. The standard version of the IR holds that immortality is necessary for any human life to be meaningful. But some people do not want to live forever in heaven, perhaps because they are not acquainted with the concept; by the current rationale, therefore, immortality is not required to reward them and hence is not necessary for their lives to be meaningful.

To deal with these problems, let us amend the desire satisfaction theory. Consider this attractive version of the desire satisfaction theory of human welfare: a person's life goes well insofar as the desires that she would have if she were functioning normally and aware of the various states of being possible for her are satisfied. To function normally involves being mentally healthy or choosing autonomously, e.g., not suffering from conditions such as neurosis, depression, duress, and adaptive preference formation. And being aware of possible states of being is a matter of being acquainted with various paths one's life could take. Putting these ideas together, this view holds that the satisfaction of only those desires that would be formed by a person who is (roughly) free and informed determines that person's welfare.

Such a view solves the two problems facing the earlier version of the desire satisfaction theory. First, since normally functioning human beings do not intrinsically desire to undergo pain, this theory does not entail that fulfilling such a desire contributes to a person's well-being. Second, since people who are sane and autonomous would invariably want eternal bliss once the idea occurred to them, this theory entails that the desire for heaven is not contingent.[11] By the present theory of well-being, then, eternal life in heaven is necessary to reward the highly virtuous (given that they would strongly desire it). And supposing it is true that life's meaning depends on being highly virtuous and receiving reward for it, we have an argument that entails the immortality requirement.

Having finally constructed a valid argument for the IR from considerations of perfect justice, it is time to enquire into whether this rationale also grounds the God-centred requirement. There is strong reason to believe that it does, for God is something that every normally functioning human being would presumably want in her life, upon acquaintance with the idea. One need not be terribly religious to admit that one would like, say, to commune with a perfect being or to live in a universe that is oriented toward a spiritual end.[12] And if mentally healthy people familiar with the concept of God would strongly want to relate to God, then the God-centred requirement follows from the claims that fulfilment of a person's strongest wants constitutes her well-being and that a person must receive well-being consequent to superior virtue for her life to be meaningful.

Recall that it is not the purpose of this essay to investigate the soundness of any argument for the IR. No doubt it would be worthwhile to ascertain whether the premises of the revised perfect justice argument are true. However, such a project is beyond the scope of this paper, the aims of which are to reconstruct the major arguments for the IR and to establish the claim that any plausible motivation for the IR is also one for holding the God-centred requirement. Let us therefore move on to the second major argument for the IR.

Ultimate Consequence

In the most widely read text on the immortality requirement, Leo Tolstoy argues that something can be worth striving for only if one faces no prospect of death.[13]

> Sooner or later there would come diseases and death (they had come already) to my dear ones and to me, and there would be nothing left but stench and worms. All my affairs, no matter what they might be, would sooner or later be forgotten, and I myself should not exist. So why should I worry about all these things?[14]

One way of putting Tolstoy's point is that life would be meaningless if nothing were worth pursuing and that nothing is worth pursuing if it will not have an 'ultimate consequence.'[15] Since a human life could apparently make a permanent difference only if it were immortal in some capacity or other, Tolstoy's rationale seems to support the IR (and to do so without supporting the God-centred requirement).

This reasoning received a decent share of attention from analytic philosophers during the 1960s. The central criticism to emerge was that death intuitively cannot undercut the worth of performing certain constructive actions. For example, Anthony Flew remarks that it would be odd to 'think of a doctor despising his profession on the Keynesian grounds that in the long run we are all dead.'[16] Such a case suggests that helping others can be worth doing, even though the helping agent will die and the helping action will have no infinite effects.

It is open to Tolstoy to deny intuitions of the sort Flew invokes, and indeed he does. For instance, with regard to helping his family, who are of course likewise mortal, Tolstoy asks, 'Why should they live? Why should I love them, why guard, raise, and watch them?'[17] However, Tolstoy would have a stronger response to Flew if he could explain why it at first seems as though it is worthwhile for a mortal to help others and why this judgement is false in the final analysis.[18]

Although the claim that our lives must have an ultimate consequence for them to be choiceworthy is eminently questionable, let us grant it. There remains a serious problem with the inferential structure of the Tolstoian argument, as it is neither deductively valid nor strongly inductive. We can accede the premise that an ultimate consequence is necessary for meaning and still deny the conclusion that immortality is necessary for meaning, for immortality is not the only way for a life to have an ultimate consequence. One's life could make a permanent difference if it made a lasting impression on other infinite things. For instance, suppose that one made a substantial contribution to God's plan and that God fondly remembered it forever. Or imagine that angels eternally sung one's praises. Or envision generations of mortal humans recounting tales of one's great deeds successively into infinity. Tolstoy seems particularly worried that his life will 'sooner or later be forgotten,' that it will seem as though he never existed or added anything to the world, but this condition could be prevented in several ways without Tolstoy's being immortal. Tolstoy's rationale therefore fails to entail that being immortal is necessary for one's life to be meaningful.

For a Tolstoian to resolve this problem, he must contend that not just any ultimate consequence is needed for constructive actions to be worthwhile. Instead, a particular kind of ultimate consequence is needed for a life to be choiceworthy, namely, one bearing on *oneself*. Now, such a view needs to be motivated, not merely asserted. Why believe that for a given project to be worth doing, it must have some eternal ramification for the person doing the project?

Here is an answer worth considering. Meaning depends on not just any sort of intrinsic value (e.g., bodily pleasure) but on a special sort of intrinsic value. Specifically, suppose that meaning depends on an infinite value. Now, if interacting with an infinite value required an immortal condition, then it would follow that meaning requires immortality. Some remarks of another immortality theorist, William Ernest Hocking, suggest this sort of view:

> The best of our experiences are normally long looked-forward-to and long remembered. . . .
> Without this natural time dimension we know we have not 'done justice' to the event: meanings
> may be seen instantly, but they are not 'realized' (by beings with our time-extended mode of

thinking) except with a certain amplitude of the process of pondering. Deprived of their due aftergrowth they fail to attain their proper value. … And if there were such a thing as 'eternal value' accessible to us mortals, it would rightly call for unlimited time for its realizing.[19]

Actions are worth doing only if they give due consideration to their objects. Giving due consideration to an 'eternal value' requires an infinite amount of time in which to honour it, part of which will involve remembering one's involvement with it. Now, if the only objects able to confer meaning on our lives have 'eternal value,' then it follows that for the actions relevant to meaning to be worth doing, one must have an eternal life. This line of thought provides a reasonable explanation of why, e.g., an infinite chain of mortal humans who remember us would not be an ultimate consequence sufficient to make our actions worth-while; *we* must not fail to honour eternal values if we want our lives to be meaningful, and this requires that *we* live forever.

So, there is now a version of the ultimate consequence rationale that supports the IR. Does this rationale also support the God-centred requirement? It appears that it does. What is an eternal value? What is the sort of value that would require an infinity to recognise? The natural answer is of course 'God.' Talk of honouring an 'eternal' or 'infinite' value points directly to the idea of communing with a perfect being. One might object that a 'bootstrap' approach would work here, i.e., that one's own immortal nature might have a superior intrinsic value requiring an infinite amount of time to honour. This claim is not implausi-ble, but it is irrelevant; the problem is that the immortality requirement gains no *unique* support from the argument that meaning requires honouring an infinite value which, in turn, requires eternal life to accomplish. The God-centred requirement is equally well sup-ported by this rationale.

Transcending Limits

Questioning the meaning of something in general appears to be a matter of asking about its relationship with other things. If we ask for the meaning of a word, we are told about its rela-tionship with other words or with objects in the world. If we ask what rising inflation means for the economy, we are told about its effects on unemployment or interest rates. Robert Nozick proposes that we likewise think of asking for the meaning of an individual's life as a matter of asking how it 'transcends limits' or 'connects with something beyond itself.'[20] And Nozick sug-gests that mortality is a boundary which, if not crossed, renders a life meaningless.

> A significant life is, in some sense, permanent; it makes a permanent difference to the world –
> it leaves traces. To be wiped out completely, traces and all, goes a long way toward destroying
> the meaning of one's life. … Attempts to find meaning in life seek to transcend the limits of an
> individual life. The narrower the limits of a life, the less meaningful it is. … Mortality is a
> temporal limit and traces are a way of going or seeping beyond that limit. To be puzzled about
> why death seems to undercut meaning is to fail to see the temporal limit itself as a limit.[21]

Many conditions that intuitively confer meaning on a life do seem to be instances of tran-scending limits. For example, finding a cure for cancer is a way of going beyond one's narrow interests, creating a great work of art is a way of connecting with complexity or beauty, and discovering the basic laws of the universe is a way of linking to reality. And it also seems true that immortality would be an instance of transcending a substantial limit, namely, the limit of time. Hence, Nozick may reasonably think that mortality is a limit the crossing of which is central to meaning.

However, this argument obviously needs to be tightened up if it is to provide strong support for the IR. Exactly which kinds of limits must one transcend in order to acquire meaning? Breaking the speed limit and pinching a stranger are ways of 'crossing boundaries,' but these are not prima facie candidates for a meaningful life. Furthermore, why believe that the limit of time is a boundary that specifically must be crossed in order for one's life to meaningful? Why would loving another person or creating a work of art not suffice?

Nozick's main strategy for specifying the relevant limits involves thinking of meaning as transcending limits that keep one from something intrinsically valuable. '(M)eaning is a transcending of the limits of your own value, a transcending of your own limited value.'[22] On this view, one must protect, produce, or respect inherently worthy objects that are beyond one's person. Unfortunately, this rendition of the transcendence argument does not yet entail the immortality requirement. Both love and creativity can constitute 'a connection with an external value' in the absence of immortality. Clearly, we need a careful specification of the intrinsic values with which a person must connect (and of how to connect with them) in order for the transcendence rationale to entail the immortality requirement.

Let us reformulate the transcendence rationale this way: a meaningful life is one that connects in the strongest possible way with intrinsic value farthest beyond the animal self. The animal self is constituted by those capacities that we share with (lower) animals. These include our being alive, experiencing pleasures and pains, and exercising perceptual capacities. These conditions might be intrinsically valuable, but they do not seem to have the sort of intrinsic value with which one must connect to acquire significance; a life is not meaningful merely for being alive or feeling pleasure. Instead, on this view, a life is meaningful for intensely linking up with intrinsic values that are qualitatively superior to our animal natures.

Such a conception of meaning plausibly gives support to the immortality requirement, for one's immortal nature itself would constitute a value farthest beyond one's animal nature. Classical theists had a number of reasons for thinking that intrinsic value supervenes on a soul that enters an atemporal realm.[23] For one, a life beyond time would have the inherent good of independence, of not being substantially confined by or dependent on other things. An atemporal spiritual entity would be free not only from decomposition, but also from a conscious point of view restricted to the moment. For another, an immortal soul manifests the intrinsic value of unity. Integrity and oneness are better than disintegration and fragmentation, and an atemporal, spiritual life amounts to the former. A being that survives its body and is beyond time would lack extension or the 'feebleness of division' (Anselm). Now, supposing that immortality so construed has a high intrinsic value, one way of intimately connecting with value far beyond one's animal self would be to *honour one's soul*. Perhaps what makes a life meaningful is coming to learn that one has a soul and taking care not to degrade it.[24] In order to connect intensely with value that is qualitatively superior to the animal self, one must not only instantiate the perfection of immortality – the most intense relationship one could have to an exceptional intrinsic good – but also treat it as more important than one's physical, sensual nature.

We have seen that the conception of meaning *qua* intense connection with intrinsic value farthest beyond one's animal nature supports the immortality requirement. But does it also support the God-centred requirement? Yes, it does. God, a perfect being, would no doubt be the highest value with which a person could relate. One could get no farther away from one's physical, sensual nature than by relating to the deity. And the most intense relation for a person to have with the divine would be to become one with it or, as in Hinduism, to realise one's extant unity with it. Hence, the present conception of meaning equally supports the view that communing with God is necessary to make one's life meaningful. Transcending one's animal nature in the strongest possible way would plausibly require that one be immortal, but this could be either because one must honour one's soul or because one must merge with God. In sum, although the revised transcendence rationale provides reason to believe the IR, it, like the previous two major arguments, provides comparable reason to believe the God-centred requirement.

Conclusion: The Fundamental Link between Immortality and God

This essay has examined three central arguments for the immortality requirement from the literature. In each case, the paper presented a thinker's basic reasoning in favour of the immortality requirement, showed that it actually fails to support the immortality requirement as it stands, and then reconstructed the rationale. Once the three rationales were revised to support the IR, they turned out to support the God-centred requirement as well. Although this essay has not addressed every possible argument for the IR, there is arguably a broad lesson to be learned here. This paper concludes by bringing out the fundamental reason why each of the major arguments for the IR is also an argument for the God-centred requirement and by suggesting that this common denominator is strong evidence for expecting other arguments for the IR to have the same implication.

Let us review the discussion. The perfect justice rationale claims that the IR follows from the view that compensatory or retributive justice is necessary for a meaningful life. We initially found it unreasonable to think that giving people what they deserve would require immortality (as opposed to a finite afterlife). This claim seemed reasonable, however, once we supposed that rewarding those who have been virtuous would require satisfying the strongest desires they would have if they were functioning normally and aware of their options. One such desire would be for eternal bliss, and another would likely be for God in one's life, making God just as necessary for positive desert. The ultimate consequence rationale maintains that a meaningful life depends on making a permanent difference to the world. It was at first difficult to grasp why one would have to be immortal in order to make a permanent difference, but this notion was easier to accept when we considered that making a particular sort of permanent difference, namely, responding proportionately to an infinite value, might be central to meaning. And since God is the most straightforward answer to the question of what constitutes an infinite value, the God-centred requirement also follows from this rationale for the IR. Finally, the transcending limits rationale holds that a meaningful life is one that overcomes certain boundaries in the right way. It was prima facie implausible to think that one would have to be immortal to transcend the kinds of limits relevant to meaning. Yet this became plausible upon taking the relevant limits to be ones that keep a person from intrinsic value that is much higher than her animal nature. Since God is no less of such a value than one's immortal nature, the God-centred requirement again follows.

In all three cases, the rationales support the IR in a straightforward way once an idealised evaluative claim is conjoined with them. The perfect justice rationale makes use of a claim about what is *best* for a human being, the ultimate consequence rationale invokes a claim about *infinite* value, and the transcending limits rationale appeals to a claim about the *highest* nature. Since meaning is an intrinsically good thing for a person to have in her life, linking meaning with immortality will require an intermediate judgement about *value*. In addition, it will require a judgement about *superlative* value since it must be of a sort that cannot obtain in any finite lifespan. And any judgement about superlative value that must be made in order to ground the IR will also ground the God-centred requirement, the view that a perfect being is central to life's meaning. That is the deep, logical reason for the tight, historical association between God and immortality in supernaturalist conceptions of meaning.

Notes

1. I have sought to analyse the sense of the question of what makes a person's life meaningful in 'The Concept of a Meaningful Life', *American Philosophical Quarterly*, 38 (2001), pp. 137–53.

2. This is one major claim in David Swenson, 'The Transforming Power of Other-worldliness', repr. in E. D. Klemke (ed.), *The Meaning of Life*, 2nd edn. (New York: Oxford University Press, 2000), ch. 3.

3. For this view, see Michael Levine, 'What Does Death Have To Do with the Meaning of Life?' *Religious Studies*, 23 (1987), pp. 457–65.

4. A term used by William Ernest Hocking, *The Meaning of Immortality in Human Experience* (New York: Harper & Brothers Publishers, 1957), pp. 74, 154.

5. For those who espouse this perspective, see Delwin Brown, 'Process Philosophy and the Question of Life's Meaning', *Religious Studies*, 7 (1971), pp. 13–29; and Charles Hartshorne, 'The Meaning of Life', *Process Studies*, 25 (1996), pp. 10–18.

6. *Ecclesiastes* 3: 19–20 and 9: 2–3 in *The Holy Bible*, New King James Version. For a recent statement, see Philip Quinn, 'How Christianity Secures Life's Meanings', in Joseph Runzo and Nancy Martin, eds., *The Meaning of*

Life in the World Religions (Oxford: Oneworld Publications, 2000), ch. 3. Note that neither text explicitly states that an *eternal* afterlife is necessary for perfect justice.

7. Although there are many ways that reward for conforming to moral rules could be administered, it might seem that only God could be the source of moral rules themselves. If moral rules were identical to God's commands, then a conception of life's meaning in terms of reward for moral excellence would support the God-centred requirement. But this point is mentioned here only to be set aside, since divine command theories (and other God-based moral views) have notorious problems, and since the divine command theory has already received substantial attention.

8. Immanuel Kant, *Critique of Practical Reason* 3rd Edition, trans. Lewis White Beck, (New York: Macmillan Publishing Company, 1993), pp. 128–9.

9. See, e.g., Plato's *Phaedo*.

10. The idea of unchangeable purity is at least part of Kant's conception of moral perfection. See his *Religion Within the Limits of Reason Alone*, trans.

Theodore Greene and Hoyt Hudson, (New York: Harper & Row Publishers, 1960), pp. 46, 57, 61, 65.

11. Some might object that a normally functioning human being could be aware of the nature of pain and intrinsically desire it (or could know of bliss and not want it for its own sake). That is, the contingency element might still be present in the amended version of the desire satisfaction theory. If so, one could revise the theory again, making human well-being in general turn on the desires of *most* human beings, suitably construed. It is surely true that most human beings would want eternal life in heaven, if they reflected on it and were not subject to 'heteronomous' influences.

12. Cf. Pascal's remark that 'the infinite abyss can be filled only by an infinite and immutable object, that is to say, only by God Himself. He alone is our true good. . . .' *Pensées* #425.

13. Leo Tolstoy, 'My Confession', trans. Leo Wiener, repr. in Klemke, *The Meaning of Life*, ch. 1.

14. Tolstoy, 'My Confession', p. 11. Cf. Bismarck's statement 'Without the hope of an afterlife, this life is not even worth the effort of getting dressed in the morning,' as quoted in Thomas V. Morris, *Making Sense of It All: Pascal and the Meaning of Life* (Grand Rapids, MI: William B. Eerdmans Publishing Company, 1992), p. 26. For a recent Tolstoian statement, see William Craig, 'The Absurdity of Life Without God', in Klemke, *The Meaning of Life*, ch. 4.

15. For someone who speaks this sort of way, see C. H. D. Clark, *Christianity and Bertrand Russell* (London: Lutterworth Press, 1958), p. 30.

16. Anthony Flew, *God and Philosophy* (New York: Harcourt, Brace, & World, Inc., 1966), p. 105.

17. Tolstoy, 'My Confession', p. 12.

18. Probably the strongest explanation is that while such activities seem to merit performance from an everyday perspective, *from a broader perspective* nothing is worth doing unless it will have a ultimate consequence. Oswald Hanfling makes this kind of point in *The Quest for Meaning* (New York: Basil Blackwell Inc., 1987), pp. 22–4. Cf. Thomas Nagel, *The View from Nowhere* (New York: Oxford University Press, 1986), ch. 11. Space precludes criticism of the point. For one who questions the authority of the objective standpoint, see David Schmidtz, 'The Meanings of Life', in Leroy Rouner, ed., *Boston University Studies in Philosophy and Religion, Volume 22; If I Should Die: Life, Death, and Immortality* (Notre Dame: University of Notre Dame Press, 2001), pp. 170–88.

19. Hocking, *The Meaning of Immortality in Human Experience*, pp. 68, 141.

20. Robert Nozick, *Philosophical Explanations* (Cambridge: Harvard University Press, 1981), ch. 6, and *The Examined Life* (New York: Simon & Schuster, 1989), ch. 15.

21. Nozick, *Philosophical Explanations*, pp. 582, 594, 595.

22. Nozick, *Philosophical Explanations*, p. 610. See also pp. 594, 611, 618.

23. The following compressed considerations can be found in rich detail in Plotinus, *The Enneads*, Anselm, *Monologion*, and *Proslogion*; and Aquinas, *Summa Contra Gentiles*, and *Summa Theologica*.

24. This is the core of the view in David Swenson, 'The Dignity of Human Life', repr. in Klemke, *The Meaning of Life*, ch. 2.

5.5

Human Extinction and the Value of Our Efforts

Brooke Alan Trisel

Discussions about nuclear weapons, the depletion of the ozone layer, and the possibility that a massive asteroid could crash into Earth, prompt us to reflect on our own individual mortality and on human extinction. And when we think about the end of humanity, it raises questions about whether our efforts have value because, if human extinction does occur, the things that we have created will decay and eventually vanish. Some claim that our efforts are pointless if humanity will cease to exist. This claim will be examined and disputed in this essay.

In recent years, there has been extensive debate regarding the question of whether we have obligations to future generations, such as an obligation to preserve the environment. To a far lesser extent, there has also been discussion about the more basic question of whether it matters how long humanity will persist. The related question of whether our efforts have value if humanity will end has received even less attention.

The human species could become extinct abruptly, with all of us dying at once or within a short time of each other. Extinction could also occur gradually. For example, if people would immediately stop having children, then we would live out our lives in a world without future generations. Humanity would become extinct over a period of 110 to 120 years – the maximum life span of someone currently alive.

If we knew that humanity would become extinct within the next few months, then we would be justified in feeling distressed about this because it would cut short our expected life span, thereby depriving us of many potential experiences. However, should we feel anguish about the possibility that humankind will become extinct long after we and our loved ones have died?

Brooke Alan Trisel (2004) "Human Extinction and the Value of Our Efforts," *Philosophical Forum*, XXXV(3): 371–91.

It is understandable why we want those that we love, including our children and friends, to continue living after we have died. Because we love them, relate to them as one existent individual to another, and empathize with their feelings and aspirations, we desire for them to live on so that they can realize their goals and experience fulfilling lives. But why should it matter whether remote future generations – faceless, abstract persons who only potentially exist and whom we will never know – will be born after we have died and will persist for as long as possible?

Ernest Partridge contends that people have a "basic need" to care for the future beyond their own lifetimes, a need that he refers to as "self transcendence."[1] He writes:

> By claiming that there is a basic human need for "self transcendence," I am proposing that, as a result of the psychodevelopmental sources of the self and the fundamental dynamics of social experience, well-functioning human beings identify with, and seek to further, the well-being, preservation, and endurance of communities, locations, causes, artifacts, institutions, ideals, and so on, that are outside themselves and that they hope will flourish beyond their own lifetimes.[2]

In attempting to support his claim, Partridge argues that there is a "desire to extend the term of one's influence and significance well beyond the term of one's lifetime – a desire evident in arrangements for posthumous publications, in bequests and wills, in perpetual trusts (such as the Nobel Prize), and so forth."[3] Partridge concludes by asserting:

> To be sure, posterity does not actually exist *now*. Even so, in a strangely abstract and metaphorical sense, posterity may extend profound favors for the living. For posterity exists as an *idea*, a potentiality, and a valid object of transpersonal devotion, concern, purpose, and commitment. Without this idea and potentiality, our lives would be confined, empty, bleak, pointless, and morally impoverished.[4]

Allen Tough makes a similar argument to Partridge when he states: "If our future is highly negative [referring to the end of humanity], then most other values and goals will lose their point."[5]

In this essay, an attempt will be made to demonstrate that the claim that our lives would be empty and pointless without future generations is greatly exaggerated. Second, it will be argued that, if we adopt a reasonable standard for judging whether our efforts are "significant," it then will not matter whether humanity will persist for an extended time.

Background on the Debate

Many people have expressed a longing for humanity to persist for as long as possible. Wilhelm Ostwald, for example, argues that the continuation of a species is a way of mitigating the death of an individual member of that species. In the context of discussing the propagation of biological organisms, he writes: "Death has here lost much of his power; many individuals may perish, but the organism as such remains alive. Only when the very last of all the offspring perishes may death be regarded as the victor."[6] Avner de-Shalit expresses a similar view insofar as he argues that the idea of future generations helps people overcome the fear of death. He writes: "We can, to a certain extent, and should immortalize the creative part of us. True, this is not a total victory over the fear [of death], nor is it a full answer. Nevertheless, if we follow this course of action, it will provide us with a certain victory."[7]

In writing about "traces," as they are now called, Ostwald indicates: "Every man leaves after his death certain things in the world changed by his influence. He may have built a house, or gained a fortune, or written a book, or begotten children."[8] He goes on to argue: "There is a very general desire in mankind to leave such impressions" and "we are not fully satisfied with the mere existence of such objective souvenirs [referring to the pyramids], but want other people to see them and realize their meaning."[9]

The principal argument advanced by those who believe that it matters how long humanity will persist is as follows: People desire to leave an enduring trace of their existence and would not be satisfied in just leaving a physical trace. People want their trace (e.g., piece of artwork) to be appreciated by other people – not just to sit on a desolate planet for countless years. Leaving an appreciable, enduring trace is dependent on the existence of future generations. Therefore, it matters, they conclude, how long humanity will continue to exist.

James Lenman convincingly argues that, from an impersonal standpoint, it does not matter whether humanity will become extinct sooner rather than later.[10] However, he does believe that this matters from a "generation-centered" perspective for reasons similar to those advanced by Partridge and de-Shalit.

It is true, as Partridge maintains, that some people do adopt goals that extend beyond the end of their lives. For example, in response to a question regarding the goal of a writer, William Faulkner remarks:

> It's – I think that a writer wants to make something that he knows that a hundred or two hundred or five hundred, a thousand years later will make people feel what they feel when they read Homer, or read Dickens or Balzac, Tolstoy … he knows he has a short span of life, that the day will come when he must pass through the wall of oblivion, and he wants to leave a scratch on that wall – Kilroy was here – that somebody a hundred, a thousand years later will see.[11]

Granted, if one's goal is to influence people for thousands of years through one's writings, then this goal could not be accomplished without the continued existence of humanity. However, the goal of leaving an enduring, appreciable trace is not important, as will be shown in a later section. Furthermore, adopting such a grandiose goal is unrealistic, especially considering the vast quantity of writings that are being produced and amassed by humanity. Although future persons may have more sophisticated technology than we do to sift through these writings, they (like us) will be limited in how much they can read. Therefore, it will be difficult for a contemporary writer to achieve the goal of influencing future persons for thousands of years.

Partridge argues that it should matter to us how long humanity will persist, but clearly this does not matter to everyone. For example, in response to the comments of an earlier presenter at a symposium, who had equated the 4.5 billion years of earth's history to once around the world in a plane, the economist Lester Thurow responded: "Do I care what happens a thousand years from now? Do I care when man gets off the airplane? And I think I basically came to the conclusion that I don't care whether man is on the airplane for another eight feet, or if man is on the airplane another three times around the earth."[12]

Thurow does not expound on why he does not care how long humanity will persist. However, for some people, a pessimistic outlook on life explains why they do not embrace the goal of achieving human immortality. According to the noted pessimist Schopenhauer: "You can also look upon our life as an episode unprofitably disturbing the blessed calm of nothingness."[13] To those who believe that nonexistence is preferable to existence or that evil outweighs the good in the world, the goal that humanity will persist for billions of years undoubtedly seems irrational and perhaps even ridiculous. From their perspective, it is unlikely that this goal could be achieved considering the destructive behavior of humankind and, even if it could be achieved, we would never know it because we would no longer be alive then. Furthermore, achieving this goal would only prolong human suffering and misery and postpone the inevitable extinction of humankind. For example, Schopenhauer writes:

> If the act of procreation were neither the outcome of a desire nor accompanied by feelings of pleasure, but a matter to be decided on the basis of purely rational considerations, is it likely the human race would still exist? Would each of us not rather have felt so much pity for the coming generation as to prefer to spare it the burden of existence, or at least not wish to take it upon himself to impose that burden upon it in cold blood?[14]

If one is miserable with one's life, then this person may wish that he or she had never been born, may assume that others also wish they had never been born, and thus may see themselves as doing future persons a favor by sparing them the "burden of existence." However, the assumption that everyone desires not to have been born must be false, because, if it were true, then there would be many more suicides than there are and people would not seek, as they do, to live as long as possible – some even wanting to live forever.

As extreme pessimism is uncommon, there must be other reasons explaining why it does not matter to some people, such as Thurow, whether humanity will endure for a long time. These reasons will become evident in the next section, where it will be demonstrated that the claim that our efforts would be pointless without future generations is an exaggeration.

Life without Future Generations

One can lead a meaningful life without personal immortality or a superior being, as many have argued.[15] If living forever, as an individual, is unnecessary for one's life to be meaningful, then this immediately raises doubt about whether it is necessary for humanity to live forever, or for a long time, for one's life to be meaningful, as some claim. It will be useful, however, to examine their arguments in more detail.

Would our lives be "pointless" without future generations as Partridge claims? "Pointless" is a vague word and Partridge does not elaborate on what he means in using this word. Therefore, before addressing the question, it is important to attain a clear understanding of the meanings of this word. "Pointless" can mean the same as "purposeless," which signifies the *absence* of a goal or purpose. Clearly, living without the prospect of future generations is not pointless, in this sense of the word, because people alive today can have and pursue goals regardless of whether there will be future generations.

"Pointless" can also mean that one has a goal, but that it no longer makes sense to continue striving to achieve this goal because conditions have changed that have made the goal irrelevant or unachievable. In this sense of the word, "pointless" has a meaning very similar to "futile." Declaring that an action or activity will be futile means that it will be impossible or highly improbable that the action, no matter how often it will be repeated, will bring about *one's envisioned goal*. Therefore, whether or not an effort is considered futile or pointless will depend, in large part, on the nature of one's goals.[16]

A few of the goals that some people have would be pointless without future generations. For example, if one's goal is to write a book that will be read by and influence others for thousands of years, then, if it becomes known that humankind will perish within six months, this individual would consider the writing of this book pointless because the envisioned goal has become unachievable. Although the goal would be pointless, it is unrealistic to adopt such a goal in the first place.

Our lives, as a whole, would be pointless without future generations only if *all* of our efforts were devoted to achieving goals directed at future persons and this is not true. Most of people's goals can be accomplished within their lifetimes. If all of our goals extended well beyond our lifetimes, then we would not fully realize *any* of our goals until long after we have died. But people do accomplish many of their goals: they graduate from college, they get married, they pursue various careers, they write books, they travel, and so on – all without future generations.

Animals preceded human life by millions of years and may continue to exist for millions of years after humanity has become extinct. Some people have goals directed at assuring that other forms of life, especially animals, will survive and flourish, regardless of how long humanity will persist. Arne Naess argues that one of the values underlying the "deep ecology" movement is the principle of "bios-pherical egalitarianism." He writes:

> The ecological field-worker acquires a deep-seated respect, or even veneration, for ways and forms of life. He reaches an understanding from within, a kind of understanding that others reserve for fellow men and for a narrow section of ways and forms of life. To the ecological field-worker, *the equal right to live and blossom* is an intuitively clear and obvious value axiom.[17]

Paul Taylor outlines a "biocentric outlook" on nature.[18] One of the four components of this outlook is that human beings are members of Earth's community of life and hold that membership on the same terms as nonhuman members. He expresses the desire to maintain the "integrity of the biosphere" for the good of human and nonhuman members of the community of life. Taylor argues that if human extinction should occur that "not only would the Earth's community of life continue to exist, but in all probability, its well-being would be enhanced."[19]

As Taylor's goal extends beyond humanity to include animals and plants, pursuing this goal would not be pointless even if humanity will become extinct because achieving this goal does not depend on the continued existence of humanity. In fact, as he argues, the continued existence of humanity actually makes it more difficult to achieve the goal that animals will survive. Those who argue that our lives would be pointless without future generations falsely assume that everyone's goals revolve around and are limited to human beings.

For the preceding reasons, it is an overstatement to claim that our efforts would be pointless without future generations. If one's goals do not extend beyond one's lifetime or are directed at nonhuman life, then it may be possible to achieve these goals even if there will be no future generations.

Wanting to influence humanity forever would be pointless without future generations, but this should not concern us. Trying to run a marathon in five minutes, and attempting to jump to the moon from Earth, are also pointless. These latter two activities are pointless because these goals exceed human capabilities and are unachievable. No matter how much effort is expended, one could never achieve these goals. Wanting to leave an everlasting trace of ourselves also exceeds human capabilities and is unachievable. If a person would try to jump to the moon or to leave a trace that will last *forever*, then this person's efforts related to these goals will be futile. However, they would not be justified in feeling distressed about this because they chose unrealistic goals, which primarily is why their efforts toward achieving these goals would be futile.

It does not concern us that we cannot jump to the moon because we understand that human beings have limits and that a jump of this magnitude far exceeds our capabilities. We accept this limitation and do not fret about it, yet some people resist accepting the limitation that they cannot leave an everlasting, appreciable trace of themselves. By accepting this limitation and adopting realistic goals, it will help assure that our efforts will not be pointless.

In addition to claiming that our lives would be pointless without future generations, Partridge also claims that our lives would be "empty" and "bleak" without future generations because purportedly we could not satisfy the desire or goal to leave an enduring trace of ourselves without them. This, however, falsely assumes that having and achieving goals are the only experiences that make living worthwhile. Even more incorrect, it assumes that being able to achieve one kind of goal, namely a goal that extends beyond one's life and is directed at future persons, is the only experience that makes life worth living.

Having and achieving goals can give us a sense of purpose, direction, and satisfaction, but these are not the only experiences that make living worthwhile. There are other commendable aspects of life, such as aesthetic appreciation and being with family and friends, which may have little or nothing to do with goal-directed activity. Therefore, it is untrue that our lives would be empty and bleak without future generations.

In contrast to those who have goals that extend beyond their lives, people who are not achievement-oriented, or are achievement-oriented but who set realistic goals, may not care whether humanity will persist for a long time. Having goals that extend beyond the end of their lives may be common among those who produce creative works such as writers and artists, but are these goals that prevalent among ordinary people, as those who long for future generations suggest? It is doubtful that individuals whose profession involves providing a service, such as delivering the mail, or caring for a patient in the hospital, really care whether they will leave a trace of their existence that will last thousands of years. Their goals and interests may not extend much, if any, beyond the point at which they, and those that they love, will cease living. Consequently, it may not matter to them whether humanity will persist for a long time.

What if there are objective values independent of human subjective evaluation, as some believe? If there are objective values, then a discrepancy could occur between what we think is important and what is important according to this objective standard. We could conclude that it does not matter how long humanity will continue to exist when it really does matter or that it does matter when it really does not.

Let us suppose that there is a god who has given us objective standards declaring what is right and wrong and what is significant and insignificant and that we have somehow discovered the following standard:

    a.   The things that human beings create are significant regardless of how long they will last.

If there were such an objective standard, then our creations would be significant regardless of what we think of them and regardless of whether future persons validate that they are significant. Even if humanity would be wiped out next month, creating things would not be pointless since the significance of these creations does not depend on how long they will last.

If there are no objective standards, as I believe, then the question becomes what criteria should be selected to decide what is and what is not significant. With the standard considered above, we do not know why this god considers our creations significant, but we do know that the length of time that our creations will last is not one of the criteria used by this god to judge significance.

The standards that we adopt are based upon our desires and goals. Reflecting their goals, some people adopt the following standard to judge significance:

    b.   My creations are significant only if they will be appreciated by others for a long time.

If people adopt this standard, then whether or not their creations are considered significant will depend on how long these creations will be appreciated which, in turn, will depend on how long humanity will last. This raises the fundamental question of whether long-lastingness should be part of a standard for judging significance. As will be argued in greater detail later, including long-lastingness as one of the criteria for judging the significance of our efforts is unreasonable and unwise.

The End of the Universe

It is important to distinguish the end of humanity from the end of the universe since the universe may continue to exist and be habitable to life for a long time after humanity becomes extinct. At a time at which a few scientists were predicting that the universe would ultimately end in "heat death" – a prediction based upon generalizing (inappropriately, some would argue) the Second Law of Thermodynamics to the whole universe – Bertrand Russell wrote the following famous words:

all the labors of the ages, all the devotion, all the inspiration, all the noonday brightness of human genius, are destined to extinction in the vast death of the solar system, and that the whole temple of man's achievement must inevitably be buried beneath the debris of a universe in ruins – all these things, if not quite beyond dispute, are yet so nearly certain that no philosophy which rejects them can hope to stand.[20]

Despite these gloomy words, Russell did not conclude that living is pointless or bleak if humanity or the universe will eventually end. However, some people do reach this conclusion.

John Barrow and Frank Tipler, in outlining the much-debated "Anthropic Cosmological Principle," and in reaction to Russell's comments quoted above, write:

Though our species is doomed, our civilization and indeed the values we care about may not be. We emphasized … that from the behavioral point of view intelligent *machines* can be regarded as people. These machines may be our ultimate heirs, our ultimate descendants, because under certain circumstances they could survive forever the extreme conditions near the Final State. Our civilization may be continued indefinitely by them, and the values of humankind may thus be transmitted to an arbitrarily distant futurity.[21]

We realize that we will die long before the universe will end. Nevertheless, some people are distressed with the thought that the universe may end one way or another. In fact, they may feel more distress thinking about the end of the universe than about the extinction of humankind. What is the explanation for this? It will be hypothesized that the level of distress that one feels about the possibility that the universe will end varies with the nature of one's goals (e.g., whether one wants to leave an everlasting trace), one's theory of value, and one's religious beliefs.

Before exploring these relations, it will be useful to clarify what the "end" of the universe means, as the "end" could be thought of in many different ways. The end of the universe could be thought of as the last event. It might also be thought of as a point at which the universe vanishes into nothingness, if one assumed this was possible. For the purposes of this discussion, the end of the universe will be defined as a point at which the universe has become irreversibly inhospitable to life and has irreversibly lost all traces of its prior states.

As discussed in the previous section, some people have goals that are not dependent on the continued existence of humanity. However, achieving these goals may be dependent on the universe having certain characteristics, such as being habitable to life. For example, it would not be possible for animals or ecosystems to survive after the extinction of humankind if the universe ends shortly after humanity does. If people think of animals as having only instrumental value to human beings, then this scenario will not concern them. However, if they believe that certain aspects of nature, such as animals, are intrinsically valuable,[22] then the destruction of the universe would signify the loss of these values.

Some people want to leave an enduring, appreciable trace and do not believe that there is a god who will outlast the universe or that there are objective values. They are consoled in believing that their friends and loved ones will persist after they have died and that they will live on in their memories and may continue to exert an influence in their lives. But if everyone else dies shortly after they do, and humanity becomes extinct, then no one would be left to remember them or to be affected by their efforts. However, if the universe has not ended, then there is a possibility and thus hopefulness, they conclude, that a trace demonstrating that they lived could be left to a nonhuman, rational species. They might imagine that another intelligent life form, either one that will come into existence on Earth in the future, or one that currently exists elsewhere on another planet, will discover the traces of their existence or adopt human values.[23] Fulfilling this desire, however, would not be possible if the universe becomes inhospitable to life, which explains why they feel distressed reflecting about the end of the universe.

In a sign of desperation to achieve quasi-immortality,[24] Barrow and Tipler suggest that our values could be "transmitted" to indestructible machines that might be able to survive the death of the universe. Would this satisfy people who seek to leave an enduring, appreciable trace? If these machines were programmed by human beings, then any appreciation these machines would have for our works would be nothing more than human commanded appreciation; the machines would "appreciate" our works because we instructed them to do so. If we program the machines to clap after reciting our writings, are they clapping for us or are we, through the machines, just clapping for ourselves? I believe that the latter answer is correct and therefore seriously doubt whether leaving a trace to a machine will satisfy anyone who wants to have their works appreciated by others.

Those who desire personal immortality despair at the thought that the universe will end,[25] which explains, in part, why they embrace the idea of a self-sufficient and eternal God. They are comforted in believing that, with God, there is hope for never-ending life even if the universe will end. However, if one has a pantheistic conception of god and worships either the universe itself or certain characteristics of the universe, such as its creative ability, and does not believe that there is a changeless reality underlying the universe, then the destruction of the universe may signify the death of god to this person.

Escalating Desires, Escalating Standards

When we adopt an imaginary perspective[26] that extends beyond the end of humanity, and look back on our achievements, some people tend to devalue these achievements. The achievements no longer seem to be of significance when viewed from this distant vantage point. For example, William Lane Craig, who argues that life has no "ultimate" significance without God and personal immortality, indicates:

> Mankind is a doomed race in a dying universe. Because the human race will eventually cease to exist, it makes no ultimate difference whether it ever did exist. … The contributions of the scientist to the advance of human knowledge, the researches of the doctor to alleviate pain and suffering, the efforts of the diplomat to secure peace in the world, the sacrifices of good men everywhere to better the lot of the human race – all these come to nothing. In the end they don't make one bit of difference, not one bit.[27]

Craig, in effect, devalues human achievements by arguing that they all "come to nothing" and make no difference. According to this reasoning, any achievements that humanity does make will cease once humanity ends and, consequently, they will not lead to further achievements or to a significant culmination that could be considered to have been the purpose of life.[28]

Historical achievements may be devalued because they may appear to lead nowhere and end in defeat when we look at them from a broad perspective. However, once this retrospective devaluation occurs, it is typically not long before one also begins to question the worth of all future efforts. For example, Miguel de Unamuno writes: "Yes, but what I work at, will not that too be lost in the end? And if it be lost, wherefore should I work at it?"[29] Similarly, the novelist Leo Tolstoy, in the midst of his well-known existential crisis, writes: "My deeds, whatever they may be, will be forgotten sooner or later, and I myself will be no more. Why, then, do anything?"[30]

What leads a person such as Tolstoy to devalue his earlier efforts (he refers to them as "delusions") and then to question the worth of *all* human efforts? This can occur when we *increase the standard* that we have previously used to evaluate whether our efforts were significant and effective. Tolstoy, in describing an earlier period in his life, indicates that, regarding the question of how we should live our lives, he believed, at that time, that "progress" was the answer. He writes: "I tried to reach intellectual perfection; I studied everything I could, everything that life gave me a chance to study. I tried to perfect my will and set up rules for myself that I endeavored to follow. …"[31]

Thus, at that point in his life, Tolstoy evaluated whether his efforts were significant based on whether improvement was occurring or, in his words, whether "Everything is developing, and I am developing. …"[32] However, later in his life, when he looks back on his many accomplishments from a broad perspective, he greatly expands his original goal, which in turn leads him to increase his original standard for judging significance – seemingly unaware that he did so. His revised goal is not simply to have created excellent works and to have made progress. If that were still the standard that he used to judge significance, then he would not belittle his accomplishments, but would uphold them. Rather, he, in effect, amends his prior standard (i.e., to make "progress") with a new condition: that his works will not be "forgotten," which is an indirect way of saying that he wants them to be remembered forever.

We may believe that longing for immortality, either for personal immortality or for our works to be remembered or appreciated forever, is irrational since immortality is unachievable. Nevertheless, the desire for long-lastingness has a way of creeping into our standards. For example, consider the following standard:

c.   If my works will be destroyed, then my efforts will have been futile.

Although not explicit, the desire for quasi-immortality is very much a part of the standard outlined above, hidden behind indirect ways of expressing our true desires and the vagueness of the word "futile." The higher one's aspirations are, the more likely it is that the efforts associated with bringing about these goals will be considered futile or ineffective. For example, if we seek to have our works last forever, then, at some point, we will probably conclude that our efforts are futile since this goal is unachievable. However, if we have more realistic aspirations, such as wanting to create an excellent work product, regardless of how long it will be appreciated by others, then we would be much less likely to conclude that our efforts at achieving this goal are futile.

If people set a goal and then accomplish the envisioned goal, they would not conclude that their efforts were ineffective or made no difference unless there is something in addition to this goal that they were seeking that remains unrealized. As argued, this additional condition that may indirectly creep into our standards is for our works to last forever, which is simply the reverse and a more direct way of saying that we do not want them to be destroyed. By rephrasing the standard to fill in the hidden information, as follows, it then becomes clear that the standard reflects the desire to achieve quasi-immortality:

c'.   If my works will be destroyed (i.e., not last forever), then my efforts will have been futile.

If one adopts the above, unreasonable standard for judging significance, then this person will likely decide, at some point, that it is not worthwhile to produce any creative works. Furthermore, they will not even consider it worth the effort to address a disvalue. For example, suppose that a young girl has fallen down a well and is in excruciating pain.[33] Soon after, the father of the child learns that the human race will perish in two weeks. If the father turned to the people around him at the top of the well, as his daughter screams in pain below, and said, "helping her is pointless since we will all be dead in two weeks," the other people around him would likely look at him with disgust and then proceed to pull the girl out of the well.

The father adopted the following unreasonable standard for judging worthwhileness by allowing his desire for long-lastingness to become part of the standard:

d.   Helping my daughter is worthwhile only if humanity will endure for more than two weeks.

This standard leads him to rationalize that no action should be taken to relieve her suffering. What would have been a reasonable standard to use for judging whether it was worthwhile to help the child? It would have been the following standard used by the people who decided to help the girl:

e.   Helping the girl is worthwhile if it will relieve her pain and suffering.

By the time a desire has been turned into a standard, it has likely become quite intense. At that point, it is no longer simply one of many desires that a person has. It may be desired more than anything else and is something that a person feels that he or she *must* have for life to be worth living. Some who have such a desire then make exaggerated claims in an attempt to defend this desire to others who may not value, as much as they do, if at all, the thing or experience that is desired. For example, they argue that if there is no immortality (i.e., if this desire for immortality cannot be satisfied), then "life is futile."[34] Just because personal immortality is unachievable does not mean that *all* of our efforts are futile. In other words, there are many goals that we can achieve, and desires that we can satisfy, even if we cannot satisfy this one desire to live forever.

The problem in allowing an unrealizable desire, such as immortality, to become part of a standard for judging whether our efforts are worthwhile or important is that it predetermines that we will fail to achieve the standard. Furthermore, it can lead us to lose sight of or discount all of the other things that matter to us besides fulfilling this one desire, as, for example, when the father concludes that helping his daughter is not worthwhile.

Since there is no way to satisfy the desire for quasi-immortality, one may fall into a state of despair, as did Tolstoy. Furthermore, because the desire may be concealed in the standard, the person may be unable to pinpoint the source of the despair and, consequently, may be unable to figure out how to overcome it. The person may believe that he or she has a new perspective on life that suddenly revealed that human endeavors are and have always been futile, when, in fact, the only thing that changed was that this person increased the standard that he or she had previously used to judge significance. Therefore, it is crucial to recognize when an unrealizable desire, such as the desire to have our works appreciated forever, has infected our standards and, when it has done so, to purge it from these standards. The original standard that we used to judge significance was likely realistic and inspiring before it became corrupted with the desire to achieve quasi-immortality.

Suppose that there is a god who created humanity and who told us that our efforts would be "significant" only if we create works that will last forever. Suppose also that humanity will not last forever and that we live in a universe that will not likely last forever. Thus, there is a clear, "objective" standard for judging whether our efforts are significant. If this were the standard handed down to us by this god, would we try to achieve the standard, or would we reject, as I believe, the standard on grounds that it is unreasonable, assuming that we were not compelled by this god to try to achieve the standard? Ironically, we are free to choose a reasonable standard to judge what is significant, yet some people unwittingly adopt, or impose upon themselves, a standard that they would reject if it had been imposed upon them by an external entity.

Leaving an Everlasting Trace Is Unimportant

As explained, the desire to have our works endure forever can creep into our standards for judging significance, which raises the following questions that should be explored. What is the ultimate goal(s) we are trying to accomplish in leaving an enduring trace? Do these goals make sense? Are they important?

Robert Nozick suggests that leaving a trace may "indicate that a person's life had a certain meaning or importance. ..."[35] He also points out that leaving a trace may be considered intrinsically important. However, he then questions whether long-lastingness should be considered important and suggests that it should not be.[36]

When people say that they would like to have an influence on future persons through their works, this sounds like a grand goal and we may be impressed, but why is this goal considered important? The importance attributed to this goal reflects two underlying relations. First, there is a relation between how challenging a goal is and how important we consider the goal; a challenging goal, such as seeking to influence future persons for hundreds of years, is considered more important than a goal that is easily met. Second, as Nozick comments on, there is a philosophic tradition that equates long-lastingness with importance; that which lasts is often valued more highly than that which does not.

Is a work product important because it endures or does it endure because it is important? Just because something may last a long time does not necessarily indicate that it is important;

long-lastingness does not lead to importance. Rather, if people consider a creation important because of the influence it had on them, or because of the contribution it made to a field of inquiry, or for other reasons, they seek to preserve the work and, consequently, it endures. Importance comes first, then long-lastingness. Thus, there is a relation between long-lastingness and importance, but the relation is the opposite of what is often thought.

As indicated in the earlier quotation from Faulkner, some suggest that they write for posterity. It is understandable if one writes for one's contemporaries and future persons or for just one's contemporaries, but it is peculiar why someone would focus solely on influencing future persons. Perhaps they believe that their creations will be ignored or undervalued by their contemporaries, for whatever reason, and that the true significance of their works will not be recognized until future persons come across them. Although there are a few exceptions (e.g., Schopenhauer), it is rare for someone's creations to be disregarded initially, but later considered important. Alternatively, they may believe that it is preferable to create works for future persons instead of for their contemporaries, but might not have or give a reason for, or have really thought about, the value judgement they are making. If they consider it more important to influence posterity than their contemporaries simply because future persons will exist at a later time, then this is strange and unjustified.

A person may have many different motivations in wanting to leave an enduring trace. The ultimate goal of a writer, for example, may be to achieve everlasting fame. Alternatively, the writer may be seeking to influence the beliefs, attitudes, and/or feelings of future persons. The writer, through insights and wisdom contained in the book, may also be seeking to help future persons cope with various problems.

Finally, if people have spent most of their lives working on projects that will be uncompleted when they die, they may want their work products to endure so that future generations can eventually complete the projects, thereby making it possible for them to achieve their goals posthumously. For example, if a team of medical researchers has worked to develop a vaccine to prevent a disease, but have not completed the work by the end of their lives, they may want their work products to endure so that future generations can eventually realize the goal of developing the vaccine so that future persons will not suffer from the disease. The researchers may want future generations to accomplish this goal that they worked toward, but may also derive a sense of pride and importance in believing that future generations will appreciate and admire the contribution they made in helping to develop the vaccine. If the researchers do not believe that their work will endure and, consequently, do not believe that it will be possible to achieve their envisioned goal of reducing human suffering by preventing this disease, then they may conclude that their efforts to develop the vaccine were unproductive and wasteful.

As outlined above, some of the reasons why people want to leave an enduring trace appear, *on the surface*, to be altruistic and others are related to satisfying their own desires. Regarding the apparent altruistic reasons, if people desire future generations so that they can accomplish goals that extend beyond the end of their lives, and if these goals are directed at helping or influencing (presumably in a positive way) future persons, then the conclusion would logically follow that they desire future generations so that they can help or influence them. But is the second premise of the argument true? We will now turn our attention to exploring this question.

If future persons currently existed, or if it were inevitable that they would exist at some point, then the goal of wanting to help or influence them would make sense and may be a worthy goal. However, future generations do not currently exist and it is not inevitable that they will exist. They may or may not be created depending on our behavior and the choices that we make. Therefore, those who desire future generations must be saying one of two things. First, they could be saying that *if future generations are created*, for whatever reasons, that they would like to help or influence them, which may reflect an altruistic motivation. On the other hand, they could be saying something quite different: that they specifically *want future generations to be created* so that they can help or influence them. If this is the reason they desire future generations, then this is quite odd, and not altruistic, but self-serving.

If a person's goal is to help or to have a positive influence on other people, then future generations are not needed to accomplish this goal. There are plenty of people around today who need help and whom we can attempt to influence how they feel or what they believe if that is our desire. Future persons are needed, however, for people to achieve goals directed at helping or influencing these future persons. But wanting people to be created so that one can then turnaround and help them cope with living, or influence how they view or relate to the world, through the traces that one has left, is a poor reason to desire future persons, if that is the real reason that a person wants humanity to endure for a long time.

Is the desire for humanity to persist for a long time reflective of an ultimate desire to influence or help future persons, through the traces that we have left, or is it mainly about wanting to have our works, and the other traces of our existence, appreciated so that we can derive a sense of importance from believing that this may occur? Let us explore this question. Many of us value the creations of our ancestors and so we assume that future generations will also value our works. Suppose that this is a false assumption. Suppose instead that people in the future did not value us or our works. Imagine that they despised our creations, including our paintings, music, and philosophic treatises. They considered our works so trivial that they destroyed them and even went so far as to make it look as if we had never existed. However, they relied on the medicines that we had created, claimed that they had created them, and these medicines helped them survive and flourish.

Under the scenario outlined above, would we still want these future persons to persist for as long as possible or would this no longer matter to us? If the latter answer is correct, as I suspect, then this suggests that the goal of wanting intelligent life to persist forever – whether it is human life or a nonhuman rational species, if it is thought that humanity will become extinct – is less about wanting to help them and more about wanting to have our works and our lives be considered important. By destroying our creations, and trivializing our existence by denying that we ever existed, these future persons would be taking away the sense of pride and importance that we derived from believing that our works would influence and be appreciated by them.

These future persons remembered us, at least collectively. Therefore, if it is true that it would no longer matter to us, under the circumstances described above, how long they will persist, then this suggests that people want more than just to be remembered by future persons. People, at least those who are achievement-oriented, want to be remembered and thought of as individuals who made a difference, meaning that the world was a better place because they lived. This would explain why obituaries typically contain not just a person's name, but also a list of the person's accomplishments.

For artists, writers, and other achievement-oriented people, the desire to have their works be considered important by future persons is much stronger than the distinct,[37] but related desire to simply be remembered. If they thought that their creations would be considered influential by future persons, but that they would eventually be forgotten, they could probably accept this. However, if they thought that future persons would lose, destroy, or ignore their work, but would remember them – unassociated from their work – then this would not likely be acceptable to them.

If people want to influence future persons, but believe that future persons will destroy their creations, then they would consider their efforts at influencing future persons pointless. Similarly, if we lived in a universe where the things that we created, such as our writings, were destroyed as soon as they were completed, without apparent reason, it would lead us to question the value of our creative pursuits. If one desired to write an essay but knew that it was certain that the essay, and all notes used in developing the essay, would be destroyed as soon as the essay was completed, would one still write the essay? This will depend on the reasons why the person is writing the essay. Writing the essay would be considered pointless if one's goal is to have the essay read by other people. In contrast, if one is writing the essay as a way to stimulate one's thinking or to clarify one's thoughts, then this person will conclude that writing the essay is not pointless even though the essay will be destroyed.

In the universe described above, where the things that we create are destroyed immediately upon their completion, our creative pursuits may still be considered worthwhile, depending upon the nature of our goals. However, if we lived in a universe where not just the things that we create are destroyed upon their completion, but all of the intermediate steps leading up to the creation are also undone, including losing any thoughts stimulated by the activity, then all of our creative endeavors would be considered futile, especially if it were certain that our efforts would be undone. People could write an essay, but it would be as if they never did it. No traces, of any kind, would remain of their efforts. No matter what their goal was in writing the essay, whether it was to stimulate their own thinking or to be read by others, their goal could never be achieved.

Fortunately, we do not live in a universe where our creations are destroyed immediately upon their completion, or all of our efforts, including intermediate advances, are undone as soon as we complete a project. Our works will not last forever, but they generally endure long enough for us to achieve our goals in creating the works. Furthermore, the achievements that we have made are not reversible. In defending his theistic views, Charles Hartshorne writes: "If the humanist does not believe in racial immortality, then he looks forward to a time when all our achievements will be exactly as if they had never been."[38] Granted, the *things* we have created will eventually vanish once human beings are no longer around to preserve them. However, *achievements are events*, not things, and events that have occurred cannot be undone or reversed. Therefore, it will continue to be true that our achievements occurred even if humanity ends. One disadvantage of having an unalterable past is that we cannot undo a wrongdoing that occurred. However, an unalterable past is also an advantage in that our achievements can never be undone, which may give some consolation to those who desire quasi-immortality.

Conclusion

Although our works will not last forever, this should not matter if we accomplished what we set out to do when we created these works. Wanting our creations to endure forever was not likely part of our goal when we created them. If we accomplish our goals and then later in life conclude that these accomplishments were of no significance, then this is a sign that a desire for long-lastingness has crept into the standards that we use to judge significance. Escalating desires can lead to escalating standards since the standards that we establish reflect our goals and desires.

Including long-lastingness as a criterion for judging the significance of our efforts is unreasonable. If one includes long-lastingness as part of the standard, then one will feel that it is necessary for humanity to persist forever. There is no need for humanity to live forever for our lives and works to be significant. If the standard that we adopt for judging significance does not include long-lastingness as part of the standard, then it will not matter whether humanity will endure for a long time.

Like Tolstoy, we may be unable to keep from wanting to have our achievements remembered forever. We may also be unable to keep from wanting our works to be appreciated forever. But we can refrain from turning these desires into standards for judging whether our efforts and accomplishments are significant. If we can keep from doing this, it will be to our advantage. Then, during those times when we look back on life from an imagined perspective that encompasses times after humanity has become extinct, we will not conclude that our efforts amounted to nothing. Rather, we will conclude that many people made remarkable accomplishments that made their lives, and possibly the lives of others, better than they would have been if these goals had never been pursued. And if we expand our evaluation, as we should, to take into account all experiences associated with living, not just goal-related experiences, we will conclude not that life was empty, but that living was worthwhile.

Notes

1. Partridge uses the term "self transcendence" to mean extending one's influence beyond one's lifetime. Others use this word in a broader sense to mean extending one's influence or help to other people, regardless of whether they are future persons and so, to avoid confusion, this word will not be used.

2. Ernest Partridge, "Why Care About the Future?" in *Responsibilities to Future Generations: Environmental Ethics*, ed. Ernest Partridge (Buffalo: Prometheus Books, 1981), 204.

3. *Ibid.*, 209.

4. *Ibid.*, 217–18.

5. Allen Tough, *Crucial Questions About the Future* (New York: UP of America, 1991), 12.

6. Wilhelm Ostwald, *Individuality and Immortality* (Boston: Houghton Mifflin Company, 1906), 14. A scholar from various disciplines is invited each year to deliver the "Ingersoll Lecture on the Immortality of Man." At the time of his lecture, which was published in the book, Ostwald was a Professor of Physical Chemistry at the University of Leipzig and a Temporary Professor at Harvard University, where he delivered the lecture.

7. Avner de-Shalit, *Why Posterity Matters: Environmental Policies and Future Generations* (London: Routledge, 1995), 38.

8. Ostwald, *op. cit.*, 53.

9. *Ibid.*, 54–5.

10. James Lenman, "On Becoming Extinct," *Pacific Philosophical Quarterly* 83 (2002), 253–69.

11. William Faulkner, *Faulkner in the University: Class Conferences at the University of Virginia, 1957–1958*, ed. Frederick L. Gwynn & Joseph L. Blotner (New York: Vintage Books, 1959), 61.

12. Lester Thurow, "Zero Economic Growth and the Distribution of Income," *The Economic Growth Controversy*, ed. Andrew Weintraub, Eli Schwartz, & J. Richard Aronson (White Plains: International Arts and Sciences Press, Inc., 1973), 141–2.

13. Arthur Schopenhauer, "On the Suffering of the World," *Essays and Aphorisms*, trans. R. J. Hollingdale (London: Penguin Books, 1970), 47.

14. *Ibid.*, 47–8.

15. See, for example, Kurt Baier, "The Meaning of Life," *The Meaning of Life*, ed. E. D. Klemke (New York: Oxford UP, 2000), 101–32. Inaugural Lecture delivered at Canberra University College, 1957.

16. For a more detailed analysis and discussion of the concept of futility, see Brooke Alan Trisel, "Futility and the Meaning of Life Debate," *Sorites* 14 (October 2002), 70–84. http://www.sorites.org/Issue_14/trisel.htm

17. Arne Naess, "The Shallow and the Deep, Long-Range Ecology Movement: A Summary," *Inquiry* 16 (1973), 95–100.

18. Paul W. Taylor, "The Ethics of Respect for Nature," *Environmental Philosophy: From Animal Rights to Radical Ecology*, ed. Michael E. Zimmerman (Upper Saddle River, NJ: Prentice-Hall, Inc. 1998), 71–86.

19. *Ibid.*, 76.

20. Bertrand Russell, "A Free Man's Worship," *Why I Am Not a Christian, and Other Essays on Religion and Related Subjects*, ed. Paul Edwards (New York: Simon and Schuster, 1957), 107. Originally published in *The Independent Review*, 1903.

21. John D. Barrow & Frank J. Tipler, *The Anthropic Cosmological Principle* (Oxford: Oxford UP, 1986), 615.

22. See, for example, Paul Taylor, *op. cit.* He argues that all living things have "inherent worth."

23. See, for example, Paul Davies, *The Last Three Minutes: Conjectures About the Ultimate Fate of The Universe* (New York: BasicBooks, 1994) for speculation such as this. Like Barrow and Tipler, the physicist Davies speculates about how it might be possible for robotic "descendants" to survive the death of the universe.

24. The term "quasi-immortality" will be used to mean leaving a trace of ourselves that will be appreciated forever.

25. See, for example, the quotation from William Lane Craig in the next section of this essay.

26. For an in-depth analysis of the external perspective, see Thomas Nagel, *The View From Nowhere* (Oxford: Oxford UP, 1986), esp. 208–31.

27. William Lane Craig, "The Absurdity of Life Without God," *The Meaning of Life*, ed. E. D. Klemke (New York: Oxford UP, 2000), 42. Originally published in *Reasonable Faith: Christian Truth and Apologetics*, 1994.

28. For a reply to the argument that life is a journey leading nowhere, see Paul Edwards, "Meaning and Value of Life," *The Encyclopedia of Philosophy*, ed. Paul Edwards (New York: Macmillan, 1967), vol. 4, 467–77. Edwards argues (p. 471) that "striving is not pointless if it achieves what it is intended to achieve even if it is without *final* consequence...." See also Thomas Nagel, "The Absurd," *The Journal of Philosophy* 63 (1971), 716–27. Nagel argues that an activity does not have to be followed by another activity to justify pursuing the first activity. Although Nagel indicates that the standard arguments for absurdity fail as arguments, he concludes (p. 718) that "they attempt to express something that is difficult to state, but fundamentally correct."

29. Miguel de Unamuno, *Tragic Sense of Life*, trans. J. E. Crawford Flitch (New York: Dover Publications, 1954), 231. English translation originally published by Macmillan and Company, Ltd., 1921.

30. Leo Tolstoy, *Confession*, trans. David Patterson (New York: W. W. Norton & Company, 1983), 30. Originally published as *Ispoved* in 1884.

31. *Ibid.*, 17.

32. *Ibid.*, 23.

33. Example adapted from one used by anonymous referee in comments.

34. See, for example, Craig, *op. cit.*, 53–4. He argues that "life is futile" without personal immortality and God.

35. Robert Nozick, *Philosophical Explanations* (Cambridge, MA: Harvard UP, 1981), 584.

36. *Ibid.*, 585.

37. Thanks to an anonymous referee for suggesting that I distinguish between the desire to be appreciated in the future and the desire simply to be remembered.

38. Charles Hartshorne, *Beyond Humanism: Essays in the Philosophy of Nature* (Lincoln, 1937; repr. Gloucester, MA: Peter Smith, 1975), 12.

5.6

Free Will, Death, and Immortality
The Role of Narrative

John Martin Fischer

Although the future is uncertain, we can at least be confident of one thing: the past is always changing. (Slavic folk saying)[1]

I. Introduction

The notion of 'narrative' is rich and suggestive, but, at the same time, vexed. The notion is invoked by philosophers and literary theorists (and others) in very different ways. Despite the confusions engendered by its multiple meanings and uses, I believe that the notion of narrative can be illuminating with respect to issues about freedom, death, immortality, and the meaning of life. Care must be taken, however, to distinguish different ideas, and to apply them appropriately.

In previous work, I have made some tentative and sketchy suggestions.[2] I have claimed that the value of acting freely, or acting in such a way as to be morally responsible, is the value of self-expression. This value is a kind of aesthetic value, or akin to an aesthetic value. When I act freely, I 'make a statement,' and the value of my free action is the value of writing a sentence in the book of my life (my narrative), rather than the value of 'making a difference' (of a certain sort) to the world. I have not suggested that artistic self-expression is the only value, or a hegemonic one; rather, the suggestion was that the value of free action is the value, whatever that is, of artistic self-expression. Further, I have suggested that our lives having the signature features of narrative does not in itself imply that immortality would necessarily be undesirable (or even unrecognizably similar to our current lives).[3]

John Martin Fischer (2005) "Free Will, Death, and Immortality: The Role of Narrative," *Philosophical Papers* 34(3): 379–403.

Here I wish to develop and tie together these ideas a bit further (although, perhaps inevitably, not as fully as I would like). I shall begin by laying out and discussing relevant aspects of the work of David Velleman on these topics.[4] I shall then argue that the value of our lives as free creatures is indeed a species of the value of artistic self-expression. More specifically, I shall contend that acting freely is what makes us the sort of creatures that live lives that have the characteristic features of narratives. Acting freely is what changes the depictions of our lives from mere characterizations to stories (or narratives). Further, I shall distinguish the claim that our lives can be explained in the distinctive manner of narrative explanation from the claim that our lives can be evaluated in the characteristic narrative fashion. Finally, I suggest that understanding our lives as narratives (in either sense) is compatible with the possibility that unending life would be attractive to human beings. Narrativity need not entail the necessity of endings.

II.   Velleman on Narrative Value and Narrative Explanation

II.1   Velleman on narrative value

Velleman argues that the overall value of our life, considered as a whole, is not determined by a function that merely adds together all of the levels of momentary well-being in our lives. Additionally, he contends that our levels of momentary well-being are not simply the marginal increment in our level of overall welfare or value. The two dimensions of value – momentary and overall – are not analyzed in terms of each other or reducible to each other.[5]

According to Velleman, we care not just about the total amount of momentary well-being in our lives, or even its temporal ordering; we care about the story of our lives, the narrative structure of our lives.[6] More carefully, the function that specifies the overall value of our lives takes into account in an important way certain characteristics that are signature features of what we take to be 'good' (in some sense) narratives.

As Velleman concedes, his point is not that we value narratives that are 'better stories' in a sense that would be of interest to potential readers of novels or (say) literary critics or reviewers. A life that makes a rather boring story might well be preferable, in terms of overall value, to a life filled with unexpected twists and turns, excitement, titillation, and tragedy. So exactly what does Velleman mean when he says that the overall value of our lives is importantly sensitive to narrative content? What are the signature features of narratives that help to shape the functions that determine the overall value of our lives?

I suggest that we begin by considering the examples Velleman employs. Velleman starts with an example of Michael Slote's:

> A given man may achieve political power and, once in power, do things of great value, after having been in the political wilderness throughout his earlier career. He may later die while still 'in harness' and fully possessed of his powers, at a decent old age. By contrast, another man may have a meteoric success in youth, attaining the same office as the first man and also achieving much good; but then lose power, while still young, never to regain it. Without hearing anything more, I think our natural, immediate reaction to these examples would be that the first man was the more fortunate ...[7]

Whereas Slote concludes from this sort of example that we have a 'time preference for goods that come late in life,' Velleman concludes that we care about the narrative content of our lives (and not just the total levels of momentary well-being, added up or even added up and weighted according to temporal position). It is a distinctive feature of narratives that later events can alter the 'meaning' or 'significance' of earlier events. In this sense narratives can have 'loops,' as Derrida (notoriously, in some quarters) contended. It is not that we can change the physico-causal past; but we can sometimes change its meaning and thus its contribution to the value of our lives overall.

Velleman says:

> Why would a person care about the placement of momentary goods on the curve that maps his changing welfare? The answer, I believe, is that an event's place in the story of one's life lends it a meaning that isn't entirely determined by its impact on one's well-being at the time. A particular electoral victory, providing a particular boost to one's current welfare, can mean either that one's early frustrations were finally over or that one's subsequent failures were not yet foreshadowed, that one enjoyed either fleeting good luck or lasting success – all depending on its placement in the trend of one's well-being. And the event's meaning is what determines its contribution to the value of one's life.
>
> … The meaning of a benefit depends not only on whether it follows or precedes hardships but also on the specific narrative relation between the goods and evils involved. Slote's politician would have experienced an improvement in his well-being whether his years of toil were capped by electoral victory or merely cut short by his winning the lottery and retiring young. But the contribution of these alternative benefits to the overall value of his life wouldn't be determined entirely by how well-off each would make him from one moment to the next. Their contribution to his life's value would also be determined by the fact that the former would be a well-earned reward, and would prove his struggles to have been a good investment, whereas the latter would be a windfall in relation to which his struggles were superfluous. Thus benefits that would effect equal improvements in his momentary well-being might contribute differently to the value of his life, by virtue of lending and borrowing different meanings in exchange with preceding events.[8]

Velleman contends that it is better to thrive as a result of learning from one's misfortunes than simply as a result of (say) winning the lottery or some other windfall. As Velleman puts it:

> A life in which one suffers a misfortune and then learns from it may find one equally well-off, at each moment, as a life in which one suffers a misfortune and then reads the encyclopedia. But the costs of the misfortune are merely offset when the value of the latter life is computed; whereas they are somehow cancelled entirely from the accounts of the former. Or rather, neither misfortune affects the value of one's life just by adding costs and benefits to a cumulative account. The effect of either misfortune on one's life is proportionate, not to its impact on one's continuing welfare, but to its import for the story. An edifying misfortune is not just offset but redeemed, by being given a meaningful place in one's progress through life.[9]

Velleman believes that the following pair of stories illustrates the same point. In both lives your first ten years of marriage are unhappy and are followed by equal amounts of contentment. But in the first life you get divorced and consider your first marriage a 'dead loss'; you just happen to meet someone else with whom you live happily (ever after!). In the second life, you learn from the troubles of your first ten years, and you save the marriage (and live happily ever after). Indeed, in the second story you think of the initial segment of the marriage as the 'foundation of your [later] happiness.' Velleman says that we would prefer the second life. He says, 'You can simply think that a dead-end relationship blots the story of one's life in a way that marital problems don't if they lead to eventual happiness.'[10]

So it seems that the primary examples suggested by Velleman of salient features of desirable narratives (in the sense relevant to the function that determines overall value of a human life) are of hard work being rewarded and learning from mistakes, rather than simply profiting (comparably) from windfalls. My suggestion is that we interpret Velleman's claim that we take narrative content into account in evaluating overall welfare as involving the idea that 'narrative content' is a shorthand for a kind (or perhaps kinds) of relationship among events of which his cases are instances. 'Narrative content' is not explained generally, but it involves the sort of relationships that are present in his cases and other, similar cases. When this sort of temporally extended pattern of events occurs, the kind of 'exchange of meaning' that is characteristic of narratives can take place.[11]

Velleman applies his claim (that human beings are distinctive insofar as the overall value of our lives is partly a function of narrative content) to issues pertaining to the badness of death. A decision about physician-assisted suicide depends at least in part on whether the individual's life would on balance be worth continuing (on some appropriate metric). Velleman says:

> The choice between heroic medical treatment and passive euthanasia is therefore frequently said to require so-called quality-of-life considerations. Whether days should be added or subtracted from a patient's life is to be judged, according to the prevalent view, by whether the days in question would be spent in a state of well-being or hardship.
>
> In my view, however, deciding when to die is not (despite the familiar saying) like deciding when to cash in one's chips – not, that is, a decision to be based on the incremental gains and losses that one stands to accumulate by staying in the game. It is rather like deciding when and how to end a story, a decision that cannot be dictated by considerations of momentary well-being. Hence a person may rationally be willing to die though he can look forward to a few more good weeks or months; and a person may rationally be unwilling to die even though he can look forward only to continued adversity. The rationality of the patient's attitude depends on whether an earlier or later death would make a better ending to his life-story.[12]

II.1a   Some reflections

The idea of employing the notion of narrative as a guide in potential cases of physician-assisted suicide is fascinating and suggestive. I think it has limitations, though. We saw above that the pertinent notion of 'better ending to his life-story' cannot be the notion of 'better' important to a reader of a work of fiction or a literary critic. But we do not have a general account of the relevant notion of narrative content and thus of 'better story' or 'better ending of the life-story.' We *do* have a set of examples, and we can intuitively recognize similar sequences of events that have the requisite 'narrative' characteristics. But I think that this will only provide guidance in some cases – by no means all.

Certainly we can say that the death of someone in the prime of her life, with many ongoing professional and personal projects underway, and no significant health problems, would be a bad ending to her story, in the relevant sense. Similarly, we can presumably say of an elderly woman who has had a full, rich life and has completed all her important life-projects, has said goodbye to her loved ones and friends and made arrangements for the disposition of her estate, and is in significant pain, that it would not be a bad thing for her to die; death now rather than later would be a better ending to her life-story. Velleman's notion of narrative content arguably does help to sort through such examples.

But there will be many other cases in which it simply does not give sufficiently definite guidance. What about a person who has completed all his life-projects, but still to some extent enjoys simply watching certain television programs or reading the newspaper. He is physically confined to a bed, but is not in intolerable or significant pain. He knows however that he has a condition that will slowly incapacitate him further, and he has decided that now is the time to die. Would death now rather than in six months or a year or two years be a better ending to his story? Are his interests in television and the newspaper sufficient to say that death now would rob him of a 'better' ending to his story? What if he did not have such interests, or any interests? That is, what if he were largely indifferent to everything, including television and the newspaper and even news of his family, and so forth? Would this make a difference, and, if so, would the narrative account suggested by Velleman entail (or help to explain) the difference in question?

The ideas that people should thrive because of their efforts, or in virtue of learning from their mistakes, do not provide sufficient guidance about the sorts of cases just sketched. Further, it is not clear how to extrapolate or extend the ideas to provide definite guidance in these and a whole range of cases. I would think that many (although certainly not all) cases of potential physician-assisted euthanasia pertain to elderly individuals who have completed the major projects of their lives, at least so far as 'projects' are understood in a fairly standard way. It is already the case that either they have learned from their mistakes or not, either they have flourished because of their efforts or not, and so forth. These considerations don't seem to help with the decision about when exactly the decision to terminate life should be made, if at all. Of course, we could try to interpret 'narrative content' in such a way as to apply to anyone with ongoing interests of any kind, but this seems a stretch; here considerations of quality of life appear to be driving our judgments, rather than considerations of narrative content or structure. Thus, whereas Velleman's idea is highly suggestive, it can give only a partial guide to the difficult decisions concerning physician-assisted suicide.[13]

Velleman also applies his insights about the significance of narrative content to the question of the distinctive badness of the death of a person. A human being can see his life as an extended sequence over time; also, he can see it as a story. A human being can thus care about the narrative structure of his life. According to Velleman, a nonhuman animal, such as a cow, cannot conceive of itself as a continuing entity – cannot even take an extended temporal perspective at all. What the animal cannot conceive it cannot care about. As Velleman puts it, '… a person can care about what his life-story is like, and a premature death can spoil the story of his life. Hence death can harm a person but it cannot harm a cow.'[14]

Velleman believes that, because a nonhuman animal cannot take a temporally extended perspective, it is incoherent to say that one sequence of moments can be better for a cow than another sequence of moments. He says, 'For a lower animal, then, momentary well-being fails not only of additivity but of cumulability by any algorithm at all. Consequently, the totality of this subject's life simply has no value for him, because he cannot care about it as such …'[15]

It is not clear to me that value (and harm) should be tied so closely to a subject's ability to conceive of the relevant thing. I do not know how to adjudicate this sort of issue. But I would simply point out that even if we granted that a cow's death deprives the cow of a sequence of future experiences (which on balance are positive), this is not the distinctive sort of value of which death can deprive a human being. That is, death can be bad for a person in a special way: it can rob a person of a good ending to his life story, whereas it cannot so rob a cow. The lives of human beings (or, more carefully, persons) have a dimension of value over and above the accumulation of momentary well-being, whereas at best this sort of accumulation exhausts the value of a cow's life. Thus death can be bad for a person in a distinctive way, even if we grant that there is a cumulative dimension to the value of a nonhuman animal's life.

Note that Velleman contends that the capacity to adopt a temporal perspective from which one can see an extended period of time is necessary for the capacity to care about the story of one's life. Thus, on Velleman's view, such a capacity is a necessary condition for the overall value of humans' lives being affected by narrative considerations.[16] I do not however believe that the capacity to take this sort of perspective is *sufficient*. Consider a human being who is being thoroughly controlled by remote-control direct stimulation of the brain, so that his choices and actions are intuitively not his own, free choices and actions. This individual may well have the normal capacity to take a more expansive temporal perspective, but the fact that he never acts freely inclines me to say that his overall level of well-being is to be determined by simply adding his momentary welfare values. For an individual who does not act freely, there is no separate dimension of value – the narrative dimension – irreducible to the intertemporal aggregation of momentary welfare. Such an individual would be 'in between' mere animals (on Velleman's account) and ordinary human beings (and other persons). That is, he would have the capacity to take the relevant temporal perspective, and yet not act freely. Thus, unlike mere animals (on Velleman's account), his momentary welfare values could be added together; but unlike ordinary human beings, he would not have a separate narrative dimension of value.

If I am correct about this supposition, then acting freely is the ingredient that gives us the distinctively narrative dimension of value. Acting freely is the feature which, when added to the others (including the capacity to take the appropriate temporal point of view and thus to care about one's story), transforms us into creatures whose lives can be evaluated by reference to salient sorts of narrative relationships.[17]

It is typically held that only a free creature – only a creature capable of acting freely – can have a meaningful life. It emerges now that acting freely is the specific ingredient that endows our lives with the distinctively narrative dimension of value. Only a creature who can act freely can affect the 'meanings' of past events by virtue of affecting the narrative relationships among various events in his life. Death robs a person of something especially important – the capacity to continue to lead a meaningful life. That is, it can now be seen that it robs a person of the capacity to continue to lead a life with a narrative dimension of value, and thus with a specific sort of meaning. It is sometimes said that death is bad because it deprives us of possible future goods. On the view I have sketched, it is also bad because it can deprive us of the possibility of changing the narrative meaning of the past.

On this sort of view (to which I am attracted), one can disagree with Velleman's claim that death cannot be bad for a cow, but still maintain that the death of a person is bad in a special way. Death arguably can be bad for the cow insofar as it deprives the cow of future pleasures (pleasures that would be part of an extended sequence that overall has considerably more pleasure than pain). But death can be bad for a person insofar as it deprives him of past goods as well as future goods: it cuts off the accumulation of momentary well-being, and it can prevent us from writing a better ending to our story (and thus vindicating our pasts).[18]

I follow Carl Ginet in holding that our freedom is the freedom to add to the given past, holding the laws of nature fixed.[19] This sort of 'fixity-of-the past' view pertains to the physico-causal events and features of the past, and not to their 'meanings.' This constraint applies to both the notion of 'freedom to do otherwise,' and the notion of 'acting freely.' Whereas we cannot go backward in physico-causal space-time and 'change the past,' we can readily go backward in narrative space-time. Whereas it is a constraint on our freedom that the physico-causal past be fixed, and that our actions be extensions of the given (physico-causal) past, it is precisely our capacity to act freely that provides the ingredient that allows for backward travel in narrative space-time.[20]

II.2   Velleman on narrative explanation

In a fascinating recent article, David Velleman has sought to give an account of narrative explanation (which, of course, is distinct from narrative value).[21] As Velleman puts it, 'A story does more than recount events; it recounts events in a way that renders them intelligible, thus conveying not just information but also understanding.'[22] Velleman seeks to describe the distinctive explanatory force of narrative, and to distinguish narrative explanation from explanation in the social and natural sciences.

Velleman says:

> This question arises for various disciplines in which narrative comes into play. For historians, it is the question whether narrating historical events conveys understanding over and above that conveyed by subsuming the same events under the generalizations of economics, political science, or sociology. For clinical psychologists, it is the question whether fitting symptomatic behaviors into a life-story adds to the understanding gained by fitting them into diagnostic categories. Even the police or the jury must ask themselves what sort of explanatory value there is in a suspect's giving his alibi in the form of a story.[23]

In providing his account of the distinctive potency of narrative explanation, Velleman builds on the work of Louis Mink and W.B. Gallie.[24] Both of these theorists emphasize the importance of characterizing events in terms of their relations to outcomes or 'endings'. Velleman says:

A narrative must move forward not only in the sense of telling one event after another but also in the sense of approaching or at least seeming to approach some conclusion to those events, some terminus, finish, or closure.

Here I should elaborate on a point ... about the difference between narrative and the artistic genres that employ it. A novel or a theater piece need not reach a conclusion or even seem to approach one. But a novel or a theatre piece need not be a work of narrative, either; it may be a work of narrative only in parts, or it may be 'of' narrative only in the sense of commenting on the requirements of narrative only by pointedly defying them. A bad story can make for a great novel (though perhaps not the sort of great novel that one likes to read). The necessity of an ending is not inherent in the aesthetics of the novel or play but in the nature of storytelling, a form of discourse that a novel or play need not employ.[25]

On Velleman's view, a narrative explains by allowing the audience to assimilate the events in the story to a familiar emotional pattern or 'cadence.' He says:

A story therefore enables its audience to assimilate events, not to familiar patterns of *how things happen*, but rather to familiar patterns of *how things feel*. These patterns are not themselves stored in discursive form, as scenarios or stories; they are stored rather in experiential, proprioceptive, and kinesthetic memory – as we might say in the muscle-memory of the heart. Although the audience may have no discursive memory of events such as those of the story, it nevertheless has an experience of *deja senti*, because its emotional sensibility naturally follows the ups and downs of the story, just as a muscle naturally follows the cycle of tension and release.

What's more, the emotion that resolves a narrative cadence lends to subsume the emotions that preceded it; the triumph felt at a happy ending is the triumph of ambitions realized and anxieties allayed; the grief felt at a tragic ending is the grief of hopes dashed or loves denied. Hence the conclusory emotion in a narrative cadence embodies not just how the audience feels about the ending; it embodies how the audience feels, at the ending, about the whole story.[26]

So, on Velleman's account, narrative explains by getting the audience to understand the relevant events because it '*knows how they feel*,' in the sense that it experiences them as leading it through a natural emotional sequence,' and also because '*it knows how it feels about them*,' in the sense that it arrives at a stable attitude toward them overall.[27]

11.2a   Some reflections

Above I distinguished two notions of 'better story' and, derivatively, 'better ending of the life-story.' One notion is, as I put it, especially relevant to potential readers of the story or critics, such as reviewers. Employing this notion, one might say that a certain story is better insofar as the ending is unpredictable, or there are unexpected and exciting twists and turns of plot, and so forth. It is clear that it cannot be this notion that is pertinent (say) to questions about physician-assisted suicide. Rather, a second notion is pertinent, and we can get a grasp on it by considering salient examples from what are considered 'good' (in the relevant sense) life-stories: persons thriving because of their efforts (and not merely because of unexpected windfalls), persons learning from their mistakes and thus flourishing (rather than deeming their mistakes 'dead-weight losses' or flourishing by lucky accidents), and so forth. It is this second notion that is relevant to questions about physician-assisted suicide.

In his paper on narrative explanation, Velleman says:

> … the question how storytelling conveys understanding is inseparable from the question what makes for a good story. Of course, a good story can be good in many accidental respects, ranging from the elegance of its diction to the personal attractions of its characters. But what makes a story good specifically as a story – what makes it a good example of storytelling, or narrative – is its excellence at a particular way of organizing events into an intelligible whole.[28]

I am not sure whether Velleman intends to be making the following sort of suggestion, or whether he would agree entirely, but I would recommend that we interpret Velleman's remarks as suggesting a way of giving more concrete content to the first notion of 'better story'. That is, I suggest that 'good story', in the sense relevant to potential readers and reviewers, is goodness in presenting a sequence of events in such a way as to have emotional resonance (that is, to map onto the natural cadence of our emotions in a natural way). The various devices of plot and literary style can be seen as ways of seeking to achieve a resonance with our natural emotional cadences – to achieve '*deja senti*' in various ways. Some such devices work considerably better than others (for individual readers and also groups of readers). The classic literary (as well as musical) forms can be considered 'tried and true' ways of evoking emotional resonances. (It then becomes the challenge of the author – or composer – to work creatively and in original ways within the structure of these forms, or perhaps to transgress the boundaries set by these forms, so as to achieve emotional resonance.) Now I certainly doubt whether the notion of 'good story' of interest to readers and reviewers of literature can be reduced to a single idea, but this suggestion can perhaps illuminate at least a central aspect of the notion.[29]

Velleman says:

> Any sequence of events, no matter how improbable, can provide material for storytelling if it completes an emotional cadence. Twins separated at birth are ideal protagonists for a story even if their eventual reunion is a fluke. A discovery due to serendipity, a tragedy narrowly averted by dumb luck, a mundane act that unforeseeably becomes the last in a life accidentally cut short – these are the stuff not only of literary storytelling but of legend, gossip, and other forms of everyday narrative. Whether a winning lottery ticket or a fatal housefire makes enough of a story to be featured on the local news depends, not on whether its causes can be told, but rather on whether the surrounding circumstances will call up feelings that can be brought to some resolution by this inexplicable stroke of good or bad fortune. So long as we feel an anxiety relieved or a hope dashed, we have the sense of hearing a story, even if we have no idea why events took the relevant turn.[30]

How exactly do these remarks fit with the point made above that the narrative value of a life in which efforts are rewarded is greater than that of a life in which one thrives by serendipity or lucky windfall? We have to distinguish between narrative understanding and narrative value. We can achieve narrative understanding, and we could even say that the story is a good story, when we are told of someone flourishing by winning the lottery. Depending on the details of the presentation, the sequence of events can resonate with an emotional cadence – the story can depict the sequence of events in such a way that it feels familiar – it feels like a recognizable human drama. Upon hearing the presentation, we are inclined to say, in our hearts, 'Ah yes …' But it does not follow that such a story depicts a life with great *narrative value*. So, for example, such a story does not depict a life with more narrative value than the story of a life of flourishing as a result of lessons learned or simply hard work. A better story in the telling need not make for a story of a life with more value. An ending that is 'better' in the sense of narrative understanding need not be 'better' in the sense of narrative value.

Return to Velleman's claim, '… the question how storytelling conveys understanding is inseparable from the question what makes for a good story.' The question of how storytelling conveys understanding is inseparable from what makes for a good story, in the sense that is relevant to readers and reviewers of literature. Further, it seems that only a life that can be explained in the distinctively narrative way is capable of having the characteristic narrative value – is capable of being evaluated through a function that is sensitive to the sorts of structural relationships sketched above. So the possibility of narrative explanation is inseparable from the possibility of narrative evaluation; being a narrative is a necessary condition for having narrative value. Of course, it does not follow from anything said thus far that the better a story is in the telling – the greater its virtues along the dimension pertinent to narrative understanding – the higher the value of the function that determines overall value of the life will be (other things equal).

As I said in the introductory section of this paper, I have suggested in previous work that the value of acting freely is the value (whatever that is) of writing a sentence in the narrative of one's life. On some approaches, acting out of character is inconsistent with the idea of one's life's having narrative structure (and admitting of narrative explanation). But I do not employ the idea of narrative in a way that would rule out free action that is 'out of character'. The situation here is a bit like the possibility of narrative explanation of flourishing as a result of a windfall, such as winning the lottery. If the storyteller is adept, the story will resonate; that is, the structure of the story will map onto the emotional memory of the 'listener' or 'reader'. As above (in the case of succeeding as a result of a lucky accident), the story of action out of character can be told in such a way that it feels familiar – it feels like a recognizable human drama. It all depends on the way the story is told, and it is a delicate matter to tell the story in such a way as to elicit an emotional response of the proper sort. Certain ways of telling the story will result in puzzlement, whereas more skillful storytelling will evoke that heartfelt, 'Ah yes …', indicating an isomorphism with a human emotional cadence. One can freely act out of character, even on an approach that invokes the importance of narrative explanation, and identities the value of acting freely with a certain sort of aesthetic value (defined in terms of narrative value).

On certain views of moral responsibility, one is morally responsible insofar as one expresses an enduring 'character trail'. This approach follows David Hume. But the basic problem with the Humean approach is that one can act freely, and be morally responsible, even when one acts out of character. The Humean may try to find some more 'complicated' character trait that is expressed in the behavior, but I believe that this trail leads inevitably to an unacceptable etiolation of the ordinary notion of 'character trait.' On this approach, it will turn out in the end that 'character traits' do not play any substantive, independent explanatory role. Despite the considerable attractions of a Humean approach to such matters, I believe that the possibility of acting out of character – and doing so freely – constitutes a significant and, indeed, insuperable problem.

On my view of acting freely and moral responsibility, one need not be expressing any sort of enduring character trait, or expressing any sort of 'commitment' or 'positive evaluation' of the relevant behavior. Rather, one is expressing oneself in the sense of writing a sentence in the narrative of one's life. If the story of one's past, and one's behavior, resonates appropriately, then one is acting freely and is morally responsible for the behavior in question. Again: it all depends on whether the storytelling is adept. In some cases the story can be told in such a way that the behavior under consideration is 'prefigured', even if it is out of character. When the behavior is in this way prefigured, the story resonates with the listener (or 'audience') in the indicated way, and the agent is morally responsible.[31]

III.   Narrative, Endings, and Immortality

On the view of narrative explanation under consideration here, a narrative must have an ending. If our lives are narratives, or have the distinctive structure of narrative, then they must have endings. On this view, we cannot be immortal (insofar as our lives are narratives or have narrative value), if our lives are indeed narratives. To imagine immortal human life is to imagine human life devoid of an essential or at least very important characteristic: having narrative structure and thus a distinctive dimension of value.

I think that, strictly speaking, this is correct. If a narrative must have an ending, then it is clear that our lives cannot have the sort of meaning that involves taking a retrospective perspective on its totality, as it were, and assigning a meaning that reflects the overall arc of the life-story. But an immortal life could have something very much like narrative meaning, strictly conceived; or, perhaps better, the relevant temporal stages or parts could be explained in the distinctive and strict narrative manner, and they could have the signature features of narrative value. Whereas the life as a whole could not be considered a narrative, the parts could be, and this would seem to render immortal life recognizably like our current human lives and also potentially desirable (in a distinctive way).[32]

The literary analogue for such a life is not the novel, but perhaps a collection of short stories. Of course, the collection needs to be infinitely large, and the short stories need to be interconnected, with the same character appearing as the protagonist. Perhaps a better analogy would be a series of novels with the same protagonist, like a mystery series with the same detective. Over time the detective's character may change, but the changes can be organic; they need not be discontinuous.[33]

Another analogy would be a 'serial' novel or even a television series. Our lives may seem to be soap operas at times. Or perhaps they are 'sitcoms'; if so, mine is in certain respects (apart from pecuniary considerations) more like Larry David's on HBO's marvelous series, *Curb Your Enthusiasm*, than Ward Cleaver's on *Leave it to Beaver*. Now, of course, all sitcoms do eventually get cancelled – *Leave it to Beaver* can only be seen in syndicated reruns. But, as far as I can see, it is not part of their distinguishing features or essence that they be so (cruelly) terminated. A serial novel, a television series, a series of mystery novels with the same detective, a collection of short stories – they all have parts that can be explained and evaluated in the characteristic narrative fashion.[34]

If I consider an apparently possible immortal human life, I can see parts of it as having the distinctive features of narrative understanding and value. Parts of the life can be explained in such a way as to achieve emotional resonance and resolution. But since the life as a whole has no ending, there is no possibility of achieving distinctively narrative understanding of the whole life. And thus there is no final answer, as it were, giving the narrative value of the life as a whole. Whereas this is indeed the case, I do not think that it renders immortal life unintelligible or unrecognizably human; nor do I think it makes it impossible for a human being to find such a life valuable and desirable. (After all, to find such a life potentially desirable does not require rank-ordering it even ordinally against other such lives, or against finite human lives. And even in a finite life, there is the problem of combining the two irreducible dimensions of value into some overall value score – the cumulative measure of momentary well-being and the narrative dimension.)

Someone might say that there is a big difference – a big and crucial difference – between merely (!) very, very long life and *infinitely* long life. It might be suggested that, although we can 'get our minds around' long life, it is a mistake to suppose that infinitely long life is relevantly similar to merely very long, finite life. The infinite, if might be said, is just fundamentally different, and thus fundamentally mysterious (and not presumably amenable to evaluation in the relevant ways).

This raises difficult and obscure questions. Consider, first, the putative Divine Attributes, such as omnipotence, omniscience, moral perfection, and so forth. It is sometimes claimed that we cannot understand these properties, since they are fundamentally different from the bounded and finite analogues in human power, knowledge, and goodness. The standard reply, of course, is that the Divine Attributes, although different from their finite analogues, are to be understood along the lines of those attributes; the relationship between the infinite and finite here is one of analogy.

Similarly, the arithmetical rules that define certain operations, such as addition, subtraction, multiplication, and division are different for infinite and finite numbers. It is sometimes supposed that, because the arithmetics are different, there must be a difference in *kind* between finite and infinite magnitudes (and thus between finite and immortal lives). Given this difference in kind, it may not even be possible to grasp or comprehend an infinitely long human life. But, again, the reply should be that, although the rules pertaining to the relevant mathematical operations are different in finite and infinite numbers, they are not totally dissimilar. Indeed, there are sufficient similarities to suggest that the relationship between these sets of rules is one of *analogy*.

But Erich Reck has raised an interesting question here:

> … one can now start to play with other mathematical facts about the infinite to create some curious questions. Suppose, e.g., that every hundred years I have one bad day (for whatever reason). Then over the span of an infinite life (say a life that is omega days long – the smallest infinite), the number of bad days will still be infinite. In fact, the number of bad days overall will be the same as the number of good days (both omega). Or to modify the example a bit: suppose you have a bad day after ten days, then the next after 100 days, then the next after

1000 days; i.e., the intervals between bad days get longer and longer. Overall, there will still be infinitely many bad days, thus the same (infinite) number as the good days. Or to turn the example around: imagine that after ten days you have your first good day of your life, then the next good day after 100 days, then the next good day after 1000 days, etc. Overall you will still have the same (infinite) number of good and bad days. These kinds of examples are used in the literature on the infinite to illustrate how different it is from the finite.[35]

In my view, the difficulties to which Reck brings our attention pertain to any attempt to quantify and aggregate welfare in the way typically employed by the function that determines overall welfare, given information about momentary welfare. These phenomena need to be addressed. But they do not pertain to the second dimension of value, the narrative dimension, which is irreducible to the first. The narrative dimension of value has to do with the structural relationships among events; it does not involve any sort of addition or mere quantitative analysis of good and bad experiences, good and bad days, and so forth. Here then is a way in which the narrative dimension of value is *better* able to address certain features of immortal life.

Similarly, consider a point raised by Borges in his short story, *The Immortal*, as described by Gustavo Llarull:

> … the immortals are fundamentally devoted to intellectual pursuits; their physical needs are very easily satisfied (they can go without food for days) and sensual pleasures do not entice them. They are immersed in thought for entire weeks, and they barely talk to each other. In this context, Borges presents an interesting episode: one of the immortals falls from a cliff.
>
> Although the other immortals know about this accident, they go to his aid *months later*. Borges suggests that what from our finite view is surely deemed as cruelty or negligence may simply be the natural expression of attitudes that have changed in virtue of the correlative change in time patterns. In an average life span of 70 years, taking 15 minutes to help someone in need may be appropriate … Now, the same proportion, for a life span of 7,000 years, yields 25 hours! Needless to say, the idea of having to wait 25 hours, or more, to be aided by my fellow immortals, when they are fully aware that I am in need of help, sounds repulsive to say the least …[36]

As Llarull points out, Borges' description need not be the reality in an immortal life. Llarull says, '… "negative" or pain-related episodes, interactions or events would *not* lose their urgency [in an immortal life]'.[37] It is clearly a mistake to think of immortal human life along the lines of an anatomical 'horizontal (or longitudinal) explosion' of ordinary, finite human life, keeping the temporal proportions fixed, as it were. Although there are perfectly good welfare-based reasons not to take the 'longitudinal explosion' model seriously, one can also invoke narrative relationships. Pain must be responded to as soon as possible, other things equal, and this fact would still obtain, in an immortal existence. It is a mistake to take a purely quantitative approach to envisaging and evaluating the relationships between finite and infinite human existence.[38]

IV. Conclusion

I have in a tentative way explored the interconnections among narrative explanation, narrative value, free will, and immortality. I have built on the fascinating and suggestive work of David Velleman. I have suggested that our acting freely is what gives our lives a distinctive kind of value – narrative value. Free Will, then, is connected to the capacity to lead a meaningful life in a quite specific way: it is the ingredient which, when added to others, endows us with a meaning over and above the cumulative value derived from adding together levels of momentary welfare. In acting freely, we are writing a sentence in the story of our lives, and the value of acting freely is thus a species of the value of artistic creativity or self-expression (understood appropriately). Finally, I have suggested that the fact that our lives are stories need not entail that they have endings, or that immortality would necessarily be unimaginable or essentially different from ordinary, finite human life. Yes, a certain sort of narrative understanding of our lives *as a whole* would be impossible in the context of immortality; but much of what we care about, and value, in our stories might remain.

Notes

1. It is well known that it is difficult to predict the future. A colleague of mine once pointed out that the situation is even worse with respect to the past: it is, he said, *impossible* to predict the past.

2. John Martin Fischer, 'Responsibility and Self-Expression,' *The Journal of Ethics*, vol. 3, no. 4 (1999): 277–97.

3. John Martin Fischer, 'Epicureanism About Death and Immortality,' *The Journal of Ethics*, vol. 10 (2006): 355–81.

4. J. David Velleman, 'Well-Being and Time,' *Pacific Philosophical Quarterly* 72 (1991), pp. 48–77.

5. J. David Velleman, 'Well-Being and Time.'

6. Cashiers in California have asked me, 'How's your day going so far?' Also, I've been implored to 'Have a great rest-of-your-day!' Of course, these sorts of thoughts, from people one does not really know, are superficial and slightly irritating. They can also reflect a mistaken view about value – or, perhaps, a focus on only one dimension of value.

     China's Chairman Mao was asked what he thought of the French Revolution. He reportedly replied. 'It is too early to tell.' This clearly goes to the opposite extreme! Aristotle more moderately urged us 'to call no man happy, until that man is dead,' alluding to an old adage going back to Herodotus' tale about King Croesus. The adage was ubiquitous in the 5th century BCE, made especially so by Sophocles, whose play, *Women of Trachis*, begins, 'There is an old saying that no man is blessed until his final day.' (Heracles dies at the end of the play, after entering as hero at the start.)

7. J. David Velleman, 'Well-Being and Time,' p. 51; the quotation is from Michael Slote, 'Goods and Lives,' in his *Goods and Virtues* (Oxford: Clarendon Press, 1983), pp. 23–4.

8. J. David Velleman, 'Well-Being and Time,' pp. 53–4.

9. J. David Velleman, 'Well-Being and Time,' pp. 54–5.

10. J. David Velleman, 'Well-Being and Time,' p. 55.

11. Whereas Velleman's contention here is appealing, it is tantalizingly underdeveloped. One problem is that there is a limited number of examples actually offered; also, as I point out in the text, Velleman does not offer any general formulaic explanation of narrative value. Perhaps not surprisingly, then, various philosophers have suggested to me that there are other potential explanations for our intuitions or judgments about various lives that are at least as plausible (as 'narrative value'). Thaddeus Metz has suggested to me that we can account for the judgments to which Velleman draws our attention by keeping in mind that stretches of one's life (or activities in these stretches) can have *instrumental* value as well as intrinsic value; thus, even a utilitarian can account for the greater value of certain lives by pointing out that stretches in certain lives (but not others) can have instrumental value. (For a discussion, see Thaddeus Metz, 'Utilitarianism and the Meaning of Life,' *Utilitas* 15 (2003), pp. 50–70.) David Hershenov has suggested that the judgments can be explained not so much by invoking narrative value, but by the moral value of staying married, the desire for (or value of) moral self-improvement, and so forth. (A skeptic about the

invocation of the notion of narrative value here, such as Hershenov, might then seek to construct examples of lives that lack the putatively relevant features – moral self-improvement, staying married, and so forth – to see if the relevant evaluations of the life stay the same.) Andrews Reath has suggested that what is significant about the cases under discussion is that they indicate that there are irreducibly *relational* goods; but this does not in itself entail anything about specifically 'narrative' value.

These matters require much more attention than I can give here. I should point out that I myself have some doubts about how to evaluate the various scenarios. For example, I do not think that it is somehow better or more valuable that a depressed individual pull out of his depression by pure strength of will, or a regimen of psychotherapy, or any other sort of extended and perhaps arduous set of activities and reflections, rather than by taking an antidepressant. Of course, if the chances of recurrence of the depression are greater if one simply takes the medication, then that counts against it. But I do not share the intuition that there is something less valuable – that it is somehow 'cheating' – to use the antidepressant (successfully). And it is not exactly clear to me how to distinguish this case, or class of cases, from those discussed by Velleman. I hope to turn to these issues in future work. Here I shall not press the worries, and take it, as a working hypothesis, that Velleman's intuitions or judgments about scenarios are plausible, and that his invocation of narrative value is explanatorily helpful.

12. J. David Velleman, 'Well-Being and Time,' p. 62.

13. This is not necessarily a criticism of Velleman, as it is unclear that he envisaged his account as providing guidance in all cases of potential physician-assisted suicide.

14. J. David Velleman, 'Well-Being and Time,' p. 71.

15. J. David Velleman, 'Well-Being and Time,' p. 71.

16. For skepticism about the necessity of this sort of capacity for the distinctive notion of 'valuing' (as opposed to merely preferring) and also for autonomy, see Agnieska Jaworska, 'Respecting the Margins of Agency: Alzheimer's Patients and the Capacity to Value,' *Philosophy and Public Affairs* 29 (1999), pp. 105–38.

17. I do not know how to prove my supposition, and I recognize that it would be good to have more to say

here. I base the claim on consideration of contexts in which we would normally suppose that there is narrative value and thus the ability of the relevant agent to affect the meanings of past events, but in which it is explicitly understood that the agent is manipulated in such a way as not to be acting freely; in this range of thought experiments, my intuition is that the agent cannot affect the meanings of the past events, and that this is precisely because he does not act freely. I hope to be able to justify this intuition (at least to some extent) in future work. I thank Ward Jones for emphasizing the need for further defense of my suggestion.

18. Of course, the past goods in question are not 'experiential' goods.

19. Carl Ginet, *On Action* (Cambridge, UK: Cambridge University Press, 1990). See, also, John Martin Fischer, *The Metaphysics of Free Will: An Essay on Control* (Cambridge, MA.: Blackwell Publishers, 1994).

20. We now have available to us a kind of 'alternative' explanation – no doubt, not the intended explanation – of the putative fact alluded to in note 1 above – that it is impossible to predict the past. If we can go backward in narrative space-time by freely acting in the future, and this free action cannot be predicted, then we also cannot predict what the narrative past will have been.

21. J. David Velleman, 'Narrative Explanation,' *Philosophical Review* 112 (2003), pp. 1–26.

22. J. David Velleman, 'Narrative Explanation,' p. 1.

23. J. David Velleman, 'Narrative Explanation,' p. 1.

24. Louis Mink, 'Philosophical Analysis and Historical Understanding,' in Brian Fay, Eugene O. Golob, and Richard T. Vann, eds., *Historical Understanding* (Ithaca: Cornell University Press, 1987), pp. 118–46; and E.B. Gallie, *Philosophy and the Historical Understanding* (London: Chatto and Windus, 1964).

25. J. David Velleman, 'Narrative Explanation,' p. 10.

26. J. David Velleman, 'Narrative Explanation,' p. 19.

27. J. David Velleman. 'Narrative Explanation,' p. 19.

28. J. David Velleman, 'Narrative Explanation.' p. 1.

29. To add just one dimension of complexity: note that a typical literary work or musical composition will not simply evoke one emotion, but many (sometimes colliding) emotions.

30. J. David Velleman, 'Narrative Explanation,' pp. 6–7.

31. I can only gesture briefly at an account of these matters here. Note that my sketch here may suggest an unintuitive 'relativization' of moral responsibility to a

particular bit of story-telling. I do not know whether this is genuinely problematic; If so, one could define acting freely and moral responsibility in terms of the 'availability' (in some sense) of a story of the right sort.

32. It is a staple of 'postmodern' critiques of 'narrative' that they posit some sort of overarching or 'totalizing' meaning. On my account of the narrative structure of an immortal life, there is no single 'grand narrative' and thus no 'totalizing meaning'; and yet there remains much to which a postmodernist could object, given that the sub-parts of the immortal life are taken to have suitable meanings.

33. In Amanda Cross's (Carolyn Heilbrunn's) delightful series of academic mystery novels, Kate Fansler (English Professor and detective extraordinaire) changes noticeably but understandably over time. As she ages, Kate is no longer the hard-drinking detective who solved the murder of the first tenured woman professor at Harvard in *Death in A Tenured Position*. In the later works, she worries about her excessive indulgence in alcohol, and seeks moderation in this and other pleasures.

The story of Heilbrun's own life, as opposed to that of her fictional professor/detective, ended rather abruptly. The *Los Angeles Times* obituary (October 15, 2003), says:

Carolyn G. Heilbrun, a distinguished feminist scholar who illuminated the female experience through erudite reinterpretations of classic English literature and in literate mystery novels written under the name Amanda Cross, was found dead in her New York City apartment Friday after an apparent suicide. She was 77.

The pioneering feminist critic had decided years earlier that she would end her life by the age of 70 to avoid the inevitable deterioration of age, but she later explained that she had let the deadline pass when her 60s proved deeply satisfying.

In *The Last Gift of Time: Life Beyond Sixty*, a book published the year she turned 71, she said she would decide each day whether to keep on living. Her son Robert told the New York Times last week that she had not been ill when she decided to kill herself.

It is almost as if Heilbrun always knew the end of her life-story, but she couldn't wait for the organic development of the plot. In any case, the details of her reasons for choosing to commit suicide when she did may remain (not inappropriately) a mystery.

34. In his classic paper. 'The Makropulos Case: Reflections on the Tedium of Immortality,' Bernard Williams argues that an immortal life would be essentially meaningless and unattractive: Williams, Bernard. *Problems of the Self* (Cambridge, UK. Cambridge University Press, 1973), pp. 82–100, reprinted in John Martin Fischer, ed., *The Metaphysics of Death* (Stanford: Stanford University Press, 1993), pp. 73–92. In my paper, 'Why Immortality is Not So Bad,' I argue against Williams' view. I suggest that the sort or immortality suggested in the text of the current paper – along the lines of a character in a series of novels or a continuing television series – could be appealing: John Martin Fischer, 'Why Immortality is Not So Bad,' *International Journal of Philosophical Studies*, vol. 2 (September 1994), pp. 257–70, reprinted in J. Feinberg, ed., *Reason and Responsibility*, 9th edn. (Wadsworth, 1996), pp. 401–9.

35. Erich Reck, personal correspondence.

36. Gustavo Llarull, 'The Problem of Immortality: A Response to Williams,' unpublished manuscript, University of California, Riverside department of philosophy.

37. Gustavo Llarull, 'The Problem of Immortality: A Response to Williams.'

38. The mistake of ignoring the crucial narrative structure of life, even infinite life, is also found in this passage from Victor Frankl: 'What would our lives be like if they were not finite in time, but infinite? If we were immortal, we could legitimately postpone every action forever. It would be of no consequence whether or not we did a thing now; every act might just as well be done tomorrow or the day after or a year from now or ten years hence. But in the face of death as absolute *finis* to our future and boundary to our possibilities, we are under the imperative of utilizing our lifetimes to the utmost, not letting the singular opportunities – whose "finite" sum constitutes the whole of life – pass by unused.' (*The Doctor and the Soul* [New York: Alfred Knopf, 1957], p. 73.)

5.7

Death, Futility, and the Proleptic Power of Narrative Ending

Joshua W. Seachris

Death and futility are among a cluster of themes that closely track discussions of life's meaning.[1] Precisely why death and futility bear such a close relationship to the meaning of life has received relatively little sustained articulation beyond the oft-repeated pessimistic claim that *cosmic* or *deep* futility supervenes upon the entirety of human existence,[2] given a naturalistic view of the ultimate fate of life, both human life as well as the universe itself, where entropy, dissolution, and death are thought to have the final word. If we and all the products of our human energies including the immediate building of a family, accomplishments, and the distant traces of progeny will some day cease to exist *forever*, then our lives and our pursuits, indeed, existence in its entirety, are deeply futile, so the argument goes.

Both defences and attempted rebuttals of the above conditional have broadly unfolded within relatively well-defined dialectical parameters. Those who accept the consequent generally do so, I think, largely by focusing on what can be called the 'staying-power intuition' (SPI). Roughly, SPI is the idea that, *ceteris paribus*, worthwhile, significant, and meaningful things *last*.[3] Though SPI is vague and subject to counter-examples in various contexts, in terms of human life, SPI requires that we leave some sort of indelible mark on reality (usually articulated in a sense requiring a doctrine of post-mortem survival that itself requires the survival of the person), something which is not possible,[4] or at minimum, highly unlikely on naturalism.

Those who reject the consequent generally make one of two (or both) moves – (i) appeal to a contrary intuition, what can be called the 'scarcity intuition' (SI) whereby life is thought to be worthwhile, significant, and meaningful – and therefore not deeply futile – precisely

Joshua W. Seachris (2011) "Death, Futility, and the Proleptic Power of Narrative Ending," *Religious Studies* 47: 141–63.

because death looms on the horizon, bringing a sense of poignant urgency and specialness to fleeting life,[5] or, more often, (ii) argue that the requirement of post-mortem survival of human beings and the fruits of their labours, extending endlessly into the future, is too strong a condition to be met in order for life to be worthwhile, significant, and meaningful.[6]

Within the dialectical parameters noted above, discussions over the perceived threat of death to living a meaningful life, as death is construed on naturalism, have been fruitful up to a point. In this context, death and futility are thought to link to the meaning of life as a threat to leading a meaningful life. While this analysis may be correct as far as it goes, it is surely a truncated story of their connection. Therefore, considerations of SPI can and should be supplemented in order to bring a more robust account of this relationship. This involves combining three claims which then provide the deeper rationale through which to understand something like SPI. These three claims are as follows:

(1)   Entire metaphysical systems (e.g. naturalism, Christian theism) can be thought of as narratives or meta-narratives,[7] narrating across the cluster of humanly deemed existentially relevant 'features' of life (e.g. origins, purpose, value, pain and suffering, and how it is all going to end).

(2)   The way a narrative ends *qua* ending, contributes to a wide range of broadly normative human responses on, possibly, emotional, aesthetic, and moral levels towards the narrative as a whole.

(3)   *Per* (1) and (2), many have concluded that naturalistic meta-narratives are characterized by deep or cosmic futility given the way they end, and the way they end is important for such normative appraisals partly because narrative ending *qua* ending is important to these appraisals.

Note carefully that the reason subsumed under (1)–(3) is importantly different from the reason anchored exclusively in a principle such as SPI where futility is thought to follow from the naturalistic meta-narrative ending, given naturalistic premises about the *nature* of that ending. In the case of (1)–(3), the reason is even more theoretically and practically fundamental – that narrative ending *qua* ending is salient in our broadly normative assessments of narratives as a whole. Hence, while judging the naturalistic meta-narrative to be irredeemably futile is, no doubt, made partly on the basis of the nature of its ending (what can be called a 'second-order futility conclusion'),[8] an important reason that the nature of the ending possesses such normative weight is that it is already anchored in the fact that narrative ending *qua* ending is thought to be normatively important (a first-order conclusion about endings in general).[9] Put simply, second-order futility conclusions, or second-order non-futility conclusions for that matter, would lose their force if something like first-order conclusions about the evaluative significance of narrative ending *qua* ending were not already in place.

Of course, introducing the concept of narrative ending presupposes an intelligible framework in which it sufficiently links up to the question of life's meaning in general and to death and futility specifically. It will only work if narrative, as a concept, appropriately relates to the meaning of life in a coherent way. In a separate work, I defend an *analytic* relationship between the question, 'What is the meaning of life?' and the concept of a narrative, whereby the question is interpreted as the request for *a meta-narrative that narrates across those elements and accompanying questions of life of greatest existential import to human beings.*[10] The relevant 'elements and accompanying questions' in need of narration largely revolve around origins, purpose, value, pain and suffering, and how life is going to end. The narrative interpretation, though, has rivals. The most common current interpretation views the question, 'What is the meaning of life?' as a place-holder or 'amalgam of logically diverse questions, some coherent and answerable, some neither.'[11] Such questions generally include those about purpose, significance, and value, among others. In these cases, meaning in life then centres on ordering one's life around valuable ends, or being subjectively attracted to objective attractiveness, or realizing one's strongest desires, among others.

Space does not allow for a re-articulation of the narrative interpretation and defence of its philosophic merits over rival theories of meaning. As such, one can introduce a weaker, *synthetic* relationship between the meaning of life and narrative in that narrative is one, among other concepts, that importantly links to issues that are largely co-extensive with the meaning of life.[12] Here, narrative occurs alongside other theories and concepts that aid us in addressing the cluster of questions and concerns found in the meaning of life context, even if none, individually, covers all of the conceptual territory. For the purposes of this paper it is sufficient to accept the following conditional: if 'the meaning of life' is best understood as a meta-narrative in the analytic sense, or if narrative is one helpful way among others for addressing central meaning-of-life issues in the synthetic sense, then either way, a compelling reason exists for why the way life ends – both human life and the universe itself – has been thought to be so relevant to broadly normative appraisals of life as a whole. As I have already developed and defended the first disjunct of the antecedent elsewhere, I will here turn my attention to the consequent.

Whether or not conclusions that life is in fact cosmically futile have philosophical merit is not my concern in this paper. Rather, I am focusing on answering the question of why futility is often thought to characterize saliently naturalistic meta-narratives in a way that moves beyond the received dialectical parameters. I am primarily interested in what I term above, a 'first-order conclusion about endings in general', which follows from the perceived normative significance of narrative ending *qua* ending. On this more fundamental level, I will argue that futility is often thought to characterize naturalistic meta-narratives because the way a narrative ends has significant proleptic power to elicit a wide range of broadly normative human responses on, possibly, emotional, aesthetic, and moral levels towards the narrative as a whole *in virtue of it being the ending.*[13]

I will first explain the rationale behind the evaluative significance of narrative ending for broadly normative appraisals of narratives as a whole. Second, I will clarify three important senses of ending, noting which is required for my argument to succeed. Third, I will propose two strategies to explain how my own proposal relates to another plausible account of the perceived connection between death and futility in a strictly naturalist world, an account Ronald Dworkin presents in chapter 6 of his *Sovereign Virtue*. Fourth, I will enlist my conclusions about the evaluative significance of narrative ending in order to frame and bring greater nuance to discussions of death and futility, and why futility is thought to follow from the nature of naturalistic meta-narrative endings. Finally, I will explore potential implications that the evaluative significance of narrative ending has for the tasks of defence and theodicy.

The Evaluative Significance of Narrative Ending

The way a narrative ends is important. Various claims have been made in support of this,[14] though I will discuss only one that is especially relevant in the immediate context. It is the claim that the way a narrative ends, in virtue of its being *the end*, has great power to elicit a wide range of broadly normative human responses on, possibly, emotional, aesthetic, and moral levels towards the narrative as a whole. This claim is important given the close connection that discussions of futility have had with the meaning of life. Conclusions of such discussions, especially those of cosmic futility, are largely connected with theses about how it is all going to end, including human life and the universe as a whole. And, it is reasonable to think that conclusions of futility are broadly normative conclusions. Furthermore, it has often been thought that naturalistic meta-narrative endings threaten the entire narrative with cosmic futility and meaninglessness, whereas theistic endings are generally thought not to pose such a threat.[15]

Why should one think that a narrative's ending has such 'retroactive' or proleptic power? Furthermore, why can, for example, the *final* emotional state instantiated in a reader subsume or overshadow the cluster of varying emotional states instantiated throughout the narrative? And what gives this final state evaluative salience out of which we then adopt a settled stance toward the narrative as a whole; why is the future privileged over the present? For, as J. David Velleman notes:

> What's more, the emotion that resolves a narrative cadence tends to subsume the emotions that preceded it: the triumph felt at a happy ending is the triumph of ambitions realized and anxieties allayed; the grief felt at a tragic ending is the grief of hopes dashed or loves denied. *Hence the conclusory emotion in a narrative cadence embodies not just how the audience feels about the ending; it embodies how the audience feels, at the ending, about the whole story.* Having passed through emotional ups and downs of the story, as one event succeeded another, the audience comes to rest in a stable attitude about the series of events in its entirety. [emphasis added][16]

This is no small point, and it seems largely correct. The ending marks the 'last word', after which nothing else can be said, either by way of remedying problems or destroying felicities that have come about within the narrative. If the last word is that hope is finally and irreversibly dashed, then grief will probably be salient at the end; if the last word is that ambitions have been realized, then triumph will probably be salient at the end. Perhaps more importantly, one cannot backtrack into a narrative, for example, where the grief felt at a tragic ending is the final word, and expect that one's emotional stance toward any specific event within the narrative will not now be affected, *in some sense*, by the ending of the narrative. The ending relevantly frames the entire story. This framing falls broadly within the normative sphere, and includes a salient emotional component. An example here will bring more clarity to the point.

Consider a case where you are dating someone. In this context, the claim under scrutiny is whether and how the end of this relationship is important for your appraisals throughout the relationship of those moments and events that compose it, as well as the relationship as a whole.[17] Here, I am referring to whether the relationship ends in something like marriage (or some culturally recognized equivalent) or dissolution, whereby each party seeks to go his or her separate way. The thought is that how it ends is very important for how you view the relationship as a whole. But in what sense is how it ends very important? Can an undesirable ending nullify the happy times in the relationship, retroactively causing them to be unhappy? This surely cannot be correct. Indeed, it is eminently reasonable to think that even if the relationship ends in dissolution, that the *pre-end* relationship cannot be fully robbed of, for example, the joy, richness, and vibrancy that once may have characterized it. Regardless of whether these realities cease, they were once present, and they cannot be nullified in this sense.[18] But what if those in the relationship know *in advance* how the relationship will end?

It seems equally plausible to think that this privileged foreknowledge will affect their appraisals *now*, in some sense, of what is presently occurring in the relationship. If the relationship is to end in dissolution, that fact will make some difference right now; if the relationship is to continue, for example, in marriage, that too will make some difference right now. Each of these endings will limit the evaluative horizon for how the relationship is appraised. Indeed, the relationship will likely mean something different, in some non-trivial way, depending upon how it will end. Furthermore, if those in the relationship want the relationship to end in marriage, then those pre-end joyful moments, while still possibly joyful, will not be as joyful as they could be. The joy experienced will be mitigated by knowledge of the coming dissolution. The joy is tainted. This may not make it cease from being joy (although it might), but surely it becomes less joyful. Once this ending is known, the present can never quite be the same as before. The settled perspective of looking back from the end saliently looms, as the present now somehow relevantly *contains* the future, though not, of course, in any strict metaphysical sense.

I think that there is an important truth here. The evaluative priority and indelibility of the final stance one takes toward a narrative as a result of the way the narrative ends provides a powerful reason for the importance of apocalyptic (ending) accounts, whether naturalistic or theistic, for how we appraise life. It is why so many have difficulty shaking conclusions of cosmic futility and meaninglessness on meta-narratives where death has the final word and love is eventually consigned, with lovers, to nothingness forever. This is partly, or largely, why so many have seen the existential (and some would argue rational) need, in order to avoid cosmic futility and retain meaningfulness, of positing an ending where life and love and other deeply held *desiderata* for a flourishing human existence have a lasting place. The general point, though, is that the way life ends is so important to us, because narrative ending itself is important to us. And, if we view life as a whole meta-narratively, it becomes clearer why we are so concerned with how it will all end. Neither naturalist nor theist can avoid the evaluative encroachment of the apocalypse into the present moment of their respective meta-narratives.

In summary, the evaluative priority attached to narrative ending resides in its being the last word, a 'word' that brings with it the finality and indelibility of a settled normative stance towards the narrative as a whole. As Christiaan Moster notes:

> The ending is a necessary part of the story, notwithstanding its open-endedness; it is not a dispensable part. It affects proleptically every part of the story; no part can be considered apart from it. … Regardless of how unexpected or incongruent the end of a story is, it is decisive for the story's meaning.[19]

And, as human beings, we are deeply interested in how the meta-narrative we inhabit is going to end. Many are searching for a specific kind of closure; the kind that allays our deepest hurts and satisfies our deepest longings. In the words of H. Porter Abbot, such closure involves 'a broad range of expectations and uncertainties that arise during the course of a narrative and that part of us, at least, hopes to resolve, or close'.[20]

A final important point lingers here; one that adds further plausibility to my use of the term 'narrative' to describe whatever it is, conceptually, that meta-narratives constructed around the cluster of issues relevant to the meaning of life are. Importantly, certain meta-narratives, naturalistic ones for example, are more like conjunctive explanations as opposed to full-blown narratives in the paradigmatic sense. But this does not mean that we should think of meta-narratives, even naturalistic ones, primarily as explanations as opposed to narratives. The reason follows from a consideration of narrative ending. For example, on naturalistic meta-narratives, the way it all ends is often, though by no means always, thought to be relevant to how we view life right now. If this is the case, then it is perhaps better to think of the meta-narrative *narratively* and not merely *explanatorily*. Importantly, we do not attach such significance or priority to the endings (or the last portion of the explanation) of non-narrative explanations.[21]

For example, in explaining how it is that water boils, each part of the explanatory account is equally important in order to fully elucidate the physical process; the last component of the explanation is no more or less important than any other part. But, on one level, this is not the case, for example, on naturalistic meta-narratives. From a detached and disinterested perspective where all one is concerned with is explaining the naturalistic meta-narrative, it is true that no component of the explanation is any more important than the others. However, from the human, existentially interested standpoint, the ending does become relevant, or at least this is where the evidence points. I think this partly shows that it is more natural to think meta-*narratively* about ultimate explanatory accounts of the world and their features and not meta-*explanatorily*. We do not attach any sort of special significance to the endings of non-narrative explanations, whereas we do to explanations that at least partially merge into the category of narrative.

The Concept of Narrative Ending

My discussion thus far of narrative ending and its evaluative significance for entire narratives invites important questions about what a narrative ending is, as well as what sense of ending is consistent, if any, with the conjunction of the general claim that narrative ending is normatively important but within meta-narratives that posit immortal life as being necessary, though not sufficient, for a meaningful life. Indeed, prima facie, it would appear that the Christian theistic meta-narrative, for example, fails to allow for the kind of view of the whole from the perspective of the end that is needed in order to appraise life as either futile or meaningful precisely because such a meta-narrative never truly ends.

Though in a slightly different context than that of the concern of this paper, John Martin Fischer notes a similar objection:

> If our lives are narratives [or in the case of my paper – life in general should be viewed meta-narratively], or have the distinctive structure of narrative, then they must have endings. On this view, we cannot be immortal (insofar as our lives are narratives or have narrative value), if our lives are indeed narratives. To imagine immortal human life is to imagine human life devoid of an essential or at least very important characteristic: having narrative structure and thus a distinctive dimension of value. … strictly speaking, this is correct. If a narrative must have an ending, then it is clear that our lives cannot have the sort of meaning that involves taking a retrospective perspective on its totality, as it were, and assigning a meaning that reflects the overall arc of the lifestory.[22]

Fischer proceeds to reject the worry by noting that although an immortal life resists final circumscription and appraisal as a whole from some absolute end, its *parts* can be thought of narratively and thus conferred with what he calls 'narrative value'. I think Fischer's point, though plausible in its own right and helpful here, can be supplemented in light of the slightly different dilemma in the present context: the problem as posed for meta-narratives about all of life, and not just narratives about an individual life.

The dilemma can be dissolved in securing a sense of ending from which to appraise life that is also consistent with immortal life. Fortunately, such a sense is available. There are at least three relevant ways of understanding the concept of ending: (i) ending as *termination*, (ii) ending as *telos*, and (iii) ending as *closure*. The first sense of ending is that of something being *finished*. Locutions such as 'the race is over', or 'I am finished with school', or 'it ceased to exist', all capture important connotations of this sense of ending. The second sense of ending tracks the notion of final causality or purpose. Ideas like 'the end of this pencil is to write', or 'the end of creation is to glorify God' are examples of this sense. Importantly, ending as *telos*, when considered within the historical context, carries additional connotations of the purposeful progression of history towards an intended end, or for that matter, the purposeful progression of the plot within a narrative toward an intended end. Finally, the third sense of ending, ending as closure, refers to a contextually anchored settled stance with respect to a 'problem' or cluster of problems emerging within a given narrative or portion of that narrative.

These three senses of ending differ conceptually, though they are compatible. For example, an intended, purposeful end might also be a termination, or it may serve as the occasion for a settled stance toward a problem having emerged in the narrative. Furthermore, when comparing ending as termination and ending as closure, it is important to note that neither the presence of ending as termination nor the presence of ending as closure is sufficient for the presence of the other. That is to say, a narrative could terminate without closure, and closure could be present without a narrative terminating, at least in one important sense. Works within the horror genre are often examples of narratives that end in the terminating sense, but lack a certain kind of closure or resolution.[23]

Conversely, closure can occur, even though the lives of the fictional characters in a narrative often presumably continue, as in *they lived happily ever after*. The post-narrative state (from the perspective of the characters, not the reader) of living happily ever after, though not an ending in the terminating sense, is still a narrative ending, because it brings an end to what J. David Velleman calls the 'emotional cadence' that a narrative evokes in its audience.[24] In these cases, ending is never cessation, at least from the characters' perspective. Rather, it is the resolution of a conflict or series of conflicts that have arisen over the course of the narrative, providing the settled stance toward the pre-end (end as closure) portion of the narrative. It is an end *of something* though not an ending in an absolute sense. Ending as closure, then, is *contextual* rather than *absolute*.

With this set of distinctions in hand, the following claims can be harmonized: (i) an ending is required in order to appraise life as either futile or meaningful, and (ii) some meta-narratives, like that of Christian theism, posit immortal life as necessary for a meaningful life and have no ending. The way out of the impasse involves two related moves. First, adopting the ending in the closure sense is sufficient for the necessary appraisal of life. And, second, contextually anchoring such closure to the portion of the meta-narrative where questions about futility and life's meaning form at least part of the plot's problem set allows for the relevant appraisal from a settled perspective, even though that perspective itself never ends in either the terminating sense or in the closure sense for that matter.[25]

If one posits an immortal life and also seeks to circumscribe all of life, including the immortal life, then one can neither invoke ending as termination nor ending as closure in order to appraise that life given that the life never ends, either in terms of termination or closure. Fischer is correct to note that this is, by definition, impossible. But to see that such ultimate termination or circumscription from some privileged vantage point of *ultimate* closure is not necessary, we must recall the target to which the charge of futility is largely directed. That target is poignantly captured in Qohelet's memorable refrain in Ecclesiastes, 'life under the sun' (Ecclesiastes, 1.3).[26] The life that people are worried is threatened by futility is the life here and now.

We worry that *this* life might be systemically futile, one where, despite all our growth in knowledge, we know so little about the vast universe we inhabit. We worry that this life, with all its pain, suffering, and hardship might be deeply futile. We worry that the loss of this life in death brings with it irredeemable futility. The target, then, of the closure-bringing vantage point is not literally all of life, if all of life also includes indefinite post-mortem existence, it is life *under the sun*, that portion of the meta-narrative where the cluster of problems associated with our common human predicament palpably remain.

The settled stance of the end, then, need not be an absolute end, just an end that includes the appropriate horizon from which to appraise that part of life whose features give rise to problems and questions about meaning and futility in the first place. That relevant horizon, in the Christian theistic meta-narrative for example, is that of the new heavens and new earth where pain and sorrow are definitively eradicated, and where tears of sadness are wiped away forever. It is the vantage point of indefectible *shalom*. This is still an end, it is still closure, though it is neither termination nor absolute closure.

And yet, the Christian theistic meta-narrative postulate of an *ending that itself never ends* is coherent precisely because the sense in which it never ends is the terminating sense, and the sense in which it does end is the closure sense, where the closure sense is contextually tied to the post-lapsarian, pre-consummation portion of Christian theism's redemptive-historical narrative. So, although it must be conceded that there can be no ultimate, settled stance from which to appraise the entire Christian theistic meta-narrative if that settled stance is meant to also circumscribe indefinite post-mortem enjoyment of the beatific vision, there *can* be a settled stance from which to appraise the portion of the meta-narrative that is itself the salient context for the problems of futility and meaning in the first place. And this kind of settled stance is sufficient to dissolve the prima facie dilemma of needing an end from which to appraise life as either meaningful or futile, but seemingly not having such an end on meta-narratives that posit immortal existence.

Death and Perceived Futility: Ronald Dworkin's Analysis

Though most accounts of why deep or cosmic futility is thought to supervene on a naturalistic narrative amount to little more than stating a deeply held intuition, there are some notable exceptions where such intuitions are conceptually augmented. One such exception is Ronald Dworkin's discussion, in chapter 6 of his *Sovereign Virtue*, of the *model of impact* within the general context of searching for a reasonable metric by which the good life can be measured. Part of his entry point into this discussion is to note the oft-repeated dilemma that eventually surfaces within discussions of life's meaning, and which is embodied in the 'staying-power intuition' (SPI) to which I alluded in the introduction:

> How can it matter what happens in the absurdly tiny space and time of a single human life? Or even in the almost equally tiny episode of all sentient life taken together? The universe is so big and has lasted so long that our best scientists struggle even to give sense to the question of how big it is or how long it has lasted. One day – any second now in the history of time – the sun will explode, and then there may be nothing left that can even wonder about how we lived. How can we reconcile these two ideas: that life is nothing and that how we live is everything?[27]

This problem is acute, at least emotionally. On the one hand, we believe that something's significance depends on proportion, meaning that nothing of infinitesimal size or scope relative to the universe as a whole can be really important. On the other hand, most of us cannot help believing that it is crucially important how we live in spite of our seeming insignificance from the vantage point of a spatially and temporally vast universe, and, furthermore, one that is, if naturalism is true, entirely unconcerned about us.

According to Dworkin, one could analyse the prospects for securing a good life through one of two primary models in light of our common human predicament: (i) the model of impact, and, the model he favours, (ii) the model of challenge.[28] I will not discuss the model of challenge, given that I am only concerned with reasonable alternative accounts for explaining the futility that is often thought to supervene on naturalistic meta-narratives. Indeed, the model of challenge is partly a response to arguments that invoke death in order to threaten the good life, and is considered immune from such arguments if one finds it plausible as an account of the good life.

The model of impact is a metric of the good life that requires a person to make a positive impact to the objective value in the world in order to secure a good life.[29] According to Dworkin, this model harmonizes with some common value judgments about the nature of the good life. For example, an inventor of a cure for a ravaging disease is thought to secure a good life, at least partly, by her helpful contribution to the world. As such, the model of impact is strongly tied to the positive *consequences* of a life, or activities partly constituting that life. However, the model does not capture what are thought to be other non-consequential features of the good life, for example, mastering a musical instrument simply for the sake of the activity done well. Some features of the good life, then, seem to be intrinsically valuable as ends in themselves, and the model of impact is weak at this point to account for these.

More relevant in the present context, if one takes the model of impact as the primary metric for measuring the good life, then futility looms threateningly on the horizon, as nothing we do will make an impact in any sort of deep, lasting, or ultimate sense in the universe as posited by naturalism. Even seemingly great impacts, like finding a cure for cancer, end up not mattering from the unconcerned, temporally distant perspective of a universe in ruins. On the model of impact, circumstances act as limitations, the most limiting of them all being a naturalistic understanding of human mortality, one that views mortality as final.[30] So, on this view, the reason futility is thought to supervene on the naturalistic meta-narrative follows from this conjunction – we often analyse the good life or a meaningful life in terms of the impact a life makes, but the nature of the universe, on naturalism, undercuts any real possibility for making a deep, lasting, or ultimate impact. It is worth noting also that this model presupposes something like SPI. Dworkin's model of impact, then, is one way of accounting for the perceived connection between futility and mortality specifically, or futility and naturalism in general.

There are two plausible strategies to explain how my own narrative proposal relates to Dworkin's account of the perceived connection between death and futility in a strictly naturalistic world. I am more interested in the second strategy, though the first is worth noting. Like theories of a meaningful life, it is likely that no one model captures every relevant dimension to the perceived connection between futility and mortality precisely because no one model may sufficiently capture what constitutes a meaningful life. If this is the case, then those who worry that a naturalistic conception of death threatens life with futility may *both* hold something like the model of impact as relevant to analysing the good life, but also think of life narratively, and thereby conclude that the way it all ends is additionally important for deciding whether or not life is futile. Therefore, it seems as though Dworkin's model of impact account and my own narrative account may not be competitors at all. Rather, they are loosely associated constructs through which we seek to understand an already enigmatic concept and the broad normative territory it encompasses, that of a meaningful life.

Second, and more importantly, I think there is a relevant sense in which accounts like Dworkin's or even Robert Nozick's – that a meaningful life is about transcending limits and mortality prohibits this[31] – actually presuppose important elements of my own account regarding the evaluative significance of narrative ending *qua* ending. Remember that the threat of futility enters on Dworkin's model of impact because death in a naturalistic world prevents a positive, deep, and ultimate impact to objective value in the world. But this raises the question: Why have we allowed death and the ultimate fate of the naturalistic universe to be that which is most salient in our appraisals of whether or not our lives make an impact, are meaningful, and avoid deep or cosmic futility? The answer, I think, resides in the prior normative significance we *already* assign to narrative endings. Indeed, I think the point about narrative endings is more basic, and is likely presupposed in the dilemma for the good life that emerges on Dworkin's model of impact. That is, it is only because we attach such evaluative significance to endings that the worries tied to the model of impact become relevant. Death prevents a significant impact only because some choose to require significant impact, in order to be significant, to be so from the perspective of the settled end. Without the perspective of the settled end already looming large, the worry about impact will not be nearly as bothersome. But we need a deeper rationale for why the perspective of the settled end itself is important, and that deeper rationale is provided by my own account which appeals to the evaluative significance of narrative ending for broadly normative appraisals of narratives as a whole.

Meta-narrative Ending, Death, and Cosmic Futility

Understanding the relationship between futility and the meaning of life in general and futility and the naturalistic meta-narrative specifically is as much about a first-order conclusion regarding the proleptic power of narrative endings in general as it is a second-order futility conclusion based upon the *nature* of naturalistic meta-narrative endings. Indeed, the reason the nature of the naturalistic meta-narrative ending is thought to be normatively important for appraising the entire narrative is first anchored in the fact that narrative ending *qua* ending is thought to be normatively important for appraising the entire narrative. Hence, judging naturalistic meta-narratives, for example, as cosmically and deeply futile is a function of both first-order and second-order conclusions in this respect. The latter would lose all of their force if the former were absent.

As already noted, it has often been claimed that cosmic or deep futility supervenes on the naturalistic meta-narrative, a meta-narrative where death has the 'final word'. Reference to cosmic futility, though, presupposes that we know what we are talking about when we refer to 'futility'. As such, the concept of futility needs unpacking. Futility supervenes upon states of affairs where two conditions obtain: (i) one aims at some desired end, and (ii) attaining that desired end is impossible for one reason or another.[32] This is largely why the case of Sisyphus has been the paradigmatic example of futility in the West. On the canonical version of the story,[33] Sisyphus never accomplishes that which he aims to accomplish; namely, ascending with his boulder to the top of the hill. On the above analysis, futility would characterize a state of affairs where I, for example, aimed to research, write, and submit this paper for publication, all in twenty-four hours. There is an extreme discrepancy between an end at which I aim, and the possibility of actually accomplishing that end. My aim, given the way the world is in terms of what it takes to accomplish the above task, is futile; it 'cannot' be done.[34]

If we take the *impossibility of attaining an aim toward which one directs effort* to be a sufficient, but not necessary, condition for the presence of futility, then futility likely comes in degrees. One aim can be more or less futile than another aim. On this analysis, the degree of futility that characterizes a state of affairs will be directly proportional to the *implausibility* (rather than impossibility) of attaining an end toward which one directs effort. For example, even though it is neither logically nor metaphysically impossible that I research, write, and submit this paper for publication in one month, it is highly unlikely. It is so unlikely, that my exerting effort to attain *this end* is more or less futile, though exerting the same effort in order to accomplish the task in, say, eight months is probably not futile.[35] But, since futility comes in degrees, researching, writing, and submitting this paper for publication in one month is less futile than my exertion of effort to have these things occur within two weeks, and more futile than my exertion of effort to see them occur within four months.

There is one further dimension of futility that is especially relevant here. The level of angst experienced in response to either *perceived* futility or *genuine* futility will be proportional to (i) the extent to which one is *invested* (emotionally, rationally, relationally, etc.) in attempting to reach some desired end, and (ii) the relative *perceived desirability* of the end at which one is aiming.[36] For example, the level of angst felt in a situation where someone confined to a wheelchair strongly desires to climb Mt Everest as part of securing a flourishing life will be much greater than someone who desires to mow her lawn (and enjoys mowing her lawn) on a day where unco-operative weather conditions prevent her from doing so. In both cases, it would be futile to undertake the desired activity, but the existential distress felt in response to this futility will be dramatically different. I will call this the 'principle of proportionality' (POP):

> POP   The existential angst attached to any putative instance of futility is directly proportional to the level of one's *investment*, broadly construed, in some desired end and the *perceived desirability* of that end.

Something like POP is salient in conclusions of cosmic futility given naturalistic premises, as those adopting such conclusions experience a high level of existential angst. Such conclusions are no doubt influenced by POP, as there is a prima facie discrepancy felt by many between the profound human investment in life, the deep-seated desire for that life to continue, and the fact that it will almost certainly not continue on naturalism.

The futility that often comes into focus in meaning-of-life discussions is analogous, though not identical, to that which emerged in the above analysis. The discrepancy component that produces futility remains the same, but the nature of the discrepancy is subtly different as already seen in my application of POP to futility within the meaning of life context. In the case of the futility that is sometimes thought to characterize life in a naturalistic universe, the futility is largely a function of the discrepancy between our deepest desires and the nature of the naturalistic world which seems to ultimately prevent these desires from being realized. Additionally, yet related, is the discrepancy on naturalism between a salient feature of the final state of affairs *where, quite literally, nothing matters*, and the current state of affairs *where lots of things seem to matter* (e.g. relationships, personal and cultural achievements, and scientific advancements, among others).

This futility or perceived futility can be thought of either strongly or weakly. In what can be called the 'strong futility conclusion' (SFC), it is thought that if the final state of affairs of the meta-narrative is one in which nothing matters, then nothing ever really mattered. SFC does have historical precedent.[37] In what can be called the 'weak futility conclusion' (WFC), it is thought that if the final state of affairs of the meta-narrative is one in which nothing matters, then the mattering or significance of things currently is in some way mitigated, either minimally or considerably, though probably not completely destroyed. There are those, of course, who reject SFC and probably WFC too.[38] In the words of C. S. Lewis, critics of SFC and WFC might contend that 'instead of criticizing the universe we may criticize our own feelings about the universe, and try to show that our sense of futility is unreasonable or improper or irrelevant'.[39] Regardless of whether or not one finds either SFC or WFC philosophically plausible, the important claim for my purposes is that both SFC and WFC should be viewed as conclusions receiving momentum from a more basic source: the evaluative importance attached to narrative ending *qua* ending.

On the above analysis of futility, one could construe human effort rather broadly to include the wide variety of activities, achievements, and relationships that partly constitute human existence. In this case, the discrepancy upon which futility is often thought to supervene is between the profound human investment and value attached to such effort, and that neither this effort nor any of its products *will last*. Again, regardless of whether this conclusion of futility is itself a reasonable one, the likely rationale for why it is often adopted (as a second-order futility conclusion) lies partly, if not largely, in the discrepancy between the ending of the naturalistic meta-narrative where nothing matters, and the middle of the meta-narrative where lots of things seem to matter. In Thomas Nagel's words, this is an 'absurdity'.[40] When human life and the activities that populate human life are viewed from a distant, detached perspective – *sub specie aeternitatis* – they seem to lose all value, worth, and significance.[41] Analogously, when those things which seem to matter now are viewed from the temporally distant perspective of death, in all its dimensions (both individual and cosmic), they seem to matter very little, if at all, from this final, settled 'point of reference' from which there is no possibility of return.[42]

If the ending of a narrative takes evaluative priority in assessments of the narrative as a whole, then a meta-narrative ending where nothing matters seems to cast a threatening shadow, either weakly or strongly, over the parts of the meta-narrative where lots of things at least seem to matter. In the same way that knowing a courting relationship will end in dissolution and not marriage will affect, in some sense, how one views the relationship right now, including one's emotional participation and response to the various dimensions of the relationship, so too might the knowledge that death, not life, that non-consciousness, not consciousness, that non-love, not love will be the final word affect the perspective we adopt towards life right now. On the naturalistic meta-narrative, nothing we do, nothing we consider valuable or worthwhile or significant, no achievement, no advances in scientific understanding, no progress, and no deep, loving relationships, in any sense, will last as part of the fabric of reality. Their marks may have been significant and felt for a season, when feelers and recognizers, or possibly inventers, of significance are around, but those marks are not indelible as they are, for example, on theistic meta-narratives.

The difference, for example, between naturalistic and Christian theistic meta-narratives with respect to their final words is the difference between entropy, decay, death, and the dissolution of conditions that make love possible, on naturalism, and resurrection, recreation, limitless fecundity, and love, on Christian theism. Naturalistic meta-narratives 'close' with complete dissolution such that it will be as if none of this ever happened. And, from this most remote and distant perspective,[43] none of this matters. It is not significant. It is not meaningful. It was, and it is no more. No-one cares. No-one is concerned. No-one remembers. Whether the final state should be able to hold such veto power over life here and now is not the point; that it does for so many is undeniable, and I have here tried to provide a plausible rationale for why this has so often been the case by grounding second-order futility conclusions tied to the nature of naturalistic meta-narrative endings in first-order conclusions about the evaluative priority of narrative ending *qua* ending for normative appraisals of narratives as a whole. We want the features of human existence to matter, and to matter deeply; we want to make an indelible mark.[44] An ending of complete dissolution does not allow for this.

In the end, whether or not one deems life to be futile on naturalistic premises will be largely a function of which perspective one adopts, that of the ending or the more immediate perspective of the present or even that portion of the universe's history that is co-extensive with human history, and therefore, a season where those who care about what matters are around to care about it. Of course, given the evaluative priority of narrative ending, it may be difficult to prevent the ending's proleptic encroachment on how we view the here and now. Those who think the ending takes priority for our evaluations of whether life is characterized by cosmic or deep futility will likely side with theists like William Lane Craig:

> If each individual person passes out of existence when he dies, then what ultimate meaning can be given to his life? Does it really matter whether he ever existed at all? It might be said that his life was important because it influenced others or affected the course of history. But this only shows a relative significance to his life, not an ultimate significance. ... Look at it from another perspective: Scientists say that the universe originated in an explosion called the 'Big Bang' about 15 billion years ago. Suppose the Big Bang had never occurred. Suppose the universe had never existed. What ultimate difference would it make? The universe is doomed to die anyway. In the end it makes no difference whether the universe ever existed or not. ... Mankind is a doomed race in a dying universe. Because the human race will eventually cease to exist, it makes no ultimate difference whether it ever did exist. ... The contributions of the scientist to the advance of human knowledge, the researches of the doctor to alleviate pain and suffering, the efforts of the diplomat to secure peace in the world, the sacrifices of good men everywhere to better the lot of the human race – all these come to nothing. In the end they don't make one bit of difference, not one bit.[45]

In such claims, Craig's implicit commitment to both SPI and SFC is clear. For human existence to avoid irredeemable futility, it must carry on in some robust sense, a sense requiring, at minimum, post-mortem survival extending endlessly into the future.[46]

Those who are suspicious of Craig's and many others' stringent conditions placed upon a worthwhile, meaningful existence will side with Brook Alan Trisel:

The higher one's aspirations are, the more likely it is that the efforts associated with bringing about these goals will be considered futile or ineffective. For example, if we seek to have our works last forever, then, at some point, we will probably conclude that our efforts are futile since this goal is unachievable. However, if we have *more realistic* aspirations … then we would be much less likely to conclude that our efforts at achieving this goal are futile. [emphasis added][47]

The kinds of cosmic futility conclusions that Trisel criticizes are largely built around what Erik J. Wielenberg refers to as 'final outcome arguments'.[48] It is thought by critics that such arguments are contingent upon a suspect assumption, namely, arbitrarily placing an undue amount of importance (perhaps all the importance!) on the final state of affairs to which life leads. But why place such priority on the future over the present or the past?[49] In the words of Thomas Nagel, 'it does not matter now that in a million years nothing we do now will matter'.[50] Of course, there may be good, principled reasons for placing normative priority on the future, but such a case will not be made here.

The important point presently is that even if such criticisms of final-outcome arguments have philosophical merit, they run up against our deep narrative proclivities as human beings, proclivities out of which we assign profound normative significance to narrative endings in virtue of them being *endings*. Indeed, the significance we attach to narrative ending will likely make it difficult for many to adopt these 'more realistic aspirations' of which Trisel spoke above toward our human efforts in the face of impending and final dissolution from which there is no possibility of return. And this is largely due to the fact that SPI and either SFC or WFC gain momentum through the evaluative significance of narrative ending *qua* ending.

Evil, Eschatology, and Narrative Ending

The evaluative priority of narrative ending in general and the way a narrative ends for broadly normative appraisals of narratives as a whole is not only helpful in providing a richer account for why death and futility so closely track discussions of the meaning of life, but may also add a helpful dimension to considerations of another issue closely linked to the meaning of life – the problem of evil. The ugly reality of pain and suffering, along with accompanying questions on philosophical, existential, and eschatological levels about such suffering, is one of a number of existentially relevant elements and accompanying questions of human existence for which we are seeking a larger narrative through which to understand and appraise such existentially relevant elements of life.

Though the problem of evil is multi-dimensional and most philosophical energy is often directed toward the theoretic aspects, those most relevant in the immediate context are the *existential* and *eschatological* dimensions.[51] Roughly, by 'existential' I mean especially the first-person, humanly centred emotive aspects of pain, suffering, and evil – largely, the feelings of angst that characterize the sufferer[52]; by 'eschatological', I mean future-oriented questions about whether pain, suffering, and evil will be, in some robust sense, redeemed and defeated.

Eschatology has occupied a prominent place in discussions of theodicy. Generally, it is thought by theists that, in some sense, the blessed final state is part of a fuller answer to the problem of evil. I think something is right about this approach, although I will not enter discussion of the specifics here. I am more concerned with a general point, which is – if the ending of a narrative takes some sort of evaluative priority for broadly normative appraisals of a narrative as a whole, then a 'good ending' to life's narrative where redemption is robustly and fully accomplished will loom large for how the entire narrative is appraised. If an ending that itself never ends is one where deep and abiding *shalom* is present for all eternity, then that state of affairs is really important for the entire meta-narrative, not just then, but also now.

This does not commit one to the utilitarian approach whereby the *eschaton* itself is somehow worth all the horrendous evil that countless millions have experienced in this life. To such a proposal, we, like Ivan Karamazov, might shudder in moral horror at the thought that the torture of even one child is worth a peaceful human destiny for all people. Of course, this might be a subtle misconstrual of what it means to say that the *eschaton* 'is worth' the pain and suffering saliently populating human history. Neither is such an approach warrant for somehow, retroactively, calling evil 'good'. That the blessed state is blessed does not retroactively erase all the pain, suffering, and evil of post-lapsarian, pre-consummation history on the Christian theistic meta-narrative.

But none of this is the point. The very general and modest claim I am advocating is simply that, given first-order conclusions about the evaluative significance of narrative ending *qua* ending, and second-order conclusions based upon the *nature* of a given ending, some measure of plausibility is brought to the practice of enlisting eschatological considerations in the projects of defence and theodicy. The final, settled stance toward life's meta-narrative from the perspective of eternal blessedness surely makes a difference for how we evaluate the elements of the meta-narrative right now. Unfortunately (for philosophers), to try and speculate during the present portion of life's meta-narrative, if it is of the theistic variety, on how possibly this might look and what kind of difference it might make is probably mitigated by the Pauline statement, 'For now we see in a mirror dimly, but then face to face' (1 Corinthians, 13.12a).[53]

Conclusion

Assessments of naturalistic meta-narratives as cosmically and deeply futile, given the way they end, will likely remain prevalent as long as we continue first to attach a significant evaluative function to narrative ending *qua* ending for broadly normative appraisals on emotional, aesthetic, and moral levels of narratives as a whole. I have argued that understanding the connection between futility and naturalistic meta-narratives solely in terms of the *nature* of their endings is truncated, and that considerations of the evaluative priority of narrative ending in general add substantially to an understanding of this connection.

A robust account of the connection, then, must not only include considerations of the staying-power intuition and strong and weak versions of the futility conclusion, but should locate them within an intelligible framework, something I have attempted to accomplish by discussing the evaluative significance of narrative ending in general. As long as our views of the world continue to be powerfully shaped by our deep seated narrative proclivities, a sense of cosmic futility will likely stubbornly persist for those who worry that we might live in a Russellian universe in which, 'buried beneath the debris of a universe in ruins',[54] lie our grandest achievements, most profound loving relationships, and our very lives themselves.

Notes

1. Others include origins, purpose, value, pain and suffering, and how life is going to end.

2. I contrast *cosmic* futility with *local* futility. The latter is futility that supervenes upon a localized state of affairs, for example, a four-year-old's aim to climb Mt Everest in a day. The entirety of existence being cosmically futile is consistent with localized aims being worthwhile and attainable.

3. SPI is nicely captured in the slogan, 'Diamonds are forever'.

4. I am, of course, not referring to *logical* impossibility, but *metaphysical* impossibility. Though, it must be admitted that, strictly speaking, one can imagine scenarios where post-mortem survival is even metaphysically possible within an exclusively naturalist ontology, for example, through successive transfers of consciousness into different material bodies, as an anonymous reviewer for this journal reminded me. Nonetheless, post-mortem survival fits much more naturally within a theistic ontology, and attempts to secure it on naturalism are tenuous at best.

5. SI is explicitly affirmed by Victor Frankl: '[D]eath itself is what makes life meaningful'; *idem The Doctor and the Soul* (New York: Alfred Knopf, 1957), 73. Also by Karl Popper: 'There are those who think that life is valueless because it comes to an end. They fail to see that the opposite argument might also be proposed: that if there were no end to life, life would have no value; that it is, in part, the ever-present danger of losing it which helps bring home to us the value of life'; *idem* 'How I see philosophy', in A. Mercier and M. Svilar (eds.) *Philosophers on Their Own Work* (Berne & Frankfurt: Peter Lang, 1977), 148.

6. This is the position of Brooke Alan Trisel in 'Human extinction and the value of our efforts', *The Philosophical Forum*, 35 (2004), 371–91, along with most contemporary naturalists. Interestingly, there are those who think that not only is post-mortem existence, extending endlessly into the future, not necessary for a worthwhile, meaningful life, but that such a state would actually *threaten* such a life. For example, see Bernard Williams's existential – as opposed to logical or metaphysical – objection to traditional accounts of post-mortem survival in his, 'The Makropulos Case: reflections on the tedium of immortality', in *idem Problems of the Self* (Cambridge: Cambridge University Press, 1973), 82–100. Importantly, (ii) additionally highlights the difference between *optimistic* and *pessimistic* naturalists. Pessimistic naturalists, along with most theists, claim that God's existence and post-mortem survival are necessary conditions for a meaningful and worthwhile life. Unlike theists, pessimistic naturalists deny that God exists, and so conclude that life is meaningless and futile. Schopenhauer, Camus, and possibly Bertrand Russell fall into this category. Optimistic naturalists, however, deny that God and post-mortem survival are necessary for a meaningful, worthwhile life. Thus, they would deny a strong version of SPI applied to human life. Most contemporary philosophical naturalists would recognize themselves as optimistic, in the sense the term is used in this context.

7. From here on, I will use the term 'meta-narrative' and not 'narrative' to describe entire metaphysical systems like naturalism and Christian theism. Interestingly, the meta-narratives of some metaphysical systems, like Christian theism for example, will possess a narrative in the paradigmatic sense of the term 'narrative', largely in virtue of such religious traditions' connection with religious texts which themselves contain an overarching redemptive story of the cosmos. In contrast, the meta-narratives of other metaphysical systems, like naturalism for example, will be narratives only in some loose and non-paradigmatic sense. For a discussion of the classification of narrative and non-narrative discourse, see Marie-Laure Ryan 'Toward a

definition of narrative', in David Herman (ed.) *The Cambridge Companion to Narrative* (Cambridge: Cambridge University Press, 2007), 22–35. Meta-narratives, or 'grand narratives' as they have been called, are 'second-order narratives which seek to narratively articulate and legitimate some concrete first-order practices or narratives'; J. M. Bernstein 'Grand narratives', in David Wood (ed.) *On Paul Ricoeur: Narrative and Interpretation* (London: Routledge, 1991), 102. New Testament Scholar, N. T. Wright, adds that such narratives are '*normative*: that is, they claim to make sense of the whole of reality'; Wright *The New Testament and the People of God*, I, *Christian Origins and the Question of God* (Minneapolis MN: Fortress Press, 1992), 41. I will not defend the concept of meta-narrative against various postmodern criticisms, though I do not share postmodernity's 'incredulity toward meta-narratives'; Jean-François Lyotard *The Postmodern Condition: A Report on Knowledge*, Geoff Bennington & Brian Massumi (trans.) (Minneapolis MN: University of Minnesota Press, 1985), xxiv.

8. The judgment might also be based upon other considerations, like whether or not one thinks objective value can be secured in an exclusively naturalistic ontology. The debate over the ontology of value, even within the naturalist camp, reveals that there is not just one naturalistic meta-narrative, even though there will be some continuity across all naturalistic meta-narratives in virtue of shared theses about the nature of reality.

9. Regardless of whether or not the endings of narratives *should* possess such influence over our broadly normative assessments of narratives as a whole (or whether or not narrative theorists and philosophers have given this literary-anthropological phenomenon enough attention), they in fact do.

10. See my paper 'The meaning of life as narrative: a new proposal for interpreting philosophy's "primary" question', *Philo*, 20 (2009), 5–23.

11. R. W. Hepburn 'Questions about the meaning of life', in E. D. Klemke (ed.) *The Meaning of Life* (Oxford: Oxford University Press, 2000), 262. Thaddeus Metz has done much helpful work on this and related issues. See his 'New developments in the meaning of life', *Philosophy Compass*, 2 (2007), 196–217; *idem* 'Recent work on the meaning of life', *Ethics*, 112 (2002),

781–814; *idem* 'The concept of a meaningful life', *American Philosophical Quarterly*, 38 (2001), 137–53; and *idem* 'Critical notice: Baier and Cottingham on the meaning of life', *Disputatio*, 19 (2005), 251–64.

12. I owe the analytic/synthetic distinction introduced in this context to the helpful suggestion of an anonymous referee for the journal.

13. A similar claim can be made for any meta-narrative. That is, meta-narrative *x*'s ending has significant proleptic power to elicit a wide range of *broadly normative* human responses on, possibly, emotional, aesthetic, and moral levels towards that meta-narrative as a whole. The *content* of the broadly normative responses will then be dependent upon *how* meta-narrative *x* ends.

14. For example, with respect to defining narrative ending, it has been proposed that a narrative's ending is largely constituted by 'scratching' or resolving an emotional 'itch' initially instantiated by the narrative's beginning and variously perpetuated throughout the narrative. See J. David Velleman 'Narrative explanation', *The Philosophical Review*, 112 (2003), 18–20. This 'scratching' is organizational and unifying, for example, like the 'tock' of a clock; the *tock*, of the clock's tick-tock, is the fictionalized ending we bestow on the sequence, thus conferring upon the space between *tick* and *tock* 'duration and meaning'. In this way, the interval between *tick* and *tock* becomes something more than the interval between *tock* and *tick*; it is transformed from mere successive *chronos* to pregnant *kairos*. See Frank Kermode *The Sense of an Ending* (Oxford: Oxford University Press, 2000), 44–6.

15. Though, theistic endings will have to contend with, among other criticisms, that of Bernard Williams mentioned in n. 6.

16. Velleman 'Narrative explanation', 19.

17. Of course, in the real world we are usually not privy to such information, but that is irrelevant to the thought-experiment.

18. It seems unreasonable to place a condition upon any instance of putative happiness that in order for it to *actually be an instance of happiness* it must satisfy some strong requirement whereby it has to be permanently stable and indefectible happiness forever.

19. Christiaan Moster 'Theodicy and eschatology', in Bruce Barber and David Neville (eds.) *Theodicy and Eschatology* (Adelaide: ATF Press, 2005), 106.

20. H. Porter Abbott *The Cambridge Introduction to Narrative* (Cambridge: Cambridge University Press, 2005), 53. Whether the desire for such closure in terms of the redemptive-eschatological vision of, say, Christian theism is mere wishful thinking or more akin to a natural desire is an interesting question, but one that I will not discuss in the present context.

21. I say 'non-narrative explanations' because narrative can be thought of as a species of explanation. For a defence of this, see Velleman 'Narrative explanation'.

22. John Martin Fischer 'Free will, death, and immortality: the role of narrative', *Philosophical Papers*, 34 (2005), 379–403.

23. Of course, one could plausibly argue that closure is present in works of horror in the sense of a settled stance, but that the settled stance itself is one of shuddering or despair.

24. Velleman 'Narrative explanation', 18–22.

25. Of course, an advocate of a meta-narrative that posits eternal life may argue that there is no longer any need of closure for the post-consummation portion of the meta-narrative, precisely because the problem set has been remedied. There may be other dilemmas for the immortal life, but perhaps this is not one of them.

26. This popular refrain occurs at least twenty-nine times in the book of Ecclesiastes. My use of the phrase is exegetically plausible, though scholars of Ecclesiastes debate its precise meaning. Unless otherwise noted, all scriptural citations will be from the English Standard Version of the Bible (Wheaton IL: Crossway Bibles, 2001).

27. Ronald Dworkin *Sovereign Virtue* (Cambridge MA: Harvard University Press, 2001), 246.

28. According to the model of challenge, a good life has the inherent value of an Aristotelian skillful performance, and thus, in contrast with the model of impact, events, achievements, and experiences can have value though they may have no impact beyond the life in which they occur; *ibid.*, 253. Death cannot nullify their value, significance, and meaningfulness, because such constructs are not functions of impact or continuation or consequence, but rather of the skilfulness of the performance(s) itself. Furthermore, the model of challenge circumvents the objection that nothing humans do in the face of the vast, unconcerned universe matters because it does not anchor value in anything other than life and the activities of life performed well.

29. Dworkin *Sovereign Virtue*, 251.

30. Cf. n. 4.

31. Robert Nozick *Philosophical Explanations* (Cambridge MA: Harvard University Press, 1981), 594–600.

32. Here, *impossible* may refer to either *logical* impossibility (e.g. me writing and not-writing at the same time and in the same sense) or *metaphysical* impossibility (e.g. me bicycling to the North Pole in 4 minutes and 45 seconds). Everything that is logically impossible is metaphysically impossible, but not everything that is metaphysically impossible is logically impossible.

33. There have been numerous alterations made to the Sisyphus story in order to test philosophical intuitions about what constitutes a futile state of affairs, and if such conclusions themselves are functions of whether one thinks valuable, worthwhile, and meaningful states of affairs should be construed as such, either subjectively or objectively. For an example of such alterations and subsequent discussion, see Richard Taylor *Good and Evil: A New Direction* (London: Macmillan, 1970), 256–68.

34. Futility, then, can be a noun, picking out some state of affairs, or it can be more of an adjective, characterizing the effort put into trying to accomplish an impossible end – e.g. a *futile* aim.

35. Whether or not effort directed at some end is futile is context relative. It will include conditions tied to external circumstances as well as conditions tied to the agent himself. For example, it may not be futile for me to research, write, and submit this paper for publication in eight months, but it would be futile for my 22-month old son, William, to do so.

36. I distinguish between *perceived* and *genuine* futility because one could be wrong about (i) whether or not some goal is attainable/unattainable, or, more subtly and relevantly in this context, (ii) whether some goal or end state of affairs needs to obtain in order to avoid futility (e.g. post-mortem survival extending endlessly into the future).

37. See, for example, possibly Qohelet (especially in Ecclesiastes 1, though debate exists about how best to interpret Qohelet's pessimistic musings in the book); Arthur Schopenhauer 'On the vanity of existence', in *Essays and Aphorisms* (London: Penguin Books, 2004), 51–4, and Leo Tolstoy 'A confession', in *Spiritual Writings* (Maryknoll NY: Orbis Books, 2006), 46–59.

38. See, for example, Trisel 'Human extinction and the value of our efforts'. This paper develops a line of

argument that casts suspicion on the intuition that nothing is now valuable or worthwhile if extinction is the final word of the universe, by highlighting a competing intuition in the following thought-experiment. Consider the case where (i) your son is on the railway track about ready to be struck by an oncoming train, and (ii) you just learn that the universe will come to an end in three days. With this knowledge of the universe's imminent demise, would you still find rescuing your son to be a valuable aim (and not simply emotionally required)? Most think the answer is yes.

39. C. S. Lewis 'De futilitate', in *idem Christian Reflections* (Grand Rapids MI: Eerdmans, 1995), 59.

40. Thomas Nagel 'The absurd', in Klemke *The Meaning of Life*, 176–85.

41. Though, in light of this absurdity, Nagel concludes that we should approach life with a sense of irony as opposed to either tragic heroism (possibly Bertrand Russell) or pessimistic despair (Camus). For Nagel, conclusions of cosmic futility are built upon an illicit assumption – that some future state of affairs detached from the first-person human perspective (because humans are no longer around) actually *matters* for states of affairs involving the first-person human perspective.

42. This phrase is a bit misleading for there will literally be *no-one* to take up this point of reference.

43. Again, there are those who argue that this most remote and distant perspective, itself, does not matter and is not relevant to appraisals of the worth, value, and meaningfulness of what goes on now in the lives of human beings. The only perspective relevant, some argue, for appraisals of the worth, value, and meaningfulness of human pursuits, projects, and relationships is *the human perspective*, and the perspective from the end may not be a perspective at all, given that *taking a perspective* entails the presence of intentionally directed consciousness. Of course, one might argue that it is relevant that we can take a perspective *now* about a state of affairs when we will no longer be able to take a perspective at all.

44. As noted in the introduction, leaving such a mark is usually articulated in a sense requiring a doctrine of post-mortem survival that itself requires the survival of the person.

45. William Lane Craig 'The absurdity of life without God', in Klemke *The Meaning of Life*, 42.

46. This, of course, makes post-mortem survival extending endlessly into the future only a necessary condition for a worthwhile, meaningful existence. Christian theists do not affirm this to be a sufficient condition. A robustly construed meaningful existence is built upon numerous doctrines that are woven into the Christian theistic meta-narrative, just one of which is post-mortem survival.

47. Trisel 'Human extinction and the value of our efforts', 384.

48. Erik J. Wielenberg *Value and Virtue in a Godless Universe* (Cambridge: Cambridge University Press, 2006), 16–31.

49. For example, see Paul Edwards, who refers to this as a 'curious and totally arbitrary preference of the future to the present'; Edwards 'The meaning of life' in Klemke *The Meaning of Life*, 140.

50. Thomas Nagel *Mortal Questions* (Cambridge: Cambridge University Press, 1979), 11.

51. There is obviously significant overlap between the philosophic and eschatological dimensions of the problem of evil.

52. In fact, I think arguments from evil receive significant motivating force, a force contributing to their perceived strength as putative instances of atheology, from the problem of evil's palpable emotional component. Compare such arguments to other atheistic arguments, for example, arguments based upon perceived incoherence among theistic divine attributes. Of course, rationally, one may think such arguments are strong; however, they have not occupied the significant place that the problem of evil has in philosophy of religion. One interpretation of this historical reality is that the problem of evil, *rationally*, is the best atheological argument. Perhaps that is the case, but I suspect that there is more to the story; that the *emotional* dimension to the problem of evil is a salient component of the problem of evil's perceived philosophical merit, a component not shared by other atheological arguments.

53. Ancient mirrors in the Graeco-Roman world were made from polished metal; thus one's reflection was considerably more 'dim' than with modern mirrors.

54. Bertrand Russell 'A free man's worship', in *idem Why I Am Not a Christian and Other Essays on Religion and Related Subjects* (New York: Simon and Schuster, 1957), 107.

5.8

Divine Hiddenness, Death, and Meaning

Paul K. Moser

In the *Phaedo*, Plato claims that "those who really apply themselves in the right way to philosophy are directly and of their own accord preparing themselves for dying and death" (64a). This claim sounds very strange to us today. If Plato is right, contemporary philosophers have failed to "apply themselves in the right way to philosophy." So, maybe contemporary philosophers aren't true footnotes to Plato after all. Maybe they have missed his main point about the point of philosophy. Even so, the important questions regarding death are not about Plato.

What has death to do with philosophy? Or, more immediately, what has death to do with *us*, with us *as persons*, regardless of whether we are philosophers? Does death have an important lesson for us, even if we are inclined to ignore its lesson? Let's begin with the obvious: death happens.

The Reality of Death

Death is the cessation of *bodily* life. Some mind-body dualists, under Plato's influence, deny that death is the cessation of *mental* life. It is, however, the end of embodied life, at least as we know it. So, when we die, others will bury or cremate our bodies, even if they don't do the same to *us*, to our souls. Mind-body dualists and materialists agree on this much: bodily death happens. They disagree, however, on whether our bodily death allows for our mental survival.

We might deny that death happens. Still, we will die. We can run but we cannot hide from death. The reality of death marks the human predicament, wherever we go in space and/or

Paul K. Moser (2007) "Divine Hiddenness, Death, and Meaning," Chapter 15 in Paul Copan and Chad Meister (eds.), *Philosophy of Religion: Classic and Contemporary Issues*, Malden, MA: Wiley-Blackwell, pp. 215–27.

time. Death is universal for humans. The reality of death is the reality of a pervasive destructive *power*. It destroys us at least physically, if not mentally and socially too. It sometimes is delayable, given the powers of modern medicine. Still, death seems unavoidable if we are left to our own resources. Its power seems immune to our best medicine and science. Death inevitably triumphs over humans and our powers.

What, if anything, is the significance of death? The answer depends on what exactly death is. One question is whether it is an *irreversible* destructive power. Is death forever? Given materialism about reality, it is: there is no coming back. If reality is uniformly material, entropy meets no lasting counterbalance, and death doesn't either. Our best physics tells us that in the long term the physical universe is destined to break down. The energy of the physical universe will naturally disperse if it is not counterbalanced. Consider, for instance, how a cube of ice will naturally melt in a heated room. The same ice cube does not ever return from its dispersion. The material world thus does not offer us, as the persons we are, a lasting alternative to death. It leaves us with dying and death, with the dispersing of bodily life. If we depend for our existence on bodily life, we too will be dispersed forever, given materialism.

Loss in Death

Given materialism, we will no longer be persons after our death. So, there is no lasting hope for *us*, regarding our future as persons. We have no lasting future; so, we have no lastingly good future. Our destiny is just the abyss of dispersed physical energy. We will then have, in the abyss, no value in ourselves because we will have ceased to exist. People who were once valuable will then no longer be valuable. We will no longer be important, or worthwhile. Our existence and value will have ceased, never to be recovered. Some people may remember us, but mere memories are not the persons we are. We ourselves will not survive in memories. We will be gone forever, dispersed and done for, given materialism.

The loss of us will be a real loss. Why? Because we now are valuable – that is, worthwhile and good – in many ways. We exemplify goodness in many respects, even though we exemplify evil too. So, our funerals will be a sad occasion for many people – not for *us*, of course, but for many others. Their sadness will correspond to the loss of us with regard to what *was* valuable about us, including our being alive. People who pretend that death is no loss at all are misguided, perhaps even self-deceived. They need a reality check from the spontaneous responses of people at funerals. One might spin the reality of death to fit a far-fetched theory, but the responses of the uninitiated at funerals are telling indeed.

Materialists might take an extreme position here. If our value as persons ceases at death, as it will given materialism, then our death is not important after all, because we aren't truly valuable. We are just insignificant energy centers waiting entropically (so to speak) to be dispersed. Such extremism is confused. The fact that we have no *lasting*, or ultimate, value, given materialism, doesn't entail that we have no value at all. We can still have *temporary* value, and we do, even though materialism makes our ultimate future bleak. Correspondingly, we can reasonably have *short-term* hope for our temporary well-being. Hope for our lasting, or ultimate, well-being would be misplaced. Materialism offers no basis for such hope.

Entropy will leave us all without hope. The final hopelessness of materialism is palpable. Lasting meaning, or purpose, is likewise excluded. Camus (1955), for example, paints a powerful portrait of life without lasting meaning.

Our ultimately hopeless destiny, given materialism, is a reality beyond our power to change. We can't save ourselves or anyone else from the abyss of final dispersion and destruction. Our intelligence, however sophisticated, can't save us. Our philosophy, however profound, can't save us. Our willful drive, however resolute, can't save us. Nor can our families, friends, colleagues, or community save us, however well-intentioned they are. Death will leave us in its cold wake, regardless of our cleverness, drive, or acquaintances. Materialism, then, is less than cheery about death. Materialists should be too, at least as long as they embrace materialism. The grave is their destiny.

Outside Help

In the face of death, we can reasonably be hopeful only if we have outside help from a power that can overcome death. This would be *outside* help, because its power would be beyond us. We lack the power of our own to overcome death. The needed help would be actual help, not merely possible help. It would offer us the actual opportunity to overcome death, to survive the destruction brought by death.

Could an *impersonal* power save us from death? This would be a power without plans, intentions, or goals. It would enable us to survive destruction by death, but it would not do so intentionally, or purposively. It would happen blindly, in the way the wind, for instance, could blindly form a three-dimensional portrait of Mother Teresa's face on the sandy shoreline of Lake Michigan. The wind *could* do this, but we cannot count on it to do so. If it happens, it is unpredictable for all practical purposes and thus beyond what we can reasonably hope for. If it were to happen for Mother Teresa (against all odds), we could not reasonably assume that it will happen for another person too. We thus wouldn't wait on the shoreline for someone's portrait to emerge from the sand. If we did, our sanity would be questioned.

Our *grounded* hope in surviving death, *if* we have such hope, requires a ground for supposing that death will be overcome by us. This ground cannot be the unpredictable vicissitudes of local wind movements. It requires a ground predictable and trustworthy by us, that is, predictable and trustworthy in practice. The announced intentions of a reliable, trustworthy personal agent would offer such a ground. We know this from everyday experience, as we often form a grounded hope on the basis of the announced intentions of other persons. For example, I reasonably hope that my return home from the campus will be timely, given that a trustworthy friend has promised to give me a ride home. This hope has a basis different in kind from the basis for my wish that the wind inscribe a human portrait on the shoreline of Lake Michigan. My hope is grounded in a good reason; my wish is not.

Let's consider the kind of outside help that would come from a trustworthy personal agent who has the power to overcome death. I have said "would come," rather than "does come," to avoid begging a likely question: namely, "*Is* there actually such help?" Another likely question is: "If there's outside help from a personal agent, why would that agent allow death to occur in the first place?" Some people hold that such an agent, if genuinely helpful, would block death from the start. Here we have the beginnings of an analogue to the so-called problem of evil for theism.

Would a superhuman personal agent allow us to undergo death even though that agent seeks to help us to overcome death? If so, why? A noteworthy answer comes from Paul's epistle to the Romans: "The creation was subjected to futility, not by its own will, but by the will of the One who subjected it, in [the One's] hope that the creation will be freed from its slavery to decay and brought into the glorious freedom of the children of God" (Rom. 8:20–21). Let's unpack this.

Paul's reference to futility echoes the writer of Ecclesiastes: "Futility of futilities! All is futility" (Eccles. 1:2; 12:8). They have in mind what is ultimately pointless, in vain, when left to its own ways. Paul thus suggests that God introduced death to show that the ways of creation on its own are ultimately futile, pointless, meaningless. In particular, as a part of creation, we humans ultimately come to naught on our own. Death leaves us with a hopeless destiny if we are left to our own resources. All of our own projects and achievements, even our philosophical labors, will meet the same fate: futility. They are all destined for the abyss, never to be revived. This seems to be nothing but bad news, but is it really?

Paul suggests that a certain hope lies behind the futility of death: God's hope of freeing people from futility to enter the family of God. Death is portrayed as a means to bring about this hope. How can death, our death, lead to life, our life? How can such loss yield such good?

Dying to Live

Death can enable a needed learning curriculum for us if it serves the teaching purposes of an agent who can overcome death for us. What might such an agent have to teach us with death, our death? We all need instruction about our desperate situation when left to our own resources. We need to learn that all of our best intentions, efforts, and achievements will ultimately be futile, meaningless, if we are on our own. Death is the intended wake-up call to this humbling lesson. It shows that we cannot think, will, or work ourselves into lasting satisfaction by our own resources. It shows that we are fragile and even ultimately hopeless on our own. Death announces that we need outside help for lasting satisfaction and meaning. It solemnly warns us who remain: if we stay to ourselves, without outside power, we are done for, forever.

The reality of death fits perfectly with the view that we are creatures intended to depend on One greater than ourselves, on One who can overcome death for us. Such depending is just trust. It is faith, *not* as guesswork or a leap beyond evidence, but as willing reliance on One whom we need to overcome death, to live lastingly. What exactly is this reliance, and how does death bear on it?

For shorthand, let's introduce talk of "God" for the One in question. The slippery word "God" is a title, not a proper name. It signifies One who not only can overcome death but also is worthy of worship, i.e., unconditional commitment and adoration as our morally impeccable Maker and Sustainer. We can use a title intelligibly, even the title "God," without begging the question whether God exists. A title can have semantic significance owing to its connotation, even if it lacks denotation. So, our use of the term "God" as a title does not automatically ignore the qualms of atheists and agnostics.

Our trusting, depending, or relying on God appropriately is just willingly counting on God as our Savior and Lord, that is, as our Redeemer and Master. In counting on God thus, I commit to God as *my* God. I thereby commit to putting God's will over my will, just as Jesus did in the Garden of Gethsemane as he prayed to God: "Not what I will, but what You will" (Mark 14:36). In trusting God, I commit to dying to my own selfish ways to live to God's ways. In short, I resolve to die to my selfishness to live to God. This entails a commitment to reject selfishness, in particular, any selfishness that involves exalting my will above God's. In selfishness, I fail to honor God as God. I put myself and my ways first. The call to faith in God is, in contrast, a call to die to selfishness in order to live to One who can overcome death for us. Whatever else it is, it is *not* a call to leap beyond evidence, as if faith in God were necessarily defective from a cognitive viewpoint. Trust in God can, in principle, be at least as cognitively good as your trusting in your best friend.

Why assume, however, that I must die to my ways to live to God? Isn't this a perversely harsh understanding of what faith in God involves? Not if my own case is at all representative of the human condition. My problem is the human problem: deep-seated selfishness, the antithesis to the unselfish love integral to God's morally impeccable character. I'm also very good at hiding my selfish ways from myself and others. I tell myself stories of how they are reasonable and even good. Our inveterate selfishness qualifies us as morally deficient and thus disqualifies us immediately as God. The title "God," requiring a morally impeccable character of its holder, does not apply to ourselves. Even so, we have the persistent tendency to play God in at least some area of our lives. We pose as Lord over at least part of our lives, particularly in areas we deem vital to our well-being. One such area concerns how we treat our enemies, that is, our acquaintances who are a clear threat to our well-being. At best, we ignore them; at worst, we seek to destroy them. Rarely do we show them unselfish forgiving love, the kind of merciful love found in the true God (see Matt. 5:43–8). The risk is, we suppose, too great, too threatening to our comfort and well-being. We thereby choose against the ways of an all-loving God. We presume to know better. We thus play God. Trust in God is the refusal to play God.

Another area where we play God concerns what is to count as suitable evidence of God's reality. We presume to be in a position, on our own, to say what kind of evidence God *must* supply regarding God's reality. We reason, in agreement with Bertrand Russell and many other philosophers: If God is real, God would be revealed in way W. For instance, God would show up with considerable fireworks or at least pomp and circumstance. God, however, is not revealed in way W. Hence, God is not real. Russell (1970) thus anticipated his preferred response if after death he met God: "God, you gave us insufficient evidence." We thereby exalt ourselves as cognitive judge, jury, and executioner over God. God, we suppose, must be revealed on *our* cognitive terms. In such cognitive idolatry (see Moser 2002), we set up our cognitive standards in ways that preclude so-called "reasonable" acknowledgment of God's reality. Our cognitive pride thus becomes suicidal. We play God to our own demise. The reality of our impending death exhibits that without the true God, we are ultimately hopeless. We are then impostors in playing God.

We must die to our playing God, if we are to live lastingly. Death is our final notice. It calls us to the stark realization that our playing God will not last but will instead lead to the grave, once and for all. In shattering us, death ultimately ruins all of our projects too. The needed power for lasting life, then, is not from us or our projects. Only pride gone blind would lead one to deny this. Even in the face of death, our selfish pride endures. In the absence of the humbling effects of death, our pride would run wild indeed. Death reveals that what is lastingly important is not from us. It exposes our core insecurity (and impotence) about life itself, that is, our insecurity about the future of our lives. We know *that* our lives will end, but we have no idea of *when* they will end. Our end could come in 20 years or it could come in 20 minutes. This indefiniteness makes for insecurity and anxiety, at least when we honestly attend to the matter. As a result, we typically divert attention in ways that lead to indifference about death and related realities.

How Not to Approach Death

Avoidance and indifference toward death threaten all of us at times, in our fear, insecurity, and weakness. Blaise Pascal writes:

> the fact that there are men indifferent to the loss of their being … is not natural. They are quite different with regard to everything else: they fear even the most insignificant things, they foresee them, feel them, and the same man who spends so many days and nights in rage over the loss of some office or over some imaginary affront to his honour is the very one who, without anxiety or emotion, knows he is going to lose everything through death. It is a monstrous thing to see in the same heart and at the same time both this sensitivity to the slightest things and this strange insensitivity to the greatest. ([1660] 1995: sec. 681)

We ignore and become indifferent to death, because we know that our own resources cannot overcome it. We know that death will triumph over us. So, we conclude, let's just resign ourselves to it. We then fail to seek the needed solution (the One who is the solution) in the right way.

Russell acknowledges the inadequacy of our own resources in the face of death, but still recommends intentional and courageous "contemplation" of our fate in death. He claims: "it remains only to cherish … the lofty thoughts that ennoble [our] little day; … to worship at the shrine that [our] own hands have built." He means the shrine that our *minds* have built. Russell also recommends that we approach the dying "to give them the pure joy of a never-tiring affection, to strengthen failing courage, to instill faith in hours of despair" ([1903] 1957: 18). Faith? In what? Russell is silent, because he has no hope-conferring object of faith to offer.

Russell's rhetoric may sound good, but he cannot deliver on it. The eternal truths he loves passionately offer no hope to the dying. How could they? They cannot overcome death for the dying. So, they are no basis for us to "instill faith in hours of despair." Russell deserves credit for facing death as an immediate problem even for philosophers. He has, however, no basis for his courage, his joy, or his faith. His faith does not yield living through dying, because his faith has no *object* of faith that can overcome death. The mere *attitude* of faith, being a psychological human state, does nothing to overcome death. Russell, then, is not helpful in solving the human plight. He offers no genuine help. He has no good news for us, the dying.

Do we want outside help? Some of us don't. Thomas Nagel claims that the existence of God poses a serious "cosmic authority problem" for us, so much so that he hopes that God does not exist. Nagel writes: "I want atheism to be true. … I hope there is no God! I don't want there to be a God; I don't want the universe to be like that" (Nagel 1997: 130). Contrast this bold attitude with the tempered attitude of the Yale surgeon, Dr Richard Selzer, who likewise is not a theist: "Probably the biggest, saddest thing about my own life is that I never had faith in God. I envy people who do. Life without faith is rather a hard proposition" (Selzer 2000). An undeniable hardship of life without God is that ultimately it all comes to naught, and we have indications of this futility of life. Selzer rightly feels the pain of life without God. Somehow, Nagel doesn't. He evidently misses the tragedy of a bypassed opportunity of a lastingly good life. Something has gone wrong.

It would be a strange, defective God who didn't pose a serious cosmic authority problem for humans. Part of the status of being *God*, after all, is that God has unique authority, or lordship, over humans. Since we humans aren't God, the true God would have authority over us and would seek to correct our profoundly selfish ways. Nagel confesses to having a fear of any religion involving God. Such fear seems widespread among humans, and all humans may share it at least at times. It stems from human fear of losing our supposed lordship over our decisions and lives. We want to be able to say, as the blindly arrogant song goes: "I did it my way." Willful children are very good at exhibiting this attitude, and adults can be too. Our attitude is: "It's my way, or no way." Human willfulness runs deeper than the reach of reason. One's willfulness, tragically, can be *consistently* suicidal. Reason is no panacea, after all. If it were, we wouldn't need God.

Our supposedly self-protective fear, confessed by Nagel, may *seem* to be for our own good. It blocks, however, our receiving a lastingly good life. Consider the existence of an all-loving God who sustains, and who alone can sustain, lastingly good life for humans. The existence of such a God is a good thing, all things considered, for us humans. Nagel hopes that there is no such God. In doing so, he hopes that something good, all things considered, for all of us does not exist. Such a hope against the reality of something good for us arises from Nagel's desire to have moral independence and authority. At least, I can't find a better diagnosis.

Nagel's desire is willful in a way that flouts good judgment. It rests on this attitude: "If I can't have my moral independence of God, even though God is all-loving and good for me, then I hope that God doesn't exist. I don't want to exist in a universe where God is the moral authority over me and others. I just won't stand for that kind of moral non-independence. If I can't be morally independent of God, then I just won't be at all." Nagel is willing to sacrifice something good for himself and others (namely, lastingly good life) for the sake of a willful desire to be morally independent of God. If, however, God is all-loving (as God is by title), this willful attitude is dangerously misguided. Its willfulness invites the needless destruction of suicide in a world blessed by the presence of an all-loving God. We thus have a case where willfulness blocks good judgment. This is a trademark of the human condition of *supposedly* self-protective fear.

Our attitudes toward God's existence are not purely cognitive in their origin and sustenance. Our *willfulness* looms large. Let's turn, then, to the role of *evidence* regarding God as the One who can overcome death for us.

Hidden Help

If God exists, God is hidden. Pascal was dead right: "… any religion which does not say that God is hidden is not true" ([1660] 1995: sec. 275). Jesus himself thanks God for hiding. After giving his disciples instructions regarding their preaching of the kingdom of God, Jesus prays as follows:

> I thank you, Father, Lord of heaven and earth, because you have hidden these things from the wise and the learned, and you have revealed them to infants. Yes, Father, this seemed good in your sight. (Luke 10:21; cf. Matt. 11:25–6; Isa. 45:15)

If an all-loving God aims to help us to overcome death, shouldn't we all receive an explicit revelation of God's reality that is beyond reasonable doubt? Wouldn't an all-loving God appear clearly to dispel doubts about God's reality and the significance of human death?

We think we know what we *should* expect of an all-loving God. As a result, we confidently set the parameters for God's reality as if they were decisive regarding God's reality. We seldom ask, however, what *God* would expect of *us*. We'll do so here. An all-loving God would promote unselfish love, and thus would not settle for our simply knowing that God exists. I could know that God exists but hate God. Indeed, my hate toward God could increase as my evidence of God's reality increases. As I get more evidence of God as a genuine moral authority over me, I could easily deepen my hate toward God. This could come from willful insistence that I be my own moral authority at least in certain areas of my life.

Hate toward God is not good for anyone, including the one who hates God. It blocks a congenial relationship between a person and the only One who can overcome death and supply lastingly good life for that person. So, an all-loving God would not promote hate toward God. For the person resolutely opposed to God, more evidence of God's reality would typically be harmful. It would intensify and solidify opposition to God. Jesus thus advises his messengers not to cast his sacred message before resolute opponents, lest they trample it under foot (Matt. 7:6). Such a mean-spirited response by Jesus' opponents would be good for no one, not even the opponents. An all-loving God seeks to break willful opposition but not typically by means of a counterproductive direct assault on it. Instead, God typically invites us in various ways to come to our senses, and then waits. Since people aren't pawns, we should not expect universal success on God's part. Because people can freely reject God's invitation, some people might not ever come around to acknowledge God, despite God's best efforts.

What of "agnostics"? They withhold judgment regarding God's existence on the basis of allegedly counterbalanced evidence. They reportedly endorse agnosticism "for reasons of evidence." Typically, however, agnostics overlook the most important evidence of God's reality: namely, the reality of God's genuinely unselfish love in Jesus and thereby in the life of a person who yields to him as Lord and thus receives God's Spirit. This kind of love prompts the apostle Paul to make the following *cognitively* relevant point: "[Christian] hope does not disappoint, because the love of God has been poured out within our hearts through the Holy Spirit who was given to us" (Rom. 5:6). Paul thus identifies a kind of evidence that saves one from disappointment in hoping in God: the presence of God's Spirit accompanied by God's unselfish love. Followers of Jesus often fail to live up to the high calling toward God's holy love, but this does not challenge the distinctive evidence just noted.

Evidence from the presence of God's Spirit is akin to the evidence from conscience regarding, for instance, the goodness of a case of self-giving kindness and the evil of a case of needless torture. Such evidence from conscience, although genuine, does not yield a non-question-begging argument against skeptics, but this is no defect in the evidence. In addition, such evidence can be suppressed by us, and we will dismiss it if we *will* to do something in conflict with it. Still, the evidence from conscience is genuine and salient. Likewise for the evidence of God's Spirit, which comes typically with the conviction in conscience that we have fallen short of God's unselfish holy ways.

Volitional factors loom large in acquiring evidence of God's reality. An all-loving God would seek to be known *as God*, for the good of humans. So, God would seek to be known as *our* God. God sent Jesus as living proof that God is for us, not against us. The self-giving sacrifice of Jesus aims to alert us to God's intervention on our behalf. In his journey from Gethsemane to Calvary, Jesus resists ("dies to") selfishness in order to live to God. He subjects his will to the unselfish will of his Father. This subjection of the will is cognitively as well as morally significant. It highlights autobiographical factors in receiving evidence of God's reality as God. As I yield to God's call to obey, as Jesus did, God emerges as *my* God, and I thereby become God's servant and child. Only in such volitional yielding on my part does God become *my* God. My firm knowledge of God as my God thus depends on volitional factors concerning me, concerning my exercise of my will in relation to God. I must yield my will in response to the convicting and redirecting intervention of God's Spirit in my conscience. I can have no firm knowledge of God as my God in a will-free manner. We tell ourselves that *if* God appeared to us in an astonishing manner, *then* we would yield to God as God. This, however, is doubtful, because we then have already set ourselves up as cognitive judge over God.

The evidence from the presence of God's Spirit does not yield a non-question-begging argument for God's reality. This is no problem, because the reality of evidence does not depend on a non-question-begging argument. For example, I do not have a non-question-begging argument for my belief that I am awake now (at least relative to an extreme skeptic's questions), but I still have good evidence that I am awake now. Whether an argument is non-question-begging varies with the questions actually raised in an exchange. Evidence itself is not exchange-relative in this way. Our *having* evidence does not entail *giving* an answer of any kind. So, we should not be troubled by our lacking a non-question-begging argument relative to an agnostic's questions. We should rather identify the evidence suited to an all-loving God who seeks volitional transformation rather than mere reasonable belief.

Commitment to the true God can yield unsurpassed explanatory value, at least in certain areas of inquiry. Such a commitment, we might argue, makes the best sense of who we are and of why we have come into existence. The reasonableness of theistic belief is thus sometimes recommended as underwritten by an inference to a best explanation. Still, the foundational evidence of God's reality is irreducibly a matter of experiencing the presence of God's personal Spirit. This presence is not an argument of any kind. It is rather God's authoritative call on a person's life. If a call promotes hate, it is not from an all-loving God. False gods compete with the true God, and they are known by the standard of unselfish love.

Some agnostics will demand that we begin with mere "existence-arguments" concerning God. This is misguided. In the case of the true God, essence, character, and value must not be bracketed for the sake of mere existence-arguments. The present approach holds these together, thereby maintaining the explanatory, psychological, and existential distinctiveness of the evidence supplied by the Jewish-Christian God. Genuine existence-evidence regarding the true God comes not as a needed preliminary to, but instead *through*, the good news of what God has done for us in Jesus, in concert with the convicting and drawing power of God's Spirit. Proper conviction of God's reality comes through the transforming working of God's personal Spirit in conjunction with the good news of what God has done for us. So, we should begin not with mere existence-evidence but rather with evidence of what God has done and is doing in terms of His gracious personal calling through the good news of Jesus. We will thus avoid the risk of being diverted to deism, mere theism, or something else less robust than the reality of the true God and Father of Jesus. We will then highlight God's gracious offer of reconciliation to all people, even unsophisticated people, via the good news of Jesus. A person doesn't have to be able to follow intricate arguments to receive evidence of God's reality. This is good news indeed.

Arguments aside, the good news of Jesus need not be lost on people raised within non-theistic traditions. The convicting and drawing power of God's Spirit can begin to transform receptive people from any tradition, even receptive people who do not yet acknowledge this Spirit as the Spirit of the risen Jesus. When the good news of Jesus actually comes to the latter people, it will, in due course, bring them to acknowledge the work of God's Spirit within them as the work of the Spirit of the risen Jesus. The good news of Jesus has its base in a power that cuts much deeper than arguments and religious traditions: the transforming power of the Spirit of the living God.

Conclusion

For the person eager to follow God's ways, the available evidence is subtle but adequate. It is subtle in order to keep people humble, free of prideful triumphalism of the kind that destroys community. In our pride, we would readily turn a conveniently available God into a self-serving commodity. This tendency prompted Jesus to say that "it's an evil generation that seeks for a sign" (Matt. 16:4). The evidence available to us fits with the curriculum of death: the aim is to teach us to trust the One who alone can save us from death and corruption.

The lesson is that we must turn from our ways to get in line with the true God. This is difficult news, because we have a hard time trusting a God we cannot see. We fear that our well-being and rationality will be at risk if we trust this invisible God. The truth of the matter is that our well-being and rationality are at risk and even doomed if we fail to trust God. Death serves as a vivid reminder. Without God as our trusted Savior, only death awaits us. As we die to our ways in order to live to God, we receive God as our Savior from death and corruption. Nothing can then extinguish us, not even death. Death leaves us, then, either with lives that are ultimately an empty tragedy or with a God subjecting this world to futility in order to save it. In sincerely hoping for the latter, we become open to a kind of evidence that will change us forever, even from death to life. If we have the courage to hope in God, we'll see that Plato was right: Philosophy done right prepares us for dying and death. It also leads to the One we need.

References

Camus, A. (1955) *The Myth of Sisyphus*, trans. J. O'Brien. New York: Knopf.

Moser, P.K. (2002) "Cognitive Idolatry and Divine Hiding." In D. Howard-Snyder and P.K. Moser (eds.), *Divine Hiddenness*. New York: Cambridge University Press.

Nagel, T. (1997) *The Last Word*. New York: Oxford University Press.

Pascal, B. ([1660] 1995) *Pensées*, trans. H. Levi. New York: Oxford University Press.

Plato (1969) *Phaedo*. In *The Last Days of Socrates*, trans. H. Tredennick. London: Penguin.

Russell, B. ([1903] 1957) "A Free Man's Worship." In *Mysticism and Logic*. Garden City, NY: Doubleday.

Russell, B. (1970) "The Talk of the Town." *New Yorker* (February 21), 29. Cited in A. Seckel (ed.) (1986) *Bertrand Russell on God and Religion*. Buffalo, NY: Prometheus.

Selzer, R. (2000) "Interview." *Teen Ink* (December).